ARISTOTLE

Selections

ARISTOTLE

Selections

Translated
with Introduction, Notes, and Glossary
by
Terence Irwin and Gail Fine
Cornell University

Hackett Publishing Company, Inc.
Indianapolis/Cambridge

19 18 17 16 15 14   5 6 7 8 9 10 11

For further information, please
address the publisher:

Hackett Publishing Company, Inc.
P.O. Box 44937
Indianapolis, Indiana 46244-0937
www.hackettpublishing.com

Text design by Dan Kirklin

Library of Congress Cataloging-in-Publication Data

Aristotle
[Selections. English. 1995]
Aristotle: selections/translated,
with introduction, notes, and glossary by
Terence Irwin and Gail Fine.
p.   cm.
Includes bibliographical references.
ISBN 0-915145-68-5 (cloth)
ISBN 0-915145-67-7 (pbk.)
1. Philosophy, Ancient.
2. Science, Ancient.
I. Irwin, Terence.
II. Fine, Gail.
III. Title
B407.F56 1995
185—dc20
95-31470
CIP

ISBN-13: 978-0-915145-68-3 (cloth)
ISBN-13: 978-0-915145-67-6 (pbk.)

to

John Ackrill

and to the memory of

Michael Woods

CONTENTS

*indicates an excerpt from the chapter or chapters marked

CONTENTS

*indicates an excerpt from the chapter or chapters marked

PREFACE

We began work on these Selections several years ago, at the suggestion of the publisher, who believed that none of the available volumes of selections from Aristotle was suitable for use in an introductory course in ancient philosophy: the available volumes either cost too much or lacked accurate translations or lacked appropriate selections. In response to suggestions by colleagues and readers, we have expanded our initial list of selections; while the volume is still intended primarily for beginners, we hope that it may also be useful in more advanced courses on Aristotle, and in courses in (for instance) religion, political science, English, or rhetoric that consider Aristotle.

Readers are advised to read the last section of the Introduction ('This Edition') before using the rest of the volume.

Our translation of the *Ethics* is extracted (with very slight alterations) from the translation by Terence Irwin (Hackett, 1985). Terence Irwin is also responsible for the *Politics*, *Poetics*, and *Rhetoric*. We bear joint responsibility, to different degrees, for the rest of the volume.

In revising the translations and notes, we have benefited from suggestions by friends and colleagues, and especially from the comments of the publisher's readers. The most recent of these readers was S. Marc Cohen, whose numerous and acute comments and suggestions greatly improved the penultimate version. The earlier readers, who remain anonymous, were also extremely helpful. John Cooper has devoted considerable time and energy to improving our translations and advising us on policy; we are very grateful for all his help. Despite the efforts of all these readers, many errors must still be present in this published version, and we will be grateful for any criticisms, suggestions, and corrections we receive.

It gives us great pleasure to dedicate this volume to John Ackrill, Emeritus Professor of the History of Philosophy in the University of Oxford and Emeritus Fellow of Brasenose College, and to the memory of Michael Woods, late Fellow of Brasenose College. Both of them have helped to raise the standard of English translations of Greek philosophical texts; John Ackrill has supervised the Clarendon Aristotle Series for many years, and Michael Woods supervised the Clarendon Plato Series until his death. Each of them has also helped both of us in many different ways with advice, encouragement, and friendship over the years.

Terence Irwin
Gail Fine

Sage School of Philosophy
Cornell University
Ithaca, New York
January 1995

ABBREVIATIONS

Works of Aristotle

The works of Aristotle are cited by abbreviations of their conventional Latin or English titles. We list both Latin and English titles below; for each treatise we translate we have used whichever title seems to be more commonly used in current English. (In many cases the English titles are mere Anglicizations rather than proper translations.) In cases where no English title is in common use, a rough translation has been placed in square brackets. More information on the titles is given in the first note to many of the treatises.

APo	Analytica Posteriora	Posterior Analytics
APr	Analytica Priora	Prior Analytics
Catg.	Categoriae	Categories
DA	De Anima	On the Soul
DC	De Caelo	On the Heavens
DI	De Interpretatione	On Interpretation
EE	Ethica Eudemia	Eudemian Ethics
EN	Ethica Nicomachea	Nicomachean Ethics
GA	De Generatione Animalium	Generation of Animals
GC	De Generatione et Corruptione	Generation and Corruption
HA	Historia Animalium	History of Animals
IA	De Incessu Animalium	Progression of Animals
MA	De Motu Animalium	Movement of Animals
Met.	Metaphysica	Metaphysics
Metr.	Meteorologica	Meteorology
MM	Magna Moralia	[Great Ethics]
PA	De Partibus Animalium	Parts of Animals
Phys.	Physica	Physics
PN	Parva Naturalia	[Short Natural Treatises]
Poet.	De Arte Poetica	Poetics
Pol.	Politica	Politics
Rhet.	Rhetorica	Rhetoric
Top.	Topica	Topics

Other abbreviations

ROT	The Revised Oxford Translation (see Further Reading, [5])
OCD	*Oxford Classical Dictionary* (Oxford, 1970)
OCT	Oxford Classical Text (see [2])
DK	Diels-Kranz (see [24])

Subscripts

English	*Greek*	*Glossary entry*
substance	*ousia*	SUBSTANCE
being$_o$	*ousia*	SUBSTANCE #1
essence$_o$	*ousia*	SUBSTANCE #2
form	*eidos*	REASON
form$_l$	*logos*	REASON #5
form$_m$	*morphē*	FORM #5
know$_e$	*epistasthai*	KNOW #1
know$_g$	*gignōskein*	KNOW #1
know$_o$	*eidenai*	KNOW #1

INTRODUCTION

1. Aristotle's life

Aristotle was born in Stagira in Macedon (now part of northern Greece) in 384 B.C. In his lifetime the kingdom of Macedon, first under Philip and then under Philip's son Alexander ('the Great'), conquered the Greek cities in Europe and Asia, and then went on to conquer the Persian Empire. The Macedonian rulers made elaborate efforts to present themselves as Greeks; they were not entirely successful in these efforts, and many Greeks regarded them as foreign invaders. Though Aristotle spent much of his adult life in Athens, he was not an Athenian citizen; he was closely linked to the kings of Macedon, and he was evidently affected by the volatile relations between the Greek cities, especially Athens, and Macedon. (The bitterly anti-Macedonian speeches of the orator Demosthenes show what some Athenians thought about Macedonians.)

Aristotle was the son of Nicomachus, a doctor who had been attached to the Macedonian court. In 367 Aristotle came to Athens, and he was a member of PLATO's[1] Academy until the death of Plato in 347. Plato's successor as head of the Academy was his nephew SPEUSIPPUS. At that time (we do not know why) Aristotle left Athens, first for Assos (in Asia Minor), where the pro-Macedonian ruler Hermeias was a patron of philosophical studies. Aristotle married Pythias, a niece of Hermeias; they had a daughter, also called Pythias. After Hermeias was killed by the Persians, Aristotle moved on to Lesbos, in the eastern Aegean, and then to Macedon, where he became tutor of Alexander. In 334 he returned to Athens and founded his own school, the Lyceum. After the death of Pythias, Aristotle formed an attachment to Herpyllis, and they had a son Nicomachus (named, following the Greek custom, after his grandfather). In 323 Alexander died; in the resulting outbreak of anti-Macedonian feeling in Athens, Aristotle left for Chalcis, on the island of Euboea, where he died in 322. In his will Aristotle directed that the bones of his wife Pythias were to be placed in his grave, in accordance

---

1. Words in CAPITALS refer to entries in the Glossary. Numbers in square brackets refer to items listed in 'Further Reading'. For abbreviations see the list of Abbreviations.

with her wishes; he also made provision for the support of Herpyllis and Nicomachus and of his daughter Pythias.[2]

These pieces of fairly reliable information have encouraged both ancient and modern writers to try to write biographies of Aristotle, tracing the development of his thought through the different periods of his life. The evidence for any detailed biographical construction, however, is lacking. The best we can do is to pick out some aspects of Aristotle's life that are probably significant for his philosophical career.

Aristotle's twenty years in Plato's Academy coincided with the writing of Plato's important later dialogues (including the *Sophist, Timaeus, Philebus, Statesman,* and *Laws*), in which Plato reconsiders many of the doctrines of his earlier dialogues, and pursues new lines of thought not explored in earlier dialogues. The exploratory and critical outlook of the Academy probably encouraged Aristotle's own philosophical growth. It would be misleading to think of him either as a disciple of a dogmatic system of 'Platonism' or as a rebel against such a system; there is no sign that Plato adhered to any such system.

We have some reason to suppose that some of the observations used in Aristotle's biological works are drawn from the eastern Aegean, and hence we have some reason to suppose that Aristotle pursued his biological research during his years away from Athens. If this is true, then the works of his later period presuppose this biological background. We might trace Aristotle's biological interests to the Academy (see Plato's *Timaeus*); he may also have acquired them from his father Nicomachus, who was a doctor.

It is reasonable to suppose that most of the Aristotelian corpus as it survives is derived from the period in which Aristotle gave lectures in the Lyceum. Some works (for instance, *On Ideas*) may have been written while Aristotle was a member of the Academy, and the *Topics* may reflect the character of dialectical debates in the Academy.

We do not know how formally the Lyceum was organized. At any rate, by the end of Aristotle's life it had become a well-established school; and his student Theophrastus succeeded him as its head.

2. Aristotle's works

The nearly complete modern English translation of Aristotle (in ROT) fills about 2450 pages. Many of his works, however, have been lost, and those that survive complete are quite different in character from many of the lost works.[3] Among the lost works are dialogues, probably similar

---

2. Aristotle's will; see ROT p. 2464.

3. Ancient lists of titles of Aristotle's works are printed in ROT p. 2386.

in character to some of Plato's dialogues, and other treatises designed for publication. Only fragments of these works survive. We have translated some passages from one work surviving only in fragments, *On Ideas*. Aristotle may refer to some of the lost works when he speaks of his POPULAR writings.[4]

The Aristotelian Corpus, as we have it, largely consists of works that appear to be closely related to Aristotle's lectures. Sometimes he seems to refer to 'visual aids' of the sort that might be present in a classroom (cf. *EN* 1107a33). Sometimes the grammatically incomplete sentences and compressed allusions suggest notes that a lecturer might expand. This is especially true, for instance, of *Met.* vii 13. One passage reads (literally translated): 'But if not, many other things result, and the third man' (1039a1–2). It is natural to suppose that Aristotle meant to explain these allusions in oral delivery. Not all the Corpus is like this, however; sometimes a particular passage or book suggests revision with a view to publication (see, e.g., *PA* i 5).

We cannot tell how many of his treatises Aristotle regarded as 'finished'. The titles of the *Eudemian* and *Nicomachean Ethics* might reflect a tradition that Eudemus (a member of the Lyceum) and Nicomachus (the son of Aristotle and Herpyllis) edited Aristotle's lectures. It is most unlikely that he intended to publish anything like our present *Metaphysics*, or even intended a course of lectures to proceed in anything like the order of the present treatise. (Parts of Book i are almost repeated in Book xiii; Book xi summarizes parts of Book iv; the authenticity of Book xi is suspected; and Book ii is probably not by Aristotle at all.)

These facts about the Corpus suggest that we ought not to treat Aristotle's treatises as finished literary works that the author intended to publish at a particular time. It may be more appropriate to compare them to different 'files' that Aristotle revised, expanded, summarized, or combined, for different teaching purposes, or when new ideas struck him. For the philosophical reader, this has both drawbacks and advantages. We may regret the fact that the treatises are not as clear and polished as they would have been if they had been revised for publication; still, we are to some degree compensated by coming closer to the philosopher's own struggles with his problems. As we watch Aristotle argue with himself, we are encouraged to argue with him.

3. The order of Aristotle's works

In approaching a philosopher's works, it is often useful to know the order in which they were written; e.g. it would be difficult to understand Kant if we did not know that his 'pre-Critical' works preceded the Critical

---

4. Selected fragments are translated in ROT pp. 2389 ff.

philosophy, and it would be difficult to understand Wittgenstein if we did not know that the *Tractatus* preceded the *Investigations*. We are forced to approach Aristotle, however, with no useful external evidence about the order of his writings. We have printed them in the order in which they appear in the Greek manuscripts. This order goes back to the Aristotelian commentators (from the first to the sixth centuries A.D.);[5] it reflects their view not about the order in which the works were written, but about the order in which they should be studied.

Speculations about the order of the works are rather controversial, but some possible indications may be these:

1. It is easier to understand the relation of the doctrine of SUBSTANCE in the *Categories* to the doctrine and argument of *Met.* vii if we suppose that the treatment in the *Categories* is earlier.

2. None of the works in the Organon (see Part 4) mentions matter. This may be because (i) Aristotle had not yet thought of it, or because (ii) he regarded it as irrelevant to the topics considered in the Organon. The first explanation is probably (though by no means indisputably) preferable; if it is correct, the works in the Organon precede the works on natural philosophy.

3. Facts about place names (see Part 1 above) suggest that some of the research resulting in some of the biological works belongs to the period that Aristotle spent away from Athens. If this is right, then it is reasonable to suppose that some of the biological works may not be the latest works in the Corpus.

Beyond these very rough considerations, it is difficult to establish anything about the order of the works without undertaking a detailed comparison of their philosophical doctrine. The literary character of the Corpus suggests, in any case, that in asking for the 'date' of a particular treatise, we may be asking an inappropriate question. If the treatises were not published, and were not intended for publication, by Aristotle, and if they are more like 'files' in which Aristotle incorporated his views from time to time, a given treatise may easily contain contributions from different dates, and these contributions may or may not be harmonious. For similar reasons, we cannot plausibly take cross-references from one work to another as evidence of the order of the works.

5. On the commentators see [10], ch. 1.

4. The contents of Aristotle's works

In the standard arrangement, the treatises are grouped as follows:[6]

1. *Catg., DI, APr, APo, Top.* These came to be known (from the second century A.D.) as the 'Organon' (see INSTRUMENT) because they deal with LOGIC (in Aristotle's broad sense), which is an instrument of philosophical thinking, not a discipline with its own specific subject matter. Aristotle himself seems to think of the *Analytics* and *Topics* as part of a single inquiry (see *Top.* 184b1n).

2. *Phys., DC, GC, Metr., DA, PN, HA, PA, MA, IA, GA.* These belong to natural philosophy, dealing with different aspects of NATURE.

3. *Met.*[7] This deals with 'first PHILOSOPHY'.

4. *EN, MM, EE, Pol.* These belong to 'practical' philosophy, which deals with ACTION rather than PRODUCTION.

5. *Rhet., Poet.* These deal with PRODUCTION rather than ACTION.[8]

A brief outline of a few of the main themes of different works in the Corpus may be useful, to give the reader some idea of what to expect.

Top. i gives a brief account of DIALECTIC, which supplies the method of argument most commonly used in Aristotle's philosophical works. Dialectical method is derived from the Socratic conversations found in Plato's dialogues, but Aristotle practices it without the dialogue form. Dialectic begins from COMMON BELIEFS, assumptions widely shared by 'the many and the wise'; it studies the puzzles arising from these beliefs, and tries to solve the puzzles. Among the common beliefs that Aristotle considers are the views of his predecessors (most elaborately in *Met.* i; cf. *DA* i, *Pol.* ii); he argues that the difficulties raised by their views help us to find better solutions.

The *Physics* is a dialectical examination of nature, *phusis*, the subject of Presocratic inquiries. Like the NATURALISTS, Aristotle wants to find the laws and regularities that make natural change intelligible; and he argues that to find the right laws, we must recognize both MATTER and FORM as CAUSES. He examines Presocratic views in *Met.* i; in *Phys.* ii and *PA* i, he

---

6. This list excludes (a) works generally agreed to be spurious that have been included in the Aristotelian Corpus; (b) the lost works; (c) the *Constitution of Athens* (probably not by Aristotle himself), which was discovered after the standard arrangement of Aristotle's works was established. All of (a) and (c), and some surviving fragments, or supposed fragments, of (b), are included in ROT.

7. On this title see PHILOSOPHY #2.

8. For Aristotle's own division of disciplines see *PA* 640a1, *Met.* 982b11, 993b20, vi 1.

presents his account of causes and his reasons for recognizing form as a cause. Aristotle argues that the ESSENCE of artifacts is their form, not simply their matter. A hammer, for instance, is not simply a lump of wood and metal, but an instrument for driving nails into wood; the function of driving nails into wood is the form that the matter has acquired by being made into a hammer. In Aristotle's view, something similar holds (though with important qualifications) for natural organisms; he argues that a plant or animal is not simply a collection of flesh, bone, and tissue, but a whole organized for a particular set of functions, and that these functions are to be identified with the form.

These claims about form and matter are the basis for Aristotle's most elaborate account of SUBSTANCE, presented in *Met*. vii–ix. Substance is introduced in the *Categories* without reference to form and matter; Aristotle identifies a particular man or particular dog, as opposed to their color, size, or shape, as substances. In the *Physics* and *De Generatione et Corruptione*, he connects his claims about substance with his views on form and matter. In the *Metaphysics* he argues that questions about substance are among the basic questions of first philosophy, and he reexamines them at length in Book vii. He argues that substance is form; he supports and clarifies his argument by explaining the relation between matter and form by reference to POTENTIALITY and ACTUALITY (Book ix). This account of ordinary perceptible, material substances is used in Book xii to develop an account of immaterial divine substance.

Aristotle's views on substance are also applied to questions about the relation of SOUL and body. Though his treatise 'On the Soul' (*De Anima*) is placed (quite reasonably) among the works on nature, the assumptions that he relies on are best understood in the light of *Met*. vii–ix. In Aristotle's view, disputes about soul and body are simply a special case of the more general disputes about form and matter; the different views of the Presocratics and of Plato need a dialectical examination. Aristotle argues that soul is substance because it is the form of a natural body, and that the body is the matter informed by the soul.

The aspects of Aristotle's philosophy mentioned so far belong mostly to metaphysics (in the modern sense of the term) and to philosophy of mind. Aristotle has no treatise devoted to epistemology, but parts of several treatises discuss questions about the nature and acquisition of KNOWLEDGE and about the relation between knowledge and PERCEPTION. In *DA* ii–iii Aristotle discusses the different senses, APPEARANCE, and UNDERSTANDING, and their contributions to knowledge. In the *Posterior Analytics* he describes the logical and epistemological structure of a completed science (as opposed to the process of empirical inquiry that leads to scientific knowledge). In *Met*. i–iv he examines the sort of knowledge that is possible for ultimate principles that cannot be defended by appeal to more ultimate principles. Aristotle's claims about the nature of knowledge also have metaphysical implications, which he examines in *Met.* vii and xiii 4 (see UNIVERSAL).

Aristotle's ethical works begin from common beliefs about morality and the puzzles that they generate. Aristotle begins with different people's conceptions of the human good, identified with HAPPINESS. He seeks to resolve puzzles by defending his own account of the nature of happiness, referring to the human FUNCTION. Here he seems to appeal to his own account of the soul to explain some of his ethical principles. Most of the rest of the *Ethics* examines the different VIRTUES and the actions that result from them; these actions, in Aristotle's view, are the ones that achieve the human good.

The *Ethics* leads directly into the *Politics*; indeed, the two treatises are parts of a single inquiry that belongs to POLITICAL SCIENCE. The *Pol.* begins with Aristotle's claims about the connection between human nature and the human good. A human being, he claims, is a political animal insofar as human capacities and aims are completely fulfilled only in a COMMUNITY; the individual's happiness must involve the good of fellow-members of a community. In the light of these claims Aristotle examines the successes and failures of actual CITIES in promoting the human good, and considers the proper design of a city that would actually realize the good of its citizens.

The selections from the *Rhetoric* and *Poetics* translated here throw some further light on Aristotle's ethical and political views. In the *Rhetoric* he considers the moral beliefs that the orator should appeal to in trying to persuade audiences or juries. In the *Poetics* he considers some of the moral issues that are raised by tragedies and the emotions that are aroused by the presentation of these issues in dramatic form. In both cases we can see some of the background presupposed by the arguments of the *Nicomachean Ethics* and *Politics*.

These are only a few of the main themes and issues discussed in the selections translated in this volume. We have sought to present both the essential readings needed for a grasp of Aristotle's general outlook and a fair selection of some of his most complex and interesting philosophical arguments. Readers should be able to form some idea of the extent of Aristotle's philosophical interests and of the arguments and discussions that assure him of a place in the first rank of philosophers.

This volume does not, however, reflect the proportions of different parts of the Aristotelian Corpus. It includes only a very small sample from the *Prior Analytics*, Aristotle's enormously influential treatise on formal logic. Nor do our selections reflect the important fact that a large proportion of the Corpus is devoted to the presentation and interpretation of detailed collections of empirical data. The biological treatises take up roughly a quarter of the entire Corpus, and large sections of the *Meteorologica* and the *Politics* contain detailed empirical argument in their respective areas. Though Aristotle can no longer be regarded as an authority on the details of zoology or meteorology, readers should remember that his philosophical inquiries rest on a broad empirical basis; they are the work of someone who regards himself not only as a philosopher, but also as an investigator into winds, tides, animal motion, and political sociology. Indeed, it would be misleading (as *PA* i and the *Politics*, for instance, show clearly) to suppose that Aristotle believes in any sharp division between his empirical and his philosophical concerns.

5. This edition

This translation is intended for students, especially those beginning the study of Aristotle, and we have tried to keep their needs in mind. The literary character of the treatises presents a translator with difficult choices. (1) Aristotle's writing is often compressed and allusive; to convey in English the impression made by Aristotle's Greek, a translator would have to produce a version that would be hard to understand without a detailed commentary. If, however, translators set out to make Aristotle readily intelligible to the English reader, they will have to expand, interpret, and paraphrase to an extent that intrudes on the role of the commentator. (2) Some of Aristotle's central philosophical terms cannot easily be translated uniformly; it is difficult, for instance, to translate *archē* (see PRINCIPLE) or *logos* (see REASON) by the same English term wherever they occur. Aristotle's arguments, however, often assume that he has been speaking about the same thing in two passages where he speaks of (for instance) an *archē*, and one is in danger of obscuring the structure of his argument if one uses different English terms in these two passages. (3) Aristotle has come to us through mediaeval Latin philosophy, and some English equivalents to Latin terms (such as 'substance', 'essence', 'accident', 'incontinence') have come to be standard renderings for some of Aristotle's Greek terms. These English terms, however, no longer convey in modern English what the mediaeval Latin terms conveyed, and so they may be misleading if they are used as substitutes for Latin in translating Greek. Still, an attempt to purge a translation of these terms derived from Latin would conceal an important thread in the history of philosophy. (4) Greek idiom differs from English. Two examples: (a) Greek tolerates longer sentences than English. Hypotactic constructions (with several long subordinate clauses) are common, but the paratactic character of modern English sometimes obliges the translator to break one complex Greek sentence into two or more English sentences. (b) It is characteristic of Greek to begin sentences with connecting particles. Concern for English style would require omitting many of these particles in a translation. Omission of them, however, may remove important information. When Aristotle connects two clauses or sentences with 'for', he normally indicates that the second clause gives some reason for what has been said in the first clause; such information about the structure of the argument is useful to the philosophical reader.

This translation tries to reproduce the details, not merely the general drift, of Aristotle's sentences and arguments, insofar as this can be done in reasonably natural English. It does not reproduce the grammatical or syntactical structure of the Greek, and it does not try to refrain from answering questions of interpretation. To this extent it does not aim at the sort of literal version that is found in some translations in the Clarendon Series. It tries, however, to give a reasonably clear picture of the structure of Aristotle's arguments and of his terminology, and to adhere to a division (necessarily imprecise) between the roles of a transla- tor and of a commentator; hence, it does not recast or paraphrase to the degree that is characteristic of some of the versions in the Oxford Translation (the one revised in ROT).[9] There are more connectives ('for', 'but', 'however', and so on) than are usual in contemporary English, and some of the sentences are more complex than a contemporary English sentence would normally be; in such cases we thought that a slight sacrifice of English idiom or custom was justified by increased clarity in conveying Aristotle's argument.

We have used bracketed supplements in cases where it seemed reason- able to point out to the reader that no precise equivalent for the bracketed words appears in the Greek text. In some cases, for instance, Aristotle's sentence has no expressed subject, because he means the subject to be understood from the context; since it is not always clear what subject is to be understood, brackets indicate the translators' decision about how to resolve the ambiguity (see, e.g., *Phys.* 192b34). In other cases the supplements are intended to clarify (see, e.g., *Phys.* 193a16). Readers should by no means suppose that everything not enclosed in brackets uncontroversially corresponds to something in Aristotle's text; they should be able to discover cases where our rendering is especially para- phrastic or controversial if they consult the notes.

Some of the decisions faced by a translator may be illustrated from the beginning of *Met.* vii 3. Here is a word-for-word, minimally interpretative version (with alternative renderings in square brackets):

> Substance [essence] is said [spoken of], if not more-wise [several- wise], at any rate in four most; for indeed the essence and the universal and the genus [kind] seem [seems] to be the substance [essence] of each, and fourth of these the subject.

9. To see the difference between two extreme attitudes to translation, readers might like to compare the Oxford Translation of *APo* (printed in [7]) with Barnes's translation (in ROT) and with Barnes's revised translation, [53].

Some of the problems arising here are these: (a) How should *ousia* be rendered? 'Essence' might seem most plausible for the first three things mentioned, but 'substance' for the subject. (b) 'More-wise' is awkward, but the more natural 'in more ways' would suggest falsely that 'in' appears in the Greek and that it is grammatically parallel to the 'in' in 'in four most'. (c) 'More-wise' suggests more than something; more than what? More than the four to be mentioned next? Or should 'several-wise' be preferred? (d) What does 'most' in 'in four most' mean? (e) Are 'essence', 'universal', and 'genus' all meant to refer to the same thing or to three different things? (f) Should the narrower sense of *genos* (genus, as opposed to species) or the broader sense (kind, whether genus or species) be preferred? (g) What should be supplied to complete the clause about the subject? Is the subject said to be 'the substance *of each thing*' or simply to be a substance?

Even to make tolerable English out of this passage, the translator must make some decisions about the questions raised above. An intelligible English version—one that conveys a reasonably clear point without constant recourse to exegetical notes—requires still more decisions. The reader can see what decisions we have made by comparing our translation of this passage with the version given above. While not every passage in Aristotle is as obscure and compressed as the one we have discussed, such obscurity and compression are by no means unusual. (For another case see *EN* 1097b16–20.)

In some cases where the same English term is used to translate more than one Greek term and it seems important to know what the Greek term is, we have resorted to subscripts (explained in the glossary and listed in the list of abbreviations). These indicate, for instance, that 'know' translates *epistasthai*, *eidenai*, and *gignōskein*, and that 'form' sometimes renders *morphē* rather than *eidos*.

The notes and glossary are essential adjuncts to the translation. The notes suggest alternative translations (in some important passages) or more literal translations (in some cases where our rendering involves some expansion or paraphrase for the sake of intelligibility). The notes also contain some very selective discussion of the course of Aristotle's argument, and some help in understanding passages that seem both difficult and important. The glossary indicates the correspondence between Greek terms and their English renderings. It also tries to explain some of Aristotle's terms and to sketch some of the philosophical doctrines and assumptions that they convey. A word in capital letters in the notes directs the reader to the relevant entry in the glossary. Asterisks in the translation also direct the reader to the glossary; they are confined to salient instances not mentioned in the notes. One way to understand Aristotle better is to look up the passages cited in the entries in the glossary and to examine them in their context. The references are not

·confined to passages included in this volume, but they are certainly not exhaustive.

Modern editions of the Greek text of Aristotle are based on the Greek manuscripts copied in the Byzantine period (mostly during the tenth century and later)[10] from manuscripts derived indirectly from the edition of Aristotle's works produced by Andronicus in the first century B.C. In the works translated here, the transmitted text is usually fairly sound, and only some books (*DA* iii, for instance) display frequent and severe textual difficulties, but smaller variations and imperfections in the manuscripts require decisions by editors and translators throughout the Corpus. We have normally translated the OCT (see [2]). In cases where no OCT has been published, we use the text specified in the first note to a particular treatise. We have tried to mention in the notes the most important places where we have deviated from the text we take as the basis for our translation. These deviations express different judgments (a) about which reading is to be preferred in cases where the manuscripts differ, or (b) about how to emend the manuscript reading in cases where it does not seem to give satisfactory sense, or (c) about whether some words are intrusions into the manuscripts, not part of what Aristotle actually wrote, or (d) about whether something has fallen out of the manuscripts and needs to be supplied, or (e) about whether the manuscripts have the text in the right order. In many cases, we have followed the OCT even when we preferred another reading, unless we thought a departure from the OCT resulted in a significant improvement.

The translation follows the division into books that is found in all editions of Aristotle. The division into books goes back to antiquity. The length of a book was determined by the requirements of ancient book production, and hence the divisions between books do not always correspond to natural divisions in the subject matter. The capitulation found in modern editions, and in our translation, has no ancient authority. The marginal numbering is derived from Bekker's edition.[11] The italicized headings are ours; they have no authority in the manuscripts. Asterisks in the translation indicate omissions. Dots indicate that not all of a given chapter has been translated. Aristotle's works are cited throughout by the abbreviated titles given in the list of abbreviations.

10. On ancient manuscripts see OCD s.v. Books, Palaeography.

11. See [1]. '1094a10', for instance, refers to line 10 of the left-hand column of page 1094 of Bekker's edition. Since Bekker's pagination is continuous, a Bekker page and line uniquely identify a particular passage. These Bekker pages and lines are standardly used to give precise references to passages in Aristotle; we have used them ourselves in the notes and glossary. Since they refer to pages and lines of the *Greek* text, they correspond only roughly to an English translation.

CATEGORIES[1]

[PRELIMINARY EXPLANATIONS]

[DIFFERENT RELATIONS BETWEEN WORDS AND THINGS]

1

If things have only a name in common, and the account of the essence$_o$[2]   *1a1*
corresponding to the name[3] is different for each, they are called homonymous. Both a man and a painted animal, for instance, are animals homonymously;[4] for these have only a name in common and the account (corresponding to the name) of the essence$_o$ is different. For if one says what
being an animal is for each of them, one will give a different account in   5
each case.

If things have both the name in common and the same account (corresponding to the name) of the essence$_o$, they are called synonymous. Both
a man and an ox, for instance, are animals <synonymously>, since each
is called animal by a common name, and the account of the essence$_o$ is
the same. For if one gives an account of each, saying what being an   10
animal is for each of them, one will give the same account.

If things are called what they are by having a name that is derived
from something else, but with a different inflection,[5] they are called

---

1. Since Aristotle does not usually use this term as the label for the ten 'categories', the traditional title of this work probably does not go back to Aristotle.
See PREDICATIONS.

2. **essence$_o$**: For this use of *ousia* see SUBSTANCE #2. Aristotle explains that the
ousia of an animal is given by an account of being an animal (for this phrase see
ESSENCE #2).

3. **corresponding to the name**: See REASON #4.

4. **Both . . . animals homonymously**: Or 'Both a man and a painting, for instance, are *zō(i)a* homonymously.' Lit. 'For instance, both the man and the
painted.' *Gegrammenon* may mean either (1) 'painting' or (2) 'thing painted in a
painting', and *zō(i)on* may mean either (1) 'picture' (of anything) or (2) 'animal'.
Our translation assumes (2).

5. **different inflection**: Aristotle means both (1) the word 'grammarian' differs
in inflection (i.e., ending) from the word 'grammar', and (2) grammarians are

15 paronymous; for example, the grammarian is so called from grammar, and the brave person from bravery.

[DIVISION OF THINGS SAID]

2

Among things said, some involve combination, while others are without combination. Things involving combination are, for instance, man runs, man wins; things without combination are, for instance, man, ox, run, wins.

[DIVISION OF BEINGS ACCORDING TO THEIR DIFFERENT RELATIONS TO A SUBJECT]

20 Among beings[6] some are said of a subject but are not in any subject; man, for instance, is said of[7] a subject, an individual man,[8] but is not in any subject. Some are in a subject but are not said of any subject.[9] (By
25 'in a subject' I mean what belongs in something, not as a part,[10] and cannot exist separately from what it is in.) For example, an individual <instance of> grammatical knowledge[11] is in a subject, the soul, but is not said of any subject; and an individual <instance of> white is in a subject, the body (for all color is in body), but is not said of any subject.
1b Some things are both said of a subject and in a subject; knowledge, for instance, is in a subject, the soul, and is said of a subject, grammatical

---

so called because of their relation to grammar. Claim (2) is not just about words; it involves the sort of asymmetrical relation that is described in 14b10–13.

6. **beings** (*onta*): Or 'things that there are' or 'existing things'.

7. **said of**: In 'G is said of F', G and F are things, not words. Aristotle is not describing a connection between the words 'the individual man' and 'man', but a connection between individual men and the species man.

8. **an individual man**: Lit. 'the some man'. See INDIVIDUAL.

9. **not said . . . subject**: If G is said of F, we can say (e.g.) of a particular man 'This is a man'. If G is in F, we cannot say (e.g.) 'This is a thin'; we need to say something further, such as 'This is a thin man'.

10. **not as a part**: Aristotle explains this contrast in 3a29–32.

11. **An individual . . . knowledge**: This might be understood as either (1) the unique instance found in (e.g.) Socrates, which differs numerically (but not necessarily qualitatively) from the unique instance found in Callias; or (2) the most fully determinate type falling under some determinable (e.g. this completely determinate shade of green in contrast to the color green). According to (2), one and the same instance of red is in two traffic lights if they are exactly the same shade of red; according to (1), there will be two instances of red. For further evidence see 2b1–6, 4a14n.

knowledge. Some things are neither in a subject nor said of a subject. This is true, for instance, of an individual man or horse; for nothing of   5 this sort is either in a subject or said of a subject.

Things that are individual[12] and numerically one[13] are, without exception,[14] not said of any subject. But nothing prevents some of them from being in a subject; for an individual <instance of> grammatical knowledge is one of the things in a subject.

[*TRANSITIVE PREDICATIONS*]

3

Whenever one thing is predicated of another as of a subject, everything   10 said of what is predicated is also said of the subject. Man, for instance, is predicated of an individual man, and animal of man; and so animal will also be predicated of an individual man, since an individual man is   15 both a man and an animal.

Genera which are different[15] and not subordinate to one another have differentiae that are different in species—for instance, the differentiae of animal and of knowledge. For footed, winged, aquatic, and biped are differentiae of animal, but none of them is a differentia of knowledge; for one sort of knowledge is not differentiated from another by being   20 biped. But if one genus is subordinate to another, nothing prevents them from having the same differentiae; for the higher genera are predicated of those below them, so that the subject will also have all the differentiae of the thing predicated.

[*THE TEN KINDS OF BEINGS*]

4

Of things said without combination, each signifies either substance or   25 quantity or quality[16] or relative or where or when or being in a position or having or acting on or being affected. To describe these in outline, here are some examples:

12. **individual**: Here this translates *atomon*; see INDIVIDUAL.

13. **numerically one**: This is characteristic of PARTICULARS. See ONE.

14. **without exception**: *haplōs*. See WITHOUT QUALIFICATION.

15. **Genera which are different**: Read *tōn heterōn genōn*.

16. **quantity or quality**: These abstract nouns translate Greek adjectives (*poson*, *poion*, lit. 'of a certain quantity', 'of a certain quality'; cf. Latin 'quantum', 'quale'). The adjectives correspond to the questions 'Of what quantity is x?' (i.e., 'How big is x?'), 'Of what quality is x?' (i.e., 'What is x like?' or 'What sort of thing

Substance:	man, horse
Quantity:	two feet long, three feet long
Quality:	white, grammatical
Relative:	double, half, larger
Where:	in the Lyceum, in the market-place
When:	yesterday, last year
Being in a position:	is lying; is sitting
Having:	has shoes on, has armor on
Acting on:	cutting, burning
Being affected:	being cut, being burned

2a (at "Where:" row)

5   None of the things just mentioned is said all by itself in any affirmation;
an affirmation results from the combination of these things with one
another. For every affirmation seems to be either true or false, whereas
10 nothing said without combination—for instance, man, white, runs,
wins—is either true or false.

[SUBSTANCE]

[PRIMARY AND SECONDARY SUBSTANCE]

5

What is called substance most fully,[17] primarily, and most of all, is what
is neither said of any subject nor in any subject—for instance, an individ-
15 ual man or horse. The species in which the things primarily called substances belong are called secondary substances, and so are their genera.
An individual man, for instance, belongs in the species man, and animal
is the genus of the species; these things, then (for instance, man and
animal), are called secondary substances.

[DIFFERENCES BETWEEN BEING SAID OF A SUBJECT AND BEING IN A SUBJECT]

20   It is evident from what has been said that if something is said of a
subject, then both its name and its account must be predicated of the
subject. For instance, man is said of a subject, an individual man, and
the name is predicated (since you will predicate man of an individual
man); moreover, the account of man will also be predicated of an individ-

---

is x?'; see QUALITY), and so on. These questions are answered by adjectives, such
as 'two feet long' (a single Greek word) or 'pale'.

17. **most fully**: See CONTROLLING. Aristotle implies that this use of 'substance'
controls the other uses; cf. 2b29, 37.

ual man (since an individual man is also a man). And so both the name   25
and the account will be predicated of the subject.

On the other hand, if something is in a subject, in most cases neither
its name nor its account is predicated of the subject.[18] In some cases the
name may well be predicated of the subject, but the account still cannot   30
be predicated. White, for instance, is in a subject, body, and is predicated
of the subject (for body is said to be white); but the account of white is
never predicated of body.[19]

[HOW OTHER THINGS DEPEND ON PRIMARY SUBSTANCES]

All other things are either said of the primary substances as subjects or   35
in them as subjects. This is evident if we examine particular cases. Animal, for instance, is predicated of man, and so also of an individual man;
for if it is not predicated of any individual man, neither is it predicated of   2b
man at all. Again, color is in body, and so also in an individual body;
for if it is not in any of the particular bodies, neither is it in body at all.

Hence all the other things are either said of the primary substances
as subjects or in them as subjects. If, then, the primary substances did   5
not exist, neither could any of the other things exist. For all the other
things are either said of these as subjects or are in these as subjects, so
that if the primary substances did not exist, neither could any of the
other things exist.

[DIFFERENCES BETWEEN SECONDARY SUBSTANCES]

Among secondary substances, the species is more a substance than the
genus, since it is nearer to the primary substance; for if someone says
what the primary substance is, it will be more informative[20] and more   10
appropriate if he mentions the species than if he mentions the genus.
It will be more informative, for instance, to say that an individual

18. **On the other . . . of the subject**: If Electra is brave, then bravery is in her,
and neither the name nor the account of bravery can be predicated of her; we
cannot say either 'Electra is bravery' or 'Electra is the virtue that controls fear'.

19. **White, for instance . . . of body**: If the table is WHITE, then the color white
(= whiteness) is in the table, and in this case the name of the color can be
predicated of the table, though the account of the color cannot be (we can say
'The table is white', but we cannot say 'The table is the lightest color'). The
Greek word *leukon*, like the English word 'white', can be used both as the name
for the quality and as an adjective characterizing the qualified subject.

20. **more informative**: *gnōrimōteron*. See KNOW #4.

man is a man than to say that he is an animal, since man is more distinctive of an individual man, while animal is more common; and it will be more informative to say that an individual tree is a tree than that it is a plant.

15   Further, the primary substances are subjects for all the other things, and all the other things are predicated of them or are in them; this is why they, most of all, are called substances. But as the primary substances are related to other things, so also is the species related to the genus; for

20   the species is a subject for the genus, since the genera are predicated of the species, whereas the species are not reciprocally predicated of the genera. And so for this reason too the species is more a substance than the genus.

Among species that are not themselves genera, however, one is no more a substance than another; for it is no more appropriate to say that

25   an individual man is a man than it is to say that an individual horse is a horse. And, similarly, among primary substances one is no more a substance than another; for an individual man is no more a substance than an individual ox is.

[WHY SECONDARY SUBSTANCES ARE SUBSTANCES]

30   It is not surprising that, after the primary substances, only their species and genera are said to be[21] secondary substances; for they are the only things predicated that reveal the primary substance. For if one says what an individual man is, it will be appropriate to mention the species or the genus, though it will be more informative to mention man than

35   animal. But it would be inappropriate to mention anything else—for instance, white or runs or any other such thing. It is not surprising, then, that species and genera are the only other things said to be substances.

Further, it is because the primary substances are subjects for every-

3a   thing else that they are said to be substances most fully. But as the primary substances are related to everything else, so also the species and genera of primary substances are related to all the other <species and genera>; for all the others are predicated of them.[22] For you will

5   call an individual man grammatical, and so you will call both man and animal grammatical;[23] and the same is true in the other cases.

21. **said to be**: sc. by Aristotle, not necessarily in ordinary usage.

22. **to all . . . of them**: Or 'to all the other things; for all the other things are predicated of them'.

23. **you will . . . grammatical**: This is a case of predicating something of a universal not universally. See *DI* 17b7.

[NO SUBSTANCE IS IN A SUBJECT]

A feature common to every substance is not being in a subject; for a
primary substance is neither said of nor in a subject. In the same way,   *10*
it is evident that secondary substances are not in a subject either; for
man is said of a subject—an individual man—but is not in a subject,
since man is not in an individual man. Similarly, animal is said of a
subject—an individual man—but animal is not in an individual man.   *15*
    Further, while things in a subject may sometimes have their name
predicated of the subject, their account can never be predicated of it.
Secondary substances, on the other hand, have both their account and
their name predicated of the subject; for you will predicate both the
account of man and the account of animal of an individual man. Hence   *20*
no substance is in a subject.
    This, however, is not distinctive of substance. The differentia is not
in a subject either; for footed and biped are said of a subject—man—
but are not in a subject, since neither footed nor biped[24] is in man.   *25*
Again, the account of the differentia is predicated of whatever subject
the differentia is said of; for instance, if footed is said of man, the account
of footed will also be predicated of man, since man is footed.
    We need not be worried that we will ever be compelled to say that
the parts of substances, being in a subject (the whole substance), are   *30*
not substances.[25] For when we spoke of things in a subject, we did not
mean things belonging in something as parts.

[PREDICATION FROM A SUBSTANCE IS SYNONYMOUS]

It is a feature of substances and differentiae that everything called from
them is so called synonymously; for all the predications from these   *35*
are predicated of either the individuals or the species. (For there is no
predication from a primary substance—since it is not said of any subject—and among secondary substances the species is predicated of an
individual, and the genus is predicated both of the species and of an
individual. Similarly, differentiae are also predicated both of the species   *3b*
and of the individuals.)[26] Now the primary substances receive the account
both of the species and of the genera, and the species receives the account
of the genus; for whatever is said of what is predicated will also be said   *5*
of the subject. Similarly, both the species and the individuals receive

24. **footed nor biped**: These are both neuter adjectives; see DIFFERENTIA.

25. **We need not . . . are not substances**: See 1a24–5, PART #4.

26. **(For there is . . . the individuals)**: This parenthesis explains the omission
of cases where something is called 'from' a primary substance; there are no such
cases, because primary substances are not predicated of anything.

the account of the differentiae; and we saw[27] that synonymous things are those that both have the name in common and also have the same account. Hence everything called from substances and differentiae is so called synonymously.

[NOT EVERY SUBSTANCE IS A THIS]

10   Every substance seems to signify[28] a this.* In the case of primary substances, it is indisputably true that each of them signifies a this; for what is revealed is an individual and is numerically one. In the case of secondary substances, it appears from the character of the name, when-
15   ever one speaks of man or animal, that they also signify a this. But this is not true. Rather, each signifies a sort of thing;[29] for the subject is not one, as the primary substance is, but man and animal are said of many things. On the other hand, it does not unqualifiedly signify a sort of thing, as white does. For white signifies nothing other than a sort of
20   thing, whereas the species and the genus demarcate a sort of substance; for they signify a substance of a certain sort.[30] One demarcates more with the genus than with the species; for in speaking of animal one encompasses more than in speaking of man.

[SUBSTANCES HAVE NO CONTRARIES]

25   It is also a feature of substances that nothing is contrary to them. For what could be contrary to a primary substance? Nothing is contrary, for instance, to an individual man; nor is anything contrary to man or animal. This is not distinctive of substance, however, but is also true of many other things—of quantity, for instance, since nothing is contrary to two
30   feet long, nor to ten, nor to anything else of this kind. One might say

27. **we saw**: in 1a6.

28. **signify**: This does not show that Aristotle is talking about words rather than nonlinguistic items. See SIGNIFY #3.

29. **a sort of thing**: *poion ti*. In the rest of this paragraph (and elsewhere; see QUALITY) Aristotle uses *poion* to refer both to secondary substance and to the category of quality. Previously (1b29) we translated *poion* as 'quality', but 'sort of thing' seems the better rendering here, since Aristotle does not mean that secondary substances are in his category of quality.

30. **substance of a certain sort**: as opposed to unqualifiedly (*haplōs*; see WITHOUT QUALIFICATION) signifying a sort of thing. When we say that x is white, we say 'what sort of thing x is' or 'what x is like', by mentioning one of its qualities; when we mention a secondary substance, we say what sort *of substance* x is (and not merely what x is like more generally).

that many is contrary to few, or large to small; but no definite quantity is contrary to any other.

[SUBSTANCE DOES NOT ADMIT OF DEGREES]

Substance does not seem to admit of more or less. By this I do not mean that one substance is no more a substance than another; for we have   35
said that one type of substance is more a substance than another.[31]
Rather, I mean that no substance is said to be more or less what it is. For example, if this substance is a man, it will not be more or less a man either than itself or than another. For one man is no more a man than another, in the way that one white thing is whiter than another, or one   4a
beautiful thing is more beautiful than another. In some cases a thing is called more or less something than itself—for example, the body which is white is said to be more white now than it was before, and the body which is hot is said to be more or less hot <than it was>. But substance   5
is not spoken of in this way; for a man is not said to be more a man now than before, nor is this said of any other substance. Thus substance does not admit of more or less.

[INDIVIDUAL SUBSTANCES ARE THE ONLY INDIVIDUALS THAT RECEIVE CONTRARIES]

It seems most distinctive of substance that numerically one and the same   10
thing[32] is able to receive contraries. In no other case could one cite something numerically one that is able to receive contraries. For example, the color that is numerically one and the same[33] will not be pale and   15
dark, nor will the action that is numerically one and the same be bad and good,[34] and the same is true of anything else that is not a substance. But a substance that is numerically one and the same is able to receive contraries. An individual man, for instance, being one and the same, becomes at one time pale, at another time dark, and hot and cold, and   20
bad and good; nothing of this sort appears in any other case.

31. **we have . . . than another**: Lit. 'it has been said that it is'. See 2a11, 2b7.

32. **numerically . . . same thing**: i.e., (in the category of substance) a primary substance.

33. **the color . . . the same**. See note on 1a25.

34. **nor will . . . and good**: Aristotle probably refers to an action token (e.g., Leonidas' last stand) rather than to an action type (e.g., standing firm in battle against heavy odds), since his claim would be false if it were applied to action types.

[AN ALLEGED COUNTER-EXAMPLE]

Someone might object, however, that statements and beliefs are like this, since the same statement seems to be both true and false. If, for instance, the statement that someone is seated is true, when he has stood up this same statement will be false. The same is true of belief; for if someone were to believe truly that someone is seated, he will believe falsely if he has the same belief about the same person when he has stood up.

But even if one were to accept this, the way in which these receive contraries is still different. For in the case of substances, a thing is able to receive contraries by itself changing; for it changed when it became cold from hot (since it altered), or dark from pale, or good from bad, and similarly in the other cases it is able to receive contraries by itself changing. But statements and beliefs themselves remain completely unchanged[35] in every way; it is because the object <they are about> changes that the contrary comes to be about them. For the statement that someone is seated remains the same, but it comes to be true at one time, false at another time, when the object has changed. The same is true of belief. Hence at least the way in which substance is able to receive contraries—by a change in itself—is distinctive of it, if indeed one were to accept it as true that beliefs and statements are also able to receive contraries.

In fact, however, this is not true. For a statement and a belief are said to be able to receive contraries not because they themselves receive something, but because something else has been affected. For it is because the object is or is not some way that the statement is said to be true or false, not because the statement itself is able to receive contraries; for, without exception, no statement or belief is changed by anything. And so, since nothing comes to be in them, they are not able to receive contraries. But substance is said to be able to receive contraries, because it receives them itself. For it receives sickness and health, or paleness and darkness; and because it itself receives each thing of this sort, it is said to be able to receive contraries.

Hence it is distinctive of substance that numerically one and the same thing is able to receive contraries. So much, then, about substance.

* * * * * * *

35. **unchanged**: In this and the next sentence 'change' translates *kinein*. In the previous sentence it translated *metaballein*. See MOTION.

[TYPES OF PRIORITY AND SIMULTANEITY [36]]

[TYPES OF PRIORITY]

12

One thing is said to be prior[37] to another in four ways. First and most   14a26
fully, in time, as when one thing is said to be older or more ancient than
another; for it is because the time is longer that it is said to be older or
more ancient. Second, what does not reciprocate in implication of being.   30
One, for instance, is prior to two; for if there are two, it follows immediately that there is one, whereas if there is one, it is not necessary that
there are two, so that from one the implication of the other's being does
not hold reciprocally; and the sort of thing that seems to be prior is that   35
from which there is no reciprocal implication of being. Third, a thing is
said to be prior in some order, as with sciences and speeches. For in the
demonstrative sciences there is prior and posterior in order, since the
elements are prior in order to the diagrams; and in grammar the letters   14b
are prior in order to the syllables. And the same is true of speeches,
since the introduction is prior in order to the exposition.

Further, apart from those mentioned, what is better and more honored
seems to be prior by nature; many people are accustomed to say that   5
those they honor and like more come first. This is, one might say, the
least strict[38] sort of priority.

There are, then, these ways of speaking of priority. There would   10
seem, however, to be another way of being prior, apart from those
mentioned. For when, among things that reciprocate in implication of
being, one is in some way the cause of the being[39] of the other, it might
reasonably be said to be naturally prior.

It is clear that there are such cases. For that a man is reciprocates in
implication of being with the true statement about him (for if a man is,   15
the statement by which we say that a man is is true; and it reciprocates,
since if the statement by which we say that a man is is true, then the
man is). The true statement, however, is in no way the cause of the

---

36. This section belongs to the 'Postpredicaments' (= *Catg.* 10–15), which probably was not originally connected to *Catg.* 1–9. This section throws some light
on Aristotle's views on PRIORITY (e.g., his claim that some substances are primary,
and hence prior to other substances).

37. **prior**: In ordinary Greek the word has a temporal sense, 'before', 'earlier'.
This probably explains why Aristotle puts temporal priority first.

38. **least strict**: lit. 'most alien'. Aristotle might mean (a) that this case is least
like genuine priority, or (b) that it is furthest from any temporal order, whereas
all the other sorts of priority he has mentioned involve some temporal aspect.

39. **being**: This might refer either to x's existence or to x's being F. See BE.

20 object's being. Rather the object is apparently in a way the cause of the statement's being true; for it is because the object is or is not that the statement is said to be true or false.

One thing, then, can be said to be prior to another in five ways.

[*TYPES OF SIMULTANEITY*]

13

Things are said to be simultaneous, without qualification and most fully,
25 if they come into being at the same time; for then neither is prior or posterior. These things are said to be simultaneous in time.

Things are simultaneous by nature if they reciprocate in implication of being and neither is at all the cause of the other's being. For example,
30 the double and the half reciprocate—for if there is a double there is a half, and if there is a half there is a double—and neither is the cause of the other's being.

Coordinates of the same genus are also said to be simultaneous by
35 nature. Those resulting from the same division are said to be coordinate to one another—for instance, winged, footed, and aquatic. These are from the same genus and coordinate to one another; for animal is divided into these—into winged, footed, and aquatic—and none of these is prior
15a or posterior, but such things seem to be simultaneous by nature. Each of these—winged, footed, aquatic—might be further divided into species; these species, then, will also be simultaneous by nature, because they are from the same genus by the same division.

5 Genera, however, are always prior to species, since they do not recip-rocate in implication of being. If there is the aquatic <species>, for instance, there is animal; but if there is animal, it is not necessary that there is the aquatic <species>.

Things are said to be simultaneous by nature, then, if either (1) they
10 reciprocate in implication of being and neither is at all the cause of the other's being, or (2) they are coordinates of the same genus. Things are said to be simultaneous without qualification if they come into being at the same time.

DE INTERPRETATIONE

[LANGUAGE, THOUGHT, AND REALITY [1]]

[THE ELEMENTS OF SIGNIFICANT THOUGHT AND DISCOURSE]

1

We must first establish what names and verbs are, then what negations,   16a
affirmations, statements, and sentences are.

Spoken sounds are symbols of affections in the soul, and written
marks are symbols of spoken sounds; and just as written marks are not   5
the same for everyone, neither are spoken sounds. But the primary
things that these signify (the affections in the soul) are the same for
everyone, and what these affections are likenesses of (actual things) are
also the same for everyone. We have discussed these questions in *On
the Soul*;[2] they belong to another inquiry.

[TRUTH AND FALSITY REQUIRE COMBINATION]

Some thoughts in the soul are neither true nor false, while others must   10
be one or the other; the same is true of spoken sounds. For falsity and
truth involve combination and division. Names and verbs by themselves,
when nothing is added (for instance, 'man' and 'pale') are like thoughts   15
without combination and separation, since they are not yet either true
or false. A sign of this is the fact that 'goatstag' signifies something but
is not yet true or false unless 'is' or 'is not' is added, either without
qualification or with reference to time.

---

1. There is no reason to suppose that Aristotle supplied the traditional title of
this work. 'Interpretation' (*hermēneia*) is used for the linguistic means of expressing or SIGNIFYING something; cf. *Top.* 166b10–16, *Poet.* 1450b14. Our heading
gives a rough idea of the contents of the treatise.

2. *On the Soul*: If this refers to the extant *DA*, it may refer to iii 3–8.

[SIMPLE AND COMPOUND NAMES]

2

20   A name is a spoken sound that is significant by convention, without time, of which no part is significant in separation. For in 'Grancourt',[3] the 'court' does not signify anything in itself, as it does in the phrase 'a grand court'. But complex names are not the same as simple ones; for
25   in simple names the part is not at all significant, whereas in complex names the part has some force but does not signify anything in separation—for instance, 'fact' in 'artifact'. I say 'by convention' because nothing is a name by nature; something is a name only if it becomes a symbol. For even inarticulate noises—of beasts, for example—reveal[4] something, but they are not names.

[INDEFINITE NAMES]

30   'Not-man' is not a name, nor is any established name[5] rightly applied to it, since neither is it a sentence or a negation. Let us call it an indefinite name.

[NAMES AND THEIR INFLECTIONS]

16b   'Philo's', 'to-Philo',[6] and the like are not names but inflections of names. The same account applies to them as to names, except that a name with 'is' or 'was' or 'will be' added is always true or false, whereas an inflection with them added is neither true nor false. For example, in 'Philo's is' or
5   'Philo's is not' nothing is yet either true or false.

[VERBS]

3

A verb is <a spoken sound> of which no part signifies separately, and which additionally signifies time; it is a sign of things said of something else. By 'additionally signifies time', I mean that, for instance, 'recovery'

---

3. **'Grancourt'**: This is not Aristotle's example (nor is 'artifact' below), but it is meant to convey the same point in English.

4. **reveal**: equivalent to SIGNIFY.

5. **established name**: See NAME.

6. **'to-Philo'**: Here and elsewhere hyphens are used to render an inflected form (here the dative case) of a single Greek word where English uses a preposition or (for tenses) an auxiliary verb.

14

is a name but 'recovers' is a verb; for it additionally signifies something's
holding now. And it is always a sign of something's holding, that is to   *10*
say, of something's holding of a subject.

I do not call 'does not recover'[7] and 'does not ail' verbs; for, although
they additionally signify time and always hold of something, there is a
difference for which there is no established name. Let us call them
indefinite verbs, since they hold of anything whether it is or is not.[8]   *15*

Similarly, 'recovered' and 'will-recover' are not verbs, but inflections
of verbs. They differ from verbs because verbs additionally signify the
present time, whereas inflections of verbs signify times outside the
present.

A verb said just by itself is a name and signifies something, since the   *20*
speaker fixes his thought and the hearer pauses; but it does not yet
signify whether something is or is not. For 'being' or 'not being' is not
a sign of an object (not even if you say 'what is' without addition);[9] for
by itself it is nothing, but it additionally signifies some combination,
which cannot be thought of without the components.   *25*

[SENTENCES AND STATEMENTS]

4

A sentence[10] is a significant spoken sound, of which some part is significant in separation as an expression, not as an affirmation. I mean that
'animal', for instance, signifies something, but not that it is or is not
(but if something is added, there will be an affirmation or negation),   *30*
whereas the single syllables of 'animal' signify nothing. Nor is the 'ice'
in 'mice' significant; here it is only a spoken sound. In the case of double
names, as was said, a part signifies, but not by itself.

Every sentence is significant, not because it is a <naturally suitable>   *17a*
instrument but, as we said, by convention. But not every sentence is a
statement; only those sentences that are true or false are statements.
Not every sentence is true or false; a prayer, for instance, is a sentence

---

7. **'does not recover'**: The Greek has the form 'not recovers'.

8. **is or is not**: Perhaps 'exists or does not exist', or 'is the case or is not the
case'. Cf. *APo* 71a12, BE #1.

9. **For being . . . without addition**: The text and interpretation are doubtful.
(1) Aristotle may be using the verb 'to be' to stand for any verb (cf. 21b6) and
pointing out that the verb 'run' (e.g.) uttered by itself does not say *what* runs
or does not run. (2) Alternatively, he may be taking the verb 'to be' as his
example, because it would be most tempting to suppose that this verb all by
itself could say that something is or is not.

10. **sentence**: See REASON #2.

but it is neither true nor false. Let us set aside these other cases, since inquiry into them is more appropriate for rhetoric or poetics; our present study concerns affirmations.

＊   ＊   ＊   ＊   ＊   ＊   ＊

[TYPES OF STATEMENTS ABOUT UNIVERSALS AND PARTICULARS]

7

17a38   Some things are universals, others are particulars. By 'universal' I mean
40   what is naturally predicated of[11] more than one thing; by 'particular',
17b   what is not. For example, man is a universal, and Callias is a particular.

Necessarily, then, when one says that something does or does not hold of something, one sometimes says this of a universal, sometimes of a particular. Now if one states universally of a universal that something
5   does or does not hold, there will be contrary statements. (By 'stating universally of a universal' I mean, for instance, 'Every man is pale', 'No man is pale'.) But when one states something of a universal, but not universally, the statements are not contrary, though contrary things may be revealed. (By 'stating of a universal but not universally', I mean, for
10   instance, 'A man is pale',[12] 'A man is not pale'. For although man is a universal, it is not used universally in the statement; for 'every' does not signify the universal, but rather signifies that it is used universally.)

In the case of what is predicated, it is not true to predicate a universal
15   universally; for there will be no affirmation in which the universal is predicated universally of what is predicated, as in, for instance, 'Every man is every animal'.

[CONTRADICTORY AND CONTRARY STATEMENTS]

I call an affirmation and a negation contradictory opposites when what one signifies universally the other signifies not universally—for instance, 'Every man is pale' and 'Not every man is pale', or 'No man is pale'
20   and 'Some man is pale'. But the universal affirmation and the universal negation—for instance, 'Every man is just' and 'No man is just'—are contrary opposites. That is why they cannot both be true at the same time, but their <contradictory> opposites may both be true about the same
25   thing—for instance, 'Not every man is pale' and 'Some man is pale'.[13]

11. **of**: *epi*. Or 'over', as in 'the one over many' (cf. *Met*. 990b13, 1035b28).

12. **'A man is pale'**: There is no indefinite article (or anything corresponding to it) in the Greek.

13. **That is why . . . pale'**: Since contraries, in contrast to contradictories, do not exhaust the possibilities, it is possible for both to be false. See OPPOSITE.

Of contradictory universal statements about a universal, one or the other must be true or false; similarly if they are about particulars—for instance, 'Socrates is pale' and 'Socrates is not pale'. But if they are about universals, but are not universal <statements>, it is not always the case   *30* that one is true, the other false. For it is true to say at the same time that a man is pale and that a man is not pale, and that a man is handsome and that a man is not handsome; for if ugly, then not handsome. And if something is becoming F, it is also not F. This might seem strange at first sight, since 'A man is not pale' might appear to signify at the same   *35* time that no man is pale;[14] but it does not signify the same, nor does it necessarily hold at the same time.

It is clear that a single affirmation has a single negation. For the negation must deny the same thing that the affirmation affirms, and   *40* deny it of the same <subject>—either of a particular or of a universal,   *18a* either universally or not universally, as, for instance, in 'Socrates is pale' and 'Socrates is not pale'. (But if something else is denied, or the same thing is denied of a different <subject>, that will not be the opposite statement but a different one.) The opposite of 'Every man is pale' is   *5* 'Not every man is pale'; of 'Some man is pale', 'No man is pale'; of 'A man is pale, 'A man is not pale'.

We have explained, then, that a single affirmation has a single negation as its contradictory opposite, and which these are; that contrary   *10* statements are different, and which these are; and that not all contradictory pairs are true or false, and why and when they are true or false.

* * * * * * *

[ARGUMENTS FOR AND AGAINST FATALISM[15]]

[TRUTH AND FALSITY IN STATEMENTS ABOUT UNIVERSALS AND PARTICULARS]

9

In the case of what is and what has been, then, it is necessary that the   *18a28* affirmation or negation be true or false. And in the case of universal   *30* statements about universals, it is always <necessary> for one to be true

14. **This might seem . . . man is pale**: This is easier to understand if we remember (cf. 17b10n) that in this and the previous sentence there is no indefinite article in the Greek.

15. This chapter discusses arguments for fatalism—the view that since everything that happens happens necessarily, it is impossible for us to affect or control what happens. Aristotle rejects this view (see 19a1–11). The chapter has aroused much dispute; in the following notes we mention only a few of the interpretative options.

and the other false; and the same is true in the case of particulars, as we have said. But in the case of universals not spoken of universally, this is not necessary; we have also discussed this.[16] But in the case of particulars that are going to be, it is not the same.[17]

[ARGUMENTS FOR FATALISM]

For if every affirmation or negation is true or false, then it is also necessary 35 that everything either is the case or is not the case. And so if[18] someone says that something will be and another denies the same thing, clearly it is necessary for one of them to speak truly, if every affirmation is true or false. For both will not be the case at the same time in such cases.

18b For if it is true to say that something is pale or not pale, it is necessary for it to be pale or not pale; and if it is pale or not pale, it was true to affirm or deny this. And if it is not the case, one speaks falsely; and if one speaks falsely, it is not the case. Hence it is necessary for the affirmation or the negation to be true or false.[19]

5 Therefore nothing either is or happens[20] by chance[21] or as chance has it; nor will it be nor not be <thus>. Rather, everything <happens> from necessity and not as chance has it, since either the affirmer or the denier speaks truly. For otherwise, it might equally well happen or not happen; for what happens as chance has it neither is nor will be any more this way than that.

16. **we have also discussed this**: See 17b29.

17. **not the same**: Lit. 'not likewise'. Aristotle might mean (i) that the previous claim ('one contradictory true, one false') is not true of future singular statements, or (ii) that it is true in a different way.

18. **And so if**: Read *hōste ei*. Some MSS read 'for if' (*ei gar*).

19. **Hence it is ... to be true or false**: This paragraph might be taken in two ways: (1) Aristotle means that it is necessary that (if p is true, then the state of affairs described by p obtains); he does not mean that if p is true, then the state of affairs described by p is necessary. The necessity governs the conditional, not its consequent (see NECESSITY #7). In the next paragraph (which seems to argue fallaciously from the necessity of the conditional to the necessity of the consequent) Aristotle articulates the fatalist's argument, which he goes on to reject. (2) In this paragraph Aristotle himself argues that if p is true, then the state of affairs described by p is necessary; he ascribes necessity to the consequent, as well as to the whole conditional. In that case the next paragraph expresses his own view.

20. **happens**: Lit. 'COMES TO BE'.

21. **chance**: *tuchē*. In this chapter *tuchē* and cognates are used broadly to cover both LUCK and CHANCE, as defined in *Phys.* 197a36–b22.

Further,[22] if something is pale now, it was true to say previously that   *10*
it would be pale, so that it was always true to say of any thing that has
happened that it would be. But if it was always true to say that it was
or would be, it could not not be, or not be going to be. But if something
cannot not happen, it is impossible for it not to happen; and what cannot
not happen necessarily happens. Everything, then, that will be will be   *15*
necessarily. Therefore, nothing will be as chance has it or by chance; for
if it is by chance it is not from necessity.

[*A MISTAKEN REPLY*]

But it is not possible to say that neither is true—that, for example, it
neither will be nor will not be. For, first, <if this is possible, then>
though the affirmation is false, the negation is not true; and though the
negation is false, it turns out <on this view> that the affirmation is not   *20*
true.

Moreover, if it is true to say that it is pale and dark,[23] both must be
the case; and if <both> will be the case[24] tomorrow, <both> must be
the case[25] tomorrow. But if it neither will nor will not be tomorrow, even
so, the sea battle, for instance, will not happen as chance has it; for in   *25*
this case, the sea battle would have to neither happen nor not happen.[26]

[*CONSEQUENCES OF FATALISM*]

These and others like them are the absurd consequences if in every
affirmation and negation (either about universals spoken of universally
or about particulars) it is necessary that one of the opposites be true and
the other false, and nothing happens as chance has it, but all things are   *30*

---

22. **Further . . .:** This introduces a second argument. Unlike the previous argument, this paragraph appeals to past truth and to the necessity of the past.

23. **pale and dark**: The fatalists insist that we cannot escape their argument by
denying the Principle of Non-Contradiction and saying that something is both
pale and dark. (Some MSS read 'pale and large'.)

24. **will be the case**: Read *huparxei*. OCT: 'must be the case'.

25. **must be the case**: Read *huparchein*. OCT: 'will be the case'.

26. **And if . . . nor not happen**: After showing that denial of the Principle of
Non-Contradiction allows us no escape from their argument, the fatalists now
point out that denial of the Principle of Excluded Middle (by saying that the sea
battle neither will nor will not happen) does not undermine their argument
either; even in these cases, they say, we must accept the move from truth to
necessity.

and happen from necessity.[27] Hence there would be no need[28] to deliberate or to take trouble, thinking that if we do this, that will be, and if we
do not, it will not be; for it might well be that ten thousand years ago one
35   person said that this would be and another denied it, so that whichever it
was true to affirm at that time will be so from necessity.

Nor does it make a difference whether or not anyone made the contradictory statements; for clearly things are thus even if someone did not
affirm it and another deny it. For it is not because of the affirming or
denying that it will be or will not be the case, nor is this any more so
19a   for ten thousand years ago than for any other time.

Hence if in the whole of time things were such that one or the other
statement was true, it was necessary for this to happen, and each thing
that happened was always such as to happen from necessity. For if
5   someone has said truly that something will happen, it cannot not happen;
and it was always true to say of something that has happened that it
would be.

[ARGUMENTS AGAINST FATALISM]

But surely this is impossible. For we see that both deliberation and action
originate things that will be; and, in general, we see in things that are
10   not always in actuality that there is the possibility both of being and of
not being; in these cases both being and not being, and hence both
happening and not happening, are possible.

We find that this is clearly true of many things. It is possible, for
instance, for this cloak to be cut up, though <in fact> it will not be cut
up but will wear out first instead. Similarly, its not being cut up is also
15   possible; for its wearing out first would not have been the case unless
its not being cut up were possible. Hence the same is true for other
things that happen, since this sort of possibility is ascribed to many of
them.

Evidently, then, not everything is or happens from necessity. Rather,
20   some things happen as chance has it, and the affirmation is no more*
true than the negation.[29] In other cases, one alternative <happens>

27. **nothing happens as ... happen from necessity**: This is alleged (by the
defenders of the argument that Aristotle has just set out) to follow from what
was said in the previous 'if . . .' clause.

28. **there would be no need**: Or perhaps 'it would not be right'.

29. **the affirmation . . . the negation**: Aristotle is probably thinking of a sentence
type, irrespective of its tense (e.g., 'It will rain (or: it rained) this year on Independence Day') whose tokens are true on some occasions (i.e., when uttered before
(or: after) 4 July in years in which it rains on 4 July) and false on others. If this

more than the other and happens usually,[30] but it is still possible for the other to happen and for the first not to happen.

It is necessary for what is, whenever it is, to be, and for what is not, whenever it is not, not to be. But not everything that is necessarily is; and not everything that is not necessarily is not. For everything's being *25* from necessity when it is is not the same as everything's being from necessity without qualification; and the same is true of what is not.[31]

The same argument also applies to contradictories. It is necessary for everything either to be or not to be, and indeed to be going to be or not be going to be. But one cannot divide <the contradictories> and say that one or the other is necessary.[32] I mean that, for instance, it is necessary for *30* there to be or not to be a sea battle tomorrow, but it is not necessary for a sea battle to happen tomorrow, nor is it <necessary> for one not to happen. It is necessary, however, for it either to happen or not to happen.

And so, since the truth of statements corresponds to how things are, it is clear that, for however many things are as chance has it and are such as to admit contraries, it is necessary for the same to be true of the *35*

---

is his point, he is not saying that a token sentence (uttered on a particular occasion) is neither true nor false.

30. **In other cases . . . not to happen**: Here and elsewhere in this chapter Aristotle adverts to his tripartite division of events and entities into those that are ALWAYS, those that are USUALLY, and those that are by CHANCE. He believes that only events in the first class are necessary; since there are events in the second and third classes, not everything is necessary, and so fatalism is false.

31. **It is necessary . . . true of what is not**: This paragraph might be understood in two ways: (1) Aristotle uncovers the fatalist's fallacy, by distinguishing necessity WITHOUT QUALIFICATION from conditional necessity. It is true to say that necessarily (when x is, x is); but we cannot validly infer from this that when x is, x necessarily is. Certainly x is conditionally necessary, in that, necessarily (when x is, x is); but x is not necessary without qualification, i.e., necessary on its own. (2) Aristotle affirms that when x is (i.e., is present), then x necessarily is. He affirms the necessity of the present and past, in contrast to the nonnecessity of the future.

These two interpretations correspond to the two interpretations of Aristotle's previous argument (see 18b4n, 19a19–20n), and imply two different views of the next paragraph.

32. **But one . . . is necessary**: From necessarily (p or not-p), we cannot infer the disjunction (either necessarily p or necessarily not-p). On 'dividing' see *Met.* 1008a19. If the first interpretation of the previous paragraph is correct, the present paragraph illustrates the fatalist's modal fallacy in a different case. If the second interpretation is correct, Aristotle seeks to show that it is true that (either there will or will not be a sea battle tomorrow), but it is neither true that there will be a sea battle nor true that there will not be a sea battle.

contradictories.[33] This is just what happens with things that neither always are nor always are not. For in these cases it is necessary for one of the contradictories to be true and the other false. It is not, however, <necessary> for this or that one <more than the other one to be true or false>. Rather, <it is true or false> as chance has it; or <in the case of things that happen usually> one is more* true than the other, but not thereby true or false <without qualification>.[34]

[CONCLUSION]

19b   Clearly, then, it is not necessary that of every affirmation and negation of opposites, one is true and one false. For what holds for things that are <always> does not also hold for things that are not <always> but are capable of being and of not being;[35] in these cases it is as we have said.

*   *   *   *   *   *   *

[POSSIBILITY AND NECESSITY]

[PUZZLES ABOUT POSSIBILITY AND NEGATION]

12

21a34   Now that we have determined these points, we should consider the
35   relation between negations and affirmations of *possible to be*[36] and *not possible to be*, and of *admitting of being* and *not admitting of being*, and about

33. **for the same . . . contradictories**: It is possible for p (e.g., it will rain here tomorrow) to be true and possible for not-p (e.g., it will not rain here tomorrow) to be true, though it is not possible for both to be true (of the same place on the same day).

34. **For in these cases . . . qualification>**: There are again two possible interpretations: (1) This is a third explanation of the fallacy. In the statement involving contradictories (p or not-p), it is necessary that one of p and not-p be true, the other false. But it does not follow that whichever of them is true is necessarily true, or that whichever of them is false is necessarily false. This third case differs from the second, in that it applies to statements whereas the second applies to states of affairs. (2) Aristotle claims that from '(p or not-p) is true' we cannot infer 'either (p is true) or (not-p is true)'. If this is our view, we will translate the last two sentences as follows: 'It is not, however, <necessary> for this or that one <to be true or false>, but rather as chance has it; or one rather than the other is true, but is not already true or false'.

35. **For what holds . . . and of not being**: Alternatively (see previous note) '<already>' might be supplied in place of '<always>'.

36. *possible to be*: Aristotle has no unambiguous device that corresponds to our inverted commas to indicate that he is talking about a sentence or phrase rather

22

what is impossible and what is necessary. For these questions raise some puzzles.

For suppose that complexes are contradictories if they are ordered in accordance with being and not being. For instance, the negation of *being* 21b *a man* is *not being a man* rather than *being a not-man*, and the negation of *being a pale man* is *not being a pale man*, rather than *being a not-pale man*. For <otherwise> if either the affirmation or the negation <of a given predicate> is true of everything, then it will be true to say that a log is 5 a not-pale man.[37] If this is true, then it follows that in cases where *being* is not added, what is said instead of *being* will have the same effect. For instance, the negation of 'a man walks' is not 'a not-man walks', but 'a man does not walk';[38] for there is no difference between saying that a man walks and saying that a man is walking.[39] 10

And so, if this is true in every case,[40] then it also follows that the negation of *possible to be* is *possible not to be*, rather than *not possible to be*. On the other hand, it seems that whatever is possible to be is also possible not to be; for whatever can be cut up or can walk can also not walk and not be cut up.[41] The reason for this is that whatever can do these things does not always actually do them, so that the negation will 15

<hr />

than what it signifies (a substance or a state of affairs). We have been sparing of inverted commas, and have used italics to reflect Aristotle's ambiguity. Cf. *Met.* 1006a31n. On possibility see POTENTIALITY #1. It is not always clear in chs. 12–13 when Aristotle is speaking of possibility (a property of statements or of states of affairs) and when he is speaking of potentiality (a property of substances).

37. **a log is a not-pale man**: We will find that instead of simply denying that a log is a pale man, we are affirming that it is a kind of man, a nonpale man. Aristotle insists that the negation cannot apply just to 'pale'.

38. **'a man does not walk'**: The order of the Greek words is 'not walks man', in which the 'not' might be taken to negate either 'man walks' ('it is not the case that a man walks') or just the verb ('it is true of a man that he does not walk').

39. **is walking**: See *Met.* 1017a27.

40. **if this is true in every case**: sc. that the negation does not attach simply to the subject term (as in 'a not-man walks'). Aristotle suggests that 'possible not to be' should negate 'possible to be' in the way 'man does not walk' negates 'man walks'. At the end of the paragraph he raises an objection to this suggestion.

41. **for whatever . . . not be cut up**: Aristotle takes 'x can walk' to be equivalent to 'it is possible that x walks'. Here he introduces 'two-sided possibility', i.e. contingency (implying that what is necessary is not possible). See POTENTIALITY #2.

also belong to it; for what can walk can also not walk, and what can be seen can also not be seen. But it is impossible for opposite assertions to be true of the same subject. Hence this <—*possible not to be*—> is not
20   the negation <of *possible to be*>. For it follows from what we have said that either the same thing is both said and negated of the same subject at the same time, or affirmation and negation do not result from the addition of *being* and *not being*.

[SOLUTION TO THE PUZZLES]

If, then, the first alternative is impossible, the second is to be chosen; hence the negation of *possible to be* is *not possible to be*. The same argument
25   also applies to *admitting of being*; for the negation of this is *not admitting of being*. And this is also true in the same way in the other cases—for instance, *necessary* and *impossible*. In the previous cases *being* and *not being* were additions, and the subjects were pale and man, whereas in
30   this case being counts as a subject, while *possible* and *admitting of being* are additions that determine possibility and impossibility in the case of being, just as in the previous cases *being* or *not being* determined truth.[42]
35   The negation of *possible not to be* is *not possible not to be*. That is why the <statements> 'it is possible to be' and 'it is possible not to be' might actually seem to follow from each other. For whatever can be can also not be; for these statements[43] do not contradict each other. But *possible*
22a   *to be* and *not possible to be* never hold at the same time, since they are opposites. Likewise, *possible not to be* and *not possible not to be* never hold at the same time. In the same way, the negation of *necessary to be* is not
5   *necessary not to be*, but *not necessary to be*; and the negation of *necessary not to be* is *not necessary not to be*. Again, the negation of *impossible to be* is not *impossible not to be*, but *not impossible to be*; and the negation of *impossible not to be* is *not impossible not to be*. And in general, as we have
10   said, one must count being and not being as the subjects, and attach these <qualifications>[44] to being and not being to produce affirmation and negation. And one must suppose the opposite expressions to be these: *possible* and *not possible*, *admitting* and *not admitting*, *impossible* and *not impossible*, *necessary* and *not necessary*, *true* and *not true*.

42. **determines truth**: i.e., truth or falsity. 'Is pale' or 'is not pale' attached to 'the man' results in a true or false statement.

43. **these statements**: sc. 'x can be (= it is possible for x to be)' and 'x can not-be (= it is possible for x not to be)'.

44. **these <qualifications>**: sc. 'possible' etc.

[THE RELATIONS BETWEEN THE MODALITIES]

13

On this basis one thing follows from another in a reasonable way. *Admit-*   15
ting of being follows from *possible to be*, and the latter follows reciprocally
from the former. Moreover, both *not impossible to be* and *not necessary to
be* follow from *possible to be*.[45] Both *not necessary not to be* and *not impossible
not to be* follow from *possible not to be* and *admitting of not being. Necessary*   20
not to be and *impossible to be* follow from *not possible to be* and *not admitting
of being. Necessary to be* and *impossible not to be* follow from *not possible not
to be* and from *not admitting of not being.* What we are saying may be
studied in the following table:

A	B	
1. possible to be	not possible to be	25
2. admitting of being	not admitting of being	
3. not impossible to be	impossible to be	
4. not necessary to be	necessary not to be	
C	D	
1. possible not to be	not possible not to be	
2. admitting of not being	not admitting of not being	30
3. not impossible not to be	impossible not to be	
4. not necessary not to be	necessary to be	

Impossible and *not impossible* follow from *admitting* and *possible*, and
from *not admitting* and *not possible*, contradictorily, but conversely. For
the negation of *impossible* follows from *possible to be*, and the affirmation   35
from the negation, i.e., *impossible to be* from *not possible to be*—for *impossible
to be* is an affirmation, whereas *not impossible* is a negation.

But we must see what is true in the case of *necessary*. It is evident,
then, that the same does not apply here, but rather the contraries follow,
whereas the contradictories are separated. For *not necessary to be* is not   22b
the negation of *necessary not to be*, since both of these admit of being true
of the same thing—for what is necessary not to be is not necessary to
be.[46]

But perhaps this arrangement of the negations of *necessary* is impossi-   10[47]

45. **Moreover . . . possible to be**: This still refers to two-sided possibility.

46. **For *not* . . . not necessary to be**: If the table were correct, then A4 and B4
would be contradictory. Since they are not in fact contradictory, the table needs
amendment, and Aristotle sets out to amend it.

47. 22b3–10 have been transposed to follow 22b28.

ble; for what is necessary to be is also possible to be. Otherwise the negation will follow, since it is necessary either to affirm or deny it,[48] so that if it is not possible to be, it is impossible to be; but then what is necessary to be will turn out to be impossible to be, which is absurd.

15 And yet, *not impossible to be* follows from *possible to be*, and *not necessary to be* follows from *not impossible to be*,[49] so that what is necessary to be turns out to be not necessary to be, which is absurd. And yet, neither *necessary to be* nor *necessary not to be* follows from *possible to be*; for in this case <—*possible to be*—>, both <being and not being> admit of

20 happening, whereas, whenever one <of *necessary* and *not necessary*> is true, <the conjunction of> those others <—*possible to be* and *possible not to be*—> will no longer be true. For something is possible to be and not to be at the same time, but if it is necessary for it to be or not to be, it will not be possible to be both.[50]

The remaining option, then, is that *not necessary not to be* follows from *possible to be*;[51] for *not necessary not to be* is also true of what is necessary to be. For this also turns out to be the contradictory to

25 what follows from *not possible to be*; for *impossible to be* and *necessary not to be* follow from *not possible to be*, and the negation of *necessary not to be* is *not necessary not to be*. These contradictories, then, also follow in the way described, and nothing impossible results if they are arranged this way.[52]

b3 The reason these do not follow in the same way as the others is that
5 *impossible* has the same force as *necessary*, when it is applied in the contrary way. For if something is impossible to be, then it is necessary— not necessary to be, but necessary not to be; and if something is impossible not to be, then it is necessary to be. And so if those follow from *possible* and *not possible* in the same way, then these follow in a contrary way, since *necessary* and *impossible* signify the same, except that, as we
10 said, they are applied conversely.

48. **since it is . . . deny it**: Aristotle appeals to the Principle of Excluded Middle (see *Met.* iv 7). Here he is discussing one-sided possibility, according to which the necessary is a subset of the possible, so that the possible includes everything that is not impossible.

49. *not necessary . . . impossible to be*: Here two-sided possibility is assumed.

50. **For something . . . be both**: If p is necessary, p is not possible (in the two-sided sense).

51. **The remaining . . . *possible to be***: We should set up the table so as to represent one-sided possibility and its relation to necessity.

52. **These . . . this way**: Aristotle suggests that C4 ('not necessary not to be') and A4 ('not necessary to be') should be exchanged; then B4 will turn out to be contradictory, as it should be, to A4.

[FURTHER QUESTIONS ABOUT POSSIBILITY AND POTENTIALITY]

One might be puzzled about whether *possible to be* follows from *necessary*   b29
to be. For if it does not follow, then its contradictory—*not possible to be*—
will follow; and if one says that this is not the contradictory, then one
must say that *possible not to be* is the contradictory; and both of these are
false of what is necessary to be. And yet, on the other hand, it seems
that whatever can be cut up can also not be cut up, and that whatever
can be can also not be,[53] so that what is necessary to be will turn out to   35
admit of not being, which is false.

It is evident, then, that not everything that can be or can walk can
also be the opposite, and that there are cases in which this <presence
of both opposites> is not true. This is true first of all in the case of things
with nonrational potentialities;[54] fire, for instance, has the potentiality to
heat, and has a nonrational potentiality. Now in the case of potentialities   23a
involving reason, the same potentiality is for more than one thing, and
indeed for contraries.[55] This is not true, however, in the case of all
nonrational potentialities, but, as we said, fire cannot both heat and not
heat. Nor is it true in the case of things that are always in actuality;[56]
but some things, even insofar as they have nonrational potentialities,
are at the same time capable of producing opposites. Our remark, how-   5
ever, was meant to make it clear that not every potentiality—not even
among potentialities of the same kind—is for opposites.

Now some potentialities are homonymous, since things are said to
be potentially something in more than one way. In one case <x is said
to have a potentiality for F> because it is true <that x is F>, in that it
is actually <F>; for instance, something is said to have a potentiality
for walking because it is walking, and in general something is said to
have a potentiality because it is already actualizing the potentiality it is   10
said to have. In another case <x is said to have a potentiality for F>
because it might actualize <the potentiality>; for instance, something
is said to have a potentiality for walking because it might walk. This
second sort of potentiality applies only to things that can be moved; the
first sort also applies to immovable things. In both cases it is true to say,
both of what is now walking and in actuality and of what might walk,   15
that <if it has the potentiality to walk or be>, it is not impossible for it
to walk or be. It is not true, then, to ascribe the second sort of potentiality

53. **cut up**: e.g., the cloak in the example of 19a12. Aristotle returns to the
puzzles that result from failure to distinguish one-sided from two-sided possibility.

54. **potentialities**: This renders *dunaton*, previously rendered by 'can'.

55. **Now in . . . contraries**: See POTENTIALITY #5.

56. **always in actuality**: i.e., necessarily actualized.

to what is necessary without qualification, but it is true to ascribe the first sort to it.

And so, since the universal follows from the partial,[57] *possible to be*—though not every sort—follows from *necessary to be*. And presumably in fact what is necessary and what is not necessary are the principles of everything's being or not being, and the other cases should be considered as following from these.

20

It is evident from what has been said, then, that what is necessarily also is in actuality, so that if everlasting things are prior, actuality is also prior to potentiality.[58] Moreover, some things—the primary substances[59]—are actualities without potentiality, while other things have potentiality; these latter are prior in nature <to the potentiality> but posterior in time.[60] Other things are never actualities but are merely potentialities.[61]

---

57. **from the partial**: The generic (e.g., animal) follows from the specific (e.g., horse).

58. **It is evident . . . to potentiality**: This paragraph summarizes some of the points in *Met*. ix 8, xii 6–7.

59. **primary substances**: These are not the individual men and horses (e.g.) that are called primary substances at *Catg*. 2a11. Aristotle discusses the everlasting primary substances in *Met*. xii 7–8.

60. **prior in nature**: The adult organism, e.g., is prior in nature to the embryo and child (by being their goal), but (in the individual case) posterior in time.

61. **Other things . . . potentialities**: See INFINITE #1.

PRIOR ANALYTICS[1]

[*DEDUCTIVE LOGIC*]

BOOK I

[*THE MAIN FEATURES OF A DEDUCTION*]

1

First we must say what the area of our inquiry is, and what we are *24a10*
inquiring into <within that area>. The area is demonstration,* and we
are inquiring into demonstrative knowledge$_e$.[2] Next we must determine
what a premiss* is, what a term is, and what a deduction* is, and what
sort of deduction is complete and what sort is incomplete. After that we
must say what it is for one thing to be included in another as a part in
a whole,[3] and what is meant by 'predicated of all' or 'predicated of none'. *15*

A premiss, then, is a sentence affirming or denying something of
something.[4] This sentence is either universal or partial[5] or indeterminate.
By 'universal' I mean belonging to every or to none. By 'partial' I mean
belonging to some or not to some or not to every. By 'indeterminate' I *20*
mean belonging or not belonging without being universal or partial (e.g.,
'knowledge of contraries is the same' or 'pleasure is not a good'[6]).

---

1. Aristotle refers to the *APr* and *APo* without distinction as the 'Analytics'
(e.g., *Met*. 1005b2, 1037b8). See LOGIC.

2. **The area . . . knowledge**: This general statement of the subject matter shows
that Aristotle thinks of the *Prior* and *Posterior Analytics* as constituting a single
inquiry. In fact he does not discuss DEMONSTRATION until the *APo*. The *APr* is
devoted to the preliminary task of analyzing deduction (since a demonstration
is a kind of deduction, 25b30).

3. **included . . . whole**: 'A part' is supplied in this formula here and afterwards.

4. **a sentence . . . of something**: On sentence (*logos*; see REASON #2) and affirmation see *DI* 16b26.

5. **partial**: *en merei*. Many translators use 'particular', but Aristotle's explanation
shows that he has in mind more than we would normally think of as particular
(i.e. singular) propositions. See PARTICULAR #2.

6. **'knowledge . . . good'**: These sentences are indeterminate because they do
not explicitly say whether they refer to all or some knowledge or pleasure.

A demonstrative premiss differs from a dialectical premiss, in that a demonstrative premiss takes one or the other side of a contradiction. For in demonstrating we do not ask <whether a premiss is true>, but

25 we take it as true; a dialectical premiss, by contrast, asks <the respondent to choose between the two sides of> a contradiction. This difference, however, does not affect the fact that both <sorts of premiss> yield a deduction; for both in demonstrating and in asking <dialectical> questions one deduces <a conclusion> by taking something to belong or not to belong to something. And so a premiss of a deduction, taken without qualification,[7] is the affirming or denying of some <attribute>

30 of some <subject> in the way described. It is a demonstrative premiss

24b11 if it is true and is reached through the original assumptions.[8] It is dialectical if (in the case of the questioner) it asks <the respondent to choose between the two sides of> a contradiction or (in the case of the one performing a deduction) it takes what appears <true> and is commonly believed, as was said in the *Topics*.[9]

What a premiss is, then, and what the difference is between a deductive, a demonstrative, and a dialectical premiss, will be stated exactly

15 in what follows. For present purposes let us take it to be adequately determined now.

By 'term'[10] I mean what a premiss is divided into—for instance, what is predicated and what it is predicated of, with being or not being added.[11] A deduction is an argument[12] in which, if p and q are assumed, then

20 something else r, different from p and q, follows necessarily by the truth of p and q.[13] By 'by the truth of p and q', I mean that r follows because of p and q, and in saying that r follows because of p and

---

7. **taken without qualification**: with reference to deduction in general, as opposed to a particular sort of deduction (demonstrative or dialectical).

8. **original assumptions**: The original (*ex archēs*) assumptions are those that constitute the origins or PRINCIPLES (*archai*) of the relevant science.

9. **Topics**: See 100a25–30.

10. **'term'**: See FORMULA #1.

11. **added**: i.e., added to the term to make up the whole premiss.

12. **argument**: Or perhaps more generally, 'discourse', *logos*. See REASON #2–3.

13. **if p and q . . . of p and q**: Lit., 'when some things have been laid down, something other than the things laid down comes about by necessity, by these things being.' Note: (1) The use of schematic letters for sentences, as here, is not Aristotelian—though he often uses them for terms. (2) Aristotle implies that more than one premiss is needed, but does not say how many are needed. (3) He often places 'by necessity' in such a way that it might apply either to the conclusion alone or to the whole deduction; see NECESSITY, #7. Here he refers to the necessity of the whole deduction.

q I mean that no term outside[14] <p and q> is needed for r to follow necessarily.

By 'complete'* deduction I mean one that needs nothing else added apart from p and q in order to make it evident that r follows necessarily from p and q.[15] By 'incomplete' I mean one that needs the addition of one   *25* or more things that are necessary through the terms already assumed, but that have not been taken <as true> through premisses.[16]

A's being included in B as a part in a whole is the same as B's being predicated of every A.[17] We say that B is predicated of every A whenever it is impossible to take any A of which B is not said;[18] and the same   *30* applies to B's being predicated of no A.

* * * * * * *

[CONDITIONS FOR A DEDUCTION]

4

Now that these points have been determined, let us say through what,   *25b26* when, and how every deduction comes about; later we will discuss demonstration. We should discuss deduction before demonstration be- cause deduction is more universal; every demonstration is a type of   *30* deduction, but not every deduction is a demonstration.

When three terms are so related to each other that the last is included in the middle as a part in a whole and the middle is either included or not included in the first as a part in a whole, then necessarily the extreme   *35* terms are related by a complete deduction.[19] (By 'middle term' I mean that it is included in another and a third is included in it, and that it

---

14. **no term outside**: i.e., no terms constituting a further premiss that does not follow from p and q.

15. **apart from p and q ... from p and q**: Lit. 'besides the things taken, to make evident the necessary'.

16. **By 'incomplete' ... through premisses**: In an incomplete, no less than in a complete, deduction r follows necessarily from p and q. But in an incomplete deduction we have not made it evident that r follows necessarily. To make this evident, we must add some further premiss s that follows from p and q (and so is not 'outside' p and q in the sense (mentioned in 24a21) that would prevent r from following from p and q), but has not been stated as an explicit premiss.

17. **A's being ... every A**: Hence, e.g., man is included in animal if and only if animal is predicated of every man (i.e., every man is an animal).

18. **not said**: Here, in contrast to *Catg.* 2a19–34, Aristotle treats 'said of' and 'predicated of' as equivalent.

19. **When three ... deduction**: On the definitions given here see DEDUCTION #2.

occurs in the middle position. By 'extremes' I mean both the term which is included in <the middle term> and the term in which <the middle term> is included.) For if A is predicated of every B, and B of every C, then necessarily A is predicated of every C (for we have already said what
40 we mean by 'predicated of every'). In the same way, if A is predicated of
26a no B, and B of every C, then A will belong to no C.

If, however, the first term follows every instance of the middle term, but the middle term belongs to no instance[20] of the last term, there will be no deduction relating the extreme terms; for nothing necessarily
5   follows by these things being true. For in such a case it is possible for the first term to belong either to every instance or to no instance of the last term, so that neither a partial nor a universal <conclusion> turns out to be necessary; and if nothing is necessary through these things, then there will be no deduction. Let the terms in the example of belonging to every instance be animal—man—horse, and let those in the example of belonging to no instance be animal—man—stone.[21]
10   Further, if the first term belongs to no instance of the middle, and the middle belongs to no instance of the last, there is no deduction in this case either. As terms in an example of belonging let us take science—line—medicine, and as terms in an example of not belonging let us take science—line—unit.[22]

If, then, the terms <belong> universally, it is clear in this figure[23] in which cases there will be a deduction and in which cases there will not;
15   and it is clear that, if there is a deduction, the terms must be related in the way we have described and that, if they are related in these ways, there will be a deduction.

Now suppose that one of the terms belongs universally, and another partially, to another term. Whenever the term belonging universally is applied to the major extreme term, either affirmatively[24] or privatively,

20. **every instance . . . no instance**: Lit. 'all the middle . . . no last'.

21. **Let the terms . . . stone**: Aristotle has in mind these examples:
   (1) Animal belongs to every man; man belongs to no horse; animal belongs to every horse. (2) Animal belongs to every man; man belongs to no stone; animal belongs to no stone.

22. **As terms . . . unit**: (1) Science belongs to no line; line belongs to no medicine; science belongs to all medicine. (2) Science belongs to no line; line belongs to no unit; science belongs to no unit.

23. **figure**: Or 'shape', or 'structure', *schēma*. Aristotle recognizes three 'figures of deduction', which are three different ways in which the middle term can appear as subject term and as predicate term so as to yield a deduction.

24. **affirmatively**: *katēgorikōs*, derived from *katēgorein*, usually translated 'to predicate'.

and the term partially belonging is applied to the minor extreme term
affirmatively, then there must be a complete deduction. But if the term   20
belonging universally is applied to the minor term, or the terms are
related in some other way, there cannot be any deduction. (By 'major
extreme term' I mean the term in which the middle term is included,
and by 'minor term' the <extreme> term included in the middle term.)
For instance, let A belong to every B, and B to some C. If 'being predicated
of every B' is understood in the way described at the beginning, then
necessarily A belongs to some C. And if A belongs to no B, but B belongs   25
to some C, then necessarily A does not belong to some C[25] (for we have
also determined what is meant by 'being predicated of no B'); and so
there will be a complete deduction. The same applies if 'B belongs to C'
is indeterminate, as long as it is affirmative; for the same deduction will   30
result whether this premiss is taken to apply partially or indeterminately.

　If the term belonging universally is applied either affirmatively or
privatively to the minor extreme term, then there will be no deduction,
whether the indeterminate or partial term is affirmative or negative.
Suppose, for instance, that A belongs or does not belong to some B, and
B belongs to every C. Let the terms, in an example of belonging, be good—   35
state—wisdom, and, in a case of not belonging, good—state—stupidity.
Again, suppose that B belongs to no C, and A either belongs or does not
belong to some B or does not belong to every B; there will be no deduction
in this case either. Let the terms <in an example of belonging> be white—
horse—swan, and <in an example of not belonging> white—horse—
raven. The same is true if 'A belongs to B' is indeterminate.

　Again, suppose that one term is applied universally, either affirma-   26b
tively or privatively, to the major extreme term, and that one is applied
privatively and partially to the minor term; there will be no deduction.
Suppose, for instance, that A belongs to every B, and B does not belong
to some C, or does not belong to every C.[26] For if the middle term does   5
not belong to some C, then <it is possible that> the first term <A>
follows all or none <of the Cs that B does not belong to>. For assume
that the terms are animal—man—white; then among the white things
of which man is not predicated take swan and snow; clearly animal is
predicated of every swan and of no snow, so that there will be no   10
deduction. Again, let A belong to no B, and let B not belong to some
C; and let the terms be inanimate—man—white; then take, among the
white things of which man is not predicated, swan and snow; for inanimate is predicated of all snow and of no swan.

25. **A does not belong to some C**: Lit. 'A not-belongs to some C', i.e. there is
some C that A does not belong to.

26. **does not belong to every C**: This must mean 'belongs to no C'.

15   Further, the statement that B does not belong to some C is indeterminate; that is, it is true if either B belongs to no C or B does not belong
to every C (because <in that case> it does not belong to some C). If
terms are taken so that B belongs to no C, then no deduction results (as
we have said before). It is evident, then, that if the terms are related in
the way we have just described, there will be no deduction; for if there
20   were one, there would have been one in the other cases also. And the
same proof will apply if the universal term is applied privatively.
       If both the relations[27] are partial (either affirmative or privative), or
if one is affirmative and one privative, or one indeterminate and one
determinate, or both are indeterminate, there will be no deduction in
25   any of these cases either. As terms common to all these cases take
animal—white—horse, and animal—white—stone.
       It is evident, then, from what has been said that if a deduction in this
figure is partial, the terms must be related in the way we have described;
for if they are related in any other way, a deduction does not result in
any of the cases. It is also clear that all the deductions in this figure are
complete, since they are all completed through the things originally
accepted, and that all problems[28] are proved through this figure; for
belonging to every, to no, to some, and not to some <are all proved
this way>. And this is the figure I call the first figure.

* * * * * * *

[THE DISCOVERY OF SUITABLE PREMISES]

30

46a3   The road <to discovery> is the same in every case, for philosophy* and
for every type of craft or <branch of> instruction. For we must survey
5   the attributes and the subjects they belong to for both terms,[29] and be
as well supplied with these as possible; and we must examine them
through the three terms, in one way for destructive argument and in
another way for constructive argument. If we argue in accordance with
the truth, we must argue from the catalogue of attributes that truly belong
10   to a subject; for dialectical deduction we must argue from premises in
accordance with belief.[30]
       We have described the principles of deductions in general terms,

27. **relations**: Lit. 'intervals', i.e., the space between the two terms in a premiss.

28. **problems**: See Top. 101b26–36.

29. **both terms**: These are the subject term and predicate term that we want to
connect in a deduction.

30. **belief**: On COMMON BELIEFS, endoxa, in dialectic see Top. 100a25–30.

saying what they are like and how we should hunt for them. We have
said this so that we do not look <indiscriminately> at everything said
about something, and so that we do not look at the same things both
in constructive and in destructive argument, or at the same things both
in constructive argument about all or some cases and in destructive
argument about all or some cases. We should look instead at a smaller   15
and determinate set of attributes, and select the ones appropriate for
each type of thing—e.g. about goodness or about knowledge.

   Most of the principles in each science are distinctive of it, and hence
it is the task of experience* to supply the principles for each area. For
instance, it is the task of astronomical experience to supply the principles
of astronomical science—for when the appearances had been adequately   20
grasped, that was how astronomical demonstrations were found; and
the same is true for every other craft or science. And so, if the attributes
in a given area have been grasped, our next task is to display the demonstrations without undue difficulty. For if our inquiry* leaves out none   25
of the attributes that really belong to the given subjects, we will be
able to find a demonstration for everything that admits of one, and
to formulate the demonstration; and if something does not admit of
demonstration,[31] we will be able to make this evident.

   We have now more or less described in general terms how premises
ought to be selected; we have provided an exact[32] discussion in our work   30
on dialectic.[33]

                    *   *   *   *   *   *   *

Book II

[INDUCTION]

23

. . . We should now point out that the figures <of deduction> that we   68b9
have mentioned are to be used not only for dialectical and demonstrative   10
deduction, but also for rhetorical deduction,[1] and indeed, speaking without qualification, for any convincing argument in any line* of inquiry.
For in every case conviction is reached either through deduction or
through induction.

31. **if something . . . demonstration**: Lit. 'that of which there is not by nature
demonstration'.

32. **exact**: *akribes*, in contrast to 'general'. See EXACT #2.

33. **work on dialectic**: See *Top.* 101a33–b4.

   1. **rhetorical deduction**: Aristotle adapts his theory of deduction in this way
in the *Rhet.*; see 1355a4–14.

15   Induction*—that is to say,[2] deduction arising from induction—is de-
ducing <a connection between> one extreme term and the middle term
through the other extreme term. If, for instance, B is the middle term
between A and C, then the deduction is the proof through C that A
belongs to B; for that is how we carry out inductions. For instance, let
20   A be having a long life, B having no bile, C a particular <kind of> thing
having a long life, e.g., man, horse, and mule. Now A belongs to C as
a whole (since every C has a long life); but B (having no bile) also belongs
to every C. If, then, C reciprocates with B, and the middle term <B>
does not extend beyond <A>, then it is necessary for A to belong to
25   B. For it has been proved previously that if two things belong to the
same thing, and the extreme term reciprocates with one of them, then
the other one of the things predicated will also belong to the one that
reciprocates. And we must understand[3] C as composed of all the particu-
30   lars; for induction is through all <the particulars>.[4]
    This sort of deduction reaches the first and immediate premisses;[5] for
in cases where there is a middle term, the deduction proceeds through
the middle term, but in cases where there is no middle term, the deduction proceeds through induction. And in a way induction is opposite to
deduction; for deduction proves through the middle term that the extreme term belongs to the third term, whereas induction proves through
35   the third term that the extreme term belongs to the middle term. By
nature the deduction through the middle term is prior and better known_g,
but to us the deduction through induction is more obvious.[6]

2. **that is to say**: Lit. just 'and'. In any case the remark is a bit misleading. In
this passage Aristotle is describing a type of deduction that uses the results of
induction; he is not describing a procedure of induction itself.

3. **understand**: See UNDERSTANDING #3.

4. **for induction . . . particulars>**: Aristotle might, but need not, be taken to
say that induction requires us to have surveyed all the instances of a given kind;
but he probably does not intend such an extreme claim. He probably means
that in order to draw a universal conclusion we must generalize from observed
instances of a kind to all the instances of the kind.

5. **premisses**: of a demonstration.

6. **more obvious**: See KNOW #2.

POSTERIOR ANALYTICS[1]

Book I

[KNOWING AND LEARNING]

[LEARNING REQUIRES PREVIOUS KNOWLEDGE]

1

All teaching and all intellectual learning result from previous knowl-
edge$_g$. This is clear if we examine all the cases; for this is how the
mathematical sciences and all crafts[2] arise. This is also true of both deductive and inductive arguments, since they both succeed in teaching because they rely on what is previously known: deductive arguments begin
with premisses we are assumed to comprehend, and inductive arguments prove the universal by relying on the fact that the particular is
already clear. Rhetorical arguments also persuade in the same way, since
they rely either on examples (and hence on induction) or on argumentations* (and hence on deduction).

Previous knowledge is needed in two ways. In some cases we must
presuppose that something is[3] (for example, that it is true that everything
is either asserted or denied truly <of a given subject>).[4] In other cases
we must comprehend what the thing spoken of is (for example, that a

71a

5

10

15

---

1. This work uses Aristotle's account of DEDUCTION (set out in the *Prior Analytics*)
to develop an account of the particular sort of deduction that constitutes a
DEMONSTRATION. Aristotle argues that genuine scientific knowledge must be
displayed in the demonstrative structure of a science. (The demonstrative structure is appropriate for scientific knowledge once it is acquired; Aristotle is not
suggesting that this is the proper method for scientific discovery, which relies
on EXPERIENCE and INDUCTION.)

2. **all crafts**: Lit. 'each of the other crafts', which probably means (in accordance
with Greek idiom) 'each of the crafts as well <as the sciences>'.

3. **that something is**: Lit. 'that (subject unexpressed) is', *hoti estin*. We render
this by 'that it is true' in 71a14 and by 'that there is such a thing' in 71a16. Cf.
93b33, *Phys.* 193a3, 217b31.

4. **that everything . . .:** The Principle of Excluded Middle must be taken for
granted. Cf. *Met.* 1005b2–5, iv 7.

triangle signifies* this); and in other cases we must do both (for example, we must both comprehend what a unit signifies and presuppose that there is such a thing). For something different is needed to make each of these things clear to us.[5]

We may also come to know that q by having previously known that p and acquiring knowledge of q at the same time <as we acquire knowledge of r>. This is how, for instance, we acquire knowledge of the cases that fall under the universal of which we possess knowledge; for we
20   previously knew$_o$ that, say, every triangle has angles equal to two right angles, but we come to know$_g$ that this figure in the semicircle is a triangle at the same time as we perform the induction <showing that this figure has two right angles>. For in some cases we learn in this way (rather than coming to know the last term through the middle);[6] this is true when we reach particulars, i.e., things not said of any subject.[7]

[DIFFERENT WAYS OF KNOWING AND NOT KNOWING [8]]

25   Before we perform the induction or the deduction, we should presumably be said to know$_e$ in one way but not in another. For if we did not know$_o$ without qualification whether <a given triangle> is, how could we know without qualification that it has two right angles? But clearly we know$_e$ it insofar as we know it universally,[9] but we do not know it without qualification. Otherwise we will face the puzzle in the Meno,
30   since we will turn out to learn either nothing or else nothing but what we <already> know$_o$.[10]

---

5. **For something . . . to us**: Alternatively: 'For they are clear to us to different degrees' (lit. 'For not in the same way is each of these clear to us').

6. **the last . . . middle**: See APr 25b32n.

7. **not said . . . subject**: Though, in Aristotle's view, a figure's having two right angles is derived from its being a triangle, and not conversely, in a particular case we may come to know the derived fact before we know the fact it is derived from.

8. By distinguishing different ways of knowing and not knowing we make it easier to see how we can learn (= acquire new knowledge) from previous knowledge. In this section Aristotle uses epistasthai and eidenai with no apparent systematic distinction.

9. **know it universally**: We know the general principle under which (in fact) this triangle falls, without recognizing that it falls under that principle.

10. **Otherwise we . . . <already> know$_o$**: Plato presents the puzzle (Meno 80a–d) as follows: (1) For any item x, either one knows x or one does not know x. (2) If one knows x, one cannot inquire into x. (3) If one does not know x, one cannot inquire into x. (4) Therefore, whether one knows or does not know x, one cannot inquire into x. Aristotle here rejects (2); he probably also rejects (3).

For we should not agree with some people's attempted solution to this puzzle. Do you or do you not know that every pair is even? When you say you do, they produce a pair that you did not think existed and hence did not think was even. They solve this puzzle by saying that one does not know that every pair is even, but rather one knows that what one knows to be a pair is even. In fact, however, <contrary to this solution,> one   71b
knows that of which one has grasped and still possesses the demonstration, and the demonstration one has grasped is not about whatever one knows to be a triangle or a number, but about every number or triangle without qualification; for <in a demonstration> a premiss is not taken to say that what you know to be a triangle or rectangle is so and so, but, on the contrary, it is taken to apply to every case.

But, I think, it is quite possible for us to know$_e$ in one way what we are learning, while being ignorant of it in another way. For what is absurd is not that we <already> know$_o$ in some way the very thing we are learning; the absurdity arises only if we already know it to the precise extent and in the precise way in which we are learning it.

[KNOWLEDGE AND DEMONSTRATION]

[KNOWLEDGE INCLUDES NECESSITY AND EXPLANATION]

2

We think we know$_e$ a thing without qualification, and not in the sophistic,   10
coincidental way,[11] whenever we think we know$_g$[12] the explanation[13] because of which the thing is <so>, know that it is the explanation of that thing, and know that it does not admit of being otherwise.[14] Clearly,

---

11. **sophistic, coincidental way**: Cf. 74b23, 75a25–32. Someone may prove separately that all scalene triangles, all isosceles triangles, and all equilateral triangles have two right angles. The conclusion that all triangles have two right angles is a coincidental result of these three proofs; the proofs do not result in knowledge$_e$ that all triangles (i.e., all triangles insofar as they are triangles) have two right angles.

12. **we think we know$_g$**: Aristotle's definition of knowledge uses epistemic verbs both in the definiens and in the definiendum. Since he uses different verbs (*gignōskein* in the definiens, *epistasthai* in the definiendum), circularity may be avoided (though it is not clear what difference he intends between the two verbs; see KNOW #1). In 100b5–17 Aristotle grounds knowledge in UNDERSTANDING.

13. **explanation**: Or 'CAUSE', *aitia*. Aristotle is thinking not only of an explanatory statement, but also of the event or state of affairs that the statement refers to.

14. **does not . . . otherwise**: In restricting knowledge$_e$ to necessary truths, Aristotle might have made a modal mistake, taking (a) necessarily, if A knows that p, then p is true, to imply that (b) if A knows that p, then p is necessarily true.

then, knowing$_e$ is something of this sort; for both those who lack knowledge and those who have it think they are in this condition, but those
15 who have the knowledge are really in it. So whatever is known without qualification cannot be otherwise.

[HENCE IT INVOLVES DEMONSTRATION]

We shall say later whether there is also some other way of knowing$_e$;[15] but we certainly say that we know through demonstration. By 'demonstration' I mean a deduction expressing knowledge; by 'expressing knowledge' I mean that having the deduction constitutes having knowledge.
20   If, then, knowing is the sort of thing we assumed it is, demonstrative knowledge must also be derived from things that are true, primary, immediate, better known$_g$ than, prior to, and explanatory of the conclusion; for this will also ensure that the principles are proper to what is being proved. For these conditions are not necessary for a deduction, but they are necessary for a demonstration, since without them a deduc-
25 tion will not produce knowledge$_e$.
        <The conclusions> must be true, then, because we cannot know what is not <true> (for example, that the diagonal is commensurate). They must be derived from <premisses> that are primary and indemonstrable, because we will have no knowledge unless we have a demonstration of these <premisses>;[16] for to have noncoincidental knowledge of something demonstrable is to have a demonstration of it.
30   They must be explanatory, better known$_g$, and prior. They must be explanatory, because we know$_e$ something whenever we know$_o$ its explanation. They must be prior if they are indeed explanatory. And they

---

Normally, however (see NECESSITY #7), he seems clear about the difference between (a) and (b). More probably, he believes that only necessary truths can provide the requisite certainty to ground knowledge claims.

15. **other way of knowing**: Sometimes Aristotle refers to our nondemonstrative grasp of the premisses of a demonstration as a higher form of *epistēmē*, 72b19–25; but in 100b5–17 he confines *epistēmē* to demonstrated knowledge, claiming that the ultimate premisses of demonstration are grasped by understanding (*nous*), not by *epistēmē*.

16. **of these <premisses>**: Probably Aristotle means that if q is our primary (i.e., ultimate) premiss for deriving p, then q must be indemonstrable; for if q were demonstrable, we could not know p without first demonstrating q (for we cannot know p without knowing q, and if q were demonstrable, we could know q only by demonstrating q). Aristotle expands this argument about indemonstrability in i 3.

must be previously known$_g$ not only in the sense that we comprehend them, but also in the sense that we know$_o$ that they are <true>.[17] Things are prior and better known$_g$ in two ways; for what is prior by nature is not the same as what is prior to us, nor is what is better known <by 72a nature> the same as what is better known to us. By 'what is prior and better known to us' I mean what is closer to perception, and by 'what is prior and better known without qualification' I mean what is further from perception.[18] What is most universal is furthest from perception, and particulars are closest to it; particular and universal are opposite to   5 each other.

[THE ELEMENTS OF A DEMONSTRATION]

Derivation from primary things is derivation from proper principles. (I mean the same by 'primary things' as I mean by 'principles'.) A principle of demonstration is an immediate premiss,* and a premiss is immediate if no others are prior to it. A premiss is one or the other part of a contradiction,[19] and it says one thing of one thing. It is dialectical if it   10 takes either part indifferently, demonstrative if it determinately takes one part because it is true.[20] A contradiction is an opposition which, in itself, has nothing in the middle. The part of the contradiction that asserts something of something is an affirmation, and the part that denies something of something is a denial.

By 'thesis' I mean an immediate principle of deduction that cannot   15 be proved, but is not needed if one is to learn anything at all. By 'axiom'* I mean a principle one needs in order to learn anything at all; for there are some things of this sort, and we usually apply the name especially to these.

If a thesis asserts one or the other part of a contradiction—for example,   20 that something is or that something is not—it is an assumption; otherwise it is a definition. For a definition is a thesis (since the arithmetician, for example, lays it down that a unit is what is indivisible in quantity), but

17. **not only . . . <true>**: See 71a11–17.

18. **By . . . I mean . . .**: Lit. 'I call (*legō*) prior . . . the things that are closer . . .' Sometimes (as below) such expressions are used to explain terminology. But in this case Aristotle is saying what things satisfy the definition of 'prior and better known', not explaining the meaning of the phrase.

19. **contradiction**: Read *antiphaseōs*, and delete *apophanseōs . . . morion*, b11–12. 'Pleasure is good' and 'Pleasure is not good' (i.e., it is not the case that pleasure is good) are the two parts of a contradiction.

20. **dialectical . . . demonstrative**: See *Top.* 100a25–b23.

it is not an assumption (since what it is to be a unit and that a unit is are not the same).[21]

[THE PREMISSES OF A DEMONSTRATION]

25   Since our conviction* and knowledge$_o$ about a thing must be based on our having the sort of deduction we call a demonstration, and since we have this sort of deduction when its premisses obtain, not only must we have previous knowledge$_g$ about all or some of the primary things, but we must also know them better. For if x makes y F, x is more F than

30   y; if, for instance, we love y because of x, x is loved more than y.[22] Hence if the primary things produce knowledge$_o$ and conviction, we must have more knowledge and conviction about them, since they also produce it about subordinate things.

       Now if we know q, we cannot have greater conviction about p than about q unless we either know p or are in some condition better than

35   knowledge about p.[23] This will result,[24] however, unless previous knowledge <of the principles> is the basis of conviction produced by demonstration; for we must have greater conviction about all or some of the principles than about the conclusion.

       If we are to have knowledge$_e$ through demonstration, then not only must we know$_g$ the principles better and have greater conviction about

72b   them than about what is proved, but we must also not find anything more convincing or better known that is opposed to the principles and allows us to deduce a mistaken conclusion contrary <to the correct one>. For no one who has knowledge$_e$ without qualification can be persuaded out of it.[25]

21. **since what . . . not the same**: A definition 'The F is G' says that if anything is F it is G; it does not assert that some definite existing thing that is F is also G.

22. **For if x . . . loved than y**: More literally: 'For in every case, a given <attribute> belongs more to that because of which <the attribute> belongs <to something else>; for instance, that because of which we love <something else> is more loved.' Cf. *Met.* 993b23–31.

23. **Now if we know. . . than knowledge about p**: More literally: 'We cannot have greater conviction about things that we neither know nor are better disposed toward than if we knew, than <we have> about things we know.'

24. **This will result**: This is the impossible situation of knowing q, having greater conviction about p, but having neither knowledge nor something better than knowledge about p.

25. **cannot be persuaded out of it**: Aristotle claims that if we could derive p from q, but could also derive the contrary of p from the contrary of q, and we

3

Some people think that because <knowledge through demonstration>   5
requires knowledge$_e$ of the primary things, there is no knowledge; others
think that there is knowledge, and that everything <knowable> is demonstrable. Neither of these views is either true or necessary.

The first party—those who assume that there is no knowledge at all—
claim that we face an infinite regress.[26] They assume that we cannot
know$_e$ posterior things because of prior things, if there are no primary
things. Their assumption is correct, since it is impossible to go through
an infinite series. If, on the other hand, the regress stops, and there are
principles, these are, in their view, unknowable$_g$, since these principles
cannot be demonstrated, and, in these people's view, demonstration is
the only way of knowing$_e$. But if we cannot know$_o$ the primary things,
then neither can we know$_e$ without qualification or fully the things
derived from them; we can know them only conditionally,[27] on the   15
assumption that we can know the primary things.

The other party agree that knowledge results only from demonstration, but they claim that it is possible to demonstrate everything, since
they take circular and reciprocal demonstration to be possible.

We reply that not all knowledge$_e$ is demonstrative, and in fact
knowledge of the immediate premises is indemonstrable. Indeed, it   20
is evident that this must be so; for if we must know the prior things
(i.e., those from which the demonstration is derived), and if eventually
the regress stops, these immediate premises must be indemonstrable.
Besides this, we also say that there is not only knowledge$_e$ but
also some origin of knowledge$_e$, which gives us knowledge$_g$ of the
definitions.

---

found the contrary of q as convincing as we found q, we would not know that
p.

26. **infinite regress**: Aristotle considers the following argument: (1) If A knows
p, A has demonstrated p. (2) One cannot demonstrate an infinite number of
things. (3) Either there are, or are not, first principles. (4) If there are no first
principles, demonstration goes on to infinity. (5) Demonstration cannot go on
to infinity. (6) If there are first principles, they cannot be demonstrated or,
therefore, known. (7) Therefore, whether or not there are first principles, there
is no knowledge.

27. **without qualification . . . conditionally**: For a similar distinction see NECES-
SITY #4.

[*CIRCULAR DEMONSTRATION IS IMPOSSIBLE*]

25   Unqualified demonstration clearly cannot be circular, if it must be derived
from what is prior and better known$_g$. For the same things cannot be
both prior and posterior to the same things at the same time, except in
different ways (so that, for example, some things are prior relative to
us, and others are prior without qualification—this is the way induction
30   makes something known$_g$.)[28] If this is so,[29] our definition of unqualified
knowledge$_o$ will be faulty, and there will be two sorts of knowledge$_o$;
or <rather> perhaps the second sort of demonstration is not unqualified
demonstration, since it is derived from what is <merely> better known$_g$
to us.[30]

Those who allow circular demonstration must concede not only the
previous point, but also that they are simply saying that something is
35   if it is. On these terms it is easy to prove anything. This is clear if
we consider three terms—for it does not matter whether we say the
demonstration turns back through many or few terms, or through few or
two. For suppose that if A is, necessarily B is, and that if B is, necessarily C
is; it follows that if A is, C will be. Suppose, then, that if A is, then B
73a   necessarily is, and if B is, A is (since this is what circular argument is),
and let A be C. In that case, to say that if B is, A is is to say that <if B
is,> C is; this <is to say> that if A is, C is.[31] But since C is the same as
5   A, it follows that those who allow circular demonstration simply say
that if A is, then A is. On these terms it is easy to prove anything.

But not even this[32] is possible, except for things that are reciprocally
predicated, such as distinctive properties. If, then, one thing is laid
down, we have proved that it is never necessary for anything else to be

28. **induction makes something known$_g$.**): because it argues from what is prior
relative to us.

29. **If this is so . . . knowledge$_o$**: If our definition of unqualified knowledge
must take account of two ways something can be prior, then we have to recognize
two sorts of unqualified knowledge, corresponding to the two sorts of priority.
In the next clause ('or <rather> perhaps . . .') Aristotle rejects this suggestion;
the definition of knowledge refers only to natural priority, not to priority to us.

30. **<merely> better known$_g$ to us**: Since the conclusion is not derived from what
is better known without qualification, the deduction cannot be an unqualified
demonstration.

31. **and this . . . C is**: Aristotle leaves unexpressed the premiss 'If A is, then B
is'; presumably it is understood from the previous sentence.

32. **not even this**: i.e., reciprocal conditional demonstration ('F is if G is, and G
is if F is'). Aristotle replies that such biconditionals are possible only with DISTINC-
TIVE properties, as in 'If x is a human being, x is capable of learning grammar,
and vice versa'.

the case. (By 'one thing' I mean that neither one term nor one thesis is enough;[33] two theses are the fewest <needed for a demonstration>,   *10* since they are also the fewest needed for a deduction.) If, then, A follows from B and C, and these follow from each other and from A, then in this way it is possible to prove all the postulates from each other in the first figure,[34] as we proved in the discussion of deduction.[35] We also   *15* proved that in the other figures, the result is either no deduction or none relevant to the things assumed. But it is not at all possible to give a circular proof of things that are not reciprocally predicated. And so, since there are few things that are reciprocally predicated in demonstrations, it is clearly empty and impossible to say that demonstration is reciprocal and that for this reason everything is demonstrable.   *20*

4

Since what is known$_e$ without qualification cannot be otherwise, what is known by demonstrative knowledge will be necessary. Demonstrative knowledge is what we have by having a demonstration; hence a demonstration is a deduction from things that are necessary. We must, then,   *25* find from what and from what sorts of things demonstrations are derived. Let us first determine what we mean by '<belonging> in every case', 'in its own right', and 'universal'.

[BELONGING IN EVERY CASE]

By '<belonging> in every case' I mean what belongs not <merely> in some cases, or at some times, as opposed to others. If, for example, animal belongs to every man, it follows that if it is true to say that this   *30* is a man, it is also true to say that he is an animal, and that if he is a man now, he is also an animal now. The same applies if it is true to say that there is a point in every line.[36] A sign of this is the fact that when we are asked whether something belongs in every case, we advance objections by asking whether it fails to belong either in some cases or at some times.

33. **is enough**: i.e., to make it necessary for anything else to be true, and so to satisfy a necessary condition for a demonstration.

34. **first figure**: See *APr* 26a13n.

35. **as we proved . . . deduction**: *APr* ii 5–7.

36. **a point in every line**: Aristotle implies that this does not mean merely that there is a point in every line that exists now, as opposed to some other time; it means that every line, at whatever time it exists, contains a point.

[INTRINSIC PROPERTIES]

A belongs to B in its own right in the following cases:

35 (a) A belongs to B in what B is, as, for example, line belongs to triangle, and point to line; for here the essence$_0$ of B is composed of A, and A is present in the account that says what B is.

(b) A belongs to B, and B itself is present in the account revealing what A is. In this way straight and curved, for instance, belong to line, 40 while odd and even, prime and compound, equilateral and oblong, 73b belong in this way to number. In all these cases either line or number is present in the account saying what <straight or odd, for example,> is. Similarly in other cases, this is what I mean by saying that A belongs to B in its own right. What belongs in neither of these ways 5 I call coincidental—as, for instance, musical or pale belongs to animal.

(c) A is not said of something else B that is the subject of A. A walker or a pale thing,[37] for example, is a walker or a pale thing by being something else;[38] but a substance—i.e., whatever signifies[39] a this*—is not what it is by being something else. I say, then, that what is not said of a subject[40] is <a thing> in its own right, whereas what is said of a 10 subject is a coincident.

(d) Moreover, in another way, if A belongs to B because of B itself, then A belongs to B in its own right; if A belongs to B, but not because of B itself, then A is coincidental to B. If, for example, lightning flashed while you were walking, that was coincidental; for the lightning was not caused by your walking but, as we say, was a coincidence.[41] If, however, A belongs to B because of B itself, then it belongs to B in its own right. If, for example, an animal was killed

37. **A walker or a pale thing**: Lit. 'the walking', 'the pale' (neuter adjectives).

38. **by being something else**: i.e., by being (e.g.) a man. Cf. 83a4–14, *Met.* 1028a24–31.

39. **signifies**: Aristotle is probably not talking about a word signifying. See SIGNIFY #3.

40. **not said of a subject**: i.e., a substance. This phrase is used in *Catg.* 1a23, 1b3–9 to pick out primary substances as well as nonsubstance individuals. Here it seems to refer to primary and secondary substances (as they are conceived in the *Catg.*) in contrast to nonsubstances, and therefore seems to be contrasted with things that belong coincidentally to a subject (= things said of a subject). Hence in this passage 'substance', 'this', '<thing> in its own right', and 'what is not said of a subject' all seem to refer to the same thing.

41. **a coincidence**: This is a case of chance (see LUCK #1), discussed in *Phys.* ii 6.

in being sacrificed,[42] the killing belongs to the sacrificing in its own   15
right, since the animal was killed because it was sacrificed, and it was
not a coincidence that the animal was killed in being sacrificed.

Hence in the case of unqualified objects of knowledge$_e$, whenever A
is said to belong to B in its own right, either because B is present in A
and A is predicated of B, or because A is present in B,[43] then A belongs
to B because of B itself and necessarily. <It belongs necessarily> either
because it is impossible for A not to belong to B or because it is impossible
for neither A nor its opposite (for example, straight and crooked, or odd   20
and even) to belong to B (for example, a line or a number).[44] For a
contrary is either a privation or a contradiction in the same genus; even,
for example, is what is not odd among numbers, insofar as this follows.[45]
Hence, if it is necessary either to affirm or to deny, then what belongs
to a subject in its own right necessarily belongs to that subject.   25
    Let this, then, be our definition of what belongs in every case and of
what belongs to something in its own right.

[UNIVERSALITY]

By 'universal' I mean what belongs to its subject in every case and in
its own right, and insofar* as it is itself. It is evident, then, that what is
universal belongs to things necessarily.[46] What belongs to the subject in
its own right is the same as what belongs to it insofar as it is itself. A
point and straightness, for instance, belong to a line in its own right,   30
since they belong to a line insofar as it is a line. Similarly, two right
angles belong to a triangle insofar as it is a triangle, since a triangle is
equal in its own right to two right angles.
    A universal belongs <to a species> whenever it is proved of an
instance that is random and primary. Having two right angles, for in-

---

42. **sacrificed**: Or 'ritually slaughtered'. The standard Greek method of animal
sacrifice was to cut the victim's throat.

43. **either because . . . present in B**: These alternatives refer, respectively, to
cases (b) and (a) described above.

44. **<It belongs . . . or a number)**: These alternatives refer, respectively, to cases
(a) and (b) described above.

45. **this follows**: from not being odd. Odd and even exhaust the possibilities
for numbers.

46. **It is evident . . . necessarily**: Aristotle takes necessity to follow from the
conjunction of the three features mentioned (in every case, in its own right, as
such); it does not follow from any one of them on its own. As he defines
UNIVERSALS here, they exist necessarily; contrast *Catg.* 14a7–10.

35 stance, is not universal to figure; for though you may prove that some figure has two right angles, you cannot prove it of any random figure, nor do you use any random figure in proving it, since a quadrilateral is a figure but does not have angles equal to two right angles. Again, a random isosceles triangle has angles equal to two right angles, but it is not the primary case, since the triangle is prior. If, then, a random

40 triangle is the primary case that is proved to have two right angles, or whatever it is, then that property belongs universally to this case primar-

74a ily, and the demonstration holds universally of this case in its own right. It holds of the other cases in a way, but not in their own right; it does not even hold universally of the isosceles triangle, but more widely.

[WHEN DO WE HAVE GENUINELY UNIVERSAL KNOWLEDGE?]

5

5 We must not fail to notice that we often turn out to be mistaken and that what we are proving does not belong primarily and universally in the way we think we are proving it to belong. We are deceived in this way in these cases: (1) We cannot find any higher <kind> apart from a particular <less general kind>. (2) We can find <such a kind>, but it is nameless, applying to things that differ in species. (3) The <kind>

10 we are proving something about is in fact a partial whole; for the demonstration will apply to the particular instances <of the partial whole>,[47] but still it will not apply universally to this <kind> primarily. I say that a demonstration applies to a given <kind> primarily, insofar as it is this <kind>, whenever it applies universally to <this kind> primarily.[48]

If, then, one were to prove that right angles do not meet, one might

15 think that the demonstration applied to this case because it holds for all right angles. This is not so, however, since this <conclusion> results not because they are equal in this <specific> way <by both being right angles>, but insofar as they are equal at all.[49]

Again, if there were no triangles other than isosceles, then <what applies to triangles insofar as they are triangles> would seem to apply to isosceles triangles insofar as they are isosceles.

47. **particular . . . whole**>: Lit. 'to the partial things', presumably referring to, say, particular isosceles triangles.

48. **(1) We cannot find . . . universally to <this kind> primarily**: The three cases mentioned in this paragraph are illustrated in the next three paragraphs, in the order 3, 1, 2.

49. **This is not . . . at all**: Two lines perpendicular to a third line do not meet, but that is not because they are both perpendicular to it, but simply because their angles of intersection are equal.

Again, <it might seem> that proportion alternates[50] in numbers insofar as they are numbers, lines insofar as they are lines, solids insofar as
they are solids, and times insofar as they are times; indeed it once used
to be proved separately <for each of these cases>. In fact it can be   20
proved by a single demonstration; but because all of these (numbers,
lengths, times, solids) do not constitute one <kind> with a name, but
differ from each other in species, they used to be taken separately. Now
it is proved universally; for it does not belong to them insofar as they
are lines or numbers, but insofar as they are this other thing that is
assumed to belong universally.   25

That is why, even if for each <kind of> triangle you prove by one
or by more than one demonstration that it has two right angles, taking
equilateral, scalene, and isosceles triangles separately, you do not
thereby know$_0$ (except in the sophistical way)[51] that the triangle has
angles equal to two right angles—not even if there is no other <kind
of> triangle apart from these. For you do not know that it belongs to a   30
triangle insofar as it is a triangle, nor that it belongs to every triangle;
you know it for every triangle taken numerically, but not for every
triangle taken as a kind—even if there is no triangle for which you do
not know it.

When, then, do you not know universally, and when do you know
without qualification? Clearly, if being a triangle were the same as being
equilateral (for each or for all), <then you would know without qualifica-
tion>.[52] But if being a triangle is not the same as being equilateral, and   35
if <having two right angles> belongs to a triangle insofar as it is a
triangle, then you do not know.

Then does having two right angles belong to a triangle insofar as it
is a triangle, or to an isosceles triangle insofar as it is isosceles? When
does it belong to a triangle primarily in respect of its being a triangle?
To what does the demonstration apply universally? It is clear that it
applies universally to F whenever it applies to F primarily, after <other
things> have been abstracted. For instance, two right angles belong to
the bronze isosceles triangle, but they still belong when being bronze
and being isosceles have been abstracted. But they do not belong when   74b
figure or limit has been abstracted. Still, these are not the first <whose
abstraction makes the property cease to belong>. Then what is the first
<whose abstraction has this result>? If it is triangle, then it is in respect

50. **alternates**: If A is to B as C is to D, then A is to C as B is to D.

51. **sophistical way**: Cf. 71b9–10.

52. **know without qualification**>: You would know that triangles as such have
two right angles by having proved that equilateral triangles have two right
angles.

of being a triangle that having two right angles belongs to the other
things too, and the demonstration applies to this universally.

[DEMONSTRATION INVOLVES INTRINSIC AND NECESSARY PROPERTIES]

6

5   We have found that demonstrative knowledge$_e$ is derived from necessary
principles (since what is known cannot be otherwise) and that what
belongs to things in their own right is necessary (for in the one case it
belongs in the essence, and in the other case it belongs in the essence
of the things predicated of it, and one or the other of the opposites
10   necessarily belongs to it). Evidently, then, demonstrative deduction will
be derived from what belongs to something in its own right; for whatever
belongs to a subject belongs to it either in its own right or coincidentally,
and coincidents are not necessary. We must either say this or else lay
it down as a principle that demonstration is of what is necessary and
15   that what is demonstrated cannot be otherwise. It follows, then, that
this deduction must be derived from necessary premisses; for nondemonstrative deduction is possible from true premisses, but not from
necessary premisses, since deduction from necessary premisses is characteristic of demonstration.

The character of the objections that are raised against demonstrations
is evidence for our claim that demonstration is from necessary premisses;
20   for we object <to an alleged demonstration> by saying that <some part
of it> is not necessary, if we think that it is possible (either in general
or for the sake of argument) for it to be otherwise. This also shows how
silly it is to think that, if the premiss is commonly believed and true,
we have the right grasp of the principles (as the sophists think, since
they assume that to know$_e$ is simply to have knowledge).[53] For a principle
25   is not something we commonly believe, but what is primary in the genus
relevant to our proofs; moreover, not every truth is proper <to the
relevant genus>.

[KNOWLEDGE REQUIRES NECESSITY]

A further argument shows that <demonstrative> deduction must be
derived from necessary premisses. When a conclusion is demonstrable,
we do not know$_e$ it if we have no account of the reason why it is true;
but A might belong to C necessarily, while B, the middle* term through

---

53. **sophists . . . knowledge):** See 71b10, 74a28, Plato, *Euthydemus* 277b. Aristotle
argues that our condition counts as knowledge only if the proposition we grasp
is actually a genuine principle; to be a genuine principle, it must have the
appropriate explanatory status.

which this conclusion was <allegedly> demonstrated, <belongs to C,   *30*
but> not necessarily. In that case we do not know$_o$ the reason <why the
conclusion is true>; for the middle term is not the reason, since it is possible
for the middle term not to be, whereas the conclusion is necessary.

Further, if we do not now know$_o$, although we have the account[54]
and we still exist, and the object still exists, and we have not forgotten,
then we did not know before either. But the middle term might cease
to exist, if it is not necessary; hence we might have the account, and we   *35*
would still exist, and the object would still exist, but we would not know,
so that we did not know previously either. If the middle term still exists,
but its nonexistence is possible, the result we have described is possible
and might arise; someone in that state cannot possibly know.

Whenever, then, the conclusion is necessary, the middle through   *75a*
which it was proved may well not be necessary; for what is necessary
can be deduced even from what is not necessary, just as a truth can be
deduced from what is not true. But whenever the middle is necessary,
the conclusion will also be necessary, just as truths always result in   *5*
truth. (For let A be said of B necessarily, and B of C <necessarily>; it
is also necessary, then, for A to belong to C <necessarily>.) But when
the conclusion is not necessary, the middle cannot be necessary either.
(For let A belong to C not necessarily, but to B necessarily; and let B   *10*
belong to C necessarily; then A will also belong to C necessarily. But it
was assumed not to.)

Since, then, what we know$_e$ demonstratively must belong necessarily,
it is clear that we must also demonstrate through a middle that is necessary. Otherwise we will not know$_e$ either the reason why or that it is
necessary for this to be; either we will think but not know$_o$ (if we take   *15*
what is not necessary to be necessary), or we will not even think it
(whether we know the fact through the middle terms or know the reason
and know it through immediate premises).

There is no demonstrative knowledge$_e$ of coincidents that do not
belong to things in their own right (according to our determination of
what belongs to things in their own right); for the conclusion cannot be   *20*
proved necessarily, since it is possible for a coincident not to belong
(this is the sort of coincident[55] I mean). Still, one might be puzzled[56]

54. **the account**: Presumably not the complete and correct account, for reasons
given at the end of i 5.

55. **the sort of coincident . . .**: i.e., not an intrinsic coincident (one belonging
to the subject in its own right) of the sort he has just described.

56. **one might be puzzled**: Aristotle answers the puzzle by pointing out that
even if the premises and conclusion are not necessary (*necessitas consequentis*; see
NECESSITY #7), nonetheless the conclusion follows necessarily from the premises
(*necessitas consequentiae*), and the right answer to dialectical questions can reveal
this.

about the point of asking questions about these things,[57] if the conclusion is not necessary; for it would make no difference if we asked any old
25 random questions and then stated the conclusion.[58] We are right to ask the questions, however, not because we assume that they make <the conclusion> necessary, but because someone who gives these answers must then necessarily affirm the conclusion and must affirm it truly, if the answers are true.

Since in each genus what belongs to something in its own right and insofar as it is a given <sort of thing> belongs necessarily, it is clear
30 that demonstrations that express knowledge_e are about, and are derived from, things that belong to a subject in its own right. For since coincidents are not necessary, we do not necessarily know_o why a conclusion <derived from them> holds, even if it holds of the subject in every case, but not in its own right (for example, deduction through signs*). For in that case you will know_e something that <in fact> belongs to something in its own right, but you will not know it <as belonging to something>
35 in its own right, nor will you know_e the reason why it belongs. (And to know the reason why is to know through the explanation.) The middle, then, must belong to the third, and the first to the middle, because of itself.

[THE PREMISSES OF DEMONSTRATION [59]]

7

It is not possible, therefore, to prove anything by crossing from one genus to another—for instance, to prove something geometrical by arith-
40 metic. For there are three elements in demonstrations: what is being demonstrated, i.e., the conclusion (this is what belongs to the genus in its own right); the axioms (i.e., the things from which the demonstration
75b proceeds); and the genus[60] that is the subject, whose attributes and coincidents in its own right[61] are revealed by the demonstration. The axioms* from which the demonstration proceeds may be the same; but

57. **questions about these things**: DIALECTICAL questions about coincidents, seeking premisses from which we can infer them.

58. **for it would make no difference . . . conclusion**: It would make no difference to the fact that the conclusion will not be necessary in any case.

59. In i 7 Aristotle argues that demonstration must be derived from the special premisses of the relevant field of study (genus), and cannot be derived from the principles of another field.

60. **the genus**: This presumably includes the basic assumptions, *hupotheseis* (72a16–17), of a science.

61. **coincidents in its own right**: Or 'intrinsic coincidents'. See COINCIDENT #2–3.

if two sciences—arithmetic and geometry, for example—have different
genera, an arithmetical demonstration cannot be applied to the coinci-   5
dents of magnitude, unless the magnitudes are numbers. (How such
application is possible in some cases will be discussed later.)[62]

A demonstration in arithmetic or in any other science includes in each
case the genus it is about; and so if a demonstration is to cross over
<from one science to another> the genus must be the same, either
without qualification or in a way. Otherwise, clearly, it cannot; for the   10
extreme and the middle* terms must belong to the same genus, since if
they do not belong to something in its own right, they will be coincidents.

That is why we cannot prove by geometry that there is one science
of contraries, or even that two cubes make a cube. Nor can we prove
by one science the truths of another, except for those pairs in which   15
one <science> is subordinate to another, as optics is to geometry, and
harmonics to arithmetic. Nor can we prove by geometry anything that
belongs to lines not insofar as they are lines and not insofar as it follows
from the distinctive principles <of that science>; <we cannot prove by
geometry,> for example, whether the straight is the most beautiful of
lines, nor whether it is contrary to the circumference, since that belongs   20
to them, not insofar as their distinctive genus belongs to them, but as
something common.

[WHAT IS DEMONSTRATED MUST BE EVERLASTING]

8

It is also evident that if the premisses of the deduction are universal,
the conclusion of such a demonstration—i.e., of a demonstration that
is so called without qualification—must also be everlasting. There is
therefore no demonstration or unqualified knowledge$_e$, but only coincidental knowledge, of perishable things,[63] because it does not hold of the   25
<kind> universally,[64] but at some time and in some way.[65] In this case,
one or the other premiss must be nonuniversal and perishable. It must
be perishable, because the conclusion will obtain whenever the premisses

---

62. **later**: 75b15, 76a9–15, 78b34–79a16.

63. **There is . . . perishable things**: On demonstration about perishable things
see *Met.* vii 15.

64. **universally**: Read *katholou*.

65. **There is therefore . . . in some way**: Aristotle probably does not mean that
there can be no demonstration about kinds of perishable things (e.g., kinds of
animals). He means that these demonstrations are primarily about properties of
the kind, and only secondarily about the perishable individuals belonging to
the kind; cf. *Met.* 1036a2–9, 1039b27–1040a7.

30 do; it must be nonuniversal, because it will be true of some of the subjects, but not of others. So one cannot deduce universally, but only that it holds now.

The same applies to definitions, since a definition is either a principle of demonstration, or a demonstration differently arranged, or some sort of conclusion of a demonstration.[66]

It is clear that demonstrations and sciences of things that often come to be—for example, eclipses of the moon—always are, insofar as they 35 are of this kind of thing; but they are particular,[67] insofar as they do not always hold. What applies to the eclipse applies in the same way to the other cases.

[PREMISSES, CONCLUSION AND GENUS]

9

Since it is evident that we cannot demonstrate anything except from its own principles, if what is being proved belongs to the subject as itself, it follows that knowing$_e$ something is not <simply> having proved it 40 from true, indemonstrable, and immediate premisses—for it is possible to give this sort of proof, as Bryson did for the squaring <of the circle>.[68] For this sort of argument proves its conclusion by reference to a common feature that will also belong to another <genus>; and so the argument 76a also applies to other things of another genus. We do not, therefore, know$_e$ the subject as itself, but only coincidentally; for otherwise the <alleged> demonstration would not also have applied to another genus.

But we know$_e$ a thing noncoincidentally when our knowledge$_g$ refers to the feature because of which <the property> belongs <to the sub- 5 ject>, and when it is derived from the principles of that <sort of subject> insofar as it is that <sort of subject>. We know, for instance, that <the triangle> has angles equal to two right angles when the feature we mentioned belongs to <the triangle> in its own right from its own principles. Hence if that feature also belongs to its subject in its own right, the middle must be in the same genus.

66. **either a . . . of a demonstration**: The relation between demonstration and definition is explained in ii 10.

67. **particular**: or 'partial', *kata meros*. Laws about eclipses are universal, not confined to this or that particular eclipse; but (in contrast to laws about, say, geometry or gravity) they are not always being exemplified, since eclipses happen only from time to time.

68. **Bryson**: See *Top.* 171b12–18.

54

Otherwise, it must be <proved> in the way in which harmonic prop-   *10*
erties are proved through arithmetic. These are proved in the same
way, but with a difference; for the fact <that is proved> belongs to the
subordinate sciences (since a distinct genus is the subject), but the reason
why belongs to the superordinate science, which has these attributes in
their own right.[69] Hence this case also makes it evident that something
cannot be demonstrated without qualification except from its own princi-   *15*
ples. But the principles of these <subordinate and superordinate sci-
ences> have the <appropriate> common feature.

[THE IMPOSSIBILITY OF A UNIVERSAL SCIENCE]

If this is evident, it is also evident that the distinctive principles of each
<genus> cannot be demonstrated; for those <principles from which
the distinctive principles will allegedly be demonstrated> will be principles of everything, and the science of them will be supreme[70] over everything. For one has fuller knowledge$_e$ when one's knowledge$_o$ is derived
from higher explanations; for knowledge$_o$ is derived from prior explana-   *20*
tions whenever it is derived from those that have no further explanations.
Hence if someone in this state has fuller, indeed the fullest, knowledge,
then that <supreme science> will also be a science to a higher,
indeed to the highest, degree. Demonstration, however, does not
apply to another genus, except in the way we have said geometrical
demonstrations apply to mechanical or optical, and arithmetical to
harmonic, demonstrations.[71]   *25*

[THE DIFFICULTY OF FINDING A GENUINE DEMONSTRATION]

It is hard to know$_g$ whether or not we know$_o$; for it is hard to know$_g$
whether our knowledge$_o$ of a thing is derived from the thing's principles
(as is required for knowledge). We suppose we have knowledge$_e$ of a
conclusion if we deduce it from true and primary premises; but that is
not enough. Rather, the conclusion and the primary premises must   *30*
<also> be in the same genus.

69. **which has . . . own right**: Odd and even, for instance, belong to number
IN THEIR OWN RIGHT. See case (b) at 73a37.

70. **supreme**: Or CONTROLLING.

71. **Demonstration, . . . harmonic, demonstrations**: Aristotle seems to reject a
universal science, because it would violate the rules about demonstration that
he has just laid down. On a universal science see *Top.* 172a11–15 and contrast
Met. iv 1–3.

[*DISTINCTIVE V. COMMON PRINCIPLES*]

10

By 'principles' in each genus I mean the things whose truth cannot be proved.[72] What the primary things, and the things derived from them, signify is assumed, and the truth of the principles must also be assumed; but the truth of the rest must be proved. For instance, we must assume
35   what a unit, or straight and a triangle, signify, and that there is such a thing as a unit[73] and a magnitude, but we must prove the other things.

Of the principles used in demonstrative science, some are distinctive of a given science and others are common. The common ones are common by analogy, since each is useful to the extent that it applies to the
40   genus falling under the science.[74] A distinctive principle is, for instance, that a line or the straight is this sort of thing. A common principle is, for instance, that if equals are removed from equals, equals are left. Each of these is adequate to the extent that it applies to a given genus; for
76b   the effect will be the same if it is not assumed to hold of everything whatever, but only of magnitudes <for the geometer>, and of numbers for the arithmetician.

* * * * * * *

[*DEMONSTRATION AND INTRINSIC PROPERTIES*]

[*PREDICATIONS AND THEIR SUBJECTS*]

22

82b37   In the case of things predicated in the what-it-is,[75] the answer is clear.[76] For if it is possible to define something or to know$_g$ the essence, but it
83a   is not possible to go through an infinite number of steps, then the things essentially predicated must be limited in number. We argue this in general as follows.

One can say truly that the pale thing is walking, or that that big thing is a log; or, on the other hand, that the log is big, or that the man is

---

72. **whose truth cannot be proved**: Lit. 'which it is not possible to prove that they are'. In the next sentence, 'the truth of the principles' = 'that they are'.

73. **that there . . . a unit**: Lit. 'that a unit is'.

74. **The common . . . science**: The principle assumed in geometry is not the unrestricted AXIOM of equals, but only the special version applying to magnitudes. Hence each so-called 'axiom' is really a group of principles.

75. **in the what-it-is**: predicated of x in what x is (x's ESSENCE).

76. **the answer** . . . Aristotle is discussing the question whether a demonstration can have an infinite number of premisses.

walking.[77] The second sort of assertion is different from the first. For   5
when I say that the pale thing is a log, I am saying that the <subject>
that is coincidentally pale is a log, not that the pale thing is the subject
for the log; for it did not become a log by being essentially pale[78] or by
being essentially some <sort of> pale thing,[79] and hence it is pale only
coincidentally. On the other hand, when I say that the log is pale, I am
not saying that some other <subject> is pale and is coincidentally a log,   10
as when I say that the musical thing is pale (i.e., that the man who is
coincidentally musical is pale). Rather, the log is the subject, and it is
this that became <pale>, not by being anything other than essentially
a log or some <sort of> log.

　　If we must legislate, let us say that speaking in the second way is predi-   15
cating, and that speaking in the first way either is not predicating at all,
or else is predicating coincidentally, not without qualification.[80] What is
predicated <without qualification> is something such as the pale thing;
<the subject> of which it is predicated is something such as the log.

[INTRINSIC VERSUS COINCIDENTAL PROPERTIES]

Let us assume, then, that what is predicated is in each case predicated
without qualification, not coincidentally, of <the subject> of which it   20
is predicated; for that is how demonstrations demonstrate. Hence, when
one thing is predicated of one <subject>, either it is predicated in the
what-it-is,[81] or it <says that the subject> has some quality or quantity,

77. **One can say truly**: . . . Aristotle offers four examples to illustrate two types
of cases: (1a) The pale thing (there is nothing corresponding to 'thing' in the
Greek) is walking (note: 'is walking' is one Greek word; cf. *Met.* 1017a24–30).
(1b) The big thing is a log. (2a) The log is big. (2b) The man is walking. He
argues that (1a) and (1b) are coincidental predications, and that (2a) and (2b)
are genuine predications.

78. **by being essentially pale**: Read *outh'hoper leukon*. Alternatively: 'by being
pale' (reading *oute leukon*).

79. **essentially some <sort of> pale thing**: Or 'some species of pale thing'. On
'essentially' (*hoper*) see ESSENCE #2 (d).

80. **coincidentally, not without qualification**: As the next paragraph shows,
Aristotle distinguishes (a) predicating coincidentally from (b) predicating a coincident of a subject. Case (b) is a genuine, unqualified predication, since it picks
out a genuine subject in its own right (e.g., the log). Case (a) is a predication
only coincidentally, insofar as it only coincidentally picks out the genuine subject
(by one of its coincidents, as, e.g., the white thing).

81. **the what-it-is**: Here Aristotle uses this as the name for the first category (see
PREDICATIONS) rather than for ESSENCE. He is thinking of different ways something
can be predicated of a substance. See SUBSTANCE #2.

or that it is relative to something, or that it is doing something or being
affected, or that it is at some place or time.

25   Further, if G signifies the substance of F, G signifies that the F of
which G is predicated is either essentially G or essentially some <sort
of> G. But if G does not signify the substance, but is said of some other
thing F that is its subject, while F is neither essentially G nor essentially
some <sort of> G, then G is a coincident—as, for instance, when pale
is said of a man.[82] For a man is neither essentially pale nor essentially
30   some <sort of> pale; presumably he is an animal, since a man is essentially an animal. And if G does not signify the substance, it must be
predicated of some subject: something can be pale only if it is pale by
being something else. (For we can forget about the Forms; for they are
idle chatter, and even if they exist they are irrelevant to the argument,
35   since demonstrations are about the sorts of things we have described.)[83]

[THERE CANNOT BE INFINITE SEQUENCES OF
INTRINSIC OR COINCIDENTAL PROPERTIES]

Moreover, if it is false that F is a quality of G and G of F, a quality of a
quality, then such reciprocal predication of F and G is impossible; it may
be true to say <that F is G and G is F> but true reciprocal predications
are not possible.
83b   For one possibility is that G is predicated of F as F's substance, by
being either the genus or the differentia of what is predicated. But we
have shown that these predications are not infinite, either upward (for
example, man is biped, biped is animal, animal is something else) or
downward (for example, animal is predicated of man, man of Callias,
5   and Callias of something else in the what-it-is).[84] For every substance of
this sort can be defined, but we cannot go through an infinite series in
thought. Hence predications cannot be infinite, since we cannot define
something of which infinitely many things are predicated. Hence things
10   will not be reciprocally predicated as genera; for if they were, each would
be some <species> of itself.

82. **of a man**: Or 'of man'. It is not clear whether the subject is a universal or
a particular.

83. **(For we can . . . described.)**: Aristotle thinks that Aristotelian universals
account adequately for the sort of knowledge for which Plato thinks it necessary
to postulate FORMS.

84. **either upward . . . what-it-is)**: Both 'animal is something else' and 'Callias
is something else in what-it-is' are impossible predications, since, on the one
hand, there is no genuine genus higher than animal, and, on the other hand,
Callias is a first substance.

Nor again can there be reciprocal predication of quality or of any of the other <nonsubstances>, unless it is coincidental; for these are all coincidents and are predicated of substances.

Nor yet are predications infinite upward. For what is predicated of each subject signifies its quality or quantity or one of those <nonsubstantial properties> or else the things in its substance; all these are limited   15
in number, and the kinds of predication[85] are limited too, since they must be either quality or quantity or relative, or acting on, or being affected, or at some place or time.

[HENCE DEMONSTRATIONS CANNOT BE INFINITELY LONG]

We assume, then, that one thing is predicated of one <subject> and that nothing other than the what-it-is is predicated of itself. For everything else is a coincident, though some are coincidents in their own   20
right,[86] some another sort. Each of them, we say, is predicated of some subject, and a coincident is not a subject. For we take every coincident to be something that is called whatever it is called by being something else; it <belongs> to something else and it <is predicated> of another thing.

Hence one thing will not be said to belong to one thing <in an   25
infinite series> either upward or downward. For <going downward> coincidents are said of the things in something's substance, which are not infinite in number; going upward, there are these <things in the substance> and their coincidents, and neither of these are infinite. There must, then, be some primary <subject> of predication, and another thing predicated of it; this sequence must stop somewhere, and there   30
must be something which is not predicated of any other prior thing and which has no other prior thing predicated of it.

This, then, is regarded as one way of demonstrating our conclusion; another is the following. Suppose there is a demonstration of something q, of which something prior, p, is predicated. If there is a demonstration of something, we cannot have any better <cognitive> state than knowl-   35
edge$_o$ about it, nor can we have knowledge$_o$ of it without demonstration. If, then, we know$_g$ q through p, but neither know$_o$ p nor have anything better than knowledge$_o$ of p, then neither will we know$_e$ q, which is known$_g$ through p. If, then, it is possible for a demonstration to yield unqualified knowledge$_o$ of something, not knowledge$_o$ given some <premisses> (i.e., conditional knowledge$_o$),[87] then the intermediate   84a

85. **kinds of predication**: See PREDICATIONS #1.

86. **coincidents in their own right**: Cf. 75a18, 75b1.

87. **conditional knowledge**: See 73b15.

predications must stop somewhere. For if they do not stop, and at each point there is something above the thing we have taken, there will be demonstration of everything. If, then, we cannot go through an infinite sequence, we will not know$_o$ by demonstration the things of which there
5   is demonstration.[88] Hence, if we have no better <cognitive> state than knowledge$_o$ of them, demonstration will not give us unqualified knowledge$_e$ of anything, but only conditional knowledge.

[A FURTHER PROOF]

From the logical point of view, these arguments might convince us on the question. From the analytical point of view,[89] the following more
10   concise argument makes it evident that in the demonstrative sciences we are examining, the things predicated cannot be infinite in number either upward or downward.

For there is demonstration of what belongs to things in their own right, and G belongs to F in its own right in one of two ways:[90] either G is present in what F is (as plurality and divisibility are present in the account of number) or else F belongs in what G is (as odd belongs to
15   number <in its own right>, since it belongs to number, and number is present in its account). Neither of these can be infinite.

<Properties> such as odd in number cannot be infinite. For there would again have to be something belonging to odd in which odd was
20   present; and if this were so, number would be the primary thing present in what belongs to it. If, then, an infinite number of such things cannot belong to one <subject>, they cannot be infinite upward, but they must all belong to the first thing, i.e., to number, and number to them, so
25   that they will be reciprocally predicated, not exceeding it.

Nor, again, can the things present in the essence be infinite; for then definition would be impossible.

88. **If, then . . . demonstration**: If we demonstrate q from p, we must either know p or have some better cognitive grasp of p (cf. 71b29–33, 72b13–15, 100b9). But there is no cognitive condition better than knowledge, and knowledge requires demonstration. Hence knowing p will depend on demonstrating the (alleged) infinite series of predications prior to p; but such a demonstration is impossible (since it would involve an infinite task; cf. 84a2). Hence, if there is an infinite series of predications prior to p, we do not know p, and so we do not know q either. Aristotle concludes that there cannot be an infinite series of predications.

89. **the analytical point of view**: In contrast to LOGICAL arguments (relying on DIALECTIC), argument in ANALYTICS relies on the special features of DEMONSTRATIVE argument.

90. **one of two ways**: Cf. 73a34–b5.

And so, if all the things predicated are said <of the subject> in its
own right, and these cannot be infinite, they will come to a halt going
upward, and hence also going downward. And if this is so, the number
of terms between any two will always be finite.   30

If this is so, then clearly demonstrations must have principles,[91] and
not everything is demonstrable, contrary to the view of those people we
mentioned at the beginning.[92] For if there are principles, it is impossible
to demonstrate everything, and impossible to have an infinite regress.
To allow either of these is to allow that all intervals <between terms>   35
are divisible, and none is immediate and indivisible; for we demonstrate
by inserting a term <between two terms>, not by adding another <from
outside>, and so if this can go on to infinity, there could be an infinite
number of intermediate terms between any two terms. But this is impossible if predications come to a stop both upward and downward; and   84b
we have proved that they do, first from the logical, and now from the
analytical point of view.

* * * * * * *

Book II

[DEMONSTRATION AND DEFINITION]

[KNOWLEDGE, DEMONSTRATION, AND DEFINITION[1]]

8

We must consider over again what is right and what is wrong in what   93a1
has been said, and what a definition is, and whether or not there is any
sort of demonstration of what something is.

Now, we say that knowing what a thing is is the same as knowing
the explanation[2] of whether it is. The argument for this is that there is   5
some explanation <of whether a thing is> and this is either the same
<as what the thing is> or something else, and if it is something else,
then it is either demonstrable or indemonstrable. If, then, it is something

---

91. **principles**: Or 'beginnings'; see PRINCIPLE #3. Aristotle means that demonstration must start somewhere.

92. **at the beginning**: 72b16.

1. Aristotle has just been setting out a number of puzzles about the relation
between demonstration and definition. He now turns to his solution, which
distinguishes different types of definition and their relation to demonstration.

2. **explanation**: See CAUSE #2. In this discussion 'cause' would sometimes be
more suitable (since Aristotle is treating substances and events, rather than
propositions, facts, or properties, as *aitiai*). We have retained 'explanation' for
the sake of uniformity with Bk i.

else and is demonstrable, the explanation must be a middle* term, and must be proved in the first figure,[3] since what is being proved is universal and affirmative.

10   One type of proof, then, would be the one examined just now—proving what something is through something else. For in proofs of what a thing is it is necessary for the middle term to be what <the thing> is, and in proofs of distinctive properties it is necessary for the middle term to be a distinctive property. Hence in one case you will, and in another case you will not, prove the essence of the same object.

15   Now this type of proof, as has been said before, is not a demonstration, but a logical* deduction of what something is.

Let us say, then, starting again from the beginning, how a demonstration is possible. In some cases we seek the reason for something when we have already grasped the fact,[4] and in other cases they both become clear at the same time; but it is never possible to come to know$_g$ the reason before the fact. It is clear, then, that in the same way we cannot

20   come to know the essence of a thing without knowing that the thing is; for it is impossible to know$_o$ what a thing is if we do not know whether the thing is.

Our grasp of whether a thing is is in some cases <merely> coincidental, while in other cases we grasp whether a thing is by grasping some aspect of the thing itself. We may grasp,[5] for instance, whether thunder is, by grasping that it is some sort of noise in the clouds;[6] whether an eclipse is, by grasping that it is some sort of deprivation of light; whether a man is, by grasping that he is some sort of animal; and whether a soul is, by grasping that it initiates its own motion.

25   In cases where we know$_o$ <only> coincidentally that a thing is, we necessarily have no grasp of what the thing is, since we do not even know that the thing is; to investigate what a thing is when we have not grasped that the thing is is to investigate nothing. But in the cases where we do grasp some <aspect of the thing itself>, it is easier <to investigate what the thing is>. And so we acquire knowledge of what the thing is to the extent that we know that the thing is.

3. **first figure**: See *APr* 26a13n.

4. **the reason . . . the fact**: Lit. 'the why (*to dihoti*) . . . the that (*to hoti*)'. Cf. *EN* 1095b7, CAUSE #2.

5. **We may grasp . . . .** : The following examples illustrate 'grasping some aspect of x itself', i.e., one of x's essential properties.

6. **that . . . clouds**: Or 'that there is some noise in the clouds'. 'Some sort' renders the rough equivalent of the indefinite article in Greek (*tis*; cf. INDIVIDUAL #4). Aristotle means that at this stage we do not yet grasp what sort of deprivation of light an eclipse is, because we do not grasp that it is the one with this specific cause.

As a case where we grasp some aspect of what a thing is, let us take
first of all the following: Let A be an eclipse, C the moon, and B blocking   30
by the earth. Then to investigate whether it is eclipsed or not is to
investigate whether B is or not. This question is just the same as the
question whether there is an account of <A>; and if there is an account
of <A>, we also say that <A> is.[7] Or perhaps we ask which of two
contradictories—for example, the triangle's having or not having two
right angles—satisfies the account.   35
When we find <the account>, we know$_o$ both the fact and the reason
at the same time, if <we reach the fact> through immediate <prem-
isses>; if <the premises are not immediate>, then we know the fact,
but not the reason. For instance, let C be the moon, A an eclipse, and
B the inability to cast a shadow at the full moon when there is nothing
apparent between us and it. Suppose, then, that B (inability to cast a   93b
shadow when there is nothing between us and it) belongs to C, and
that A (being eclipsed) belongs to B. In that case it is clear that the moon
has been eclipsed, but it is not thereby clear why it has been eclipsed;
we know$_o$ that there is an eclipse, but we do not know what it is.
If it is clear that A belongs to C, then <to investigate> why it belongs
is to investigate what B is—whether it is the blocking <by the earth>   5
or the rotation of the moon or its extinguishing. And this is the account
of one extreme term—in this case the account of A, since an eclipse is
a blocking by the earth.
<Or take another example:> What is thunder? Extinguishing of fire
in a cloud. Why does it thunder? Because the fire is extinguished in the
cloud. Let C be a cloud, A thunder, B extinguishing of fire. Then B   10
belongs to C, a cloud (since the fire is extinguished in it), and A, the
noise, belongs to B; and in fact B is the account of A, the first extreme
term. And if there is a further middle term <explaining> B, this will be
found from the remaining accounts <of A>.[8]   15
We have said, then, how one grasps the what-it-is, and how it comes
to be known$_g$. And so it turns out that though the what-it-is is neither
deduced nor demonstrated, still it is made clear through deduction and
demonstration.[9] Hence, in the case where the explanation of a thing is
something other than the thing, a demonstration is required for knowl-

---

7. **and if . . . <A> is**: Once we know that the moon's failure to give light is
caused by the earth's blocking light from the sun, we incorporate that knowledge
in our account of an eclipse, and we say that there is an eclipse.

8. **remaining accounts**: The other explanations needed are parts of the definition
of thunder.

9. **And so . . . demonstration**: Even though a conclusion of a demonstration
is not itself a definition, it shows us how to formulate a definition that incorpo-
rates the explanation stated in the premises of the demonstration.

20 edge$_g$ of what the thing is, even though there is no demonstration of what the thing is, as we also said in setting out the puzzles.[10]

9

Some things have something else as their explanation, while other things do not; and so it is clear that in some cases the what-it-is is immediate and a principle. In these cases we must assume (or make evident in some other way) both that it is and what it is—as the students of arithmetic do, 25 since they assume both what the unit is and that it is. In the other cases—those that have a middle term, and where something else is the explanation of their essence$_o$—it is possible, as we said, to make clear what something is through demonstration, even though the what-it-is is not demonstrated.

[NOMINAL DEFINITIONS]

10

30 Since a definition is said to be an account of the what-it-is, it is evident that one type will be an account of what a name or some other name-like account signifies[11]—for example, what triangle signifies. When we have grasped that <a thing> is <this>,[12] we investigate why it is; but it is difficult to grasp in this way <why a thing is>, given that we do not know$_o$ that the thing is.[13] The reason for this difficulty has been mentioned before: <if we know only what a thing's name signifies>, we do not even know whether or not the thing is, unless <we know this> coincidentally.[14] (An account is unified in either of two ways—

10. **setting out the puzzles**: This was done in ii 3.

11. **an account of . . . account signifies**: This is often (though not by Aristotle) called a 'nominal definition'.

12. **When we . . . is <this>**: Or: 'when we have grasped that a thing exists' (lit. 'having which, that it is').

13. **but it is difficult . . . the thing is**: Or 'But it is difficult to have this sort of grasp <i.e., the sort we get through a nominal definition> about things whose existence we do not know'. This might be taken to mean (contrary to our supplements) that we cannot grasp a nominal definition of x without knowing that x exists.

14. **<if we know . . . know this> coincidentally**: According to our translation and supplements, knowledge of x's nominal definition does not supply knowledge of whether x is (exists)—if we knew what triangle signifies and also happened to know that triangles exist, the second piece of knowledge would be coincidental to the first. Both knowledge of x's nominal definition and knowledge

either by connection, like the *Iliad*, or by revealing one <property> of one <subject> noncoincidentally.[15])

[*THE DIFFERENCE BETWEEN REAL DEFINITION AND DEMONSTRATION*]

This, then, is one definition of definition; another sort of definition is an account revealing why something is.[16] Hence the first type of definition signifies but does not prove, whereas the second type will clearly be a sort of demonstration of what something is, but differently arranged— for saying why it thunders is different from saying what thunder is. We will answer the first question by saying 'Because fire is extinguished in the clouds'. And what is thunder? A noise of fire being extinguished in the clouds. These are two different statements, then, of the same account; the first is a continuous demonstration,[17] the second a definition. More-over, a definition of thunder is noise in the clouds, which is the conclusion of a demonstration of what it is. In contrast to this, the definition of something immediate[18] is an indemonstrable positing of what it is.

One sort of definition, then, is an indemonstrable account of the what-it-is; a second is a deduction of the what-it-is, differing in arrangement from a demonstration; and a third is the conclusion of a demonstration of the what-it-is.

What we have said, then, has made it evident, first, in what way the what-it-is is demonstrable and in what way it is not, and what things are demonstrable and what things are not; secondly, in how many ways a definition is spoken of, in what way it proves the what-it-is and in what way it does not, and what things have definitions and what things do not; and, thirdly, how definition is related to demonstration, and in what way there can be both definition and demonstration of the same thing and in what way there cannot.

94a

5

10

15

---

that x exists are needed for knowledge of why x is. A different conclusion emerges from other accounts of these two sentences (see previous two notes).

15. **An account . . . noncoincidentally**: Cf. *Met.* 1030a9n.

16. **another sort . . . something is**: This is often called (though not by Aristotle), a 'real', as opposed to a 'nominal', definition.

17. **continuous demonstration**: Perhaps Aristotle means that a demonstration is extended but uninterrupted, and so continuous, as a line is. A line ABC is continuous, because the segments AB and BC share B; similarly, a demonstration contains different propositions (the premisses and the conclusion) that share some of the same terms. A definition, by contrast, is a single proposition.

18. **something immediate**: This would be appropriate to an ultimate premiss of demonstration, and therefore not open to further demonstration.

* * * * * * *

[*THE ULTIMATE PRINCIPLES OF DEMONSTRATION*]

[*KNOWLEDGE OF FIRST PRINCIPLES IS NOT INNATE*]

19

99b15 It is evident, then, what deduction and demonstration are and how they come about; the same holds for demonstrative knowledge$_e$, since it is the same <as demonstration>. But how do we come to know$_g$ principles, and what state knows$_g$ them?[19] This will be clear from the following argument, if we first state the puzzles.

20 We said before that we cannot know$_e$ through demonstration without knowing$_g$ the first, immediate principles.[20] But one might be puzzled about whether knowledge$_g$ of the immediate principles is or is not the same <as knowledge of truths derived from them>; whether there is

25 knowledge$_e$ of each, or knowledge of one but something else of the other; and whether the states are acquired rather than <innately> present or are <innately> present in us without our noticing them.[21]

It would be absurd if we had the principles <innately>; for then we would possess knowledge$_g$[22] that is more exact than demonstration, but without noticing it. If, on the other hand, we acquire the principles and do not previously possess them, how could we know$_g$ and learn them

30 from no prior knowledge? That is impossible, as we also said in the case of demonstration. Evidently, then, we can neither possess the principles <innately> nor acquire them if we are ignorant and possess no state <of knowledge>. Hence we must have some <suitable> potentiality, but not one that is at a level of exactness superior to that of the knowledge we acquire.[23]

19. **But how ... knows$_g$ them?**: Aristotle returns to a question he raised in i 3, in arguing that demonstrative knowledge$_e$ has to rely on a cognitive grasp of principles that cannot be demonstrated. In this chapter he identifies this nondemonstrative cognitive grasp with UNDERSTANDING.

20. **We said ... principles**: See 72b18–25.

21. **and not <innately> ... noticing them**: Cf. Plato, *Meno* 81a–86c.

22. **knowledge**: Lit. 'knowledges', i.e., pieces of knowledge.

23. **but not ... acquire**: Lit. 'but not to have such a one as will be more honorable than these in respect of exactness'. It must be less exact than the acquired cognitive states, since otherwise it would face the objection just raised against innate knowledge of ultimate principles.

[*THE GROWTH OF OUR KNOWLEDGE OF UNIVERSALS*]

All animals evidently have <such a potentiality>, since they have the   35
innate discriminative* potentiality called perception. Some animals that
have perception (though not all of them) also retain <in memory> what
they perceive; those that do not retain it have no knowledge_g outside
perception (either none at all or none about what is not retained), but
those that do retain it keep what they have perceived in their souls   100a
even after they have perceived. When this has happened many times a
<further> difference arises: in some, but not all, cases, a rational ac-
count[24] arises from the retention of perceptions.

From perception, then, as we say, memory arises, and from repeated
memory of the same thing experience arises; for a number of memories   5
make up one experience. From experience, or <rather> from the whole
universal that has settled in the soul—the one apart* from the many,
whatever is present as one and the same in all of them—arises a principle
of craft (if it is about what comes to be) or of science (if it is about what
is).[25]

Hence the relevant states are not <innate> in us in any determinate   10
character and do not arise from states that have a better grasp on knowl-
edge_g; rather, they arise from perception. It is like what happens in a
battle when there is a retreat: first one soldier makes a stand, then a
second, then another, until they reach a starting point.[26] The soul's
nature gives it a potentiality to be affected in this way.

Let us state again, then, what we stated, but not perspicuously, before.   15
When one of the undifferentiated things[27] makes a stand, that is the first
universal in the soul; for though one perceives the particular, perception

24. **rational account**: *logos*. In referring to a *logos*, Aristotle may mean to explain
(1) the acquisition of universal concepts (e.g., the concept of horse) from perception (e.g., of particular horses) or (2) the acquisition of knowledge of universal
truths (e.g., that horses have four legs) from perception (e.g., that this horse
has four legs, that horse . . . etc.) or (3) both (1) and (2). On perception, memory
and knowledge cf. *Met*. 980a21–981a12.

25. **arises a . . . what is)**: CRAFTS are productive, whereas sciences (see KNOW
#3) are theoretical.

26. **It is like . . . starting point**: Aristotle exploits the different uses of '*archē*';
see PRINCIPLE #3. When soldiers rally and gather to make a stand, they reach a
starting point (*archē*), which provides a beginning (*archē*) for a new advance.
Similarly, perceptions 'gather' until they produce a starting point (*archē*), which
is a suitable principle (*archē*) for demonstrations explaining the facts initially
grasped by perception.

27. **undifferentiated things**: Probably these are the lowest species (e.g., man),
not further differentiated into species. It is less probable that Aristotle refers to
particular perceptible things.

100b   is of the universal—of man, for instance, not of Callias the man.[28] Again, in these <universals something else> makes a stand, until what has no parts and is universal makes a stand—first, for example, a certain sort of animal makes a stand, until animal does, and in this <universal> something else makes a stand in the same way. Clearly, then, we must
5   come to know$_g$ the first things[29] by induction; for that is also how perception produces the universal in us.[30]

[WE GRASP BASIC PRINCIPLES BY UNDERSTANDING]

Among our intellectual states that grasp the truth, some—knowledge$_e$ and understanding[31]—are always true, whereas others—for example, belief and reasoning—admit of being false; and understanding is the only sort of state that is more exact than knowledge$_e$. Since the principles of demonstration are better known$_g$ <than the conclusions derived from
10   them>, and since all knowledge$_e$ requires an account,[32] it follows that we can have no knowledge$_e$ of the principles. Since only understanding can be truer than knowledge$_e$, we must have understanding of the principles.

The same conclusion follows from the further point that since the principle of a demonstration is not a demonstration, the principle of knowledge$_e$ is not knowledge$_e$. If, then, the only sort of state apart
15   from knowledge$_e$ that is <always> true is understanding, understanding must be the principle of knowledge$_e$. The principle,[33] then, will grasp the principle, and, similarly, all knowledge$_e$ will grasp its object.

28. **though one . . . Callias the man**: Though we perceive Callias, we perceive him *as* something (tall, pale, a man etc.), and the property we are aware of when we perceive him is a universal.

29. **first things**: These are the most determinate universals, e.g., man. Probably they are the same as the 'undifferentiated things' mentioned in 100a16.

30. **induction . . . in us**: The process leading from perception of particulars (e.g., particular men) to the point where a universal (e.g., man) 'makes a stand' is inductive.

31. **understanding**: See UNDERSTANDING #3. Here it is the state that grasps ultimate first principles as such, without any further account. This is the sort of cognitive grasp that was demanded in i 3, to avoid a circle or infinite regress of justification. We have knowledge$_g$ of the first principles, and indeed they are better known$_g$ than the conclusions derived from them; but we have no knowledge$_e$ of the principles, since knowledge$_e$ requires DEMONSTRATION and the first principles are indemonstrable.

32. **an account**: Contrast i 3.

33. **The principle**: i.e., understanding. Aristotle again relies on the use of *archē* for 'starting point'.

TOPICS[1]

BOOK I

[THE THEORY AND PRACTICE OF DIALECTIC]

[DIALECTIC AND DEDUCTION]

1

The purpose of our discussion[2] is to discover a line* of inquiry that will   *100a18*
allow us to reason deductively* from common* beliefs on any problem   *20*
proposed to us, and to give an account ourselves[3] without saying anything contradictory. First, then, we must say what a deduction is and
what different types of it there are, so that we can grasp what dialectical
deduction is—for this is what we are looking for in our proposed discussion.

A deduction, then, is an argument[4] in which, if p and q are assumed,   *25*
then something else r, different from p and q, follows necessarily through
p and q.[5] It is a demonstration whenever the deduction proceeds from
true and primary premisses or our knowledge_g of the premisses is originally derived from primary and true premisses.[6] A dialectical deduction   *30*
is the one that proceeds from common beliefs.

The premisses that are true and primary are those that produce convic-   *100b*

---

1. The *Topics* is about *topoi*, 'places' (hence 'commonplaces'). See 163b20–31.
'Places' probably refers to a technique for remembering a list of items by correlat-
ing them with a previously learned grid or list of places. Hence the dialectical
'places' are common forms of argument to be remembered for use in dialectical
discussions. See also *Rhet.* 1395b22, 1396b21.

2. **discussion**: Or 'treatise', *pragmateia*.

3. **give an account ourselves**: i.e., as respondents in a dialectical discussion.

4. **argument**: or 'discourse', *logos*. See REASON #3.

5. **if p and q ... p and q**: Lit., 'when some things have been laid down,
something other than the things laid down comes about by necessity, through
the things laid down'. On this definition of DEDUCTION see *APr* 24b18n.

6. **or our ... premisses**: Lit. 'or whenever it proceeds from things of the sort
that have the origin of knowledge about them through some primary and true
things'.

20 tion* not through other things, but through themselves.[7] For in the principles of knowledge_e we must not search further for the reason why; rather, each of the principles must be credible itself in its own right.

The common beliefs are the things believed by everyone or by most people or by the wise (and among the wise by all or by most or by those most known and commonly recognized[8]). A contentious* deduction is
25 one proceeding from apparent common beliefs that are not really common beliefs, or one apparently proceeding from real or apparent common beliefs. <We speak of 'apparent' common beliefs,> because not everything that appears to be a common belief really is one; for none of the things called common beliefs has the appearance entirely on the surface.[9] On this point they differ from what happens in the case of the principles
30 of contentious arguments. For in the latter case the nature of the falsity is especially clear straightaway to those with even a little ability to trace
101a consequences.[10] The first kind of deduction that we have called contentious, then, should indeed count as a genuine deduction, whereas the other kind is a contentious deduction, but not a genuine deduction, since it appears to make a deduction, but does not actually do so.[11]
5 Further, apart from all the types of deduction just mentioned, there are fallacious arguments that start from premises that are proper to a given science, as happens in the case of geometry and cognate sciences. For this type of argument would seem to be different from the types of
10 deduction previously mentioned; for someone who draws the wrong diagram deduces a conclusion neither from true and primary premises nor from common beliefs. He does not fall into either class, since he does not accept what is believed by all, or by most people, or by the wise (either all or most or the most commonly recognized of these), but produces his deduction by accepting things that are proper* to the science
15 but are not true. For example, he produces his fallacious argument[12] either by describing the semicircles wrongly or by drawing lines wrongly.

These, then, are, in outline, the types of deduction. In general, both
20 in all the cases we have discussed and in all those to be discussed

7. **through themselves**: These premises are described in *APo* 100b5–17.

8. **commonly recognized**: *endoxos*. 'Common beliefs' translates *endoxa*.

9. **has . . . surface**: The appearance, *phainomenon* or *phantasia*, stating the real content of the common belief, is not always obvious at first sight.

10. **even a little . . . consequences**: Or perhaps 'able to see the details (lit. small points)'.

11. **The first . . . make one**: The first kind of CONTENTIOUS deductive argument argues validly from premises that are not genuine common beliefs. The second begins from real or apparent common beliefs and argues invalidly from them.

12. **fallacious argument**: Aristotle is thinking of attempts to square the circle.

later, this degree of determinateness is to be taken as adequate. For <in undertaking this discussion> the account we decide to give on any subject is not an exact* account, but enough for us to describe it in outline. We assume that the ability to recognize these things in some way is entirely adequate for the proposed line of inquiry.

[THE USES OF DIALECTIC]

2

Our next task is to say what areas, and how many, there are in which our discussion is useful. It is useful, then, for three purposes—for training, for encounters, and for the philosophical sciences.

Its usefulness for training is immediately evident; for if we have a line of inquiry, we will more easily be able to take on a question proposed   25
to us. It is useful for encounters,[13] because once we have catalogued the beliefs of the many, our approach to them will begin from their own views, not from other people's, and we will redirect them whenever they appear to us to be wrong. It is useful for the philosophical sciences, because the ability to survey the puzzles on each side of a question   35
makes it easier to notice what is true and false. Moreover it is useful for finding the primary things in each science.[14] For from the principles proper to the science proposed for discussion nothing can be derived about the principles themselves, since the principles are primary among all <the truths contained in the science>; instead they must be discussed   101b
through the common beliefs in a given area. This is distinctive of dialectic, or more proper to it than to anything else; for since it cross-examines, it provides a way toward the principles of all lines of inquiry.

[THE PROPER AIM OF THE DIALECTICIAN]

3

We will have grasped the line of inquiry completely once our grasp is   5
similar to one's grasp of rhetoric, medicine, and similar capacities—and this is to achieve what we decide on from among the things that are possible. For the orator or doctor will not succeed in all circumstances[15]

13. **encounters**: Cf. *Rhet.* 1355a28.

14. **Moreover . . . science**: Probably this is part of the third function of dialectic; but it may be intended as a fourth function, added as an afterthought.

15. **in all circumstances**: Lit. 'from every way'.

10   in persuading or healing; rather, we will ascribe an adequate grasp of
      the science to him if he omits nothing that is possible.[16]

      [THE ELEMENTS OF DIALECTIC]

      4

      First, then, we should study what this line of inquiry consists of. If we
      find what sorts of things and how many things the arguments are di-
      rected to, what their sources are, and how we are to be well supplied
      with them, we will adequately fulfill the task before us.
           The sources of arguments are equal in number to, and indeed are
15   identical to, the subjects of deductions. For arguments are constructed
      from premisses,* and deductions are about problems; and every premiss
      and every problem reveals either a distinctive property or a genus or a
      coincident (for the differentia should be classified together with the
      genus, since it is generic in character). And since the distinctive property
20   in some cases signifies the essence and in other cases does not, let us
      take it to be divided into the two types previously mentioned; let us call
      the type signifying the essence the formula,*[17] and the other type the
      distinctive property (using for it the name[18] that is <sometimes> applied
      to them both indiscriminately[19]).
           It is clear, then, from what we have said that in accordance with this
25   division, everything turns out to be one of these four—either a definition
      or a distinctive property or a genus or a coincident.[20] No one should
      suppose, however, that we mean that each of them, spoken of by itself,
      is a premiss or a problem. Rather, we mean that from these both problems
      and premisses are constructed.
30   A problem differs from a premiss in its manner of expression; for if
      one says 'Is biped land animal the definition of man?' or 'Is animal the
      genus of man?', then we have a premiss. If, however, one says 'Is biped
      land animal the definition of man, or not?', we have a problem; and the

      16. **rather we . . . possible**: The competent doctor tries to do everything proper
      to the craft in order to heal; he is no less competent if, through no fault of his
      own, the craft does not produce the desired result. Cf. *Rhet.* 1355b10–14.

      17. **formula**: Aristotle is not necessarily thinking, or thinking exclusively, of a
      linguistic expression (see SIGNIFY). He may instead, or also, be thinking of what
      is defined by the linguistic expression—e.g., of biped animal as well as 'biped
      animal'.

      18. **the name**: Aristotle proposes to confine the name 'distinctive property',
      idion, to nonessential properties.

      19. **that is . . . indiscriminately**: Lit. 'according to the common naming of them'.

      20. **these four . . . coincident**: They are traditionally called the four 'predicables'.

same is true in the other cases. It is not surprising, then, that problems   *35*
and premisses are equal in number; for a problem can be formed from
every premiss by changing the manner of expression.[21]

[THE MAIN CONCEPTS USED IN DIALECTICAL QUESTIONS]

5

We must say, then, what a definition, a distinctive property, a genus,
and a coincident are.

A definition is an account[22] that signifies the essence. One provides
either an account to replace a name or an account to replace an account—   *102a*
for it is also possible to define some of the things signified by an account.
Those who merely provide a name, whatever it is, clearly do not provide
the definition of the thing, since every definition is an account. Still, this   *5*
sort of thing—for example, 'the fine is the fitting'[23]—should also be
counted as definitory. In the same way one should also count as definitory a question such as 'Are perception and knowledge$_e$ the same or
different?'; for most of the discussion about definition is occupied with
whether things are the same or different. Speaking without qualification,
we may count as definitory everything that falls under the same line of   *10*
inquiry that includes definition.

It is clear immediately that all the things just mentioned meet this
condition. For if we are able to argue dialectically that things are the
same and that they are different, we will in the same way be well supplied
to take on definitions;[24] for once we have shown that two things are not
the same, we will have undermined the <attempted> definition. The   *15*
converse of this point, however, does not hold; for showing that two
things are the same is not enough to establish a definition, whereas
showing that two things are not the same is enough to destroy a definition.

A distinctive* property is one that does not reveal what the subject

21. **for a problem . . . expression**: Aristotle distinguishes problems (explicitly
posing alternatives) from PREMISSES, to indicate the order of dialectical inquiry.
We construct a deduction by taking one of the alternatives in the problem, stating
it as a premiss (as a question), and then trying to deduce it (in indicative form)
from common beliefs.

22. **account**: *logos*. See REASON #4–5. This is not necessarily (see 101b22n) a
linguistic expression (though here the contrast with names suggests that this is
what Aristotle has in mind).

23. **'the fine is the fitting'**: Aristotle objects that this provides a single word
('fitting') instead of a *logos* as a definition.

24. **take on**: especially for the purpose of attacking them.

20

is, though it belongs only to that subject and is reciprocally predicated of it. It is distinctive of man, for instance, to be receptive of grammatical knowledge; for if someone is a man, he is receptive of grammatical knowledge, and if someone is receptive of grammatical knowledge, he is a man. For no one counts as a distinctive property what admits of belonging to something else—for instance, no one counts being asleep as a distinctive property of a man, even if at some time it happens to belong only to him. If, then, something of this sort were to be called a distinctive property, it would be called distinctive not without qualification, but at a time, or in relation to something; being on the right, for instance, is distinctive of something at a particular time, while being a biped is distinctive of one thing in relation to another—of man, for instance, in relation to horse and dog. It is clear that nothing that admits of belonging to something else is reciprocally predicated of its subject; it is not necessary, for instance, that what is asleep is a man.

25

30

A genus* is what is essentially predicated[25] of a plurality of things differing in species. Let us count as essentially predicated whatever it is appropriate to mention if we are asked what a given thing is; when we are asked what man is, for instance, it is appropriate to say that it is an animal. It is also relevant to the genus to say whether two things are in the same genus, or each is in a different genus, since this also falls under the same line of inquiry as the genus. If, for instance, we argue dialectically that animal is the genus of man, and also of ox, we will have argued that they are in the same genus; and if we prove that something is the genus of one thing but not of another, we will have argued that these two things are not in the same genus.

35

102b

5

A coincident* is what though it is none of these things—neither a definition nor a distinctive property nor a genus—belongs to the subject. Again, it is whatever admits both of belonging and of not belonging to one and the same subject. Being seated, for instance, admits both of belonging and of not belonging to one and the same subject, and so does being pale, since the same subject may easily be pale at one time and not pale at another. The second of these two definitions of coincident is better. For if the first is stated, we will not understand it unless we first know what a definition, a distinctive property, and a genus are; the second, however, is sufficient in its own right for our knowing$_g$ what is meant.

10

15

Let us also add to the <class of> coincidents the comparisons between things whose descriptions are derived in some way from the coincident. These include, for instance, the question whether the fine or the advantageous is more choiceworthy, or whether the life of virtue or the life of

25. **essentially predicated**: Lit. 'predicated in the what-it-is'.

gratification is pleasanter, and any other questions similar to these. For
in all such cases the question proves to be about whether the thing   *20*
predicated is more <properly> a coincident of the one subject or of the
other.

It is immediately clear that a coincident may easily be distinctive of
a subject at a particular time and in relation to a particular thing. Whenever, for instance, someone is the only one seated, being seated, which
is a coincident, is distinctive at that time; and when he is not the only
one seated, being seated is distinctive of him in relation to those not
seated. Hence a coincident may easily turn out to be distinctive in relation   *25*
to a particular thing and at a particular time, but it is not a distinctive
property without qualification.

*　*　*　*　*　*　*

[THE CATEGORIES]

9

Next, then, we must determine the genera of predications* in which the   *103b20*
four things previously mentioned belong. These are ten in number: what-
it-is, quantity, quality,[26] relative, when, where, being placed, having,
acting on, being affected. For in every case the coincident, the genus,
the distinctive property, and the definition will be in one of these predica- *25*
tions; for all the premisses involving these four things signify either
what-it-is or quantity or quality or one of the other predications.

It is immediately clear that whoever signifies the what-it-is sometimes
signifies substance, sometimes quantity, sometimes quality, sometimes
one of the other predications.[27] Whenever, for instance, a man[28] is pre-   *30*
sented and one says that the thing presented is a man or that it is an
animal, one says what it is and signifies a substance. When a pale color
is presented and one says that the thing presented is pale or that it is a
color, one says what it is and signifies a quality. Likewise, if a yard's
length is presented and one says that the thing presented is a yard's
length, one says what it is and signifies a quantity. The same is also   *35*
true in the other cases. For if any of these things is said about itself or
its genus is said about it, then it signifies[29] what-it-is; but whenever it

26. **quantity, quality**: The abstract nouns translate Greek adjectives. See *Catg.*
1b26n.

27. **It is . . . predications**: Here 'what-it-is' applies to all categories. Just above
it seemed to be a name for the category of substance. Cf. *Met.* 1028b36–b2.

28. **a man**: i.e., an individual man. Or perhaps 'man', i.e., the species.

29. **it signifies**: Or 'one signifies'.

is asserted of something else, it does not signify what-it-is, but quantity or quality or one of the other predications.

These, then, are the subjects and the components of the arguments. Next we must say how we are to find arguments, and how we are to get a good supply of them.

104a

[THE USE OF COMMON BELIEFS]

10

First, then, let us determine what a dialectical premiss is and what a dialectical problem is; for not every premiss or problem should be counted as dialectical. For no one with any sense would propose something that no one believes or something that is apparent to all or most people; in the second case no puzzle arises, and in the first case no one would put it forward.

A dialectical premiss asks about something that is commonly believed, either by everyone, or by most people, or by the wise (all, or most, or the best known), and that is not in conflict with common beliefs[30]—for one might put forward what is believed by the wise, as long as it is not contrary to the beliefs of the many.

Dialectical premisses also include those that are similar to the common beliefs, and the denials of the contraries of what seem to be common beliefs, and as many beliefs as accord with the crafts that have been found. If, for instance, it is a common belief that one and the same science grasps contraries, it might also appear to be a common belief that one and the same sense grasps contraries. If it is a common belief that grammatical science is a single science, then it might also appear to be a common belief that flute-playing science is a single science; and if, on the contrary, it is a common belief that there is more than one science of grammar, then it might also appear to be a common belief that there is more than one science of flute-playing—for all these would seem to be similar and akin.

Similarly, the denials of things contrary to the common beliefs will appear to be common beliefs. If, for instance, it is a common belief that one ought to treat one's friends well, then it is a common belief that one ought not to treat them badly. In this case the contrary is the claim that one ought to treat one's friends badly, and the denial is the claim that one ought not to treat them badly. The same is true of the claim that if one ought to treat one's friends well, one ought not to treat one's enemies

30. **in conflict with common beliefs**: *paradoxos*. Cf. the comment on Socrates' view about incontinence, *EN* 1145b27.

well. This also involves denial of contraries; for the contrary is the claim that one ought to treat one's enemies well.

Further, the contrary of the contrary in a comparison will also appear a common belief—for instance, if one ought to treat one's friends well, one ought also to treat one's enemies badly. Treating one's friends well   *30* might appear contrary to treating one's enemies badly—we will say, however, whether or not this is really so, in our discussion of contraries.[31]

It is also clear that whatever beliefs are in accordance with crafts are dialectical premises. For one might put forward what is believed by those who have examined the question—as the doctor thinks, for instance, on medical questions, and as the geometer thinks on geometrical questions, and so on in the other cases.

* * * * * * *

[INDUCTIVE AND DEDUCTIVE ARGUMENT]

12

Now that these points have been determined, we should distinguish   *105a10* the different types of dialectical argument. One type is induction,* one deduction. What deduction is we have said previously. Induction is a transition from the particulars to the universal. For instance, if the one who knows$_e$ is the best pilot and the best charioteer, then in general the   *15* one who knows is best in a given area. Induction is more persuasive and more perspicuous, better known$_g$ on the basis of perception, and shared with the many. Deduction, on the other hand, is more forceful, and more effective against people who go in for contradicting <other people's views>.[32]

* * * * * * *

BOOK VI

[DEFINITIONS]

4

. . . Whether or not someone has defined and stated the essence is to   *141a24* be examined on the following grounds.   *25*

First, we should see whether he has constructed the definition out of things that are prior and better known$_g$. For a formula[1] is supplied to

---

31. **discussion of contraries**: *Top.* ii 7.

32. **people . . . views>**: Plato's *Euthydemus* is an encounter with such people.

 1. **formula**: *horos.* This seems to be used interchangeably with 'definition', *horismos*, in this chapter.

give knowledge, and we gain knowledge not from just any old thing,

30   but from things that are prior and better known,[2] as is true in demonstrations—for that is the character of all teaching and learning. Hence it is apparent that whoever fails to define through these things has not given a definition at all.

If this is not so, there will be more than one definition of the same thing. For <if we recognize definitions that are not through prior and better-known things,> it is clear that someone who uses prior and better-known things has also given a definition—in fact a better one; and so both would be formulae of the same thing. Such a thing does not seem

35   <possible>, however. For each being has just one essence;[3] and so, if there is more than one definition of the same thing, the essence revealed by each of the definitions will be the same as the thing defined, whereas

141b   in fact they are not the same, since the definitions are different. Clearly, then, someone who has not given a definition through prior and better-known things has not given a definition.

The objection that the formula has not been stated through better-known things can be understood in either of two ways: either <that it is composed> of things less well known without qualification, or <that

5   it is composed> of things less well known to us—for either case may arise. The prior* is better known without qualification than the posterior. The point, for instance, is better known than the line, and the line than the plane, and the plane than the solid, just as the unit is better known than the number (since the unit is prior to any number and is the principle of number); the same is true of the letter and the syllable. <In the case

10   of what is better known> to us, by contrast, the opposite is sometimes true; for the solid is more readily available to perception than the other things, and the plane more than the line, and the line more than the point. For most people come to know_g these <more readily perceptible> things first, since any sort of intellect can learn about them, whereas it takes a superior and exact* intellect to learn about the things that are

15   naturally prior.

Without qualification, then, it is better to seek knowledge_g of the posterior things through the prior things, since that is a more scientific[4] procedure. Still, in dealing with people who are incapable of acquiring knowledge through these prior things, it is presumably necessary to construct an account through the things known to them. Definitions of

20   this sort include those of the point, the line, and the plane. For all these

---

2. **prior and better known**: See KNOW #2.

3. **essence**: *hoper estin.* See ESSENCE #2.

4. **more scientific**: i.e., more characteristic of knowledge_e. See KNOWLEDGE #1.

reveal the prior things through the posterior—it is said that a point is the limit of a line, a line of a surface, and a surface of a solid.

We must realize, however, that someone who offers this sort of definition cannot possibly reveal the essence of the thing being defined, unless the same thing turns out to be both better known to us and better known   *25* without qualification. For a correct definition must be given through the genus and the differentiae, and these are better known without qualification and prior to the species; for the destruction of the genus and differentia involves the destruction of the species, so that they are prior to it.[5] They are also better known. For it is necessary that if the   *30* species is known, the genus and differentia are known (for example, someone who knows man also knows both animal and terrestrial), but it is not necessary that if the genus or the differentia is known, the species is also known; and so the species is less well known.

Moreover, those who claim that these definitions based on what is   *35* known to each person are really definitions[6] will end up saying that there are many definitions of the same thing. For in fact different things are better known to different people, not the same things to everyone; and so a different definition will have to be provided for each person,   *142a* if definitions ought to be constructed from the things known to each person.

Further, different things are better known to the same people at different times. Originally perceptibles are better known <than things grasped by intellect>, but when people become more exact, it is the other way round. Hence those who assert that a definition should be provided   *5* through the things better known to a given group of people do not always have to provide the same definition for the same person.

It is clear, then, that we should not give definitions through such things, but through things that are better known without qualification. For this is the only way that there will turn out to be one and the same definition for each thing. And presumably what is known without qualification is not what is known to everyone, but what is   *10* known to those in a good intellectual condition, just as what is healthy without qualification is what is healthy for those in a good bodily condition.[7]

We must, then, work out all of these points exactly and use them advantageously in dialectical argument. . . .

---

5. **prior to it**: This is a partial statement of conditions for natural priority. The next two sentences give a full statement of conditions for priority in knowledge. See PRIOR #1.

6. **are really definitions**: Or perhaps 'accord with truth'.

7. **just as . . . condition**: Cf. *Met.* 1010b3–9n.

* * * * * * *

Book IX[1]

[PLATO'S 'THIRD MAN' ARGUMENT]

22

178b36   . . . There is also the argument that there is a third man apart* from man himself[2] and the particular men. For man and everything common signify not a this,* but this sort of thing[3] or a quantity or a relative or something else of that kind. The same applies to the question about
179a   whether Coriscus and musical Coriscus are the same or different;[4] for the former signifies a this, and the latter this sort of thing, so that it cannot be isolated.[5]

The source of the third man, however, is not the isolation <of man>,
5   but the concession that it is essentially[6] a this. For being essentially what man is cannot be a this, as Callias is. And even if someone were to say that what is isolated is not essentially a this, but essentially a sort of thing, it will make no difference. For there will still be a one—for instance, man—apart* from the many.

It is clear, then, that one ought not to grant that what is predicated in common of all things <of a given kind> is a this; rather one should
10   grant that it signifies* either a sort of thing or a relative or a quantity or something of that kind.

* * * * * * *

[THE PROGRESS OF DIALECTICAL THEORY]

34

183a37   . . . Our plan was to find an ability to form deductions from the most commonly accepted beliefs available on any question proposed
183b   to us. For this is the task both of dialectic in its own right and of

---

1. Book ix of the *Topics* is traditionally entitled *De Sophisticis Elenchis,* 'On Sophistical Refutations'. See SOPHIST. The discussion of Plato's Third Man Argument (see FORM (PLATONIC) #3) included here occurs in a discussion of fallacies arising from misleading forms of expression.

2. **man himself**: i.e., the Platonic Form.

3. **this sort of thing**: *toionde.* This term and *poion* (translated 'a sort of thing') are sometimes usd to refer to secondary substance, but sometimes to refer to QUALITY. It is not clear which use Aristotle has in mind in this passage.

4. **Coriscus . . . different**: Cf. *Met.* 1004b2, 1032a4.

5. **isolated**: Cf. *Met.* 1031b21.

6. **essentially**: See ESSENCE #2.

testing.[7] We must also, however, prepare ourselves in advance[8] for it because of its closeness to sophistry, so that we shall be able not only to test dialectically, but also to <argue> as people who know$_o$. This was why we laid down not only the previously mentioned task for our discussion—to be able to get someone else to give an account <as a result of our testing him>—but also the task of defending a position dialectically through the most commonly accepted beliefs possible, when we are required to give an account ourselves. We have stated the reason for this.[9] Indeed, this was why Socrates* used to ask questions, but not to answer them; for he used to admit that he did not know.

We have made it clear above what our arguments are aimed at, and what their sources are, and where we can get a good supply of these sources. Further, we have described ways to ask questions, and ways to arrange every type of questioning, and the lines of answering and dissolution to be directed at deductions. We have also clarified the other things that belong to the same line of inquiry into arguments. In addition, we have gone through fallacious arguments, as we said before. It is apparent, then, that our plan has adequately reached its completion.

We must also, however, take note of the actual situation of this sort of discussion. What happens in the case of all discoveries is that the later workers take over the results of their predecessors' labor, and advance them gradually; the original discoverers usually make only a little progress, but this is far more useful than the later growth resulting from these discoveries. For presumably in every case the beginning is, as they say, the greatest part,[10] and that is why it is also the most difficult part; for the unequalled importance of its effects is proportional to the smallness of its bulk and hence to the difficulty of seeing it. And once the origin has been found, it is easier to add and to develop the rest.

This has already happened in the case of rhetorical speeches, and indeed of practically all the other crafts. Those who found the origins made an extremely small advance, whereas the people who are eminent now took it over, as in a relay, from many predecessors who had gradually improved it, and in that way have developed it further. Teisias came after the first practitioners, after Teisias came Thrasymachus, and after him Theodorus; and many others have developed many parts of it. For this reason it is not at all surprising that this craft has achieved some considerable scope.

7. **testing**: See DIALECTIC.

8. **prepare ourselves in advance**: Text and sense uncertain.

9. **the reason for this**: 165a19.

10. **the beginning**: See PRINCIPLE #1. For the proverb alluded to here cf. *EN* 1098b7.

35   In our present discussion, by contrast, it was not true that some work had been done and some remained to be done; on the contrary, nothing at all had been done. The education* provided by the paid practitioners of contentious argument was similar to Gorgias' practice. For just as some people handed out rhetorical speeches to be learned by heart, in the same way others handed out the contentious arguments that they

184a   thought would be used most often in arguments with other people. Hence their teaching of their pupils was quick, but quite without any craft. For although they supposed that they were educating people, what they gave them were the products of a craft, not the craft itself. It is as

5   though someone were to claim that he would pass on a science[11] for relieving wear on the feet, and then did not teach the shoemaking craft or any other way of being able to produce such relief, but gave them shoes of many kinds and of varying quality; such a person has done something to meet a need, but he has not passed on any craft.

          Moreover, in the area of rhetoric there were already many things said

184b   for a long time; but in the area of deduction[12] nothing at all was available to us before we worked it out by investigation and practice over a long time.

          If you survey our work, realizing that this was the situation we began from, and if our line* of inquiry appears to have reached adequate results

5   in comparison with the treatments of other subjects that have been developed by tradition, then the remaining task for you, our audience, is to be considerate toward the omissions in our line of inquiry, and to appreciate greatly what has been discovered.

11. **science**: This passage brings out the connection between science (*epistēmē*; see KNOW #1) and finding the CAUSE or explanation; see *Met.* i 1.

12. **deduction**: This may suggest that Aristotle intends these reflections on his discoveries to apply to the general discussion of deduction in the *Analytics* as well as to the discussion of dialectic in the *Topics*.

PHYSICS[1]

Book I

[THE METHOD OF INQUIRY]

[KNOWLEDGE OF PRINCIPLES]

1

In every line* of inquiry into something that has principles[2] or causes   *184a10*
or elements, we achieve knowledge$_o$—that is, scientific knowledge$_e$—
by knowing$_g$ them; for we think we know$_g$ a thing when we know its
primary causes and primary principles, all the way to its elements.
Clearly, then, it is also true in the science of nature that our first task is   *15*
to determine the principles.

   The natural path is to start from what is better known$_g$ and more
perspicuous* to us, and to advance to what is more perspicuous and
better known by nature; for what is better known to us is not the same
as what is better known without qualification. We must advance in this
way, then, from what is less perspicuous by nature but more perspicuous   *20*
to us, to what is more perspicuous and better known by nature.[3]

[UNIVERSALS AND PARTICULARS]

The things that, most of all, are initially clear and perspicuous to us
are inarticulate wholes; later, as we articulate them, the elements and
principles come to be known$_g$ from them. We must, then, advance from

---

   1. This title (unlike, e.g., *Catg.*) seems to go back to Aristotle himself. He refers
to all or parts of the *Physics* as *ta phusika*, i.e., 'the work on NATURE (*phusis*)'. The
title may be partly inspired by the treatises of the Presocratic NATURALISTS 'On
Nature'. Aristotle discusses some of their views in Bk i; at the beginning of Bk
ii he explains how he understands 'nature'.

   2. **principles**: 'Origins' would often be appropriate in Bk i (see PRINCIPLE); but
to display the connection of thought, we have kept 'principles' throughout.

   3. **We must advance . . . known by nature**: See KNOW #2.

25   universals to particulars;[4] for the whole is better known in perception, and the universal is a sort of whole, since it includes many things as

184b   parts. The same is true, in a way, of names in relation to their accounts. For a name—for instance, 'circle'—signifies a sort of whole and signifies indefinitely, whereas the definition <of a circle> articulates it by stating the particular <properties>.[5] Again, children begin by calling all men 'father' and all women 'mother'; only later do they distinguish different men and different women.

* * * * * * *

[THE GENERAL PRINCIPLES OF COMING TO BE]

[COMING TO BE IS NOT A RANDOM PROCESS, BUT INVOLVES CONTRARIES]

5[6]

188a31   We must first of all grasp the fact that nothing that exists is naturally such as to act or be affected in just any old way[7] by the agency of just any old thing; nor does something come to be just any old thing[8] from

35   just any old thing, unless you consider coincidents. For how could <something> come to be pale from being musical,[9] unless musical were a coincident[10] of the not-pale or the dark thing?[11] Rather, something

---

4. **from universals to particulars**: This is how we clarify very general principles that we do not fully understand at the start. Contrast *APo* 72a4 (which describes INDUCTION).

5. **For . . . <properties>**: We may be able to use the name 'circle' roughly correctly (so that we are usually able to identify actual circles), without having a clear conception of the properties constitutive of being a circle. We get a clear conception from the definition. See PARTICULAR #2.

6. In i 2–4 Aristotle discusses (1) arguments of the Eleatics (see PARMENIDES, MELISSUS) against the reality of COMING TO BE and (2) views of other Presocratics on the sorts of principles needed to account for coming to be. He rejects (1) and now offers his own account of the principles considered in (2).

7. **just any old way**: See LUCK #2.

8. **nor does . . . old thing**: Because of the ambiguity of 'COMING TO BE' this phrase might also be rendered (less probably) 'nor does any old thing come to be'. The same is true in the rest of the chapter.

9. **from being musical**: Lit. 'out of musical' (and so on in all such expressions in i 5–9).

10. **coincident**: A man, e.g., is a pale thing, and this pale thing is COINCIDENTALLY musical (since being musical is not ESSENTIAL to it); cf. *Met.* 1017a7–13.

11. **the not-pale or the dark thing**: Aristotle uses just the neuter definite article and adjective, which might refer either to the quality or to the subject that has it. Cf. 189b35n, *GC* 318a31n, *Met.* 1031b22–28.

comes to be pale from being not-pale—and not simply from being not-pale, but from being dark or something between dark and pale. Similarly, *188b* something becomes musical from being not-musical, and not from just any old way of being not-musical but from being unmusical or from being something (if there is anything) between musical and unmusical.[12]

Nor, on the other hand, does anything perish primarily into just any old thing. The pale thing, for instance, does not perish into the musical thing (unless it does so coincidentally), but into the not-pale thing, and *5* not into just any old not-pale thing, but into the dark thing or into something between pale and dark.[13] In the same way the musical thing perishes into the not-musical thing, and not into just any old not-musical thing, but into the unmusical thing or into something between musical and unmusical.

The same is also true in the other cases, since the same account applies to things that are not simple but composite;[14] but we do not notice that *10* this is so, because there is no name for the opposite condition in each case. For whatever is ordered must necessarily come to be from something disordered, and what is disordered from something ordered, and whatever is ordered must necessarily perish into disorder, and not into just any old disorder, but into the one opposed to that order. *15*

It makes no difference whether we speak of order or arrangement or combination, since it is evident that the same account applies to them all. Now, a house, a statue, and any other <artifact> comes to be in the same way. For a house comes to be from these <bricks etc.> which were not combined, but dispersed in this way; and a statue, or whatever is shaped, comes to be from shapelessness; and each of these is a case *20* of arrangement or combination.

If, then, this is true, everything that comes to be or perishes does so from one contrary into the other, or from or into the intermediate. And

12. **not from . . . unmusical**: If something that was pale and nonmusical becomes musical, it does not do so because it was previously pale, or because it was nonmusical in some other way; in order to become musical, it must have had the right sort of contrary (or intermediate) property that made it capable of the relevant change (in this case it must have been unmusical). See OPPOSITE.

13. **between pale and dark**: If Socrates was pale and becomes dark, and is musical throughout this change, we can describe the termini of the change by their proper characteristics ('the pale thing perished into the dark thing') or we can describe one or the other of them by a coincidental property ('the pale thing perished into the musical thing [i.e., the dark thing that was coincidentally musical]').

14. **but composite**: A statue is a composite of bronze (e.g.) and a certain shape. Aristotle believes that here also we must recognize an opposite, not the opposite of the statue or the bronze, but of the shape; this is what he calls 'shapelessness' (188b20).

25 the intermediates are from the contraries, as, for instance, colors are from pale and dark. And so all the things that come to be naturally are either contraries or from contraries. . . .[15]

* * * * * * *

[IN ADDITION TO CONTRARIES, COMING TO BE REQUIRES A SUBJECT]

6

189a27 . . . The following puzzle might arise if we do not assume some other nature as subject for the contraries. For we see[16] that contraries are not
30 the substance of anything that is, and a principle must not be said of any subject; for if it were, then the <alleged> principle would itself have a principle, since a subject seems[17] to be a principle of, and prior to, what is predicated of it. Further, we say that one substance is not contrary to another.[18] How, then, could a nonsubstance be prior to a substance?
35 That is why someone who takes both the previous argument[19] and
189b this one to be correct must, if he is to retain them both, assume a third thing as subject, as those theorists do who take the whole universe to be some one nature—water, fire, or something intermediate. And in fact something intermediate seems more reasonable, since fire, earth, air, and water are essentially[20] involved with contrarieties. . . .

* * * * * * *

[COMING TO BE IN GENERAL: SIMPLE AND COMPOUND]

7

189b30 Let us, then, give our own account[21] of coming to be, in the following way. And first let us deal with all of coming to be; for the natural

15. In the rest of i 5, Aristotle argues that the various Presocratic views confirm his conclusion.

16. **we see**: One of Aristotle's appeals to PERCEPTION in a rather wide sense, including APPEARANCES in general.

17. **seems**: See COMMON BELIEFS.

18. **one substance . . . another**: Cf. *Catg.* 3b24–32.

19. **the previous argument**: In i 5 Aristotle suggested that principles must include contraries. He now argues that contraries cannot be the only principles there are.

20. **essentially**: Lit. 'already'.

21. **our own account**: At the end of i 6 Aristotle asks whether there are two or three 'elements' (i.e., principles), and he now promises to answer that question. He answers it at 190b29.

procedure is to speak first about what is common to every case, and then to study what is special to each case.

When we say that something comes to be one thing from being another and different thing, we are speaking about either simple or compound things. What I mean is this: It is possible that a man comes to be musical, that the not-musical thing[22] comes to be musical, and that the not-musical man comes to be a musical man. By 'simple thing coming to be <F>' I mean the man and the not-musical thing; and by 'simple thing that comes into being'[23] I mean the musical thing. By 'compound' I mean both the thing that comes into being and what comes to be that thing, whenever we say that the not-musical man comes to be a musical man.

In one type of case we say not only that something comes to be F, but also that it comes to be F *from* being G;[24] for instance, <the man not only comes to be musical, but also comes to be> musical from being not-musical. But we do not say this for all <properties>; for <the man> did not come to be musical from being a man, but rather the man came to be musical.

When something comes to be F (in the sense in which we say a simple thing comes to be <something>), in some cases it remains when it comes to be F, and in other cases it does not remain. The man, for instance, remains a man and is still a man when he comes to be musical, whereas the not-musical or unmusical thing, either simple or compound, does not remain.[25]

[ALL COMING TO BE REQUIRES A SUBJECT]

Now that we have made these distinctions, here is something we can grasp from every case of coming to be, if we look at them all in the way described. In every case there must be some subject that comes to be <something>; even if it is one* in number, it is not one in form,* since

35

190a

5

10

15

22. **not-musical thing**: As before (see 188a36n), 'thing' is a supplement here and in the rest of this discussion.

23. **thing that comes into being'**: This refers to the product of the coming to be—in this case, to the musical thing that comes into being as a result of the man becoming musical.

24. **not only . . . being G**: Or: 'not only that it comes to be, but also that it comes to be from F'. See 188a33n. The second rendering is less likely, since Aristotle seems to introduce 'F comes to be' (i.e., comes to be without qualification) for the first time at 190a31. We have supplied the dummy letters ('F', etc.); Aristotle uses either nothing (leaving the reference to be gathered from the context) or demonstrative pronouns ('this comes to be this', etc.).

25. **The man, . . . does not remain**: This sentence refers to the three cases mentioned in 189b34–190a1.

being a man is not the same as being an unmusical thing.[26] (By 'in form' I mean the same as 'in account'.) One thing <that comes to be> remains, and one does not remain. The thing that is not opposite[27] remains, since
20 the man remains; but the not-musical thing, or the unmusical thing, does not remain. Nor does the thing compounded from both (for instance, the unmusical man) remain.

We say that something comes to be F from being G, but not that the G comes to be F,[28] more often in cases where G does not remain; for instance, we say that <a man> comes to be musical from being unmusical, but not that <the unmusical comes to be musical> from a man. Still, sometimes we speak in the same way in cases where G remains;
25 we say, for instance, that a statue comes to be from bronze, but not that the bronze comes to be a statue.[29] If, however, something comes to be F from being G, where G is opposite to F and G does not remain, we speak in both ways, saying both that something comes to be F from being G and that the G comes to be F; for it is true both that the man comes to be musical from being unmusical and that the unmusical one comes to be musical. That is why we also say the same about the com-
30 pound: we say both that the musical man comes to be musical from being an unmusical man and that the unmusical man comes to be musical.

[THE COMING TO BE OF SUBSTANCES]

Things are said to come to be in many ways, and some things are said not to come to be, but to come to be something; only substances are said to come to be without* qualification. In the other cases it is evident that there must be some subject that comes to be <something>; for in fact, when <something> comes to be of some quantity or quality, or
35 relative to another, or somewhere, something is the subject <underlying the change>, because a substance is the only thing that is never said of
190b any other subject, whereas everything else is said of a substance.[30]

26. **being a man . . . being an unmusical thing**: On 'being F' and 'being G' see ESSENCE #2.

27. **not opposite**: sc. to the thing that comes into being.

28. **but not that the G comes to be F**: The text in a21–22 is uncertain, and the interpretation is uncertain up to 'comes to be a statue', a26.

29. **but . . . statue**: Lit. just 'not the bronze [noun] statue'. Cf. *Met.* 1033a5–23, 1049a18–27.

30. **said of a substance**: Aristotle uses 'said of a subject' more broadly here than in *Catg.* 1a21. In the *Catg.* the phrase is confined to the predication of essential properties. Here (and elsewhere; cf. *Met.* 1017b24, 1028b26) it also includes nonessential properties (and so includes the cases where the *Catg.* speaks of being 'in a subject'). On substance and subject see SUBJECT.

However, substances—the things that are without qualification[31]—also come to be from some subject. This will become evident if we examine it. For in every case there is something that is a subject from which the thing that comes to be comes to be, as plants and animals come to be from seed.   5

Some of the things that come to be without qualification do so by change of figure (for instance, a statue);[32] some by addition (for instance, growing things); some by subtraction (for instance, Hermes from the stone); some by composition (for instance, a house); some by alteration (for instance, things changing in accordance with their matter). It is evident that everything that comes to be in this way comes to be from   10
a subject.

And so it is clear from what has been said that, in every case, what comes to be is composite: there is something that comes into being and something that comes to be this. And this latter thing is of two sorts: either the subject or the opposite. I mean, for instance, that the unmusical is opposite, and the man is subject; and that the lack of figure, shape,   15
and order is the opposite, and the bronze, stone, or gold is the subject.

Suppose, then, that there are indeed causes and principles of natural things, from which they primarily are and have come to be—not come to be coincidentally, but come to be what each thing is called in accordance with its essence$_o$.[33] It evidently follows that everything comes to   20
be from the subject and the shape.[34] For in a way the musical man is composed from man and musical, since you will analyze him into their accounts. It is clear, then, that whatever comes to be does so from these things.

The subject is one in number but two in form.[35] Man, gold, and matter*   25
in general, is countable, since it is a this[36] more <than the privation is>, and what comes to be comes to be from it not coincidentally. The privation—the contrariety—is a coincident. The form is one—for instance, structure, musicality, or anything else predicated in this way.

31. **are without qualification**: They are not merely qualities (etc.) of some further subject. Cf. *APo* 83a8–14, *Met.* 1028a30.

32. **statue**: On artifacts as substances see CRAFT.

33. **not come . . . its essence$_o$**: These are the causes of its coming to be (for example) a tree, not of its (coincidentally) coming to be liable to be struck by lightning.

34. **shape**: Here *morphē* is the physical shape, though at 190b28 it is closely connected with form, *eidos*. See FORM #4.

35. **two in form**: i.e., two in being—the matter and the privation.

36. **is a this**: Here being a this (see THIS #3) is connected with being a definite identifiable particular.

Hence we should say that in one way there are two principles, and that
30   in another way there are three.[37] In one way they are contraries—if, for
instance, one were to speak of the musical and the unmusical, or the
hot and the cold, or the ordered and the disordered. But in another way
they are not contraries, since contraries cannot be affected by each other.[38]
This <puzzle about how becoming is possible> is also solved by the
35   fact that the subject is something different, since it is not a contrary.

Hence, in a way the principles are no more numerous than the contraries, but, one might say, they are two in number. On the other hand,
191a   because they differ in being, they are not two in every way, but three;[39]
for being man is different from being unmusical, and being shapeless
is different from being bronze.

We have said, then, how many principles are relevant to the coming
to be of natural things, and we have described the different ways they
5   should be counted.[40] And it is clear that some subject must underlie
the contraries, and that there must be two contraries. In another way,
however, there need not be two; for just one of the contraries is enough,
by its absence or presence, to produce the thing.

The nature that is subject[41] is knowable$_e$ by analogy. For as bronze is
10   to a statue, or wood is to a bed, or as the shapeless before it acquires a
shape is to anything else that has a shape, so the nature that is subject
is to a substance, a this, and a being.[42]

This, then, is one principle; it is not one or a being in the way a this
is. Another principle is the one specified by the account,[43] and a third
is the contrary of this, the privation. The way in which these are two,
15   and the way in which they are more than two, has been stated above.

37. **Hence . . . are three**: See 189b30n.

38. **contraries. . . each other**: And so if there were only contraries, becoming
would be impossible.

39. **On the other . . . three**: The two things are subject and form. The third
thing is the privation, which is different from the subject in form, but not in
number.

40. **different . . . counted**: Lit. 'in what way how many' (referring to the difference between being one in number and being one in form).

41. **the nature that is subject**: Or 'the underlying nature', probably just a periph-
rasis for 'the subject'.

42. **a substance, a this, and a being**: Probably all three refer to the same thing.
For THIS cf. 190b25 (where, unusually, Aristotle apparently suggests that matter
is a this). Probably 'being' refers to being without qualification; see 190b2n.

43. **account**: This says what the statue, etc. is, and so specifies the FORM.

First, then, it was said that only the contraries were principles.[44] Later we added that something further is needed as subject and that there must be three principles. And from what we have said now it is evident how the contraries differ, how the principles are related to one another, and what the subject is. It is not yet clear, however, whether the form *20* or the subject is substance.[45] Still, it is clear that there are three principles, and in what way there are three, and what sorts of things they are. This, then, should allow us to observe how many principles there are, and what they are.

[A PUZZLE ABOUT THE IMPOSSIBILITY OF COMING TO BE]

8

This is also the only solution to the puzzle raised by the earlier philoso- phers, as we shall now explain. Those who were the first to search for *25* the truth philosophically and for the nature of beings were diverted and, so to speak, pushed off the track by inexperience. They say that nothing that is either comes to be or perishes. For, they say, what comes to be must come to be either from what is or from what is not, and coming to be is impossible in both cases; for what is cannot come to be (since it already is), while nothing can come to be from what is not (since there must be some subject). And then, having reached this result, they make things worse by going on to say that there is no plurality, but only being itself.[46]

[SOLUTION TO THE PUZZLE]

They accepted this belief for the reason mentioned. We reply as follows: The claim that something comes to be from what is or from what is not, *30* or that what is or what is not acts on something or is acted on or comes to be anything whatever, is in one way no different from the claim that, *191b* for instance, a doctor acts on something or is acted on, or is or comes to be something from being a doctor. We say this about a doctor in two ways; and so, clearly, we also speak in two ways when we say that something is or comes to be something from what is, and that what is is acting on something or being acted on.

44. **First . . . principles.**: This is a summary of i 5–7.

45. **whether . . . substance**: It is surprising that Aristotle considers only the matter and the form, and omits the statue (which might seem to be a compound of matter and form) as a candidate for being substance. See further *Met.* vii 3, 10–11, 1042a26–31, FORM.

46. **being itself**: i.e., the essence of being. This is the monist doctrine that Aristotle ascribes to PARMENIDES (discussed in i 2).

Now a doctor builds a house, not insofar as he is a doctor, but insofar
as he is a housebuilder; and he becomes pale, not insofar as he is a
doctor, but insofar as he is dark.[47] But he practices medicine, or loses
his medical knowledge, insofar as he is a doctor. We speak in the fullest
sense of a doctor acting on something or being acted on, or coming to
be something, from being a doctor, if it is insofar as he is a doctor that
he is acted on in this way or produces these things or comes to be these
things. So it is also clear that coming to be from what is not signifies
this: coming to be from it insofar as it is not.

The early philosophers failed to draw this distinction and gave up
the question. This ignorance led them into more serious ignorance—
so serious that they thought nothing else <besides what already is>
either is or comes to be, and so they did away with all coming to
be.

We agree with them in saying that nothing comes to be without
qualification from what is not, but we say that things come to be in a
way—for instance, coincidentally—from what is not. For something
comes to be from the privation, which in itself is not and which does
not belong to the thing <when it has come to be>. But this causes
surprise, and it seems impossible that something should come to be in
this way[48] from what is not.

Similarly, there is no coming to be, except coincidentally, from what
is, or of what is. But coincidentally what is also comes to be, in the same
way as if animal came to be from animal and a certain animal from a
certain animal. Suppose, for instance, that a dog came to be from a
horse.[49] For the dog would come to be not only from a certain animal,
but also from animal, though not insofar as it is animal (for that is
already present). But if a certain <sort of> animal is to come to be, not
coincidentally, it will not be from animal; and if a certain thing that is
<is to come to be>, it will not be from what is, nor from what is not.
For we have said what 'from what is not' signifies—i.e., insofar as it is

---

47. **Now a doctor . . . is dark**: Aristotle relies on his distinction between intrinsic
and coincidental CAUSES.

48. **in this way**: i.e., coincidentally.

49. **Suppose . . . from a horse**: Read *kuōn ex hippou*. (OCT: 'Suppose that a dog
came to be from a dog or a horse from a horse'.) Text and interpretation uncertain.
Aristotle appears to be considering an imaginary case of a horse turning into a
dog. In this case, he says, it would not be accurate to say that the dog comes
to be from an animal. The horse is the subject of the coming to be, not because
it is a horse or an animal (as Aristotle puts it, not INSOFAR AS it is an animal),
but because (we imagine) it provides matter suitable for the coming to be of a
dog (just as it is not qua animal that it provides suitable upholstery for a couch).

not. Further, we are not doing away with <the principle that> everything is or is not.[50]

This is one way <of solving this puzzle>. Another is <to note> that
the same things can be spoken of in accordance with potentiality and
actuality; this is discussed more exactly elsewhere.[51]

[THE IMPORTANCE OF UNDERSTANDING THE SUBJECT UNDERLYING CHANGE]

And so, as we have said, we have solved the puzzles that compelled   30
people to do away with some of the things we have mentioned. For this
is why earlier thinkers were also diverted from the road leading them
to <an understanding of> coming to be, perishing, and change in general. For if they had seen this nature <of the subject>, that would have
cured all their ignorance.

9

Admittedly other people touched on the nature of the subject, but did   35
not grasp it adequately. For first they agree that a thing comes to be
without qualification from what is not and that to this extent Parmenides   192a
is right;[52] but then it appears to them that if a thing is one in number,
it is also only one in potentiality—whereas in fact the two are very
different.

For we say that matter and privation are different and that matter is
coincidentally a not-being, whereas the privation is a not-being in its   5
own right. Moreover, we say that matter is close <to being substance>
and in a way is substance, whereas the privation is not substance in any
way. Previous thinkers,[53] however, identify both the great and the small

50. **Further . . . is not**: The statue, e.g., comes to be from the bronze, which is
(i.e., exists), but also is not (is not statue-shaped, when it still has the privation),
and comes to be coincidentally from the privation (since the bronze is coincidentally shapeless before it is shaped).

51. **elsewhere**: See *Met.* ix (though Aristotle need not be referring specifically
to this work). Aristotle means that we can say that the subject of coming to be
is POTENTIALLY the thing that results from the change.

52. **Parmenides is right**: He believed that (i) becoming requires becoming from
what is not, and (ii) becoming from what is not is impossible, and so inferred
(iii) becoming is impossible. Aristotle accepts (i) (suitably understood, in the
way he has specified) but rejects (ii), and so rejects (iii).

53. **Previous thinkers**: This apparently refers to the 'unwritten doctrines' of
PLATO. The plural is probably to be explained by Aristotle's apparent tendency
to use a vague plural on some occasions when in fact he has only one person
in mind (cf. *Met.* 1078b11 with 987a32–b7, and *EN* 1096a13).

10 (taken both together or each separately) with what is not, so that their conception of the three things involved must be quite different from ours. For they got as far as seeing that there must be some nature that is the subject, but they take this to be one—for even though someone takes it to be a pair (calling it the great and small), he still does the same thing <in taking it to be one>, since he overlooked the other nature.[54]

For the nature that remains[55] is a joint cause, together with the form$_m$, of what comes to be, as a mother is;[56] but the other part of the contrariety[57] 15 might often appear not to be at all, if one focuses on its evildoing aspect. For we say that one principle is divine, good, and an object of striving, while a second is contrary to the first, and the third naturally strives for the first and tends toward it in accordance with its own nature. In their 20 view,[58] by contrast, the contrary tends toward its own destruction. In fact, however, the form cannot strive for itself, since it does not lack <itself>; nor does the contrary strive for it, since contraries destroy each other. Hence what strives for the form must be the matter. It is as though the female strove to be male, or the ugly to be beautiful—except that 25 <the matter> is not ugly or female in its own right, but coincidentally.[59]

The <matter> perishes and comes to be in a way, and in a way it does not.[60] For as that in which <the privation is present> it perishes in its own right, since what perishes—the privation—is present in this; but as what is potentially <formed, the matter> does not come to be or perish in its own right, but must be without coming to be or perishing. For if it was coming to be, there has to be some primary subject from 30 which it was coming to be and which is present in it; and this is the very nature of matter. And so <if we assume that the matter comes to be,> it will already be before it has come to be—for by 'matter' I mean a thing's primary subject, from which the thing comes to be and which

54. **for even . . . nature**: Plato (referred to as 'someone') overlooked the privation as something distinct from the subject and the form. He characterizes the subject as 'the great and small', mentioning two opposites; but he does not recognize the sense in which subject, privation, and form are three principles.

55. **nature that remains**: i.e., matter.

56. **mother**: On reproduction see FORM #6.

57. **the other part of the contrariety**: i.e., the privation.

58. **In their view**: i.e., the Platonists' view.

59. **coincidentally**: only insofar as it has the privation, which is coincidental to it.

60. **The <matter> . . . does not**: The following argument shows that in every case of coming to be there is some matter that, in that process, does not come to be (and correspondingly for perishing). It does not show that there is some matter that never comes to be or perishes. Cf. *Met.* 1033a14–b10.

is present in the thing noncoincidentally. And on the other hand, if the matter perishes, it will come finally to <matter>, so that <if we assume that the matter perishes>, it will have perished before it has perished.

An exact* determination of questions about the formal principle—whether it is one or many, and what it is in each case—is a task for first philosophy*, and so we may put it off to that occasion.[61] Natural and *192b* perishable forms, however, will be discussed in the following exposition.

We have now determined, then, that there are principles, what they are, and how many they are. Let us now continue, after first making a fresh start.

BOOK II

[NATURE AS MATTER AND AS FORM]

[THE DIFFERENCE BETWEEN NATURAL AND NONNATURAL OBJECTS]

1

Some existing things are natural,[1] while others are due to other causes. *192b8* Those that are natural are animals and their parts, plants, and the simple *10* bodies,[2] such as earth, fire, air and water; for we say that these things and things of this sort are natural.[3] All these things evidently differ from those that are not naturally constituted, since each of them has within itself[4] a principle* of motion[5] and stability in place, in growth and decay, *15* or in alteration.

In contrast to these, a bed, a cloak, or any other <artifact>—insofar as it is described as such, <i.e., as a bed, a cloak, or whatever>, and to the extent that it is a product of a craft—has no innate impulse to change; but insofar as it is coincidentally made of stone or earth or a *20* mixture of these, it has an innate impulse to change, and just to that

61. **we may . . . occasion**: Such an inquiry is found in *Met.* vii–ix, xii.

1. **natural**: *phusei*, also translated 'by nature'.

2. **simple bodies**: On the natural motions of the elements see NATURE #1.

3. **for we say . . . are natural**: Aristotle appeals to what we ordinarily say, since he wants to show that his use of 'nature' covers the things that COMMON BELIEFS recognize as natural.

4. **within itself**: This does not imply that they do not also have an external source of their motions. Animals, for example, are moved not only by their internal principles but also by external forces and stimuli.

5. **motion**: This renders *kinēsis*. 'Change' renders *metabolē*. Aristotle does not seem to intend any distinction between the two in this context, though elsewhere he does; see MOTION.

extent. This is because a nature[6] is a type of principle and cause of motion and stability within those things to which it primarily belongs in their own right and not coincidentally.* (By 'not coincidentally' I mean, for instance, the following: Someone who is a doctor might cause himself to be healthy, but it is not insofar as he is being healed that he has the medical science; on the contrary, it is coincidental that the same person is a doctor and is being healed, and that is why the two characteristics are sometimes separated from each other.)[7]

The same is true of everything else that is produced, since no such thing has within itself the principle of its own production. In some things (for instance, a house or any other product of handicraft) the principle comes from outside, and it is within other things. In other things (those that might turn out to be coincidental causes for themselves) the principle is within them, but not in their own right.

[WHATEVER HAS A NATURE IS A SUBSTANCE]

A nature, then, is what we have said; and the things that have a nature are those that have this sort of principle. All these things are substances;[8] for <a substance> is a sort of subject, and a nature is invariably in a subject.[9] The things that are in accordance with nature include both these and whatever belongs to them in their own right, as travelling upward belongs to fire—for this neither is nor has a nature, but is natural and in accordance with nature. We have said, then, what nature is, and what is natural and in accordance with nature.

[THERE IS NO DOUBT OF THE EXISTENCE OF NATURE]

To attempt to prove that there is such a thing as nature would be ridiculous;[10] for it is evident that there are many things of the sort we have described. To prove what is evident from what is not evident betrays an inability to discriminate what is known$_g$ because of itself[11] from what

6. **a nature**: Or perhaps just 'nature'. See NATURE #2–3.

7. **(By 'not coincidentally'. . . from each other.)**: If there were some explanatory connection between S's needing to be cured and S's being a doctor (as there is, e.g., between a plant's need for water and its having roots), then being a doctor would be noncoincidentally connected with S's needing to be cured.

8. **substances**: Lit. 'substance'.

9. **subject**: On substance and subject see 190a36, SUBSTANCE.

10. **that there is . . . ridiculous**: Aristotle refers to the question 'whether it is'; cf. APo 71a12n.

11. **known$_g$ because of itself**: Cf. APr 64b35. Top. 100b1–2, APo ii 19.

is not. (It is clearly possible to suffer from this inability: someone blind from birth might still make deductions about colors.)[12] And so such people are bound to argue about <mere> names and to understand nothing.

[SOME PEOPLE THINK THAT NATURE IS MATTER]

Some people think that the nature and substance of a natural thing is   10
the primary[13] constituent present in it, having no order in its own right, so that the nature of a bed, for instance, <would be> the wood, and the nature of a statue <would be> the bronze.[14] A sign of this, according to Antiphon, is the fact that, if you were to bury a bed and the rotting residue were to become able to sprout, the result would be wood, not a bed. He thinks that this is because the conventional arrangement, i.e.,   15
the craft <making the wood into a bed>, is a <mere> coincident of the wood, whereas the substance is what remains continuously while it is affected in these ways. And if each of these things is related to something else in the same way (bronze and gold, for instance, to water; bones and wood to earth; and so on with anything else),[15] that thing is their   20
nature and substance.[16]

   This is why some people say that fire or earth or air or water is the nature of the things that exist; some say it is some of these, others say it is all of them. For whenever any of these people supposed one, or more than one, of these things to be <the primary constituent>, he takes this or these to be all the substance there is, and he takes everything   25
else to be attributes, states, and conditions of these things; and each of these is held to be everlasting, since they do not change from themselves, but the other things come to be and are destroyed an unlimited number of times.

   This, then, is one way we speak of a nature: as the primary matter

---

12. **someone blind . . . colors)**: Though colors are evident to the senses, a blind person has to reach conclusions about them from other evidence.

13. **primary**: Here and in 193a29 'primary' refers to proximate rather than prime matter. See MATTER #2–3.

14. **the nature of a bed . . . the bronze**: These people do not mean that beds are natural objects, but that if they were natural objects, their nature would be the wood.

15. **(bronze . . . else)**: Water and earth are two of the four basic material elements (cf. 192b10) that are persisting subjects of change, producing more complex types of matter (bronze, gold, etc.). See GC ii 3–5.

16. **substance**: Aristotle might be thinking of substance as basic subject, or of substance as essence, or (most probably) of both.

30   that is a subject for each thing that has within itself a principle of motion
     and change.

     [BUT FORM IS NATURE TOO]

     In another way the nature is the shape, i.e., the form[17] in accordance
     with the account. For just as we speak of craftsmanship in what is in
     accordance with craft and is crafted, so also we speak of nature in what
     is in accordance with nature and is natural. But if something were only
35   potentially a bed and still lacked the form of a bed, we would not yet
     speak of craftsmanship or of a product in accordance with craft; nor
     would we say the corresponding thing about anything that is constituted
193b naturally. For what is only potentially flesh or bone does not have its
     nature, and is not naturally flesh or bone, until it acquires the form in
     accordance with the account by which we define flesh or bone and say
     what it is. In another way, then, the nature is the shape and form of
5   things that have within themselves a principle of motion; this form is not
     separable except in account.[18] (What is composed of form and matter—for
     instance, a man—is not a nature, but is natural.)
         Indeed, the form is the nature more* than the matter is. For something
     is called <flesh, bone, and so on> when it is actually so, more than
     when it is only potentially so. Further, a man comes to be from a man,[19]
     but not a bed from a bed. In fact that is why some say that the nature
10   of the bed is not the shape but the wood, because if it were to sprout
     the result would be wood, not a bed. If this shows that the wood is the
     nature, then the shape is also the nature, since a man comes to be from
     a man. Further, nature, as applied to coming to be, is really a road
     toward nature;[20] it is not like medical treatment, which is a road not
15   toward medical science, but toward health. For medical treatment neces-
     sarily proceeds *from* medical science, not *toward* medical science. But
     nature <as coming to be> is not related to nature in this way; rather,
     what is growing, insofar as it is growing, proceeds from something
     toward something <else>. What is it, then, that grows? Not what it is
     growing from, but what it is growing into.[21] Therefore, the shape is the
     nature.

     17. **shape, i.e., the form**: See FORM #5.

     18. **separable . . . in account**: See SEPARABLE #3.

     19. **a man comes to be from a man**: See FORM #6.

     20. **road toward nature**: See NATURE #1.

     21. **What is it . . . growing into**: The process of growth is described with refer-
     ence to the goal rather than to the beginning. We say 'the tree (= the goal) is
     growing', when the sapling is getting bigger.

Shape and nature are spoken of in two ways; for the privation is also form in a way. We must consider later[22] whether or not there is a privation and a contrary in unqualified coming to be.[23]   20

[UNLIKE THE MATHEMATICIAN, THE STUDENT OF NATURE STUDIES MATTER]

2

Since we have distinguished the different ways we speak of nature, we should next consider how the mathematician differs from the student of nature; for natural bodies certainly have surfaces, solids, lengths, and   25
points, which are what the mathematician studies.[24] We should also consider whether astronomy is different from or a part of the study of nature; for it would be absurd if a student of nature ought to know what the sun or moon is but need not know any of their coincidents in their own right[25]—especially since it is evident that students of nature also discuss the shape of the sun and moon, and specifically whether or not   30
the earth and the world are spherical.[26]

These things are certainly the concern of both the mathematician and the student of nature. But the mathematician is not concerned with them insofar as each is the limit of a natural body, and he does not study the coincidents of a natural body insofar as they belong to a natural body. That is why he also separates these coincidents;[27] for they are separable* in thought from motion, and his separating them makes no difference   35
and results in no falsehood.[28]

Those who say there are Ideas do not notice that they do this too; for they separate natural objects, though these are less separable than   194a
mathematical objects. This would be clear if one tried to state the formulae of both natural and mathematical objects—of the things themselves

22. **later**: Perhaps *Phys.* v 1.

23. **for the privation . . . coming to be**: The privation is the arrangement of the matter before the change; hence it is contrary to the form, which is the arrangement of the matter after the change. On coming to be see i 7–8.

24. **for natural . . . studies**: This explains why the difference between the mathematician and the student of nature is not completely obvious—since, from one point of view, they study the same things.

25. **coincidents in their own right**: These are the proper concern of DEMONSTRATION. See COINCIDENT #3.

26. **for it would . . . spherical**: This explains why astronomy might seem to be part of the study of nature.

27. **these coincidents**: i.e., the geometrical properties that he studies.

28. **and his . . . no falsehood**: See ABSTRACTION.

5   and of their coincidents. For odd and even, straight and curved, and
also number, line, and point do not involve motion, whereas flesh,
bones, and man do—we speak of them as we speak of the snub nose,
not as we speak of the curved.[29]

This is also clear[30] from the parts of mathematics that are more related
to the study of nature—for instance, optics, harmonics, and astronomy.
10 These are in a way the reverse of geometry; for geometry investigates
natural lines, but not insofar as they are natural,[31] whereas optics investigates mathematical lines, but insofar as they are natural, not insofar as
they are mathematical.[32]

[LIKE THE CRAFTSMAN, HOWEVER, HE STUDIES FORM AS WELL AS MATTER]

Since we speak of nature in two ways—both as form and as matter—
we should study it as though we were investigating what snubness is,
and so we should study natural objects neither independently of their
15 matter nor <simply> insofar as they have matter. For indeed, since
there are these two types of nature, there might be a puzzle about which
one the student of nature should study.[33] Perhaps the compound of the
two? If so, then also each of them. Then is it the same or a different
discipline that knows$_g$ each one of them?

If we judge by the early thinkers, the student of nature would seem
20 to study <only> matter, since Empedocles and Democritus touched
only slightly on form and essence. Craft, however, imitates nature,[34]
and the same science knows$_o$ both the form and the matter up to a point.
The doctor, for instance, knows health, and also the bile and phlegm in
which health <is realized>; similarly, the housebuilder knows both the
25 form of the house and that its matter is bricks and wood; and the same

29. **we speak . . . the curved**: To speak of them as we speak of **the snub** is to
speak of them as involving matter. See SNUB. On separated Ideas see FORMS #3.

30. **This is also clear**: i.e., the impossibility of studying natural objects in the
abstract way preferred by believers in Platonic Ideas.

31. **not insofar as they are natural**: but simply insofar as they are lines with
these geometrical properties.

32. **not . . . mathematical**: Aristotle answers the question he raised in 193b25–
26 about the relation between astronomy and the study of nature. He argues
that astronomy must depend partly on the study of nature; it cannot be purely
mathematical, since it is concerned with the physical, not merely the geometrical,
properties of the heavenly bodies.

33. **a puzzle . . . study**: For this puzzle cf. DA 403a27, PA 641a22.

34. **Craft . . . nature**: See 199a15.

is true in the other cases. The science of nature, therefore, must also know$_g$ both types of nature.

Moreover the same discipline studies both what something is for*— i.e., the end—and whatever is for the end. Nature is an end and what something is for; for whenever a continuous motion has some end this   *30* sort of terminus is also what the motion is for. That is why it was ludicrous for the poet to say 'He has reached the end he was born for';[35] it was ludicrous because by 'end' we mean not every terminus but only the best one.

For crafts produce their matter (some by producing it without qualifi- cation, others by making it suitable for their work);[36] and we use all <matter> as being for our sake,[37] since we are also an end in a way.   *35* (For what something is for is of two sorts,[38] as we said in *On Philosophy*.[39])

There are two crafts[40] that control the matter and involve knowledge$_g$:   *194b* the craft that uses <the matter> and the craft that directs this productive craft. Hence the using craft also directs in a way, but with the difference that the directing craft knows the form, whereas the productive craft[41] knows the matter. For instance, the pilot knows what sort of form the   *5* rudder has, and he prescribes <how to produce it>, whereas the boat- builder knows what sort of wood and what sorts of motions are needed to make it. With products of a craft, then, we produce the matter for the sake of the product; with natural things, the matter is already present.

Further, matter is relative*; for there is one <sort of> matter for one form, and another for another.[42]

How much, then, must the student of nature know$_o$ about form and   *10* what-it-is? Perhaps as much as the doctor knows about sinews, or the smith about bronze—enough to know what something is for. And he

35. **That . . . born for'**: A remark about someone's death.

36. **For crafts . . . work)**: This shows that they study both end and means, as the previous paragraph suggested. In distinguishing production WITHOUT QUALIFICATION (e.g., painters making their own paint or canvas) from making the matter suitable (e.g., writers sharpening their pencils before writing), Aristotle explains in what sense he means that crafts produce their matter.

37. **as being for our sake**: This might mean 'as we would if it were for our sake', or 'because we believe it is for our sake' or perhaps 'because it is for our sake'.

38. **two sorts**: See FOR SOMETHING #5.

39. *On Philosophy*: A work of Aristotle's that survives only in fragments. See ROT pp. 2389–97.

40. **two crafts**: Cf. *Met.* 981a30.

41. **productive craft**: Or perhaps '<that directs> by being productive'.

42. **Further . . . another**: Hence to know about the appropriate sort of matter, we have to know about the relevant form.

must confine himself to things that are separable[43] in form but are in matter—for a man is born from a man and the sun. But it is a task for
15 first philosophy[44] to determine what is separable[45] and what the separable is like.

[CAUSE AND CHANCE]

[THE FOUR CAUSES]

3

Now that we have determined these points, we should consider how many and what sorts of causes* there are. For our inquiry aims at knowledge$_o$; and we think we know something only when we find the reason
20 why it is so,[46] i.e., when we find its primary cause. Clearly, then, we must also find the reason why in the case of coming to be, perishing, and every sort of natural change, so that when we know their principles we can try to refer whatever we are searching for to these principles.

In one way, then, that from which, as a <constituent> present in it,
25 a thing comes to be is said to be that thing's cause—for instance, the bronze and silver, and their genera, are causes of the statue and the bowl.

In another way, the form—i.e., the pattern*—is a cause. The form is the account (and the genera of the account) of the essence (for instance, the cause of an octave is the ratio[47] two to one, and in general number[48]), and the parts that are in the account.
30 Further, the source of the primary principle of change or stability[49] is

43. **separable**: i.e., (probably) SEPARABLE in definition.

44. **for first philosophy**: Hence it is not a task for the study of nature. See PHILOSOPHY.

45. **separable**: i.e., (probably) SEPARABLE in being, capable of existing without what it is separable from.

46. **the reason why it is so**: Lit. 'the why'.

47. **account . . . ratio**: Both terms render *logos*. See REASON #6.

48. **and in general number**: An example of one of the genera of an account (since number is more generic than the specific ratio 2:1). The genus, like the account itself (in the nonlinguistic sense of 'account'; see REASON #5), may be regarded as the formal cause.

49. **the source . . . stability**: Lit. 'that from which the primary PRINCIPLE of change or stability <comes>'. Sometimes Aristotle refers to the moving (or 'efficient' cause) more briefly, omitting 'that from which' from the formula. The fuller formula may be intended to distinguish the substance (e.g., the person who decided to go for a walk) from the principle within the substance (in this case, the person's decision to go for a walk).

a cause. For instance, the adviser is a cause <of the action>, and a father is a cause of his child; and in general the producer is a cause of the product, and the initiator of the change is a cause of what is changed.

Further, something's end—i.e., what it is for—is its cause, as health is of walking. For why does he walk? We say, 'To be healthy'; and in saying this we think we have provided the cause. The same is true of   35
all the intermediate steps that are for the end, where something else has initiated the motion, as, for example, slimming, purging, drugs, or   195a
instruments are for health; all of these are for the end, though they differ in that some are activities,[50] while others are instruments.

We may take these, then, to be the ways we speak of causes.

[THE SAME THING MAY HAVE MORE THAN ONE CAUSE]

Since causes are spoken of in many ways, there are many noncoincidental   5
causes of the same thing. Both the sculpting craft and the bronze, for instance, are causes of the statue, not insofar as it is something else, but insofar as it is a statue. But they are not causes in the same way: the bronze is a cause as matter, the sculpting craft as the source of the motion. Some things are causes of each other: hard work, for instance, is the cause of fitness, and fitness of hard work. But they are not causes   10
in the same way: fitness is what the hard work is for, whereas hard work is the principle of motion. Further, the same thing is the cause of contraries; for sometimes if a thing's presence causes F, that thing is also, by its absence, taken to cause the contrary of F, so that, for instance, if a pilot's presence would have caused the safety of a ship, we take his absence to have caused the shipwreck.   15

All the causes just mentioned are of four especially evident types: (1) Letters are the cause of syllables, matter of artifacts,[51] fire and such things of bodies, parts of the whole, and the assumptions of the conclusion,[52] as that out of which. In each of these cases one thing[53]—for instance, the parts—is cause as subject, while (2) the other thing—the whole, the   20
composition, and the form—is cause as essence. (3) The seed, the doctor, the adviser and, in general, the producer, are all sources of the principle of change or stability. (4) In other cases, one thing is a cause of other things by being the end and the good. For what the other things are for

50. **activities**: *ergon*. See FUNCTION.

51. **matter of artifacts**: Perhaps Aristotle refers to the use of '*hulē*' for timber. See MATTER #1.

52. **the assumptions of the conclusion**: in a DEDUCTION. The conclusion has the premises contained in it; see *Met.* 1014a35–b2.

53. **one thing**: e.g., letters, fire.

25   is taken to be[54] the best and their end—it does not matter <for present
purposes> whether we call it the good or the apparent good.[55] These,
then, are the number of kinds of causes there are.

[DIFFERENT WAYS OF SPECIFYING CAUSES]

Although there are many types of causes, they are fewer when they are
arranged under heads. For causes are spoken of in many ways, and
even among causes of the same type, some are prior and others posterior.
30   For example, the cause of health is a doctor and <speaking more gener-
ally> a craftsman, and the cause of an octave is the double and <speaking
more generally> number; in every case the inclusive causes are posterior
to the particular.[56]

Further, some things and their genera are coincidental causes. Polycleitus and the sculptor, for instance, are causes of the statue in different
35   ways, because being Polycleitus is coincidental to the sculptor.[57] What
includes the coincident[58] is also a cause—if, for example, the man or,
195b   quite generally, the animal is a cause of the statue. Some coincidental
causes are more remote[59] or more proximate than others; if, for instance,
the pale man or the musician were said to be the cause of the statue <it
would be a more remote cause than Polycleitus is>.

We may speak of any <moving> cause, whether proper or coinciden-
5   tal, either as having a potentiality or as actualizing it; for instance, we
may say either that the housebuilder, or that the housebuilder actually
building, is causing the house to be built.

Similar things may also be said about the things of which the causes
are causes. For example, we may speak of the cause of this statue, or
of a statue, or of an image in general; or of this bronze, or of bronze,
10   or of matter in general. The same is true of coincidents. We may speak
in this same way of combinations[60]—of Polycleitus the sculptor, for instance, instead of Polycleitus or a sculptor.

54. **is taken to be**: Or perhaps 'tends to be'.

55. **the good or the apparent good**: For the difference see *DA* 433a28, *EN* 1113a22–
24.

56. **particular**: i.e., more determinate. See PARTICULAR #2.

57. **because being . . . the sculptor**: i.e., the fact that he is Polycleitus does not
explain his having made the statue. See CAUSE #5.

58. **What includes the coincident**: The various properties that are coincidental
to being a sculptor (e.g., being tall, being witty) are included among the properties
of this man and (still more generally) this animal.

59. **more remote**: Cf. *Met*. 1014a5.

60. **of combinations**: i.e., combinations of proper and coincidental causes, or
combinations of proper and coincidental things caused.

Still, all these ways amount to six, each spoken of in two ways. For there is (1) the particular and (2) the genus, and (3) the coincident and (4) the genus of the coincident; and these may be spoken of either (5) in combination or (6) simply. Each of these may be either active or potential. The difference is the following. Active and particular causes exist and cease to exist simultaneously with the things they cause, so that, for instance, this one practicing medicine exists simultaneously with this one being made healthy, and in the same way this one housebuilding exists simultaneously with this thing being built into a house.[61] But this is not true of every cause that is potential; for the house and the housebuilder do not perish simultaneously.

Here as elsewhere, we must always seek the most precise[62] cause. A man, for example, is building because he is a builder, and he is a builder insofar as he has the building craft; his building craft, then, is the prior cause, and the same is true in all cases. Further, we must seek genera as causes of genera, and particulars as causes of particulars; a sculptor, for instance, is the cause of a statue, but this sculptor of this statue. And we must seek a potentiality as the cause of a potential effect, and something actualizing a potentiality as the cause of an actual effect.

This, then, is an adequate determination of the number of causes, and of the ways in which they are causes.

[LUCK AND CHANCE]

4

Luck* and chance are also said to be causes, and many things are said to be and to come to be because of them. We must, then, investigate how luck and chance are included in the causes we have mentioned, whether luck is or is not the same as chance, and, in general, what they are.

[DOUBTS ABOUT THE EXISTENCE OF LUCK ARE UNJUSTIFIED]

Some people even wonder whether luck and chance exist.[63] For they say that nothing results from luck; rather, everything that is said to result from chance or luck has some definite cause. If, for instance, as a result of luck someone comes to the market-place and finds the person he

---

61. **Active and . . . a house**: Aristotle thinks of an active cause as a substance in a particular condition (e.g., the builder in the condition of building), not as an event (the building engaged in by the builder) or a fact (the fact that the builder is building).

62. **most precise**: Or perhaps 'highest' (lit. 'most extreme').

63. **whether . . . exist**: On 'whether it is' see 193a3n.

5   wanted to meet but did not expect,[64] they say the cause is his wanting
to go to market. Similarly, for every other supposed result of luck, they
say it is possible to find some cause other than luck. For if there were
such a thing as luck, it would appear truly strange and puzzling that
none of the early philosophers who discussed the causes of coming to
10   be and perishing ever determined anything about luck; in fact it would
seem that they also thought that nothing results from luck. But this too
is surprising; for surely many things come to be and exist as a result of
luck and chance. Though people know perfectly well that everything
that comes to be can be referred to some cause, as the old argument
15   doing away with luck says, everyone nonetheless says that some of
these things result from luck and that others do not.

That is why[65] the early philosophers should have mentioned luck in
some way or other. But they certainly did not think luck was among the
causes they recognized—for instance, love or strife or mind or fire or
anything else of that sort. In either case, then, it is strange, whether
they supposed there was no such thing as luck, or supposed there was
20   such a thing but omitted to discuss it. It is especially strange considering
that they sometimes appeal to luck. Empedocles, for example, appeals
to luck when he says that air is separated out on top, not always but as
luck has it; at least, he says in his cosmogony that 'it happened to run
that way at that time, but often otherwise'.[66] And he says that most of
the parts of animals[67] result from luck.

[THE ROLE OF CHANCE IN COSMOLOGY]

25   Other people make chance the cause of our heaven* and of all worlds. For
they say that the vortex, and the motion that dispersed and established
everything in its present order, resulted from chance.[68] And this is cer-
30   tainly quite amazing. For animals and plants, they say, neither are nor
come to be from luck, but rather nature or mind or something of that
sort is the cause, since it is not just any old thing[69] that comes to be from
a given type of seed, but an olive-tree comes from one type, and a man
from another; and yet they say that the heaven and the most divine of

64. **as a result of luck . . . did not expect**: The lucky thing is the conjunction
of the two events (the creditor's being there and the debtor's being there).

65. **That is why**: sc. since luck is so widely recognized as a cause.

66. **'it happened . . . otherwise'**: Empedocles DK 31 B 53.

67. **parts of animals**: See 198b32.

68. **Other people . . . from chance**: Aristotle is thinking especially of the Atomists. See DEMOCRITUS.

69. **just any old thing**: See LUCK #2.

visible things result from chance and have no cause of the sort that   35
animals and plants have.

If this is so, it deserves attention, and something might well have
been said about it. For in addition to the other strange aspects of what   196b
they say, it is even stranger to say all this when they see that nothing
in the heaven results from chance, whereas many things happen as a
result of luck to things whose existence is not itself a result of luck.[70]
Surely the contrary would have been likely.   5

Other people suppose that luck is a cause, but they take it to be divine
and superhuman, and therefore obscure to the human mind.

And so we must consider chance and luck, and determine what each
is, and whether they are the same or different, and see how they fit into
the causes we have distinguished.

[THE NATURE OF LUCKY EVENTS]

5

First, then, we see that some things always,[71] others usually, come about   10
in the same way. Evidently luck and the result of luck are not said to
be the cause of either of these things—either of what is of necessity and
always or of what is usually. But since apart from these there is a third
sort of event[72] which everyone says results from luck, it is evident that   15
there is such a thing as luck and chance; for we know that this third
sort of event results from luck and that the results of luck are of this
sort.

Further, some events are for something and others are not. Among
the former, some are in accordance with a decision* while others are
not, but both sorts are for something. And so it is clear that even among   20
events that are neither necessary nor usual there are some that admit
of being for something. (Events that are for something include both the
actions that result[73] from thought and also the results of nature.) This,
then, is the sort of event that we regard as a result of luck, whenever

70. **whereas . . . of luck:** Aristotle takes it to be obvious that some chance
events (e.g., the meeting in the market-place) happen to natural organisms,
even though, in the Atomists' view, these organisms are not themselves products
of chance. By contrast, he thinks it is obvious that nothing is a matter of chance
(since everything is necessary) in the motions of the heavens, even though the
heavens are, in the Atomists' view, the product of chance.

71. **always:** Used in a modal sense; see ALWAYS #2.

72. **event:** Lit. 'thing coming to be'.

73. **that result:** Reading *an prachthē(i)*. Alternatively (reading *an prachtheiē*) 'that
might result'.

25 an event of that sort comes about coincidentally.[74] For just as some things are something in their own right, and others are something coincidentally, so also it is possible for a cause to be of either sort. For example, the cause of a house is, in its own right, the housebuilder, but coincidentally the pale or musical thing.[75] Hence the cause in its own right is determinate, but the coincidental cause is indeterminate, since one thing might have an unlimited number of coincidents.[76]

30 As has been said, then, whenever this <coincidental causation> occurs among events of the sort that are for something[77] the events <that have these coincidental causes> are said to result from chance and luck. The difference between chance and luck will be determined later; we may take it as evident for the moment that both are found among events of the sort that are for something.

For instance, A would have come when B was collecting subscriptions, in order to recover the debt from B, if A had known <B would be 35 there>.[78] In fact, however, A did not come in order to do this; it was a coincidence that A came <when B happened to be there>, and so met

74. **This, then . . . coincidentally**: Aristotle speaks of an event type (e.g., meeting in the market-place, which has many tokens) having a final cause when it is characteristically and USUALLY true that its tokens (e.g. these people meeting in the market-place on this occasion) have a final cause. He does not mean that if an event type has a final cause, every token of the type must have the same final cause; on the contrary, lucky events are just those tokens that do not have the final cause that is characteristic of the type.

75. **For example . . . musical thing**: The builder qua builder is the intrinsic cause (cause in its own right) of the house qua house. But since the builder is coincidentally a pale thing, the pale thing is a coincidental cause of the house. If the house also (coincidentally, not because anyone intended it) blocks out the neighbors' sunlight, the builder (pale thing, etc.) is a coincidental cause of the thing blocking the neighbors' sunlight. On coincidental causes cf. 195a32.

76. **unlimited number of coincidents**: Cf. *Met.* 1026b3.

77. **events of the sort that are for something**: Lit. 'things coming to be for something'. Here again (cf. 196b23n) the difference between event-types and event-tokens is important. An event of the type 'meeting one's debtor in the market-place' is of the type that usually has tokens coming about for some end, because they result from a decision to find one's debtor. When a particular token of this type is a matter of luck, it does not result from a decision to find one's debtor.

78. **For instance . . . would be there>**: The example Aristotle has in mind seems to be this: A wants to collect a debt from B; one day A comes to the market-place for some other reason (e.g., wanting to sell his olives) and meets B who happens to be there at the same time collecting subscriptions for a club of which B is the treasurer. It is not always clear in this passage whether 'collect' refers to A's collecting the debt from B or to B's collecting subscriptions for his club.

B in order to collect the debt[79]—given that A neither usually nor of   197a
necessity frequents the place <for that purpose>. The end—collecting
the debt[80]—is not a cause <of A's action> in A, but it is the sort of thing
that one decides to do and that results from thought. And in this case
A's coming is said to result from luck; but if A always or usually frequented the place because he had decided to and for the purpose of
collecting the debt, then <A's being there when B was there> would   5
not result from luck.

[HOW LUCK IS A CAUSE: EXPLANATION OF CURRENT BELIEFS]

Clearly, then, luck is a coincidental cause found among events of the
sort that are for something, and specifically among those of the sort that
are in accordance with a decision. Hence thought (since decision requires
thought) and luck concern the same things.

Now the causes whose results might be matters of luck are bound to
be indeterminate. That is why luck also seems to be something indeterminate and obscure to human beings, and why, in one way, it might seem   10
that nothing results from luck. For, as we might reasonably expect, all
these claims are correct. For in one way things do result from luck, since
they are coincidental results and luck is a coincidental cause. But luck
is not the unqualified <and hence noncoincidental> cause of anything.
The <unqualified> cause of a house, for instance, is a housebuilder,
and the coincidental cause a flute-player; and the man's coming and   15
collecting the debt, without having come to collect it, has an indefinite
number of coincidental causes—he might have come because he wished
to see someone, or was going to court or to the theatre.

It is also correct to say that luck is contrary to reason. For rational
judgment tells us what is always or usually the case, whereas luck is   20
found in events that happen neither always nor usually. And so, since
causes of this sort are indeterminate, luck is also indeterminate.

Still, in some cases one might be puzzled about whether just any old
thing might be a cause of a lucky outcome.[81] Surely the wind or the
sun's warmth, but not someone's haircut, might be the cause of his

---

79. **it was a coincidence . . . the debt**: Text and interpretation uncertain. Lit. 'it
was a coincidence that he came and did this for the sake of collecting'. 'In order
to collect the debt' states not A's reason for being in the market-place at this
time, but A's purpose once he had coincidentally found B in the market-place.

80. **The end . . . debt**: This is the end A pursues when he has coincidentally
met B. In this case it is not, as it normally would be, the final cause of A's being
where B is.

81. **a lucky outcome**: Lit. 'luck'.

health; for some coincidental causes are closer than others to what they cause.[82]

25   Luck is called good when something good results, bad when something bad results; it is called good and bad fortune[83] when the results are large. That is why someone who just misses great evil or good as well <as someone who has it> is fortunate or unfortunate; for we think

30 of him as already having <the great evil or good>, since the near miss seems to us to be no distance.[84] Further, it is reasonable* that good fortune is unstable; for luck is unstable, since no result of luck can be either always or usually the case.

    As we have said, then, both luck and chance are coincidental causes,

35 found in events of the sort that are neither without exception nor usual, and specifically in events of this sort that might be for something.[85]

[THE DIFFERENCE BETWEEN LUCK AND CHANCE]

6

Chance is not the same as luck, since it extends more widely; for results

197b of luck also result from chance, but not all results of chance result from luck. For luck and its results are found in things that are capable of being fortunate and in general capable of action, and that is why luck must concern what is achievable by action. A sign of this is the fact that good

5 fortune seems to be the same or nearly the same as being happy, and being happy is a sort of action, since it is doing well in action.[86] Hence what cannot act cannot do anything by luck either.[87] Hence neither inanimate things nor beasts nor children do anything by luck, because

---

82. **Surely the wind . . . they cause**: Someone gets a haircut (not for the sake of his health), which exposes him to wind and sun, which happen to be good for his health. The wind and the sun are less remote coincidental causes than the haircut is.

83. **good and bad fortune**: See LUCK #3.

84. **for we . . . no distance**: Although in fact he is no better or worse off than he was, we speak of him as though he were better off (or worse off), because of his narrow escape (or his unfortunate near miss).

85. **events of the sort . . . for something**: A simplified paraphrase. More literally: 'things that are capable of coming about not without exception (haplōs) nor usually, and among however many of these might come about for something'.

86. **doing well in action**: See EN 1139b3. On good luck and happiness see EN 1099b6–8.

87. **Hence what . . . luck either**: Aristotle does not always confine tuchē to the area of rational action. See LUCK #2.

they are incapable of decision.[88] Nor do they have good or bad fortune, except by a <mere> similarity—as Protarchus[89] said that the stones from   *10* which altars are made are fortunate, because they are honored, while their fellows are trodden underfoot. Still, even these things are affected by the results of luck in a way, whenever an agent affects them by some lucky action; but otherwise they are not.

Chance, on the other hand, applies both to animals other than man and to many inanimate things. We say, for instance, that the horse came   *15* by chance, since it was saved because it came but did not come in order to be saved. And the tripod fell by chance, because it did not fall in order to be sat on, although it was left standing[90] in order to be sat on.

Hence it is evident that among types of events that are for something (speaking without qualification), we say that a particular event of such a type results from chance if it has an external cause and the actual result is not what it is for:[91] and we say that it results from luck if it results   *20* from chance and is an event of the sort that is decided on by an agent who is capable of decision.[92] A sign of this is the fact that we say an event is pointless[93] if it <is of the sort that> is for some result but <in this case> that result is not what it is for. If, for instance, walking is for evacuating the bowels, but when he walked on this occasion it was not <for that reason>, then we say that he walked pointlessly and that his   *25* walking is pointless. We assume that an event is pointless if it is naturally

---

88. **decision**: DECISION is needed for ACTION in the restricted sense.

89. **Protarchus**: An orator and pupil of Gorgias; cf. Plato, *Philebus* 58a.

90. **left standing**: Presumably it had fallen upright by chance in a convenient place.

91. **if it . . . it is for**: Literally, 'among things coming to be for the sake of something without qualification, whenever those whose cause is external come to be not for the sake of what results, then we say they are from chance'. If an event type has a final cause (is 'for something'), it does not follow that every token of the type also has a final cause; see 196b29n. For this use of WITHOUT QUALIFICATION cf. *EN* 1110a19.

92. **the sort . . . decision**: On this particular occasion, however, it did not happen because it was what the agent had decided to do.

93. **pointless**: *matēn*. If 'in vain' (i.e., unsuccessful; see NATURE #6) is the right rendering, the passage should be translated: '. . . if the result that it was done for does not come about. If, for instance, walking is for evacuating the bowels, but when he walked, he did not succeed in doing this, we say that he walked in vain and that his walking was in vain. We assume that something is done in vain if it is naturally for something else, but does not succeed in achieving the result that it is naturally for'.

for something else,[94] but does not succeed in <being for> what it is
naturally for. For if someone said that his washing himself was pointless
because the sun was not eclipsed, he would be ridiculous, since washing
is not for producing eclipses. So also, then, an event happens by chance

30　(as the name suggests) whenever it is pointless.[95] For the stone did not
fall in order to hit someone; it fell by chance, because it might have
fallen because someone threw it to hit someone.

　　The separation of chance from luck is sharpest in natural events. For

35　if an event is contrary to nature, we regard it as a result of chance, not
of luck. But even this is different from <other cases of chance; the other
cases> have an external cause, but <events contrary to nature> have
an internal cause.[96]

[HOW LUCK AND CHANCE ARE RELATED TO THE FOUR CAUSES]

198a　We have said, then, what chance and luck are and how they differ. Each
of them falls under the sort of cause that is the source of the principle
of motion. For in every case they are either among natural causes or

5　among those resulting from thought, and the number of these is indeterminate.

　　Chance and luck are causes of events <of the sort> that mind or
nature might have caused, in cases where <particular> events <of this
sort> have some coincidental cause. Now nothing coincidental is prior
to anything that is in its own right; hence clearly no coincidental cause

10　is prior to something that is a cause in its own right. Chance and luck
are therefore posterior to mind and nature. And so however true it might
be that chance is the cause of the heavens, still it is necessary for mind
and nature to be prior causes of this universe and of many other things.

[CONNECTIONS BETWEEN THE FOUR CAUSES]

7

It is clear, then, that there are causes, and that there are as many different

15　types as we say there are; for the reason why something is so includes
all these different types <of causes>. For we refer the ultimate reason

94. **it is naturally for something else**: i.e., is an event of the sort that is for
something else.

95. **by chance (*automaton*) . . . pointless**: *matēn*. Aristotle appeals to supposed
etymology.

96. **an internal cause**: Aristotle is thinking of events that are contrary to nature
(i.e., contrary to the USUAL course of nature) because of something unusual in
the matter of the organism.

why (1) in the case of unmoved things, to the what-it-is (for instance, in mathematics; for there we refer ultimately to the definition of straight or commensurate or something else), or (2) to what first initiated the motion (for instance, why did they go to war?—because the other side *20* raided them), or (3) to what it is for (for instance, in order to set themselves up as rulers), or (4) in the case of things that come to be, to the matter.

It is evident, then, that these are the causes and that this is their number. Since there are four of them, the student of nature ought to know₀ them all; and in order to give the sort of reason that is appropriate for the study of nature,[97] he must trace it back to all the causes—to the matter, the form, what initiated the motion, and what something is for. The last three often amount to one; for what something is and what it *25* is for are one, and the first source of the motion is the same in species as these, since a man generates a man;[98] and the same is true generally of things that initiate motion by being in motion.

Things that initiate motion without being in motion are outside the scope of the study of nature.[99] For although they initiate motion, they do not do so by having motion or a principle of motion within themselves, but they are unmoved. Hence there are three inquiries: one about what *30* is unmoved, one about what is in motion but imperishable, and one about what is perishable.

And so the reason why is given by referring to the matter, to the what-it-is, and to what first initiated the motion. For in cases of coming to be, this is the normal way of examining the causes—by asking what comes to be after what, and what first acted or was acted on, and so on *35* in order in every case.

Two sorts of principles initiate motion naturally.[100] One of these principles is not itself natural, since it has no principle of motion within itself; *198b* this is true of whatever initiates motion without itself being in motion— for instance, what is entirely without motion (i.e., the first of all beings) and also the what-it-is (i.e., the form[101]), since this is the end and what

97. **that is . . . of nature**: Lit. 'naturally'. Aristotle refers to his view that different disciplines have their special PRINCIPLES. See LOGICAL, DISTINCTIVE.

98. **a man generates a man**: See FORM #6.

99. **Things that . . . nature**: The unmoved mover is discussed in *Phys.* viii.

100. **Two sorts . . . naturally**: This paragraph is an explanation appended to the mention in the previous paragraph of the cause that initiates motion.

101. **the form**: This is an unmoved mover, not because it is completely unmoved, but because its explanatory role in a particular change does not consist in its being in motion (e.g., the form of the adult organism, but not the motion of the form, explains the growth of the developing organism).

something is for. And so, since natural processes[102] are for something, this cause too must be known$_o$.

5   The reason why should be stated in all these ways. For instance, (1) this necessarily results from that (either without exception or usually); (2) if this is to be (as the conclusion from the premises); (3) that this is the essence; and (4) because it is better thus—not unqualifiedly better, but better in relation to the essence$_o$ of a given thing.

[FINAL CAUSES AND NECESSITY IN NATURE]

[AN OBJECTION TO FINAL CAUSES IN NATURE]

8

10   We must first say why nature is among the causes that are for something, and then how necessity applies to natural things. For everyone refers things to necessity, saying that since the hot, the cold, and each element have a certain nature, certain other things are and come to be of necessity.

15   For if they mention any cause other than necessity (as one thinker mentions love or strife, and another mentions mind[103]), they just touch on it, then let it go.

A puzzle now arises: why not suppose that nature acts not for something or because it is better, but of necessity?[104] Zeus's rain does not fall in order to make the grain grow, but of necessity. For it is necessary that what has been drawn up is cooled, and that what has been cooled

20   and become water comes down, and it is coincidental that this makes the grain grow. Similarly, if someone's grain is spoiled on the threshing floor, it does not rain in order to spoil the grain, and the spoilage is coincidental.[105]

Why not suppose, then, that the same is true of the parts of natural organisms? On this view, it is of necessity that, for example, the front

25   teeth grow sharp and well adapted for biting, and the back ones broad and useful for chewing food; this <useful> result was coincidental, not what they were for. The same will be true of all the other parts that seem to be for something. On this view, then, whenever all the parts

102. **natural processes**: Lit. 'nature'.

103. **one thinker** . . . **mentions mind**: See EMPEDOCLES, ANAXAGORAS.

104. **of necessity**: The reference in the previous paragraph to thinkers who appeal to no other causes than necessity suggests that 'but of necessity' means 'but only of necessity'. Aristotle need not be denying that the growth of organisms happens of necessity; he may simply mean to affirm that it is also for something.

105. **it does not rain** . . . **coincidental**: In these cases, as opposed to those mentioned in the next paragraph, the correlation between the event (rain falling) and the benefit (crops growing) is not even regular.

came about coincidentally as though they were for something, these   *30*
animals survived, since their constitution, though coming about by
chance, made them suitable <for survival>. Other animals, however,
were differently constituted and so were destroyed; indeed they are still
being destroyed, as Empedocles says of the man-headed calves.[106]

[REPLY TO THE OBJECTION]

This argument, then, and others like it, might puzzle someone. In fact,
however, it is impossible for things to be like this. For these <teeth and
other parts> and all natural things come to be as they do either always   *35*
or usually, whereas no result of luck or chance comes to be either always
or usually. (For we do not regard frequent winter rain or a summer heat   *199a*
wave, but only summer rain or a winter heat wave, as a result of luck
or coincidence.) If, then, these[107] seem either to be coincidental results
or to be for something, and they cannot be coincidental or chance results,   *5*
they are for something. Now surely all such things are natural, as even
those making these claims <about necessity> would agree. We find,
then, among things that come to be and are by nature, things that are
for something.

[ARGUMENTS FROM CRAFT TO NATURE]

Further, whenever <some sequence of actions> has an end, the whole
sequence of earlier and later actions is directed toward the end.[108] Surely

---

106. **man-headed calves**: Empedocles DK 31 B 61.

107. **If, then, these**: 'These' might refer (a) to all natural things including, e.g., the
winter rain mentioned in the previous sentence, or (b) to the 'these' mentioned in
198b34, which were teeth and other parts of organisms. If Aristotle means (a),
then he argues that all natural things are for something; if he means (b), then
he argues only that the natural things mentioned in the previous paragraph
(those that 'appear to be for something') are for something. If (b) is right, the
parenthesis in the previous sentence ('For we do not . . . coincidence') explains
only the claim that what is usual is not coincidental; it does not claim that
everything that occurs always or usually in the same way (including, e.g., frequent winter rain) is for something. If (a) is right, the parenthesis cites frequent
winter rain as an example of something that is for something. Probably Aristotle
intends (b); elsewhere, at least, he restricts the scope of final causation more
narrowly than (a) would suggest (cf. *Met.* 1044b9–12).

108. **Further, whenever . . . toward the end**: Lit., 'Further, in those things in
which there is some end, for its sake the earlier things and the things following
them in order are done.' Aristotle means that if I aim to build a house, my end
guides my further choice to lay the foundations before I put on the roof. The
end explains each step in the process, not just the process as a whole.

10   what is true of action[109] is also true of nature, and what is true of nature
        is true of each action, if nothing prevents it.[110] Now actions are for
        something; therefore, natural sequences are for something. For example,
        if a house came to be naturally, it would come to be just as it actually
15   does by craft,[111] and if natural things came to be not only naturally but
        also by craft, they would come to be just as they do naturally; one thing,
        then, is what the other is for. In general, craft either completes the work
        that nature is unable to complete or imitates nature. If, then, the products
        of a craft[112] are for something, clearly the products of nature are also for
        something; for there is the same relation of later stages to earlier in
        productions of a craft and in productions of nature.
20   This is most evident in the case of animals other than man, since they
        use neither craft nor inquiry nor deliberation in producing things—
        indeed this is why some people are puzzled about whether spiders,
        ants, and other such things operate by understanding or in some other
        way. If we advance little by little along the same lines, it is evident that
25   even in plants things come to be that promote the end—leaves, for
        instance, grow for the protection of the fruit. If, then, a swallow makes
        its nest and a spider its web both naturally and for some end, and if
        plants grow leaves for the sake of the fruit, and send roots down rather
        than up for the sake of nourishment, it evidently follows that this sort
30   of cause is among things that come to be and are by nature. And since
        nature is of two sorts, nature as matter and nature as form, and the
        form is the end, and since everything else is for the end, the form must
        be what things are for.[113]

[APPARENT IRREGULARITIES IN NATURE]

        Errors occur even in productions of craft; grammarians, for instance,
35   have written incorrectly, and doctors have given the wrong medicine.
199b   Clearly, then, errors are also possible in productions of nature.

109. **action**: Aristotle is not thinking of all sequences of movements, but only
of those rational human ACTIONS (including productions) that have an END (*telos*),
i.e., are goal-directed.

110. **if nothing prevents it**: Aristotle recognizes exceptions to final-causal regularities. See USUAL #3.

111. **just as . . . craft**: i.e., it would also have a goal-directed sequence (not
necessarily including the same stages in the same order).

112. **the products of a craft**: Lit. (here and in what follows) 'the things in accordance with (*kata*) a craft'.

113. **the form must . . . are for**: This passage shows how ch. 8 is meant to
support the claim in 193a30 that an organism's form is its nature; for Aristotle

In some productions by crafts, the correct action is for something, and in cases of error the attempt is for something but misses the mark. The same will be true, then, of natural things; freaks will be errors, missing what they are for. Hence in the original formations of things, a defective principle would also have brought the <man-headed> calves into being, if they were unable to reach any definite term and end—just as, in the actual state of things, <freaks> come to be when the seed is defective. Further, it is necessary for the seed to come into being first, and not the animal straightaway; in fact the 'all-natured first'[114] was seed.

Further, in plants as well as in animals things happen for something, though in a less articulate way. Then what about plants? Did olive-headed vines keep coming into being, as he says <man-headed> calves did? Surely not—that is absurd—but surely they would have to have come into being, if the animals did.

Further, <on Empedocles' view> coming to be would also have to be merely a matter of chance among seeds. But whoever says this does away entirely with nature and natural things. For things are natural when they are moved continuously from some principle in themselves and so arrive at some end. From each principle comes, not the same thing in each case, but not just any old thing either; in every case it proceeds to the same <end>, if nothing prevents it.

Now certainly both the end that a process is for and the process that is for this end might also result from luck. We say, for instance, that a friend in a foreign country came by luck and paid the ransom and then went away, when he did the action as though he had come in order to do it, though in fact that was not what he came to do. This end is achieved coincidentally, since (as we said before) luck is one of the coincidental causes. But whenever the end results always or usually, it is neither coincidental nor a result of luck. And in natural things that is how it is in every case, unless something prevents it.

[FINAL CAUSES DO NOT REQUIRE DELIBERATION]

Besides, it is strange for people to think there is no end unless they see an agent initiating the motion by deliberation. Even crafts do not deliberate. Moreover, if the shipbuilding craft were in the wood, it would produce a ship in the same way that nature would. And so if what something is for is present in craft, it is also present in nature. This is clearest when a doctor applies medical treatment to himself—that is what nature is like.

---

has argued that the form is a final cause, and therefore an internal principle of motion (cf. 192b13).

114. **'all-natured first'**: Empedocles DK 31 B 61–62.

It is evident, then, that nature is a cause, and in fact the sort of cause that is for something.

9

35 Is the necessity present <in nature only> conditional,[115] or is it also unqualified?

200a The sort of necessity that is ascribed nowadays to things that come to be is the sort there would be if someone supposed that a wall came into being of necessity. On this view, heavy things naturally move downward, and light things upward, and that is why the stones and the foundations are below, while the earth is above because of its lightness,

5 and the wooden logs are on the very top because they are lightest of all.

Nonetheless, though the wall certainly requires these things, it did not come to be because of them (except insofar as they are its material cause), but in order to give shelter and protection.

The same is true in all other cases that are for something: although they require things that have a necessary nature, they do not come to be because of these things (except insofar as they are the material cause),

10 but for some end. For instance, why does a saw have such and such features?[116] In order to perform this function, and for this end. But this end cannot come to be unless the saw is made of iron; and so it is necessary for it to be made of iron if there is to be a saw performing its function. What is necessary, then, is conditional,[117] but not <necessary>

15 as an end; for necessity is in the matter, whereas the end is in the form₁.

Necessity is found both in mathematics and in things that come to be naturally, and to some extent the two cases are similar. For instance, since the straight is what it is,[118] it is necessary for a triangle to have angles equal to two right angles. It is not because the triangle has angles equal to two right angles that the straight is what it is; but if the triangle does not have angles equal to two right angles, the straight will not be what it is either.

115. **conditional**: See NECESSARY #4.
116. **why . . . features?**: i.e., why is it hard, durable, etc.?
117. **conditional**: sc. on the assumption that the end is to be achieved.
118. **the straight is what it is**: This refers to the formal cause.

The reverse is true in the case of things that come to be for an end: if the end is or will be, then the previous things are or will be too. Just as, in the mathematical case, if the conclusion <about the triangle> is false, the principle[119] <about the straight> will not be true either, so also in nature if the <materials> do not exist, the end that the process is for will not come about either. For the end is also a principle; it is a principle not of the action, but of the reasoning.[120] (In the mathematical case <also> the principle is the principle of the reasoning, since in this case there is no action.)

And so, if there is to be a house, it is necessary for these things to come to be or to be present; and in general, the matter that is for something must exist (for example, bricks and stones if there is to be a house). The end, however, does not exist because of these things, except insofar as they are the material cause, nor will it come about because of them; still, in general, the end (the house or the saw) requires them (the stones or the iron). Similarly, in the mathematical case the principles require the triangle to have two right angles.

[BOTH MATTER AND FINAL CAUSES CONCERN THE STUDENT OF NATURE]

Evidently, then, necessity in natural things belongs to the material cause and to the motions of matter. The student of nature should mention both causes, but more especially what something is for, since this is the cause of the matter, whereas the matter is not the cause of the end. The end is what something is for, and the principle comes from the definition and the form$_1$.

The same is true in productions of craft. For instance, since a house is this sort of thing, these things must come to be and be present of necessity; and since health is this, these things must come to be and be present of necessity. In the same way, if a man is this, these things must come to be and be present of necessity; and if these, then these.

But presumably necessity is present in the form$_1$ as well <as in the matter>. Suppose, for instance, that we define the function of sawing as a certain sort of cutting; this sort of cutting requires a saw with teeth of a certain sort, and these require a saw made of iron.[121] For the form$_1$, as well as the matter, has parts in it as matter of the form$_1$.

119. **the principle**: i.e., (in the mathematical case) the premiss.

120. **of reasoning**: In the case of final causes, this is reasoning about how to achieve the end.

121. **this sort of cutting requires . . . and these require . . . iron**: These two requirements express unqualified necessity (it is necessary, irrespective of any end, that only teeth of a certain kind will cut). See PA 642a31–b4. On material parts and definitions see PART.

Book III

[MOTION]

1

200b12 Since nature is a principle of motion* and change, and since our line* of inquiry is about nature, we must find out what motion is; for if we
15 do not know_g what it is, neither can we know what nature is. Once we have determined what motion is, we should try the same approach to the things that come next in order.[1]

Motion seems to be continuous, and the first thing discerned in the continuous is the infinite.[2] That is why those who define the continuous
20 often turn out to be relying on the account of the infinite as well, since they assume that what is infinitely divisible is continuous. Moreover, it seems impossible for there to be motion without place, void, and time.

It is clear, then, both because of these <connections> and because these things are common to everything and universal, that we should undertake a discussion of each of them, since the study of special topics
25 comes after the study of common topics; and first, as we said, we should discuss motion.

[THE DEFINITION OF MOTION]

Some things are only in actuality,[3] and others are in potentiality and in actuality—thises*, or quantities, or qualities, or one of the other predications* of being. Among relatives, some are spoken of with reference to
30 excess and deficiency, and others with reference to acting and being affected, and in general with reference to initiating motion and to being moved—for what initiates motion initiates it in what is moved, and what is moved is moved by what initiates motion.

There is no motion apart* from things <that are moved>. For what changes always does so either in substance or in quantity or in quality
35 or in place, and we claim that there is nothing that is common and
201a applies to all of these—i.e., is neither a this nor a quantity nor a quality nor any of the other things predicated.[4] Hence there is no motion or

---

1. **in order**: Aristotle goes on to describe the program of Bks iii–iv, in what he takes to be the logical order.

2. **first thing . . . infinite**: because of the definitional connection that Aristotle goes on to mention.

3. **actuality**: *entelecheia*. In this chapter both *energeia* and *entelecheia* are translated by 'actuality', since no difference seems to be intended. See ACTUALITY #1.

4. **things predicated**: See PREDICATIONS.

change of anything apart from the things mentioned, since there is
nothing apart from these things.

Each of these things belongs to everything in <one of> two ways.[5]
This is true, for instance, of the this, which in some cases is form$_m$
and in other cases privation;[6] of quality, which in some cases is pale   5
and in other cases dark; and of quantity, which in some cases is
complete and in other cases incomplete. It is true in the same way
of local motion,[7] which in some cases is upward and in other cases
is downward, or <in other words> where some things are light and
others heavy. Hence there are as many kinds of motion and change
as there are of being.

In each kind of thing we distinguish what is actually F from what is   10
potentially F.[8] Hence the actuality of what is F potentially, insofar as it
is F potentially, is motion. The actuality of the alterable, for instance,
insofar as it is alterable, is alteration; the actuality of what is capable of
growing or its opposite, decaying (since there is no name that covers
both), is growing or decaying; the actuality of what is capable of coming
to be or perishing is coming to be or perishing; the actuality of what is   15
capable of local movement is local movement. That this is what motion
is is clear from the following. Whenever the buildable, insofar* as we
say it is buildable,[9] is in actuality, it is being built, and this is building.
The same applies to learning, curing, rolling, jumping, ripening, and
ageing.

In some cases, the same things are both in potentiality and in   20
actuality, though not at the same time or in the same way, but rather
they are, for instance, actually hot and potentially cold. It follows
that many things will both act on and be affected by each other,
since everything of this sort will be capable both of acting and of
being affected. Hence what naturally initiates motion is also moveable;
for everything of this sort initiates motion by itself being moved.   25

5. **two ways**: These are the contraries that constitute the starting point and
terminus of change in the different categories.

6. **which in . . . privation**: This is explained in *Phys.* i 5, 7.

7. **local motion**: See TRAVEL.

8. **actually F . . . potentially F**: In the following discussion 'F' is added to make
the form of Aristotle's definition clear, in conformity with his explanation below.

9. **insofar . . . buildable**: This clause (explained in 201a29) seeks to distinguish
(i) the actuality that is to be identified with the process of building from (ii) the
actuality that is the completed house (which is also an actuality of the buildable,
i.e., the realization of a capacity of the bricks and stones).

Hence some people even believe that whatever initiates motion is itself moved. The truth about this, however, will be clear from other considerations; for in fact there is something that initiates motion without being moveable.[10] In any case, the actuality of what is potentially F, whenever, being in actuality, it is active[11]—not insofar as it is itself, but insofar as it is moveable—is motion.

30   By 'insofar as' I mean the following: Though bronze is potentially a statue, it is not the actuality of bronze, insofar as it is bronze, that is motion. For being bronze is not the same as being potentially something; for if they were the same without qualification, i.e.,[12] in definition, the actuality of bronze insofar as it is bronze would be motion, but in

35 fact, as we have said, they are not the same. This point is clear in the case of contraries. For being potentially healthy is not the same

201b as being potentially ill;[13] if they were the same, then being ill and being healthy would also be the same. Rather, the subject (whether it is moisture or blood) that is healthy and ill <at different times> is one and the same. The two potentialities, therefore, <of F insofar as it is F, and of F insofar as it is moveable> are not the same, just as color and the visible are not the same; and so it is evident that

5 the actuality of what is potentially F, insofar as it is potentially F, is motion.[14]

   It is clear, then, that this actuality is motion, and that something is in fact in motion just when the actuality is this one, and neither earlier nor later. For it is possible for something—for instance, the buildable—to be at one time actual and at another not, and the actuality of the

10 buildable, insofar as it is buildable, is building. For the actuality is either the <process of> building or the house; but when the house exists, it is no longer buildable,[15] whereas what is being built is something buildable; necessarily, then, the actuality is <the process of> building. Now, building is a type of motion; moreover, the same account will also fit the

15 other cases of motion.

10. **without being moveable**: Or 'without being moved'. The ending represented by '-able' is sometimes ambiguous between these two readings. On the unmoved mover see viii 5.

11. **active**: *energein*, cognate with *energeia*.

12. **i.e.**: Or 'and'.

13. **being potentially . . . ill**: Aristotle is describing a case where the F and the G are the same, but their being is not the same. See ESSENCE #2.

14. **the actuality . . . motion**: On this definition see MOTION #2.

15. **it is no longer buildable**: Or 'the buildable no longer exists'.

[OTHER VIEWS OF MOTION]

2

That this account is correct is clear both from what other people say
about motion and from the fact that it is not easy to define it in any
other way. For motion and change cannot be assigned to any other
genus, as is clear if we examine what some people assign them to. They   20
assert that motion is difference, or inequality, or what is not; but none
of these—different things or unequal things or things that are not—is
necessarily in motion, and change is no more into these or from these
than it is from their opposites.

The reason why they assign motion to these genera is that motion   25
seems to be something indefinite, and the principles in the second column[16] are indefinite because they are privative; for none of them is a
this, or of any quality, or any of the other predications.* The reason why
motion seems to be indefinite is that it cannot be assigned either to the
potentiality or to the actuality of beings. For neither what potentially   30
has a given quantity nor what actually has it is necessarily in motion.
Moreover, motion seems to be some sort of actuality, but an incomplete
one; this is because the potential, of which motion is an actuality, is
incomplete. This, then, is why it is difficult to grasp what motion is; for
it has to be assigned either to privation or to potentiality or to unqualified   35
actuality, but none of these appears possible.

The remaining option, then, is the way <of understanding motion>   202a
that we have described: to say that it is a sort of actuality, and, in fact,
the sort we have mentioned,[17] which is difficult to notice but possible
to be.

As we have said, everything that initiates motion is also moved,
provided that it has a potentiality to be moved and that its lack of motion
is rest (for, in the case of things that undergo motion, lack of motion is   5
rest).[18] For to act on this sort of thing <i.e., something moveable), insofar
as it is of this sort, is just what it is to move it. <The agent> does this
by contact, so that it is itself acted on at the same time. That is why
motion is the actuality of the moveable insofar as it is moveable; this
comes about by contact with the mover,[19] so that <the mover> is also
acted on at the same time. In each case the mover will bring some form—
either a this or of this quality or of this quantity—that will be the principle   10

16. **second column**: On the columns of opposites see *Met*. 1004b27n.

17. **mentioned**: See 201a27.

18. **for lack . . . motion**: Aristotle is distinguishing moved movers (which are
said to be at rest when they are not in motion) from unmoved movers (which
are not in motion, but are not said to be at rest). See viii 5.

19. **mover**: i.e., what initiates motion. See MOTION #1.

and cause of motion whenever the mover initiates motion; for instance, an actual man makes something else actually a man from being potentially a man.

[PUZZLES ARISING FROM THE DEFINITION]

3

It is also evident how to answer the puzzle, by saying that the motion is in the thing moved.[20] For it is the actuality of the thing moved, brought
15   about by the agency of the mover. The actuality of the mover is not different from this; for there must be an actuality of both mover and thing moved, since the mover is an initiator of motion by its potentiality, and it initiates motion by its actuality, but it is the thing moved that it brings to actuality. And so both mover and moved have one actuality, in the way in which the same interval is the interval from one to two and the interval from two to one, and <the same road> is the uphill
20   and the downhill <road>. For these things are one, but their account is not one;[21] and the same applies to the mover and the thing moved.

This, however, raises a logical* puzzle. For presumably there must be some actuality of the agent and of what is acted on. The former actuality is *acting on* something, and the latter actuality is *being acted on*; and the achievement[22] and end of the former is an action, and of the
25   latter a way of being acted on. Both of these actualities, then, are motions; if, then, they are different, what are they in?

Either both are in the thing that is affected and moved, or else the acting is in the agent and the being acted on is in the thing acted on. (If this being acted on is <also> to be called acting, then acting will be homonymous.)[23] But now, if this is so, then the motion will be in the
30   mover, since the same account applies to the mover and to the thing moved <as applies to the agent and to the thing acted on>. And so either the mover will be moved or it will have motion and yet not be moved.

20. **puzzle . . . moved**: Aristotle has not actually mentioned the puzzle he alludes to here, about whether motion is in the mover or in the thing moved.

21. **For . . . not one**: See ESSENCE #2.

22. **achievement**: Or 'work', *ergon*. Here the *ergon* is the outcome. See FUNCTION.

23. **(If . . . homonymous)**: Aristotle's point is clearest if we think of 'doing' in English. I might say either (a) that the only thing I 'did' was to be hit by a falling rock, or (b) that I *did* nothing, but just happened to be in the way. In (a) 'do' is used in the weak sense (marked by the use of quotation marks) that Aristotle sets aside in this parenthesis. In (b) 'do' is used in a stronger sense (marked by the use of italics); the stronger sense is the one Aristotle is trying to explain.

Suppose that, on the contrary, both the acting and the being acted on in the thing that is moved and acted on, and that both teaching and learning, being two <motions>, are in the learner. In that case, first of all, the actuality of a given <subject> will not be in that <subject>. Secondly, it is absurd that <the thing acted on> should undergo two motions at the same time. For what will be the two alterations of one   35 <subject> into one form? That is impossible.

Suppose, then, that the actuality <of the mover and the thing moved> are one. But it is unreasonable for two things that are different in form   202b to have one and the same actuality. Moreover if <the processes of> teaching and learning, or <the processes of> acting and being acted on, are the same, then to teach will be the same as to learn, and to act on will be the same as to be acted on, so that it will be necessary for the one teaching to be learning <everything that he is teaching>, and for   5 the agent to be acted on <by its own action>.

[ANSWERS TO THE PUZZLES]

Perhaps, however, it is not absurd for the actuality of one thing to be in another thing; for teaching is the actuality of what is capable of teaching, but in some subject <acted on>. It is not cut off, but is the actuality of this <agent> in this <thing acted on>.[24] And perhaps it is not impossible for two things to have one and the same actuality—not in such a way that the actuality is one in being, but in the way in which the   10 potential is related to the actual.

Nor is it necessary for the one teaching to be learning, even if acting and being acted on are the same, given that they are not the same in such a way that one and the same account states the essence of both, as it does for cape and cloak; rather, they are the same in the way in which the road from Thebes to Athens is the same as the road from Athens to Thebes, as has been said before.[25] For if things are <merely>   15 the same in some way, it does not follow that all the same things belong to them; this follows only if their being is the same.[26]

Moreover, even if <the process of> teaching is the same thing as learning, it does not follow that to teach is the same as to learn, just as,

24. **not cut . . . acted on**>: Teaching is properly described not simply as 'an action of a teacher', but as 'an action of a teacher acting on a learner'.

25. **said before**: See 202a18–20.

26. **For if . . . is the same**: On sameness see ONE, ESSENCE #2. 'Not all the same things belong' to the Athens-Thebes road and to the Thebes-Athens road: the first essentially has the direction Athens-Thebes, not Thebes-Athens, and the second essentially has the direction Thebes-Athens, not Athens-Thebes.

even if there is one interval between the two things separated by it, it does not follow that to be separated by the interval from here to there is one and the same as to be separated by the interval from there to here.[27] And, to speak generally, <the process of teaching> is not the
20 same thing in the full sense[28] as learning, nor is acting the same <in the full sense> as being acted on. What is one is the motion to which both the properties <of being a teaching and being a learning> belong. For being the actuality of this <subject> in that one is different in account from being the actuality of that <subject> by the agency of this one.

We have said, then, what motion is, both in general and in particular
25 cases. For it is clear how each species of it will be defined. Alteration, for instance, will be the actuality of the alterable insofar as it is alterable. To make it still better known$_g$: <motion will be> the actuality of what has the potentiality for acting and being acted on, insofar as it has that potentiality. This is true without qualification, and again in particular cases—for instance in building or healing. The same account will be given of each of the other types of motion.

* * * * * * *

Book IV

[TIME]

[PUZZLES ABOUT THE REALITY OF TIME]

10

217b29 The next topic to be considered, after those that have been discussed,
30 is time. First of all, it is a good thing to expound the puzzles, using the more popular* arguments as well <as the more specialized ones>. In the first place, is time something that is or something that is not?[1] Next, what is its nature?

The following arguments might arouse the suspicion that either time is not at all, or else it scarcely is, and is in some obscure way.

(1) Part of it has been and is not, and another part of it is still to come and
218a is not yet. Now time—both infinite time and any time you care to take[2]—is composed of these parts; but it might seem impossible for a <whole> to have any share in being$_o$ if it is composed of parts that are not.

27. **to be separated . . . here**: Aristotle thinks of the direction as being essential to the properties of 'to be separated . . .', just as he took it to be essential to the Athens-Thebes road.

28. **full sense**: See CONTROLLING.

1. **something . . . is not**: For the question 'whether it is' cf. *APo* 71a12n.

2. **any time you care to take**: i.e., any length of time including the present moment and extending as far as you like on each side.

(2) Moreover, if something that has parts is, then either all or some   5
of its parts must be whenever <the whole> is. But time has parts, and
some of these have been, and others are still to come.[3] But the now is
not a part; for the part measures the whole, and the whole must be
composed of the parts, whereas time does not seem to be composed of
nows.

(3) Further, it is not easy to see whether the now, which appears to
distinguish the past from the future, (a) remains one and the same on   10
every occasion, or (b) is a different thing on different occasions. (b) For
if it is different on every occasion, and different parts in time are not
simultaneous (unless one includes and the other is included, as a shorter
time is included in a longer), and if something that is not now and
previously was must have perished sometime, then neither are the nows   15
simultaneous, but in every case the previous one must have perished.
It cannot have perished in itself, because it was then; on the other hand,
a previous now cannot have perished in a later now. For let us agree
that nows cannot be next to one another, just as a point cannot be next
to a point.[4] If, then, the <previous> now has not perished in the next   20
now, but in another one, then it is simultaneous with the nows in
between them,[5] which are infinitely many;[6] and this is impossible. (a)
Nor, on the other hand, can the now possibly remain the same on every
occasion. For nothing divisible and finite has <just> one limit, whether
it is continuous in one direction or in more than one. The now, however,
is a limit, and it is possible to take a limited <length of> time.[7] Further,   25

3. **But time . . . not a part**: If the past and the future do not exist, then time
exists only if some other part of time exists. But there is nothing more to time
besides the past and future, except the present; and so the present must be a
part of time if time exists. But the present is not a part of time; and so there is
no part of time that exists; and so time does not exist. Aristotle's term 'the now',
to nun, covers (i) the present in contrast to the past and future and (ii) an instant
in contrast to a length of time.

4. **nows cannot . . . to a point**: Since a point has no extension, we cannot say,
for instance, that the left hand edge of point B is next to (and hence in a different
place from) the right hand edge of point A and that the right hand edge of B is
next to the left hand edge of point C; for in that case B (and therefore A and C)
would have to be extended.

5. **between them**: between this now and the now in which this now supposedly
perishes.

6. **infinitely many**: since every length is infinitely divisible. See INFINITE
#1–2.

7. **limited . . . time**: Every length of time requires two limits, and hence requires
two nows to bound it; hence there cannot be one and the same now at both
boundaries.

if being simultaneous in time, neither before nor after, is being in one and the same now, it follows that if the time before and the time after are in some one now, then what happened ten thousand years ago is simultaneous with what happened today, and nothing is either before

30   or after anything else.

So much, then, for our exposition of the puzzles about the properties of time.

[DIFFERENT VIEWS ON THE NATURE OF TIME]

What time is and what its nature is are left equally obscure both by what our predecessors have handed down and by our own previous

218b   discussion. For some say (1) that it is the motion of the whole <heaven>, and others say (2) that it is the sphere itself. (1) On the other hand <in opposition to the first view>, a part of the <heavenly> revolution is also a time, but not a revolution—for whatever part we take is a part of a revolution, not a revolution. Moreover, if there were more than one

5   heaven,* time would be the motion of any one of them equally, so that there would be many <different> times simultaneously. (2) People who said that time is the sphere of the whole universe believed this because everything is both in time and in the sphere of the whole universe. But this view is so naive that it is not worth examining its impossible consequences.

10   Time seems most of all to be motion and some sort of change;[8] and hence this should be examined. Now the change and motion of a given thing is present only in the thing that changes, or in any place where the thing in motion and change happens to be. Time, by contrast, is equally everywhere, and accompanies everything. Further, change is

15   faster or slower, but time is not. For slow and fast are defined[9] by time, fast as what is moved much in little time, and slow as what is moved little in much time; time, by contrast, is not defined by time, neither as so much time nor as a certain sort of time.

It is apparent, then, that time is not motion (we assume that it does

20   not matter at present whether we speak of motion or of change).[10]

8. **Time seems . . . change.**: This is a third common view, not mentioned in the initial description of two views.

9. **defined**: The same word (*horizein*) is also translated 'mark' in the rest of the discussion of time. See FORMULA #1.

10. **(we assume . . . change)**: On the distinction between motion and change see MOTION #1.

[*THE CONNECTION BETWEEN TIME AND MOTION*]

11

Nor, on the other hand, is time independent of[11] change; for whenever
our thoughts do not change at all, or we do not notice the change, it
does not seem to us that time has passed. In the story this is what
happens to those who sleep in the heroes' temple in Sardinia, whenever   *25*
they wake up; they combine the earlier now with the later now and
make them one, removing what comes between the two nows because
they have not noticed it. Hence, just as there would be no time if the
now were not different but one and the same, so also there does not
seem to be any time coming between <the nows> because, though the
now is different, we do not notice that it is. We suppose, then, that
there is no time whenever we do not mark any change, but the soul   *30*
appears to remain in one indivisible <now>. Whenever, on the other
hand, we notice and mark a change, that is when we say time has
passed. It is evident, therefore, that time is not independent of motion   *219a*
and change.
    And so it is evident that time is neither motion nor independent of
motion. And since we are inquiring into what time is, we should begin
from this fact about it and find what feature of motion[12] it is. For we
notice time if and only if[13] we notice motion. Even if it is dark, and
nothing affects us through the body, but there is some motion in the   *5*
soul, that is all it takes for us to believe that some time has also passed.
Moreover, whenever any time seems to have passed, it thereby seems
that some motion has also occurred. And so time is either motion or
some feature of motion. Since, therefore, it is not motion, it must be   *10*
some feature of motion.
    Since everything in motion is in motion from one thing to another,[14]
and every magnitude is continuous, motion is also continuous. For motion is continuous because magnitude is continuous, and time is continuous because motion is continuous; for the quantity of time that has
passed always seems to correspond to the quantity of change.   *15*
    Before and after belong primarily to place, and there they belong to
position. And since before and after belong to magnitude, they must

---

11. **independent of**: Or 'without'. Our translation reflects the fact that Aristotle
intends the modal claim that time cannot exist without motion (not simply that
it does not exist without motion).

12. **what feature of motion**: Lit. 'what thing belonging to motion'.

13. **if and only if**: Lit. 'at the same time as' (*hama*, often used with a purely
logical sense).

14. **from one thing to another**: and hence over some magnitude.

20   also belong to motion, in an analogous way. But further, before and
after also belong to time, since in every case motion and time imply each
other.[15] Before and after in motion are the same in subject as motion,[16]
but their being is different <from it>, and is not motion.

Further, we also come to know$_g$ time whenever we mark motion, mark-
25   ing it by before and after. And we say that time has passed whenever we
notice before and after in motion. We mark before and after by appre-
hending that they are different and that something else is between them.
For whenever we understand that the extremities are different from the
middle, and the soul says there are two nows, one before and one after,
that is when we say that there is time, and this is what we say it is. For
30   what is marked by the now seems to be time; let us assume this is correct.

[THE DEFINITION OF TIME]

And so, whenever we notice the now as one, neither as before and after
in motion <and hence as two> nor as the same thing belonging to
something before and something after, no time seems to have passed,
because there seems to have been no motion. But whenever we notice
219b the before and after, then we say that there is time. For this is what time
is: the number of motion in respect of before and after.[17]

Time, then, is not motion; it is what makes motion have number.[18]
A sign of this is the fact that we discriminate more and less by number,
5   and discriminate more and less motion by time. It follows that time is
some sort of number. Number, however, is of two types. Both what is
counted[19] and countable and what we count it by are called number.
Time, then, is what is counted, not what we count with. What we count
with and what is counted are different.[20]

10   And just as motion is different on every occasion, so also is time. All
the time that is simultaneous is the same; for the now is the same subject,
though its being is different, and the now marks time, insofar as <time>
is before and after.

15. **since . . . each other**: Lit. 'since one of them always follows the other'.

16. **same . . . as motion**: Text and translation doubtful. A more literal translation:
'The before and after in motion, as regards that being which <it is before and
after>, is motion'. Motion and the temporal before-and-after are one in number
but two in being (see ESSENCE #2), since time is an aspect of motion.

17. **in respect of before and after**: One part of a motion is before or after another
by a measurable distance insofar as it is earlier or later in time.

18. **what makes motion have number**: Lit. 'that qua which motion has number'.

19. **counted**: 'Count', *arithmein*, is cognate with *arithmos*, 'number'.

20. **What we . . . are different**: See NUMBER.

[THE NATURE OF THE NOW]

The now is in a way the same, in a way not the same; for insofar as it occurs on different occasions, it is different (for this is what it is for it to be a now), but the subject of the now is the same.[21] For, as we said   *15* before, motion corresponds to magnitude; and time, we are saying now, corresponds to motion. And what is true of a point is also true of the travelling thing by which we come to know$_g$ motion and what is before and after in it. This is the same in subject—for what corresponds to a point is[22] a stone or something else of that sort—but it is different in   *20* account. It is similar to the cases where the sophists* think that, for instance, Coriscus in the Lyceum is different from Coriscus in the market-place.[23] This <travelling thing>, then, is different[24] by being in different places.

The now, then, corresponds to the travelling thing, just as time corresponds to motion. For the travelling thing gives us knowledge of the before and after in motion, and the now is what makes the before and   *25* after countable. Hence in this case also the subject of the now is the same—for it is the before and after in motion; but its being is different— for the now is what makes the before and after countable.

And this now is best known. For we also come to know motion because of the thing in motion, and travel because of the thing travelling;   *30* for the thing travelling is a this, but the motion is not. In a way, then, the now is always the same, and in a way it is not; for the same is true of the thing travelling.

[THE CONNECTION BETWEEN TIME AND THE NOW]

It is also apparent that if time were not, the now would not be, and that   *220a* if the now were not, time would not be. For just as the travelling thing and its travel imply each other, so also do the number of the thing and the number of its travel. For time is the number of the travel, and the now corresponds to the travelling thing, as a sort of unit of a number.[25]

21. **But the subject . . . same**: It is always the present, but it is present at different times and hence is different presents.

22. **for what corresponds to a point is . . . .** : Read *hē stigmē*. Lit. 'the point is . . . '

23. **the sophists . . . market-place**: They do not realize that the 'two Coriscuses' are merely different 'in being'. See ESSENCE #2, *Met.* 1032a8n.

24. **is different**: i.e., different in being.

25. **as a sort of unit of a number**: Aristotle probably does not mean that the now is straightforwardly a unit for measuring lengths of time (such units are minutes, seconds etc.). He probably means that two different nows bound a

5   The now, then, makes time continuous and also makes it divisible; for this also corresponds to travel and the travelling thing. For there also the motion, i.e., the travel, is one, because of the object travelling, since this object is one—not one in subject (since this might not ensure unity of motion),[26] but in account; and this is what marks the motion that is before and after.

10   In this respect too <the now> corresponds, in a way, to a point. For a point also both makes a length continuous and marks <different lengths>, since it is the end of one length and the beginning of another. But when we take a point this way, using one point as two, we must come to a stop, if the same point is to be both the beginning <of one length> and the end <of another>. But the now is always different because of the motion of the thing travelling.

15   And so time is number, not as the number of the same point (because it is both beginning and end),[27] but rather as the extremes <are the number of> a line, and not as parts. This is true for the reasons we have given—since we use the middle point as two, and the result is that we come to a stop;[28] and moreover it is evident that the now is no part

20 of time, and the division is no part of a motion, just as a point is no part of a line, but, on the contrary, the parts of one line must be two lines.[29] And so, insofar as the now is a limit, it is not time, but a coincident of it; and insofar as it numbers, it is number. For limits belong only to that of which they are limits, but a number is a number both of these horses (for instance, ten of them) and of other things.

25   It is apparent, then, that time is the number of motion in respect of

---

length of time, and the now is the unit of these (i.e., it is what these two are two of).

26. **since this . . . motion**: Lit. 'for then it might fail'. The unity of a motion is not ensured simply by the fact that one body moves (since it might stop moving, and then begin a different motion), but only by the 'account'—i.e., 'one body moving continuously from this place to that place'.

27. **both beginning and end**: and thereby counted as two.

28. **since we use . . . a stop**: If the sense in which the nows (at different times) are two were simply the sense in which the same point is treated as two 'in being' when it is the end of one segment of a line and the beginning of another, then we would not capture the sense in which the two nows, different in being, correspond to different times.

29. **the parts . . . two lines**: Suppose that a line A is divided into two proper parts B and C. If both B and C are points, then neither has any length, and so A has no length, and so is not a line. If B is a line and C is a point, then the whole line A is longer than B only by a point; and since a point has no length, A cannot be longer than B. Hence any proper part of a line must be a line.

before and after, and that it is continuous, since what it belongs to is continuous.

*   *   *   *   *   *   *

[*TIME DEPENDS ON SOUL*]

14

. . . A puzzle arises about whether there would be time if there were   *223a21*
no soul. For if it is impossible for there to be anyone who counts, it is
also impossible for there to be anything countable, and so plainly there
will be no number either; for number is either what is counted or what
is countable.   *25*

If nothing else besides soul, and <more specifically> the understanding in the soul, is naturally capable of counting, then it is impossible for
there to be time if there is no soul. All there would be would be the
subject of time, if, that is to say, it is possible for there to be motion
without soul. Before and after belong to motion, and time is these insofar
as they are countable. . . .

*   *   *   *   *   *   *

Book VI

[*ZENO'S PARADOXES*]

[*INFINITE DIVISIBILITY*[1]]

2

. . . It is evident that if time is continuous, then so is magnitude, if one   *233a13*
covers half of a given distance in half the time, and, in general, less of   *15*
a distance in less time; for the time and the magnitude will have the
same divisions. And if either is infinite, then so is the other, and in
whatever way either is infinite, the other is infinite in the same way. If,
for instance, time is infinitely long,[2] then so is length; if time is infinitely
divisible,[3] then so is length; and if time is infinite in both ways, then   *20*
magnitude is also infinite in both ways.

That is why Zeno's argument makes a false assumption in saying that
it is impossible for something to traverse infinitely many things or to
touch each of infinitely many things in turn in a finite time. For both
length and time, and in general everything continuous, are said to be   *25*

1. This preliminary discussion in vi 2 anticipates the fuller treatment of Zeno
in vi 9.

2. **infinitely long**: Lit. 'infinite in its extremities'.

3. **infinitely divisible**: Lit. 'infinite in division'.

infinite in two ways—either infinitely divisible or infinitely long. If, then, they are infinite in quantity, then it is impossible to touch them all in a finite time; but if they are <only> infinitely divisible, it is possible to touch them—and in fact this is the way in which time is infinite. . . .

* * * * * * *

[*ZENO'S ERROR*]

9

239b5 Zeno argues fallaciously. If, he says, in every case a thing is at rest when it occupies a space equal <to itself>, and in every case what is travelling is in the now, then it follows[4] that the travelling arrow is not in motion. This is false; for time is not composed of indivisible nows,[5] any more than any other magnitude is.

[*THE BISECTION*]

10 Zeno has four arguments about motion, and they cause trouble to some-one trying to solve them.

According to the first argument, nothing is in motion, because the travelling object must first reach the halfway mark before it reaches the end. We have examined this argument in our previous discussion.[6]

[*THE ACHILLES*]

15 The second argument is the one called the Achilles.[7] According to this, the slowest runner will never be caught, while it is running, by the fastest; for the pursuer must first reach the place where the leader has left, so that the slower must always be some distance ahead.

This argument is the same as the bisection, except that it differs insofar
20 as it divides, instead of bisecting, whatever magnitude you care to take. The conclusion that the slower runner is not overtaken results from the

4. **then it follows**: since in any given now the arrow occupies a space equal to itself.

5. **for time . . . indivisible nows**: Aristotle accepts (1) In any now the arrow travels no distance. But he rejects the inference to (2) In the smallest part of the time during which it is travelling, the arrow travels no distance. For he denies that the now is a part of time; in his view, every part of time is a length of time, during which the arrow travels some distance.

6. **previous discussion**: in vi 2.

7. **Achilles**: the fastest runner among the Greeks at Troy.

argument by the same method as in the bisection. For in both arguments the result is failure to arrive at the end because the magnitude is divided in some way. But in the Achilles it is added that even the fastest runner (this is the dramatic element added) will not reach the end in its pursuit   *25* of the slowest.

[ANSWER TO THE FIRST TWO ARGUMENTS]

And so the solution must be the same <as that of the bisection>. To claim that the leader is not overtaken is false. Certainly it is not overtaken while it is in the lead, but it is overtaken nonetheless, if you grant that it is possible to traverse a finite distance.

[THE FLYING ARROW]

These, then, are the first two arguments. The third is the one we have   *30* mentioned, that the arrow is at rest while it travels. This conclusion results from supposing that time is composed of nows; for if this is not conceded, the deduction will not go through.

[THE MOVING BLOCKS]

In the fourth argument, blocks of equal size are moving past each other in a stadium, from opposite ends, one lot beginning from the starting line[8] of the stadium, the other lot from the far end,[9] moving at equal   *35* speed. The conclusion, according to Zeno, is that half the time is equal   *240a* to double the time.

The error in this argument is the assumption that equal magnitudes moving at equal speeds, one past a moving object, the other past a stationary object, travel by in an equal time. This assumption is false.

Suppose, for instance,[10] that AA are the stationary equal blocks; that   *5* BB are the blocks, equal in number and size to AA, beginning from the middle; and that CC are the ones, equal in number and size to the preceding, and travelling at equal speed to BB, beginning from the end. The result, then, is that <as the Bs and Cs> move past each other, the

---

8. **starting line**: Lit. 'end'.

9. **far end**: Lit. 'middle'. Cf. *EN* 1095b1. Aristotle is thinking of a Greek stadium, in which the 'middle' point is (what we would call) the far end of the stadium (beginning from a starting point at one end), since the far end is the middle point in a complete circuit of the stadium.

10. **Suppose . . .** : This paragraph states Zeno's argument. Text and interpretation uncertain.

10   first B reaches the last <C>, and the first C <reaches the last B>. But
a further result is that the <first> C has passed all the Bs,[11] while the
<first> B has passed half <the As>; hence the time taken <by the first
B> must be half <the time taken by the first C>, since each takes an
equal <time> to pass each block. Further, at this same time the first B
15   will have passed all the Cs; for the first C and the first B will reach the
opposite extremes of the stadium at the same time, because both take
equal time to pass the As.

This, then, is the argument. The false move in it is the one we have
mentioned.

[OTHER OBJECTIONS TO MOTION]

Nor will we find anything impossible in change involving contradicto-
20   ries. I mean, for instance, that we need not agree that if something is
passing from not-pale to pale and is in neither condition, then it is neither
pale nor not pale. For if something is not wholly in either condition, it
does not follow that it will be called neither pale nor not pale; for we
call something pale or not pale, not because that is how the whole of it
is, but because that is how most, or the most important, of its parts are;
25   not being in this condition <at all> is different from not being wholly
in it.

The same is true of being and not being, and of the other contradictory
pairs. For it is necessary for a subject to be in one or the other of the
opposed conditions, but not necessary that at every time it should be
wholly in the one or in the other.
30   The same is true of the circle, the sphere, and generally of things that
move within their own area. <It is argued> that they will turn out to
be at rest, since during some length of time the whole and its parts will
be in the same place, and so it will be both at rest and in motion at the
same time. <In reply we say that> first of all, the parts are not in the
240b   same place for any <length of> time. Second, the whole also changes
to a different place. For the circumference beginning from A is not the
same as that beginning from B or C or any of the other points, except
in the way that the musical man is the same as the man, because it
5   coincides. And so one circumference is always changing into another
and never comes to rest. The same applies to a sphere and to anything
else that moves within its own area.

*   *   *   *   *   *   *

11. **the Bs**: retaining *ta B*, deleted in OCT.

Book VIII

[MOTION AND THE UNMOVED MOVER]

[MOTION CANNOT HAVE HAD A BEGINNING]

1

Has motion ever come to be without having previously been? And does *250b11*
it perish in turn, in such a way that nothing is any longer in motion?
Or did it not come to be at all, and does it never perish, so that it always
was and always will be? Is this something immortal and ceaseless that
belongs to things that exist, a sort of life for everything constituted by *15*
nature?

All those who discuss nature say that there is motion, because they
are constructing a world order, and all their study concerns coming to
be and perishing, which cannot exist unless there is motion. All those
who say that there are infinitely many worlds,[1] and that some come to
be and others perish, say that there is always motion, since the coming *20*
to be and perishing of the worlds necessarily involves motion. But those
who say that there is one world, either everlasting or not, also make
corresponding assumptions about motion.

If, then, it is possible that at some time nothing is in motion, this
must happen in <one of> two ways. One is the way described by
Anaxagoras, who says that everything had been together and at rest for *25*
infinite time, until mind initiated motion in them and parted them. The
other way is the one described by Empedocles, who says that things are
in motion and at rest in turn; they are in motion when love makes one
out of many or strife makes many out of one, and at rest in the times
in between. He says: 'Thus insofar as one has learned to come from *30*
many, or again many arise when one divides, that is how they come to *251a*
be and have no rest during their lives. But insofar as these things never
cease alternating, that is how they always are <at some time> unmoved
in their circle <of becoming>.' For in 'insofar as these things never cease
alternating', we must take him to mean that they alternate from the one
motion to the other.

We must, therefore, examine the truth of these matters; for finding *5*
the truth about them is relevant not only to our study of nature, but
also to the line of inquiry about the first principle.*

Let us begin from what we have previously determined in our study
of nature.[2] We say, then, that motion is the actuality of the moveable *10*
insofar as it is moveable. Hence there must be things with the potential-

---

1. **All those . . . worlds**: See DEMOCRITUS.

2. **study of nature**: in iii 1.

ity* for each kind of motion. And even apart from the definition of motion, everyone would agree that it is necessary for what is moved to be what has a potentiality for each type of motion; what is altered, for
15 instance, is alterable, and what travels is what is potentially changed from place to place. And so something must also be combustible before it is burned, and capable of burning before it burns anything. It is necessary, then, that things <with the relevant potentialities> either come to be, having once not been, or else are everlasting.

If, then, each moveable thing came into being, it is necessary that, before whatever motion we take, some other change and motion came
20 about, bringing into being the thing that has the potentiality for being moved or for initiating motion. If they were always previously in being, but there was no motion, that immediately appears unreasonable as soon as we consider it, and must appear even more unreasonable when we take the argument further. For suppose that some things have a potentiality for being moved, and others for initiating motion, and at
25 one time there is a first mover, and something that is moved, but at another time there is not, and everything is at rest. In that case the thing <at rest> must change earlier; for there was some cause of its being at rest, since rest is the privation of motion. And so, <on this supposition,> there will be a previous change before the first change.

Some things initiate motion of only one sort, while others initiate
30 contrary motions. Fire, for instance, heats but does not cool, whereas there seems to be a single science of contraries. Even in the <first> case there appears to be something similar; for a cold thing heats by having, in a way, turned aside and departed, just as a scientific expert makes an error willingly whenever he uses the science in the wrong way.[3]
251b But at any rate, if we take the things that have a potentiality for acting and for being affected, or those that have a potentiality for initiating motion and those that have a potentiality for being moved, these do not have these potentialities <to do what they do> irrespective of their condition, but <to do it only> in the right condition and when they come close to each other.[4] And so, whenever they come close, one thing initiates the motion and the other is moved, whenever they are in the condition specifying the potentiality of the one thing to initiate motion
5 and the potentiality of the other thing to be moved.[5]

If, then, something has not always been in motion, clearly things were not in the condition in which the one thing has the potentiality to be moved and the other has the potentiality to initiate motion, but rather

3. **just as . . . wrong way**: On potentialities for contraries cf. *Met*. 1046b4–24.

4. **these are . . . each other**: See POTENTIALITY #3.

5. **whenever they are . . . to be moved**: Lit. 'when there obtains the way in which the one is an initiator of motion and the other is moveable'.

one or the other of them had to change <before there could be motion>. For this has to come about in the case of relatives;* if, for instance, x was not double y and now is double y, then either x or y or both must change. Hence, <on the supposition that at one time there was no motion>, there must be a change before the first change.   10

Further, how can there be before and after if there is no time? And how can there be time if there is no motion? If, then, time is in fact the number of motion or itself some sort of motion,[6] it follows that if there is always time, motion must also be everlasting. And in fact all <the philosophers> except one evidently agree about time, since they say it does not come to be.[7] Indeed this is the reason Democritus gives to show   15 that it is not possible for everything to have come to be; for time, he says, does not come to be. Plato is the only one who regards time as having come to be; for he says it is together with the heaven,* and he says the heaven came to be.[8]

Let us agree, then, that it is impossible for time to be or to be thought   20 of without the now, and that the now is a sort of midpoint, containing both a beginning and an end together—the beginning of future time and the end of past time. It necessarily follows that there is always time. For the extreme end of the last <length of> time we take[9] will be in some now, since there is nothing in time that we can take apart* from a now;   25 and so, since the now is both a beginning and an end, there must in every case be time on each side of it.[10] But if there is time, it is apparent that there must also be motion, if time is some attribute of motion. . . .

* * * * * * *

[WHATEVER IS IN MOTION IS MOVED BY SOMETHING]

4

Among things that initiate or undergo motion[11] some do so coinciden-   254b7 tally, others in their own right. The things that initiate or undergo motion coincidentally are those that do so by belonging to things that initiate or undergo motion, or by having a part that initiates or undergoes it.   10

6. **If, then . . . sort of motion**: Aristotle refers back to the account of time in iv 11.

7. **does not come to be**: Or 'cannot come to be'. On Aristotle's ambiguous term *agenētos* see *PA* 644b23n.

8. **Plato . . . came to be**: See *Timaeus* 28b, 38b.

9. **For the extreme . . . we take**: as we go back to the supposedly earliest time.

10. **there must . . . side of it**: Hence there must be some time earlier than the supposedly earliest time.

11. **initiate or undergo motion**: See MOTION #1.

The things that initiate or undergo motion in their own right are those
that do so not by belonging to what does so or by having a part that
does so.

Among the things initiating or undergoing motion in their own right,
some initiate or undergo it by their own agency,[12] some by the agency
of something else; and some things initiate or undergo motion naturally,
others by force and contrary to their nature.[13]

15   For what is moved by its own agency is moved naturally.[14] This is
true, for instance, of each kind of animal. For an animal is moved by its
own agency, and if something has the principle of its motion within itself,
we say it is moved naturally. Hence the whole animal initiates its own
motion naturally; but it is possible for its body to be moved either naturally
20   or contrary to its nature—for it makes a difference what sort of motion it
is in fact undergoing, and what sorts of elements compose it.

Among the things moved by the agency of something else, some
are moved naturally, others contrary to their nature—as, for instance,
earthen things are moved upward and fire downward <contrary to their
nature>. In addition, the parts of animals are often moved contrary to
their nature—<that is to say,> contrary to their <natural> positions
25   and types of motion.

The things moved contrary to their nature make it most apparent that
what is moved is moved by the agency of something; for it is clear that
they are moved by the agency of something else. After these, <the
clearest cases> are those among the things moved naturally that are
moved by their own agency—animals, for instance. For the point that
is unclear is not whether the animal is moved by the agency of something,
but how to distinguish the <part> of the animal that initiates the motion
30   from the part that undergoes it. For it would seem that in animals, just
as in boats and <in general> in things not naturally constituted, the
<part> that initiates motion is divided from the <part> that undergoes
it. The same is true for everything that initiates its own motion.

[MOTION IN LIFELESS THINGS AND IN LIVING THINGS]

A special puzzle arises about the remaining part of the last division. For
35   among the things moved by something else we took some to be moved

12. **by their own agency**: Lit. 'by (*hupo*) themselves'. The preposition *hupo* normally indicates a higher degree of agency than the instrumental dative (usually
rendered 'by').

13. **contrary to their nature**: Here and afterwards 'their' is supplied.

14. **For what . . . naturally**: It does not follow that all its motion is what Aristotle
calls 'natural motion' when he speaks of the elements. An animal, e.g., can
make its body move upward contrary to the natural tendency of its matter.

contrary to their nature; and the remaining ones, in contrast to these, we take to be moved naturally. These are the things—for instance, light and heavy things—that would raise a puzzle about what agency they are moved by. For when these things are moved into the places opposite <to their proper places>, they are moved by force; but when they are moved into their proper places (light things, for instance, are moved upward and heavy things downward), it is no longer evident, as it is whenever they are moved contrary to their nature, what agency they are moved by.

For it is impossible to say that they are moved by their own agency. For this is a feature of living things, distinctive of things that have souls; and <if light and heavy things were moved by their own agency>, they would also be able to stop themselves moving. I mean that, for instance, if something is a cause of its own walking, then it is also a cause of its not walking.[15] And so, if it were up to[16] fire to travel upward, it would also clearly be up to it to travel downward.

Further, it is unreasonable for these things to undergo only one motion by their own agency, if they really initiate motion in themselves. . . .

*   *   *   *   *   *   *

[THERE MUST BE UNMOVED MOVERS]

5

<Everything that is moved is moved by something.> This is true in two ways. For either (1) B initiates motion in A not because of B itself, but because of something else C that initiates motion in B, or (2) B initiates motion in A because of B itself. In the second case this is true either (2a) because B is the first thing immediately preceding A, or (2b) because B initiates the motion in A through a number of intermediaries.[17] For instance, <in case (2b)> the stick initiates motion in the stone, and the stick is moved by the agency of the hand, which is moved by the agency of the man; he <is set in motion, but> not[18] by being moved by the agency of some further thing. We say that both the last and the first mover[19] initiate motion, but the first mover does so to a higher degree.

15. **if something . . . not walking**: If something can on some occasions cause itself to walk, then it can on some occasions also cause itself not to walk.

16. **up to**: Cf. *EN* 1113b7.

17. **either (2a) . . . intermediaries**: Lit: 'as the first mover after the last thing, or through a number of things'.

18. **he <is set in motion, but> not**: Or 'he <initiates motion,> not . . . '.

19. **mover**: i.e., the initiator of motion. In this example the first mover is the man, and the last mover is the stick.

. . . For the first mover initiates motion in the last mover, but the last does not initiate motion in the first. Moreover, without the first mover the last mover will not initiate motion, but the first will initiate it without the last; the stick, for instance, will not move <the stone> unless the man moves <the stick>.[20]

It is necessary, then, for whatever is moved to be moved by the agency of some mover, either by the agency of a mover that is in turn moved by the agency of something else moving it or by the agency of a mover that is not moved by the agency of something else moving it. And if it is moved by the agency of something else moving it, there must be some first mover that is not moved by the agency of something else; and if this is the character of the first mover, it is not necessary for there to be another mover.[21] For it is impossible to have an infinite series of movers each of which initiates motion and is moved by the agency of something else; for there is no first term in an infinite series.[22]

[HENCE THERE MUST BE SELF-MOVERS]

If, then, everything that is moved is moved by the agency of something, and if the first mover is moved, but not by the agency of something else, then it necessarily follows that it is moved by its own agency.

Moreover, it is also possible to carry out the same argument in the following way. Every mover moves something and moves it by means of something; for it moves something either by means of itself or by means of something else. The man, for instance, initiates motion either himself or by means of the stick; again, either the wind itself knocked

20. **the stick . . . moves <the stick>**: whereas the man can move the stone with something other than a stick.

21. **And if . . . another mover**: Alternatively: 'And if (i) it is moved by the agency of something else moving it, there must be some first mover that is not moved by the agency of something else. If, on the other hand, (ii) this is the character of the first mover, it is not necessary for there to be another mover.' This alternative assumes that the last occurrence of 'first mover' refers to the immediate mover (= case 2a above, where there is no intermediary), rather than to the first mover in a series that includes intermediate movers (the reference of 'first mover' in the rest of the passage).

22. **for there is no first term in an infinite series**: It is agreed that the series comes to an end in one direction (with the motion of, e.g., the stone); and so it is infinite only if there is no first member in the other direction (when we go from the immediate mover to its immediate mover, and so on). Since such an infinite series has no first member, an infinite series of movers cannot include any first mover; but we have agreed in case (2b) that we need a first mover, e.g., the man; hence an infinite series of moved movers is impossible.

the thing over, or the stone pushed by the wind knocked it over. But if   *25*
C moves A by means of B, then B cannot move A unless there is something else that initiates motion by means of itself.[23] But if C initiates
motion by means of itself, there need not be anything else B by means
of which C initiates motion. And if there is something else B by means
of which C initiates motion, then there is something that initiates motion
not by means of something <else>, but by means of itself—otherwise
there will be an infinite regress.

If, then, something initiates motion by being moved, we must come
to a stop, and not go on to infinity. For if the stick initiates motion by   *30*
being moved by the hand, the hand moves the stick, and if something
else initiates motion by means of the hand, then there is something else
that moves the hand. And so, in each case when one thing moves another
by means of something, there must be something prior that initiates
motion in itself by means of itself. If, then, this is moved, but what
moves it is not something else, it must initiate motion in itself.   *256b*

And so this argument also shows that either what is moved is moved
immediately by what initiates motion in itself or eventually we come to
a mover of this sort. . . .

* * * * * * *

[THERE MUST BE AN EVERLASTING UNMOVED MOVER]

6

Since motion must be everlasting and must never fail, there must be some   *258b10*
everlasting first mover, one or more than one. The question whether each
of the unmoved movers[24] is everlasting is irrelevant to this argument;
but it will be clear in the following way that there must be something
that is itself unmoved and outside all change, either unqualified or coinci-   *15*
dental, but initiates motion in something else.

Let us suppose, then, if you like, that in the case of some things it is
possible for them to be at one time and not to be at another without any
coming to be or perishing—for if something has no parts, but it is at
one time and is not at another time, perhaps it is necessary for it to be   *20*
at one time and not to be at another without changing.[25] Let us also

23. **But if C . . . by means of itself**: Lit. 'But it is impossible for something by
means of which a mover initiates motion to initiate motion without a mover that
initiates motion by means of itself.'

24. **unmoved movers**: i.e., SOULS.

25. **without changing**: i.e. without undergoing any process of change. See *Met.*
1033b5–8n.

suppose that, among the principles that are unmoved but initiate motion, it is possible for some to be at one time and not to be at another time.

Still, this is not possible for every principle of that sort; for it is clear that there is something that causes the self-movers to be at one time and not to be at another time. For every self-mover necessarily has some magnitude, if nothing that lacks parts is moved; but from what we have said it is not necessary for every mover to have magnitude. Hence the cause explaining why some things come to be and other things perish, and in a continuous sequence, cannot be any of the things that are unmoved but do not always exist; nor can some things be the cause of some <parts of the sequence> and other things the cause of other <parts>; for neither any one of them nor all of them together is the cause explaining why the sequence is everlasting and continuous. For the sequence is everlasting and necessary, whereas all these movers are infinitely many and they do not all exist at the same time.

It is clear, then, that however many unmoved movers and self-movers perish and are succeeded by others, so that one unmoved mover moves one thing and another moves another, still there is something that embraces them all and is apart* from each of them, which is the cause explaining why some exist and some do not exist, and why the change is continuous. This is the cause of motion in these <other movers>, and these are the cause of motion in the other things.

If, then, motion is everlasting, the first mover is also everlasting, if there is just one; and if there are more than one, there are more than one everlasting movers. But we must suppose there is one rather than many, and a finite rather than an infinite number. For in every case where the results <of either assumption> are the same, we should assume a finite number <of causes>; for among natural things what is finite and better must exist rather <than its opposite> if this is possible. And one mover is sufficient; it will be first and everlasting among the unmoved things, and the principle of motion for the other things. . . .

* * * * * * *

[FURTHER DISCUSSION OF ZENO ON BISECTION]

8

263a15   . . . That solution[26] is adequate relative to the questioner—for the question was whether it is possible to traverse or count infinitely many things in a finite <time>; but it is not adequate for the actual facts and for finding the truth. For suppose one sets aside questions about length

26. **That solution** . . . : Aristotle has just restated Zeno's argument about bisection, and the answer to it that was given in vi 9.

and about whether it is possible to traverse infinitely many things in a   *20*
finite time, and asks the question about time itself (since time has infinitely many divisions); then that previous solution is no longer adequate.[27] Rather, we must give the true answer that we gave in our
argument just now.

For if we divide a continuous length into two halves, we treat the
single point as two, since it makes a beginning <of one half> and an   *25*
end <of the other>. And that is what we do by counting, as well as by
dividing into halves. But if this is the way we divide, then neither a line
nor a motion will be continuous; for a continuous motion is of something
continuous, and in something continuous infinitely many halves are
indeed present—but potentially present, not actually present.[28] If we
produce them in actuality, we do not produce a continuous motion but   *30*
bring it to a halt. This evidently results in the case of counting the halves;
for one necessarily counts just one point as two, since it will be the end   *263b*
of one half and the beginning of the other, if we count not the one
continuous line, but the two halves.

And so, in reply to someone asking the question whether it is possible
to traverse infinitely many things in time or in length, we say that in   *5*
one way it is possible, and in another way it is not. For if the infinitely
many things are in actuality, it is not possible to traverse them, but if
they are in potentiality, it is possible.[29] For someone in continuous motion
has traversed infinitely many things coincidentally, but not without qualification; for the line is coincidentally infinitely many halves, but its
essence and being are different from this. . . .[30]

27. **For suppose one sets . . . no longer adequate**: The new question is: How
can there be a finite length of time between any two points of time, if any length
of time contains infinitely many times?

28. **potentially present, not actually present**: On infinity and potentiality see
INFINITE #1.

29. **For if . . . is possible**: If a division of an infinitely divisible length were (per
impossibile) completed, then an infinitely long time would be needed to traverse
the infinite number of lengths that would result from the completed division.
In a finite time we can traverse the whole of a finite line that is infinitely divisible
(though not divided) into parts.

30. **For someone . . . different from this**: It is true of the line coincidentally that
it can be bisected without limit, but it is not defined as something infinite.

DE GENERATIONE ET CORRUPTIONE[1]

Book I

[DIFFERENT TYPES OF CHANGE]

[PREVIOUS PHILOSOPHERS DISAGREE ABOUT THE DIFFERENCE BETWEEN ALTERATION AND COMING TO BE]

1

314a We must distinguish the causes and accounts of coming* to be and perishing that are common to everything that comes to be and perishes naturally. We must also ask what growth and alteration* are and whether

5 alteration and coming to be should be taken to have the same nature, or separate natures that correspond to their distinct names.

Some of the early <philosophers> say that what is called unqualified coming to be is <really nothing but> alteration, while others say that alteration is different from coming to be. For those who say that the whole universe is some one thing and make everything come to be

10 from one thing have to say that <so-called> coming to be is <really> alteration, and that what <allegedly> comes to be in the full sense[2] is <really only> altered. But those who say that matter is more than one thing—for instance, Empedocles, Anaxagoras, Leucippus—have to say that coming to be and alteration are different.

And yet <among these pluralists> Anaxagoras misunderstood his own statements.[3] At any rate, he says that coming to be and perishing

15 are the same as alteration, even though, like others, he says that there are many elements. For Empedocles says that there are four bodily

---

1. This traditional title (i.e., 'On (unqualified) COMING TO BE and perishing') may be derived from Aristotle's reference at *Meteor.* 338a24. Text: H. H. Joachim (Oxford, 1922).

2. **full sense**: *kuriōs* (see CONTROLLING #2), here equivalent to UNQUALIFIED.

3. **And yet . . . statements**: Aristotle considers an apparent exception to his claim in the previous paragraph.

146

elements, but that the total number of elements, including the <two>
sources of motion, is six,[4] while Anaxagoras, Leucippus and Democritus
say that the elements are unlimited <in number>. For the elements that
Anaxagoras recognizes are uniform[5] things—for instance, bone, flesh,
marrow, and everything else whose parts are synonymous* with the   20
whole. Democritus and Leucippus, by contrast, say that everything else
is composed of indivisible bodies that are infinite both in number and
in shapes, and that <differences in> these components and <in> their
position and arrangement make the compounds different from each
other. For the views of Anaxagoras and his supporters are evidently   25
contrary to those of Empedocles and his supporters. For Empedocles
says that fire, water, air, and earth, rather than flesh, bone, and similar
uniform things, are <the only> four elements and that only these are
simple, whereas Anaxagoras and his supporters say that these <uniform
things> are simple and elemental, while earth, fire, water, and air are
compounds—for these four, they say, are a common seed-bed of the   314b
uniform things.

Those, then, who constitute everything out of some one thing must
say that <so-called> coming to be and perishing are <nothing but>
alteration. For in their view, in every <change> the subject remains one
and the same;[6] and that is the sort of thing that we say is altered. On
the other hand, those who recognize more than one kind of thing must   5
distinguish alteration from coming to be; for when things <of different
kinds> are combined there is coming to be, and when they are dissolved
there is perishing. That is why Empedocles also speaks in this way,
when he says 'There is no birth of anything, but only mixture and the
dissolution of things that have been mixed'.[7]

It is clear, then, that this account fits their assumption,[8] and that this   10
is what they actually say. But they must also distinguish alteration from
coming to be; yet their own statements make this impossible. It is easy
to see that we are right about this. For just as we see a substance re-

4. **For Empedocles . . . is six**: Empedocles is someone who thinks there are
many elements. His two sources of motion are Love and Strife; see EMPEDOCLES
#1.

5. **uniform**: See PART #1.

6. **one and the same**: Cf. *Met.* 983b6–18.

7. **That is why . . . mixed'**: Empedocles wants to deny that there is any coming
to be. But in recognizing that there is mixture and dissolution of compounds of
different elements (i.e., that these compounds come into and go out of existence)
he implies the reality of coming to be. On 'birth', *phusis*, see NATURE #1.

8. **their assumption**: i.e., the assumption that there is more than one basic
constituent.

15 maining stable while its size changes (this is called growth and decay), so also we see alteration; and yet the views of those who recognize more than one principle* make alteration impossible. For the attributes that we take to be <gained or lost> when something is altered—i.e., hot and cold, pale and dark, dry and wet, soft and hard, etc.—are differentiae
20 of the elements.[9] Empedocles also says this: 'The sun is pale to the eye and hot all over, but rain is dark and cold throughout' (and he distinguishes the other <elements> in the same way). If, then, water cannot come to be from fire, or earth from water, then neither will anything be dark from being pale, or hard from being soft; and the same
25 argument applies to the other cases. But we agreed that this is what alteration is.[10]

Hence it is also evident that in every case we must assume a single matter for the contraries <involved in change>, whether the change involves place, or growth and decay, or alteration. Moreover, the existence of this matter and of alteration are equally necessary; for if there
315a is any alteration, it follows both that the subject is a single element and also that all the <contraries> that allow change into each other have a single matter. And equally, if the subject is one, there is such a thing as alteration. . . .

* * * * * * *

[PUZZLES ABOUT COMING TO BE]

3

317a32 Now that we have determined these points, the next question is this: Does anything come to be without qualification[11] or perish, or does nothing come to be in the full sense, so that in each case a thing comes
35 to be F from being G[12]—comes to be healthy, for instance, from being sick and sick from being healthy, or comes to be small from being large
317b and large from being small, and everything else in the same way? For if there is such a thing as unqualified coming to be, then something would come to be without qualification from what it is not, so that it will be true to say that not being belongs to some things. For a thing

9. **differentiae of the elements**: If they are DIFFERENTIAE, they must be essential properties of the elements. Since alteration involves only nonessential properties, these differentiae cannot enter into alteration.

10. **this is what alteration is**: It is something's becoming dark from being pale, etc.

11. **without qualification**: haplōs, equivalent to 'in the full sense', kuriōs, as in 314a10.

12. **F from being G**: Lit. 'something from something'.

comes to be F from what is not F (for instance, not pale or not beautiful),   5
and a thing comes to be without qualification from what is-not without
qualification.

Now, 'without qualification' signifies either what is primary in a given
predication* of being, or what is universal and includes everything. If,
then, <'not-being without qualification' signifies not being> the primary
thing, then substance will come to be from nonsubstance; but if a thing
is not a substance and a this*,[13] then clearly it has none of the other
predications either—for instance, quality, quantity, or location—for if it   10
had, attributes would be separable from substance. Alternatively, if
<'not-being without qualification' signifies> not being at all, it will be
the universal negation of everything, so that what comes to be <without
qualification> will have to come to be from nothing.[14]

The puzzles about this issue have been thoroughly examined, and
the <necessary> distinctions[15] drawn more fully, in other discussions;[16]
but we should also state the points concisely here. In one way, something   15
comes to be <without qualification> from what is-not without qualification, but in another way it comes to be, in every case, from what is. For
something that is F potentially, but is not F actually, must precede <any
coming to be of F>, and this is spoken of in both ways <as being and
as not being>.

But even when these distinctions have been drawn, a further question
is remarkably puzzling, and we must go back to it again: How can there
be unqualified coming to be, either from what potentially is or in any   20
other way? For it is a puzzling question whether there is any coming to
be of a substance and a this, rather than <merely> of a quality or quantity
or location (and the same applies to perishing). For if something[17] comes
to be, then clearly there will be some potential but not actual substance

13. **and a this**: Here and in 317b20 the 'and' may be equivalent to 'i.e.'.

14. **come to be from nothing**: Aristotle refers to the puzzle about coming to be
that he mentions at *Phys.* 191a23–33. We may be willing to agree that qualified
coming to be (i.e., alteration, etc.) is possible, because it does not involve coming
to be from what is-not without qualification, but only the coming to be of what
is F (the musical man) from what is not F (the unmusical man). But if some type
of coming to be is different from qualified coming to be because it involves the
coming to be of a new SUBSTANCE (cf. *Phys.* 190a31–b1), does it not involve
coming to be from nothing (from what is-not without qualification)? This is the
puzzle that Aristotle tries to resolve.

15. **distinctions**: *dihorizein*: See DETERMINE.

16. **other discussions**: See *Phys.* 191a33–b27.

17. **something**: Aristotle uses 'something' to refer to SUBSTANCE. Cf. 318a15,
319a25.

25   from which <the substance> will come to be and into which the <sub-
stance> will have to change when it perishes. Will this, then, actually
have any of the other things (quantity, quality, or location) if it is only
potentially a this and a being, and is neither a this nor a being without
qualification? For if it has none of these actually, but has all of them
potentially, then it turns out that what lacks all these sorts of being
is separable, and moreover that something comes to be from nothing
30   preceding it—the very thing that always most alarmed the earliest philosophers. If, on the other hand, it is not a this or a substance but has one
of the other <predications> we mentioned, then, as we said, attributes
will turn out to be separable from substance.
       We must, therefore, work on these questions as much as we can. We
35   must also ask what is the cause of there always being coming to be,
both unqualified coming to be and coming to be in a particular respect.[18]
318a   One sort of cause* is the one we call the source of the principle* of
motion, and one sort is matter. Here we ought to discuss the second
sort of cause; for we have discussed the first sort earlier, in the treatment
of motion,[19] where we said that one sort of <principle of motion> is
5   unmoved for all time, and the other sort is always in motion. A consideration of the first sort of cause is a task for a different and prior <branch
of> philosophy;* and later we will discuss the <principle> that initiates
motion in other things by being in continuous motion itself, and say
which particular thing of this sort is the cause.[20] But for now let us
10   discuss the material cause, explaining why perishing and coming to be
never fail in nature. For, presumably, in making this clear we will also
make clear both the answer to the present puzzle and the right account
of unqualified perishing and coming to be.
       It is puzzling enough to know what causes the continuity of coming
15   to be, if what perishes passes into what is not and what is not is nothing—
since what is not neither is something[21] nor has any quality, quantity,
or location. If, then, at every time something that is is passing away,
why has everything not been used up and vanished long ago, if it is
indeed true that there was only a limited amount from which everything
coming to be comes to be? For surely the reason that coming to be does
not fail is not that there is an infinite source from which things come to
20   be. That view is impossible; for since nothing is infinite in actuality, and
something can be infinite in potentiality only by division, it follows that
division into ever smaller things is the only type of coming to be that

18. **in a particular respect**: Lit. 'partial'.
19. **the treatment of motion**: i.e., *Phys.* viii 6.
20. **and later . . . cause**: See ii 10.
21. **something**: Cf. 317b23n.

never fails—and that is not what we see happen.[22] Alternatively, then, does the fact that the perishing of F[23] is the coming to be of G, and the coming to be of F is the perishing of G, explain why change is necessarily   25 ceaseless?

[AN ACCOUNT OF UNQUALIFIED COMING TO BE]

This, then, should be regarded as an adequate explanation for all cases, of why coming to be and perishing belong to each being alike.[24] If, however, we agree that the coming to be of F is the perishing of G, and   30 the perishing of F is the coming to be of G, we must reconsider why we say that some things come to be or perish without qualification, whereas others do so only with some qualification; for we need to give some account of this. For sometimes we say that a thing is now perishing without qualification, not that F is perishing, and that one event is an unqualified coming to be, and another an unqualified perishing. Moreover, sometimes the F comes to be G, but the F does not come to be without qualification;[25] for we say, for instance, that the learner comes to be expert, not that he comes to be without qualification.   35

Now we often draw a distinction by saying that some things signify   318b a this,[26] and others do not; and this is why our present question arises. For it all depends on what the subject is changing into; presumably, for instance, turning into fire is both an unqualified coming to be and the perishing of something (for instance, of earth), whereas the coming to   5 be of earth is both a sort of coming to be (not an unqualified coming to

22. **For since . . . see happen**: If the continuity of coming to be required something INFINITE, then, since (in Aristotle's view) only divisibility is infinite, continuous coming to be would involve the coming to be of smaller and smaller things. Since this is not what happens, the appeal to something infinite to explain continuous coming to be must be rejected. Aristotle believes that infinity is to be explained by reference to POTENTIALITY.

23. **perishing of F**: We have used 'F' and 'G' where Aristotle simply uses 'this'. He might be referring either to (e.g.) pale or to the pale thing (cf. *Phys.* 189b35n).

24. **This, then, should . . . each being alike**: The reciprocal relation between coming to be and perishing (secured by the nature of the matter) is needed to secure the permanence of change.

25. **the F comes . . . qualification**: In this sentence Aristotle uses 'this' where we have 'the F' and 'the G'. His example suggests that here at least the subject is (e.g.) the pale thing that comes to be dark.

26. **signify a this**: In this chapter 'this' is applied both (a) to the category of substance, and (b) to the positive property as opposed to the negative (e.g., to the form rather than the privation). Aristotle does not argue that (a) and (b) coincide.

be) and an unqualified perishing (for instance, of fire). This is Parmenides' view when he mentions two things <that something can change into>, and asserts that what is is fire and that what is not is earth.[27] (It does not matter whether we assume fire and earth or other such things, since we are inquiring about the type, not the subject, of the change.)

10 Turning into what is-not without qualification, therefore, is <unqualified> perishing, and turning into what is without qualification is unqualified coming to be. And so one of the two elements that mark the distinction (whether they are fire and earth, or other things) will be what is, and the other will be what is not.[28]

[COMING TO BE AND MATTER]

This, then, is one way to distinguish unqualified from qualified coming to be or perishing. Another way appeals to the character of the matter.
15 For if the differentiae of a type of matter signify a this to a higher degree, what they signify is itself a substance to a higher degree; if they signify a privation, what they signify is not-being. If heat, for instance, is a <positive> predication and form, and cold a privation, and these differentiate earth and fire, <then fire will be being and earth not-being>.

Most people, however, are more inclined to believe that <coming to be and perishing> are distinguished by whether <the product> is
20 perceptible or not: whenever there is a change into perceptible matter, they say it is a coming to be, and when it is into imperceptible matter, they say it is a perishing. For they distinguish being from not-being by whether something is perceived or not, just as what is known is what is and what is not known is what is not—for perception <in their view>
25 counts as knowledge. Hence, just as they think they are alive and have their being by perceiving or being capable of it, so they think things have their being <by being perceived or by being perceptible>. In a way, then, they are on the track of the truth, though what they actually say is not true.

In reality, then, unqualified coming to be and perishing turn out to be different from what they are commonly believed to be. For from the point of view of perception, wind and air are beings to a lesser extent
30 <than earth is>. Hence people say that what perishes without qualifica-

27. **This is Parmenides' . . . is earth**: Aristotle refers to PARMENIDES' 'Way of Opinion'. He suggests that Parmenides regards fire as a this, and so refers to it as 'what is', and refers to water as 'what is not' because he believes it is not a this.

28. **what is . . . what is not**: These are not the existent and the nonexistent, but the positive and the negative. Cf. *Phys.* 188b12–15, 192a3–6, *Met.* 1032b3n.

tion perishes by changing into one of them, and that something comes to be <without qualification> when something changes into what is tangible (i.e., earth). In reality, however, each of them is more of a this and a form than earth is.

We have explained, then, why there is unqualified coming to be that is also something's perishing, and unqualified perishing that is also something's coming to be. The reason is that there are different types   35 of matter, so that the matter out of which and that into which <the change occurs> may be either substance and nonsubstance, or sub-   319a stances to different degrees, or more and less perceptible.

[COMING TO BE AND THE CATEGORIES]

But why are some things said to come to be without qualification, and others said merely to come to be F, in other cases besides those in which things come to be from each other in the way we have described? For   5 so far we have only determined why we do not speak in the same way of coming to be and perishing in all cases of things that change into each other, even though every coming to be is the perishing of something else and every perishing is the coming to be of something else. But our further question raises a different puzzle, about why the learner is said   10 merely to come to be expert, not to come to be without qualification, whereas <a plant> growing <from a seed> is said to come to be <without qualification>.

These cases, then, are distinguished by reference to the predications;* for some things signify a this, some quality,[29] some quantity. Whatever does not signify a substance,[30] then, is said to come to be F, not to come to be without qualification. Still, in every case we speak of coming to be in <only the positive> one of the two columns;* for instance, we   15 recognize a coming to be in the case of substance if fire rather than earth comes to be, and in the case of quality if someone comes to be expert rather than inexpert.

We have said, then, why some things do and others do not come to be without qualification, both in general and also in the case of substances themselves. We have also explained why the subject is the material cause of the continuity of coming to be—because it is capable of changing   20 from one contrary to another, and in every case where substances are involved, the coming to be of one thing is the perishing of another, and the perishing of one thing is the coming to be of another.

Nor should we be puzzled about why there is coming to be even

29. **quality**: Lit. 'such'. See QUALITY.

30. **a substance**: Here 'SUBSTANCE' and 'THIS' seem to be used equivalently.

though things are always being destroyed. For just as people speak of
unqualified perishing whenever a thing passes into something imperceptible and into what is not,[31] so also they speak of coming to be from
25   what is not, whenever a thing comes to be from something imperceptible.
And so whether or not the subject is something,[32] a thing comes to be
from what is not, so that things come to be from what is not and likewise
perish into what is not. It is not surprising, then, that coming to be
never ceases; for coming to be is the perishing of what is not, and
30   perishing is the coming to be of what is not.

  But is what is-not without qualification also one of a pair of contraries?
For instance, is earth (i.e., the heavy) a thing that is not, and is fire (i.e.,
the light) a thing that is, or is earth also a thing that is, and is the common
319b   matter of earth and air a thing that is not? And is the matter of each one
different, or <must it be the same, since otherwise> they would not
come to be from each other and from their contraries? For the contraries
are present in these—in fire, earth, water, and air. Or is it in a way the
same and in a way different? <Apparently so;> for the subject, whatever
it may be <at a particular time> is the same <subject>, but what it
is <at different times> is not the same.[33] So much, then, for these
questions.

[THE DIFFERENCE BETWEEN ALTERATION AND UNQUALIFIED COMING TO BE]

4

5   Let us now describe the difference between coming to be and alteration,
since we say that these changes are different from each other.
  A subject is different from an attribute that is by its nature said of the
10   subject, and each of these may change. Alteration occurs whenever the
subject, being perceptible, remains but changes in its attributes, these
being either contraries or intermediates. A body, for instance, is at one
time healthy and at another time sick, still remaining the same <body>;
and the bronze is at one time round and at another time angular, still
remaining the same <bronze>.
15   But whenever the whole <subject> changes and something perceptible does not remain as the same subject[34] (as, for instance, blood comes

31. **what is not**: This is what people usually (but erroneously, in Aristotle's
view) call it.

32. **something**: i.e., a substance. See 317b23n.

33. **but what . . . not the same**: See ESSENCE #2.

34. **something perceptible . . . subject**: This might mean either (a) there is some
perceptible thing that does not remain as subject, or (b) there is no perceptible
subject that remains. While (a) leaves open the possibility that some perceptible

to be from the whole seed, or air from <the whole of the> water, or water from the whole of the air), then this is a case of the coming to be of one thing, <for instance, the blood>, and the perishing of the other, <for instance, the seed>. This is so especially if the change is from something imperceptible to something perceptible (perceptible by touch, or by all the senses)—whenever, for instance, water comes to be, or   20
perishes into air (since air is fairly imperceptible).

In such cases <of unqualified coming to be>, sometimes the same attribute (which is one of a pair of contraries) that belongs to the thing that has perished remains in the thing that has come to be, when water, for instance, comes to be from air, if both are transparent or cold. But in these cases the thing resulting from the change must not itself be an attribute of this <attribute that remains>—if it were, the change would be an alteration. Suppose that a musical man, for instance, perished,   25
and an unmusical man came to be, and the man remains as the same thing. If, then, musicality and unmusicality were not attributes of the man in their own right,[35] it would have been a coming to be of the unmusical and a perishing of the musical.[36] In fact, however, each of these is an attribute of the thing that remains; that is why they are attributes of the man, and it is <only> a coming to be or perishing   30
of the musical or unmusical man. That is why such cases count as alterations.

A change between contrary quantities, then, is growth or decay; between contrary places it is locomotion; and between contrary attributes and qualities it is alteration. But when nothing remains that has <the   320a
contrary resulting from the change> as its attribute or as any sort of coincident,* the change is a coming to be, and <its contrary> is a perishing.

Matter is most of all and most fully the subject that admits the <unqualified> coming to be and perishing <of another thing>; but the subject for the other types of change is also matter in a way, since every   5
subject admits <its proper> contraries.

Let this, then, be our account of whether or not there is coming to be and in what way there is, and of alteration.

*   *   *   *   *   *   *

---

subject remains (as long as some other perceptible subject does not remain), (b) rules out this possibility. Normally Aristotle's account of unqualified coming to be requires only (a).

35. **attributes in their own right**: This is the second sense of IN ITS OWN RIGHT distinguished at *APo* 73a34–b24.

36. **of the unmusical . . . of the musical**: Lit. 'of the one . . . of the other'.

[*GROWTH: THE ROLE OF MATTER AND FORM*]

5

321a29 . . . One might also be puzzled about what grows. Is it the thing to which something is added? If, for instance, someone grows in his shin, is it the shin, rather than the food by which it grows, that is bigger? Why, then, have both not grown, since what has grown and that by which it grows have both increased—just as, when you mix wine with water, each component alike is increased?

Perhaps the reason is that the substance of the leg, not of the food,
35 remains. For in the other case also we refer to the mixture by its dominant
321b component[37]—as wine, for instance, since the mixture as a whole performs the function of wine, not of water. The same is true of alteration; if <the subject> continues to be flesh, i.e., to be what it is, and it now possesses some intrinsic attribute that it did not previously possess, then
5 this subject has been altered, and that by which it has been altered has sometimes itself been affected, sometimes not. But what initiates the alteration, i.e., the principle of the motion, is in <the subject> that grows or is altered; for what initiates the motion is in <one or the other of> these. For though sometimes the body that enters as well as the body that feeds on it may become greater (if, for instance, after entering,
10 it becomes wind,[38] still, once it has been affected this way, it has perished, and what initiates the motion is not in this).

Since we have examined the puzzle adequately, we must also try to find a solution of it.[39] We must retain the beliefs that something grows when it remains and has something added, and decays when <it remains and> has something removed; that every perceptible particle has become
15 bigger or smaller; that the body contains no void;[40] that no two magnitudes are in the same place; and that nothing grows by <the addition of> something incorporeal.

To grasp the cause <of growth> we must draw some distinctions. First, a nonuniform part grows by the growth of uniform parts, since it is
20 composed of them. Second, flesh and bone and each of these <uniform> parts, like the other things that have form in matter, have two aspects, since both matter and form are called flesh or bone. It is possible, then, for something, insofar as it is form, to grow in every part by the addition

37. **we refer . . . component**: Or 'we say that the dominant component in the mixture has grown'.

38. **becomes wind**: in a case of flatulence.

39. **Since . . . solution of it**: See DIALECTIC.

40. **contains no void**: Lit. 'is not void'.

of something; but insofar as it is matter, this is not possible.[41] For we must take it to be similar to measuring water with the same measure, where what comes to be is always one thing after another. Similarly, when the matter of flesh grows, not every single part of it receives addition, but rather one <part> flows out and another is added; every part of the shape and the form, however, receives addition.

It is clearer in the case of the nonuniform parts—for instance, a hand—that the growth is proportional <in every part>. For here it is clearer than it is in the case of flesh and the <other> uniform parts that the matter is different from the form; and that is why a dead body would more readily seem to have flesh and bone than to have a hand or an arm.[42]

In a way, then, every <part> of the flesh has grown, and in a way it has not; for insofar as it is form, every part has received addition, but insofar as it is matter, it has not. But the whole has become bigger by the addition of something (i.e., food) that is contrary[43] and by <the added matter> changing into the same form—as if, for instance, wet were added to dry and after having been added, it changed and became dry. For in a way like grows by like, and in a way unlike by unlike.

*   *   *   *   *   *   *

The form, as a sort of channel,[44] is a kind of potentiality in the matter. If, then, matter is added that is potentially a channel and that also has quantity potentially, then these channels will get bigger. But if it is no longer able to do this —just as more and more water mixed in wine eventually makes the wine watery and turns it to water—then it will make the quantity decay; but the form still remains.[45]

41. **It is possible . . . not possible**: On the role of form in growth see FORM #2.

42. **and that is . . . an arm**: Aristotle appeals to his doctrine of HOMONYMY about dead organs and their parts; see MATTER #5. Though it is easier to suppose that a dead organism has flesh than to suppose that it has arms, it is still, in Aristotle's view, mistaken, if we are thinking of flesh as form rather than as matter.

43. **contrary**: Read *enantiou*.

44. **channel**: Lit. 'pipe' (*aulos*, a reed instrument). This analogy, together with the analogy of the measure for successive quantities of water, suggests the role that Aristotle sees for form in growth. It is not a single determinate shape (as his comparisons of form with the shape of a statue, e.g., might suggest), but the property of the subject (or the subject insofar as it has this property; cf. *Met.* 1035a8) that explains the order and goal-directed character of growth.

45. **the form still remains**: The persistence of the same form is necessary and sufficient for the persistence of an organism, though the organism may be more or less capable of efficient use of the matter it takes in.

*   *   *   *   *   *   *

Book II

[MATTER AND CHANGE]

[THE FOUR ELEMENTARY QUALITIES]

2

329b7   Since we are seeking the principles of perceptible body, that is to say,
of tangible body, and since what is tangible is what is perceived by the
sense of touch, it is evident that not all contrary properties, but only
10   contrary tangible properties, constitute forms and principles of bodies;
for <primary bodies> are distinguished not only by having contrary
properties but specifically by having contrary tangible properties. That
is why neither paleness and darkness nor sweetness and bitterness nor,
equally, any of the other pairs of perceptible contraries constitute any
15   element. Admittedly, since sight is prior to touch, the <visible> subject
is also prior; but it is not an attribute of tangible body insofar as it is
tangible, but insofar as it is something else that may indeed be naturally
prior.[1]

Among the tangible properties themselves, we must first distinguish
the primary differentiae and pairs of contraries. The pairs of contraries
20   corresponding to touch are these: hot and cold, dry and wet, heavy
and light, hard and soft, sticky and brittle, rough and smooth, coarse
and fine. Among these, heavy and light neither act nor are affected;
for these are not called what they are called by acting on or by being
affected by anything else, whereas the elements must be capable of
mutual action and affection, since they combine and change into each
25   other.

Hot and cold, dry and wet, however, are so called insofar as they
either act or are affected. Hot is what holds together things of the
same kind; for dispersal, which is said to be the action of fire, is
really holding together things of the same kind, since the result of
30   the dispersal is the removal of the foreign things. Cold is what brings
and holds together both things of the same kind and things of different
kinds. Wet is what is not confined by any limit of its own, but is
easily confined within <another> limit. Dry is what is easily confined
within its own limit, but is hard to confine within <another> limit. . . .

1. **Admittedly . . . naturally prior**: Aristotle thinks sight is more informative
and valuable than touch, and to that extent PRIOR to it (on this sort of priority
cf. *Catg.* 14b3). On sight see *Met.* 980a23–27. On touch see *DA* 423b27–30.

* * * * * * *

[THE ELEMENTARY BODIES ARE NOT THE SAME AS THE STANDARD 'FOUR ELEMENTS']

3

. . . Fire, earth, and the other things we have mentioned[2] are not simple,   *330b22*
but mixed. The simple bodies are similar to these, but they are not the
same. If, for instance, there is a simple body that is similar to fire, it is
fiery but not fire, and the one similar to air is airy, and so on. Fire is a   *25*
predominance of heat, just as ice is a predominance of cold; for freezing
and boiling are types of predominance—of cold and heat, respectively.
If, then, ice is the freezing of what is wet and cold, fire is the boiling of
what is dry and hot—that is why nothing comes to be from ice or from
fire. . . .

* * * * * * *

[HOW THE FOUR ELEMENTS CHANGE INTO EACH OTHER]

4

We have previously determined that the simple bodies come to be from   *331a7*
one another. Moreover, perception makes this evident; for if they did
not, there would be no alteration, since alteration involves the attributes   *10*
of tangible things. We must, then, describe the way they change into
each other, and consider whether each of them can come to be from
every other one, or only some can, and others cannot.

It is evident that all of them naturally change into each other; for
coming to be begins from one contrary and ends in the other, and each   *15*
element has some quality contrary to a quality of each of the others,
since their differentiae are contraries. For some <elements>—fire and
water—have both properties contrary <to each other> (since fire is dry
and hot, and water is wet and cold), while others—air and water—have
only one property contrary <to that of the other element>, (since air is   *20*
wet and hot, and water is wet and cold).

In general, therefore, it is evident that each <element> naturally
comes to be from each of the others. It is easy to see how this is so when
we come to particular cases; for each will come from each, but the
process will be quicker or slower, and harder or easier. For if bodies
have corresponding qualities, change from one to the other is quick;   *25*
otherwise it is slow, since one quality changes more easily than many.
Air, for instance, will come from fire when just one quality changes; for

2. **Fire . . . mentioned**: i.e., the recognized 'four elements'.

30   fire is hot and dry, and air hot and wet, so that if the dry is overcome by the wet, air will result. Again, water will result from air if the hot is overcome by the cold; for air is hot and wet, and water is cold and wet, so that if the hot changes, water will result. . . .

*   *   *   *   *   *   *

5

332a3   But let us also consider the following points about <the elements>. If
5   fire, earth, and so on are, as some people think, the matter of natural bodies, there must be either one or two or more than two of them. Now they cannot all be one—for instance, they cannot all be air or all water or all fire or all earth—since change is into contraries. For if they are all air, then, since this will remain, there will be alteration, not coming to
10   be; and besides, it does not seem to happen in such a way that water would at the same time be air or any other <element>. There will therefore be some contrariety and differentia of which <water will have one member> and some <element> will have the other member, as fire, for instance, has heat. Nor again is fire hot air; for in that case <the change from air to fire> would be an alteration, but this is not what it
15   appears to be. Moreover, if air came from fire, it would come from hot changing into its contrary, so that this contrary would be present in air, and air would be something cold. Hence fire cannot be hot air, since that would make the same thing both hot and cold.[3]

    Both <air and fire>, then, must be some other thing that is the same for both, i.e., some other matter common to them.[4] The same argument
20   applies to all the elements, showing that there is no one of them from which everything comes.

    Nor again is there anything else apart from these—something intermediate, for instance, between air and water (coarser than air, but finer than water) or between fire and air (coarser than fire but finer than air). For this intermediate element will be air and fire (respectively) when a contrariety is added to it; but since one of a pair of contraries is a privation,
25   the intermediate element cannot exist alone at any time (as some people

---

    3. **Hence fire . . . both hot and cold**: Aristotle is considering the suggestion that air is the basic SUBJECT, and that air becomes fire simply by being heated. He argues that if this were possible, then (1) the process would be a mere alteration, which it clearly is not; (2) air would come to be from fire by being cooled, so that air would be (at one time) hot and (at another time) cold, which is inconsistent with the definition of air as essentially hot (see 331a30).

    4. **matter common to them**: This is usually taken to refer to 'prime matter'; see MATTER #3.

say the indefinite and all-inclusive does).[5] It is therefore one or another of the elements, or nothing.

If, then, nothing (or nothing perceptible at least) is prior to these elements, they will be everything. They must, then, either always remain without changing into each other, or else change into each other; if they change, then either all of them do, or else some do and some do not, as Plato wrote in the *Timaeus*.[6] We have shown previously that they   30 must change into each other, and that one does not come to be from another equally quickly in each case, because those that have a corresponding property come to be more quickly from each other, and those that have none come to be more slowly.

If, then, the elements change within just one pair of contraries, there   35 must be two of them; for the matter, being imperceptible and inseparable, is intermediate between them. But since we see that there are more than   332b two elements, there must also be at least two pairs of contraries; and if there are two <pairs of contraries>, there must be, as in fact there appear to be, four elements, not three. For that is the number of combinations <of qualities>; though there are six <describable combinations>, two of them cannot occur because they are contrary to one another. . . .   5

* * * * * * *

[THE CAUSES OF COMING TO BE]

[ALL FOUR CAUSES MUST BE RECOGNIZED]

9

Since some things come to be and perish, and coming to be takes place   335a24 in the middle region <of the universe>, we must discuss quite generally   25 the number and nature of the principles of all coming to be; for once we find the universal principles, it will be easier to study the particular cases. There are as many principles, and they are of the same type, <for perishable things> as for eternal and primary things; for one principle   30 is the material principle, and the second is the formal$_m$.[7] The third must

5. **For this intermediate . . . all-inclusive does).**: If the alleged intermediate thing can acquire one of the contraries (e.g., hot, characteristic of fire), it must previously have had the privation (in this case cold, characteristic of air); hence it cannot have had (as alleged) some quality intermediate between the privation and the positive quality. Cf *Phys.* 188a30–b8 (which seems to raise a difficulty for Aristotle's argument here). 'The indefinite' probably refers to ANAXIMANDER.

6. **in the** *Timaeus*: See 54b–d.

7. **the material . . . the formal$_m$**: Lit. 'the principle as matter . . . the principle as shape'.

also be present; for just as the first two are insufficient in primary things, so they are insufficient to produce coming to be.

The material cause* of things that come to be is what is capable of being and not being. For some things—such as eternal things—necessarily are,
35 and some things necessarily are not; it is impossible for the first of these
335b not to be, and impossible for the second to be (since it is impossible for them to be otherwise, contrary to necessity). Other things are capable of both being and not being. This, then,[8] is what comes to be and perishes, since it at one time is and at another time is not. Coming to
5 be and perishing, then, must occur in what is capable of being and not being; and so this is the material cause of what comes to be. The final cause is the shape and form; this is the account of a thing's substance.

But the third cause must still be added, and though everyone dreams
10 about it no one actually states it.[9] Rather, some people took the nature of the Forms to be a sufficient cause for coming to be, as Socrates in the *Phaedo*[10] does. For after attacking other people for having had nothing to offer, he assumes that one class of beings are Forms, the other participants in Forms, and that something is said to be insofar as <it has> the
15 Form, to come to be insofar as it acquires the Form, and to perish insofar as it loses the Form. In that case, then, he must think the Forms are causes both of coming to be and of perishing.[11] Others, however, think matter itself <is the cause of coming to be>, since they say that motion proceeds from it.

Neither side is right, however. For if the Forms are causes, why do they not in every case generate continuously, but instead sometimes generate
20 and sometimes do not, even though the Form and the participants are present in every case? Further, in some cases we observe that something else is the cause; for it is the doctor who imparts health, and the scientific expert who imparts scientific knowledge$_e$, though health, scientific knowledge, and the participants <already> exist. The same is true of all other results achieved by <the actualization of> a potentiality.[12]

8. **This, then**: sc., what is capable of being and not being.

9. **no one actually states it**: On the neglect of the moving cause see *Met.* 984a16–b1.

10. **in the** *Phaedo*: 96–105.

11. **In that case . . . of perishing**: According to our translation, this is Aristotle's reason for attributing to Socrates the (implicit) view that Forms are causes of becoming. An alternative translation: 'In that case the Forms must (he thinks) . . .'; in that case Aristotle would be claiming to report the reason that Socrates actually gives for thinking that the Forms are causes of becoming.

12. **For if the Forms . . . a potentiality**: To explain how different things participate in some Forms, but not in others, we must suppose that something else besides the Forms is a cause of coming to be.

If someone were to say that matter generates by its motion, that   *25*
answer would be more appropriate to the study of nature than the
answer mentioning the Form. For what initiates alteration and change
of shape is more of a cause of generation; and in every case of coming
to be, from nature or from craft, we habitually regard the thing that
initiates motion as the producer. These people, however, are also wrong.
For it is characteristic of matter to be affected and moved, whereas   *30*
initiating motion and producing are characteristic of a different potentiality. This is clear both for craft and for nature; for the water does not
produce an animal from itself all by itself, and it is not the wood but
the craft that produces a bed.

These people also, then, are wrong, both for this reason and also
because they omit the more controlling* cause, since they do away with   *35*
the essence and the form$_m$. Further, the potentialities they attribute to   *336a*
bodies to explain why they generate are too instrumental, since they do
away with the formal cause. For they say that it is the nature of hot to
disperse and of cold to combine, and the nature of each of the other   *5*
things to act on something else or to be affected by something else; they
suppose, then, that from these and through these <material processes>
all the other things come to be and perish. In fact, however, fire itself
is also evidently moved and affected. Besides, what they are doing is
similar to someone attributing the cause of things that come to be to a
saw or to another instrument; for <they neglect the fact that> to split   *10*
the wood someone must use the saw, and to smooth the wood someone
must use the plane, and so on in the other cases. And so, however true
it might be that fire acts on things and initiates motion, these people
neglect the further question of how it does so—namely, in a way inferior
to an instrument.

We have previously discussed causes in general, and now we have
reached a determination about matter and form.

[*WHY COMING TO BE NEVER CEASES*]

10

Further, since we have shown that local motion is everlasting, it necessar-   *15*
ily follows that coming to be goes on continuously; for the local motion
will produce coming to be without interruption, by bringing the generator[13] closer and further away. At the same time it is clear that we were
right in our previous claim that local motion, rather than coming to be,   *20*
is the primary type of change. For it is far more reasonable <to suppose>
that something that is causes the coming to be of something that is
not than <to suppose> that something that is not causes the being of

13. **the generator**: i.e., the sun.

something that is; and what engages in local motion is a being, whereas what is coming to be is not a being,[14] so that local motion is also prior to coming to be.

25 Now, we assume and have shown that things undergo both coming to be and perishing continuously, and we say that local motion is the cause of coming to be. It evidently follows that if there is only one type of local motion, it is impossible for both coming to be and perishing to occur, since they are contraries; for the same thing in the same condition always by nature produces the same result. And so <on this supposi-tion> either there will always be coming to be or there will always be

30 perishing. Rather, there must be more than one type of motion, and the motions must be contrary, either in <the direction of> the local motion or by their nonuniformity; for contrary effects have contrary causes.

Hence it is not the primary type of local motion, but local motion along the inclined circle, that is the cause of coming to be and perishing;[15] for here we find both continuous motion and two types of motion. For

336b if both coming to be and perishing are always to be continuous, some-thing must always be in motion, so that these changes will not fail; moreover, there must be two types of motions, so that not only one of these changes occurs.

The cause of the continuity is the local motion of the whole, and the cause of the approach and withdrawal <of the sun> is the inclined

5 motion; for the result is that it sometimes goes further away and some-times comes closer. And since the distance is unequal, the motion is nonuniform. And so if it generates by approaching and being close, this same thing destroys by withdrawing and being distant, and if it generates by its frequent approach, it destroys by its frequent withdrawal, since

10 contrary effects have contrary causes, and natural perishing and coming to be take equal time. That is why both the times and the lives of each kind of living thing have some <definite> numerical length and are distinguished by this. For everything has <its proper> order, and every life and every time is measured by a period, but not all are measured by the same period; rather, some are measured by a shorter period,

15 others by a longer—for some the measure is a year, for others a longer or a shorter period.

What is found in perception also evidently agrees with our argu-

14. **is not a being**: i.e., insofar as x is (in the process of) coming to be, x does not yet exist.

15. **Hence it is not . . . perishing**: The primary type of local motion is the movement of the extreme outer sphere with the fixed stars. Motion along the inclined circle is inclined at an angle to the motion of the outer sphere; it is the annual movement of the sun closer to and further from particular places on the surface of the earth.

ments.[16] For we see that coming to be occurs when the sun approach-
es, and wasting away occurs when it withdraws, and both take equal
time, since natural coming to be and perishing take equal time. But it   *20*
often turns out that things perish in a shorter time, because of the way
things are mixed together.[17] For since the matter is nonuniform and not
everywhere the same, the cases of coming to be must necessarily also be
nonuniform, some slower and some quicker. Hence it turns out that
because[18] one set of things comes to be, another set of things perishes.

But, as we have said, coming to be and perishing will always be   *25*
continuous and will never fail, because of the cause we have mentioned.
And it is reasonable that this comes about. For we say that in everything
nature always tends toward what is better; and being is better than not
being (we have described elsewhere the number of ways in which being   *30*
is spoken of); but being cannot be present in everything, since <some
things> are distant from the principle. The god*, therefore, completed[19]
the whole universe in the way that was left open, by making coming to
be uninterrupted; for that was the way to make being as connected as
possible, since incessant coming to be is closest to <continuous>
being$_o$.[20] The cause of this, as we have often said, is circular motion, since   *337a*
it is the only one that is continuous.

Hence all the other things that change into each other because of the
ways they are affected and because of their potentialities—the simple
bodies, for instance—imitate circular motion. For when air comes to be   *5*
from water, and fire from air, and again water from fire, we say that
coming to be has gone round in a circle, because it comes back again to
the beginning. Hence motion in a straight line is also continuous insofar
as it imitates motion in a circle. . . .

*   *   *   *   *   *   *

[CONDITIONAL AND UNQUALIFIED NECESSITY]

11

In things that are moved continuously, in the course of coming to be or   *337a34*
alteration or change in general, we see that one thing follows another   *35*
in coming to be and in being, in such a way that <the sequence> never   *337b*

---

16. **What is . . . arguments**: On this contrast between APPEARANCES and DEDUCTION
see REASON #3.

17. **mixed together**: Text uncertain.

18. **that because**: Read *dia tēn toutōn*.

19. **completed**: Lit. 'filled out' or 'fulfilled'.

20. **being . . . being$_o$**: 'Being' translates first *einai* and then *ousia*, which seem
to be used equivalently here. See SUBSTANCE #1.

fails. We must, then, consider whether there is anything that necessarily will be, or there is nothing of that sort, in which case everything admits of not coming to be. For it is clear that some things admit of not coming to be, and indeed this in itself explains why 'will be' and 'is going to be' are different. For if it is true to say of something that it will be, then it must at some time be true to say of it that it is; but if it is now true to say of something that it is going to be, it is quite possible for it not to come to be—for someone might be going to walk, but still not walk.[21] And in general, since among things that are some also admit of not being, clearly the same will be true of things that come to be, and their coming to be will not be necessary.

Then is the same true of everything? Or, on the contrary, are there some things whose coming to be is necessary without qualification? And is the same true of coming to be as of being, where some things are capable of not being and some are not capable of not being? Is it[22] necessary, for instance, for the solstices to come to be and impossible for them not to admit of coming to be?

Let us grant that the earlier must come to be if the later is to be; if, for instance, a house <is to be>, a foundation <must come to be>, and if this <is to be>, then mud <must also come to be>.[23] Then is it also true that if a foundation has come to be, it is necessary for a house to come to be? Perhaps in this case it is not necessary, if it is not also necessary without qualification for <the house> to come to be. If this is <necessary without qualification>, then it is also necessary, once a foundation has come to be, for a house to come to be. For we agreed that the earlier is related to the later in such a way that if the later is to be, the earlier necessarily precedes it. If, then, it is necessary for the later to come to be, it is necessary for the earlier also; and if it is necessary for the earlier, then it is also necessary for the later—not, however, because of the earlier, but because it was assumed from the beginning that the later necessarily would be.[24] And so in those cases where the

21. **for someone . . . not walk**: Aristotle distinguishes 'x will F' (the ordinary future tense of a verb) from 'x is going to (or 'is about to', *mellein*) F'. If yesterday the phone rang and I said, 'I'm going to (I'm about to) answer the phone', but I tripped and fell before I answered the phone, what I said was nonetheless true. If, however, I said yesterday, 'I'll answer the phone', but then I tripped before I could do it, then what I said was false.

22. **Is it . . . :** Read *ara* (interrogative).

23. **if, for instance . . . then mud . . . :** On this conditional necessity see NECES-SITY #4.

24. **not, however, because . . . necessarily would be**: From (1) It is necessary without qualification for the house to come to be, Aristotle allows us to infer (2) It is necessary that (if the foundations have come to be, the house will come to be). But he points out that the antecedent of the conditional in (2) is redundant

later necessarily is, it also holds good in the other direction; and in each
of these cases, when the earlier has come to be, it is necessary for the   25
later to come to be.

Now, if the series is to continue infinitely downward <toward the
future>, it will not be necessary without qualification, but only conditionally necessary, for this later thing to come to be. For at every stage it is
necessary for there to be something later because of which it is necessary
for this <earlier> thing to come to be; and so, if an infinite series has
no principle,[25] there will be no primary <later> thing because of which   30
it is necessary for <the earlier thing> to come to be.

Moreover, even in finite series it will not be possible to say truly that
it is necessary without qualification for a thing (for instance, a house)
to come to be whenever a foundation comes to be. For when <the
foundation> comes to be, then, if it is not necessary for this <house>
always to be, it will turn out that what admits of not always being always
is.[26] But <this result is unacceptable; the house> must, in its coming to
be, always be, if its coming to be is necessary. For what necessarily is   35
thereby always is, since what necessarily is cannot possibly not be; and   338a
so if it is necessary, it is everlasting, and if everlasting, then necessary.[27]
Hence if something's coming to be is necessary, that thing's coming to
be is everlasting, and if it is everlasting, it is necessary.

[NECESSITY IN COMING TO BE]

If, then, a thing's coming to be is necessary without qualification, it is   5
necessary for it to go in a circle and return to the beginning. For coming
to be must be either finite or not; if not, it must be either linear or circular.
But <one> of these <is ruled out; for> it cannot be linear, because
there will be no way for it to have a principle, whether we take it
downward (as future events) or upward (as past events). But coming to

---

and does not explain why the consequent is necessary without qualification; its
unqualified necessity follows from (1) alone.

25. **principle**: Here Aristotle alludes to the use of *archē* for an 'origin' or 'beginning'. In this case the 'origin' is actually the last member in the series (the end
or goal) that necessitates the earlier members. Here, however, the series is
infinite, and so it has no end; hence it has no *archē*.

26. **it will turn out . . . always is**: This will be the consequence if it is assumed
that it is necessary without qualification for the house to come to be. Aristotle
assumes that the house is not in fact unqualifiedly necessitated, and he points
out that this assumption conflicts with the claim that once the foundations have
come to be, the coming to be of the house is necessary without qualification.

27. **For what necessarily . . . then necessary**: On this connection between 'always' and 'necessarily' see ALWAYS #2.

10 be must have a principle, although it is not itself finite,[28] and this principle must be everlasting; hence coming to be must be circular. It must, then, be convertible so that if, for instance, this is necessary, then so is the earlier thing, and if the earlier thing is necessary, then the later thing must also come to be. And this always goes on continuously; for the same is true whether it goes on through two stages or through many.

15 Unqualified necessity is present, therefore, in circular motion and coming to be. If the sequence is circular, it is necessary for each thing to come to be and to have come to be; and if this is necessary, their coming to be is circular.

This is reasonable, since it was also evident on other grounds that circular motion—i.e., the motion of the heaven*—is everlasting, because

338b all its motions and all the motions caused by its motion necessarily come to be and will be. For if what is moved in a circle is always initiating motion in another thing, the motion of the other things <set in motion at different times> must also necessarily be in a circle. Since, for instance, the highest local motion is circular, the sun is moved in this way; and

5 since this is so, the coming to be of the seasons is circular and turns back to the beginning; and since these come to be in this way, the things below them also come to be in this way.

Why, then, do some things evidently come to be in this way (so that, for instance, the coming to be of water and air is circular, so that if there is cloud, it must rain, and if it rains there must be cloud), whereas men

10 and animals do not turn back to themselves in such a way that the same man comes to be again? For it is not necessary, if your father came to be, for you to come to be, but it is necessary, if you came to be, for him to have come to be; and this coming to be seems to be linear.

The starting point for investigating this problem is again the question whether everything comes back to the beginning in the same way, or some things come back numerically, others only specifically.[29] Those

15 whose substance undergoes motion but is imperishable will evidently be numerically the same, since the character of a motion follows from the character of what is moved. But things whose substance is, on the contrary, perishable will necessarily come back to the beginning, not numerically, but specifically. Hence, when water comes to be from air, and air from water, what comes to be is specifically, not numerically, the same; and even if these things are numerically the same, this is not true of those things whose substance comes to be and is the sort of substance that admits of not being.

28. **not itself finite**: Text uncertain.

29. **numerically . . . specifically**: On numerical v. specific oneness and sameness see ONE. On recurrence see *DA* 415a27–b7.

DE ANIMA[1]

BOOK I

[INTRODUCTION TO THE STUDY OF THE SOUL]

[PROBLEMS OF METHOD]

1

We suppose that knowing$_o$[2] is fine and honorable, and that one type of   *402a*
knowing is finer and more honorable than another either because it is
more exact or because it is concerned with better and more wonderful
things. On both grounds, we might reasonably place inquiry* into the
soul in the first rank. Moreover, knowledge$_g$ of it seems to make an   *5*
important contribution to <knowledge of> the truth as a whole, and
especially to the <knowledge of> nature, since the soul is a sort of
principle of animals.[3] We seek to study and know the nature and essence$_o$
of the soul, and then all of its coincidents; some of these seem to be
distinctive attributes of the soul, while others also seem to belong to   *10*
animals because they have souls.

And yet it is altogether in every way a most difficult task to reach
any conviction about the soul. For, as in many other areas of study, we
are seeking the essence$_o$ and the what-it-is; and so someone might perhaps think some single line* of inquiry is appropriate for every case
where we want to know the substance—just as demonstration suits all   *15*
coincidents that are distinctive of a given subject.[4] On this view, then,
we should seek this single line of inquiry. If, however, no single line of
inquiry is suitable for the what-it-is, our task turns out to be still more
difficult, since in that case we must discover how to study each area.
But even if it is evident whether demonstration or division or some   *20*
further line of inquiry is the right one, the question of where to begin

---

1. i.e., 'On the Soul'. Aristotle himself uses this title (or description) at *DI* 16a8.

2. **knowing$_o$:** In these three paragraphs Aristotle uses 'know$_o$' and 'know$_g$' with
no clear difference in sense. See KNOW.

3. **principle of animals:** This common belief mentions only animal souls. Later
Aristotle assumes that plants have souls too. See 413a25.

4. **demonstration . . . subject:** See *APo* 75b1.

our investigation causes many puzzles and confusions; for different things—for instance, numbers and surfaces—have different principles.

[THE INITIAL QUESTIONS]

First of all, presumably, we must determine the soul's genus and what it is. Is it, in other words, a this and a substance, or a quality, or a
25 quantity, or something in one of the other predications* that we have distinguished? Further, is it something potential or is it more of an
402b actuality? That makes quite a bit of difference. We should also examine whether it is divisible into parts or has no parts. Do all souls belong to the same species or not? If not, do they differ in species, or in genus? As things are, those who discuss and investigate the soul would seem
5 to examine only the human soul.[5] Nor should we forget to ask whether there is just one account of the soul, as there is of animal, or a different account for each type of soul—for instance, of horse, dog, man, god— so that the universal animal either is nothing or else is posterior to these.[6] The same will apply to any other common thing predicated.

Further, if there are not many types of soul, but <one type of soul
10 with many> parts, must we begin by investigating the whole soul, or by investigating the parts? It is also difficult to determine which parts differ in nature from each other and whether we should begin by investigating the parts or their functions. Should we, for instance, begin with understanding, perceiving, and so on, or with the part that understands and the part that perceives? And if we should begin with the functions,
15 we might be puzzled anew about whether we should investigate the corresponding objects before the functions—the object of perception, for instance, before perceiving, and the object of understanding before understanding.

[ESSENCE, COINCIDENT, AND DEFINITION]

It would indeed seem useful to know_g the what-it-is, in order to study the causes of the coincidents of substances. In mathematics, for instance, it is useful to know what straight and curved are or what a line and a
20 surface are, in order to notice how many right angles the angles of a triangle are equal to. Conversely, however, the <knowledge of the>

5. **only the human soul**: Hence they do not raise the question about the nature of the difference between different types of soul.

6. **so that . . . to these**: This is a consequence of the second alternative (that there is a different account for each type of soul), and hence it is not Aristotle's own view.

coincidents is also very important for knowing₀ the what-it-is. For we can state the essence₀ best once we can describe how all or most of the coincidents appear to be;[7] for since the what-it-is is the principle of all demonstration, a definition will clearly be dialectical and empty[8] unless it results in knowledge₉, or at least in ready conjecture, about the coincidents.

[THE RELATION OF PSYCHIC STATES TO THE BODY]

A further puzzle arises about whether all the affections[9] of the soul also belong to what has the soul or there is also some affection that is distinctive of the soul itself. We must find the answer, but it is not easy.

In most cases (for instance, being angry or confident, having an appetite, or perceiving in general), it appears that without the body the soul neither is affected nor acts. Understanding, more than the other affections, would seem to be distinctive <of the soul>; but if it is also some sort of appearance[10] or requires appearance, then understanding also requires a body. And so if some function or affection of the soul is distinctive of it, then the soul would be separable; but if not, then it would not be separable. Similarly, the straight, insofar as it is straight, has many coincidents—for instance, that it touches a bronze sphere at a point—but if it is separated, it will not touch the sphere in this way; for it is inseparable, given that in every case it requires some body.[11]

In fact, all the affections of the soul—emotion, gentleness, fear, pity, confidence, and, further, joy, loving, and hating—would seem to require a body, since whenever we have them the body is affected in some way. An indication of this is the fact that sometimes, though something severe and obvious affects us, we are not provoked or frightened; and sometimes we are moved by something small and faint, if the body is swelling and in the condition that accompanies anger. It is still more evident that

7. **appear to be**: Lit. 'according to the appearance'. Aristotle is setting out the APPEARANCES or COMMON BELIEFS (*endoxa*).

8. **dialectical and empty**: Aristotle regards them as purely LOGICAL arguments and accounts that do not say anything specific enough about the relevant subject matter.

9. **affections**: *pathē*. *Pathos* is often most appropriately rendered by 'ATTRIBUTE'. But in this section the connection with being affected (*paschein*) is especially close; hence 'affection' has been preferred.

10. **some sort of appearance**: i.e., a state of being appeared to (in which it is true that x appears F to me). See APPEARANCE #2.

11. **requires some body**: Hence if the soul requires some body, the same will be true of it as of the straight. On mathematical objects see ABSTRACTION.

sometimes, though nothing frightening is happening, people are affected just as a frightened person is.[12]

25   If this is so, then clearly affections are forms₁ that involve matter. Hence the formulae will be, for instance:[13] 'Being angry is a certain motion of this sort of body or part or potentiality by this agency for this end'. Hence study of the soul—either every sort or this sort[14]—turns out to be a task for the student of nature.

[PROBLEMS OF DEFINITION]

The student of nature and the dialectician would give different defini-
30   tions of each of these affections—of anger, for instance. The dialectician would define it as a desire to inflict pain in return for pain, or something of that sort, whereas the student of nature would define it as a boiling
403b   of the blood and of the hot <element> around the heart. The student of nature describes the matter, whereas the dialectician describes the form and the account: for desire, for instance, is the form₁ of the thing, but its existence requires this sort of matter. Similarly, the account of a
5   house is of this sort—that it is a shelter preventing destruction by wind, rain, or heat; someone else[15] will say that it is stones, bricks, and timber; and someone else will say that it is the form in these <stones, for instance,> for the sake of this end. Who, then, is the <real> student of nature—the one who is concerned with the matter but is ignorant of the account, or the one who is concerned only with the account? Or is the <real> student of nature more properly the one who mentions both form and matter? If so, then what is each of the first two?
10   Perhaps in fact no one is concerned with the inseparable affections of matter but not concerned with them insofar as they are separable.[16] Rather, the student of nature is concerned with all the actions and af-fections of this sort of body[17] and this sort of matter; what is not of this sort concerns someone else, perhaps a craftsman (for instance, a
15   carpenter or a doctor). Inseparable affections, insofar as they are not

12. **affected . . . person is**: The appropriate bodily condition—whether or not the external stimulus is appropriate—is necessary for the psychic state.

13. **will be, for instance**: Or perhaps 'will be such (sc. involving matter). For instance . . . '.

14. **this sort**: i.e., the sort that requires a body. On the role of the student of nature cf. *Phys.* 194a15, *PA* 641a29.

15. **someone else**: Or perhaps 'another account'.

16. **separable**: i.e., separable in account. See SEPARABLE #3.

17. **this sort of body**: This is a natural body, in contrast to the artifacts that are mentioned next.

affections of this sort of body but <are considered> by abstraction, concern the mathematician; insofar as they are separated, they concern first philosophy.*

We should return to where our discussion began. We were saying, then, that the affections of the soul (for instance, emotion and fear) are, insofar as they are affections of the soul, inseparable[18] (unlike surface and line) from the natural matter of animals.

[THE MAIN CHARACTERISTICS OF SOULS]

2

In our examination of the soul, we must both set out the puzzles that   20
are to be solved after we have made progress, and at the same time collect the views of all the previous thinkers who have expressed views on the soul, so that we can accept whatever is correct in their views and avoid whatever is mistaken. The right starting point for our investigation is to set out the features that most commonly seem to belong naturally   25
to the soul.

What has a soul, then, seems to differ in two most characteristic ways from what lacks a soul—motion and perception. These are also roughly the two features of the soul that have been handed down by our predecessors; for some say that the soul is what most characteristically and primarily initiates motion. . . .[19]

*   *   *   *   *   *   *

[HOW CAN THE SOUL BE IN MOTION?]

3

First we should discuss motion. For presumably it is not merely false to   405b31
say that the essence$_o$ of the soul is as described by people who say that   406a
the soul is what sets itself in motion or what is capable of doing so, but it is also impossible for motion to belong to the soul.

Now, we have previously said that not everything that initiates motion must itself be in motion.[20] Moreover, something may be in motion in either of two ways—either because of something else or in its own right.   5
By 'because of something else' I mean things that are in motion because

18. **inseparable**: They cannot exist without matter, though they are SEPARABLE in account and definition. See further *Met.* vii 10–11.

19. The remaining selections from Book i are extracts from Aristotle's discussion of different views of the soul favored by his predecessors.

20. **not everything . . . in motion**: On unmoved movers see *Phys.* viii 5.

they are in something that is in motion—as sailors are, for instance. For they are not in motion in the same way as the boat is—for the boat is in motion in its own right, whereas they are in motion because they are in something that is in motion. This is clear if we consider the parts; for the proper motion of the feet is walking, and this is also <the proper

10   motion> of a man, but the sailors are not walking in this situation. Since, then, being in motion is spoken of in these two ways, we are now examining whether the soul is in motion, and shares in motion, in its own right. . . .

*   *   *   *   *   *   *

406b15   Some people say that the soul is itself in motion and thereby initiates the same sort of motion in the body that it belongs to. This is what Democritus says, in terms rather similar to those used by Philippus the comic poet. For Philippus says that Daedalus set the wooden statue of

20   Aphrodite in motion, by pouring in quicksilver. Democritus says the same sort of thing; for he says that the indivisible spheres[21] are in motion, because it is in their nature never to be at rest, and that they drag along the whole body and set it in motion.

In reply we will ask whether the same thing causes the body to come to rest. It is difficult, or actually impossible, to say how it will do this.

25   In general, this is not how the soul appears to initiate motion in the animal; rather it appears to initiate motion through some sort of decision and thought. . . .

*   *   *   *   *   *   *

[THE RELATION BETWEEN BODY AND SOUL]

407b13   This account[22] and most accounts of the soul have an absurd result, since
15   they attach the soul to a body and place it in a body, with no further determination about the cause <of the attachment> or the condition of the body. But this <further determination> would seem to be needed; for the association <of this soul and this body> explains why one acts and the other is affected and why one initiates motion and the other is in motion—and none of these applies to the relation between just any* old soul and body.

21. **indivisible spheres**: These are the atoms that (according to Democritus) constitute the soul.

22. **This account**: Aristotle has just been discussing Plato's account in the *Timaeus*.

These people, however, merely undertake to say what sort of thing   20
the soul is; they determine nothing further about the body that is to
receive it. They speak as though it were possible, as in the Pythagorean
stories, for just any old soul to be inserted into any old body, whereas
in fact each body seems to have its own distinctive form and shape.[23]
What they say is like saying that carpentry gets inserted into flutes; in   25
fact a craft must use suitable instruments, and equally the soul must use
a suitable body.

[CAN THE SOUL BE AN ATTUNEMENT OF THE BODY?]

4

There is also another view about the soul that has been handed down,
one that many find no less persuasive than those we have mentioned
and one that has also been scrutinized in popular discussions.[24] People   30
say that the soul is some sort of attunement;[25] for, they say, an attunement
is a blending and combination of contraries, and the body results from
a combination of contraries.

   An attunement, however, is some sort of ratio[26] or combination of
the things mixed together, and the soul cannot be either of these. Further,
an attunement does not initiate motion, whereas practically everyone   408a
takes this to be most characteristic of the soul. It is more in tune with[27]
the facts to speak of attunement in the case of health and of bodily
excellences in general than in the case of the soul. This would be evident
if one tried to assign the actions and affections of the soul to some sort   5
of attunement; for it is hard to attune them to it. . . .

*   *   *   *   *   *   *

[CAN THE SOUL BE IN MOTION?]

We say that the soul feels pain or enjoyment, and confidence or fear,   408b
and also that it is angry or perceives or thinks; and all of these seem to
be motions. Hence one might infer that the soul is in motion; but this   5
does not necessarily follow.

23. **its own . . . shape**: This makes it suitable for only one sort of soul.

24. **popular discussions**: Perhaps this refers to Aristotle's own *Eudemus*, of which
only fragments survive (ROT p. 2400), some of them discussing the attunement
theory. See POPULAR.

25. **attunement**, *harmonia*. See Plato, *Phaedo* 86b–d.

26. **ratio**: Or 'account', *logos*. See REASON #6.

27. **more in tune**: *harmozein*. Like 'hard to attune' below, this is a pun on *harmonia*.

For let us by all means grant that feeling pain, feeling enjoyment, and thinking are motions, and that to be in these conditions is to be moved, and that the soul initiates the motion—so that to be angry or afraid, for instance, is for the heart to undergo this motion, while thinking is presumably a motion of this part or of something else, and this comes about in some cases by the local motion of some things, in other cases by alteration (to say which things and what sort of motion requires another discussion). Still, to say that the soul is angry is like saying that the soul weaves or builds houses. For presumably it is better to say, not that the soul feels pity or learns or thinks, but that the human being does so by the soul. And this is true not because the motion is in the soul, but because sometimes it reaches as far as the soul, and sometimes it begins from the soul. Perception, for instance, begins from these <external> things <and reaches as far as the soul>, while recollection begins from the soul and extends to the motions or to the traces remaining in the sense-organs. . . .

*   *   *   *   *   *   *

Book II

[DEFINITION OF THE SOUL]

[SUBSTANCE AS FORM, MATTER, AND COMPOUND]

1

So much for the views on the soul that our predecessors have handed down. Let us now return and make a new start, trying to determine what the soul is and what account of it best applies to all souls in common.

We say, then, that one kind of being is substance. One sort of substance is matter,[1] which is not a this in its own right; another sort is shape or form, which makes <matter> a this;[2] and the third sort is the compound of matter and form. Matter is potentiality, and form is actuality; actuality is either, for instance, <the state of> knowing or <the activity of> attending <to what one knows>.[3]

---

1. **One sort . . . matter**: Lit. 'of this <i.e., substance> one <sort? part? aspect?> is <substance?> as matter'.

2. **which makes <matter> a this**: Lit. 'according to which already (or 'by now') it (or 'something') is called a this' or 'according to which already a this is spoken of'.

3. **attending**: i.e., actually thinking of what one knows. See STUDY #1.

[*NATURAL BODIES ARE SUBSTANCES AS COMPOUNDS,*
SOULS AS FORM AND FIRST ACTUALITY]

What seem to be substances most of all are bodies, and especially natural bodies, since these are the sources[4] of the others. Some natural bodies are alive and some are not—by 'life' I mean self-nourishment, growth, and decay.[5]

It follows that every living natural body is a substance and, <more precisely,> substance as compound.[6] But since every such body is also this sort of body—i.e., the sort that is alive—the soul cannot be a body, since the body <is substance> as subject and matter and is not said of a subject. The soul, then, must be substance as the form of a natural body that is potentially alive. Now, substance is actuality; hence the soul will be the actuality of this specific sort of body.

Actuality is spoken of in two ways—one corresponding to <the state of> knowing$_e$ and the other to attending to <what one knows>. Evidently, then, the soul is the same sort of actuality that knowing is. For both being asleep and being awake require the presence of the soul; being awake corresponds to attending and being asleep to the state of inactive knowing. Moreover, in the same subject the state of knowing precedes the activity. Hence the soul is the first actuality[7] of a natural body that is potentially alive.

The sort of natural body that is potentially alive[8] is an organic one. The parts of plants are also organs,* though altogether simple ones; the leaf, for instance, is a shelter for the shell, and the shell for the fruit, and similarly the roots correspond to a mouth, since both draw in food.[9] And so, if we must give an account common to every sort of soul, we will say that the soul is the first actuality of a natural organic body.

Hence we need not ask whether the soul and body are one, any more than we need to ask this about the wax and the seal[10] or, in general,

15

20

25

412b

5

4. **sources**: *archai*. See PRINCIPLE #2. Aristotle means that artifacts are made from natural bodies; cf. *Phys.* 192b19.

5. **self-. . . decay**. 'Self-' governs 'growth' and 'decay' as well as 'nourishment', since in living creatures these all have an internal *archē*. See MOTION #3, *Phys.* viii 5.

6. **as compound**: It is a compound of body and life.

7. **first actuality**: Aristotle applies this term to the state exemplified by having knowledge, contrasted with attending to what one knows.

8. **The sort . . . alive**: Only bodies that are actually alive have the relevant potentiality for being alive. Cf. 412b25, *Met.* 1048b37–1049a18.

9. **correspond . . . food**: The common function is the basis for the analogy.

10. **seal**: Or perhaps 'shape'.

about the matter and the thing of which it is the matter.[11] For while one and being are spoken of in several ways, the actuality <and what it actualizes> are fully one.[12]

10   We have said in general, then, that the soul is substance that corresponds to the account; and this <sort of substance> is the essence of this sort of body. Suppose some instrument*—an axe, for instance— were a natural body; then being an axe would be its substance,[13] and its soul would also be this <i.e., being an axe>; and if this substance were
15   separated from it, it would no longer be an axe, except homonymously. In fact, however, it is an axe;[14] for the soul is not the essence and form₁ of this sort of body but of the specific sort of natural body that has in itself a principle of motion and rest.

    We must also study this point by applying it to the parts <of living things>.[15] If the eye, for instance, were an animal, sight would be its
20   soul. For sight is the eye's substance that corresponds to the account, while the eye is the matter of sight; if an eye loses its sight, it is no longer an eye, except homonymously, as a stone eye or a painted eye is.[16] We must apply this point about the part to the whole living body; for what holds for the relation of part <of the faculty of perception> to part <of the body> holds equally for the relation of the whole <faculty
25   of> perception to the whole perceptive body, insofar as it is perceptive. The sort of body that is potentially alive is not the one that has lost its soul[17] but the one that has it; and the seed or the fruit is potentially this sort of body.

    Being awake, then, is a <second> actuality, corresponding to cutting
413a   or seeing. The soul is <a first> actuality, corresponding to <the faculty of> sight and to the potentiality of the instrument <to cut>; and the

11. **of which it is the matter**: Here the form is conceived as itself having matter. On unity cf. *Met.* 1045b17–23.

12. **the actuality . . . one**: Or perhaps: 'The full (or strict; see CONTROLLING #4) sense <of 'one'> is that of actuality'.

13. **substance**: Or 'essence₀' (and in the rest of this and the next paragraph). Aristotle assumes a connection between ESSENCE (*ti ēn einai*) and SUBSTANCE. Cf. 415b11n, SUBSTANCE #2.

14. **it is an axe**: Since it is an artifact, it has no soul.

15. **We must . . . living things>**: This is a second comparison with nonsubstances, after the comparison with artifacts. Cf. *EN* 1097b30.

16. **painted eye is**: This sort of matter does not survive the loss of its form. See MATTER #5.

17. **lost its soul**: This sort of matter, in contrast to the organs mentioned above, survives the loss of the form. See MATTER #5.

body is potentially this. And as an eye is the pupil plus sight, so an animal is soul plus body.

[SOME PARTS OF THE SOUL MAY BE SEPARABLE FROM THE BODY]

It is clear, then, that the soul is not separable* from the body. At least, some parts of it are not, if it is divisible into parts; for the actuality of   5
some <parts of the soul> is <the actuality> of the parts <of the body> themselves. Still, some <parts of the soul> might well not be actualities of any body and might therefore be separable. Moreover, it is still unclear whether the soul is the actuality of the body in the way a sailor is of a ship.[18]

Let this, then, be our outline definition and sketch of the soul.   10

[CRITERIA FOR A DEFINITION]

2

Since what is perspicuous* and better known$_g$ from the point of view of reason emerges from what is less perspicuous but more evident, we must start again and apply this approach to the soul. For the defining account must not confine itself, as most definitions do, to showing the   15
fact; it must also include and indicate its cause.[19] The accounts that are customarily stated in formulae are like conclusions, so that if we ask, for instance, what squaring is, we are told that it is making an equilateral rectangle equal to an oblong rectangle. This sort of formula is an account of the conclusion, whereas the one that defines squaring as the finding of the mean states the cause of the fact.   20

[DIFFERENT FORMS OF LIFE]

To begin our examination, then, we say that living is what distinguishes things with souls from things without souls. Living is spoken of in several ways—for instance, understanding, perception, locomotion and rest, and also the motion involved in nourishment, and decay and   25
growth. And so whatever has even one of these is said to be alive.

This is why all plants as well <as animals> seem to be alive, since they evidently have an internal potentiality and principle through which

---

18. **sailor . . . ship**: Interpretation doubtful. Perhaps Aristotle means: just as a sailor ceases to be a sailor when he leaves the ship, so also the intellectual part of the soul survives the body, but is no longer a soul or part of a soul. See 413b24, 415a11, 430a22.

19. **For the defining . . . its cause**: See DEFINITION #2.

they both grow and decay in contrary directions. For they grow up and down and in all directions alike, not just up rather than down;[20] they
30   are continually nourished, and they stay alive as long as they can absorb nourishment. This <sort of life> can be separated from the others, but in mortal things the others cannot be separated from it. This is evident in the case of plants, since they have no other potentiality of the soul.
413b   This principle, then, is what makes something alive. What makes something an animal is primarily perception; for whatever has perception, even without motion or locomotion, is said to be an animal, not simply to be alive. Touch is the primary type of perception belonging
5   to all animals, and it can be separated from the other senses, just as the nutritive <potentiality> can be separated from touch and the other senses.

[THE PARTS OF THE SOUL]

The part of the soul that belongs to plants as well as to animals is called
10   nutritive; and all animals evidently have the sense of touch. Later we will state the explanation of each of these facts.[21] For now let us confine ourselves to saying that the soul is the principle of the <potentialities> we have mentioned—for nutrition, perception, understanding, and motion—and is defined by them.
    Is each of these a soul or a part of a soul? And if a part, is it the sort
15   that is separable only in account, or is it also separable in place? In some cases the answer is easily seen, but some parts raise a puzzle. For some plants[22] are evidently still alive when they are cut <from one plant> and are separated from each other; for, we assume, the soul in each plant is actually one but potentially more than one. And we see that the
20   same is also true of other differentiae of the soul. <This is clear> in the case of insects that are cut in two. For each part has both perception and locomotion; if it has perception, then it also has appearance and desire. For if it has perception, then it has pain and pleasure,[23] and if it has these, then it necessarily also has appetite.
25   So far, however, nothing is evident about understanding and the potentiality for theoretical study. It would seem to be a different kind

20. **For they . . . than down**: Hence the motion involved in growth cannot simply be explained by reference to the motion of the material elements constituting the organism.

21. **explanation . . . facts**: A final-causal explanation is given in iii 12.

22. **For some plants . . .** : This paragraph gives evidence to suggest that some parts of the soul cannot be separated in place.

23. **then . . . pleasure**: If it has these it must have appearance.

of soul,[24] and to be the only part that admits of being separated,[25] just as the everlasting <admits of being separated> from the perishable.

It evidently follows, however, that the other parts of the soul are not separable, as some say they are. But they evidently differ in account; for perceiving is different from believing, and hence being the perceptive   30 part is different from being the believing part, and so on for each of the other parts mentioned.

Further, animals are differentiated by the fact that some of them have all of these parts, some have some of them, and some have only one; we should investigate the reason for this later. Practically the same is   414a true of the senses: some animals have all of them, some have some of them, and some have only the most necessary one, touch.

[ANOTHER APPROACH TO THE DEFINITION OF THE SOUL]

When we say we live and perceive by something, we speak in two   5 ways,[26] just as we do when we say we know$_e$ by something. For we say we know either by knowledge or by the soul, since we say we know by each of these; and similarly, we are healthy in one way by health, in another way by some part or the whole of the body. In these cases, knowledge or health is a sort of shape and form, i.e., an account[27] and a sort of actuality of what is receptive of knowledge or health; for the   10 actuality of the agent seems to occur in the thing that is acted on and suitably disposed.

Now the soul is that by which we primarily[28] live, perceive, and think, and so it will be an account and a form, not matter and subject. For substance, as we said, is spoken of in three ways, as form, matter, and   15 the compound of both; of these, matter is potentiality, form actuality. Since, therefore, the compound of body and soul is ensouled, body is not the actuality of soul, but the soul is the actuality of some sort of body.[29]

24. **different kind of soul**: Or perhaps 'different kind (*genos*) of thing from soul'.

25. **and the . . . separated**: Read *endechesthai*, 413b26. OCT: 'and it is the only part that admits of being separated'.

26. **two ways**: These refer to the formal and to the efficient cause.

27. **account**: *logos*. Here Aristotle actually seems to refer to what the account is an account of. See REASON #5. 'Form$_l$' would be appropriate here and in 414a13 below, if 'form' (*eidos*) did not occur in the immediate context.

28. **primarily**: This corresponds to the formal cause illustrated above, since being alive is a functional, not a material, property.

29. **Since, therefore . . . of body**: Since the soul is what primarily (as formal cause) makes the body alive, and since it is actuality, it is form.

[THE RELATION OF SOUL TO BODY]

20   This vindicates the view of those who think that the soul is not a body
but requires a body; for it is not a body, but it belongs to a body, and
for that reason it is present in a body, and in this sort of body. Our
predecessors were wrong, then, in trying to fit the soul into a body
without further determining the proper sort of body, even though it
25   appears that not just any old thing receives any old thing.[30] Our view,
however, is quite reasonable, since a thing's actuality naturally comes
to be in what has the potentiality for it, i.e., in the proper matter.

It is evident from this, then, that the soul is a certain sort of actuality
and form₁ of what has the potentiality to be of this sort.

[THE DIFFERENT PARTS OF THE SOUL]

3

As we said, some things have all the potentialities of the soul that were
30   previously mentioned, while other things have some of these potentialities, and others have only one. The potentialities we mentioned were
those for nutrition,[31] perception, desire, locomotion, and understanding.
414b   Plants have only the nutritive part. Other things have the nutritive part
and also the perceptive part, and if they have the perceptive part, they
also have the desiring part. For desire includes appetite, emotion, and
wish; but all animals have at least the sense of touch, and whatever has
5   any perception has pleasure and pain and finds things pleasant or painful. Whatever finds things pleasant and painful also has appetite, since
appetite is desire for what is pleasant.

Further, animals have the perception of nourishment; for touch is
perception of nourishment, since all living things are nourished by things
that are dry and wet and hot and cold, and touch is the perception
of these. Animals are nourished by other objects of perception[32] only
10   coincidentally, since neither sound nor color nor smell contributes anything to nourishment, and flavor is an object of touch. Now, hunger
and thirst are appetites for the dry and hot, and the wet and cold,
respectively, while flavor is a sort of pleasant relish belonging to these.[33]

We must make these points clear later on. For now let us confine

30. **it appears . . . old thing**: Cf. 407b21.

31. **for nutrition**: Lit. 'the nutritive' (neuter adjective). The same phrases are
translated by 'nutritive part', etc., below. Aristotle evidently intends no distinction between potentialities and parts of the soul.

32. **other objects of perception**: Read *tois d'allois tōn aisthētōn*.

33. **Now . . . to these**: Hence the sense of touch implies these appetites.

ourselves to saying that living things that have touch also have desire.   *15*
Whether they all have appearance is not clear,[34] and must be considered
later.

Besides these parts, some things have the locomotive part. Others—
human beings, for instance, and any thinking being that is different
from, or superior to, a human being[35]—also have the thinking part and
understanding.*

[A COMPLETE ACCOUNT OF THE SOUL MUST DESCRIBE THESE PARTS]

Clearly, then, soul will have one single account in the same way that   *20*
figure has; for just as figure is nothing apart* from the triangle and the
figures that follow in order, so equally the soul is nothing apart from
those <potentialities> we have mentioned. Still, in the case of figures
we can find a common account that fits all of them and is distinctive of
none; the same is true for the souls we have mentioned. It is ridiculous,   *25*
then, in these and other such cases, to seek a common account that is
not distinctive of any being and does not fit the proper and indivisible
species, if we neglect[36] this <distinctive> account. Hence[37] we must ask   *32*
what the soul of each particular <kind of thing>—for instance, a plant,
a human being, or a beast—is.   *33*

What is true of the soul is similar to what is true of figure; for in both   *28*
cases the earlier is invariably present potentially in its successor—for
instance, the triangle in the square, and the nutritive in the perceptive.
We must consider why they are in this order. For the perceptive part   *415a*
requires the nutritive, but in plants the nutritive is separated from the
perceptive. Again, each of the other senses requires touch, whereas
touch is found without the other senses, since many animals lack sight,   *5*
hearing, and smell. Among things that perceive, some but not all have
the locomotive part. Finally and most rarely, some have reasoning and
thinking. For perishable things that have reasoning also have all the
other parts of the soul; but not all of those that have each of the other   *10*
parts also have reasoning—on the contrary, some animals lack appear-

34. **Whether . . . is not clear**: It is puzzling that Aristotle thinks this is still
unclear, given his remarks in 413b22–24 above. See also 428a8, 434a5–11.

35. **any thinking . . . human being**: Or: 'anything else that is similar or superior
to a human being'.

36. **if we neglect**: Lit. just 'neglecting'. Aristotle is not rejecting a general account
as impossible or useless; he is just saying that it needs to be supplemented by
accounts of the different types of soul. See DEFINITION #7.

37. **Hence . . . beast—is**: 414b32–33 have been transposed to 414b28.

ance, while some live by appearance alone.[38] Theoretical intellect requires a different account.

Clearly, then, the account of each of these parts of the soul is also the most proper account of <each type of> soul.

[NUTRITION AND GENERATION]

4

15 If we are to examine these <parts of the soul>, we must find what each of them is and then investigate the next questions and those that follow. And if we ought to say what, for instance, the understanding or the perceptive or the nutritive part is, we should first say what it is to understand or perceive, since actualities and actions are prior in account 20 to potentialities. If this is so, and if in addition the objects corresponding to the actualities are prior to them and so must[39] be studied first, then we must, for the same reason, begin by determining the objects corresponding to nutrition, sense, and understanding. And so we should first discuss nourishment and generation; for the nutritive soul belongs to other living things as well as <to plants>, and it is the first and most 25 widely shared potentiality of the soul, the one that makes all living things alive.

Its functions are generation and the use of nourishment. For the most natural of all functions for a living thing, if it is complete and not defective and does not come to be by chance,[40] is to produce another thing of the same sort as itself (an animal, if it is an animal, and a plant, if it is a plant), in order to share as far as it can in the everlasting and divine. 415b For this is the end they all strive for,[41] and for its sake they do every action that accords with nature. (What something is for is of two types— the goal and the beneficiary.)[42] These living things cannot share in the everlasting and divine by continuously existing, since no perishable thing can remain numerically one and the same; hence they share in it as far 5 as they can, to different degrees, and what remains is not the <parent>

38. **appearance alone**: i.e., without reason. For Aristotle's different claims about appearance see 414b16n above.

39. **and so must . . .**: Read *kai dei*.

40. **by chance**: Or 'spontaneously', *automaton* (see LUCK #4), i.e., without parents.

41. **strive for**: or 'desire', *oregesthai*. Literal desire would not apply to plants, which are meant to be included in this remark.

42. **the goal and the beneficiary**: See FOR SOMETHING #4. Here Aristotle is concerned with the goal, and in 415b20–21 below with the beneficiary.

itself, but something else of the same sort[43] as <the parent>—something that is specifically, not numerically, one*[44] with <the parent>.

[THE SOUL IS A FORMAL, EFFICIENT, AND FINAL CAUSE]

The soul is the cause and principle of the living body. Now, causes are spoken of in many ways, and the soul is a cause in three of the ways distinguished—as the source of motion, as what something is for, and as the substance[45] of ensouled bodies.   10

It is clearly the cause as substance; for a thing's substance is the cause of its being, and the being of living things is their living, the cause and principle of which is soul. Moreover, the actuality is the form₁ of what is potentially.[46]

The soul is evidently also a cause by being what something is for.   15
For just as productive thought aims at something, so does nature, and what it aims at is its end. In living things[47] the natural end is the soul; for all natural bodies, of plants no less than of animals, are organs of the soul, since they are for the sake of the soul. (The end for the sake   20
of which is of two types, either the goal or the beneficiary.)

Moreover, the soul is also the source of locomotion, though not all living things have this potentiality. Alteration and growth also depend on the soul; for perception seems to be some kind of alteration, and   25
nothing that lacks a soul perceives. The same applies to growth and decay; for nothing either decays or grows naturally without being nourished, and nothing that has no share of life is nourished.

[NUTRITION AND GENERATION SHOW THE DIFFERENT WAYS THE SOUL IS A CAUSE]

Empedocles is wrong when he adds that plants grow by putting down roots because earth naturally moves downward, and that plants grow   416a
by extending upward because fire naturally moves upward. His conception of up and down is wrong. For up and down are not the same for each particular <sort of> thing as they are for the universe as a whole; in fact, if we ought to call organs the same or different in accordance   5

43. **of the same sort**: *hoion*, cognate with *poion*. See QUALITY.

44. **specifically . . . one**: Or 'one in form' (*eidos*). Cf. *Met.* 1033a8.

45. **substance**: Or 'essence₀'. Cf. 412b13n, SUBSTANCE #2.

46. **the form₁ of what is potentially**: Aristotle takes it for granted that the form is substance and that the soul is the actuality.

47. **living things**: Read *zōsin*. OCT: 'animals'.

with their functions, a plant's roots correspond to an animal's head.[48]
Besides, what is it that holds the fire and earth together when they
are moving in contrary directions? For they will be torn apart unless
something prevents it; whatever prevents it will be the soul, the cause
of growing and being nourished.

10   Some think the nature of fire is the unqualified cause of nourishment
and growth, since it is the only body that is evidently nourished and
grows, and hence one might suppose that it also performs this function
in both plants and animals. In fact, however, fire is a sort of joint cause,
15   but not the unqualified cause; it is the soul, rather than fire, that is the
unqualified cause. For while fire grows without limit, as long as there
is fuel, the size and growth of everything naturally constituted has a
limit and form$_1$,[49] which are characteristic of soul, not of fire—i.e., of the
form$_1$ rather than of the matter.

[DIFFERENT ACCOUNTS OF NOURISHMENT TURN OUT TO BE CONSISTENT]

Since one and the same potentiality of the soul is both nutritive and
20   generative, we must first determine the facts about nutrition; for this is
the function that distinguishes the nutritive potentiality from others.

Contrary seems to nourish contrary, not in every case, but only when
they not only come to be but also grow from each other; for many things
25   come to be from each other (healthy from sick, for instance) without
gaining any quantity. And not even those contraries that grow seem to
nourish each other in the same way; water, for instance, nourishes fire,
but fire does not nourish water. It seems to be true, then, of the simple
bodies more than of other things, that one thing nourishes and the other
is nourished.

30   A puzzle arises: while some say that like nourishes like, just as (they
say) like grows by like, others, as we have said, hold the opposite view,
that contrary nourishes contrary; for, they say, like is unaffected by like,
but nourishment changes and is digested, and everything changes into
35   its opposite or into the intermediate. Moreover, nourishment is affected
by the thing nourished, whereas the thing nourished is unaffected by
416b   the nourishment—just as the matter is affected by the carpenter, who
is unaffected by it and merely changes from inactivity to activity.[50]

It matters for this question whether nourishment is the first or last

48. **if we . . . animal's head**: Hence the growth of a plant's roots corresponds
to an animal's growing taller.

49. **form$_1$**: See REASON #6.

50. **activity**: *energeia*, usually rendered 'actuality'.

thing added.[51] Perhaps it is both, if undigested nourishment is added   5
first, and digested nourishment last. If so, then it would be possible
to speak of nourishment in both ways; for insofar as nourishment is
undigested, contrary nourishes contrary, and insofar as it has been digested, like nourishes like. Evidently, then, each view is in a way both
correct and incorrect.

Since nothing is nourished except what has a share of life, the ensouled   10
body, insofar as it is ensouled, is what is nourished. Nourishment,
therefore, is also relative, not coincidentally, to an ensouled thing. However, nourishing something is not the same as making it grow; for
an ensouled thing is caused to grow insofar as it has some quantity,
but it is nourished insofar as it is a this and a substance.[52] For it
preserves its substance and exists as long as it is nourished; and what   15
it generates is not itself, but something else of the same sort—for its
own substance already exists, and a thing does not generate, but
preserves, itself.

Hence this sort of principle in the soul is a potentiality of the sort that
preserves the ensouled thing, insofar as it is ensouled, and nourishment
equips it for its actuality; and so if it has been deprived of nourishment   20
it cannot exist. Further,[53] since a thing's end rightly determines what   23
we should call it, and in this case the end is the generation of another
thing of the same sort, this first soul will be the generative soul, generat-   25
ing another thing of the same sort.

We must distinguish three things—what is nourished, what it is nour-   20
ished by, and what nourishes. What nourishes is this first soul, what is
nourished is the ensouled body, and what it is nourished by is the
nourishment. What the soul nourishes by is of two types—just as what
we steer by is both the hand and the rudder: the first both initiates
motion and undergoes it, and the second simply undergoes it.[54] Since all
nourishment must be digestible and the hot element produces digestion,
every ensouled thing contains heat.

This, then, is an outline of what nutrition is; we should describe it   30
more clearly later in the discussions proper to it.[55]

51. **last thing added**: To the organism that is nourished.

52. **substance**: The growth counts as nutrition insofar as it keeps some form,
and hence some substance, in being.

53. **Further, since . . . same sort**: 416b23–25 are transposed to 416b20.

54. **just as what we steer . . . undergoes it**: On different types of movers see
Phys. viii 5.

55. **discussions proper to it**: Aristotle's treatise on nutrition has been lost.

[PERCEPTION]

[PERCEPTION AS MOTION]

5

Now that we have determined this, let us discuss perception in general.
Perception occurs in being moved and affected, as we have said, since
it seems to be a type of alteration.[56] Some also say that like is affected
by like; we have said in our general discussion of acting and being
affected[57] how this is or is not possible.

A puzzle arises about why we do not perceive the senses themselves,
and about why they do not produce perception without external objects,
despite the presence of fire,[58] earth, and the other elements, whose
intrinsic or coincidental properties are the things that are perceived.
Clearly, then, the perceptive part is <what it is> by merely potential,
not actual, <perceiving>, and so it does not perceive <without an
external object>—just as what is combustible is not burned all by itself
without something to burn it, since otherwise it would burn itself with
no need of actual fire.

We speak of perceiving in two ways; for we say that something sees
or hears both in the case of something that has the potentiality for seeing
or hearing, even though it is asleep at the time, and in the case of
something that is actually seeing or hearing at the time. It follows that
perception is also spoken of in two ways, as potential and as actual, and
in the same way both what is potentially perceived and what is actually
perceived are called objects of perception.

First, then, let us speak as though the actuality were the same as
being affected and moved—for motion is in fact a sort of actuality, though
an incomplete one, as we have said elsewhere.[59] Now, everything is
affected and moved by an agent[60] that has the relevant property in
actuality,[61] so that in a way like is affected by like, and in a way unlike
by unlike—for what is being affected is unlike the agent, but when it
has been affected it is like the agent.

35
417a

5

10

15

20

---

56. **a type of alteration**: Aristotle gradually modifies this claim. See 417b2–16.

57. **we have ... affected**: See *GC* i 7.

58. **presence of fire**: It is present in the body, and specifically in the sense-organ.

59. **said elsewhere**: See *Phys.* iii 1.

60. **agent**: Or 'producer', *poioun*.

61. **that has ... actuality**: What is acted on by an agent that is actually F is
changed from not being F to being actually F.

[DIFFERENT TYPES OF POTENTIALITY]

We must also distinguish types of potentiality and actuality, since just now we were speaking of them without qualification. One way in which someone might know$_e$ is the way we have in mind in saying that a man knows because man is a kind of thing that knows and has knowledge; another way is the way we have in mind in saying that someone who   25
has grammatical knowledge knows. These knowers have different sorts of potentiality—the first has a potentiality because he has the right sort of genus and matter, whereas the second has a potentiality because he has the potentiality to attend to something when he wishes, if nothing external prevents it.[62] A third sort <of knower> is someone who is attending to something at the time, actualizing his knowledge and fully knowing (for instance) this A. In the first and second case we pass from   30
potentially to actually knowing; but in the first case we do so by being altered through learning, and by frequent changes from the contrary state, while in the second case—where we pass from having arithmetical or grammatical knowledge without actualizing it, to actualizing it—we   417b
do so in another way.

Further, there is not just one way of being affected. On the contrary, one way of being affected is a destruction of contrary by contrary, while the other way is more properly preservation, not destruction, of a potential F by an actual F, when the potential F is <not contrary, but> like the actual F, in the way that a potentiality is like its actuality. For the   5
second case—where the possessor of knowledge comes to attend to what he knows—either is not a case of alteration at all (since the addition leads to <the knowledge> itself and to the actuality) or is a different kind of alteration. That is why we should not say that the intelligent subject is altered in exercising his intelligence, just as we should not say that the builder is altered in <actually> building.

First, then, when an understanding and intelligent subject is led from   10
potentiality to actuality, we should not call this teaching but give it some other name. Again, if a subject with potential knowledge learns and acquires knowledge from a teacher with actual knowledge, then we should say either, as we said, that this is not a case of being affected, or that there are two ways of being altered, one of which is a change   15
into a condition of deprivation, and the other of which is a change into possession of a state and into <the fulfilllment of the subject's> nature.[63]

62. **the potentiality . . . prevents it**: See POTENTIALITY #3. The second type of potentiality seems to be the 'first actuality' of 412a10, 22.

63. **Again, . . . nature**: In the previous sentence Aristotle has contrasted actualizing one's knowledge (when one attends to what one already knows) with teaching. In this sentence he contrasts teaching with a mere alteration.

[PERCEPTION AS POTENTIALITY AND ACTUALITY]

In the perceiver, the first change[64] is produced by its parent; and at birth it possesses perception corresponding to <the second type of> knowledge. We speak of actual perceiving in a way that corresponds to attending,[65] except that the visible, audible, and other perceptible objects that produce the actuality are external. This is because actual perception is of particulars, while knowledge[e][66] is of universals, which are, in a way, in the soul itself;[67] hence it is up to us to think whenever we want to, but it is not up to us to perceive whenever we want to, since perception requires the presence of its object. The same is true for the types of knowledge[e] that are about perceptible things, and for the same reason— namely that perceptible things are particulars and external.

There may be an opportunity to explain these points more perspicuously* another time, but for the moment let us be content with the distinctions we have made. There are different types of potentiality: One is what is meant in saying that a child is potentially a general. A second is what is meant in attributing the potentiality to someone of the right age, and <this second type> applies to the perceptive part. Since the difference between these cases has no name, though our distinctions have shown that they are different, and in what ways, we have to use 'being affected' and 'being altered' as though they were the strictly correct[68] names.

The perceiver is potentially what the perceptible object actually is already, as we have said. When it is being affected, then, it is unlike the object; but when it has been affected it has been made like the object and has acquired its quality.[69]

64. **first change**: This change results in the genus and matter that are suitable for perception (as opposed to the genus and matter of, say, a plant).

65. **attending**: to what one knows, in the third way of knowing.

66. **knowledge[e]**: This is the appropriate epistemic term for KNOWLEDGE of UNIVERSALS. In 417b26 below, however, it is not confined to universals, but applies to perceptible particulars.

67. **universals . . . itself**: Aristotle normally seems to assume that UNIVERSALS have extra-mental existence. This remark is consistent with that assumption, if 'in a way' is emphasized strongly.

68. **strictly correct**: See CONTROLLING #2.

69. **it has been . . . its quality**: This account of perception as involving similarity is qualified later; see 424a1n.

[PROPER, COMMON, AND COINCIDENTAL OBJECTS OF PERCEPTION]

6

We should first discuss the objects of perception,[70] taking each sense in turn. An object of perception is spoken of in three ways: two types are perceived intrinsically, and one coincidentally. One type of intrinsic object is proper[71] to each sense; the other type is common to all the senses.

    By 'proper object' I mean the one that cannot be perceived by another sense and about which we cannot be deceived.[72] Sight, for instance, is of color; hearing of sound; taste of flavor; and touch has a number of different objects. At any rate, each sense discriminates* among its proper objects, and a sense is not deceived about whether, for instance, something is a color or a sound, but it can be deceived about whether or where the colored or sounding thing is. These objects, then, are said to be proper to each sense.

    Motion, rest, number, shape, and size are the common objects, since they are not proper to any one sense, but are common to them all—a certain sort of motion, for instance, is perceptible by both touch and sight.

    Something is said to be coincidentally perceptible if, for instance, the pale <thing> is the son of Diares. For we perceive the son of Diares coincidentally, since he coincides with the pale thing we perceive, and hence we are not affected at all by the perceptible object insofar as it is <the son of Diares>.[73]

    Among the intrinsic objects of perception, the proper objects are most properly perceptible, and the essence of each sense is by nature relative to these.

10

15

20

25

* * * * * * *

[PERCEPTION REQUIRES SUITABLE ORGANS]

11

  . . . The objects of touch are the differentiae of body insofar as it is body, i.e., those that distinguish the elements—hot, cold, dry, and wet; we have discussed these earlier in what we said about the elements.[74] Their

423b27

30

70. **objects of perception**: *aisthēton*. Or 'perceptibles' or 'sensibles' (hence 'proper (common) sensibles').

71. **proper**: See DISTINCTIVE #3.

72. **cannot be deceived**: See *Met*. 1010b2n.

73. **in so far . . . Diares>**: We are not aware of it as the son of Diares, but only insofar as it is an object of sight.

74. **about the elements**: See *GC* ii 2–3.

424a tactile sense-organ, the primary seat of the sense called touch, is the
part that has these qualities potentially. For perceiving is a way of being
affected; hence the agent causes the thing that is affected, which potentially has the quality that the agent has, to have that quality actually.[75]

Hence we do not perceive anything that is as dry or wet, or hard or
soft, <as the organ>, but only the excesses in either direction, because
5   the sense is a sort of intermediate condition between the contraries in
objects of perception. And that is why a sense discriminates among its
objects; for what is intermediate discriminates, since in relation to each
extreme it becomes the other extreme. And just as what is going to
perceive both pale and dark must be actually neither pale nor dark but
potentially both, and similarly in the other cases, so also in the case of
10   touch, <what is going to perceive the contraries> must be neither hot
nor cold.

Further, just as we found that sight in a way perceives both the visible
and the invisible, and similarly the other senses perceive the opposites,
so also touch perceives the tangible and the intangible. What is intangible
is either something that either has altogether very few of the differentiat-
ing properties of tangibles—air, for instance—or has an excess of tangible
15   qualities—for instance, things that destroy <the sense>.

We have spoken in outline, then, of the senses, one by one.

[PERCEPTION IS RECEPTION OF FORM WITHOUT MATTER]

12

A general point to be grasped is that each sense receives the perceptible
forms without the matter.[76] Wax, for instance, receives the design on a
20   signet ring without the iron or gold; it acquires the design in the gold
or bronze, but not insofar as the design is gold or bronze. Similarly,
each sense is affected by the thing that has color or flavor or sound, but
not insofar as it is said to be that thing <for instance, a horse>, but

75. **which potentially has . . . quality actually**: This general formula for perception includes a claim about potentiality and actuality that qualifies the claim
about similarity at 418a5 above. Not every case of x's being similar to y actualizes
a potentiality in x; see POTENTIALITY #3.

76. **perceptible forms without the matter**: This formula restricts the sense in
which the perceiver becomes 'like' the object (see 417a18–20) and explains the
sense in which the perceiver is potentially what the object is actually. Perception
absorbs only the 'perceptible' form, which is not the form that makes a particular
man a man, but the form that makes him perceptible. On the 'form in the soul'
without matter see *Met.* 1032b1.

insofar as it has a given quality <for instance, color> and in accordance with the form₁ <of the sense>.

The primary sense-organ is the seat of this sort of potentiality. Hence   *25*
the organ and the potentiality are one, but their being is different.⁷⁷ For
though <the sense-organ> that perceives is of some magnitude, being
perceptive is not, and <so> the sense is not something with magnitude
but is a <specific sort of> form₁ and potentiality of the organ.

It is also evident from this why excesses in objects of perception   *30*
destroy the sense-organs. For if the motion is too strong for the sense-
organ, then the form₁, i.e., the sense, is destroyed, just as the harmony
and tension are destroyed if the strings of an instrument are struck
heavily.

This also makes it evident why plants do not perceive, even though
they have one part of soul, and are affected in some ways by objects of
touch, since they are chilled and heated. The reason is that they lack a   *424b*
<suitable> intermediate condition and a principle suitable for receiving
the form of perceptible things; instead, they are affected <by the form>
with the matter.

A puzzle arises about whether something that cannot smell can be at
all affected by odor, or something that cannot see can be affected by   *5*
color, and so on for the other cases. If the object of smell is odor,
then anything produced by odor must be <the act of> smelling; hence
nothing that is incapable of smelling anything can be affected by odor
(the same applies to the other cases), and any such thing must be affected
insofar as it is a perceiver. A further argument makes the same conclusion
clear. For a body is affected neither by light and darkness nor by sound   *10*
nor by odor, but only by their subject, as, for instance, the air that comes
with the thunder splits the log.

On the other hand, tangible <qualities> and flavors affect bodies;
otherwise, what would affect and alter soulless things? Then will the
other objects of perception also affect bodies? Perhaps not every body
is liable to be affected by odor and sound, and those that are affected   *15*
are indefinite and impermanent—air, for instance, since it acquires an
odor as though affected in some way.

Then what is there to smelling, apart* from being affected? Perhaps
smelling is <not only being affected, but> also perceiving, while air
that is affected <by odor>, by contrast, soon becomes an object of
perception <not a perceiver>.⁷⁸

77. **their being is different**: See ESSENCE #2.

78. **becomes . . . perceiver>**: It does not become a perceiver because it does not
receive the form without the matter.

* * * * * * *

BOOK III

[CONNECTIONS BETWEEN THE SENSES]

[THE COMMON SENSE]

1

425a14   . . . Nor can there be any proper sense-organ for the common objects
    15   of perception, namely those we perceive coincidentally by each sense[1]—
         for instance, motion, rest, shape, magnitude, number, unity. For we
         perceive all these by perceiving motion. For instance, we perceive magni-
         tude by motion, and so we also perceive shape by motion, since shape
         is a kind of magnitude; we perceive what is at rest by the absence of
         motion; we perceive number both by the absence of continuity and by
    20   the proper objects of perception, since each sense perceives one thing.
         And so it is clear that there cannot be any proper sense for any of
         these—for motion, for instance. For if there were, then <the way we
         perceive them by the proper senses> would be the way we in fact
         perceive the sweet by sight. <We perceive the sweet by sight> because
         in fact we have a perception of both, and by this we recognize them at
         the same time when they occur together. If this were not so, we would
         not perceive <the objects of one sense by another sense> in any way
    25   except coincidentally;[2] for instance, we see the son of Cleon, not because
         he is the son of Cleon, but because he is pale and the pale thing is
         coincidentally the son of Cleon.
         We have a common, noncoincidental, perception, however, of the
         common objects of perception. Hence they are not proper objects of any
         sense; for if they were, we would not perceive them in any way except
         the <coincidental> way just mentioned.

[HOW THE SENSES PERCEIVE ONE ANOTHER'S OBJECTS]

    30   The senses perceive one another's proper objects coincidentally, not
         insofar as each one is the sense it is,[3] but insofar as they are one sense.
         <The senses perceive one another's objects coincidentally> whenever
 425b   we perceive the same thing at the same time <with different senses>.
         This happens, for instance, whenever we perceive that bile is bitter and

    1. **coincidentally by each sense**: We do not, however, perceive them merely
coincidentally by all the senses together.

    2. **coincidentally**: Cf. 418a20.

    3. **insofar as they are one sense**: Lit. 'insofar as they are themselves'. It is not
(e.g.) the function of sight qua sight to perceive shape.

yellow—for surely it is not some further <sense besides sight and taste> that says the two[4] are one. That is why we are deceived and if something is yellow, we suppose it is bile. . . .[5]

* * * * * * *

[HOW WE PERCEIVE THAT WE PERCEIVE]

2

Since we perceive that we are seeing and hearing, it must be either sight   *425b12*
or a different sense by which we perceive that we are seeing. <In the
second case> the same sense will perceive both sight and the color
that is the <external> subject,[6] so that either there will be two senses
perceiving the same thing,[7] or else the sense will perceive itself. Again,   *15*
if the sense that perceives sight is different <from sight itself>, then
either it will go on without limit or there will be some sense that perceives
itself, so that one ought to make this claim about the first sense.[8]

Still, a puzzle arises. If perceiving by sight is seeing and if what we
see is color or something colored, then if we are seeing, the first case
of seeing will be colored.

It is evident, then, that perceiving by sight is not just one thing; for   *20*
indeed, whenever we are not seeing, we discriminate light and darkness,
but not in the same way. Moreover what sees is in fact colored in a way;
for a sense-organ receives the object of perception without its matter.
That is why, even when the objects of perception have gone away,
perceptions and appearances are still present in the sense-organs.   *25*

[THE ACTUALITY OF PERCEPTION IS THE SAME AS THE ACTUALITY OF ITS OBJECT]

The actuality of the object of perception and of the sense are one and
the same, but their being is not the same. I mean, for instance, that the
actual sound and the actual hearing <are one and the same>; for it is

4. **the two**: The bitter thing and the yellow thing.

5. **suppose . . . bile**: We do this because we assume that it is also bitter.

6. **<external> subject**: See SUBJECT #5.

7. **two . . . same thing**: This will happen if both sight and the additional sense
perceive color as their proper object.

8. **one ought . . . first sense**: If we postulate a further sense in order to avoid
saying that a sense can perceive itself, then even so we must eventually recognize
a sense that perceives itself, on pain of an infinite regress.

30   possible to have <the sense of> hearing without <actually> hearing, and what has sound is not always making a sound. But whenever what has the potentiality to hear is actually hearing, and what has the potentiality to sound is sounding, then actual hearing and actual sounding occur

426a   at the same time, so that we would say that one thing is a case of hearing and the other a case of sounding.

If, then, the motion and the action[9] are in the thing affected, both the sounding and the actual hearing must be in the <sense> that has the potentiality. For the actuality of what acts on something and initiates

5   motion in it comes to be in the thing affected—that is why what initiates motion need not be set in motion itself. Now, the actuality of what has the potentiality to sound is sound or sounding, while the actuality of what has a potentiality for hearing is hearing or listening;[10] for hearing is of two sorts, and so is sound.

The same account applies to the other senses and their objects. For

10   just as both acting on something and being affected are in the thing affected, not in the thing acting on it, so also both the actuality of the object of perception and the actuality of the perceiver are in the perceiver. In some cases, however, the two actualities have different names, as sounding and hearing have, while in other cases one of them has no name; for the actuality of sight is called seeing, whereas the actuality of color has no name, and the actuality of what has the potentiality to taste

15   is called tasting, whereas the actuality of flavor has no name.

And since the actuality of the object of perception and of what has the potentiality for perceiving are one, but their being is different, it follows that hearing and sounding (spoken of in this way), flavor and tasting, and so on, must all perish or remain in being at the same time. But this is not necessary for the things said to have the relevant potentiality.

20   In fact the earlier naturalists were wrong on this point, in supposing that nothing was pale or dark without sight, and that there was no flavor without taste. For in a way they were correct, but in a way incorrect. For perception and its object are spoken of in two ways, as potential

25   and as actual; in the case <of the actuality> what they say is correct, but in the case <of the potentiality> it is not. They, however, spoke without qualification about things that are not spoken of without qualification. . . .

*   *   *   *   *   *   *

9. **action**: Or 'production', *poiēsis*, i.e., the external body's acting on the sense.

10. **hearing or listening**: These two Greek words correspond to 'sight' and 'seeing'.

[APPEARANCE [11]]

[APPEARANCE CONTRASTED WITH PERCEPTION]

3

. . . If appearance* is that in virtue of which some object appears to us,[12]   428a1
in contrast to what is so called metaphorically, then is it one of those
potentialities or states in virtue of which we discriminate and attain truth
or falsity? These are perception, belief, knowledge$_e$, and understanding.   5
It is clear as follows that appearance is not the same as perception.
For perception is either a potentiality, such as sight, or an actuality, such
as seeing; but we have appearances when we have neither of these—
in dreams, for instance. Moreover, perception is present in every <ani-
mal>, but appearance is not.[13] If they were the same in actuality, then
it would be possible for all beasts to have appearance, whereas in fact   10
it does not seem possible <for all>; ants or bees, for instance, and grubs
<do not have it>.[14] Further, perceptions are always true, whereas most
appearances are false. Again, whenever we are actually perceiving accurately, we do not say that this appears to us <to be> a man; we are
more inclined to say <that something appears to be so> in cases where
we do not see clearly whether something is true or false. Further, as we   15
were saying before, sights appear to us even when we have our eyes
closed.

[APPEARANCE CONTRASTED WITH BELIEF]

The remaining question is whether appearance is belief; for belief may
also be either true or false. Belief, however, implies conviction—since   20
one cannot believe things if one does not find them convincing—whereas
no beasts have conviction, though many have appearance. Further, belief
implies conviction, conviction implies being persuaded, and persuasion
implies reason, whereas no beasts have reason, though some have appearance.
It is evident, then, that appearance is neither belief that involves   25
perception, nor belief that is produced through perception, nor a combi-

11. **appearance**: This might also be translated 'imagination' in this chapter.

12. **object appears to us**: Lit. 'some object-of-appearance (*phantasma*) arises for
us'.

13. **Moreover . . . appearance is not**: Cf. 414b15n.

14. **ants or . . . have it>**: Text uncertain. A plausible emendation: 'ants or bees,
for instance, <have it>, but grubs do not'.

nation of belief and perception.[15] This is so both for the reasons given and also because <on this view> belief will not be about anything other than the thing, if there is one, that is the object of perception.

30

428b

I mean, for instance, that the combination of a belief about the pale and a perception of the pale will turn out to be appearance; for surely it will not be the combination of a belief about the good and a perception of the pale—for appearance will be having a belief noncoincidentally about the very thing one perceives. In fact, however, we sometimes have false appearances about the same things at the same time as we have a true supposition about them, as when, for instance, the sun appears a foot across, even though we are convinced that it is bigger than the inhabited world.

5

It turns out, then, <on the view being considered> that either we have lost the true belief we had, even though the thing still exists and we have neither forgotten our belief nor been persuaded to change it, or else, if we still have the true belief, the same belief must at the same time be both true and false. But in fact it could have become false only if the thing changed without our noticing it. It follows, then, that appearance cannot be any of these things, nor a product of them.

[THE RELATION OF APPEARANCE TO PERCEPTION]

10

It is possible, however, when one thing has been set in motion, for a second thing to be set in motion by the first. Moreover, appearance seems to be a sort of motion, to involve perception, to be present in things that have perception, and to be about the objects of perception. Now, it is also possible for motion to result from actual perception, and this motion must be similar to the perception.

15

Hence this motion cannot occur without perception or in things that do not have perception. Things that have appearance act and are affected in many ways in accordance with it, and it can be either true or false. . . .

*   *   *   *   *   *   *

[*UNDERSTANDING*]

[UNDERSTANDING COMPARED WITH PERCEPTION]

4

429a10

Now we must consider the part by which the soul has knowledge$_g$ and intelligence, and ask whether it is separable, or it is not separable in magnitude but only in account;[16] and what its differentia is, and how understanding comes about.

---

15. **neither belief . . . and perception**: Contrast Plato, *Sophist* 264ab.

16. **not separable . . . account**: See SEPARABLE #3.

Now, if understanding[17] is like perceiving, it consists either in being affected by the object of intellect or in something else of the same sort. *15* Hence the intellect must be unaffected, but receptive of the form; it must have the quality <of the object> potentially, not actually; and it must be related to its object as the perceiving part is related to the objects of perception.

Hence the intellect, since it understands all things,[18] must be unmixed, in order, as Anaxagoras says, to 'master' them (i.e., to know$_g$ them); for *20* the intrusion of any foreign thing would hinder and obstruct it. And so it has no nature except this—that it is potential. Hence the part of the soul called intellect (by which I mean that by which the soul thinks and supposes) is not actually, before it understands, any of the things there are. It is also unreasonable, then, for intellect to be mixed with the body, *25* since it would then acquire some quality (for instance, hot or cold) or even, like the perceiving part, have some organ, whereas in fact it has none.

And so those who say that the soul is a place of forms are right, except that it is the intellectual soul, not the whole soul, which is— potentially, not actually—the forms.

The condition of the sense-organ and of the faculty of perception *30* makes it evident that the perceiving part and the intellectual part are unaffected in different ways. For after a sense perceives something very *429b* perceptible, it cannot perceive; after hearing very loud sounds, for instance, it cannot hear sound, and after seeing vivid colors or smelling strong odors, it cannot see or smell. But whenever intellect understands something that is very intelligible, it understands more, not less, about inferior objects;[19] for intellect is separable, whereas the perceiving part *5* requires a body.

When the intellect becomes each thing <that it understands>, as it does when someone is said to have actual knowledge$_e$ (this comes about whenever someone is able to actualize his knowledge through himself), even then it is still potential in a way, though not in the same way as before it learned or discovered; and then it is capable of understanding itself.[20]

---

17. **understanding**: In this chapter *noein* is rendered 'understand', and the term for the relevant faculty, *nous*, by 'intellect'. See UNDERSTANDING #2. 'Thought' and 'thinking' are reserved for *dianoia* and *dianoeisthai*. See *APo* 100b8n.

18. **understands all things**: i.e., is capable of understanding all kinds of things (it is not restricted to knowledge of birds as opposed to numbers).

19. **For after a sense . . . inferior objects**: We do not, for instance, find it more difficult to measure a room after thinking about complex geometry.

20. **understanding itself**: Reading *de hauton*. OCT: 'it is capable of understanding through itself'.

[THE OBJECTS OF UNDERSTANDING]

10   Magnitude is different from being magnitude and water from being water;[21] and the same applies in many other cases too, though not in all, since in some cases the thing is the same as its being.[22] It follows that to discriminate being flesh we use something different, or something in a different state, from what we use in discriminating flesh; for flesh requires matter, and, like the snub,* it is this <form> in this <matter>.
15   Hence to discriminate the hot and the cold and the things of which flesh is some sort of form₁, we use the perceptive part; but to discriminate being flesh, we use something else that is either separable <from body> or related to it as a formerly bent line is related to the straight line it has become.

   Further, if we turn to things whose being depends on abstraction,* the straight is similar to the snub, since it requires something continuous.
20   But if being straight is different from the straight, then so is the essence of straight (duality, let us say) different from the straight, and therefore to discriminate it we use something different, or something in a different state. In general, then, the <separability> of intellect corresponds to the way in which objects are separable from matter.

[PUZZLES ABOUT INTELLECT AND UNDERSTANDING]

   A puzzle arises. If intellect is simple and unaffected, having, as Anaxa-
25   goras says, nothing in common with anything, then how can it under- stand, if understanding consists in being affected? For it seems that two things must have something in common if one is to affect the other. Again, is intellect itself an object of intellect? For if nothing other <than itself> makes it an object of intellect, and if all objects of intellect are one in species, then the other objects of intellect will also be intellect; alternatively, it will need something mixed into it, to make it an object
30   of intellect in the same way as the other objects of intellect are.[23]
   On the other hand, our previous discussion of ways of being affected because of something in common has shown that the intellect is in a way potentially the objects of intellect, but before it understands them,
430a   it is none of them actually. Its potentiality is that of a writing tablet with nothing actually written on it—which is also true of intellect.
   Further, intellect itself is an object of intellect in the same way as its

21. **being water**: This translates *to einai* with the dative; see ESSENCE #2. In this chapter 'essence' renders *to ti ēn einai*.

22. **the thing is the same as its being**: See *Met.* 1036a1.

23. The next two paragraphs set out the account of thinking and being affected that is meant to solve the puzzles of this paragraph.

objects are. For in the case of things without matter, the understanding part and its object are one,[24] since actual knowledge$_e$[25] and its object are   5
the same. (We should investigate why it is not <engaged in the activity of> understanding all the time.) In things that have matter, each object of intellect is potentially present; hence intellect will not be in them (since it is a potentiality for being such things without their matter), but it will be an object of intellect.

[PASSIVE V. PRODUCTIVE INTELLECT [26]]

5

In the whole of nature each kind of thing has something as its matter,   10
which is potentially all the things in the kind, and something else as the cause and producer, which produces them all—for instance, the craft in relation to its matter. These differences, then, must also be found in the soul. One sort of intellect corresponds to matter, by becoming all things.   15
Another sort corresponds to the producer by producing all things[27] in the way that a state,[28] such as light, produces things—for in a way light makes potential colors into actual colors. This second sort of intellect is separable, unaffected,[29] and unmixed, since its essence$_o$ is actuality.

For in every case the producer is more valuable than the thing affected, and the principle is more valuable than the matter. Actual knowledge$_e$ 20
is the same as its object; potential knowledge is temporally prior in an individual <knower>, but in general it is not even temporally prior. But <productive intellect> does not understand at one time and not at another.

24. **the understanding . . . are one**: Cf. *Met.* 1072b18–21.

25. **actual knowledge**: Lit. 'attending (or 'contemplating', *theōrētikē*) knowledge', when we are actually attending to what we know; see 412a11n, 22, 417b5.

26. The text, translation, and interpretation of this chapter are all extremely doubtful. There are disputes about whether a numerically distinct productive intellect belongs to each individual soul or there is one productive intellect common to all souls, about the role of productive intellect in thought, and about its dependence on or independence of the senses and the body.

27. **One sort . . . producing all things**: Lit. 'One intellect is such by becoming all things, one by producing all things'.

28. **a state**: A state, *hexis*, is contrasted with some process of change. Light makes things visible simply by shining on them, not by undergoing any change in the course of shining on them. Aristotle may suggest that productive intellect is more like a permanent feature of intellect than like a potentiality that is activated at one time and not at another.

29. **unaffected**: Or perhaps 'impassible' (i.e., incapable of being affected).

Only when it has been separated is it precisely what it is, all by itself. And this alone is immortal and everlasting. But <when it is separated>³⁰ we do not remember, because this <productive intellect> is unaffected,³¹

25   whereas the intellect that is affected is perishable. And without this <productive intellect>³² nothing understands.

*   *   *   *   *   *   *

[DESIRE AND ACTION]

[THE ROLE OF THOUGHT AND DESIRE IN PRODUCING ACTION]

10

433a9   There are apparently two parts that move us—both intellect and desire*,
10   if we take appearance to be a kind of understanding.³³ For many people follow their appearances against their knowledge$_e$,³⁴ and the other animals have appearance but lack understanding and reasoning. Both intellect and desire, then, move us from place to place. This is the intellect
15   that reasons for some goal and is concerned with action; its <concern with an> end distinguishes it from theoretical intellect. All desire also aims at some goal; for the object of desire is the starting point³⁵ of intellect concerned with action, and the last stage <of our reasoning> is the starting point of action.

Hence it is reasonable to regard these two things—desire, and thought concerned with action—as the movers.³⁶ For the object of desire moves
20   us, and thought moves us because its starting point is the object of desire. Moreover, whenever appearance moves us, it requires desire.

And so there is one mover, the desiring part. For if there were two—

---

30. <when it is separated>: Or perhaps: <when it is embodied>.

31. this <productive . . . unaffected: We cannot remember without being affected.

32. without this <productive intellect>: Or perhaps 'without this <passive intellect>'.

33. if we take . . . understanding: In that case we will classify appearance under intellect.

34. For many . . . knowledge: And so if we do not recognize appearance as a kind of thought, we will have to recognize a third mover.

35. starting point: *archē*. See PRINCIPLE #2.

36. movers: i.e., initiators of MOTION. See *Phys.* viii 4–5.

intellect and desire—they would move us insofar as they had a common form. In fact, however, intellect evidently does not move anything without desire,[37] since wish is desire, and any motion in accordance with reasoning is in accordance with wish; desire, on the other hand, also *25* moves us against reasoning, since appetite is a kind of desire. Now, intellect is always correct, but desire and appearance may be either correct or incorrect. Hence in every case the mover is the object of desire, but the object of desire is either the good or the apparent good[38]—not every sort of good, but the good that is achievable in action. What is achievable in action admits of being otherwise.   *30*

Evidently, then, the potentiality of the soul that moves us is the one called desire. People who divide the soul into parts—if they divide it *433b* into separate parts corresponding to the different potentialities[39]—will find very many of them—the nutritive, perceptive, intellectual, and deliberative parts, and, moreover, the desiring part; for the difference between these parts is greater than the one between the appetitive and emotional parts.

[CONFLICTING DESIRES]

Desires that are contrary to each other arise, however, when reason and *5* appetite are contrary, which happens in subjects that perceive time. For intellect urges us to draw back because of what is to come, while appetite <urges us on> because of what is present; for the pleasant thing that is present appears both unqualifiedly pleasant and unqualifiedly good, because we do not see what is to come.   *10*

Hence the mover is one in species—the desiring part, insofar as it is desiring. Indeed, the first mover of all is the object of desire, since it moves us without being moved, by being present to understanding or appearance. But the movers are numerically more than one.[40]

37. **does not move anything without desire**: On the roles of thought and desire see *EN* 1139a35.

38. **the good or the apparent good**: Cf. *EN* iii 4.

39. **People who . . . emotional parts**: If we suppose that different potentialities pick out different SEPARABLE parts (i.e., parts capable of existing without any other parts of the soul), we will introduce too many separable parts. This does not mean that the division into parts (not necessarily separable) is illegitimate; cf. *EN* i 13.

40. **numerically more than one**: This is contrasted with being 'ONE in species' or 'one in form', *eidos*, i.e., one in kind. Cf. 415b7n.

[HOW DESIRE RESULTS IN ACTION]

We must distinguish three things—the mover, its instrument,[41] and the
15   subject moved. There are two types of movers: the unmoved mover[42]
and the moved mover. The unmoved mover is the good achievable in
action, and the moved mover is the desiring part; for the thing that is
moved is moved insofar as it desires, and desire, insofar as it is actual,
is a sort of motion. The thing moved is the animal. When we reach the
instrument by which desire moves, we reach something bodily, and so
20   we should study it when we study the functions common to soul and
body.[43]

To summarize for the present: What moves something as an instrument is found where the same thing is both the starting point and the
last stage. In the hinge-joint, for instance, the convex is last, and hence
at rest, while the concave is the starting point, and hence is moved.
25   These are different in account, though they are spatially inseparable.[44]
For since everything is moved by pushing and pulling, something must
remain at rest, as in a circle, and the motion must originate from this.

In general, then, as we have said, an animal moves itself insofar as
it has desire. For desire needs appearance; and appearance is either
30   rational appearance or the perceptual appearance that other animals
share <with human beings>.

[THE CONNECTION BETWEEN DESIRE AND APPEARANCE]

11

434a   We should also consider what moves incomplete animals, whose only
form of perception is touch. Can they have appearance and appetite, or
not? For they evidently have pleasure and pain; if they have these,
they must have appetite. But how could they have appearance?[45] Well,
5   perhaps, just as they are moved indeterminately, so also they have
appearance and appetite, but have them indeterminately.

Now, the other animals as well <as human beings> also have perceptual appearance, as we have said, but <only> reasoning animals have
deliberative appearance. For when we come to the question whether

41. **its instrument**: Lit. 'that by which it moves something'.

42. **unmoved mover**: See *Phys.* viii 5.

43. **functions common to soul and body**: These are discussed in the shorter
biological treatises called the *Parva Naturalia*, and in the *MA*.

44. **different . . . inseparable**: See SEPARABLE #3.

45. **But how . . . appearance?**: For previous comments on this question see
414b16n.

one is to do this or that, we come to a task for reasoning. And <in this case> one must measure by one <standard>, since one pursues the greater <good>. And so one is able to make one object of appearance   10
out of many.[46] And this is why <nonrational animals> do not seem to have belief; it is because they lack the <appearance> resulting from reasoning.

[CONFLICTS BETWEEN DESIRES]

That is why desire lacks the deliberative part.[47] And sometimes one desire overcomes and moves another, while sometimes the second over-comes and moves the first, like one sphere moving another, whenever incontinence[48] occurs. By nature the <desire> that is superior is domi-   15
nant in every case and moves <the agent>, and so it turns out that three motions[49] are initiated <in the agent>. The part that has knowledge, stays at rest and is not moved.

One sort of supposition and statement is universal, while another is about what is particular;[50] for the first says that this sort of agent ought to do this sort of thing, and the second says that this is this sort of thing and I am this sort of agent. Hence the second belief, not the universal   20
belief, initiates motion; or <rather> both initiate motion, but the first does so by being more at rest, in contrast to the second.

46. **to make one . . . many**: We can (1) consider the advantages and disadvantages of doing x and (2) consider the advantages and disadvantages of doing y. As a result of this we can (3) form one appearance incorporating the comparative advantages and disadvantages of doing x and doing y.

47. **desire lacks . . . part**: Desire by itself does not imply deliberation. In the next sentence Aristotle appears to be contrasting desires that rest on deliberation with desires that do not.

48. **incontinence**: Cf. *EN* i 13, vii 3.

49. **motions**: Lit. 'locomotions'.

50. **One sort of supposition . . . particular**: See DEDUCTION #4.

DE PARTIBUS ANIMALIUM[1]

Book I

[INTRODUCTION TO THE STUDY OF NATURE]

[THE IMPORTANCE OF GENERAL EDUCATION]

1

639a In every sort of study and line* of inquiry, more humble and more honorable* alike, there appear to be two sorts of competence. One of 5 these is rightly called scientific knowledge$_e$ of the subject, and the other is a certain type of education;* for it is characteristic of an educated person to be able to reach a judgment based on a sound estimate of when people expound their conclusions in the right or wrong way. For this is in fact what we take to be characteristic of a generally educated person, and this is the sort of ability that we identify with being educated. 10 We expect one and the same individual with this general education to be able to judge in practically all subjects; but if someone <is educated in some narrower area>, we take him to have this ability <only> for some determinate area—for it is possible for someone to have the ability of an educated person about a restricted area.[2]

Clearly, then, in inquiry* into nature as elsewhere, there must be standards[3] of this sort that we can refer to in deciding whether to accept 15 the way in which a conclusion is proved, apart from whether or not the conclusion is true.

1. 'On the parts of animals'. Text: A. L. Peck (London, 1937). The actual study of the parts of animals begins in Book ii. The chapters translated from Book i are a general discussion of the methods and value of biological studies. These are questions that should concern the EDUCATED person described in the first paragraph.

2. **for it is . . . area**: Aristotle has distinguished (1) the scientific KNOWLEDGE of an expert in a given area from (2) the EDUCATED critic's ability to judge what the expert says. He now divides (2) into (2a) the ability of someone who can judge every area of expertise, and (2b) the critic's ability applied to some specific area.

3. **standards**: See FORMULA #3.

[*THE RIGHT ORDER OF STUDY*]

Should we, for instance, consider each single substance[4]—the nature of man, for instance, or ox or any other <species>, taking them one at a time—and determine what belongs to it in its own right? Or should we begin with the coincidents[5] that belong to them all insofar as they have some common property? For often the same properties— *20* for instance, sleep, breathing, growth, shrinkage, death, and all the other attributes and conditions of this sort—belong to many different kinds[6] of things.

For, as things are, the right way to discuss these questions is unclear and indeterminate. Evidently, if we discuss them one species[7] at a time, we will repeat ourselves on many topics. For in fact each of the properties *25* mentioned actually belongs to horses, dogs, and human beings; and so, if we describe the coincidents one species at a time, we will be compelled to describe the same things many times over—in the case of each property that belongs to specifically different[8] animals but is not itself different in each species. Presumably, though, there are also properties that have *30* the same predicate but differ specifically in the different species. The *639b* mobility[9] of animals, for instance, is apparently not specifically one, since flying, swimming, walking, and creeping differ from one another.

Hence we should consider the right way to examine such questions: Should we begin by studying a whole genus in common before going *5* on to study the special properties of the different species? Or should we study the particular species one at a time? For, as things are, this has not been determined.

Another question that has not been determined is this: Should the student of nature follow the procedure of the mathematician who proves truths about astronomy? If he does, he will first study the appearances* about animals and about the parts of each type of animal, and then go *10* on to state the reason why and the causes. Or should he follow some other procedure?

---

4. **substance**: This refers to the 'secondary SUBSTANCE' described in *Catg.* 2a14.

5. **coincidents**: These include 'coincidents in their own right'. See COINCIDENT #2.

6. **kinds**: *genos*, usually rendered 'genus', but here applied to species.

7. **species**: We supply 'species' throughout this paragraph, since the next paragraph implies that Aristotle has had species in mind.

8. **specifically different**: See ONE #1.

9. **mobility**: Or 'progression'. We can apply this single term to the way animals move around (and so we can apply 'the same predicate'), but we must recognize that it is specifically different in different animals.

[THE RIGHT METHOD OF STUDY]

Further, we see that natural coming to be has more than one cause—
for instance, both the cause that is for* something and the cause that is
the source of the principle of motion. We must, then, also determine
15   which is primary and which is secondary among these.

The primary cause is apparently the one that we say is for something.
For this is the form$_1$,[10] and the form$_1$ is the principle, both in the products
of craft and equally in naturally constituted things. For the doctor or the
builder begins by focussing, by thought or perception, on the definition[11]
of health or a house, and goes on to supply the forms$_1$ and the causes of
each thing he produces, explaining why it should be produced in this way.
20   And, moreover, what something is for—i.e, the fine result—is more fully
present in the products of nature than in the products of craft.

[DIFFERENT TYPES OF NECESSITY]

Further, what is of necessity is not present in the same way in everything
that is in accordance with nature. Practically all <students of nature>,
however, try to refer their accounts back to what is of necessity, without
having distinguished the different ways necessity is spoken of.[12]
25   Unqualified necessity[13] belongs to everlasting things, whereas conditional necessity belongs to everything that comes to be, just as it belongs
to the products of crafts—to a house, for instance, and to anything else
of that sort. In such cases it is necessary for the right sort of matter to
be present if there is to be a house or some other end; first this must
come to be and be moved, then this, and so on in order in the same
30   way, until it reaches the end for which a thing comes to be and is.[14] And
640a   the same is true of what comes to be by nature.

[THE RIGHT METHOD OF DEMONSTRATION]

The appropriate type of demonstration and necessity, however, is not
the same in the study of nature as it is in the theoretical sciences;[15] we
have discussed this in another work. For in the latter case the principle

10. **form$_1$**: What the craftsman has in his soul is the 'form without the matter',
i.e., the *logos* of the product he means to produce. See FORM #7.

11. **focussing . . . on the definition**: Lit. 'by defining'—but Aristotle does not
mean that it is the doctor's task to decide what health is.

12. **without having . . . spoken of**: These other people ignore the significance
of HOMONYMY.

13. **Unqualified necessity**: See NECESSITY #4.

14. **In such cases . . . and is**: Cf. *Phys.* 200a5–15.

15. **theoretical sciences**: *theōrētikai*, i.e., those concerned only with STUDY, *theōria*.

we begin from[16] is what something is, but in the former case it is what
will be. For since F (for instance, health or a man) is of this sort, it is   5
necessary for G to be or to come to be,[17] whereas it is not true that since
G is or has come to be, F is or will be of necessity. Nor can you combine
the necessity of such demonstration for ever, so as to say that since one
thing is, another thing is. In another work[18] we have discussed both
these questions, and also the sorts of things that are necessary, and in
what cases necessities are reciprocal, and why.   10

[THE RESULT SHOULD BE STUDIED BEFORE THE PROCESS THAT LEADS TO IT]

We must also consider whether we should follow the procedure of our
predecessors, by studying how a thing naturally comes to be rather than
how it is. For it matters quite a bit which procedure we follow.

Now, it would seem that in the case of coming to be we should begin
from how things are; for, just as we said before, we must begin with
the appearances about a given kind of thing and then go on to state   15
their causes. For in the case of building also, this comes about because
the form of a house is of this sort, whereas it is not true that a house is
of this sort because this is how it comes to be; for coming to be is for
the sake of being$_o$,[19] but being$_o$ is not for the sake of coming to be.

That is why Empedocles was wrong to say that many things belong   20
to animals because they came about coincidentally in the course of the
animals' coming to be. He says, for instance, that the backbone has
vertebrae because of the coincidence that the foetus got twisted and the
backbone was broken. He did not know, first, that the seed resulting in
the animal must already have the right potentiality, and, secondly, that
the producer is prior in time as well as in account—for a human being   25
generates a human being, so that the character of the parent explains
the way in which the offspring comes to be.

The same point applies to the <natural> things that seem to come
to be by chance, as it also does in the case of things produced by craft.[20]

16. **the principle we begin from**: This translates *archē*, which refers both to the
starting point and to the basic principle of our DEMONSTRATION. See PRINCIPLE
#3. In this case the principle is a statement of what something is, i.e., of its
ESSENCE.

17. **For . . . come to be**: An example in which 'what will be' is the principle.

18. **In another work**: *GC* ii 11.

19. **being$_o$**: *ousia*. Aristotle uses this as the abstract noun corresponding to 'be'
in contrast to 'become', *gignesthai*.

20. **The same point . . . craft.**: A rather compressed note. Perhaps the point is
that since chance (*to automaton*; see LUCK #4) processes with results similar to
those of craft imitate the procedure of a craft, it is still appropriate in these cases
to study the result before the process. Cf. *Met.* 1034b4.

For some things—for instance, health—are the same when they come
30   to be by chance as when they come to be from craft. In those cases,
then, where the producer comes first (in statue-making, for instance),
the product does not come to be by chance. The craft is the account
(without the matter) of the product;[21] and the same is true for things
resulting from luck,* since how they come to be corresponds to the
character of the craft.

Hence the best thing to say is that since being a human being is this,
35   this is why he has these parts, since it is impossible for him to be without
these parts. If we cannot say this, we must come as close as we can,
and say either that it was quite impossible any other way or that it is
640b   done well this way. And these <means to the end> follow: since this
is the character of the product, it is necessary for the coming to be to
have this character and to happen in this way—that is why first this
part comes to be, and then this part. And the same is true equally in
5   the case of everything that is naturally constituted.

[WE MUST STUDY THE FORMAL CAUSE, NOT ONLY THE MATERIAL CAUSE]

The early philosophers,[22] the first to study nature, investigated the material principle and cause, to see what it is and of what sort, how the
whole universe comes to be from it, and what initiates the motion. <In
their view>, strife, for instance, or love, or mind, or chance initiates the
motion, and the matter that is the subject necessarily has a certain sort
10   of nature; fire, for instance, has a hot and light nature, earth a cold and
heavy nature. This, indeed, is their account of how the world order
comes into being.

They give the same sort of account of how animals and plants come
into being. On their account, for example, the flowing of water in the
body results in the coming to be of the stomach and of every receptacle
15   for food and waste, and the flow of air results in the breaking open of
the nostrils. Air and water are the matter of <living> bodies, since all
<these philosophers> constitute nature from <elementary> bodies of
this sort.

If, however, human beings and animals and their parts are natural,
20   then we should discuss flesh, bone, blood, and all the uniform parts,[23]
and equally all the nonuniform parts, for instance, face, hand, and foot;

21. **account . . . product**: See FORM #7.

22. **The early philosophers**: These are the NATURALISTS discussed in *Met.* i 3.

23. **we should . . . uniform parts**: And hence we should not confine ourselves
to discussing their elementary constituents, as the early philosophers did. On
uniform and nonuniform parts see PART #1–2.

and we should ask what gives each of them its character, and what potentiality is involved.

For it is not enough to say what constituents each of these parts is made of—of fire or earth, for instance. If we were speaking of a bed or any other <artifact>, we would try to distinguish its form rather than   25
its matter (for instance, bronze or wood), or at any rate <the relevant matter> would be the matter of the compound. For a bed is this form in this matter, or this matter of this sort.[24] And so we ought to speak of the thing's figure and the sort of character it has[25] as well <as of its matter>, since the nature corresponding to the form_m is more important[26]
than the material nature.   30

If, then, an animal and its parts have their being by having their figure[27] and color, what Democritus says will turn out to be right, since this is what he seems to suppose. At any rate he says it is clear to everyone what the human form_m is, on the assumption that a human being is known_g by his <visible> figure and his color. <This is false>, however, <since> a dead human being has the same <visible> shape and figure that the living human being has, but still it is not a human   35
being. Further, it is impossible for something <with the right figure and color> to be a hand, if it is not in the right condition—if, for instance, it is a bronze or wooden hand; in that case it can be a hand only homony-   641a
mously,[28] just as the doctor <painted in a picture is a doctor only homon-ymously>. For it will lack the potentiality to perform the function of a hand, just as the painted doctor or stone flute lacks the potentiality to perform the function of a doctor or flute. Similarly, none of the parts of a dead human being is any longer the relevant sort of part—an eye or   5
a hand, for instance.

Hence Democritus' claim lacks the appropriate qualifications; it is no better than a carpenter claiming that a wooden hand is a hand. For such a claim is typical of the naturalists'* account of the coming to be and the causes of something's figure. For suppose we ask, 'What potentialities produced this?' Presumably the carpenter will mention an axe or an   10
auger, whereas the naturalist will mention air and earth. The carpenter, however, gives the better answer.[29] For he will not suppose that it is

---

24. **this form . . . this sort**: Lit. 'this in this or this such'. Cf. *Met.* 1036b23–24, QUALITY.

25. **figure**: Here and in 641a8 the FIGURE seems to be the FORM. On 'form_m' see FORM #5.

26. **important**: See CONTROLLING.

27. **figure**: In this paragraph, the FIGURE seems to be the perceptible shape.

28. **only homonymously**: On this claim about HOMONYMY see MATTER #5.

29. **better answer**: Cf. *Phys.* 199b34–200a7.

enough to say that when his tool struck the wood, this part became
hollow and this part plane. He will also mention the cause that explains
why and for what end he struck this sort of blow—that is to say, in
15   order to produce this or that sort of shape.

It is clear, then, that the natural philosophers are wrong, and that we
must say that an animal has the <formal> character we have described.
We must say, both about the animal itself and about each of its parts,
what it is and what sort of thing it is, just as we also speak of the form
of the bed.

[SINCE WE MUST STUDY THE FORMAL CAUSE, WE MUST STUDY THE SOUL]

Now, this form is either the soul[30] or a part of the soul, or requires the
soul. At any rate, when the soul has left, the animal no longer exists,
20   and none of its parts remains the same, except in figure,[31] like the things
in stories that are turned to stone. If this is so, it is the task of the student
of nature[32] to discuss and to know₀ about the soul—if not about all soul,
then about the soul insofar as it makes the animal the sort of thing it is.
He should know what the soul is, or what the relevant part of it is, and
25   he should know about the coincidents that belong to it insofar as it has
this sort of substance.

This is especially important because nature is, and is spoken of, in
two ways, as matter and as substance. Now, substance is both the cause
initiating motion and the end; and the soul, all or part of it, is both sorts
of cause of the animal.[33] Hence, for this reason also, the student of nature
30   should discuss the soul more than the matter, to the extent that the
<animal's> matter is its nature because of the soul, rather than the
other way round—for the wood is a bed or a tripod because it is one
potentially.[34]

Reflection on what we have said might raise a puzzle about whether

30. **Now, this form is either the soul**: Lit. 'If this . . . '. The whole sentence is part
of the if-clause, which is resumed (after the explanatory parenthesis beginning at
'At any rate. . . ') at 'If this is so', in the next sentence. But Aristotle clearly
accepts the content of the if-clause.

31. **figure**: the perceptible shape.

32. **student of nature**: *phusikos*. On this task cf. DA 404a24–b19.

33. **the soul . . . cause of the animal**: On the soul as cause cf. DA ii 415b8–28.

34. **potentially**: Aristotle implies that the wood of an actual bed is only potentially
a bed. For this claim about MATTER and potentiality cf. POTENTIALITY #4, DA
412a19–21, 27–28, b25–27, Met. 1049a15–18.

the study of nature should consider all soul, or only some.[35] If it considers   *35*
all soul, then there will be no branch of philosophy apart from the science
of nature. For since understanding* grasps the objects of understanding,   *641b*
the study of nature will be knowledge_g of everything. For if two correlatives fall under the same study, as perception and its object do, and if
understanding and its object are correlatives, then the same study will
be concerned both with understanding and with its object.

Perhaps, however, not all soul, and not every part of soul, is a principle   *5*
of motion. Rather, perhaps the principle of growth is the same part as
in plants, the principle of alteration is the perceiving part, and the principle of local motion is some other part[36] distinct from understanding,
since local motion is found in other animals as well as in human beings,
but understanding is not found in any of them. It is clear, then, that we
should not discuss all soul; for it is not all soul, but only one or more   *10*
parts of it, that is nature.

[NATURAL PROCESSES HAVE FINAL CAUSES]

Further, it is impossible for natural science to study any product of
abstraction,* because nature produces everything for something.[37] For
it is apparent that, just as craft is present in artifacts, so also in natural
things themselves there is another cause and principle of this sort, which
we get, as we get the hot and the cold, from the whole universe. Hence   *15*
it is more plausible to suppose that the heaven* has come to be by such
a cause (if indeed it has come to be at all) and remains in being because
of it, than to suppose this about mortal animals. For what is ordered
and determinate is far more apparent in the heavens than in us, whereas   *20*
variations from one time to another and matters of chance are more
apparent in mortal things.

Some other people, however, hold that whereas every animal comes
to be and remains in being by nature, the heaven was constituted as it

35. **all . . . some**: This might mean (a) the whole of the (human) soul or only
some part of it or (b) every type of soul or only some types of soul and not
others. 641b9–10 suggests that (a) is the primary contrast; but Aristotle probably
has both contrasts in mind, since the division of types of soul ultimately rests
on the division of parts (cf. *DA* 414b28–415a13).

36. **some other part**: Presumably the desiring part. For this division of parts of
the soul cf. *DA* 413b11–414a3.

37. **Further, it is . . . for something**: For this connection between final causes
in biology and the essentially material character of natural organisms cf. *Met.*
1035b22–24, 1036b28–32.

25

30

is from luck and chance. They say this even though nothing at all resulting from luck and disorder is apparent in the heaven.[38]

Again, whenever some end is apparent toward which a motion progresses if nothing impedes, we say that the motion is for the end. Hence it is evident that there is something of this sort, which we call nature. For not just any old thing comes to be from a given type of seed, but this sort of thing from this sort of seed; nor does any old body produce any old seed. Hence the <body> that the seed comes from is the principle that produces the seed that comes from it. For this happens naturally—at any rate, the body grows naturally from the seed.

35

642a

But prior still is what it is the seed of. For the seed is a case of becoming, and the end is being$_o$. And what produces the seed is prior both to the seed and to what comes from the seed. For it is a seed in two ways—as the seed produced by something and as the seed of something.[39] For in fact it is the seed of what produced it (for instance, a horse), and also the seed of what comes to be from it (for instance, a mule), but it is not the seed of both in the same way; it is the seed of each in the way just described. Moreover, the seed is potentially[40] <the organism>, and we know how potentiality is related to actuality.

[FINAL CAUSES AND NECESSITY]

5

There are, then, two causes—what something is for and what is of necessity (since many things come to be because it is necessary <for them to come to be>). And presumably a puzzle might arise about the sort of necessity that is meant by those who speak of what is of necessity; for neither of the two types defined in our treatises on philosophy[41] can apply to this case.

10

There is a third type, however, in things that come to be. For we speak of food as necessary in neither of these two ways, but because an organism cannot exist without it. This, one might say, is conditional necessity.[42] For instance, since an axe is needed for splitting wood, it is necessary for it to be hard; and in that case it is necessary for it to be made of iron.[43] In the same way, the body is also an instrument,* since

38. **They say . . . heaven**: Cf. *Phys.* 196a24–b5.

39. **For it is . . . seed of something**: For these two ways cf. *Met.* 1072b30–1073a3.

40. **the seed is potentially**: For a more elaborate statement see *Met.* 1048b37–1049a18.

41. **our treatises on philosophy**: It is not clear what work Aristotle refers to.

42. **conditional necessity**: This has already been introduced at 639b24. See NECESSITY #4.

43. **since an axe . . . of iron**: Cf. *Phys.* 200a11–15.

each of its parts, and the whole likewise, is for something; it is necessary, then, for it to be of this sort and to be composed of things of this sort, if what it is for is to result.

It is clear, then, that there are two types of cause and that in what   15
we say we must either find both of them or, alternatively, try to make it clear, at any rate, that we cannot find both.[44] It is also clear that people who do not do this might be said to tell us nothing about nature; for nature is a principle more than matter is.

[PREVIOUS NATURAL PHILOSOPHERS WERE ONLY DIMLY AWARE OF FORMAL AND FINAL CAUSES]

Sometimes, indeed, Empedocles is led by the truth itself,[45] and stumbles on the right sort of cause, and is compelled to say that the form$_1$ is a   20
thing's substance and nature. When, for instance, he expounds what bone is, he does not say that it is one, two, three, or all of its elements, but that it is the form$_1$ of their mixture. It is clear, then, that flesh and every other part of that sort have this character.

The reason our predecessors did not discover this character is that   25
they did not grasp the essence or the practice of defining substance. Democritus[46] was the first to make some contact with them, but that was all he did—and not because he supposed it to be necessary for the study of nature, but because the facts themselves carried him away <from his own views>. In the time of Socrates,[47] this <concern with essence and definition> grew, but investigation into nature stopped, and philosophers turned away to studying the virtue that is relevant to   30
the conduct of life, and to political study.

[THE PROPER EXPOSITION OF THE TWO TYPES OF CAUSES]

Our proof should be on these lines—that respiration, for instance, is for this, but this comes about because of these things of necessity. Necessity sometimes signifies that if that end is to result, it is necessary for these things to be; and sometimes that they are so by nature.[48] <In the second   35
case> it is necessary, for instance, for the hot to go out and to come back in when it meets resistance, and for the air to flow in. This is all

44. **try to . . . both**: Read *dēlon ge peirasthai poiein, dēlon*.

45. **led by the truth itself**: Cf. *Phys.* 188b29–30, *Met.* 986b31.

46. **Democritus**: See DEMOCRITUS #2.

47. **Socrates**: Cf. *Met.* 1078b17–23.

48. **they are so by nature**: This refers to 'unqualified necessity', introduced above at 639b24.

642b necessary; and when the hot that is inside resists as cooling goes on, the air outside enters or leaves.

This, then, is the procedure of our line* of inquiry, and these are the sorts of things whose causes we must find.

* * * * * * *

[THE VALUE OF NATURAL PHILOSOPHY]

5

644b22 Among the substances constituted by nature, some, we say, neither come to be nor perish[49] for all time, and others share in coming to be
25 and perishing. It turns out that we have fewer ways of studying the first type of substances, honorable[50] and divine though they are; for very few things indeed are apparent in perception to give us a basis for inquiry into what we would like to know about these things. We are better
30 supplied, however, with opportunities for knowledge$_g$ about perishable plants and animals, since we live among them. For someone willing to undertake the appropriate labor can discover many of the facts about each kind of plant and animal.

Each of the two types of substance has some appeal. For even though we have little contact with the divine substances, still their honorable nature makes it pleasanter to know them than to know all the things
35 around us—just as a chance glimpse of some small part of someone we
645a love is pleasanter than an exact view of many other great things. On the other hand, since we can know$_e$ better and know more about the substances around us, the knowledge of them has some superiority. Further, the fact that they are closer to us and more akin to our nature compensates to some degree for <the superior attraction of> philosophy about divine things.

5 We have finished our discussion of divine things,[51] saying what appears to us.[52] The remaining task, then, is to speak of animal nature, whether more or less honorable, leaving nothing out, as far as possible. For even though some of the animals we study are unattractive to perception, still the nature that has produced them provides amazing pleasures
10 for those who are capable of knowing$_g$ the causes and are naturally

49. **neither . . . nor perish**: Or 'can neither come to be nor perish'. Aristotle's terms *agenētos* and *aphthartos* are ambiguous, as words ending in -*tos* often are. See *Phys.* 251b15n, SEPARABLE #1.

50. **honorable**: See HONOR.

51. **divine things**: in the *De Caelo*.

52. **appears to us**: See APPEARANCES. Aristotle indicates the tentativeness of his views. See *Met.* 1074a16.

philosophers.* For in studying representations of them, we also delight in studying the painter's or sculptor's craft that has produced them; how absurd it would be, then, not to like studying those naturally constituted things themselves, provided, of course, that we are able to notice the 15 causes.

That is why we must avoid childish complaints about examining the less honorable animals; for in all natural things there is something admirable.* The story goes that when some strangers wanted to see Heracleitus, they stopped on their way in, since they saw him warming himself at the oven;[53] but he kept urging them, 'Come in, and don't worry; for 20 there are gods here also.' In the same way, then, we must go forward without embarrassment with our search into each type of animal, assuming that there is something natural and fine in each of them.

For <processes> that are for something and are not a matter of luck are most characteristic of the products of nature; and the end for which 25 these things are constituted or have come to be counts as something admirable. And anyone who regards the study of other animals as dishonorable ought to take the same view about himself; for one is bound to feel great distaste at the constituents of the human species[54]—blood, 30 flesh, bones, veins, and parts of that sort.

Similarly, when someone is discussing some part or equipment, we should not suppose that he is drawing attention <simply> to the matter, or that he is concerned with it for its own sake; he is concerned with the form$_m$ as a whole. In the case of a house, for instance, <we are concerned with the form>, not with the bricks, mud, and wood. So 35 also, in studying nature we are concerned with the composite structure and with the substance as a whole, not with the things that are never found in separation from their substance.[55]

53. **warming himself at the oven**: Perhaps a euphemism for going to the lavatory.

54. **species**: *genos*, usually translated 'genus'.

55. **never found . . . substance**: On the type of matter that is inseparable from the organism that it constitutes see MATTER #5.

DE MOTU ANIMALIUM[1]

[THOUGHT, DESIRE, AND ACTION]

7

701a7 How is it that thought[2] sometimes results in action or motion, and
sometimes does not? What happens would seem to be more or less the
10 same as when one thinks and deduces about immobile things.[3] In this
latter case, however, the goal is <a proposition that we> study; for when
one has thought the two premisses, one has thought and composed the
conclusion. In the former case, by contrast, the conclusion from the two
premisses becomes the action.

For example, whenever someone thinks that every man should walk,
15 and he is himself a man, at once he walks. And if he thinks that no man
should walk now, and he is himself a man, at once he stays where he
is. And he does each of these things unless something prevents him
<from doing it> or compels him <to do something else. Or take another
example:> 'I should make something good, and a house is something
good.' At once he makes a house. 'I need a covering, and a cloak is a
covering; I need a cloak. What I need I should make; I need a cloak; I
20 should make a cloak.' And the conclusion, 'I should make a cloak', is
an action.[4]

The action begins from a principle:[5] 'To make a cloak I must first do

---

1. 'On the movement of animals'. Text: E. S. Forster (London, 1937). This is
one of Aristotle's short biological treatises. This chapter deals with thought,
desire, and practical inference; see DEDUCTION #4.

2. **thought**: See UNDERSTANDING.

3. **immobile things**: in theoretical sciences.

4. **is an action**: Possible interpretations: (a) It becomes an action (i.e., it is acted
on; see above). (b) It describes an action. (c) There is really no propositional
conclusion, but only an action, resulting from the combination of the two premisses. The previous example makes (c) unlikely.

5. **principle**: See PRINCIPLE #3.

A, and to do A I must do B', and at once he does B.[6] It is evident, then, that the conclusion is the action; the premisses leading to production proceed through two sorts of things—through the good and through the possible.   25

But in this case, as in some types of questioning,[7] thought does not pause to examine the obvious second premiss at all. If, for instance, walking is good for a man, someone does not linger over <the thought> that he is a man. And that is why whatever is done without rational calculation is done quickly. For whenever someone is actually aware[8] of the object of his desire by perception or appearance or thought, he acts   30 at once; for the actualized desire turns out to replace questioning or thought. 'I should drink', says appetite. 'And this is drinkable', says perception or appearance. At once he drinks.

This, then, is the way in which animals have an impulse toward motion and action; the last cause[9] of motion is desire, and this results   35 either from perception or from appearance or thought. And among agents that desire to act, some produce or act because of appetite or emotion, some because of wish.[10]   701b

The way in which animals are set in motion is similar to the case of puppets,[11] which are set in motion by a small motion, when the strings are released and strike one another. It is also similar to <a child's> wagon; the child himself who is riding on it moves it straight ahead, and yet it is moved in a circle because its wheels are unequal in size—   5 for the smaller wheel acts as a center, as is also true in the case of the cylinders <in puppets>. For animals have organs[12] of the same sort— <that is> the nature of their sinews and bones. The bones correspond to the wooden <pegs in the puppet>, and the sinews correspond to

---

6. **To make . . . does B.**: Lit. 'if there is to be a cloak, then necessarily this first, and if this, then this, and at once he does this.' In this example B—the thing I can do here and now—is the proximate PRINCIPLE of the action. Cf. *EN* 1139a31, 1147a24–31.

7. **types of questioning**: In DIALECTICAL question-and-answer the questioner need not explicitly put a question in cases where the answer is obvious.

8. **actually aware**: Lit. 'is actual by perception'. Cf. *DA* 417a21–29.

9. **last cause**: i.e., the last one we come to in thought. It is the proximate cause of motion; hence it is the 'first cause' previously mentioned. Aristotle refers to the desire for this particular thing.

10. **because of wish**: Reading *dia boulēsin*. MSS: *di' orexin ē boulēsin* ('because of desire or wish').

11. **puppets**: *automata*. See LUCK #4.

12. **organs**: *organa*. See INSTRUMENT.

10   the strings whose loosening and releasing results in the \<puppet's\>
motion.

Now, in the puppets and wagons there is no alteration;* for if the
internal wheels \<in the wagons\> were to become smaller and again
larger, \<the wagon\> would still have the same circular motion.[13] But
in an animal the same thing is able to grow bigger and smaller and to
15   change shape, as its parts expand because of heat and contract again
because of cold, and are \<thus\> altered.

These alterations are initiated by appearances,* perceptions, and
thoughts. For perceptions are, as such, a kind of alteration, while appearance and thought have the same power as their objects. For in a way
20   the form grasped by thought—of hot or cold or pleasant or frightening—
in fact has the character of the thing whose form it is;[14] and that is
why the \<mere\> thought \<that something is frightening\>[15] results in
shuddering and fear. And all these affections[16] are also alterations. As
a result of \<these\> alterations, some things in the body expand and
some contract.[17]

25   Now, it is clear that a small change occurring at the starting point[18]
produces large and numerous differences at a distance—just as a tiny
shift of a boat's rudder results in a large shift of the prow. Further,
whenever there is an alteration in the area of the heart—even in an
imperceptibly small part of it—corresponding to the degree of heating
or chilling or some other affection of that sort, it produces a large difference in the body through blushing, pallor, shudderings, tremblings, and
their contraries.

13. **for if . . . motion**: The qualitative changes would make no difference.

14. **in fact has . . . form it is**: On the similarity of the form grasped in perception
to the external object see *DA* 417a18–20, 418a3–6.

15. **thought . . . frightening\>**: Or perhaps 'thought of something frightening'.

16. **affections**: Or 'ways of being affected'. See ATTRIBUTE #3.

17. **As a result . . . expand**: Lit. 'things being altered, some things in the body
expand', or perhaps 'some things in the body being altered, some things expand'.

18. **starting point**: See PRINCIPLE #1.

METAPHYSICS[1]

Book I

[THE SCIENCE OF FIRST CAUSES]

[SCIENCE AND CRAFT GROW FROM SENSE-PERCEPTION, MEMORY, AND EXPERIENCE]

1

All human beings by nature desire to know$_o$. A sign of this is our liking   *980a21*
for the senses; for even apart from their usefulness we like them for
themselves—especially the sense of sight, since we choose seeing above
practically all the others, not only as an aid to action, but also when we
have no intention of acting. The reason is that sight, more than any   *25*
of the other senses, gives us knowledge$_g$ of things and clarifies many
differences among them.

    Animals possess sense-perception by nature at birth. In some but not
all of these, perception results in memory, making them more intelligent   *980b*
and better at learning than those that cannot remember. Some animals[2]
that cannot hear sounds (for instance, bees and similar kinds of animal)
are intelligent but do not learn; those that both perceive sounds and   *25*
have memory also learn.

    Nonhuman animals live by appearances and memories but have little
share in experience, whereas human beings also live by craft[3] and reasoning. In human beings experience results from memory, since many memories of the same thing result in the potentiality for a single experience.[4]   *981a*
Experience seems to be quite like science and craft, and indeed human
beings attain science and craft through experience; for, as Polus[5]

---

1. On this title see PHILOSOPHY #2.

2. **Some . . . also learn**: This explains why INTELLIGENCE (here used in a rather
reduced sense) and the capacity to learn are not the same.

3. **craft**: 'CRAFT', like 'knowledge', applies both to a cognitive state and to what
is grasped by someone in that state.

4. **experience**: See *APo* 100a3–6.

5. **Polus**: A rhetorical theorist of the mid-fifth century, and a pupil of Gorgias.
He is a character in Plato's *Gorgias*.

5 correctly says, experience has produced craft, but inexperience only
luck.[6]

A craft arises when many thoughts that arise from experience result
in one universal view* about similar things.[7] For the view that in this
illness this treatment benefited Callias, Socrates, and others, in many
10 particular cases, is characteristic of experience, but the view that it benefited everyone of a certain sort (marked out by a single kind)[8] suffering
from a certain disease (for instance, phlegmatic or bilious people when
burning with fever) is characteristic of craft.

[CRAFT IS SUPERIOR TO EXPERIENCE BECAUSE IT KNOWS CAUSES]

For practical purposes, experience seems no worse than craft; indeed
we even see that experienced people are actually more successful than
15 those who have a rational account but lack experience.[9] The reason is
that experience is knowledge$_g$ of particulars, whereas craft is knowledge
of universals. Moreover, each action and event concerns a particular; in
medical treatment, for instance, we do not heal man (except coinciden-
20 tally) but Callias or Socrates or some other individual[10] who is coincidentally a man.[11] If, then, someone has a rational account but lacks experience, and knows$_g$ the universal but not the particular falling under it,
he will often give the wrong treatment, since treatment is applied to the
particular.
25 Nonetheless, we attribute knowing$_o$ and comprehending to craft more
than to experience, and we suppose that craftsmen are wiser than experienced people, on the assumption that in every case knowledge$_o$, rather
than experience, implies wisdom. This is because craftsmen know$_o$ the
cause, but <merely> experienced people do not; for experienced people
know$_o$ the fact that something is so but not the reason why it is so,[12]
30 whereas craftsmen know$_g$ the reason why, i.e., the cause.

6. **luck**: i.e., good LUCK (the best that one can hope for without craft-
knowledge).

7. **craft . . . similar things**: On craft and UNIVERSALS cf. *Rhet.* 1356b30–35.

8. **kind**: *eidos*.

9. **we even . . . without experience**: On the usefulness of experience cf. *EN*
1141b14–22.

10. **some other individual**: Lit. 'someone else spoken of in this way'.

11. **coincidentally a man**: i.e., coincidentally from the point of view of healing.
Aristotle does not mean that being a man is a COINCIDENTAL property of Socrates.

12. **that . . . why**: Cf. *APo* 93a16, *EN* 1095b6.

[KNOWLEDGE OF CAUSES IS CHARACTERISTIC OF WISDOM]

That is why we believe that the master craftsmen[13] in a given craft are more honorable, know$_o$ more, and are wiser than the manual craftsmen, because they know$_o$ the causes of what is produced. The manual craftsmen, we think, are like inanimate things that produce without knowing$_o$ what they produce, in the way that, for instance, fire burns; the latter produce their products by a natural tendency, while the manual craftsmen produce theirs because of habit. We assume, then, that some craftsmen are wiser than others not because they are better in practice, but because they have a rational account and know$_g$ the causes.　　981b

　　5

And in general, a sign that distinguishes those who know$_o$ from those who do not is their ability to teach. Hence we think craft, rather than experience, is knowledge$_e$, since craftsmen can teach, while merely experienced people cannot.　　10

Further, we do not think any of the senses is wisdom,* even though they are the most authoritative ways of knowing$_g$ particulars. They do not tell us why anything is so; for instance, they do not tell us why fire is hot, but only that it is hot.

[THEORETICAL WISDOM IS CHARACTERISTICALLY PURSUED FOR ITS OWN SAKE]

It is not surprising, then, that in the earliest times anyone who discovered any craft that went beyond the perceptions common to all was admired* not only because he discovered something useful, but also for being a wise person, superior to others. Later on, as more crafts were discovered—some related to necessities, others to <leisuretime> pursuits—those who discovered these latter crafts were in every case taken to be wiser than the others, because their sciences did not aim at practical utility. Hence, finally, after all these crafts had been established, the sciences that aim neither at pleasure nor at necessities were discovered, initially in the places where people had leisure. This is why mathematical crafts arose first in Egypt; for there the priestly class were allowed to be at leisure.　　15　　20　　25

The difference between craft and science and other similar sorts of things has been discussed in the Ethics.[14] The point of our present discussion is to show that in everyone's view any discipline deserving the name of wisdom must describe[15] the first causes, i.e., the principles.* And so, as we said earlier, the experienced person seems to be wiser　　30

13. **master craftsmen**: Cf. *Phys.* 194a33–b7.

14. **the *Ethics***: See *EN* vi 2.

15. **any discipline . . . must describe**: Lit. 'what is called "wisdom" describes'.

982a than those who have just any old perception; the craftsman seems to be wiser than those with nothing more than experience; the master craftsman wiser than the manual craftsman; and the purely theoretical[16] sciences wiser than the productive sciences. It is clear, then, that wisdom is knowledge$_e$ of certain sorts of principles and causes.

[COMMON BELIEFS ABOUT WISDOM AND THE WISE PERSON]

2

5 Since this is the science we are seeking, we should consider what sorts of causes and principles wisdom is the science of. Perhaps this will become clearer if we consider our views about the wise person. First, we suppose that he has knowledge$_e$ about all things as far as possible, without, however, having it about each particular <kind of thing>.

10 Next, the one who is capable of knowing$_g$ difficult things, i.e., things not easily known by human beings, is the wise person; for sense-perception is common to everyone, and that is why it is easy and not characteristic of wisdom. Further, someone is wiser in a given science if he is more exact,* and a better teacher of the causes. Again, if one of two sciences

15 is choiceworthy for itself—<purely> for the sake of knowing$_o$ it—and the other is choiceworthy <only> for the sake of its results, the first has a better claim to be wisdom than the second. Moreover, the superior science has a better claim than the subordinate science; for the wise person must give orders, not take them, and those who are less wise

20 must follow his orders, not he theirs. These, then, are our views about wisdom and wise people.

[THE SCIENCE OF THE HIGHEST PRINCIPLES FITS THESE COMMON BELIEFS]

Of these features, we suppose that knowledge$_e$ about everything necessarily belongs to the one who has the best claim to universal science; for he in a way[17] knows$_o$ everything that is a subject for a science. These most universal things are also just about the most difficult for human

25 beings to know$_g$, since they are furthest from perceptions.[18] Further, the most exact sciences are those that, more than the others, study the first things; for the sciences that are derived from fewer principles (for instance, arithmetic) are more exact than those (for instance, geometry)

16. **theoretical**: See STUDY #3.

17. **in a way**: This qualification is added to show that the wise person's knowledge is not an encyclopedic collection of particular facts.

18. **furthest from perceptions**: Cf. *APo* 72a1–5.

that require further principles. Moreover, the science that studies the
causes is more of a teacher, since teachers are those who state some-   30
thing's causes. Besides, knowledge$_o$ and science for their own sake are
most characteristic of the science of the most appropriate object of
knowledge$_e$. For one who chooses knowledge$_e$ for its own sake will
choose above all the science that is a science to the highest degree. This   982b
science is the science of the most appropriate objects of knowledge$_e$;
these objects are the first things, i.e., the causes, since we know$_g$ the
subordinate things because of these and from these, not the other way
round. Further, the most superior science—the one that is superior to   5
any subordinate science—is the one that knows$_g$ the end for which a
given thing should be done; this end is something's good, and in general
the end is what is best in every sort of nature.[19]

From everything that has been said, then, we find that the name
under discussion, <i.e.,'wisdom'>, applies to the same science; for we
find that wisdom must study the first principles and causes, and the   10
good, the end, is one of the causes.[20]

[WISDOM IS THE RESULT OF WONDER, NOT OF NEED, AND IS PURSUED FOR ITS OWN SAKE, NOT FOR SOME FURTHER USE]

The fact that this science is not productive is also clear from those who
first engaged in philosophy.* For human beings originally began philosophy, as they do now, because of wonder, at first because they wondered
at the strange things in front of them, and later because, advancing little
by little, they found greater things puzzling—what happens to the moon,   15
the sun and the stars, how the universe comes to be. Someone who
wonders and is puzzled thinks he is ignorant (this is why the myth-
lover is also a philosopher in a way, since myth is composed of wonders);
since, then, they engaged in philosophy to escape ignorance, they were   20
evidently pursuing scientific knowledge for the sake of knowing$_o$, not
for any further use.

What actually happened is evidence for this view. For it was only
when practically everything required for necessities and for ease and
<leisuretime> pursuits was supplied that they began to seek this sort
of understanding;[21] clearly, then, we do not seek it for some further use.   25
Just as we describe a free* person as one who exists for his own sake

19. **every sort of nature**: Aristotle assumes that the science that knows the causes
knows this end. Less probably, 'nature as a whole'.

20. **for we find . . . causes**: And so the study of the good comes under the study
of the causes.

21. **understanding**: *phronēsis*. See INTELLIGENCE.

and not for someone else's,[22] so we also describe this as the only free science, since it is the only one that exists for its own sake.

[IT IS THEREFORE A PREEMINENTLY DIVINE SCIENCE]

30 Hence the possession of this science might justifiably be thought to be beyond human capacity. For in many ways human nature is in slavery, so that, as Simonides says, 'the god alone would have this privilege', and it is unfitting for human beings to transgress their own level in their search for the science. If there actually is something in what the poets
983a say, and the divine nature is spiteful,* divine spite would be likely in this case, and all those who go too far would suffer misfortunes. The divine nature, however, cannot be spiteful: as the proverb says, 'Poets tell many lies'.[23]

Nor ought we to take any science to be more honorable than this one,
5 since the most divine science is also the most honorable, and this science that we are describing is the most divine. It alone is most divine in two ways: for the divine science <may be understood> as (i) the one that a god more than anyone else would be expected to have, or as (ii) the science of divine things. Only this science <of first causes> satisfies both conditions <for being divine>. For (i) the god[24] seems to be among the causes of all things, and to be some sort of principle, and (ii) this is
10 the sort of science that the god, alone or more than anyone else, would be expected to have. Hence all the other sciences are more necessary than this one, but none is better.

[WISDOM BOTH ARISES FROM WONDER, AND REMOVES WONDER]

However, the possession of this science must in a way leave us in a condition contrary to the one we were in when we began our search. For, as we said, everyone begins from wonder that something is the
15 way it is, as they wonder at toys that move spontaneously,[25] or the turnings of the sun, or the incommensurability of the diagonal (for people who have not yet studied the cause are filled with wonder that there is something that is not measured by the smallest length). But we must end up in the contrary and (according to the proverb) the better state, the one that people achieve by learning <the cause> in these other cases

22. **free . . . someone else's**: The FREE person is contrasted with the SLAVE.

23. **The divine . . . lies'**: For this reply to criticisms of pursuits above the human level cf. *EN* 1177b31; Plato, *Epin.* 988ab, *Laws* 821ab.

24. **the god**: See GOD #2.

25. **toys that move spontaneously**: *ta automata.* See CHANCE.

as well—for nothing would be more amazing to a geometer than if the   *20*
diagonal turned out to be commensurable.

We have described, then, the nature of the science we are seeking,
and the goal that our search and our whole line of inquiry must reach.

[SURVEY OF PREVIOUS PHILOSOPHERS: THE PRESOCRATICS[26]]

[THE FOUR CAUSES]

3

It is evident, then, that we must acquire knowledge$_e$ of the original causes,
since we say we know$_o$ a thing whenever we think we know$_g$ its primary   *25*
cause. Causes are spoken of in four ways. One of these, we say, is the
being$_o$ and essence; for the reason why is traced back ultimately to the
account, and the primary reason why is the cause and principle.[27] Another
is the matter and subject. A third is the source of the principle of motion.[28]   *30*
The fourth is what something is for,* i.e., the good—the opposite to the
third cause, since it is the end[29] of all coming to be and motion.

We have studied these causes adequately in our work on nature.[30]
Still, let us also enlist those who previously took up the investigation of   *983b*
beings and pursued philosophical study about the truth; for it is clear
that they also mention causes and principles of some sort. A discussion
of their views, then, will advance our present line of inquiry; for either   *5*
we shall find some other kind of cause or we shall be more convinced
about those we have just mentioned.

[THE MATERIAL CAUSE]

Most of the first philosophers, then, thought that the only principles of
all things were material. For, they say, there is some <subject> that all

---

26. In this section Aristotle wants to see whether he is justified in recognizing
his standard four CAUSES. He tests his claims, as he often does, by examining
COMMON BELIEFS; in this case he considers the views of the 'wise', turning to a
survey of earlier philosophers.

27. **for the reason. . . and principle**: The 'ultimate' and the 'primary' cause are
probably identified with the proximate cause (not the cause furthest from the
effect, but the one closest and most appropriate to it). Cf. 1044b1, *Phys.* 195b21.
On the use of 'account' to pick out the formal cause see REASON #4.

28. **source . . . motion**: See *Phys.* 194b29n.

29. **since it is the end**: Hence it is the opposite of the source, i.e., beginning,
of motion.

30. **on nature**: See *Phys.* ii 3.

10 beings come from, the first thing they come to be from and the last thing they perish into, the substance remaining throughout but changing in respect of its attributes. This, they say, is the element and the principle of beings. And for this reason they think that nothing either comes to be or is destroyed, on the assumption that this nature <that is the subject> persists in every change, just as we say that Socrates does not come to be without qualification when he comes to be good or musical,

15 and that he is not destroyed when he loses these states (because the subject, Socrates himself, remains)[31]—so also they say that nothing else either comes to be or perishes without qualification (for there must be some nature, either one or more than one, that persists while everything else comes to be from it).[32]

But they do not all agree about the number or type of this material

20 principle. Thales, the originator of this sort of philosophy, says it is water (that is why he also declared that the earth rests on water). Presumably he reached this view from seeing that what nourishes all things is wet and that the hot itself comes from the wet and is kept alive by it (and what

25 all things come to be from is their principle).[33] He also reached this view because he thought that the seeds of all things have a wet nature (and water is the principle of the nature of wet things).

Some people think that even those who first gave accounts of the gods in very ancient times, long before the present, accepted this view

30 about nature. For the ancients made Oceanus and Tethys the parents of coming to be and described the oath of the gods as water, which they called Styx; for what is oldest is most honored, and what is most honored

984a is the oath.[34] It is perhaps unclear whether this belief about nature is in fact old or even ancient, but at any rate this is what Thales is said to have declared about the first cause. (No one would think of including

5 Hippon among these philosophers, given the triviality of his thought.)

Anaximenes and Diogenes take air to be both prior to water and

31. **just as we . . . remains)**: This is being compared both to what precedes and to what follows.

32. **(for there must . . . comes to be from it)**: This is an explanatory comment by Aristotle; he does not imply that the monists explicitly state it as their reason. On monism and the persisting SUBJECT cf. GC 314b1–6.

33. **(and what . . . their principle)**: This again is a comment of Aristotle's, not represented as an explicit claim by Thales. The same is true of the parenthesis in the next sentence.

34. **is the oath**: The gods' oath is taken to establish the boundaries of their different areas of influence; hence it is connected with the river Styx, which marked the boundary of the underworld. The argument from mythology is meant to support the claim that water is oldest, and hence the origin (or PRINCIPLE: *archē*).

also the primary principle of all the simple bodies, while Hippasus of Metapontium and Heracleitus of Ephesus say this about fire. Empedocles takes the four bodies to be principles, adding earth as a fourth to the ones mentioned. These, he says, always remain, and do not come to   *10* be, except insofar as they come to be more or fewer, being combined into one and dispersed from one into many.

Anaxagoras of Clazomenae, who was older than Empedocles but wrote later, says that the principles are unlimited; for he says that practically all the uniform things[35] (for instance, water or fire) come to be and are destroyed only in the ways we have mentioned, by being combined   *15* and dispersed; they do not come to be or get destroyed in any other way, but always remain.

[THE MOVING CAUSE [36]]

If one went by these views, one might suppose that the material cause is the only sort of cause. But as people thus advanced, reality itself showed them the way and compelled them to search. For however true it might be that all coming to be and perishing is from one (or more   *20* than one) thing, still, *why* does this happen, and what is the cause? For certainly the subject does not produce change in itself. I mean, for instance, neither the wood nor the bronze causes itself to change, nor does the wood itself produce a bed, or the bronze a statue, but something   *25* else causes the change. And to search for this is (in our view) to search for the second principle—the source of the principle of motion.

Those who were the very first to undertake this line of inquiry into nature, who said that the subject is one, were quite satisfied with this. But at least some[37] of those who said that the subject is one, as though   *30* defeated by this search <for an explanation of change>, said that the one, i.e., nature as a whole, is immobile, not only as regards coming to be and perishing (that was an old belief agreed on by all), but also as regards every other sort of change.[38] This view is distinctive of them.   984b

35. **uniform things**: Lit. 'things with parts similar to the wholes', *homoiomerē*. See PART.

36. Some of the early naturalists made progress toward the discovery of the moving cause but did not explicitly recognize it; Aristotle argues that the difficulties they faced show that they need to recognize this further cause.

37. **some**: the Eleatics, especially PARMENIDES in his 'Way of Truth'.

38. **that the one . . . change**: Aristotle might have either of two points in mind: (1) The Eleatics noticed that it is impossible to explain change within the constraints of a single, material, causal principle, but then they drew the erroneous conclusion that change is impossible, instead of the correct conclusion that more

Of those who said that the universe is one element, none managed to notice this <second> cause, unless Parmenides did; he noticed it only insofar as he posited not only one cause, but also in a way two causes.[39] Indeed those who recognize more than one element—for instance, hot and cold, or fire and earth—make it easier to state <the cause that initiates motion>, since they regard fire as having a nature that initiates motion, and water, earth, and other such things as having natures contrary to this.

After these sorts of principles were proposed by these people, other people found them inadequate to generate the nature of beings; once again, as we said, it was as though the truth itself compelled them, and so they began to search for the next sort of principle.[40] For presumably it is unlikely that fire or earth or anything else of that sort would cause some things to be in a good and fine state and would cause other things to come to be in that state, and unlikely that people would think so; still, it was unsatisfactory to entrust so great a result to chance and luck. And so when one of them said that mind is present (in nature just as in animals) as the cause of the world order and of all its arrangement, he seemed like a sober person, and his predecessors seemed like babblers in comparison. We know that Anaxagoras evidently made a start on giving such accounts, but an earlier statement of them is ascribed to Hermotimus of Clazomenae. Those who held this view posited a principle of beings that is at once both the cause of things' turning out well and the sort of cause that is the source of motion for beings.

[EARLY GLIMPSES OF THE MOVING CAUSE]

4

One might suspect that the first to search for this sort of cause was Hesiod and anyone else who counted desire[41] or appetite among beings as a principle, as Parmenides, for instance, also did. For he too, in describing the coming to be of the whole universe, says: 'Desire was the

---

than one causal principle must be recognized. (2) The Eleatics supposed that if there could be no coming to be or perishing, there could be no change of any sort.

39. **two causes**: This refers to PARMENIDES' 'Way of Opinion (doxa)'.

40. **the next sort of principle**: the moving cause. This and the next paragraphs describe another reason for thinking there should be a moving cause distinct from the material cause. They do not describe the explicit discovery of the final cause; for, in Aristotle's view, the Presocratics did not discover the final cause, though they had some inkling of it in their remarks on the moving cause.

41. **desire**: erōs. Used especially for sexual attraction.

first of all the gods she devised'.[42] And Hesiod says: 'Before everything else that came to be, there was chaos, and then the broad-fronted earth, and desire, preeminent among all the immortals.'[43] He assumes that there must be some cause among beings to initiate motion in things and to bring them together. Let us leave it till later to determine which of these people was the first <to discover this sort of cause>.

Moreover, the contraries of good things (i.e., disorder and ugliness no less than order and beauty) were also apparent in nature, and bad things were apparently more numerous than good things, and base things more numerous than beautiful things. For this reason someone else introduced love and strife so that each of them would be the cause of one of these two sorts of things. For if we follow Empedocles' argument, and do not confine ourselves to his mumbling way of expressing it, but attend to what he has in mind, we will find that love is the cause of good things, and strife of bad. And so, if one were to claim that in a way Empedocles said—indeed was the first to say—that the good and the bad are principles, one would perhaps be right, if the cause of all goods is the good itself.

These people, then, as we say, evidently made this much progress in fastening on two of the four causes that we distinguished in our work on nature—the matter and the principle of motion. But they did so dimly and not at all perspicuously. They were like unskilled boxers in fights, who, in the course of moving around, often land good punches, but are not guided by knowledge; in the same way these thinkers would seem not to know what they are saying, since they evidently make practically no use of these causes, except to a slight degree.

Anaxagoras, for instance, uses mind as an artificial contrivance[44] for the production of the universe; it is when he is puzzled about the cause of something's being necessarily as it is that he drags in mind, but in other cases he recognizes anything but mind as the cause of things that come to be. Empedocles, admittedly, uses these causes more than Anaxagoras does, but he too still makes insufficient use of them, and he does not succeed in using them consistently. At any rate, he often makes love draw things apart, and strife draw them together. For when-

42. **'Desire was. . . devised'**: From Parmenides' 'Way of Opinion'. The subject of 'she' is probably Aphrodite, the goddess of sexual desire and love.

43. **'Before . . . immortals'**: An inaccurate quotation (probably, like many of Aristotle's quotations, from memory) of Hesiod, *Theogony* 116–20.

44. **artificial contrivance**: Lit. 'machine'. Aristotle probably alludes to the theatrical device of the 'god from the machine' (deus ex machina), brought out on a crane above the stage at the end of the play to provide an artificially tidy ending. Cf. *Poet.* 1454a39–b3.

ever strife scatters the universe into its elements, all the fire is gathered into one, and so is each of the other elements; and whenever love brings things back together again into one, the parts from each element are necessarily scattered again.[45]

30 Empedocles, then, went beyond his predecessors. He was the first to distinguish this cause and to introduce it; he did not take the principle of motion to be one, but assumed different and contrary principles. Moreover, he was the first to say that there are four material elements.

985b In fact, though, he does not use all four, but treats them as two, treating fire in its own right as one nature, and its opposites—earth, air, and water—as together constituting another; this may be gathered from studying his poems. As we say, then, this is how many principles he recognized, and this is what he said about them.

5 Leucippus and his colleague Democritus, on the other hand, say that the elements are the full and the empty, and that, of these, the full and solid is what is, and the empty is what is not. That is why they also say that what is is no more of a being than what is not, because body is no
10 more of a being than the empty is.[46] They take these to be the material causes of beings.

Those who take the substance that is the subject to be one explain how everything else comes to be by referring to the ways in which the subject is affected, taking the rare and the dense to be the principle of the ways it is affected. In the same way, Leucippus and Democritus take the differentiae[47] to be the causes of the other things. They say, however,
15 that there are three of these differentiae—shape, order, and position. For they say that what is is differentiated only by rhythm, touching, and turning.[48] Of these rhythm is shape, touching is order, and turning

45. **For whenever . . . scattered again**: This shows that Empedocles is inconsistent in claiming that what draws things together is the cause of what is good. For what draws things together (in the course of dissolution into the elements, when different bits of each element combine with each other) is sometimes the cause of something bad. Moreover, what draws things apart (in the course of the formation of compound bodies, when one bit of fire goes to this compound body, and another bit to that one) is sometimes the cause of something good.

46. **because . . . empty is**: i.e., both are beings. Read *tou kenou to sōma*. (OCT: 'because the empty <is no more a being> than body <is>'.) This whole sentence illustrates the use of *einai* ('to BE') both for what is (something or other) and for what is (= exists). The void 'is not' insofar as it lacks the properties of bodies (the atoms), but the Atomists insist that it exists.

47. **differentiae**: of the atoms, the solid bodies referred to in general terms as 'the full'.

48. **rhythm, touching, and turning**: These are the Atomists' own terms, which Aristotle explains; the illustration using letters (*stoicheia*, also translated 'ELEMENTS'; cf. 1041b15) is probably theirs too.

is position; for A differs from N in shape, AN from NA in order, and
Z from N in position. Like the other <naturalists>, however, they were   20
too lazy to take up the question about motion and to ask from what
source and in what way it arises in beings.

This, then, would seem to be the extent, as we say, of the earlier
thinkers' search for these two causes.

* * * * * * *

[CRITICISMS OF PLATO]

[ORIGINS OF THE THEORY OF IDEAS [49]]

6

Plato's work came after the philosophical views we have mentioned;[50]   987a29
it agreed with them in most ways, but it also had distinctive features   30
setting it apart from the philosophy of the Italians. For in his youth Plato
first became familiar with Cratylus and with the Heracleitean beliefs that
all perceptible things are always flowing and that there is no knowledge$_e$
of them; he held these views later too. Socrates, on the other hand, was   987b
concerned with ethics and not at all with nature as a whole; he was
seeking the universal in ethics and was the first to turn his thought to
definitions. Plato agreed with Socrates, but because of his Heracleitean
views he took these definitions to apply not to perceptible things but to   5
other things; for, he thought, the common formula could not be of any
of the perceptible things, since they are always changing. Beings of this
sort <that definitions are of>, then, he called Ideas, and he said that
perceptible things are apart* from these, and are all called after them,
since the things with the same names[51] as the Forms are what they are[52]   10
by participation in them.

In speaking of 'participation' he changed only the name; for the Pythagoreans say that things are what they are by imitating numbers, and
Plato (changing the name) said they are what they are by participating
<in Forms>. But they left it to others to investigate what it is to partici-
pate in or to imitate Forms.

49. For other accounts of Plato and the Theory of Ideas (or Forms) see FORM
(PLATONIC) # 2.

50. **views we have mentioned**: Aristotle has been discussing the Eleatics and
Pythagoreans, whom he calls the 'Italians'.

51. **with the same names**: *homōnuma*. Here and in 990b6 this term probably just
means literally 'having the same name as', rather than HOMONYMOUS in Aristotle's
technical sense (implying a different definition).

52. **are what they are**: Lit. just 'are', and hence perhaps 'exist' (and also in the
rest of the paragraph).

[*IDEAS, MATHEMATICAL OBJECTS, AND NUMBERS*]

15   Further, he says that, apart from perceptible things and Forms, there
are also mathematical objects in between. These differ from perceptible
things in being everlasting and immobile; they differ from Forms in that
there are many of the same kind, whereas there is only one Form for
each kind of thing.[53]

Since the Forms are the causes of other things, he thought that their
20   elements are the elements of all beings. The great and the small, then,
as matter, and the one, as substance, are principles; for Forms come
from these, by participating in the one. And yet he said, agreeing with
the Pythagoreans, that the one is substance, and that it is not said to be
one by being something else.[54] He also agreed with them in saying that
25   numbers are the causes of the being₀ of other things; but in positing a
duality instead of treating the indefinite[55] as one, and in taking the great
and small to constitute the indefinite, he held a distinctive view of his
own. Moreover, in his view numbers exist apart from perceptible things;
whereas the Pythagoreans take the objects themselves to be numbers,
and do not place mathematical objects between perceptible things and
Forms.

30   His claim that the one and numbers exist apart from the other objects
(in contrast to the Pythagorean view) and his introduction of the Forms
were the result of his investigation of arguments; for none of his predecessors engaged in dialectic. He made the other nature <besides the
One> a duality because he thought that numbers (except the primes)
988a   could be neatly produced from the duality, as though from something
malleable.

What actually happens, though, is the contrary of this, and it is implau-
sible to think it would happen in the way they <the Platonists> say.
For in their view many things are made out of the matter, but the Form
generates only once; in fact, however, only one table is apparently made
out of one <bit of> matter, whereas the agent who applies the form,
5   though he is one, makes many tables. Similarly, in the case of male and
female, the female is impregnated from one copulation, whereas the
male impregnates many females. And yet these things[56] are imitations
of those principles <that they believe in>.

---

53. **there is only one Form for each kind of thing**: Lit. 'each Form itself is only
one'.

54. **it is not . . . something else**: Cf. *APo* 83a13.

55. **indefinite**: See INFINITE #3.

56. **these things**: matter and form.

[PLATO CONSIDERED ONLY TWO OF THE FOUR CAUSES]

This, then, was what Plato determined about the questions we are investigating. It is evident from what has been said that he used only two causes, the cause involving the what-it-is and the material cause; for the   *10* Forms are causes of the what-it-is of other things, and the one is the cause of the what-it-is of Forms. The nature of the matter that is the subject for the Forms (in the case of perceptible things) and for the one (in the case of Forms) is also evident: it is the duality, the great and the small. Further, he has assigned the cause of good and bad to the ele-   *15* ments, one to each, as we say some earlier philosophers, such as Empedocles and Anaxagoras, also sought to do.

*　*　*　*　*　*　*

[THE IDEAS SIMPLY MULTIPLY THE NUMBER OF THINGS TO BE EXPLAINED [57]*]*

9

. . . As for those who posited Ideas, the first objection is that in seeking   *990a34* to grasp the causes of the beings in this world,[58] they introduced different   *990b* things, equal in number to them. It is as though someone wanted to count things and thought he could not do it if there were fewer of them, but could do it if he added more. For the Forms they resorted to in their   *5* search for the causes of things in this world are practically equal in number to—or at any rate are no fewer than—the things in this world. For take each <kind of> thing that has a one over many, both substances and nonsubstances, both things in this world and everlasting things; in each case there is some <one over many> that has the same name[59] <as the many>.

57. In chs. 7–8 Aristotle criticizes the treatment of the four causes by philosophers before Plato. In ch. 9 he criticizes Plato's Theory of Ideas.

58. **the beings in this world**: Lit. 'these beings here'.

59. **same name**: See 987b10n. Platonic Forms are (in Aristotle's view) similar to the corresponding sensible things (so that the Form of just, e.g., is simply another just thing, and the Form of man is simply another man; cf. *EN* 1096a34–b5). In Aristotle's view, a universal corresponding to the predicate 'F' should not simply be another instance of something that 'F' applies to.

[THE ARGUMENTS FOR FORMS FAIL]

Further, none of the proofs we[60] offer to show that there are Forms
10   appears to succeed; for some of them are invalid,[61] while some also yield
Forms of things that we think have no Forms.[62] For the arguments from
the sciences yield Forms of all the things of which there are sciences;
the one over many yields Forms even of negations; and the argument
from thinking about something that has perished yields Forms of things
15   that perish, since there is an appearance[63] of these. Further, among the
more accurate arguments, some produce Ideas of relatives,[64] whereas
we deny that these are a kind of things that are in their own right;[65]
others introduce the Third Man.[66]

[THE THEORY OF FORMS CONFLICTS WITH OTHER PLATONIST DOCTRINES]

And in general the arguments for Forms undermine the existence of
things that matter more to us than the existence of the Ideas does. For
20   they imply that number, not duality, is first and that what is relative is
prior to what is in its own right, and they lead to all the other <unaccept-
able> conclusions that some people have been led to believe by following
the beliefs about the Ideas, even though these beliefs conflict with their
own principles.
    Further, the reasoning that leads us to say that there are Ideas also

60. we: Aristotle thinks of himself as one of the Platonic school, though he does
not endorse their position. In xiii 4 he uses 'they' in a passage parallel to this
one; the variation between first and third person does not seem to be significant.
In the rest of this chapter 'we' and 'our' also refers to the Platonists, not to
Aristotle's independent views. The arguments for Forms summarized here are
derived from On Ideas, where they are presented more fully.

61. are invalid: Lit. 'do not yield a necessary deduction'.

62. while some . . . no Forms: This might mean: (1) 'and some yield Forms of
things that we think have no Forms as well <as of things that we think have
Forms>' or (2) 'and some in addition <to being invalid> also yield Forms of
things that we think have no Forms'.

63. appearance: phantasma, usually rendered 'object of appearance'.

64. relatives: RELATIVES include large, small, equal. See On Ideas.

65. whereas we . . . their own right: Lit. 'of which we say there is no in-its-
own-right kind'. The translation takes things that are in their own right to be
SUBSTANCES; in Aristotle's view, the argument in question implies that some
Forms are (impossibly) both RELATIVES and substances. An alternative rendering
would be: 'we deny that these constitute a kind in its own right', i.e., relatives
do not constitute a genuine kind.

66. the Third Man: See FORM (PLATONIC) #2.

yields Forms of many other things as well as of substances. For a thought   *25*
is one not only in the case of substances but also in other cases; there
are sciences of other things as well as of substance; and thousands of
other such difficulties arise.

On the other hand, it is necessary, and follows from the beliefs about
Forms, that if things can participate in Forms, only substances can have
Ideas; for a thing does not participate in a Form coincidentally, but insofar   *30*
as it is not said of a subject. (If, for instance, something participates in
the Double itself, it also participates in the Everlasting, but coincidentally,
since it is coincidental that the Double is everlasting.) Hence the Forms
will be substances.[67] But the same things signify substances among the   *991a*
Forms as in this world—otherwise what will the claim that there is
something apart from these things, the one over many, amount to?[68]
And if the Idea and the things participating in it have the same form,
they will have something in common—for why should <what it is to
be> two be one and the same thing in all the perishable twos and in all
the many everlasting twos, but not one and the same thing in the Two   *5*
itself and in some particular two? But if they do not have the same form,
they will be <merely> homonymous; it will be like calling both Callias
and a wooden <statue>[69] a man, when one has observed no common
<nature> that they share.

[THE IDEAS CANNOT EXPLAIN PERCEPTIBLE THINGS]

One might be especially puzzled about what on earth Forms contribute
to perceptible things, either to those that are everlasting or to those that   *10*

67. **Hence . . . substances**: Aristotle may mean something like this: A particular
does not participate in a Form insofar as that Form is merely a coincident of
some other subject; for in that case everything double would also be everlasting,
since being everlasting is a coincident of the Form of Double. But if Double (e.g.)
were merely a coincident of some further Form (which would follow if it were
a nonsubstance), particulars could not participate in Double (any more than they
participate in Everlasting). And so a particular must participate in a Form insofar
as the Form is something in its own right, i.e., a substance.

68. **But the same . . . amount to?**: Aristotle seems to use the conclusion of the
previous paragraph to raise an objection: the Forms will simply reduplicate the
perceptible things to be explained (the Form of man is simply another man, etc.;
see 990a34 and note). This is one of the Platonic views that result in the Third
Man regress (see FORM (PLATONIC) #2). If the Platonists deny that the Forms are
similar to perceptible things in the way Aristotle claims, he thinks they are
caught on the other horn of a dilemma, which he presents in the next paragraph.

69. **a wooden <statue>**: Lit. 'the wood', referring to a statue of Callias. Callias
and his statue are (in Aristotle's view, not Plato's) merely homonymous (see

come to be and perish; for they cause neither motion nor any change in them. Nor do they contribute to knowledge$_e$ of other things, since they are not their substance—if they were, they would be in the other things.[70] Nor do they contribute to the being of other things, since Forms are not present in the things that participate in them. For if they were

15   present, they might perhaps be thought to be causes, as white is if it is mixed in a white object. This argument was first stated by Anaxagoras and then by Eudoxus and certain others. It is easily upset, since it is easy to collect many impossible consequences that challenge such a belief.

20   Nor can the other things be from Forms in any of the ways things are normally said to be from something. And to say that Forms are patterns* and that other things participate in them is empty talk, mere poetic metaphors. For what is it that looks to the Ideas when it produces things? And it is possible for one thing to be, or to come to be, like

25   another without being copied from it, so that whether or not Socrates exists someone like Socrates might come to be; and clearly the same would be true even if Socrates were everlasting. Further, there will be many patterns of the same thing, hence many Forms; the Forms of man, for instance, will be Animal and Biped as well as Man-itself. Further,

30   the Forms will be patterns not only of perceptible things, but also of themselves—the genus, for instance, of its species—so that the same

991b   thing will be both pattern and copy.

Further, it would seem impossible for a substance to be separate from what it is the substance of. How, then, if the Ideas are the substances of things, could they be separate from them?

According to the *Phaedo*,[71] the Forms are the causes both of being and

5   of coming to be. But what participates in the Forms does not come to be, even if the Forms exist, unless something initiates the motion. And in addition to these <natural things>, many things—for instance, a house or a ring—which in our view have no Forms,[72] come to be. Hence it is clearly also possible for the <natural> things to be and to come to be because of causes of the sort just mentioned.[73]

10   Further, if the Forms are numbers, how can they be causes? Is it because beings are other numbers, so that one number, for instance, is

---

HOMONYMY #2, MATTER), since they do not share the same nature (the nature of a human being).

70. **if they were . . . other things**: Cf. perhaps 1038b14–15, 1040b16.

71. *Phaedo*: See Plato, *Phaedo* 100a–105c.

72. **have no Forms**: because they are artifacts. Cf. perhaps 1070a13–20.

73. **causes of the sort just mentioned**: those that initiate change without any Forms.

238

man, another is Socrates, and another is Callias? If so, why are one lot
of numbers causes of the other lot? It makes no difference if the Forms
are everlasting and the other things are not.[74] But if it is because things
in this world—for instance, a harmony—are ratios of numbers, it is clear
that the things of which they are ratios are some one <kind of> thing.
But if there is this one thing, i.e., the matter, then evidently the numbers   15
themselves will also be ratios of one thing to another. If, for instance,
Callias is a numerical ratio of fire, earth, water, and air, then his Idea
will also be the number of certain other subjects. And Man-itself, even
if it is in some way numerical, will nonetheless be a numerical ratio of   20
certain things, not <properly> a number.[75] This argument,[76] then, does
not show that any Idea is a number.

* * * * * * *

[THE PLATONISTS HAVE THE WRONG CONCEPTION OF A UNIVERSAL SCIENCE]

. . . In general, it is impossible to find the elements of beings without   992b18
distinguishing the ways they are spoken of, since in fact beings are
spoken of in many ways. It is especially impossible to find them if we   20
search in this way[77] for the sorts of elements that compose beings. For
what elements compose acting or being affected or the straight? Presumably these cannot be found; at most the elements of substances can be
found. Hence it is incorrect either to seek the elements of all beings or
to think one has found them.

    And how could one even learn the elements of all things? For clearly   25
one cannot begin with previous knowledge$_g$.[78] If, for instance, we are
learning geometry, we may have previous knowledge$_o$ of other things

---

74. **If so, why . . . things are not**: i.e., why are one lot of numbers (the Forms)
causes of the other lot (the perceptible things) rather than the other way round?
The mere fact that Forms are everlasting and the other things are not does not
seem to justify the claim that the Forms are explanatory.

75. **even if . . . a number**: Lit. 'whether or not it is a number of some kind, will
nonetheless be a ratio of certain things in numbers, and not a number.' Aristotle
distinguishes the number of things that are counted (e.g., three cows) from the
number that counts them (in this case the number three); see NUMBER. He argues
that even if the Forms are numbers in the first sense (by being shown to be
numerical ratios), they have not been shown to be numbers in the second sense.

76. **This argument**: the one based on the claim that things in this world are
ratios.

77. **in this way**: Along the lines favored by Platonists.

78. **knowledge$_g$**: This presumably has a fairly weak sense here; cf. APo 71a11–
17.

<outside geometry>, but we know$_g$ nothing about the subject matter of the science we are to learn about; the same is true in other cases. Hence if there is some science of all things, such as some say there is,
30   we could not have previous knowledge$_g$ of anything before we learn this science. And yet all learning, either through demonstration or through definitions, relies on previous knowledge$_g$ of either all or some things; for one must previously know$_o$ the elements of the definition, and they must be well known$_g$; the same is true for learning through induction.
993a   Then is this science actually innate? If so, it is remarkable that we manage not to notice[79] that we possess the supreme science.

Further, how is one to acquire knowledge$_g$ of the elements, and how is this knowledge to be made clear? For there is a puzzle here too, since
5   our answers might be disputed, as in the case of certain syllables; for some say that ZA is from S, D, and A, while others say it is a different sound, and none of the well-known$_g$ ones.

Further, how could one know$_g$ perceptible things without perception? And yet one would have to, if the elements composing all things are
10   indeed the same, as complex sounds are <composed of> their proper elements.

*   *   *   *   *   *   *

BOOK II[1]

[THE STUDY OF PHILOSOPHY]

1

993a30   To study the truth is in one way difficult and in another way easy. A sign of this is the fact that no one is capable of reaching the truth
993b   adequately, but on the other hand not everyone completely fails to attain it. Everyone has something to say about nature, and though each person on his own contributes nothing or only a little to the truth, all together contribute quite a lot. Truth, then, seems to be like the door in the
5   proverb, a target we cannot miss, and in this way it is easy to study; but it is possible to possess a whole and still to be unable to find a part,[2] and this shows what is difficult about studying the truth.

There can be two sorts of difficulty,[3] and in this case, presumably,

79. **not to notice**: Cf. *APo* 99b25–30.

1. This book may not be entirely by Aristotle; in any case it seems to be a fragment inserted into the *Metaphysics*.

2. **but it is . . . a part**: Cf. *Phys.* 184a21–b14.

3. **two sorts of difficulty**: It may be in us or in the objects themselves. See KNOW #2.

the cause of the difficulty is in us, not in the objects. For what happens
to bats' eyes when they meet the daylight also happens to the intellect   *10*
in our soul when it meets the things that are naturally most evident of
all.

We ought to be grateful not only to those whose beliefs we share
but also to those whose views are more superficial; for they have also
contributed something, since they have prepared the way for us to reach
the right state. For certainly we would have lacked much of lyric poetry   *15*
if there had been no Timotheus, but without Phrynis there would have
been no Timotheus.[4] The same is true in the case of those who have
held views on the truth: only some of them passed on to us beliefs that
we accept, but other thinkers caused these thinkers to arise.

It is correct to call philosophy* knowledge_e of the truth, since the end   *20*
of theoretical knowledge is truth. On the other hand, the end of practical
knowledge is some practical achievement;[5] for if those who are concerned
with action also investigate how things are, they do not study the cause
in its own right but only the cause relative to this <end> and for this
occasion.

We do not know_o the truth unless we know the cause. Now, in any
class of F things, x is the most F if it is by x that Fness, the synonymous   *25*
property, belongs to the other Fs;[6] fire, for instance, is the hottest thing
because it is the cause of heat in other hot things. And so what is truer
is in each case whatever causes the things derived from it to be true.
That is why the principles of things that always are must be truest, since
they are not true <only> at a particular time, nor is there any cause of
their being, but rather they cause other things to be. And so, to the   *30*
extent to which a thing has being, to that extent it has truth.

*   *   *   *   *   *   *

Book III

[*THE PROBLEMS OF PHILOSOPHY*]

[*THE IMPORTANCE OF STUDYING PUZZLES*]

1

In approaching the science we are searching for, we must begin by going   *995a24*
through the questions that require us first to raise puzzles*. These include   *25*
all the questions on which different people have held different views

4. **without ... Timotheus**: Timotheus was a first-rate, Phrynis a second-rate
lyric poet.

5. **practical achievement**: *ergon*. See FUNCTION.

6. **Now, in any ... other Fs**: Cf. *APo* 72a29–30.

about these things,[1] and also any further questions that may have been overlooked. If we want to be in a position to make progress,[2] our first task is to explore the puzzles well. For we will be in a position to make progress later on only if we free ourselves from our earlier puzzles by solving them; but we cannot free ourselves if we do not know$_g$ we are being held captive. When our mind is puzzled, that shows that our subject matter is holding us captive. For being puzzled is rather like being captives: in both cases we are unable to go forward.

30

We must, then, complete a study of all the difficulties before we go any further. For (in addition to the reasons just mentioned) those who do not explore the puzzles before they start their search are like people who do not know$_g$ where to go, and, moreover, they do not know whether or not they have found what they were searching for;[3] for the goal is unclear to them, but clear to someone who has raised the puzzles in advance. Moreover, one is bound to be better equipped for making a judgment* if one has previously listened to all the disputing arguments, like different sides presenting their cases.

35

995b

[PUZZLES ABOUT THE NATURE AND SCOPE OF WISDOM]

5

(1) The first puzzle is among the ones we raised in our preliminary discussions: Is the study of the causes a task for one science or for more than one?

(2) Is it the only task of this science to examine the primary principles of substance, or should it also consider the principles from which everyone proves things? Should it, for instance, consider whether or not it is possible to affirm and deny one and the same thing at the same time, and other such principles?[4]

10

(3) If the science is about substance, is there one science about all substances, or more than one science about substances? If more than one, then are they all of the same kind, or are some of them types of wisdom and others to be called something else?

[PUZZLES ABOUT THE OBJECT OF THE SCIENCE]

(4) And here is a question we must definitely investigate: Should we say that there are only perceptible substances, or also others apart from

15

1. **these things**: the matters discussed in Bk i.

2. **to be . . . make progress**: Lit. to be in a condition of *euporia*, opposed to 'puzzle', *aporia*. See DIALECTIC.

3. **like people . . . searching for**: Cf. Plato, *Meno* 80d5–8.

4. **it is possible . . . principles?**: These are AXIOMS.

them? And are these other substances of just one kind or of more than one kind (as in the view of those who count as substances both Forms and mathematical objects between Forms and perceptible things)?

We should, then, as we say, inquire into these questions.

(5) We should also inquire into whether our study is confined to substances or is also concerned with the coincidents* in their own right   20 of substances in their own right. Moreover, what about same, different, like, unlike, contrariety, prior and posterior, and all other such things— all the things that dialecticians try to examine, proceeding from nothing but common beliefs? Whose task is it to study all these things? And   25 what about *their* coincidents in their own right? Must we consider not only what each of them is, but also whether, for instance, one thing has <only> one contrary?

[PUZZLES ABOUT THE PRINCIPLES TO BE STUDIED BY THE SCIENCE]

(6) Are the principles and elements the kinds,[5] or are they the <parts> present in a given thing, those into which the thing is divided?

(7) If the principles are kinds, are they the last kinds, those applying to individuals,* or the first kinds?[6] For instance, is it animal or man that   30 is a principle? Which of them is more entitled to count as something apart* from the particular?[7]

(8) Above all we should investigate and consider whether or not there is something that is a cause in its own right and is apart from matter, and, if there is, whether or not it is separable. Is there only one such cause, or more than one? Is there or is there not something apart from the compound? (By 'compound' I mean <what there is> whenever   35 something is predicated of matter.) Or is this true of some compounds and not of others?[8] And which beings are of this sort?   996a

(9) Are the principles—both those in the accounts and those in the subject[9]—limited in number, or in species?

5. **kinds**: *genos*, usually rendered 'GENUS'. Here it covers both species and genera.

6. **are they . . . first kinds?**: The last kinds are the lowest, most determinate species (e.g., man); see FORM #8. The first kinds are the highest GENERA.

7. **Which of . . . the particular?**: This is probably a partial explanation of the previous sentence.

8. **Or is . . . others?**: Aristotle is asking whether some compounds have components that can exist apart from the compound, so that the components are SEPARABLE.

9. **both . . . subject**: i.e., both formal and material causes.

(10) Are the principles of perishable things the same as or different from those of imperishable things? Are all principles imperishable, or are the principles of perishable things perishable?

5   (11) The question that is hardest and most puzzling of all is this: Are one and being the substance of beings, as the Pythagoreans and Plato used to say, and not <properties of> something else?[10] Or is this wrong, and is something else their subject? (Empedocles says it is love, someone else that it is fire, another that it is water or air.)

10   (12) Are the principles universals or particulars?[11]

(13) Does their being consist in potentiality or in actuality? And is their potentiality and actuality different from the sort found in motion? These questions are quite puzzling.

(14) Further, are numbers, lengths, figures, and points substances of 15 any sort, or not? If they are, are they separated from perceptible things or present in them?

In all these cases, not only is it difficult to be in a position to make progress toward the truth, but it is also by no means easy to explore the puzzles well in a discussion.

*   *   *   *   *   *   *

BOOK IV

[THE SCIENCE OF BEING]

[THE PHILOSOPHER STUDIES BEING INSOFAR AS IT IS BEING]

1

1003a21   There is a science that studies being insofar as it is being,[1] and also the properties of being in its own right. It is not the same as any of the so-called special sciences. For none of them considers being quite generally, insofar as it is being; rather, each of them cuts off some part of being 25 and studies the relevant coincident[2] of that part, as, for instance, the mathematical sciences do.

Since we are seeking the principles, i.e., the highest causes, clearly

---

10. **not . . . else?**: Cf. *APo* 83a24–32.

11. **particulars?**: Lit. 'as particulars among objects'.

1. **insofar as**: Aristotle is not referring to some special kind of being (as though something had the properties of being insofar as it is being, but not the properties of any specific sort of being). He is thinking of ordinary beings studied with reference to the properties that belong to them INSOFAR AS they are beings. Cf. 1004b5–17.

2. **coincident**: This is the intrinsic COINCIDENT.

they must be the causes of the nature of some subject as it is in its own right.[3] If, then, those who were seeking the elements of beings were also seeking these highest principles, the elements must also be the   *30* elements of being not coincidentally, but insofar as it is being. That is why[4] we also[5] ought to find the first causes of being insofar as it is being.

[THE PHILOSOPHER STUDIES SUBSTANCE AS THE PRIMARY TYPE OF BEING]

2

Being is spoken of in many ways, but always with reference to one thing—i.e., to some one nature—and not homonymously.[6] Everything   *35* healthy, for instance, is spoken of with reference to health—one thing because it preserves health, another because it produces health, another because it indicates health, another because it can receive health. Simi-   *1003b* larly, the medical is spoken of with reference to medical science; for one thing is called medical because it has the medical science, another because it is naturally suited to medical science, another because it is the function of medical science, and we shall find other things spoken of in ways similar to these.

Similarly, then, being is spoken of in many ways, but in all cases it   *5* is spoken of with reference to one principle. For some things are called beings because they are substances, others because they are attributes of substance, others because they are a road to substance, or because they are perishings or privations or qualities of substance, or productive or generative of substance or of things spoken of with reference to it, or because they are negations of one of these or of substance. This is   *10* why we also say that not being is—i.e., is not being.

A single science studies all healthy things, and the same applies in the other cases. For it is not only things that are spoken of in accordance with one <common property> that are studied by a single science; the same is true of things that are spoken of with reference to one nature, since these things are also, in a way, spoken of in accordance with one   *15*

3. **causes . . . own right**: Lit. 'causes of some nature in its own right' or perhaps 'must belong to some . . .'. If they did not meet this condition, they would not be the *highest* causes; they would be only coincidental causes, which depend on further causes applying to the subject in its own right. (Something causes Socrates to be pale only if something prior causes him to be a man.)

4. **That is why**: sc. since the highest causes are the elements of being.

5. **we also**: sc. we as well as the Platonists who looked for the elements of being (992b18).

6. **not homonymously**: This probably means what is expressed elsewhere by 'not *merely* homonymously'. See HOMONYMOUS #3.

<common property>.[7] Clearly, then, it is also the task of a single science to study beings insofar as they are beings.

In every case the dominant concern of a science is with its primary object, the one on which the others depend and because of which they are spoken of as they are. If, then, this primary object is substance, the philosopher must grasp the principles and causes of substances.

[THE PHILOSOPHER STUDIES THE SPECIES OF BEING [8]]

1004a2   There are as many parts of philosophy as there are <types of> sub-
           stances, and so there must be a first philosophy, and a second philosophy
5   following it; for being is divided immediately into genera, which is why
           the sciences will also conform to these. For the philosopher is spoken
           of in the same way as the mathematician is; for mathematical science
           also has parts, and in mathematics there is a first and a second science
           and others succeeding in order.
1003b19   For every single genus there is a single <sort of> perception and a
20   single science; there is, for instance, a single grammatical science, and
           it studies all the <types of> sounds. Hence it is also the task of a science
           that is one in genus to study all the species of being insofar as it is being;
           it is the task of the species of that science to study the species <of being>.

[THE PHILOSOPHER STUDIES BOTH BEING AND UNITY, AND ALSO THEIR
OPPOSITES]

           Being and unity[9] are the same and a single nature, since they imply each
           other, as principle and cause do, though they are not one and the same
25   in the sense of being revealed by the same account[10] (though indeed it
           does not matter if we take them to have the same account; that would
           be even more suitable for our purpose). For one man is the same as a
           man, and moreover a man who is is the same as a man, and 'he is a
           man and a man who is'[11] reveals nothing different by the repetition in

7. **these things ... property>**: Contrast APo 85b11, 97b36, 99a7, which de-
mands synonymous predication in scientific demonstrations.

8. The following paragraph consists of 1004a2–9 transposed to an apparently
more suitable place.

9. **unity**: hen, also translated by 'one'.

10. **they are not ... account**: Aristotle refers to his standard formula, 'The F
and the G are the same thing, but different in being' (i.e., different in account).
See ESSENCE #2.

11. **For one man ... man who is'**: Read heis anthrōpos <kai anthrōpos> in b26
and estin anthrōpos kai estin ōn anthrōpos in b28. OCT: 'For one man is the same
as a man who is and a man, and 'he is one man and one man who is'...'

what is said, since clearly a man and a man who is are separated neither
in coming to be nor in perishing. The same also applies to unity.[12] It is   *30*
evident, then, that in these cases the addition <of 'one'> reveals the
same thing <as 'is' reveals>, and that unity is nothing different from
being. Moreover, the substance of a thing is noncoincidentally one thing;
and similarly it is essentially[13] some being.

It follows that there are as many species of being as of unity. Hence
it is a task for a science that is the same in genus to study the what-it-   *35*
is about these species—for instance, about same, similar and other such
things. Practically all the contraries are referred to this principle; our   *1004a*
study of these in the Selection of Contraries[14] will suffice.[15]

It is the task of one science to study opposites, and plurality is the   *10*
opposite of unity. It is also the task of one science to study negation
and privation, since in both cases we study the one thing of which it is
the negation or the privation. For either we say without qualification
that something does not belong to the subject, or we say that it does
not belong to some genus of the subject.[16] In the latter case a differentia
is added apart from what is in the negation—for the negation is the   *15*
absence of that property, but the privation also involves some nature
that is the subject of which the privation is said.

And so it is also the task of the science we have mentioned to know
about the contraries of the things we have mentioned—different, unlike,
unequal, and everything else that is spoken of either with respect to these
or with respect to plurality and unity. Contrariety is also one of these; for   *20*
it is a type of difference, and difference is a type of otherness. And so,
since unity is spoken of in many ways, these will also be spoken of in many
ways; but still it is the task of a single science to know them all. For the
mere fact that things are spoken of in many ways does not imply that they
cannot be studied by one and the same science; different sciences are required only if it is true both that the things have no one <common prop-
erty> and that their accounts are not referred to one thing.   *25*

---

12. **the same . . . unity**: In 'he is a man and one man', 'one man' reveals nothing
different from what 'man' reveals (i.e., SIGNIFIES).

13. **essentially**: *hoper*. See ESSENCE #2(c).

14. **Selection of Contraries**: Perhaps this is a separate treatise, now lost.

15. For 1004a2–9 (which follows here in the mss) see above before 1003b19.

16. **For either . . . genus of the subject**: The first case is the negation, and
the second the PRIVATION, as the next sentence explains. The privative term
'unmusical' and the positive term 'musical' refer to the same genus, i.e., the
sort of thing that is capable of being musical; but the negative 'not musical' also
refers to (e.g.) prime numbers, which are not the sort of thing that could be
musical and hence are not unmusical either.

[THE PHILOSOPHER STUDIES ALL THE ATTRIBUTES OF BEING AS SUCH]

Since in each case everything is referred to the primary thing (for instance, everything that is called one is referred to the primary unity),
this is also what we ought to say about same, different, and contraries.
And so we should first distinguish how many ways each thing is spoken
of, and then show how each of the things we have distinguished is
30   spoken of with reference to the primary thing in each predication; for
some things will be spoken of as they are because they have that primary
thing, others because they produce it, others in other such ways.

Evidently, then, it is the task of a single science to take account both
of these things and of substance (this was one of the questions that
1004b   raised puzzles),[17] and it is the philosopher's task to be able to study all
<these> things. For if this is not his task, who will consider whether
Socrates is the same as seated Socrates,[18] or whether one thing has
<just> one contrary, or what contrariety is, or how many ways it is
spoken of? And the same is true for other questions of that sort.
5   We have found, then, that these are attributes of unity insofar as it
is unity, and of being insofar as it is being; each is an attribute of unity
and being in their own right, not insofar as they are numbers or lines
or fire.[19] Hence it is clearly the task of that science <of being> to know
both what being and unity are, and also their coincidents. The mistake
of those who currently consider these questions is not that they fail to
practise philosophy but that, although substance is prior, they comprehend nothing about it.[20]
10   There are attributes distinctive of number insofar as it is number (for
instance, oddness and evenness, commensurability and inequality, being
more and being less), and these belong to numbers both in their own
right and in relation to one another. Likewise there are other attributes
distinctive of the solid, both moved and unmoved, and <of the moved>,
15   both weightless and having weight. In the same way, then, there are

17. **raised puzzles)**: See 997a25.

18. **whether . . . seated Socrates**: On this puzzle cf. *Met.* 1032a8n.

19. **of unity . . . or fire**: The beings that we discuss may in fact be mathematical
or physical objects, but this is irrelevant, since we do not argue from or about
their specifically mathematical or physical properties. This is another way of
explaining what is implied by considering beings INSOFAR AS they are beings.

20. **comprehend nothing about it**: Hence they do not study the attributes of
substance correctly. For they do not realize that the properties they study are
in fact attributes of substance, and they have the wrong conception of substance
in the first place. Perhaps Aristotle is referring to the 'students of nature' whom
he mentions later, at 1005a31.

also some attributes distinctive of being insofar as it is being, and it is the philosopher's task to investigate the truth about these.

Here is a sign <to show that it is his task>. Dialecticians and sophists assume the same guise as the philosopher. For sophistic has the appearance of wisdom, though nothing more, and dialecticians practise dialectic about all things; being is common to all things, and clearly they practise dialectic about all things because all things are proper to philosophy. For sophistic and dialectic treat the same genus as philosophy, but philosophy differs from dialectic in the type of power it has, and it differs from sophistic in its decision about how to live.[21] Dialectic tests[22] in the area where philosophy achieves knowledge, while sophistic has the appearance <of knowledge>, but not the reality.

Further, one column* of contraries is privation, and all contraries are referred to being and not being, and to unity and plurality—for instance, stability belongs to unity, motion to plurality. And practically everyone agrees that beings and substance are composed of contraries. At any rate, they all say that the principles are contrary; for some say that they are the odd and even, some that they are the hot and cold, some that they are the determinate and indeterminate, others that they are love and strife. All the other contraries are also evidently referred to unity and plurality (let us assume this referral), and the principles recognized by others fall completely under unity and plurality as their genera.

This also makes it evident, then, that it is the task of a single science to study being insofar as it is being; for all things are either contraries or composed of contraries, and unity and plurality are principles of the contraries. Unity and plurality belong to one science, whether or not they are spoken of as having one <common property> (and presumably in fact they are not). Even if unity is indeed spoken of in many ways, still the nonprimary unities will be spoken of with reference to the primary unity; the same applies to the contraries. This is true even if being or unity is neither universal and the same over them all nor separable; and presumably it is neither of these, but rather some <beings and unities> are spoken of with reference to one thing, and others in succession. That is why[23] it is not the geometer's task to study what a contrary is or what completeness is, or to study unity, or being, or same, or different, but only to study them on the basis of an assumption.[24]

21. **how to live**: The SOPHIST chooses to pursue the appearance rather than the reality of knowledge

22. **Dialectic tests**: On 'testing' (*peirastikē*) see DIALECTIC.

23. **That is why**: since these are questions for the science of being.

24. **on the basis of an assumption**: The ASSUMPTION states the definition of the property in question, and the geometer takes the definition for granted.

Clearly, then, it is the task of a single science to study both being insofar as it is being and also the things that belong to it insofar as it is
15   being. And clearly the same science studies not only substances but also their attributes—both those we have mentioned and also prior and posterior, genus and species, whole and part, and the other things of this sort.

[*THE PHILOSOPHER STUDIES THE PRINCIPLES OF INFERENCE,
ESPECIALLY THE FIRMEST PRINCIPLES*]

3

We ought to say whether it is the task of one and the same science or
20   of different sciences to study both the axioms* (as they are called in mathematics) and substance.[25] Evidently it is also the task of one and the same science—the philosopher's—to examine these, since these belong to all beings and are not distinctive of one genus in separation from the others.

Every scientist uses the axioms because they belong to being insofar
25   as it is being, and each genus is a being. But each uses them to the extent he needs them, and that is however far the genus about which he presents his demonstrations extends. Clearly, then, the axioms belong to all things insofar as they are beings (for this is what all things have in common);[26] and so it is also the task of the one who knows being insofar as it is being to study the axioms.

This is why none of those who investigate a special area—for instance,
30   a geometer or an arithmetician—undertakes to say anything about whether or not the axioms are true. The ones who did so were some of the students of nature; and it is not surprising that they did this, since they were the only ones who thought they were examining the whole of nature and examining being. In fact, however, there is someone still higher than the student of nature, since nature is only one kind of being;
35   and so investigating these axioms will also be a task of this universal
1005b scientist,[27] the one who studies primary substance. The study of nature is also a type of wisdom, but not the primary type.

Now, some of those who argue about when a conclusion should properly be accepted as true object that one should not accept <principles

25. **We ought . . . substance**: Aristotle answers the puzzle raised at *Met.* 996b26.

26. **what all things have in common)**: If the axioms are to apply to all things, they must apply to them in virtue of some property that all things share; but the only property that all things share is that they are all beings; hence the axioms must apply to all things qua beings.

27. **universal scientist**: Read *tou katholou.*

that have not been demonstrated>. They do this because they lack education in analytics;[28] for someone who comes <to the science of being> must already know$_e$ about analytics and not ask about it when   5
he studies <the science of being>.

Clearly, then, study of the principles of deductions is also a task for the philosopher—i.e., for the one who studies the nature of all substance. Whoever has the best claim to knowledge$_g$ of a given genus ought to be able to state the firmest principles of his subject matter; hence whoever   10
has the best claim to knowledge of beings insofar as they are beings should be able to state the firmest principles of all things. This person[29] is the philosopher.

[THE PHILOSOPHER STUDIES THE PRINCIPLE OF NONCONTRADICTION,
SINCE IT IS THE FIRMEST PRINCIPLE]

The firmest principle of all is one about which it is impossible to be mistaken. For this sort of principle must be known$_g$ best (for what we make mistakes about is invariably what we do not know),[30] and it cannot be an assumption. For a principle that we must already possess in order   15
to understand anything at all about beings is not an assumption;[31] and what we must know in order to know anything at all is a principle we must already possess. Clearly, then, this sort of principle is the firmest of all.

Let us next say what this principle is: that it is impossible for the same thing both to belong and not to belong at the same time to the same   20
thing and in the same respect (and let us assume we have drawn all the further distinctions that might be drawn to meet logical complaints).[32]

28. **Now, some . . . in analytics**: The translation includes supplementation derived from 1006a5–8, to make the point clearer. Lit. 'As for as many things as those people undertake who speak about the truth, in what way it should be accepted, they do this because of lack of education. . .'. Education in ANALYTICS (i.e., in the nature of DEDUCTION and DEMONSTRATION, as set out in Aristotle's *Analytics*) would have taught them that it is not appropriate to demand a demonstration of first principles.

29. **This person**: i.e., the one with the best claim to knowledge of beings insofar as they are beings.

30. **do not know)**: The firmest principle, however, is the one we cannot be mistaken about.

31. **For a . . . an assumption**: This is because an ASSUMPTION is a PRINCIPLE of a special science, not of all knowledge.

32. **logical complaints)**: See LOGIC. Here Aristotle refers to the various counterexamples that might be offered against versions of the Principle of Noncontradiction (PNC) that do not include suitable qualifications.

This, then, is the firmest principle of all, since it has the distinguishing feature previously mentioned.[33]

25   For it is impossible for anyone to suppose that the same thing is and is not, though some people take Heracleitus to say this; for what one says need not be what one supposes to be true.[34] For it is impossible for contraries to belong at the same time to the same thing (and let us assume that the customary further distinctions are added to this statement). But what is contrary to a belief is the belief in its contradictory. Hence evi-
30   dently it is impossible for the same person at the same time to suppose that the same thing is and is not, since someone who makes this mistake would have contrary beliefs at the same time. This is why all those who demonstrate refer back to this belief as ultimate;[35] for this is by nature the principle of all the other axioms as well.

[DEFENCE OF THE PRINCIPLE OF NONCONTRADICTION]

[THE PRINCIPLE CAN BE DEFENDED BY ARGUMENT,
THOUGH NOT BY DEMONSTRATION]

4

35   There are some people, however, who, as we said, themselves affirm
1006a   not only that it is possible for the same thing to be and not to be but also that they believe this; many students of nature also make use of this claim. But we have just now found that it is impossible for the same thing to be and not to be at the same time, and through this we showed
5   that this is the firmest principle of all.

Now, some people actually demand that we demonstrate even this, but their demand is the result of lack of education; for we lack education if we do not know$_g$ what we should and should not seek to have demonstrated. For in general it is impossible to demonstrate everything, since there would be an infinite regress, and so even then there would be no
10   demonstration; and if there are some things of which we must not seek a demonstration, these people could not say what principle is more appropriately left without demonstration than this one <the Principle of Noncontradiction>.

Still, even about this <denial of the Principle of Noncontradiction>

33. **previously mentioned**: i.e., that one cannot be mistaken about it.

34. **for . . . supposes to be true**: This explains why, even if Heracleitus sincerely asserted the denial of PNC, it would not follow that he believed the denial.

35. **as ultimate**: They do not explicitly mention it, but they rely on it. If they did not, then a demonstration that x is F would not rule out x's not being F.

it is possible to demonstrate by refutation that it is impossible,[36] if only the disputant speaks of something.[37] If he speaks of nothing, it is ridiculous for us to seek to engage in rational discourse[38] with someone who does not engage in rational discourse about anything, insofar as he does not engage in it;[39] for insofar as he does not engage in any rational discourse, he is like a plant. It should be noticed, though, that demonstration by refutation is different from demonstration. For in attempting to demonstrate <the Principle of Noncontradiction>, someone might seem to beg the question;[40] but if the respondent is responsible <for speaking of something>, it will be a refutation, not a demonstration.

Now the starting point[41] for all such things is not the demand that the respondent speak of something either as being or as not being (for someone might perhaps suppose that this would be begging the question),[42] but the demand that he signify something[43] both to himself and to another. For he must do this if he speaks of something; for otherwise he does not engage in any rational discourse either with himself or with another. And if he grants this, there will be a demonstration <by

36. **Still, even . . . impossible**: Hence PNC turns out not to be wholly indemonstrable in every sense. A 'demonstration by refutation' does not argue from a prior and better-known principle (for this demand on demonstration cf. *APo* 71b21), and so it differs from an ordinary demonstration.

37. **speaks of something**: Or 'says something'. See SAY. It is often difficult to decide whether to render *legein* by 'say' (followed by a that-clause) or by 'speak of' (applied to a nonlinguistic item); and it is especially difficult in this chapter.

38. **rational discourse**: *logos*. Aristotle exploits the use of *logos* both for speech and for the REASON that underlies it.

39. **insofar . . . in it**: If I do not concede that I am speaking of something, you cannot treat the sounds I utter as constituting rational discourse, and so you have no reason to believe that any sounds I might utter when you ask me questions are intended to answer your questions.

40. **beg the question**: In order to demonstrate a conclusion (rather than its denial), we must assume that the first premiss is true and therefore its negation its false. To assume this is just to assume the truth of PNC.

41. **starting point**: See PRINCIPLE #3.

42. **(for someone . . . the question)**: It might be thought question-begging if you offered me the mutually exclusive options of saying that x is or that x is not. For, if I reject PNC, I will deny that these are mutually exclusive options.

43. **signify something**: Probably Aristotle is assuming, in the argument of this chapter, that (e.g.) 'man' signifies man, i.e., rational animal (a nonlinguistic item). Alternatively, he might be taken to assume that what 'man' signifies is 'rational animal' (the sense of the word). See SIGNIFY; cf. 1006a12n on 'speaking of'.

25   refutation>, since something will be definite as soon as he grants this.[44]
In allowing this it is he, not the demonstrator, who is responsible <for
something's being definite>; for in rejecting rational discourse, he allows
it.[45] Moreover, in conceding this he has conceded that something is true
apart from demonstration, so that not everything will be F and not F.

[ARGUMENTS FOR THE PRINCIPLE OF NONCONTRADICTION:
(1) THE REQUIREMENTS OF SIGNIFICATION]

30   First of all, clearly this much is true, that the name[46] signifies being or
not being this, so that not everything will be F and not F.

[(2) SIGNIFYING SOMETHING RELIES ON THE PRINCIPLE OF NONCONTRADICTION]

Further, if 'man'[47] signifies one thing, let this be biped animal. By 'signifying one thing' I mean that if a man is this, then if anything is a man,
its being a man is this.[48] If someone says that 'man' signifies more than

44. **something . . . grants this**: It is fixed and definite (and hence not open to
simultaneous denial) that the objector to PNC has spoken of something (e.g.,
of man, in the example that follows). In saying that x is both F and not F, the
opponent must be speaking of one and the same subject x, which he asserts to
be both F and not F. Hence he must satisfy the necessary conditions for speaking
of one and the same subject.

45. **he allows it**: For after all he claims to *assert* that one and the same subject
x is both F and not F (not just to utter these sounds).

46. **the name**: This is probably the name that the opponent is assumed to have
used in signifying something.

47. **'man'**: In this passage it is often difficult to know where quotation marks
should be used. We have used them only where Aristotle uses the neuter article
with the noun (of whatever gender; e.g., *to anthrōpos*) as a device for quoting
(he also uses it for other purposes; cf. *Met.* 1030a1). This may result in our
inserting too few quotation marks. An alternative would be to use quotation
marks every time Aristotle says one thing signifies another, but that might result
in too many quotation marks. At any rate, he believes that nonlinguistic items
also SIGNIFY; and so the use of 'signify' does not necessarily indicate that he is
talking about words.

48. **if a man . . . a man is this**: Translation and interpretation uncertain. Probably
this means: 'If a man is this (sc. biped animal), then if x is a man, this (sc. biped
animal) is x's being a man (i.e., what it is for x to be a man)'. If 'man' did not
signify one thing, then it would not be true that what it is to be a man is the
same for everything that is a man. An alternative translation: 'If this is a man,
then if something is a man, this will be being a man'. A further source of difficulty
is the fact that *anthrōpos*, translated 'a man', might also be translated 'man'. (The

one thing, that makes no difference, provided that he says it signifies a   *1006b*
definite number of things; for if he says that, a different name can be
assigned to each account. Suppose, for instance, he says that 'man'
signifies many things, not just one, and that biped animal is the account
of one of the things signified, but there are also several other accounts,[49]
though a definite number of them. His saying this makes no difference,   *5*
since a different name can be assigned to correspond to each account.[50]
If, however, a different name is not assigned, and he says the name
signifies an indeterminate number of things, then evidently there will
be no rational discourse. For to signify no one thing is to signify nothing,
and if names do not signify, then rational discussion[51] with one another,
and indeed even with oneself, is destroyed (for we cannot think without   *10*
thinking of one thing, and if we can think, then one name can be assigned
to this one thing we are thinking of).[52]

Suppose, then, that, as we said at the beginning, the name signifies
something and some one thing; it follows that being a man[53] cannot
signify essentially not being man, if 'man' not only signifies about one
thing but also signifies one thing. For we do not suppose that signifying   *15*
one thing is merely signifying about one thing; if it were merely that,
then 'musical thing', 'pale thing', and 'man' would also signify one thing,
and so <being musical, being pale, and being a man> would all be one,
since they would be synonymous.[54]

Further, it will not be possible for the same thing to be and not to be,
except by homonymy of the sort that would arise if, for instance, others   *20*
called not a man the one whom we call a man. The puzzle, however, is

---

Greek has no indefinite article.) It is often difficult in this argument to know
whether the subject Aristotle is thinking of is a particular or a universal, and
whether he intends the argument to apply to both sorts of subject (cf. 1007b20n
below).

49. **other accounts**: for the other things signified.

50. **since . . . account**: OCT deletes this.

51. **rational discussion**: *dialegesthai*, cognate with *dialektikē*. See DIALECTIC.

52. **(for we . . . thinking of)**: This explains the remark about rational discourse
with oneself.

53. **being a man**: On such phrases see ESSENCE #2.

54. **For we do not . . . synonymous**: 'Musical thing', 'pale thing', and 'man' all
signify about one thing (namely, the one subject who is a man, pale, and musical).
If we did not distinguish signifying one thing from signifying about one thing,
then not only would 'man' and 'not man' signify one thing, which follows from
the previous discussion, but (even worse) 'musical', 'pale', and 'man' would
also signify one and the same thing. In that case they would all have the same
definition, and hence would be SYNONYMOUS.

not about whether the same thing at the same time can both be and not be a man in name, but about whether this is possible in actual fact.

25

30

Now, if 'man' and 'not man' do not signify something different, then plainly neither does not being a man signify something different from what being a man signifies, and so being a man will be not being a man, since they will be one thing. For being one signifies being as cloak and cape are, i.e., having one account;[55] and if <man and not man> are one, then being a man and not being a man will signify one thing. It has been shown, however, that they signify different things. Necessarily, therefore, if it is true to say of something that it is a man, it is a biped animal, since this, we saw, is what 'man' signifies. And if this is necessary, then it is not possible for the same thing in that case not to be a biped animal; for 'necessary for it to be' signifies precisely that it is impossible for it not to be. Hence it cannot be at the same time true to say that the same thing is a man and is not a man.

1007a

5

The same also applies to not being a man. For being a man and not being a man signify something different, if being a pale thing and being a man are different; for not being a man is much more opposed <than being pale is to being a man>, and therefore it signifies something different.[56] If the respondent also says that 'pale' signifies the same one thing <that 'man' signifies>, we will tell him again, as we did before, that this will make all things, not merely opposites, one. And if this is not possible,[57] then the conclusion that was drawn earlier still follows, as long as he answers the question he is being asked.

10

If we ask him the question without qualification,[58] but he adds the negations, then he is not answering the question he is being asked. For although it is quite possible for the same thing to be a man and pale and a thousand other things, still the question was whether it is true to say that this is a man or not; and so he should answer with what signifies one thing, not adding that this thing is also pale and large.[59] For it is

55. **having one account**: On identity see ONE, ESSENCE #2.

56. **for not being . . . different**: Saying that man is pale is not the same as saying that man is man; and so Aristotle infers that saying that man is not man cannot be the same as saying that man is man.

57. **And . . . possible**: If 'all things were one' (i.e., everything signified the same), then 'x is F and not F' would be equivalent to 'x is F and F', and so would not violate PNC. The opponent, however, must take 'x is F and not F' to violate PNC, since otherwise he cannot state his thesis.

58. **without qualification**: i.e., without the irrelevant additions that he insists on inserting.

59. **also pale and large**: These are ways of being not man (i.e., something other than man). Aristotle argues that they do not falsify the claim that the subject in question is man (or a man).

impossible to list the coincidents, since they are indeterminate; and so   *15*
he should list either all or none of them. Similarly, then, even if the
same thing is a thousand times a man and not a man, still the question
was whether it is a man, and the answer should not add that it is also
at the same time not a man. He should not add this unless he should
also add the other coincidents, all the things it is or is not; but if he adds
these, he is not engaged in rational discussion.[60]   *20*

[(3) THE OPPONENTS MUST DENY THE EXISTENCE OF SUBSTANCE]

And in general our opponents do away with substance and essence; for
they must say that everything is coincidental and that there is no such
thing as being essentially a man or being essentially an animal. For if
there is such a thing as being essentially a man, it will not be being not
a man or not being a man; but these are the negations of being a man.[61]   *25*
For, as we saw, one thing is signified, and this is the substance of
something. Now, to signify a thing's substance is to signify that being
that thing is nothing other <than its substance>; but if the thing's being
essentially a man is being essentially not a man or essentially not being a
man, then being that thing will be something other <than its substance>.
Hence they must say that nothing has the sort of account <that signifies   *30*
substance>, but everything is coincidental. For precisely this[62] is the
difference between substance and coincident; for pale is a coincident of
a man because, though a man is pale, he is not essentially pale.[63]
    If everything is spoken of coincidentally, nothing will be the primary
subject of which <something is predicated>, since in every case the   *35*
coincident signifies a predication of some subject. Hence the predication *1007b*
must go on with no determinate limit; but this is impossible, since no
more than two things are combined <in a predication>. For no coincident is a coincident of a coincident, except insofar as both are coincidents
of the same <subject> (for instance, the pale is musical and the musical
pale because both are coincidents of the man[64]); but what makes Socrates *5*
musical is not this, that both <Socrates and the musical> are coincidents

60. **rational discussion**: *dialegesthai*. Cf. 'rational discourse' (*logos*) in 1006a14.

61. **negations of being a man:** Hence it should be possible for them to be true
of being a man, if PNC is false.

62. **precisely this**: This is the feature specified in the fourth sentence of this
paragraph ('Now, to signify . . . <than its substance>').

63. **for pale . . . essentially pale**: F is a COINCIDENT of x if it is possible for x to
be not F, but F is x's SUBSTANCE only if it is not possible for x to be not F. Since
the opponents believe that each of x's properties can be denied of x, they must
believe that all of x's properties are coincidental.

64. **the pale . . . of the man**: See 1017a7–22.

of something else. Hence some things are called coincidents in this way,[65] and others in the other way.[66]

And so things that are called coincidents in the way in which the pale is a coincident of Socrates cannot form an indeterminate upward series (so that, for instance, something else would be a coincident of the pale that is a coincident of Socrates); for these together do not amount to one thing. Nor yet can something else—the musical, for instance—be a coincident of the pale, since it is no more a coincident of the pale than the pale is of it. Moreover, we have distinguished the things that are coincidents in this way from those that are coincidents in the way in which the musical is a coincident of Socrates, and we have found that the coincident is a coincident of the coincident in the first case, but not in the second.[67]

Hence not everything is spoken of by coincidence. In this way too, then, there is something signifying substance. And if this is so, it is shown that contradictories cannot be predicated at the same time.

[(4) THEY CANNOT DISTINGUISH ONE THING FROM ANOTHER]

Moreover, if all contradictories are true of the same thing at the same time, then clearly all things will be one. For the same thing will be a warship, a wall, and a man,[68] if it is possible both to affirm and to deny anything of everything—as those who state the argument of Protagoras must say. For if a man seems to someone not to be a warship, then clearly he is not a warship; then he is also a warship, if the contradictory is true;[69] and so the result is that, as Anaxagoras said, all things are together, so that no one thing truly belongs <to anything>.[70] Hence

65. **in this way**: i.e., as the pale is a coincident of Socrates.

66. **in the other way**: i.e., as the pale is a coincident of the musical because both are coincidents of Socrates.

67. **in the first . . . second**: In the first case we can say that a coincident is a coincident of a coincident (e.g., that the musical is a coincident of the pale)—though only because both are coincidents of something else (the man).

68. **a warship, a wall, and a man**: Or 'warship, wall, and man'. The same choice must be in the next sentence. It is not clear in either sentence whether the argument is about particulars (saying that this man is also a wall and a warship) or universals (saying that being a man is also being a wall and being a warship). Cf. 1006a32–4n above.

69. **For if a man . . . contradictory is true**: This is meant to explain why the supporters of Protagoras must say that the same thing is a warship, wall, and man.

70. **no one . . . anything>**: Whenever any property belongs, every other property does too. Alternative translation: 'nothing is truly one'.

they would seem to be speaking of the indefinite, and though they think
they are speaking of what is, they are really speaking of what is not; for
the indefinite is what potentially is but actually is not.[71]

Further, they must affirm or deny every property of every subject;   *30*
for it is absurd if it is true to say <as our opponents claim> that F is
not F, but not true to say that F is not G, even though G does not belong
to F.[72] If, for instance, it is true to say that a man is not a man, then clearly
he is also either a warship or not a warship; and so if the affirmation <of
warship> is true, the negation must also be true. If, alternatively, the   *35*
affirmation <of warship> does not belong, at least its negation must
belong more than the negation of man does; if, then, the negation of   *1008a*
man belongs, so does the negation of warship, and if this belongs, so
does the affirmation.

[(5) THEY MUST DENY THE PRINCIPLE OF EXCLUDED MIDDLE [73]]

These are the results, then, for those who give this argument. It also
results that it is not necessary either to affirm or to deny. For if it is true
that he is a man and not a man, then clearly he will also be neither a   *5*
man nor not a man. For each of the affirmations has a negation; and if
one of the affirmations has two components, it will be opposed by one
negation <that also has two components>.[74]

[(6) THEY REFUTE THEMSELVES]

Moreover, either this <rejection of the Principle of Noncontradiction>
holds for everything (so that everything is also pale and not pale, and
being and not being, and similarly for the other affirmations and nega-   *10*
tions), or it does not hold for everything, but holds for some affirmations
and negations and not for others. If it does not hold for all of them,

---

71. **for the indefinite . . . is not**: If x is not definitely F or G, then it is capable
of becoming F or becoming G, by becoming more definite, but it is not actually
F or actually G.

72. **for it is absurd . . . to F**: Lit. 'for it is absurd if a thing's own negation
belongs to it, but the negation of something else not belonging to it does not
belong to it.'

73. On the Principle of Excluded Middle see AXIOM.

74. **For each . . . components>**: The affirmation with two components is 'He is
a man and not a man', which opponents of PNC must accept. Since they reject
PNC, they must also accept the negation of this compound affirmation. The
negation is the compound 'He is neither a man nor not a man'; and this negation
conflicts with the Principle of Excluded Middle.

then the exceptions will be agreed on. But if it holds for all, then once again either the negation is true of everything of which the affirmation is true and the affirmation is true of everything of which the negation is true, or else the negation is true of everything of which the affirmation is true but the affirmation is not true of everything of which the negation is true.

15   If this last claim is true, then something will be fixed as not being, and this will be a firm belief; and if not being is something firm and known$_g$, the opposed affirmation will be still better known. But if it is also true to affirm whatever it is true to deny, then necessarily either it

20   is true to divide[75] and say, for instance, that it is pale and again that it is not pale, or it is not.

It is not true to divide and say it, then he is not really *saying*[76] these things, and nothing has any being—and how could things that are not utter sounds or walk? And all things will be one, as we also said before,

25   and the same thing will be man, god, warship, and stone, and the contradictories of these; for if they are true of each thing in the same way, there will be no difference between one thing and another, since, if there were any difference, this fact would be true and would be distinctive of the thing it belonged to.

Similarly, if it is possible to divide and speak truly, we reach the result we mentioned. Moreover, it follows that everyone speaks truly and

30   everyone speaks falsely, and that he agrees that he himself speaks falsely. And at the same time it is evident that if we attempt to examine what he says, there is nothing to examine; for he speaks of nothing, because he speaks neither thus nor not thus, but both thus and not thus, and then again he denies both, saying that it is neither thus nor not thus— for if he did not deny both, something would thereby be definite.

[*(7) THEY IGNORE THE MEANING OF 'TRUE' AND 'FALSE'*]

35   Further, if the negation is false whenever the affirmation is true, and the affirmation is false whenever the negation is true, then it will not

1008b   be possible both to affirm and to deny the same thing truly. But presum-

75. **divide**: i.e., affirming the two parts of the conjunction separately. For 'division' applied to disjunctions and to conditionals see *DI* 18b29. The next two paragraphs present the opponent with a dilemma.

76. **not saying**: If the opponent utters (1) 'x is F and not F' but is not willing to divide (1) into (2) 'x is F' and (3) 'x is not F', then he cannot be taken to be asserting a conjunction, and so he cannot after all be asserting (1); he will merely be uttering the sounds.

ably he might say that this was the very point proposed for discussion at the beginning.⁷⁷

[(8) THEY CANNOT SAY ANYTHING]

Further, is someone speaking falsely if he supposes that something is some way or that it is not, and speaking truly if he supposes both? If he speaks truly in the second case, then what is being said in the statement that such is the nature of beings? If he does not speak truly, but   5
speaks more* truly than the one who supposes the other thing, then beings will be some way, and this will be true and not also not true at the same time. And if all alike speak both falsely and truly, then anyone of whom this is true cannot utter or say anything; for at the same time he says this and not this. But if he supposes nothing, but thinks this no   10
more than he does not think this, how is his state any different from a plant's?

[(9) THEIR ACTIONS SHOW THAT THEY ACCEPT
THE PRINCIPLE OF NONCONTRADICTION]

From this it is especially evident that no one at all, including those giving this argument, is in this condition. For why, when he thinks he ought   15
to walk toward Megara, does he walk toward it, instead of staying where he is? And why does he not get up in the morning and walk straight into a wall or a pit, whichever it happens to be? Why does he instead evidently take care to avoid it, on the assumption that he does not think falling in is both good and not good? Clearly, then, he supposes one thing is better and the other is not better. If so, he must also suppose   20
that one thing is a man and another is not a man, and that one thing is sweet and another is not sweet. For if he thinks it is better to drink water and see a man, and then he seeks them, he does not seek and suppose all things indiscriminately, which he would have to do if the same thing were alike both a man and not a man. But in fact, as was said, everyone evidently takes care to avoid some things and not others.   25

It would seem, then, that everyone supposes that things are some way without qualification;⁷⁸ even if they do not suppose this about everything, they at least suppose it about the better and the worse. And if this supposition* counts as belief rather than knowledgeₑ, one should pay all the more attention to truth, just as one should pay more attention

---

77. **he might . . . beginning**: He might object that the appeal to the meaning of 'true' and 'false' begs the question at issue.

78. **without qualification**: so that they are not also not that way.

30   to health when one is sick than when one is healthy; for indeed someone
      who has a belief is not in a healthy condition in relation to the truth,
      compared to someone with knowledge.

[(10) IF APPROXIMATION TO TRUTH IS POSSIBLE, THE PRINCIPLE OF NONCONTRADICTION MUST BE TRUE]

      Further, however true it might be that everything is thus and not thus,
      nonetheless the more and less is in the nature of beings. For we would
      not say that two and three are even to the same degree, or that the one
35   who thinks four are five is mistaken to the same degree as someone
      who thinks four are a thousand. If they are not mistaken to the same
      degree, then clearly one of them is less mistaken, so that he speaks more
1009a truly. Now if what is more F is nearer to being F, then there will be
      some truth to which the more true is nearer; and even if there is not,
      still at least in this case something is firmer and has more of the character
      of the truth. In that case, we are rid of the extreme argument that
      prevents us from having anything definite[79] in thought.

[PHILOSOPHY AS KNOWLEDGE OF OBJECTIVE REALITY]

[PROTAGORAS AND THE DENIAL OF THE PRINCIPLE OF NONCONTRADICTION]

      5

5   The argument of Protagoras[80] arises from the same belief <that leads to
      the denial of the Principle of Noncontradiction>, and each view must
      be true or false if the other is. For if everything that seems and appears
      is true, everything must at the same time be true and false. For many
10   people suppose things contrary to other people and think those who do
      not believe what they believe have false beliefs; hence the same things
      must both be and not be. And if this is so, then whatever seems must
      be true. For those who believe falsely and those who believe truly believe
15   opposite things; and so, if beings are <opposite ways at the same time>,
      everyone will have true beliefs. Clearly, then, both arguments are based
      on the same line of thought.
         But not everyone who holds these views requires the same treatment;
      rather, some need persuasion, while others need force. For those who
      supposed this because they were puzzled are easily cured of their igno-
20   rance; for our approach to them should focus on their line of thought,

---

79. **having anything definite**: Lit. 'defining anything' (*horizein*, cognate with
horismos, 'DEFINITION').

80. **The argument of Protagoras**: Cf. Plato, *Theaetetus* 152a.

not on the argument <they actually give>.[81] But those who state it for the sake of argument must be cured by refutation of their argument in their utterance and in their words.[82]

Those who are really puzzled have reached their belief from perceptible things. They have reached their belief that contradictory and contrary belong <to the same subject> at the same time, because they see that contraries come to be from the same thing, and they infer that since   *25* what is not cannot come to be, the thing from which the contraries came was previously both contraries alike. This is the point of Anaxagoras' statement that everything is mixed in everything and of what Democritus says—for he says that the empty and the full belong to every part alike, and that one of these is being and one is not being.   *30*

Our reply to those who suppose as they do on this basis is that in a way what they say is correct, but in a way they are mistaken. For in fact being is spoken of in two ways, so that in one way it is possible, and in another way it is not possible, for something to come to be from what is not.[83] Similarly, it is possible for the same thing at the same time both to be and not to be, but not in the same respect; for it is possible for the   *35* same thing at the same time to have contrary properties potentially, but not to have them actually. Further, we will demand that they recognize the existence of another sort of substance, to which neither motion nor perishing nor coming to be belongs at all.[84]

[THE BELIEF IN THE TRUTH OF APPEARANCES, AND CONCLUSIONS ABOUT CHANGE]

Similarly, some people have been led to believe in the truth of appear-   *1009b* ances because of perceptible things. In their view, one ought not to judge the truth of something by the large or small number <of people who believe it>.[85] But the same thing seems sweet to some who taste it, bitter to others, so that if all were sick or all insane except for two or   *5*

81. **for our . . . give**>: They are convinced by an argument that rests on mistaken assumptions; hence we must refute these assumptions.

82. **But those who state . . . their words**: These are the people who were said to need force.

83. **in one way . . . what is not**: See *Phys.* 187a27, 191a23–b4.

84. **another sort . . . belongs at all**: See 1010a25–35.

85. **the truth . . . believe it**>: This general principle is applied to the examples that follow. Mere numbers do not determine truth; but in cases of conflicting appearances (the proponents of this argument suggest) there is nothing to choose between the two appearances, except that more people believe one than believe the other; hence we have no ground for supposing that one appearance is really true and the other is really false. See Plato, *Theaetetus* 152bc, 154a, 158a–e.

three healthy or sane people, these two or three, not the majority, would seem to be sick or insane. Further, many of the other animals have appearances* contrary to ours about the same things, and even for each one of us in relation to himself things do not always seem the same as far as perception goes. It is unclear, then, which appearances are true or false; for one lot are no more true than another lot, but all are true or false alike. This is why Democritus says that either nothing is true or, at any rate, what is true is unclear to us.

10

In general, the reason they say that what appears in perception must be true is that they suppose both that perception is understanding[86] and that it is <simply> alteration.[87] For this is how Empedocles, Democritus, and all the others (we may say)[88] have been trapped by such beliefs. Empedocles, for instance, says that when one's state changes, one's understanding also changes: 'For man's cunning increases in relation to what is present'. And elsewhere he says: 'To the extent that their nature was altered, to that extent understanding presented altered things to them.' Parmenides, in the same way, affirms: 'Whatever the state of the mixture of their much-bent limbs, so is the state of mind present to men. For the nature of the limbs, in each and every man, is precisely what understands; what predominates is thought.' A saying of Anaxagoras to some of his companions is also recorded, that 'beings will be for them such as they suppose them to be'. People say that even Homer evidently had this belief, because he says that Hector was knocked out of his wits by a blow and lay 'with his understanding knowing other things'; they take him to mean that even those with deranged understanding have understanding, though not about the same things. It is clear, then, that if both <the normal and the deranged states have> understanding, then beings are also at the same time both thus and not thus.

15

20

25

30

This result, indeed, is the hardest to accept. For if those who more than anyone else have seen such truth as it is possible to see—those who more than anyone else search for it and love it—if they believe and affirm such views about truth, how can we expect beginners in philosophy not to lose heart? The search for truth would be a wild goose chase.

1010a

86. **understanding**: *phronēsis*, usually translated by 'INTELLIGENCE'.

87. **alteration**: i.e., merely a bodily process. For Aristotle's criticism of this view of perception see *DA* 416b32–417a20, 424b3–18. These people think perception is true, but they recognize that bodily conditions change in different circumstances; hence they infer that perception, and hence truth, varies according to these changes in circumstances.

88. **(we may say)**: Aristotle often uses this or a similar phrase to apologize for a possible exaggeration that does not affect his main point; cf. 1028b7, *Pol.* 1323a20, 1328b16, *Rhet.* 1354a12.

They reached this view because they were investigating the truth about beings and supposed that the only beings were perceptible things; in these, however, there is much of the nature of the indeterminate, i.e., of the sort of being we have described.[89] Hence it is not surprising   5 that they say what they say, but what they say is not true. (This is a more appropriate comment than Epicharmus' comment on Xenophanes.)

Further, since they saw that all of this nature around us is in motion and that nothing true can be said about what is changing, they said it is impossible to say anything true about what undergoes every sort of change in every respect. From this view there blossomed the most ex-   10 treme of the views we have mentioned, that of the self-styled Heracleitizers. This was the sort of view held by Cratylus, who ended up thinking he must say nothing, and only moved his finger.[90] He criticized Heracleitus for saying one could not step into the same river twice; for Cratylus thought one could not do it even once.   15

[REPLIES TO THE ARGUMENTS ABOUT CHANGE]

We also reply to this argument as follows. Though they do have some argument for their view that what is changing, when it is changing, is not, still this is at any rate disputable. For what is losing something has some of what is being lost, and some of what is coming to be must already be. And in general, if something is perishing, there must be   20 something that it is; and if something is coming to be, there must be something from which it comes to be and something that generates it, and this does not go on without limit.

But let us leave these arguments aside and insist that a change in <a subject's> quantity is not the same as a change in the sort of thing <the subject is>. Hence, even if we concede that something is unstable in quantity, still we know_g each thing by its form.[91]   25

Further, those who suppose <that everything changes> should also be criticized for something else. The things that they saw <constantly changing> are a minority even of perceptible things, but they declared that the same <constant change> was true of the whole universe. In

89. **we have described**: See 1009a32; both contraries are (potentially) present together.

90. **moved his finger**: Presumably he did this to point at things, since he did not think they were stable enough to apply any words to them.

91. **we know_g . . . form**: Hence a subject cannot always be changing in respect of the sort of thing it is. Aristotle identifies FORM (or species: *eidos*), with the sort of thing (*poion*) a subject is. See QUALITY, *Catg.* 3b13–23, 4a10–21; Plato, *Theaetetus* 182cd.

30   fact it is only the area of the perceptible universe around us that is in constant destruction and generation, and this is an insignificant part of the whole universe. And so it would be more just to acquit this part <of the world from constant change> because of the other part than to condemn the other part <for constant change> because of these things. Again, clearly we shall also say in response to these people what we said before;[92] for they should be shown and persuaded that there is some unmoved nature.

35   In any case, to say that things simultaneously are and are not is to imply that they are at rest rather than that they are moving; for there is

1010b nothing for anything to change into, since everything belongs to everything.

[REPLIES TO ARGUMENTS ABOUT THE TRUTH OF APPEARANCES]

As for the truth, we say that not everything that appears is true. First, even if perception, at least of its proper objects,[93] is not false, still, appearance is not the same as perception.

5   Further, one may justifiably be surprised if they are puzzled by such questions as these: 'Are magnitudes and colors such as they appear to be to observers from a distance or such as they appear to be to observers close at hand? Are they such as they appear to be to healthy people or such as they appear to be to sick people? Are things heavier if they appear so to feeble people or if they appear so to vigorous people? Are things true if they appear so to people asleep or if they appear so to people awake?'[94] For it is evident that at any rate they do not really think

10   <the appearances of the dreamer are true>—certainly no one who is in Libya and one night supposes <in a dream> that he is in Athens goes off toward the Odeion.[95]

Further, as for the future, as Plato[96] says, the belief of a doctor and of an ignorant person surely are not equally authoritative[97] about, for instance, whether someone is or is not going to be healthy.

15   Further, among perceptions themselves, a sense's perception of the object of another sense is less authoritative than its perception of its

92. **said before**: See 1009a36–38.

93. **proper objects**: See *DA* 418a7–16, 428b17–20.

94. **Are things true . . . awake?'**: For this test cf. *Top.* 142a9, *EE* 1248b26–34, *EN* 1173b20.

95. **goes off toward the Odeion**: sc. when he wakes up. The Odeion is a building in Athens.

96. **Plato**: See *Theaetetus* 178bc.

97. **authoritative**: See CONTROLLING.

own proper object, and its perception of a neighboring object is less authoritative than the perception of its own object. In the case of color it is sight, not taste, that is authoritative, and in the case of flavor it is taste, not sight; and none of these senses ever says that the same thing at the same time is both thus and not thus. And even when different times are involved, there is no dispute about the <perceptible> attribute   20
but only about that <subject> of which the attribute is a coincident. I mean, for instance, that the same wine might seem sweet at one time but not at another, if it or the body <of the perceiver> had changed; but what sweetness is, whenever it is present, has never yet changed— one always has the truth about it, and whatever is to be sweet is necessar-   25
ily of this sort.

And yet this is eliminated by all these arguments: just as nothing has a substance, so also nothing is of necessity. For what is necessary cannot be both one way and another, and so if something is thus of necessity, it will not be both thus and not thus.   30

And in general, if there are only perceptible things, nothing would exist unless animate things existed, since without them there would be no perception. Now presumably it is true that <without animate things> there would be neither perceptible things nor perceivings, since this is a way in which a perceiver is affected; but there must be subjects that cause perception and that exist whether or not they are perceived. For   35
perception is certainly not of itself; on the contrary, there is also something else apart* from the perception, which is necessarily prior to perception. For what initiates a motion is naturally prior to what is moved,   1011a
and this is just as true even if what initiates the motion and what is moved are spoken of in relation to each other.[98]

[SOME PUZZLES REFLECT IGNORANCE OF THE APPROPRIATE SORTS OF ARGUMENTS]

6

Some people, however, including some who are persuaded by these <puzzles about the senses> and some who merely put forward these arguments, are puzzled. For they ask who is to discriminate which   5
people are healthy and, in general, who is to discriminate correctly about anything. But being puzzled about these sorts of questions is like being puzzled about whether we are now awake or asleep.

All such puzzles have the same force. For those who raise them demand to be given an argument for everything, since they seek a principle, and seek to reach it through demonstration; for it is evident   10

98. **For what initiates . . . to each other**: On the PRIORITY of the perceptible object to perception see DA 425a15–26.

in their actions that at any rate they are not really persuaded <by their puzzles>.[99] But as we said, this is what happens to them; for they search for an argument for things for which there is no argument. For the starting point[100] of demonstration is not a demonstration.

15   These people might easily be persuaded of this, since it is not hard to grasp. But those who will be satisfied with nothing less than an argument that forces them <to change their mind> ask for the impossible; for they demand <that we refute them by> stating contrary things <to what they say>, but then they at once state contrary things[101] <in rejecting the Principle of Noncontradiction>.

[OUR OPPONENTS RESTRICT THEIR POSITION TO AVOID REFUTATION]

If, however, not everything is relative* to something, but there are also some things that are in their own right, then not everything that appears will be true; for whatever appears appears to someone, and so those 20 who say that whatever appears is true make all beings relative to something. Hence those who ask for an argument that forces them, and at the same time present their view for examination, should be careful; they should say that <what is true> is not what appears but what appears to someone, and when it appears, and insofar as, and how it appears.

    If they present their view for examination but do not state it in these 25 terms, they will soon find themselves contradicting themselves. For it is possible for the same thing to appear to the same perceiver to be honey according to sight but not according to taste, and, since we have two eyes, it is possible for different things to appear to the sight of each, if their sight is dissimilar.[102] For we must reply to those who say, for 30 reasons mentioned previously, that what appears is true, and hence that everything is equally true and false; for the same things, they say, do not always appear to everyone or even always to the same person, but

---

    99. **for it is evident . . . puzzles>**: This is intended to support Aristotle's claim that they are demanding an argument for argument's sake and are not expressing a genuine doubt.

    100. **starting point**: See PRINCIPLE #3.

    101. **for they . . . contrary things**: Since they do not regard a proof of not-p as a refutation of p, or as any reason to stop asserting p (given their rejection of PNC), it is not clear what they can regard as an adequate refutation of anything. Hence they ask for the impossible.

    102. **For it is possible . . . is dissimilar**: And so, unless the opponents add the qualifications mentioned in the previous paragraph, they will undermine their own claim that what is true is what appears.

contraries often appear at the same time—when the fingers are crossed, for instance, touch says there are two things, but sight says there is one. We reply that still, these contraries do not appear to the same sense in the same respect, in the same way, and at the same time; and hence this[103] would be true.

35

1011b

[OBJECTIONS TO AN EXTREME POSITION]

Presumably this is why those who argue for the sake of argument, not because they are puzzled, must say that this is not true, but is true *to* someone.[104] As we said before, they must make everything relative to something—both to belief and to perception—so that nothing either has or will come to be without someone's first having the belief that it is so. But if something has come to be or will come to be <without someone first believing it>, then it is clear that not everything is relative to belief.

5

Again, if something is one, it is one relative to one thing, or to something definite; and if the same thing is both half and equal, still, the equal is not relative to the double. If, then, relative to a believer, the same thing is both a man and an object of belief, then it is not the believer, but the object of belief, that will be a man. And if everything is relative to a believer, believers will be relative to things that are unlimited[105] in kind.

10

[CONCLUSION]

Let this suffice, then, to show that the firmest belief of all is the belief that opposite affirmations cannot be true at the same time; to show what results for those who say that they are true; and to show why they say this.

15

Since it is impossible for a contradiction to be true at the same time about the same thing, neither, evidently, can contraries belong at the same time to the same thing. For one of the contraries is, no less, a privation (a privation of substance), and a privation is a negation about some definite genus. If, then, it is impossible to affirm and deny truly at the same time, it is also impossible for contraries to belong at the same time—unless either they both belong <only> in a way or one belongs <only> in a way and the other belongs without qualification.

20

103. **this**: The claim that contraries cannot be true, with the qualifications just mentioned.

104. **to someone**: Or 'for someone'.

105. **unlimited**: See INFINITE.

* * * * * * *

BOOK V

[MAJOR PHILOSOPHICAL TERMS AND THEIR VARIOUS USES [1]]

[BEING]

[(1) PREDICATIVE BEING]

7

1017a7 Being is spoken of both coincidentally and in its own right. It is spoken
of coincidentally when we say, for instance, that the just one[2] is musical,
10 the man is musical, and the musician is a man; this is just like saying
that a musician builds, because being musical is coincidental to the
builder, or being a builder to the musician—for the F being G signifies
G being coincidental to the F.[3] That is how it is in the cases mentioned,
15 whenever we say that the man is musical, or that the musician is a man,
or that the pale one is musical, or that the musician is pale. <In the
third case> it is because both are coincidental to the same thing; <in
the first case> it is because <the coincident—musical, for instance—>
is coincidental to the thing that is <for instance, the man. In the second
case> the musical <thing> is a man because the musical is coincidental
to the man—this is the way in which the not-pale is said to be, because
it is coincidental to something that is.

20 The things that are said to be coincidentally, then, are so called either
because each of two things belongs to the same thing that is, or because
the first belongs to the second, a thing that is, or because the second is
predicated of the first, the first belongs to the second, and the second
is a thing that is.[4]

The things that are said to be in their own right are all those that are
signified by the types of predication;[5] for they are said to be in as many

---

1. Though the contents of this book are relevant to the rest of the *Metaphysics*,
it is not clear that it was originally intended to stand at this place in the treatise.
Each chapter contains a short discussion of one of the important terms that
Aristotle says are 'said in many ways' (see HOMONYMY).

2. **the just one**: Aristotle uses a masculine article and adjective, as he does in
'the musician' and 'the pale one'. 'Musical <thing>' below represents the neuter
article and adjective.

3. **for F . . . coincidental to F**: See 1007b2–16.

4. **or because . . . that is**: Lit. 'or because that is, to which belongs that of
which it is predicated'. The man, for instance, is predicated of the musician, the
musician belongs to the man, and the man is.

5. **types of predication**: See PREDICATIONS.

ways as there are ways of signifying being. Among things predicated,   *25*
some signify what-it-is, some quality, some quantity, some relative, some
acting, some being acted on, some where, some when; and so being
signifies the same as each of these. For there is no difference between
'a man is flourishing'⁶ and 'a man flourishes', or between 'a man is
walking (or cutting)' and 'a man walks (or cuts)', and the same is true   *30*
in the other cases.

[(2) BEING AS TRUTH]

Further, being and 'is' signify that something is true; and not being
signifies that something is not true but false, in affirmation and negation
alike. For example, that Socrates is musical signifies that this is true,
and that Socrates is not-pale signifies that this is true, while that a   *35*
diagonal is not commensurable signifies that this is false.⁷

[(3) POTENTIAL AND ACTUAL BEING]

Being and what is also signify that some of the things mentioned are   *1017b*
potentially, others actually. We say, for instance, that something *is* a
thing that sees, both if it potentially sees and if it actually sees. Similarly,
we say that something knows_e both if it is capable of exercising its
knowledge and if it is exercising it; we say that something rests both if   *5*
it is at rest at the time and if it is capable of being at rest.
    The same is true of substances. We say that Hermes *is* in the stone,
and the half-line <in the line, because they are in it potentially> and
that what is unripe is grain <because it is grain potentially>.⁸ We must
determine elsewhere⁹ the conditions in which something has or does
not yet have a potentiality.

6. **'a man is flourishing'**: Greek does not standardly use the verb 'to be' with
a present participle (as in 'is walking'), as English does, to form the present
imperfect tense. Hence when Aristotle uses this construction (*esti badizōn*) here,
he explains that it signifies the same as the normal present tense verb (*badizei*).
Cf. *DI* 21b9.

7. **and that Socrates ... this is false**: The hyphen in 'not-pale' is meant to
capture Aristotle's point that the negation is attached to the adjective. In the
last part of the sentence the negation is attached to the 'is'. Cf. *DI* 21a38–b3.

8. **We say that ... potentially>**: Cf. *Met.* 1048a32–35.

9. **elsewhere**: *Met.* 1048b37–1049a17.

8

10 The things called substances[10] are, first, the simple bodies (earth, fire, water, and everything like that) and in general bodies and the things composed from them (animals and divine things and their parts). All these things are said to be substances because they are not said of a subject, but the other things are said of them.

15 In another way, that which, by being present in things that are not said of a subject, is the cause of their being—for instance, the soul for an animal—is called substance.

Further, the parts present in such things, defining them and signifying a this, the things with whose destruction the whole is destroyed, are called substances; for instance, the body is destroyed with the destruction

20 of the plane (as some people say), and the plane with the destruction of the line. And in general it seems to some people that number is this sort of thing, since if it is destroyed nothing exists, and it defines all things.

Further, the essence, whose account is a definition, is also said to be the substance of a thing.

It turns out, then, that substance is spoken of in two ways.[11] It is both the ultimate subject, which is no longer said of anything else, and

25 whatever, being a this,*[12] is also separable—this is true of the shape, i.e., the form, of a thing.

Book VII

[THE STUDY OF SUBSTANCE]

[SUBSTANCE IS THE PRIMARY TYPE OF BEING]

1

1028a10 Being is spoken of in many ways, which we distinguished previously in the work on how many ways things are spoken of.[1] For one <type of being> signifies what-it-is and a this; another signifies quality, or quantity, or any of the other things predicated in this way. But while being is spoken of in this many ways, it is evident that among these the

15 primary being is the what-it-is, which signifies substance. For whenever

---

10. **things called substances**: For these examples cf. vii 2, 16, viii 1.

11. **two ways**: Cf. 1028b32–36, 1038b1–8, 1042a25–31, 1049a27–36.

12. **a this**: For this claim see 1028a12, 1029a27–28, 1039a1.

1. **in the work . . . spoken of**: See *Met.* v 7 above.

we say what quality this has,[2] we call it good or bad, not six feet long or a man, whereas whenever we say what it is, we call it a man or a god, not pale or hot or six feet long; and the other things[3] are called beings by belonging to this type of being—some as quantities, some as qualities, some as affections, some in some other such way.   20

That is why someone might actually be puzzled about whether walking, flourishing, or sitting signifies a being;[4] for none of these is in its own right[5] nor is any of them capable of being separated from substance, but it is more* true that the walking or sitting or flourishing thing is a   25 being (if indeed it is a being). This latter type of thing is apparently more of a being because it has some definite subject—the substance and the particular—which is discerned[6] in such a predication; for this subject is implied in speaking of the good or sitting thing. Clearly, then, it is because of substance that each of those other things is also a being,[7] so   30 that what is in the primary way[8]—what is not something,[9] but is without qualification a being—is substance.

[HOW SUBSTANCE IS PRIMARY]

Now the primary is so spoken of in many ways, but still, substance is primary in every way: in nature, in account, and in knowledge$_g$.[10] For none of the other things predicated is separable, but only substance. Substance is also primary in account, since its account is necessarily   35 present in the account of each thing. Moreover, we think we know a

2. **this has**: Aristotle treats a THIS, mentioned in 1028a12 above, as the SUBJECT about which the different questions are asked.

3. **the other things**: the things in the other categories. See PREDICATIONS.

4. **signifies a being**: Read *on sēmainei*. OCT: 'is a being or not a being'.

5. **is in its own right**: Nonsubstances such as qualities are not beings except insofar as they belong to something else (a substance), and hence are not beings IN THEIR OWN RIGHT. Cf. *APo* 83a30–32.

6. **discerned**: Cf. *Phys.* 200b17.

7. **is also a being**: Lit. just 'is'.

8. **what is in the primary way**: Cf. 1045b27.

9. **what is not something**: i.e., what is not something *else*, as the sitting thing is something else, e.g., a man. (Or 'what is not a certain sort of being'.) In speaking of being WITHOUT QUALIFICATION Aristotle probably means to convey the same point as he conveyed above by saying that substance is a being IN ITS OWN RIGHT.

10. **in nature ... knowledge$_g$**: Read *kai phusei kai logō(i) kai gnōsei*. OCT: 'in account, in knowledge, and in time'. See PRIOR. The next three sentences explain how substance is prior in each of the three ways just distinguished.

1028b thing most of all whenever we know what, for instance, man or fire is, rather than when we know its quality or quantity or place; for indeed we know each of these only when we know *what* the quantity or the quality *is*.[11]

[THE OLD PUZZLE ABOUT BEING IS REALLY ABOUT SUBSTANCE]

Indeed, the old question—always pursued from long ago till now, and always raising puzzles—'What is being?' is just the question 'What is
5   substance?'. For it is substance that some say is one and others say is more than one, some saying that it is limited in number, others that it is unlimited. And so we too must make it our main, our primary, indeed (we may say)[12] our only, task to study what it is that is in this way.

[CANDIDATES FOR SUBSTANCE]

2

The most evident examples of substances seem to be bodies. That is
10 why we say that animals and plants and their parts are substances, and also natural bodies, such as fire, water, earth, and all such things, and whatever is either a part of these or composed of all or some of them— for instance, the universe and its parts, the stars, moon, and sun. But we ought to consider: Are these the only substances there are, or are
15 there also others? Or are only some of these things substances, or some of these and also some other things? Or are none of these things sub- stances, but only some other things?
    Some people think that the limits of a body—for instance, a surface, a line, a point, and a unit—are substances, and are so to a higher degree than a body and a solid. Further, some think there are no substances apart from perceptible things, while to others it seems that there are also everlasting substances, which are more numerous and are beings
20 to a higher degree. Plato, for example, thinks that Forms and mathemati- cals[13] are two <types of> substances, and that the substance of percepti- ble bodies is a third <type>. Speusippus posits even more substances, beginning with the one, and posits a principle for each <type of> sub- stance—one for numbers, another for magnitudes, and then another for soul; and in this way he multiplies the <types of> substances. Some

11. **when we know . . . is**: On the connection between substance and what-it- is see *Top.* 103b22, 27–28, SUBSTANCE #2.

12. **(we may say)**: See 1009b16n.

13. **mathematicals**: Cf. 987b14.

say that Forms and numbers have the same nature, and that everything   25
else comes after them—lines, planes, and everything else, extending to
the substance of the universe and to perceptible things.

We must consider, then, which of these views are correct or incorrect;
what substances there are; whether or not there are any substances
apart from perceptible substances, and in what way these perceptible
substances are <substances>; and whether or not there is any separable   30
substance apart from perceptible ones, and, if there is, why there is,
and in what way it is <substance>. But before doing this, we must first
sketch what substance is.

[SUBSTANCE AS SUBJECT]

[THE MAIN CRITERIA FOR SUBSTANCE]

3

Substance is spoken of, if not in several[14] ways, at any rate in four main
cases.[15] For the essence, the universal and the genus seem to be the   35
substance of a given thing, and the fourth of these cases is the subject.[16]

[SUBSTANCE IS THE FIRST SUBJECT]

Now, the subject is that of which the other things are said, but which
is not itself in turn said of any other thing;[17] hence we must first determine   1029a
what it is, since the primary subject seems to be substance most of all.

What is spoken of in this way <as the primary subject> is in one
way the matter,[18] in another way the form$_m$, and in a third way the thing

---

14. **several**: Or 'more'.

15. **in four main cases**: Aristotle seems to intend to distinguish this from 'being
spoken of in many ways' (i.e., having different definitions). These seem to be
four main widely-accepted criteria for being a substance.

16. **and the fourth . . . subject**: Aristotle does not say (as he said of the first
three cases) that the subject is the substance *of* anything.

17. **the other things . . . any other thing**: Aristotle might be referring either to
(i) some given range of other things or to (ii) all other things. If he means (i),
he is defining a 'relative' subject (so that F is the subject of G and H if and only
if G and H are said of F, but F is not said of G or H); if he means (ii), he is
defining an 'absolute' subject, i.e., a subject of all properties. Probably he intends
(i).

18. **the matter**: As the example shows, Aristotle seems to intend the matter of
a particular object (e.g., a statue), rather than matter in general (as we speak of
'matter and energy'). Hence we have retained the definite article.

5   composed of these. (By the matter I mean, for example, the bronze; by
the form$_m$ I mean the figure and character;[19] and by the thing composed
of them I mean the statue, i.e., the compound.) And so if the form is
prior to the matter, and more[20] of a being, it will also, by the same
argument, be prior to the thing composed of both.

We have now said in outline, then, what substance is: it is what is
not said of a subject but has the other things said of it.

[*THIS ANSWER SEEMS TO MAKE MATTER THE ONLY SUBSTANCE*]

However, we must not confine ourselves to this answer. For it is inade-
10   quate: for, first, it is itself unclear; and further, the matter turns out to
be substance.[21] For if the matter is not substance, it is hard to see what
other substance there is; for when all the other things are removed,
nothing <but the matter> evidently remains.[22] For the other things are
affections, products, and potentialities of bodies; and length, breadth,
15   and depth[23] are kinds of quantities but not substances (for quantity is
not substance), but the primary <subject> to which these belong is
more of a substance than they are. But when length, breadth, and depth
are abstracted,[24] we see that nothing is left, except whatever is determined by these. And so, if we examine it in this way, the matter necessarily appears as the only substance.

20   By matter I mean what is spoken of in its own right neither as being
something, nor as having some quantity, nor as having any of the other
things by which being is determined. For there is something of which
each of these is predicated, something whose being is different from
that of each of the things predicated; for the other things are predicated
of the substance, and the substance is predicated of the matter. And so

19. **figure and character**: Lit. 'FIGURE of the character'.

20. **more**: The translation of *mallon* (see MORE) makes a considerable difference
to what we think of Aristotle's claims about matter in this chapter; see 1029a15,
29.

21. **turns out to be substance**: This might be (i) an identity statement ('matter =
substance'), so that the unwelcome consequence is that matter is the only
substance, or (ii) a predication ('matter is a substance'), so that the unwelcome
consequence is that matter is included among substances at all. The following
argument and Aristotle's comments on it make (i) more probable; see 1029a27n.

22. **nothing ... evidently remains**: This is ambiguous between (a) 'It is not
evident that anything <but the matter> remains' and (b) 'It is evident that nothing
<but the matter> remains'. The weaker claim (a) is all that is needed for the ar-
gument.

23. **length, breadth, and depth**: These are the essential properties of bodies.

24. **abstracted**: See ABSTRACTION #3.

the last thing is in its own right neither something nor of some quantity nor any other <of the things mentioned>;[25] nor is it <in its own right>   *25* the negations of these, since what we have said implies that the negations as well <as the positive properties> belong to it <only> coincidentally.[26]

[BUT THIS RESULT IS IMPOSSIBLE, AND HENCE WE MUST EXAMINE FORM]

And so, if we study it from this point of view, the result is that the matter is substance;[27] but that is impossible. For being separable and being a this seem to belong to substance most of all; that is why the form and the <compound> of both <matter and form> would seem to be substance more than the matter is.   *30*

And so the substance composed of both—I mean composed of the matter and the form$_m$—should be set aside, since it is posterior to the other two, and clear. The matter is also evident in a way. We must, then, consider the third type of substance, since it is the most puzzling.

Since some of the perceptible substances are agreed to be substances,   *1029b* we should begin our search with these.

[SUBSTANCE AS ESSENCE]

[WE SHOULD STUDY FORM BY STUDYING ESSENCE]

4

Since we began by distinguishing the things by which we define substance and since essence seems to be one of these, we ought to study it.[28] For it is useful to advance toward what is better known, since this is how anyone succeeds in learning, by advancing through what is less

25. **neither something . . . mentioned>**: These are the different categories (see PREDICATIONS). For the use of 'something' for substance cf. GC 318a15.

26. **the negations . . . coincidentally.** Matter lacks any essential properties falling into the different categories. A given lump of bronze is neither essentially six feet long nor essentially not six feet long, since it could remain the same lump of bronze in either case.

27. **the matter is substance**: Probably (in the light of 'appears as the only substance' in a19) this is intended to be an identity statement. This suggests (see note on 1029a10) that what Aristotle regards as impossible is the claim that something's matter is the only substance, not the claim that the matter is one substance among others. He implicitly accepts this second claim at 1029a32.

28. **. . . to study it**: The OCT transposes the rest of this paragraph to the end of ch. 3. If we retain the mss order, Aristotle claims that the study of essence is the best approach to the study of form, because it is better KNOWN to us.

5 well known$_g$[29] by nature to what is better known. In questions about action, our task is to advance from what is good to ourselves, and so to make what is good without reservation[30] good to ourselves; in the same way, then, we should advance from what is better known to ourselves, and so make what is well known by nature well known to ourselves. Admittedly, what is well known and known first to any given type of

10 person is often only slightly known and has little or no hold on being; still, we must begin from what is poorly known but known by us and try to come to know what is known without reservation, by advancing, as has been said, through the very things that are known to us.

[*WHAT IS ESSENCE?*]

First let us make some logical[31] remarks about it. The essence of a thing

15 is what the thing is said to be in its own right. For being you[32] is not the same as being a musician, since you are not a musician in your own right; hence your essence is what you are in your own right.

Nor indeed is your essence all of what you are in your own right. For a thing's essence is not what belongs to it in its own right in the way that pale belongs in its own right to a surface; for being a surface[33] is not the same as being pale. But neither is a thing's essence the same as the combination of the thing and what belongs in its own right to it[34]—for instance, being a pale surface, since here surface is added.[35] It

20 follows that the account of a thing's essence is the account that describes

29. **well known$_g$**: This translates *gnōrimon* (which might also be rendered 'familiar' when what is 'well known to us' is in question). 'Known' by itself renders *gnōston*.

30. **without reservation**: *holōs*, usually rendered by 'IN GENERAL'. Here its force is similar to that of 'WITHOUT QUALIFICATION'.

31. **logical remarks**: See LOGICAL. Here (and probably also in 1030a25, 27, 29) Aristotle probably has in mind a discussion of the relation between essence and definition, with no attempt to connect the concept of essence with the ontological constraints that make some things count as beings to a higher degree than others. Later in the chapter (at 1030a2, 25) Aristotle explains the relevance of these ontological considerations to questions about essence.

32. **being you**: In this chapter 'being x' translates phrases of the form *to x einai*, which in vii 6 are translated by 'the essence of x'. See ESSENCE #2.

33. **being a surface**: The indefinite article makes more natural English, but corresponds to nothing in the Greek. The Greek leaves open the question whether Aristotle has in mind the essences of particulars or of universals.

34. **But neither . . . own right to it**: Lit. 'But neither what is out of both'.

35. **surface is added**: Aristotle considers a definition of surface as 'pale surface'; here the definition repeats what is to be defined.

but does not mention the thing; and so if being a pale surface is the same as being a smooth surface, being pale and being smooth are one and the same.

[DO COMPOSITES HAVE ESSENCES?]

There are composites <not only among substances but> also in the other predications, since each of these (for instance, quality, quantity, when, where, and motion) has a subject;[36] hence we should ask whether   25 there is an account of the essence of each of these composites, and whether an essence belongs to them—to a pale man, for instance—as well as to substances. Let us, then, call this composite 'cloak'.* What is being a cloak?

One might object, however, that a cloak is not spoken of in its own right either.[37] <We reply:> There are two ways in which we speak of what is not in its own right: one way is from addition, the other is not.   30 In the first case, something is said <not to be in its own right> because the thing to be defined is added to something else—if, for instance, one gave the account of pale man as a definition of pale. In the second case, something is said not to be in its own right because something else is added to it—if, for instance, 'cloak' signified a pale man, but one were to define cloak as pale. A pale man, then, is pale, but is not what being   1030a pale is.[38]

[ONLY SUBSTANCES HAVE ESSENCES IN THE PRIMARY WAY]

But is being a cloak an essence at all?[39] Perhaps not. For an essence is what something essentially is,[40] but whenever one thing is said of another, the

36. **has a subject**: Hence some composites are composed of a substance (as subject) and a nonsubstance; these are the composites that Aristotle goes on to discuss.

37. **a cloak . . . own right either**: Hence (the objector suggests) a cloak cannot have an essence.

38. **A pale man . . . pale is**: Hence, both the accounts of the essence of a pale man that were just offered turn out to be wrong. In the first case the attempted definition includes too much, and so pale is not pale man in its own right (since the definition of pale as 'pale man' is wrong). In the second case the attempted definition includes too little, and so pale is not cloak in its own right (for since cloak is pale *man*, a definition of cloak as 'pale' would be wrong).

39. **But. . . at all?**: In this paragraph Aristotle seems to introduce ontological, and no longer purely LOGICAL (see note on 1029b13), considerations into the argument.

40. **what something essentially is**: Read *hoper ti*. (OCT: 'what a this essentially is'.) On *hoper* see ESSENTIALLY.

5   composite of the two is not essentially a this; the pale man, for instance,
is not essentially a this, since only a substance is a this. Hence the things
that have an essence are those whose account is a definition. But the
mere fact that a name and an account signify the same thing does not
imply that the account is a definition. If it did, then all accounts would
be formulae* (since for every account, we can find a name that signifies
10   the same), so that even the *Iliad* would be a definition.[41] Rather, an
account is a definition <only> if it is of some primary thing; primary
things are those that are spoken of in a way that does not consist in one
thing's being said of another.[42] Hence essence will belong only to species
of a genus and to nothing else,[43] since <only> these seem to be spoken
of in a way that does not consist in one thing's participating in another,
or in one thing's being an attribute or coincident of another.[44] Admittedly,
15   everything else <besides members of a species>, if it has a name, will
also have an account saying what it signifies (i.e., that this belongs to
this) or, instead of an unqualified account,[45] a more exact one; but nothing
else will have a definition or essence.

[NONSUBSTANCES HAVE ESSENCES IN A SECONDARY WAY]

Perhaps, however, definitions, like what-it-is, are spoken of in several
ways. For in fact what-it-is in one way signifies substance and a this,
20   and in another way signifies each of the things predicated—quantity,
quality, and all the rest. For just as being[46] belongs to them all—not
in the same way, but to substance primarily and to the other things

41. **so that . . . definition**: We could say that 'Sing, Muse, of the wrath of Achilles
. . .' is the definition corresponding to the name 'Iliad'. Cf. 1045a12, *APo* 93b35.

42. **in a . . . of another**: Lit. 'not by one thing being said of another'. Aristotle
implies that only a this passes this test.

43. **Hence essence . . . to nothing else**: Two possible interpretations: (1) Essences
are found only within species and genera (of substances), i.e., only members
of these substantial species and genera have essences. (2) Species and genera
(as opposed to individual members of them) are the only things that have
essences. While (1) involves reading more into the Greek, it is easier to see
how (1) follows from the previous argument than to see how (2) follows. The
supplement in the next sentence assumes (1); if (2) is assumed, then '<besides
species>' should be supplied.

44. **in a way . . . coincident of another**: Lit. 'not by sharing or attribute, nor by
coincidence'.

45. **unqualified**: This sort of account lacks the necessary qualifications, and so
is less EXACT than an account that includes them.

46. **being**: Lit. 'the is'. The phrase anticipates 'the what-it-is' just below.

derivatively—so also the what-it-is belongs without qualification to substance and derivatively to the other things. For we might ask what a quality is, so that quality is also a what-it-is, though not without qualification; just as some people say, speaking logically,[47] that not-being is (not that it is without qualification, but that it is not-being), so also we say what a quality is.[48]

We must certainly consider what ought to be said[49] about a particular question, but we must consider no less how things really are.[50] That is why, in this case, since what is said is evident <we must consider how things are>. We find that essence, like what-it-is, belongs primarily and without qualification to substance, and derivatively to the other things, where it will be the essence of quality or quantity, not the essence without qualification. For we must say that these <nonsubstances> are beings either homonymously or by addition and subtraction,[51] as we say that what is not known is known <not to be known>. The right answer is that they are beings neither homonymously nor in the same way. What is medical, for instance, is spoken of with reference to one and the same thing, not by being one and the same thing, but not homonymously either—for a body, a procedure, and an instrument are called medical neither homonymously nor by having one <nature>, but with reference to one thing. The same applies to beings.

It does not matter which alternative we accept:[52] in either case substances evidently have a definition and essence of the primary type, i.e., a definition and essence without qualification. Certainly other beings also have definitions and essences, but not primarily. For if we accept this view of definition, not every name that signifies the same as an account will necessarily have a definition corresponding to it; rather, in order to be a definition, the account must be of the right type, namely an account of something that is one—and something that is one not merely by continuity (like the *Iliad*, or like things that are tied together)

25

30

35

1030b

5

47. **speaking logically**: See 1029b13n. The parenthesis that follows explains how the 'logical' remark avoids ontological claims.

48. **so . . . quality is**: Lit. 'so also a quality'. We say what quality it is, not what it is without qualification. On being WITHOUT QUALIFICATION see 1028a31n.

49. **what ought to be said**: This is a description of a purely LOGICAL inquiry; see 1029b13n.

50. **how things really are**: This introduces ontological questions, resting on the questions about substance.

51. **either homonymously ... subtraction**: 'Homonymy' probably refers to 'mere homonymy'; see HOMONYMOUS #3. For the contrast with 'addition and subtraction' and for 'with reference to one thing' cf. 1003a33–b10.

52. **which alternative we accept**: Homonymy, or addition and subtraction.

10 but that is one in one of the ways in which one is spoken of. Now, one is spoken of in the same ways as being,[53] and one type of being signifies a this, another quantity, another quality. That is why there will also be an account and a definition of the pale man, but not in the way that there is of pale and of the substance.

[THE COMBINATION OF A SUBJECT AND AN ESSENTIALLY
DEPENDENT PROPERTY HAS NO ESSENCE]

5

If someone says that an account that involves addition is not a definition,
15 a puzzle arises about which things that are coupled, rather than simple, have definitions. For coupled things have to be explained by addition.[54] I mean, for instance, that as well as nose and concavity there is also snubness, which is composed of the two and is spoken of as the one in the other <i.e., concavity in nose>. For concavity, i.e., snubness,[55] is
20 not a coincidental attribute of the nose, but belongs to the nose in its own right; nor does it belong in the way that pale belongs to Callias or to man (i.e., because Callias is pale, and being a man is a coincident of his). Rather, snubness belongs to nose as male[56] belongs to animal, and as equal belongs to quantity, and as everything said to belong in its own right belongs to its subject. Such things are all those in which either the account or the name of the <subject> of which this is an attribute
25 belongs. These are things that cannot be explained separately <from their subject>; pale, for instance, can be explained without man, but female cannot be explained without animal. Hence either none of these <coupled things> has an essence and definition, or else, if they do, they have them in another way, as we have said.

53. **Now, one . . . as being**: See 1003b22–32. The demand that the object of definition should be one leads us back to the claim that the primary object of definition is a substance (since substance is a unity of the primary sort, just as it is a being of the primary sort).

54. **by addition**: And so, if addition precludes definition, apparently these composites ('coupled things') have no definition. Aristotle presents two objections to the view that they have essences: (1) Their definition is not of a single thing (1030b17–28). (2) A definition of a composite involves an infinite regress (1030b28–1031a1). The conclusion that composites such as SNUB have definitions only in a secondary way is important; for Aristotle returns to the example of snubness (which he takes as—in some sense—a pattern for natural substances) in vii 10–11.

55. **concavity, i.e., snubness**: Text uncertain. Probably both terms are intended to refer to the same property.

56. **male**: For this sort of coincident see APo 73a37, Met. 1058a29–36.

There is a further puzzle about these things. For if a snub nose and a concave nose are the same thing, then snub and concave will be the same thing. If, however, they are not the same (for we cannot speak of   *30* snub without the thing of which snub is an attribute in its own right, since snub is concavity in nose[57]), then either we cannot speak of snub nose, or else we will speak of the same thing twice, concave nose nose (since a snub nose will be a concave nose nose). It is absurd, then, for   *35* such a thing to have an essence; for if it has an essence, then a snub nose nose will contain yet another <nose>, and so there will be an   *1031a* infinite regress.

Clearly, then, only substances have definitions. For if the other things predicated also have definitions, they must have them by addition. Odd, for instance, has this sort of definition, since odd implies number; similarly, female implies animal. ('By addition' refers to cases like these, where we turn out to speak of the same thing twice.) Nor, in that case,   *5* will coupled things—odd number, for instance—have definitions; but we overlook this because the accounts are not stated exactly. If, however, these things also have formulae, then either they have them in another way, or, as we said earlier, we should say that definitions and essences   *10* are spoken of in many ways, so that in one way only substances have definitions and essences but in another way nonsubstances also have them.

Clearly, then, a definition is the account of the essence, and only substances have essences, or else they have them most of all, primarily and without qualification.

[*THE RELATION OF SUBJECTS TO THEIR ESSENCES*]

6

We should investigate whether a thing is the same as or different from   *15* its essence. For this is useful for our investigation of substance; for a thing seems to be nothing other than its own substance, and something's substance is said to be its essence.

In the case of things spoken of coincidentally, a thing might seem to   *20* be different from its essence; a pale man, for instance, is different from being a pale man. For if it is the same, then being a man is the same as being a pale man; for, they say, a man is the same as a pale man, so that being a pale man is the same as being a man.[58]

---

57. **for we cannot . . . concavity in nose**: The argument takes it for granted that we can speak of concave without nose.

58. **as being a man**: But this conclusion is false; hence it seems that pale man is not the same as its essence.

25   Perhaps, however, it is not necessary for things to be the same if one
is a coincident of the other, since the extreme terms are not the same
in the same way.[59] But presumably it might seem to follow that the
extremes, the coincidental things, turn out to be the same—for instance,
being pale and being musical. In fact, however, it seems not to follow.[60]

[*THE RELATION OF PLATONIC FORMS TO THEIR ESSENCES*]

But is it necessary for things spoken of in their own right to be the same
as their essences? For instance, what about substances of the sort some
30   say Ideas are, ones that have no other substances or natures prior to
them? If the good itself <the Idea> is different from the essence of good,[61]
and the animal itself from the essence of animal, and the being itself from
1031b   the essence of being, then there will be further substances, natures, and
Ideas apart from those mentioned, and these will be prior substances and
substances to a higher degree, if essence is substance.[62]
        If, then, <the Ideas and the essences> are severed from each other,
it follows that <the Ideas> will not be known$_e$ and that <the essences>
5   will not be beings. (By 'severed' I mean that the essence of good does
not belong to the good itself, and being good does not belong to the
essence of good.)[63] For we know$_e$ a thing whenever we know$_g$ its essence.[64] Further, what applies to good applies equally to the other essences, so that if the essence of good is not good, then neither will the
essence of being be, nor the essence of one be one. But since all essences

59. **in the same way**: For instance, the way in which man is the same as pale
man is different from the way in which man is the same as being man. The first
case is a case of merely coincidental identity.

60. **But presumably ... seems not to follow**: The conclusion (that coincidental
things such as pale man are not the same as their essences) follows if we assume
that pale man and musical man are the same as man. Since Aristotle believes that
this assumption is false, he rejects this particular argument for the conclusion. He
believes, however, that the conclusion (properly understood) is correct, and
hence that a sound argument for it can be given; see 1032a22.

61. **the essence of good**: Or 'being good' (*to agathō(i) einai*). This is meant to pick
out the essence (*to ti ēn einai*).

62. **then there will ... essence is substance**: Aristotle uses Platonic Ideas to
argue (in the next paragraph) that noncoincidental things must be identical to
their essences.

63. **(By 'severed' ... essence of good.)**: Aristotle explains that by 'severed' he
means something more than he means in speaking of the Platonic Ideas as
SEPARABLE.

64. **know$_g$ its essence**: And so, if the Idea of good is severed from the essence
of good, we do not know the Idea, since in that case it has no essence.

alike either are or are not, it follows that, if not even the essence of being   *10*
is a being, none of the other essences is a being either. Moreover, if the
essence of good does not belong to a given thing, that thing is not good.[65]

The good, then, is necessarily one with the essence of good, and the
fine with the essence of fine. The same applies to all the primary things,
those spoken of in their own right, not insofar as they belong to something else.[66] For if this is true <i.e., that something is a primary being>,
it already implies <that the primary being is identical to its essence>,
even if it is not a Form—though presumably <the conclusion> is all the   *15*
more <necessary> if the thing is a Form.

Further, if the Ideas are what some people say they are, then clearly
the subject will not be substance. For Ideas must be substances, but not
by <being predicated> of a subject, since <if they were predicated of
a subject>, they would exist <only> by being participated in.[67]

From these arguments, then, we find that a thing itself and its essence
are noncoincidentally one and the same, and that knowing$_e$ a thing is   *20*
knowing$_e$ its essence; and so even isolating the Forms shows that[68] a
thing and its essence must be some one thing.

[THINGS SPOKEN OF IN THEIR OWN RIGHT ARE THE SAME AS THEIR ESSENCES]

But because what is spoken of coincidentally—for instance, the musical
or the pale—signifies two things, it is not true to say that it is the same
as its essence. For the pale signifies both the subject of which pale is a   *25*
coincident and the coincident;[69] and so in a way it is the same as its
essence, and in a way it is not the same—for <the pale> is not the same
as man or as pale man, but it is the same as the attribute.

We can also see that it is absurd <for something not to be the same
as its essence>, if we give a name to each essence; for apart from that
essence there will be another essence as well—for instance, another   *30*
essence will be the essence of the essence of horse. But why not let some
things be essences at once, going no further, since essence is substance?

65. **the thing is not good**: And so the Idea of good will not be good.

66. **insofar ... something else**: Lit. 'in accordance with something else'.

67. **by being participated in**: Hence, they would be inseparable from the things
participating in them, contrary to the Platonist view.

68. **isolating the Forms shows that ...**: Lit. 'in accordance with isolation'. For
isolation and the Theory of FORMS see *Top.* 179a3.

69. **the pale ... coincident**: We can use 'the pale' (neuter article + adjective)
to refer (i) to the man who is pale (i.e., to the pale thing) or (ii) to his quality
(i.e. his paleness). On this double use of the neuter adjective see *Phys.* 188a36n,
189b35, *Met.* 1028a24.

Moreover, not only is <a thing> one <with its essence>, but their
account is also the same; for one and being one are noncoincidentally
one. Moreover, if there is another essence, the essences will go on to
infinity; for one thing will be the essence of the one, and another will
5   be the one, so that the same argument will also apply in their case.

Clearly, then, in the case of the primary things, those spoken of in
their own right, a thing and its essence are one and the same. And it is
evident that the sophistical refutations aimed against this position are
all resolved in the same way as is the puzzle of whether[70] Socrates and
being Socrates are the same; for there is no difference in the premisses
from which one would ask the questions[71] or in the premisses from
10   which one would find a solution.

We have said, then, in what way something's essence is the same as
the thing, and in what way it is not.

[THE ROLE OF FORM AND MATTER IN CHANGE[72]]

[DIFFERENT TYPES OF COMING TO BE]

7

Among things that come to be, some come to be by nature, some by
craft, and some by chance, but they all come to be by some agent and
from something, and come to be something. (By 'comes to be something'
15   I mean something in any of the predications*; for things come to be
either this or of some quantity or quality or somewhere.) Things that
have natural comings to be are those whose coming to be is from nature.
What they come to be from is what we call matter; the agent is something
that is by nature; and the something they come to be is a man or a plant[73]
20   or anything of the sort we say are substances most of all.

Everything that comes to be by nature or craft has matter; for these
things can both be and not be, and what has this potentiality is a thing's
matter.

70. **that resolves the puzzle of whether**: Lit. 'and whether'. On these sophistical
refutations cf. *Met.* 1004b2, *Top.* 133b15 (on whether Socrates is the same as
seated Socrates; apparently they are not, since some properties seem to belong
to one but not to the other), *Phys.* 219b20.

71. **the questions**: The sophistical questions and the question about Socrates.

72. Chs. 7–9 may not have originally been intended to be a part of Bk vii, but
they are relevant to the main topics of the book; they introduce questions about
form, matter, and coming to be, which Aristotle discusses in his reconsideration
of substance and essence in chs. 10–11.

73. **a man or a plant**: Or 'man or plant'. The same question arises in the paragraph
after the next ('In general . . . or an animal').

In general, both what something comes to be from and what it becomes is a nature; for what comes to be has a nature—a plant or an animal, for instance. Moreover, the agent is the nature that is spoken of with reference to form, and this nature is the same in form <as the nature of what comes to be>,[74] but it is in another <particular>, since a man   25
generates a man. Things that come to be because of nature, then, come to be in this way.

The other comings to be are called productions; these are all from either craft or potentiality or thought. Some productions also come to be from chance or luck, similarly to the way in which things come about   30
from chance or luck[75] among things that come to be from nature; for in the latter case too the same things that <usually> come to be from a seed also <sometimes> come to be without any seed. We must investigate these cases later.

[THE ROLE OF FORM IN PRODUCTION]

Things that come to be from craft are those whose form is in the soul.[76]   1032b
(By 'form' I mean a thing's essence and primary substance.) For even contraries have the same form in a way, since the substance of a privation[77] is the substance opposed to it, so that health, for instance, is the substance of disease because disease results from the absence of health;   5
and health is the account in the soul and the knowledge$_e$.[78]

What is healthy comes into being when the producer has had the following sort of thought: since health is this, then if something is to be healthy, it must have this (for instance, a uniform condition of the body), and if it is to have this, it must have heat.[79] This is how he thinks at each stage, until he leads the process back to the last thing, which is what he can produce himself; and then the motion from here on toward   10
health is called a production. And so it turns out that in a way health comes to be from health, and a house from a house—the one that has matter from the one without matter. For the medical or housebuilding <knowledge> is the form of health or house, and substance without matter is what I call the essence.

74. **the same . . . to be>**: The generator is the same in species ('form') as the particular thing that comes into being as a result of the generation.

75. **chance or luck**: For the distinction between them see LUCK #1.

76. **in the soul**: The soul of the producer. See FORM #7.

77. **substance of a privation**: This is the positive characteristic opposed to the privation. Cf. 1042b2–3, GC 318b14–16 and note.

78. **the knowledge$_e$**: knowledge of how to produce health. This knowledge is 'the form (or account, *logos*) in the soul'.

79. **since health . . . heat**: See DEDUCTION #4.

15   One sort of coming to be and motion is called thinking, another
production. Thinking is the motion that proceeds from the principle,
i.e., the form; and production is the motion that proceeds from the last
stage of thinking. Each of the other things—those in between[80]—comes
to be in the same way. I mean, for instance, that if this <body> is to
be healthy, its bodily condition must be made uniform. What, then, is
20   it to be made uniform? This. <The body> will have this if it is warmed.
What is it to be warmed? This. But this is potentially present. And now
he has reached what is up to himself.
    If the motion toward health comes from craft, the producer that is its
principle is the form in the soul; if it comes from chance, it comes from
25   whatever is the principle of the production if the producer exercises a
craft.[81] In medical treatment, for instance, the principle is presumably
from warming, which the doctor produces by rubbing; heat in the body,
then, either is a part of health or is followed, directly or in several stages,
by something that is part of health. This last thing producing the part
<of health> is in a way itself also a part of health,[82] just as the last thing
(for instance, stones) is a part of the house, and part of the product in
30   other cases. Hence, as is said, nothing can come to be unless something
1033a   is previously present. Evidently, then, some part will have to be present;
for the matter is a part, since it is present in the product, and it comes
to be the product.
    But is <the matter> also one of the things in the account? We speak
in both ways when we say what bronze circles are. For we speak of the
matter when we say that the circle is bronze, and of the form when we
say that it is this sort of shape; shape is the genus into which it is
5   primarily placed. The bronze circle, then, has the matter in its account.

[THE RELATION BETWEEN THE MATTER AND THE PRODUCT]

Some things that come to be from matter, once they have come to be,
are called not that, but of-that;[83] the statue, for instance, is called of-

80. **those in between**: They come between the beginning of the thinking and
the end of the production.

81. **if it comes from chance . . . a craft**: A condition (e.g., warming) that sometimes results from the exercise of a craft sometimes comes about without being
produced by a craft (e.g., if I happen to get warm without any intervention by
a doctor) and produces the effect (health) that would result from the exercise of
the craft.

82. **is . . . of health**: Read *kai auto pōs meros*, 1032b29. OCT: 'is itself thus a part
of health'.

83. **of-that**: Or 'thaten', e.g., wooden, woollen, etc., as opposed to wood, wool,
etc. Cf. 1049a18.

stone, not stone, and similarly the healthy man is not called that from which he has come to be. The reason for this is that a thing comes to be from its privation, or from its subject which we call the matter. For   10
instance, the man as well as the sick one comes to be healthy, but he is said to have come to be from the privation rather than the subject, so that he is said to have become healthy from having been sick, rather than from having been a man; that is why the healthy one is said to be a man, not to be sick, and the man is said to be healthy, <not sick>. But in cases where the privation—the privation of some definite shape in bronze, for instance, or of a house in bricks and   15
timbers—is unclear and nameless, the product seems to come to be from this <matter>, as in the first case <the man became healthy> from having been sick.[84]

   That is why, just as in the first case the product is not called by the name of that <privation> from which it came to be, so also in the second case the statue is not called wood, but rather the name is varied and the statue is called of-wood, not wood, or of-bronze, not bronze, or of-stone, not stone, and the house is of-bricks, not bricks. For if we look at it   20
closely, we would not say without qualification, in this case any more than in the other, that a statue comes to be from wood, or a house from bricks; for that from which something comes to be must change and not remain when the thing comes to be.[85] This, then, is why we speak in this way.

[BOTH THE FORM AND THE MATTER MUST EXIST BEFORE SOMETHING COMES TO BE]

8

What comes to be, then, does so by some agent (i.e., the source of the   25
principle of the coming to be) and from something (not the privation but the matter; we have now determined the sense in which we say

84. **But in cases . . . been sick**: In 'a man becomes healthy from being sick', the privation is clear and has a name ('sick'), and so the product comes to be from this privation rather than from the subject. In 'the house comes to be from bricks', the privation has no recognized name (in *Phys.* 188b10–21, 190b5, Aristotle coins terms such as 'shapelessness'), and so we say that the product comes from the matter that is the subject. The first case is a case of qualified, the second a case of unqualified, coming to be; see COME TO BE #1.

85. **For if we . . . comes to be**: Aristotle notes that the product does not come simply from the matter. For the product cannot come into existence unless the matter changes, i.e., unless it changes from having the privation to having the form. Here also, then, we must recognize both the subject of coming to be and the privation. This is a further reason for saying that a statue is wooden, not wood (since it requires the wood to be in a certain condition, and so cannot be simply wood).

30   this) and becomes something (a sphere or a circle or whatever else it may be). And just as <the producer> does not produce the subject—the bronze—neither does he produce the sphere, unless he does so coincidentally, because he produces the bronze sphere and it is a sphere; for to produce a this is to produce a this from a subject in general.[86]

    Let me explain. To make the bronze round is not to produce the round or the sphere, but to produce one thing, this form, in another thing; for

1033b   if someone produces the form, he must produce it from another thing, since another thing must have been the subject. For instance, he produces the bronze sphere, and this is so because he produces this, which is a sphere, from this subject, which is bronze; and if he also produces this form itself, i.e., sphere, clearly he will produce it in the same way,[87]

5   and then comings into being will go back to infinity.

    Evidently, then, the form (or whatever the shape in the perceptible thing ought to be called) and the essence (i.e., what comes to be in something else by the agency of craft, nature, or potentiality) does not come into being and there is no coming to be of it.[88] But the producer does make a bronze sphere to be; for he produces it from bronze and

10   sphere—he produces this form in this subject, and the product is a bronze sphere.

    If the essence of sphere in general is to have a coming to be,[89] this essence will be something from something; for in each case what is coming to be must be divisible into this (i.e., matter) and this (i.e., form). Now, if the sphere is the figure whose circumference is everywhere

15   equidistant from the center, one aspect of it is the matter that the product is in, the other is the form in that matter, and the whole thing—the bronze sphere, for instance—is what has come to be. It is evident, then, that what is called substance as form[90] does not come to be, but the compound substance, which is called substance insofar as it is substance as form,[91] does come to be. It is also evident that matter is present in

---

86. **from a subject in general**: Obscure. Perhaps it means: 'from something that is a subject, but not a definite particular' (since matter is not a definite particular; cf. 1033b11, 26).

87. **in the same way**: From preexisting form and matter.

88. **does not come into being and there is no coming to be of it**: This is not a mere repetition. See COME TO BE #4.

89. **If the essence . . . coming to be**: The rest of the paragraph argues that the essence cannot have a coming to be (since comings to be all require matter).

90. **substance as form**: Read *hōs eidos ousia*. OCT: 'called form or substance'.

91. **in so . . . form**: Or 'in accordance with this <substance as form> that it has'. Lit. 'which is spoken of in accordance with this <substance>'.

everything that comes to be, and that one aspect of the product is this matter and the other is this form.[92]   *20*

[PLATONIC IDEAS ARE USELESS FOR EXPLAINING COMING TO BE]

Is there, then, some sphere apart* from these <perceptible ones>, or a house apart from bricks? If there were, then surely there could never have been any coming to be of any this.[93] Rather, <sphere, for instance,> signifies this sort of thing;[94] it is not a this and something definite.[95] On the contrary, one produces or generates this sort of thing from this <matter>, and when it has been generated, it is *this* thing of this sort. This whole thing—for instance, Callias or Socrates—corresponds to this   *25* bronze sphere, while man and animal correspond to bronze sphere in general.

It is evident, then, that the forms, construed as some people habitually construe them, as things apart from particulars, are useless as causes, at any rate of comings to be and of substances; this role, at any rate, is no reason for these forms to be substances in their own right.   *30*

In some cases, generator and generated are evidently also of the same sort, but they are not the same thing—they are one in form,[96] not one in number. This is true of natural things (for instance, a man generates a man[97]), except in cases where something contrary to nature comes about, so that a horse, for instance, generates a mule.[98] And even in these cases something similar is true;[99] for the nearest genus, whatever

92. **and that one . . . this form**: Lit. 'and one is this, and the other is this'.

93. **If there were . . . any this**: The possibility of the process of coming to be requires forms that, in contrast to Platonic Ideas, are not SEPARATED from matter. Aristotle criticizes Platonic Ideas as being useless for explaining coming to be; see also 991b3–9.

94. **this sort of thing**: *toionde*. See QUALITY.

95. **a this and something definite**: Here 'and' perhaps = 'i.e.'. Aristotle implies that something that is not a this cannot exist apart from particulars.

96. **one in form**: This refers to the species form, which appears to be a universal (since it is common to Socrates and Callias). It is open to dispute whether Socrates also has his own particular form numerically different from Callias' particular form. See FORM #9.

97. **a man generates a man**: Cf. *Phys.* 193b8, 198a26.

98. **mule**: Greek uses the same term, *hēmionos*, for English 'mule' and 'hinny'; the latter is intended here.

99. **something similar is true**: It is true to some degree that the generator has the same form as the generated, since they both share the more generic features common to horses and asses.

1034a   is common to horse and ass, has no name, but is presumably both, as
         a mule is.
             Evidently, then, there is no need to set up a form as a pattern*. For
         if we sought such forms anywhere, it would be in natural generation,
         since natural things are substances most of all;[100] but in fact the generator
5   is sufficient to produce the thing and to be the cause of the form in the
         matter. And the whole—this sort of form in this flesh and bones—is
         Callias or Socrates; and they differ because of matter, since their matter
         is different, but they are the same in form, since the form is indivisible.[101]

         [HOW THINGS COME TO BE BY CHANCE AS WELL AS BY CRAFT]

         9

         A puzzle might arise about why some things—for instance, health—
10   come to be both by craft and also from chance, while others—for instance,
         houses—do not. The reason is as follows. The matter that is the principle
         of production and coming to be from craft, and that has some part of
         the product present in it, in some cases can be moved by its own agency,
         and in other cases cannot. In some cases of the first sort, the matter can
         be moved <by its own agency> in a particular way <required for a
15   certain kind of product>, and in other such cases it cannot; for many
         things are capable of being moved by their own agency, but not in a
         particular way (for instance, dancing). Hence things with matter of this
         second sort—stones, for instance—cannot be moved in a particular
         way[102] except by something else, but in another way they can be moved
         by their own agency. That is why in some cases the result requires a
         craftsman, but in other cases it does not; in these cases the movers will
20   be agents that have no craft but can themselves be moved, either by
         other agents that have no craft or from a part <of the eventual product>.
             It is also clear from what we have said that in a way every <product
         of craft> comes to be, just as natural things do, from something with
         the same name[103] (for instance, a house from a house, insofar as it is
         produced by mind, since the craft <of building> is the form), or from
25   a part with the same name, or from something that has a part <of the
         product>. This is true if it does not come to be coincidentally; for the

100. **substances most of all**: Hence, if we do not need Platonic Ideas in this
case, we do not need them anywhere.

101. **the same . . . indivisible**: Again (cf. 1033b32n above) *eidos*, translated by
'form', refers to the species form.

102. **a particular way**: The way that is needed, for instance, for building a house.
This is why houses do not come into being spontaneously from stones.

103. **with the same name**: *homōnumon*. See HOMONYMOUS #1.

first cause in its own right of the production is a part of the product. Heat in the motion, for example, produces heat in the body, and this heat is either health or a part of it or is followed by a part of health or by health itself; that is why it is also said to produce <health>, because it produces that on which health follows and in which it coincides.   30

And so, just as in deductions, substance is the principle of everything; for deductions begin from what-it-is, and comings to be are from this too.[104]

[CHANCE IN NATURAL COMING TO BE]

Naturally constituted things are similar to the products of craft. For the seed produces in the same way as the efforts of craft do; for it has the   1034b
form potentially, and in a way the parent providing the seed has the same name as the offspring. For one must not expect all offspring to come to be in the way a man comes to be from a man[105]—even here, indeed, a female comes to be from a male. The offspring has the same name if it is not defective; hence a mule's parent is not a mule <since mules are defective>.

Things that come to be by chance (just as in the case of crafts) are   5
those whose matter can on some occasions also be moved by its own agency with the motion that the seed <usually> initiates in it; unless this is true of the matter, things cannot come to be except from the parents.

[THE COMING TO BE OF NONSUBSTANCES]

Our argument not only shows that form cannot come to be in the case of substance, but it also applies equally to all the primary <genera>— to quantity, quality, and the other predications. For it is the bronze   10
sphere, not sphere or bronze, that comes to be, and the same applies to bronze, if it comes to be; for in every case the matter and the form must previously exist. This is true both for what-it-is and also for quality, quantity, and each of the other predications; for what comes to be is not a quality, but wood of some quality, and not a quantity, but wood or   15
animal of some quantity.

However, a distinctive feature of substance may be noticed from these cases, that it must be produced by another actual substance preceding

---

104. **for deductions . . . this too**: Deductions (or, more exactly, DEMONSTRATIONS) begin with a statement of the essence. See PRINCIPLE #3, *DA* 402b25.

105. **For . . . from a man**: This explains why the claim in the previous sentence is true only with the restrictions and qualifications that are mentioned here.

it (for instance, by an animal, if an animal comes to be), whereas a quality or quantity needs only a potential quality or quantity to precede it.

[FORM, ESSENCE, AND DEFINITION]

[WHEN ARE THE PARTS OF A WHOLE PARTS OF ITS ESSENCE?]

10

20   A definition is an account, and every account has parts; and a part of the account corresponds to a part of the thing defined in the way in which the whole account corresponds to the whole thing defined. Hence a puzzle arises about whether or not the account of the parts must be present in the account of the whole. For in some cases the accounts of the parts evidently are present and in some cases they evidently are

25   not;[106] the account of a circle, for instance, does not include that of the segments, but the account of a syllable includes that of the letters,[107] even though the circle is divided into its segments just as the syllable is divided into its letters.

Moreover, if a part is prior to a whole, and an acute angle is part of a right angle, and a finger of an animal, then an acute angle would be

30   prior to a right angle, and a finger to a man. In fact, however, the whole seems to be prior, since the account of the part refers to the whole, and the whole is prior by being independent.[108]

[DIFFERENT TYPES OF PARTS]

Alternatively, perhaps a part is spoken of in many ways, and a quantitative measure is only one type of part; leaving this type aside, we should examine the parts that compose substance.

1035a   If, then, there is matter, form, and the compound of these, and matter, form, and the compound of them are all substance, then it follows that in one way matter is also called a part of something, but in another way it is not, and in this second way only the components of the account[109] of the form are parts. For example, flesh is not a part of concavity (since

---

106. **For in some cases . . . evidently are not**: Or 'For the accounts of some parts evidently are present, and the accounts of other parts evidently are not.'

107. **letters**: *stoicheia*. See ELEMENT.

108. **independent**: Lit. 'by being without one another'. In these cases the whole can exist without the part, but the converse is not true. This clause refers to natural PRIORITY (of the whole to a *single* part, not of the whole to the sum of its parts). The previous clause refers to priority in definition.

109. **account**: See REASON #5.

it is the matter in which concavity comes to be), but it is a part of   5
snubness. Again, bronze is a part of the compound statue, but not a
part of the statue spoken of as form. For it is the form of the statue—
i.e., the statue insofar as it has form—and never the material aspect in
its own right, that should be spoken of as the statue.[110]

[SOME DEFINITIONS INCLUDE ONLY PARTS OF THE FORM,
WHILE OTHERS INCLUDE MATERIAL PARTS]

This is why the account of a circle does not include that of the segments,   10
whereas the account of a syllable does include that of the letters; for the
letters are not matter, but parts of the account of the form, while the
segments are parts as matter in which the form comes to be. Still, the
segments are nearer to the form than bronze is to the circle in the cases
where circularity comes to be in bronze.

In a way, however, not every sort of letters—for instance, those in   15
wax or those in air—will be included in the account of the syllable; for
these also <like the bronze in the circle> are a part of the syllable as its
perceptible matter. For if a line is divided and perishes into halves, or
a man into bones, sinews, and bits of flesh, it does not follow that these
compose the whole as parts of the substance, but only that they compose   20
it as its matter. They are parts of the compound, but when we come to
the form, which is what the account is of, they are not parts of it; that
is why they are not included in accounts either.

Hence the account of some things will include that of these material
parts, but the account of other things, if it is not of something combined
with matter, must not[111] include it. For this reason, the principles composing a given thing are, in some but not all cases, the material parts into
which it perishes.   25

If, then, something—for instance, the snub or the bronze circle—is
form and matter combined, then it perishes into these <material parts>,
and matter is a part of it. But if something is without matter, not combined
with it, so that its account is only of the form, then it does not perish—
either not at all, or at least not in this way.[112] Hence these <material   30
parts> are parts and principles of things combined with matter, but
neither parts nor principles of the form.

110. **For it is the form . . . the statue**: Lit. 'For the form and insofar as it has
form should be called a given thing, but the material should never in its own
right be called'.

111. **must not**: Or 'need not'.

112. **in this way**: By dissolution into material parts.

1035b
That is why[113] the clay statue perishes into clay, the ball into bronze, and Callias into flesh and bones. Moreover, the circle perishes into its segments, because one type of circle is combined with matter; for the circle spoken of without qualification and the particular circle are called circles homonymously,* because the particular[114] has no distinctive name.

[NOT ALL PARTS OF A WHOLE ARE PARTS OF ITS ESSENCE]

We have now given the true answer, but let us take up the question again, and state the answer more perspicuously. Parts of the account—
5 i.e., the things into which the account is divided—are, either all or some of them, prior to the whole. The account of the right angle, by contrast, does not include that of the acute angle, but, on the contrary, that of the acute angle includes[115] that of the right angle; for we use the right angle in defining the acute, which is <defined as> less than a right angle. This is also the relation of the circle to a semi-circle, since the
10 semi-circle is defined by the circle. Similarly, a finger is defined by reference to the whole, since this sort of part of a man is a finger.

And so all the material parts—i.e., those into which the whole is divided as its matter—are posterior to it, but the parts that are parts of the account and of the substance corresponding to the account are, either all or some of them, prior to the whole.
15 Now, an animal's soul—the substance of what is ensouled—is the substance corresponding to the account; it is the form and essence of the right sort of body.[116] At any rate, a proper definition of each part[117] requires reference to its function, and this function requires perception.[118] Hence the parts of the soul, either all or some of them, are prior to the compound animal, and the same is true in the case of the particular.
20 The body and its parts are posterior to this substance <i.e., the soul>, and its parts are the matter into which the compound, but not this substance, is divided. In a way they are prior to the compound, but in

113. **That is why**: These things perish because they include matter.

114. **the particular**: This is the material particular ring (which is 'combined with matter'). The Greek 'kuklos' is used both for 'circle' and for 'ring'; hence Aristotle remarks that it is homonymous ('ring' is the distinctive name in English that Greek lacks).

115. **does not include . . . includes**: Lit. 'is not divided into . . . is divided into'.

116. **right sort of body**: Lit. 'such a body', i.e., a living body with suitable organs. Cf. 1036b30, DA 412a16. In 'at any rate . . . ' Aristotle explains this claim.

117. **each part**: Retain to meros, deleted in OCT.

118. **requires perception**: Hence it requires soul.

a way they are not, since they cannot exist when they are separated; for a finger is not an animal's finger in all conditions—on the contrary, a *25* dead finger is only homonymously a finger.[119] Some of them are simultaneous,[120] if they are the controlling parts, those on which the account and the substance primarily depend[121]—the heart or the brain, for instance (for it does not matter which of the two it is).

[PARTS OF UNIVERSALS AND OF PARTICULARS]

Now, man or horse or anything else that applies in this way to particulars, but universally,[122] is not a substance, but a sort of compound of this account and this matter as universal. When we come to particulars, *30* Socrates is composed of ultimate matter,[123] and the same is true in the other cases.

A part may be either of the form (by 'form' I mean the essence), or of the compound of the form and the matter, or of the matter itself. But only parts of the form are parts of the account, and the account is of the universal; for being circle[124] is the same as circle, and being soul is the *1036a* same as soul. But a compound such as this particular circle, either perceptible (for instance, bronze or wooden) or intelligible[125] (for instance, a mathematical object), has[126] no definition, but we know₈ it with the *5* help of understanding or perception. When it has departed from actual understanding or perception, it is unclear whether or not it exists; but still, we always speak of it and know it by means of the universal account, whereas the matter is unknowable in its own right.

One sort of matter is perceptible, another intelligible. Examples of *10*

119. **only homonymously a finger**: For this principle about homonymy see 1036b30, HOMONYMOUS, MATTER, PART.

120. **simultaneous**: Neither prior nor posterior to the compound of soul and body.

121. **depend**: Lit. 'are in'.

122. **applies ... universally**: The universal applies to particulars, but does not apply to just one particular to the exclusion of others (as 'Socrates' does); it applies to all particulars of a given sort.

123. **ultimate matter**: This probably refers not to 'prime matter' (see MATTER #3), but simply to a particular bit of matter, which is 'ultimate' because it is last in the series passing from greater universality to greater particularity; cf. *EN* 1143b3.

124. **being circle**: For the use of this phrase for the essence cf. 1029b14n.

125. **intelligible**: *noēton*, i.e., an object of *nous*, UNDERSTANDING.

126. **But a compound ... has**: Lit. 'But when we come to the compound and some one of the particulars, either perceptible ones or intelligible (by "intelligible" I mean mathematical, by "perceptible" bronze or wooden ones)—this has ...'.

perceptible matter are, for instance, bronze and wood, and all matter that is capable of motion; intelligible matter is the matter present in perceptible things (as, for instance, mathematical objects are present in them), but not insofar as they are perceptible.[127]

[PARTS OF THE FORM]

15

We have now stated the facts about whole and part and about prior and posterior. If someone asks whether the right angle, or circle, or animal is prior to the parts composing it, i.e., the parts into which it is divided, or whether, alternatively, the parts are prior to the whole, we must answer that neither is true without qualification.

For suppose first that the soul is the animal, or rather the ensouled thing,[128] or that a thing's soul is the thing itself, that being circle is the circle, and that being right angle, i.e., the essence₀ of the right angle, is the right angle. In that case, we should say that <the particular compound>—both the bronze right angle including <perceptible> matter

20

and the right angle in particular lines—is posterior to the things in the account and to one sort of right angle,[129] and that the right angle without matter is posterior to the things in its account, but prior to the parts in the particular. We should <add these conditions and> not give an unqualified answer. Suppose, alternatively, that the soul is not the animal but different from it. In this case too we should say that some things

25

are <prior> and some are not, as we have said.

[SOME, BUT NOT ALL, MATERIAL PARTS ARE PARTS OF THE FORM]

11

Not surprisingly, a further puzzle arises: What sorts of parts are parts of the form, and what sorts are parts of the combined thing, not of the form? If this is not clear, we cannot define anything; for definition is of the universal and of the form. If, then, it is not evident which sorts of

30

parts count as matter and which do not, it will not be evident what an account is either.

In cases where something evidently occurs in different kinds of things, as a circle, for instance, is found in bronze, stone, and wood, it seems clear that the bronze or stone (for instance) is not part of the substance of a circle, because a circle is <also found> separated from it. Even if

127. **but not . . . perceptible**: On mathematical objects see ABSTRACTION.

128. **ensouled thing**: This includes plants, not just animals. See SOUL #1.

129. **one sort of right angle**: i.e., the form.

it is not seen to be separated, the case may still be similar to those just   35
mentioned.[130] This would be true if, for example, all the circles that were   1036b
seen were bronze; for it would still be true that the bronze is not part
of the form <of circle>, even though it is hard to remove the bronze in
thought. Now the form of man, for instance, always appears in flesh
and bones, and in parts of this sort. Does it follow that these are also   5
parts of the form and the account? Perhaps not; perhaps they are only
matter, and we are incapable of separating them from the form because
it does not also occur in other <sorts of material parts>.

Since this sort of thing seems to be possible, but it is unclear when
<it is possible>, some people are puzzled even when they come to a
circle or a triangle. They suppose that it is not suitably defined by lines
and by the continuous, and that we speak of these in the same way as   10
we were speaking of the flesh and bones of a man, or the bronze or
stone of a statue.[131] Hence they reduce everything to numbers, and say
that the account of the line is the account of the two.

Those who talk about the Ideas also <offer accounts.> Some of them
say that the dyad is line-itself; others say that it is the form of line since,   15
they say, in some cases—for instance, dyad and the form of dyad—the
form is the same as the thing whose form it is, but in the case of the
line it is not. The result is that there is one form for many things whose
form appears different (this was also the result of the Pythagorean view);
and then it is possible to make this form the one form of all things, and   20
to make nothing else a form. On this argument, however, all things will
be one.[132]

We have said, then, that questions about definitions raise a puzzle,
and why they raise it. That is why[133] this reduction of everything <to
numbers and Forms> and the abstracting of matter goes too far; for
presumably some things are <essentially> this form in this matter, or
these material parts with this form.[134] And Socrates the Younger was   25

---

130. **Even if . . . mentioned**: Even if x is not actually separated from y, y need
not be part of the account of x.

131. **They suppose . . . of a statue**: They suppose that lines are simply the matter
of a triangle, as bronze is the matter of a statue, and so they infer that the
definition of triangle does not mention lines. They over-generalize the point
made in the previous paragraph.

132. **will be one**: This is because they will all have the same form.

133. **That is why**: The puzzles about definition show that the process of ABSTRAC-
TION can be taken too far. Hence they show that the error involved in the
reduction to Forms and numbers is the error of excessive abstraction.

134. **this form . . . this form**: Lit. 'this in this or these in this condition'. Cf. *PA*
640b27.

wrong in his habitual comparison of an animal <and its parts with circle and bronze>.[135] For his comparison leads us away from the truth; it makes us suppose that a man can exist without his parts, as a circle can exist without bronze. But in fact the two cases are not similar; for an animal is a perceiver,[136] and cannot be defined without reference to
30   motion, and therefore to parts in the right condition.[137] For a hand is not a part of a man in just any condition, but only when it is capable of fulfilling its function, and hence only when it is ensouled—when it is not ensouled, it is not a part <of a man>.

[PERCEPTIBLE AND INTELLIGIBLE MATTER]

But in the case of mathematical objects, why are accounts <of parts>—for instance, of semicircles—not parts of accounts <of wholes>—for
35   instance, of circles? For these are not perceptible.[138] But perhaps this makes no difference; for some nonperceptible things have matter too,
1037a and in fact everything that is not an essence and form itself in its own right, but a this, has some sort of matter. Hence these semicircles will not be parts of the universal circle, but they will be parts of particular circles, as we said before; for one sort of matter is perceptible, one sort
5   intelligible.[139]

[FORM AND COMPOUND; PARTICULAR AND UNIVERSAL]

It is also clear that the soul is the primary substance, the body is matter, and man or animal is composed of the two as universal. As for Socrates or Coriscus, if <Socrates'> soul[140] is also Socrates, he is spoken of in two ways; for some speak of him as soul, some as the compound. But
10   if he is without qualification this soul and this body, then what was said about the universal also applies to the particular.[141]

135. **And Socrates ... and bronze>**: Aristotle now rejects the argument put forward in 1036b3–7.

136. **perceiver**: Read *aisthētikon*. OCT: 'perceptible'.

137. **in the right condition**: Lit. 'in a certain condition'. Aristotle returns to the point in 1035b23–7 about parts and their relation to the form.

138. **are not perceptible**: Hence the previous arguments about perceptible matter apparently do not apply.

139. **intelligible**: See MATTER #6.

140. **<Socrates'> soul**: Lit. 'the soul'. Probably (not certainly) Aristotle is thinking of a particular soul (and therefore of a particular form); see FORM #9.

141. **what was said ... particular**: Lit. 'as the universal, also the particular'.

[PERCEPTIBLE AND NONPERCEPTIBLE SUBSTANCE]

We must postpone an investigation of whether there is another sort of matter apart from the matter of these <perceptible> substances, and whether we must search for some other sort of substance—for instance, numbers or something of the sort. For we also have this in view in trying to determine* <the answers to questions> about perceptible substances as well <as nonperceptible substances>, since in a way the study of nature, i.e., second philosophy, has the task of studying perceptible sub-   *15* stances.[142] For the student of nature must know not only about matter but also, and even more, about the substance corresponding to the account.

[THE UNITY OF DEFINITION]

We must also postpone an investigation of the way in which the things in the account are parts of the definition, and of why the definition is one account. For it is clear that the thing defined is one. But what makes   *20* it one, given that it has parts?

[SUMMARY OF CONCLUSIONS ABOUT FORM AND ESSENCE]

We have said generally, then, about all cases, what the essence is;[143] in what way it is itself in its own right; why in some cases the account of the essence includes the parts of the thing defined and in some cases it does not; and that in the account of substance the parts that are matter   *25* will not be present, because they are parts of the compound substance, not of the substance corresponding to the account.

The compound substance has an account in one way, but in another way it has none. Taken together with matter, it has no account, since that is indefinable;[144] but it has an account corresponding to the primary substance, so that the account of man, for instance, is the account of soul. For <the primary> substance is the form present in the thing, and the compound substance is spoken of as composed of the form and the   *30* matter. Concavity, for instance, <is a form of this sort>; for snub* nose and snubness are composed of concavity and nose (for nose will be present twice in these). And the compound substance (for instance snub nose or Callias) will also have matter in it.

142. **For we have . . . substances**: Aristotle anticipates the argument of Bks xii–xiv (which was already anticipated in the puzzles of Bk iii). On first and second philosophy see PHILOSOPHY.

143. **what the essence is**: Aristotle claims to have completed the inquiry into essence that he began in vii 4.

144. **that is indefinable**: This might refer either to matter or to the compound.

1037b   We have also said that in some cases, as in the case of primary substances, a thing and its essence are the same; curvature, for instance, is
the same as being curvature, if curvature is primary.[145] (By 'primary
substance' I mean the substance that is so called not because x is in y
and y is the subject of x by being the matter of x.) But if a thing is <a
5   substance> by being matter or by being combined with matter, it is
not the same as its essence. Nor, however,[146] are they one <only>
coincidentally, as Socrates and the musical are; for these are the same
<only> coincidentally.[147]

[HOW IS THE SUBSTANCE THAT WE DEFINE ONE THING, NOT MANY?]

12

Let us now first discuss the aspect of definition that was not discussed
10   in the *Analytics*,[148] since the puzzle that was stated there is useful for
our arguments about substance. The puzzle I mean is the following: We
say that the account, for instance biped animal (taking this to be the
account of man), is the definition of something, man; why, then, is man
one thing, not more than one—both animal and biped?
15   For man and pale are more than one thing if the one does not belong
to the other. But they are one thing if pale belongs to man, i.e., the
subject, man, has the attribute <pale>; for in that case one thing results,
and the pale man exists. But in our present case <of biped animal>,
one thing does not participate in another.[149] For the genus does not seem
20   to participate in the differentiae; if it did, the same thing would have to
participate in contraries at the same time, since the differentiae that
divide the genus are contraries. The argument is the same even if the
genus participates in the differentiae, if the differentiae are many—for
instance terrestrial, biped, wingless. For why are these one thing,[150] not
many things? Surely it is not because they are all present <in one sub-
ject>; for if that were enough, all <the differentiae> would amount to
one thing.[151]

145. **curvature, for instance . . . is primary**: Deleted in OCT.

146. **Nor, however**: Read *oude kata*. OCT: 'not even if they are. . .'.

147. **as Socrates . . . coincidentally**: See vii 6, esp. 1031a21, ONE.

148. *Analytics*: See APo 92a29.

149. **one thing does not participate in another**: Aristotle confines 'participation'
to nonessential properties; man, for instance, participates in pale.

150. **one thing**: i.e., a terrestrial, biped, wingless animal.

151. **all <the differentiae> . . . one thing**: This is taken to follow from the fact
that they all belong to the genus. Or 'all <the attributes of the subject> . . .'.

Moreover, all the things in the definition must amount to one thing.   *25*
For since a definition is one account and an account of substance, it
must be an account of some one thing; for in fact, as we say, substance
signifies some one thing and a this.

[DIVISION OF A GENUS INTO DIFFERENTIAE]

First we must examine definitions reached by divisions. For there is
nothing else in a definition except the genus that is mentioned first and   *30*
the differentiae; the other genera are in fact the first genus plus the
differentiae combined with it. The first genus, for instance, is animal,
the next is biped animal, and then wingless biped animal; the same
applies if it is spoken of through more differentiae. And in general, since   *1038a*
it does not matter if the genus is spoken of through many or through
few things, neither does it matter if it is spoken of through few or through
two; one of the two is the differentia, the other the genus (in biped
animal, for instance, animal is the genus and biped is the differentia).   *5*

Suppose, then, that the genus is nothing at all apart from its species;
or suppose that it is something apart from them, but <only> as matter
(sound, for instance, is genus and matter, and the differentiae make the
species—i.e., the letters—from sound). In either case it is evident that
the definition is the account composed of the differentiae.

But further, the genus must be divided by the differentia of the differentia;[152] since footed, for instance, is a differentia of animal, we must   *10*
know the differentia of footed animal insofar as it is footed. Hence, if
we speak correctly, we must not say that one division of the footed is
winged and the other wingless; if we do say that, it is because we cannot
do better. Instead we should say that one division is cloven-footed, and
the other noncloven footed; for these are differentiae of foot, since cloven-   *15*
footedness is a type of footedness. And in each case we mean to proceed
in this way, until we reach the undifferentiated <species>; then we will
have found as many species of foot as there are differentiae, and the
types of footed animals will be equal in number to the differentiae.

[HOW THE SUBSTANCE WE DEFINE IS ONE]

If this is so, then it is evident that <only> the last differentia will be
the substance and the definition of the thing, if we must avoid repeating   *20*
the same thing many times in formulae; for that is redundant. Such

---

152. **the genus . . . of the differentia**: Read *tē(i) tēs diaphoras diaphora(i)*. OCT:
'we must also divide the differentia of the differentia'.

redundancy indeed results;[153] for whenever we say that something is a two-footed footed animal, we have said exactly that it is an animal with feet with two feet, and if we divide two-footed by its own proper differentia, we will say the same thing over and over as many times as

25   there are differentiae. If, then, we take a differentia of the differentia, the last single differentia will be the species[154] and the substance. But if we take <alleged> differentiae that are coincidental—if, for instance, the footed is divided into pale and dark—then there will be as many of them as there are stages of division.

     Evidently, then, the definition is the account composed of the differ-

30   entiae, and in fact, following the correct procedure, it is the account composed of the last differentia. This would be clear if we rearranged this sort of definition, in the case of man, for instance, and called him animal two-footed footed; for once the two-footed has been mentioned, the footed is redundant. But there is no order in substance; surely we must not think that one substance is posterior and another prior.

35   So much, then, for our first discussion of the sorts of definitions reached by divisions.

[SUBSTANCE, FORM, AND UNIVERSAL]

[CAN A UNIVERSAL BE A SUBSTANCE?]

13

1038b   Since we are investigating substance, let us return to it again. Just as the subject and the essence[155] are said to be substance, so too is the universal. We have discussed the first two of these, namely essence and

5   subject; we have seen that something is a subject in one of two ways, either by being a this (as an animal is the subject for its attributes) or as matter is the subject for the actuality. But some also think that the universal is a cause and principle more than anything else is; that is why we should also discuss the universal.[156]

153. **Such redundancy indeed results**: It results unless we recognize that the last differentia is the definition.

154. **species**: *eidos*. Or 'form'.

155. **the subject and the essence**: OCT adds: 'and the thing composed of these'. Aristotle returns to the criteria for substance that he mentioned at 1028b33.

156. **But some . . . universal**: Some think the universal is the best candidate for being a cause and a principle; moreover, being a cause and principle is clearly connected with being a substance (as Aristotle himself makes clear in vii 17); hence the universal has a good prima facie claim to count as a substance.

[A UNIVERSAL CANNOT BE THE SUBSTANCE OF THE THINGS IT IS PREDICATED OF]

For it would seem impossible for anything spoken of universally to be
substance. For, first, the substance of a thing is the substance that is   *10*
distinctive of it, which does not belong to anything else, whereas the
universal is common; for what is called universal is what naturally belongs to more than one thing. Then which thing's substance will the
universal be?[157] For it must be the substance either of all or of none of
them. It cannot be the substance of all; but if it is the substance of one
of them, then the others will be this one too, since things that have one
substance also have one essence and are themselves one.[158]   *15*

[SUBSTANCE IS SUBJECT, HENCE NOT UNIVERSAL]

Further, what is called substance is what is not said of a subject,[159]
whereas every universal is said of a subject.

*[IF A UNIVERSAL IS SUBSTANCE, IT CANNOT BE A COMPONENT OF
SOMETHING'S ESSENCE]*

Now, suppose someone says: 'Admittedly, a universal cannot belong to
something as its essence. Still, it is present in the essence, as animal is
present in man and horse.' Surely it is clear that it will be some account
of <the essence it is present in>.[160] It does not matter even if it is not
an account of everything in the substance; for this <universal> will still   *20*
be the substance of something, as man is of the man in which it is present.
And so the result will be the same once again; for <the universal>—for

157. **which thing's . . . be?**: The universal F belongs to many particular Fs. If
it is their substance, it must be the substance of one, or of some, or of all of
them. But, Aristotle argues, none of these options seems satisfactory.

158. **since things . . . are themselves one**: If, then, the universal is the substance
of all its instances, all its instances will be one (given the principle stated in
1038b10–12). Hence the universal must be the substance of none of its instances.
Alternative rendering: 'since things that have one substance and [or 'i.e.'] one
essence are themselves one'.

159. **not said of a subject**: Aristotle appeals again to the conception of substance
as a subject; cf. 1028b36, 1029a8. He allows, however, that it is predicated of
one sort of subject; see 1029a23.

160. **it will be . . . present in>**: Alternatively: 'there is some account of <the
universal>'.

instance, animal—will be the substance of whatever it is present in by being its distinctive property.[161]

25   Further, it is both impossible and absurd for a this and substance, if it is composite, to be composed not from substances and not from a this, but from a sort of thing;[162] for it will follow that a nonsubstance, a sort of thing, will be prior* to substance, to a this. But that is impossible; for attributes cannot be prior to substance, either in account or in time or in knowledge[163]—for if they were, they would also be separable*.

30   Moreover,[164] a substance will be present in <the substance> Socrates, so that <the universal> will be the substance of two things.

In general, if a man and things spoken of in this way[165] are substances, it follows that nothing in their account is the substance of any of them or exists separately from them or in anything else. I mean, for instance, that there is no animal, or anything else mentioned in the accounts, apart* from the particular animals.[166]

[A UNIVERSAL CANNOT BE A THIS, AND SO CANNOT BE A SUBSTANCE]

35   If we study them in this way, then, it is evident that nothing that belongs
1039a universally is a substance and that what is predicated in common signi- fies this sort of thing,[167] not a this. If it is a this, then many <difficulties> result, including the Third Man.

[OUR DISTINCTION BETWEEN ACTUALITY AND POTENTIALITY EXPLAINS WHY UNIVERSALS CANNOT BE SUBSTANCES]

Further, our conclusion can also be made clear from the following points. Substance cannot be composed of substances that are actually present

161. **for <the . . . property**: And so all animals will be one, by the first argument against universal substances. Read *hoion to zō(i)on, en hō(i) hōs idion huparchei.* OCT: 'for it will be the substance of that species in which it is present . . . '.

162. **sort of thing**: *poion.* Or 'such'. See 1039a2n, QUALITY.

163. **in knowledge**: Read *gnōsei.* OCT: 'in coming to be'.

164. **Moreover . . .**: This will follow on the assumption that the universal is present in the substance of its subject.

165. **a man**: i.e., a particular man. Alternatively, 'man', i.e. the species. Our decision on this point will require a corresponding interpretation of 'and things spoken of in this way'.

166. **apart from the particular animals**: Or 'apart from the various species of animals'.

167. **this sort of thing**: *toionde.* This is cognate with *poion* in 1038b25. See QUALITY. On the Third Man see FORM (PLATONIC) #3.

in it; for things that are actually two in this way are never actually one,   5
but if they are potentially two they are <actually> one. A double line,
for instance, is composed of halves that are <only> potentially two
things; for the actuality separates them.[168] And so if substance is one, it
will not be composed of substances that are actually[169] present in it.
Democritus is right about actuality, when he says that one cannot come   10
to be from two, or two from one; he says this because he regards the
indivisible magnitudes[170] as the substances. Clearly, then, the same will
apply in the case of number if, as some say, number is a combination
of units; for either the pair is not one or else a unit is not actually in it.

This conclusion, however, raises a puzzle. For if no substance can be   15
composed of universals (because a universal signifies this sort of thing,
not a this) and if no substance can be composed of substances actually
present in it, then it follows that every substance will be incomposite,
so that none will have any account. And yet, it seems to everyone, and
we have said much earlier,[171] that substances alone, or most of all, have   20
formulae, whereas now they too turn out not to have them. And so
either nothing will have a definition or else in a way things will have
definitions, and in a way they will not. What this means will be clearer
from what follows.

[THE IMPOSSIBILITY OF SEPARATED PLATONIC IDEAS]

14

It is also evident from this what results for those who both say that the   25
Ideas are separate substances[172] and also, at the same time, take a Form
to be composed of genus and differentiae. For if there are Forms, and
if animal is in man and horse, then it is either numerically one and the
same in both or numerically different in each. (For clearly it is one in
account; a statement of the account will state the same thing in each   30
case.) If, then, there is some man himself in his own right that is a
this and separated, each of his components—for instance, animal and

---

168. **the actuality separates them**: If they are to be actually two, they must be
separated.

169. **actually**: Lit. 'in this way'.

170. **indivisible magnitudes**: None of these Democritean atoms is potentially
two.

171. **much earlier**: 1030a2–27.

172. **separate substances**: Aristotle assumes that if Ideas are separate substances,
they must be particulars. This assumption underlies many of his objections to
Ideas.

biped—must also signify a this and be separable and a substance; and so this is also true of animal.

[A GENERIC IDEA CANNOT BE THE SAME IN DIFFERENT SPECIES]

1039b
If the animal in horse is one and the same as the animal in man, as you are one and the same as yourself, then how will this one[173] thing that is in separate things be one, and why will this animal not be separate from itself as well?

Further, if it is to participate in two-footed and many-footed, then something impossible follows; for contraries will belong simultaneously to it, though it is one and a this. But if it is not to participate in them, what is meant by saying that animal is two-footed or footed? Presumably <we might be told> they are combined and in contact or mixed; but all such answers are absurd.

5

[NOR CAN IT BE DIFFERENT IN DIFFERENT SPECIES]

Suppose, alternatively, that animal is different in each <species>; then there will be practically an unlimited number of things whose substance is animal, since man is noncoincidentally composed of animal.

10
Further, animal itself will be many things. For the animal in each <species> is substance, because <the species> is not called <animal> by reference to anything else—if it were, then that other thing would be a component of man and would be its genus.

Further, all the elements composing man will be Ideas; but nothing will be the Idea of one thing and the substance of another (for that would be impossible). Hence animal itself will be each one of the animals in the different <species of> animals.[174]

Further, what is that <animal in each species> composed of, and how will it be composed of animal itself? Or how can the animal <in each species>, whose substance is this animal itself, be something apart from animal itself?

15

[THERE ARE EVEN WORSE PROBLEMS IN THE RELATION OF IDEAS TO PARTICULARS]

Further, in the case of perceptible things, these and even more absurd results follow. If, then, this cannot be how things are, clearly there are no Forms of perceptible things in the way some say there are.

173. **how will this one**: Read *pōs to hen*. OCT: 'how will this thing that is in separate . . .'.

174. **animals**: Hence the generic Idea, Animal Itself, will be many, and so will not be numerically one (as it should be if it is a separate substance).

[DIFFICULTIES ABOUT PARTICULAR SUBSTANCES]

15

We have found that the compound and the form₁ are different sorts of   20
substance; I mean that the first sort of substance is substance by being
the form₁ combined with matter, and the second sort is the form₁ without
qualification. Now, all the substances spoken of as compounds perish,
since all of them also come to be; but the form₁ does not perish in such
a way that it is ever <in the process of> perishing, since neither is it
ever <in the process of> coming to be. For it is the essence of this   25
house, not the essence of house, that is <in the process of> coming to
be, whereas forms₁ are and are not without <any process of> coming
to be and perishing, since we have shown that no one generates or
produces them.¹⁷⁵

[THEY ARE PERISHABLE AND HENCE ALLOW NEITHER DEFINITION NOR KNOWLEDGE]

For this reason there is neither definition nor demonstration about particular perceptible substances, because they have matter whose nature
admits of both being and not being; that is why all <perceptible> particu-   30
lars are perishable.

Now, demonstrations and definitions that express knowledgeₑ are of
necessary things.¹⁷⁶ And just as knowledge cannot be knowledge at one
time and ignorance at another, but what admits of such variation is
belief, so also neither demonstration nor definition admits of such variation; belief is what is concerned with what admits of being otherwise.   1040a
It clearly follows that there will be neither definition nor demonstration
of these <particular perceptible things>. For whenever perishing things
pass from perception, they are unclear to those with knowledge, and
though the accounts still remain in the souls of those with knowledge,
there will be neither definition nor demonstration <about perceptible   5
things>. That is why, whenever anyone who looks for a formula is
defining a particular, he ought to realize that the definition can in every
case be undermined, since particulars cannot be defined.

175. **whereas forms₁ . . . produces them**: On the distinction drawn here see
COME TO BE #4. Probably Aristotle means that (a) a given form at one time is
(when it is embodied in matter) and at another time is not (when its material
embodiment perishes); but he might mean that (b) some forms (e.g., horse and
sheep) are and some (e.g., unicorn) are not.

176. **Now . . . necessary things**: Or (assuming a different text): 'Now, demonstrations are of necessary things, and definitions express knowledgeₑ'.

[SINCE PLATONIC IDEAS ARE PARTICULARS, THEY ARE INDEFINABLE]

Nor, indeed, can Ideas be defined. For Ideas are particulars, they say,
10 and separable. But accounts must be composed of names, and the definer
will not make a <new> name (since it would be unknown); yet each
of the established names is common to all <the particulars of a given
kind>, and so they must also belong to something else <as well as to
a given particular>. If, for instance, someone defines you, he will say
you are a thin or pale animal, or something else that belongs to something
else as well as to you.

Someone might say: 'Even though each name <in the definition>
15 belongs separately to many things, still it is possible that all together
belong only to this.'[177] We should answer, first, that biped animal, for
instance, belongs both to animal and to biped—indeed, this must be so
with everlasting things, since they are prior to and parts of the composite
thing. Moreover, they are also separable if man is separable; for either
20 none of the three is separable or both animal and biped are. And so if
none of them is separable, the genus will not exist apart from the species;
but if the genus is separable, so is the differentia. Moreover, <animal
and biped> are prior in being <to biped animal>, and therefore they
are not destroyed when it is.

Further, if Ideas are composed of Ideas (for the things they are composed of are less composite), then the components of the Idea—for
instance, animal and biped—will also have to be predicated of many
25 things. If they are not, how will they be known? For there will be an
Idea which cannot be predicated of more than one thing. But that does
not seem to be so; on the contrary, every Idea can, it seems, be participated in.[178]

[DIFFICULTIES IN DEFINING PARTICULARS]

As has been said, then, we fail to notice that everlasting things <that
are particulars> are indefinable. This is especially true in the case of
those that are unique—for instance, the sun and the moon. For some-
30 times people not only go wrong by adding the sorts of things (for instance, going around the earth, or being hidden at night) that can be
removed from the sun without its ceasing to be the sun. (For <this sort
of definition implies that> if it stops going around or shows at night,

177. **only to this**: And so, if such an individuating description can be given, it
seems that a particular can be defined.

178. **can . . . participated in**: Or 'seems to be participated in'. Aristotle suggests
that the claim that Ideas are particulars conflicts with the claim that they can be
participated in (since, in his view, only universals can be participated in).

it will no longer be the sun; but that is absurd, since the sun signifies a certain substance.) They also <sometimes go wrong by mentioning only the features> that can be found in something else as well. If, for instance, something else of this sort comes to be, then clearly, <according to the alleged definition>, it will also have to be the sun, and in that case the   1040b account will be common <to the two>. But in fact the sun is a particular, as Cleon and Socrates are.

<These objections show why Ideas are indefinable.> For why does none of those <who believe in Ideas> present a formula of any Idea? If they tried to do so, the truth of what we have just said would become clear.

[SOME APPARENT SUBSTANCES, BOTH PARTICULARS AND UNIVERSALS, LACK THE APPROPRIATE SORT OF UNITY]

16

It is evident that even among the substances that are generally recognized   5 to be such,[179] most are potentialities. These include the parts of animals (for none of them is separated <as long as they remain parts of animals>; whenever they are separated, they all exist as matter),[180] and also earth, fire, and air. For none of these is one, but each is a sort of heap, until they are worked up[181] and some one thing comes to be from them.   10

One would be most inclined to suppose that the parts of ensouled things that are closely <associated with> the soul are beings both in actuality and in potentiality; for they have principles of motion from some source in their joints, which is why some animals keep on living when they are divided. But nonetheless, all these things exist <only> in potentiality. They exist as long as they are one and continuous by   15 nature, rather than by force or by growing together (that sort of thing is a deformity).

Now, one is spoken of in the same ways as being is; and the substance of one thing is one, and things whose substance is numerically one are numerically one. Evidently, then, neither one nor being can be the substance of things, just as being an element or being a principle cannot <be the substance of things>; rather, we ask 'What then is the princi-   20 ple?', so that we may refer <the thing> to something better known. Among these things, then, being and one are substance to a higher

179. **the substances . . . such**: Or: 'the things that seem to be substances'.

180. **(for none . . . as matter)**: Aristotle refers to his doctrine of HOMONYMY; see 1035b23, 1036b30.

181. **worked up**: Lit. 'cooked' or 'concocted'. Aristotle often uses this term for the processes involved in nutrition (incorporating food into the body).

degree than principle, element, and cause are; but even being and one are not substance, since nothing else common is substance either. For substance belongs only to itself and to what has it, the thing whose
25   substance it is. Moreover, one thing would not be[182] in many places at once, but what is common exists in many places at once. Hence clearly no universal is found separately apart from particulars.

But those who say there are Forms are right in one way, in separating them, if they are indeed substances; but in another way they are wrong,
30   because they say that the one over many is a Form.[183] The reason is that they cannot describe these imperishable substances apart from particular and perceptible substances, and so they make them the same in kind[184] as perishable things (since these are the substances we know$_o$); they speak of man itself and horse itself, adding to perceptibles the word 'itself'.[185]

1041a   And yet even if we had not seen the stars, nonetheless, I think, they would have been everlasting substances apart from those we know; and so, as things are, it is equally true that even if we do not know what nonperceptible substances there are, there must presumably be some.

It is clear, then, that nothing said universally is a substance, and that
5   no substance is composed of substances.

[SUBSTANCE AS CAUSE AND ESSENCE]

17

But let us make a sort of new beginning, and say over again what, and what sort of thing, substance should be said to be; for presumably our answer will also make things clear about the substance that is separated from perceptible substances. Since, then, substance is some sort of princi-
10   ple and cause, we should proceed from here.

In every case, we search* for the reason why by asking why one thing belongs to another. For if we ask why a musical man is a musical man, either we are searching for what we have mentioned—for instance, why the man is musical—or else we are searching for something else. Now,
15   to ask why something is itself is to search for nothing. For that <it is so> and its being so—I mean, for instance, that the moon is eclipsed— must be clear already; and the answer 'because it is itself' is one account

182. **would not be**: Perhaps this means 'cannot be'.

183. **because . . . Form**: The one over many is a universal, and (Aristotle has argued) no universal can be separated.

184. **kind**: *eidos*.

185. **they speak . . . 'itself'**: Cf. the objection that the theory of Ideas simply multiplies familiar entities, 990a33–b8n.

and one cause applying to every case, to why a man is a man or a musician a musician. Perhaps, however, someone might answer 'because each thing is indivisible from itself, since this is what it is to be one'. But this is a short answer common to all cases.   20

We might, however, ask why a man is this sort of animal. Here, then, we are clearly not asking why something that is a man is a man. We are asking, then, why one thing belongs to another; that it does belong must already be clear, since otherwise we are searching for nothing. For instance, when we ask why it thunders, we are asking why there is a noise   25
in the clouds; here we ask why one thing belongs to another. Similarly, we ask why these things—for instance, bricks and stones—are a house.

Evidently, then, we are searching for the cause; and this is the essence, to speak from a logical point of view.[186] In some cases—for instance, presumably, a house or a bed—the cause[187] is what something is for; sometimes it is what first initiated the motion, since this is also a cause.   30
We search for the latter type of cause in the case of coming to be and perishing; in the case of being as well <as in the case of coming to be> we search for the former type of cause.[188]

[*ESSENCE IS SUBSTANCE AND FORM*]

What we are searching for is most easily overlooked when one thing is not said of another (as when we ask, for instance, what a man is),   1041b
because we speak without qualification and do not specify that we are asking why these things are this thing.[189] Instead of speaking without qualification, we must articulate our question before we search, since otherwise we will not have distinguished a genuine search from a search for nothing. Since we must take it as given that the subject exists, clearly   5
we search for why the matter is something. We ask, for instance, 'Why are these things a house?' Because the essence of house belongs to them. Similarly, a man is this, or rather is this body having this. Hence we search for the cause on account of which the matter is something, i.e., for the form;[190] and this cause is the substance.

186. **this is ... view**: See 1029b13n, LOGICAL. OCT deletes these words.

187. **the cause**: Or perhaps 'the essence'.

188. **the former type**: The final cause; see FOR SOMETHING.

189. **why these things are this thing**: We answer the question 'What is a man?' by rephrasing it as 'Why are these things (the flesh, bones etc.) a man?'. The answer to this 'Why?' question (giving the form of man) also answers the 'What?' question.

190. **i.e., for the form**: Deleted by OCT.

10   Evidently, then, there is neither searching nor teaching about incomposite things; the approach to them is different from searching.

[THE FORM CANNOT BE ONE OF THE MATERIAL CONSTITUENTS OR COMPOSED OF THEM]

Now, a composite is composed of something in such a way that the whole thing is one, not as a heap is, but as a syllable is. A syllable is not the same as its letters[191]—for instance, B and A are not the same thing as BA, nor is flesh fire and earth. For when the components

15   are dispersed, the flesh or syllable no longer exists, though the letters or the fire and earth still do. Hence the syllable is something, and not only the vowel and the consonant but some further thing; and similarly, flesh is not only fire and earth, or the hot and cold, but some further thing.

20   Now suppose that this further thing must be either an element or composed of elements. If it is an element, there will be the same argument over again; for flesh will be composed of this <new element>, plus fire and earth, plus some further thing, so that it will go on without limit. If the further thing is composed of an element, it is clearly not composed of just one (otherwise it would itself be this one), but of more than one;

25   and then we will repeat the same argument about it as about flesh or a syllable.[192]

It would seem, however, that this further thing is something, and not an element, and that it is the cause of one thing's being flesh and another thing's being a syllable, and similarly in the other cases.

[SUBSTANCE IS FORM AND NATURE]

Now this is the substance of a given thing; for this is the primary cause of the thing's being <what it is>. Some things are not substances,

30   but the things that are substances are naturally constituted; hence this nature—the one that is not an element but a principle—will apparently be substance. An element is what is present in something as the matter into which the thing is divided—for instance, the A and the B in the syllable.

191. **letters**: *stoicheion*. Also translated 'ELEMENT'; cf. 985b15n.

192. **a syllable**: The further thing must be composed of elements plus something else; and what is the something else composed of? We again have an infinite regress.

Book VIII

[FURTHER QUESTIONS ON SUBSTANCE AND FORM]

[SUMMARY OF THE ARGUMENT ABOUT SUBSTANCE]

1

We must, then, draw the conclusions from what has been said, gather   1042a3
together the main points, and so complete the discussion. Here, then,
is what we have said:[1]   5

(1) We are searching for the causes, principles, and elements of substances.

(2) Some substances are agreed by everyone to be substances, while
some people have held distinctive views of their own about some other
things <that they count as substances>. The agreed substances are the
natural ones—for instance, fire, earth, water, air, and the other simple
bodies, then plants and their parts, animals and their parts, and, finally,   10
the heaven* and its parts. In some people's distinctive views, Forms and
mathematical objects are substances.[2]

(3) Some arguments imply that the essence is substance, others that
the subject is substance.[3] Other arguments imply that the genus is substance more than the species are, and that the universal is substance more
than the particulars are. The Ideas are closely related to the universal   15
and the genus, since the same argument makes all of them seem to be
substances.[4]

(4) Since the essence is substance and a definition is an account of
the essence, we have discussed definition and what is in its own right.[5]

(5) Since a definition is an account and an account has parts, we also
had to consider what a part is,[6] to see what sorts of parts are parts of   20
the substance, and what sorts are not, and whether the same parts <that
are parts of the substance> are also parts of the definition.[7]

---

1. **what we have said**: The numbered points that follow summarize the argument of Bk vii; only vii 7–9 do not seem to be mentioned.

2. **Some substances . . . are substances**: Point (2) recapitulates vii 2.

3. **Some arguments . . . subject is substance**: Or (less probably, in view of vii
3–6) 'Other arguments imply that the essence and the subject are substances.'

4. **Some arguments . . . to be substances**: For the different possibilities mentioned in (3) see 1028b33–36, 1038b1–8.

5. **Since the essence . . . own right**: For (4) see vii 4–6.

6. **to consider what a part is**: Lit. 'to see about part'.

7. **Since a definition . . . of the definition**: With (5) cf. vii 10–11.

(6) Further, neither the universal nor the genus is substance.[8]

(7) We should examine Ideas and mathematical objects later, since some say that these are substances apart from perceptible substances.[9]

[SUBSTANCE AS SUBJECT]

25 For now, let us proceed with a discussion of the agreed substances; these are the perceptible ones, and all perceptible substances have matter.

The subject is substance. In one way, matter <is a subject>.[10] (By 'matter' I mean what is potentially but not actually a this.) In another way, the account and the form$_m$, which, being a this, is separable in
30 account, <is a subject>. The third <sort of subject> is the composite of these two. Only it comes to be and perishes, and it is separable without qualification; for among substances that correspond to the account some are <separable without qualification> and some are not.

[SUBSTANCE AS MATTER]

Now, clearly matter as well <as form and compound> is substance; for in all changes between opposites there is some subject for the change. Changes in place, for instance, have a subject that is here at one time,
35 elsewhere at another time; those involving growth have one that is this size at one time, smaller or bigger at another time; changes involving
1042b alteration have one that is, <for instance,> healthy at one time, sick at another time. Similarly, changes involving substance have a subject that is at one time in <process of> coming to be, at another time in <process of> perishing, and at one time is the sort of subject that is a this and at another time is the sort of subject that corresponds to a privation.*[11]

Coming to be and perishing imply all the other sorts of change, but
5 one or two of the other sorts do not imply this sort. For if something has matter for change in place, it need not also have matter for coming to be and perishing. The difference between unqualified and qualified coming to be has been described in the works on nature.[12]

---

8. **Further . . . is substance**: With (6) cf. vii 13–16.

9. **We should . . . perceptible substances**: The question in (7) was raised at 1037a10.

10. **<is a subject>**: Less probably, '<is a substance>'. The same question arises in the rest of the paragraph.

11. **subject . . . privation**: i.e., matter (e.g., the unshaped bronze).

12. **works on nature**: See *Phys*. i 7, COMING TO BE.

[SUBSTANCE AS ACTUALITY]

2

The substance that is subject and matter is agreed; this is the substance   10
that is something potentially. It remains, then, to describe the substance
of perceptible things that is actuality.

[DIFFERENT CONDITIONS OF MATTER CORRESPOND TO DIFFERENT ACTUALITIES]

Democritus would seem to think that there are three differentiae; in his
view, the body that is the subject—the matter—is one and the same,
but <perceptible things> differ either by 'balance', i.e., figure,* or by
'turning', i.e., position, or by 'contact', i.e., arrangement.[13] It is evident,   15
however, that there are many differentiae. For things are differentiated[14]
by the way their matter is combined (blended together, for instance, as
honey-water is); or tied together (for instance, a bundle); or glued (for
instance, a book); or nailed (for instance, a box); or by more than one
of these; or by having a specific position (a threshold or a lintel, for
instance, since their differentia is being in a certain position); or by a   20
specific time (for instance, dinner and breakfast); or by a specific place
(for instance, the winds); or by having different perceptible attributes
(for instance, hardness or softness, thickness or thinness, dryness or
wetness), either some or all of them, and, in general, by excess or defi-   25
ciency <of them>.

Clearly, then, 'is' is also said in just as many ways.[15] Something is a
threshold, for instance, because it has this position, and its being a
threshold signifies its having this position; and similarly, being ice signifies <water's> having solidified in this way. The being of some things
will be defined by all of these things—by some things being mixed, some
blended, some bound together, some solidified, and some (a hand or   30
foot, for instance) having the other differentiae.

We must grasp, then, what kinds of differentiae there are, since they
will be the principles of <a thing's> being <what it is>. For instance,
things differentiated by more and less, or thick and thin, or by other
such things, are all differentiated by excess and deficiency; things differ-   35
entiated by shape, or by roughness and smoothness, are all differentiated

13. **'balance'** . . . **arrangement**: Aristotle seems to quote Democritus' actual terms
(marked here by quotation marks), which he then explains.

14. **differentiated**: Lit. 'spoken of'. Aristotle means that they are distinguished
by their different definitions.

15. **'is'** . . . **ways**: When we say that x is F, the 'is' refers to the different relations
just mentioned.

1043a   by straight and bent; and the being of other things will be being mixed,[16]
           and their not being will be the opposite.

[HENCE WE UNDERSTAND HOW SUBSTANCE IS ACTUALITY]

It is evident from what we have said, then, that if substance is the cause
of a thing's being, we should seek the cause of the being of each of these
things in these <differentiae>. Although none of these <differentiae>
is substance even when combined <with matter>, still <the differentia>

5   is in each case analogous to substance; and just as in substances what
is predicated of the matter is the actuality itself, so also in other definitions
what is predicated is what is closest to being the actuality.[17] If, for instance, we have to define a threshold, we will say it is wood or stone
in this position; we will define a house as bricks and timber in this
position (or in some cases we mention the end as well). If we have to

10   define ice, we will say it is water frozen or solidified in this way; we
will say harmony is this sort of blending of high and low; and the same
is true in the other cases.
      It is evident from this that each different sort of matter has a different
actuality and account. For in some cases the actuality is the composition,
in some it is the mixture, and in others one of the other things we have
mentioned.

[DIFFERENT WAYS OF DEFINING SUBSTANCES [18]]

15   That is why some people who offer definitions say what a house is by
saying it is stones, bricks, and timber; in saying this, they speak of what
is potentially a house, since these things are matter. Others say that a
house is a container sheltering possessions and <living> bodies (or add
something else of that sort); in saying this, they speak of the actuality.
Others combine the matter and the actuality; in doing this, they speak
of the third sort of substance, which is composed of the first two. For

20   the account giving the differentiae would seem to be the account of the
form and the actuality, and the one giving the constituents present in
the house would seem to be more an account of the matter. The same
is true of the sorts of formulae that Archytas used to accept; for these
are accounts of the composite. What, for instance, is calm weather? Quiet
in a large expanse of air; for air is the matter, and quiet is the actuality

16. **being mixed**: Read *to memichthai*. OCT: 'by being mixed'.

17. **is what . . . actuality**: Lit. 'is most of all the actuality'.

18. The distinctions drawn in this section are relevant to the questions discussed
in vii 10–11.

of the substance. What is calm? Smoothness of sea; the material subject   *25*
is the sea, and the actuality and form$_m$ is the smoothness.

It is evident from what we have said, then, both what perceptible
substance is and what sort of being it has; for one sort is substance as
matter, another is substance as form$_m$ and actuality, and the third is the
substance that is composed of these.

[A NAME MAY SIGNIFY SUBSTANCE AS FORM OR AS COMPOUND]

3

We must realize that it is not always obvious whether a name signifies   *30*
the composite substance or signifies the actuality and form$_m$. Does a
house, for instance, signify[19] the combination (that it is a shelter composed of bricks and stone in this position) or does it signify the actuality
and form (that it is a shelter)? Is a line twoness in length, or twoness?
Is an animal a soul in a body, or a soul—since soul is the substance and   *35*
actuality of the right sort of body?[20] Now, animal might belong to both
form and compound; if it does, it will be spoken of not in one account
<applying to both>, but with reference to one thing.[21]

Although this question makes a difference in another area, it makes no
difference to the search for perceptible substance;[22] for the essence belongs   *1043b*
to the form and actuality. For soul and being soul are the same, whereas
man and being man are not the same, unless the soul is also to be called
the man. In the latter case, <being man> is the same as one thing, <i.e.,
soul>, but not the same as the other, <i.e., soul plus body>.[23]

[THE FORM IS NOT A FURTHER COMPONENT OF A SUBSTANCE]

It is evident when we investigate that a syllable is not composed of letters   *5*
plus composition,[24] and that a house is not bricks plus composition. And

19. **signify**: Aristotle passes from saying what the word 'house' SIGNIFIES to
saying what a house signifies, without indicating that he sees any important
difference.

20. **right sort of body**: Lit. 'a certain body'.

21. **with reference to one thing**: See 1003a33, HOMONYMY.

22. **Although . . . substance**: Aristotle does not explain why this is so. Perhaps
his view is connected with his claim that the essence of a natural organism
includes the right sort of matter, 1036b21–32.

23. **In the latter . . . plus body>**: Or perhaps: 'Thus x and being x are in some
cases the same, in other cases not the same'. Lit. 'Thus to one, but not to the
other (or: to another).'

24. **a syllable . . . composition**: This question was raised in vii 17.

this is correct; for neither composition nor mixture is composed of the things of which it is composition or mixture.[25] The same is true in other cases. If, for instance, a threshold is <what it is> because of its position,

10   the threshold is composed of the position, but the position is not composed of the threshold; nor is a man animal plus two-footed. On the contrary, there must be something beyond these <elements>, if they are matter; this other thing is neither an element nor composed of elements, but it is what people <mistakenly> exclude when they speak <only> of the matter. If this, then, is the cause of being, and <the cause of being> is substance,[26] then in speaking of this they speak of the substance itself.

[PERISHABLE AND IMPERISHABLE FORM]

15   This substance must either be everlasting or else be perishable without <being in process of> perishing[27] and have come to be without <being in process of> coming to be. It has been proved and shown elsewhere[28] that no one produces or generates the form; what is produced is a this, and what comes to be is what is composed <of form and matter>.

It is not yet clear whether the substances of perishable things are separable. In some cases, however, this is clearly impossible—for in-

20   stance, in the case of such things as house or utensil, which cannot exist apart from the particulars. Now, presumably these are not substances at all, and neither is anything else that is not constituted by nature; for one might take nature to be the only substance found in perishable things.[29]

[FORMS ARE NOT COMPONENTS]

Hence the puzzle which used to be raised by the followers of Antisthenes

25   and equally uneducated[30] people is quite relevant. Essence, in their view,

25. **for neither . . . or mixture**: Aristotle uses 'composition' and 'mixture' not for the thing resulting from mixing or compounding (as in 'sticky mixture' or 'ugly composition'), but for the formal aspects (for instance, the proportion in which sand and cement must be mixed to produce concrete) that must be distinguished from the material aspects.

26. **and <the . . . substance**: Read *ousia touto*. OCT: 'and of substance'.

27. **perishable . . . perishing**. See COMING TO BE #4.

28. **elsewhere**: 1033a24–b19.

29. **for one . . . perishable things**: For the suggestion that artifacts are not substances cf. 1041b28–36.

30. **uneducated**: They do not know the appropriate questions to ask in different areas of inquiry. See 1006a6, EDUCATION.

is indefinable, since <they say> a formula is a long account; and, <they suppose>, though one can teach what sort of thing something is, one cannot define anything. One cannot say what silver is, for instance, though one can say that it is the sort of thing tin is. Hence, <on this view>, a formula and account is possible for one sort of substance— the compound—whether it is perceptible or intelligible; but definition 30 is no longer possible when we come to the primary parts of the compound substance, since a defining account signifies something of something, and one <aspect> must be material and the other formal$_m$.

It is also evident why, if substances are in a way numbers, they are so <as wholes>, and not (as some say) as aggregates of units. For a definition is a sort of number; for it is divisible, indeed divisible into 35 indivisibles, since accounts are not infinite; and number is this sort of thing.[31] Just as the removal or addition of a component, however small, from the number makes it no longer the same number but a different one, so also such removal or addition does away with a definition and 1044a essence. For indeed the number must be what makes something one number,[32] but these people cannot state what makes it one. For either it is not <one> but a sort of heap,[33] or else it is indeed <one>, and 5 they should say what makes one from many. The definition is also one, but, for the same reasons, they cannot state <what makes it one>.

And this result is no surprise. For by the same argument substance is one in this way,[34] not, as some say, by being a sort of unit or point; rather, each substance is a sort of actuality and nature. And just as a 10 number does not admit more or less, neither does the substance that corresponds to the form; the only sort of substance, if any, that admits more or less is the substance that is combined with the matter.

Let this, then, be a sufficient determination of the ways in which the things spoken of as substances can and cannot come to be and perish, and about the reduction of things to numbers.

*   *   *   *   *   *   *

31. **and number . . . thing**: It is composed of units that are not divisible into further units.

32. **For indeed . . . one number**: For Aristotle's distinction between the number that counts and the number that is counted see NUMBER. A group of, say, four things counts as one group of four (rather than two groups of two or four groups of one) because the definition of 'four' applies to it; but we cannot understand how this is so if we regard the definition as corresponding to some further component besides the four things we are considering.

33. **heap**: See 1040b9, 1041b12.

34. **in this way**: As one composed of many.

6

1045a7   Let us now return to the puzzle we mentioned[35] about definitions and
          about numbers, namely about the cause of their being one. If something
10   has several parts, but all together it is not a sort of heap, but, on the
          contrary, the whole is something apart from the parts, then there is a
          cause of its being one, since, even among bodies, in some cases the
          cause of being one is contact, and in others it is viscosity or some other
          such attribute.

          A definition is an account that is one, not by being tied together (like
          the *Iliad*),[36] but by being of one thing. What, then, is it that makes man
15   one? Why is he one, and not more than one—animal and two-footed,
          for instance—especially if, as some say, there is some animal itself and
          two-footed itself?[37] For why is man not these things themselves? If so,
          men will exist by participating, not in one thing (man), but in two (animal
20   and two-footed); and in general, man would be more than one (animal
          and two-footed) and not one.

          Now, it is evident that it is impossible to explain and solve the puzzle
          if one continues to define and to speak as they normally do. But if,
          as we say, one thing is matter and another is form$_m$, and the one is
          <something> potentially, the other actually, then what we are searching
25   for no longer seems to be a puzzle. For this puzzle is the same as the
          question whether the round bronze is the formula of cloak.* <If it is,>
          then this name <'cloak'> is a sign of the account, and so what we are
          searching for is what causes the round and the bronze to be one. There
          no longer appears to be a puzzle, then, because one of them is the
          matter, and the other is the form$_m$.

30   What, then, causes something that is potentially to be actually? That
          is to say, what is the cause apart from the agent that produced it (in the
          case of things that come to be)? There is no cause other than <the fact
          that> the potential sphere is an actual sphere;[38] this is the essence of
          both <the potential and the actual sphere>.

          Some matter is intelligible,[39] some perceptible; and in every account
35   one part is the matter, one the actuality.

35. **the puzzle we mentioned**: See vii 12, 17, viii 3.

36. *Iliad*: Cf. 1030a9.

37. **animal itself and two-footed itself**: i.e., the Platonic FORMS.

38. **There is . . . actual sphere**: Or: 'Nothing else is the cause of <the fact that>
the potential sphere is an actual sphere.'

39. **Some matter is intelligible**: See 1037a4, MATTER #6.

If something has neither intelligible nor perceptible matter, it is   *1045b*
thereby essentially one thing, just as it is also essentially a being—a this,
a quality, a quantity; this is why neither being nor one is present in
definitions. Moreover, the essence of these things is thereby one thing,
just as it is also a being. Hence none of these things has any other cause   5
than being one or being a being;[40] for each is some being and some one
<thing> immediately <by its own nature>, not by being in the genus
of being or of one, and not in such a way that <being and one> are
separable apart from particulars.[41]

[OUR ACCOUNT OF FORM AND MATTER SOLVES THE PUZZLES]

This puzzle leads some to speak of participating and to be puzzled about
its cause and about what it is. Others speak of communion: Lycophron,   10
for instance, says that knowledge is a communion of knowing and the
soul. Others say that life is a compounding or tying together of the soul
with the body. But the same thing can be said about all these attempts.
For according to them being healthy, for instance, will also be a communion or tying together or compounding of soul and health; and the
bronze's being a triangle will be a compounding of bronze and triangle;   15
and something's being pale will be a compounding of surface and paleness. The reason they say these things is that they are searching for an
account that makes potentiality and actuality one, and <in doing so>
they are searching for the differentia.[42]
    In fact, however, as we have said, the ultimate matter[43] and the form
are one and the same; the matter <is something> potentially, and the
form <is that thing> actually. Hence <to search for what causes them
to be one> is like searching for the cause of one and of being one. For   20
each thing <that has matter and form> is some one thing; and what is
potentially and what is actually are in a way one. And so nothing else
causes <them to be one>, unless something has initiated the motion
from potentiality to actuality. Anything that lacks matter is without
qualification some one thing essentially.

40. **than . . . a being**. Or: 'of being one or of being a being'.

41. **not by being . . . particulars**: Aristotle rejects a Platonic account of one and
being.

42. **searching for the differentia**: Or: 'seeking the difference between them'.

43. **ultimate matter**: See 1035b30n.

Book IX

[SUMMARY OF PREVIOUS DISCUSSION. BEING AS POTENTIALITY AND ACTUALITY]

1

1045b27   We have now discussed what is in the primary way,[1] the being to which
30   all the other predications* of being are referred, namely substance. For
it is the account of substance that determines that the other things—
quantity, quality, and the other things spoken of in this way—are called
beings;[2] for, as we said in the first discussion,[3] they all have the account
of substance.

   Now being is spoken of in one way as either what, or quality, or
quantity; and in another way in accordance with potentiality* and realization,[4] and in accordance with activity.[5] Let us, then, also discuss potenti-
35   ality and realization.

[DIFFERENT TYPES OF POTENTIALITY]

First let us discuss the type of potentiality that is so called most fully,[6]
1046a   though it is not the most useful for our present purpose; for potentiality
and actuality extend more widely than the type spoken of only in connection with motion.[7] After we have spoken of this type of potentiality, we
5   will define actuality, and in the course of doing so we will also clarify
the other types of potentiality.

   We have determined elsewhere[8] that potentiality and being potential
are spoken of in many ways. Let us ignore all those potentialities that
are so called <merely> homonymously;[9] for some things are called

---

1. **what is in the primary way**: Cf. 1028a30n.

2. **For it is . . . beings**: Lit. 'For in accordance with the account of substance
the other things . . . are called beings'.

3. **first discussion**: This might refer to 1003a38–b10 or to 1028a29–b2.

4. **realization**: See ACTUALITY #1.

5. **activity**: *ergon*, usually translated 'FUNCTION'.

6. **most fully**: See CONTROLLING. This is the sort of potentiality by reference to
which we understand the other sorts, because it displays all the features of
which only some are found in the other sorts of potentiality.

7. **the type . . . motion**: i.e., the one most fully so called.

8. **elsewhere**: In v 12.

9. **Let us . . . homonymously**: Aristotle speaks of HOMONYMY here when he
has a mere similarity in mind. In the next paragraph he turns to the cases of

potentialities from some <mere> similarity—in geometry, for instance, we say that some things are or are not powers[10] of other things, by being or not being related to them in some way.

[THE RELATION OF DIFFERENT TYPES OF POTENTIALITIES TO THE PRIMARY TYPE]

All potentialities that are spoken of with reference to the same form are principles of some sort and are called potentialities with reference to one   10
primary sort of potentiality. This primary sort is a principle of change either in another subject or in the subject of the potentiality itself insofar as this subject is another thing.[11]

For one sort of potentiality is a potentiality for being affected. This is the principle of change in the very subject that is affected, causing this subject to be affected by the agency of another thing,[12] or <by its own agency> insofar as it is another thing. Another sort of potentiality is a state of being unaffected by deterioration or perishing by the agency of a principle initiating change—either another thing or itself insofar as it is another thing. For the account of the primary sort of potentiality is   15
present in all these formulae.[13]

Again, these potentialities are called potentialities either for merely acting on or being affected, or for acting on or being affected well. Hence the accounts of the potentialities of the first sort are also present in a way in the accounts of those of the second sort.

Evidently, then, in a way the potentiality for acting on and for being   20
acted on is one. For a thing is potentially <something> either by itself having the potentiality for being being acted on or by something else's having the potentiality to be acted on by it. In a way, however, the two potentialities are evidently different. For one sort of potentiality is in the subject acted on; for it is because this thing has some principle in it, and matter is also a sort of principle, that what is acted on is acted on, and one thing is acted on by another (what is oily, for instance, is combustible,   25

---

potentiality that, while spoken of in many ways, have a genuine connection, because of their relation to the primary case of potentiality.

10. **powers**: *Dunamis* is applied in Greek, as 'power' is in English, to numbers.

11. **either in . . . another thing**: If, e.g., you kick my shin, you initiate a change in another thing (in me). If I kick my own shin, I initiate (by kicking) a change in myself insofar as I am another thing (something with a shin vulnerable to being kicked).

12. **by the agency of another thing**: 'Agent' and 'agency' indicate the preposition *hupo*, used for the efficient CAUSE.

13. **is present**: Hence these sorts of potentiality illustrate the point that the others are so called with reference to the primary type.

what is pliable in a certain way is crushable, and so on). The other sort of potentiality is in the producer; heat, for instance, is present in the producer of heat, and the building craft in the builder. Hence insofar as something is naturally unified, it is not acted on at all by itself, since it is one and not something else.

30   Lack of potentiality or what lacks potentiality is the privation that is contrary to this sort of potentiality. Hence every potentiality is for the same thing and in the same respect[14] as the corresponding lack of potentiality. Privation is spoken of in many ways. We ascribe it to what does not have something, and also to what would naturally have something but does not have it—either if it does not have it at all or if it does not have it when it would naturally have it (either because it does not have it in a given way (for instance, completely) or because it

35   does not have it at all). In some cases, if things would naturally have something and are without it as a result of force,* we say that they have been deprived.

[RATIONAL AND NONRATIONAL POTENTIALITIES ARE
DIFFERENTLY RELATED TO CONTRARY ACTUALITIES]

2

Some principles of this sort are present in inanimate things, while others
1046b   are present in animate things, both in the soul and in the rational part of the soul; clearly, then, some potentialities will be nonrational and others will involve reason. Hence all crafts—i.e., the productive sciences—are potentialities; for they originate change in another thing or in the subject itself insofar as it is another thing.[15]

5   Every potentiality that involves reason is a potentiality for either one of a pair of contraries,[16] whereas every nonrational potentiality is a potentiality for just one contrary; the hot, for instance, can produce only heat, whereas medical knowledge[17] can produce either illness or health. This is because knowledge_e is a rational account,[18] and the same rational account reveals both the object <proper to the potentiality> and its privation* (though not in the same way), so that in a way it is the

10   knowledge of both contraries, but in a way it is the knowledge of the

14. **same respect**: Since x qua F has the potentiality for G, the corresponding privation will be x's inability qua F for G.

15. **another thing**: For instance, the doctor, qua doctor, cures herself, qua patient.

16. **Every . . . pair of contraries**: Cf. *Phys.* 251a30.

17. **knowledge**: In this passage both 'knowledge' and 'science' render *epistēmē*.

18. **rational account**: *logos*. See REASON.

proper object[19] rather than of the privation. And so every such science must also be of contraries, but in its own right each science must be the knowledge of the proper object, and not in its own right the knowledge of the privation. For the rational account is of the proper object in its own right, and of the privation coincidentally, in a way; for it reveals the contrary by denial and removal, since the contrary is the primary   15
privation, and the privation is the removal of the proper object.

Since contraries do not occur in the same thing, and since knowledge is a potentiality insofar as it includes reason, and the soul has a principle of motion, it follows that, whereas a producer of health produces only health, a producer of heat produces only heat, and a producer of cold produces only cold, a knower$_e$ produces both contraries. For the rational   20
account is of both (though not in the same way), and it is present in a soul, which has a principle of motion. And so it will initiate both motions from the same principle, by connecting them with one and the same account. Hence a rational potentiality produces contraries,[20] since they are included under one principle, the account.

It is also evident that the potentiality of acting well or being acted on   25
well implies the potentiality of merely acting or being acted on, but the latter potentiality does not always imply the former. For whatever acts well necessarily also acts, but what acts does not necessarily act well.

* * * * * * *

[INNATE VERSUS RATIONAL POTENTIALITIES]

5

All potentialities[21] either are innate (for instance, the senses) or depend   1047b31
on habit (for instance, flute-playing) or on learning (for instance, the crafts). If a potentiality depends on habit and reason, we must actualize it before we can possess it;[22] but this does not hold for potentialities that   35
are not of this sort, or for potentialities for being acted on.

19. **the proper object**: Lit. 'what obtains'. This is the positive property (health, etc.), as opposed to the PRIVATION.

20. **produces contraries**: Delete *tois aneu logou dunatois*. OCT: 'produce things contrary to those thing with nonrational potentialities'.

21. **All potentialities**: The classification here does not indicate a satisfactory place for potentialities acquired by habituation in nonrational subjects.

22. **we must . . . possess it**: Cf. *EN* ii 4.

[*DIFFERENT TYPES OF POTENTIALITIES REQUIRE DIFFERENT CONDITIONS*
FOR THEIR ACTUALIZATION]

1048a   Now, whatever has a potentiality has a potentiality to do something, to
do it at some time, and to do it in some way (and however many other
conditions must be present in the definition). Further, some things have
a potentiality to initiate motion in accordance with reason, and their
potentialities involve reason; other things are nonrational, and their
potentialities lack reason. Hence the former sort of potentialities must
5   be in animate things, whereas the latter sort may be in both animate
and inanimate things.
     In the case of nonrational potentialities, it is necessary that whenever
the agent and the thing acted on meet in the conditions suitable for their
potentialities,[23] the one acts and the other is acted on. But this is not
necessary in the case of rational potentialities. For whereas each nonrational potentiality acts in <only> one way, each rational potentiality acts
in contrary ways; and so <if rational potentialities were necesarily actualized whenever the agent and the thing acted on meet,> each would act
10   in contrary ways at the same time, which is impossible. Something else,
then, namely desire or decision, must control the action; for when the
agent has an overriding[24] desire for one alternative, that is how it will
act, whenever it is in the conditions suitable for its potentiality and meets
the thing that is acted on. Necessarily, then, when anything with a
rational potentiality desires to act in a way for which it has a potentiality,
15   and it is in the conditions suitable for the potentiality, it acts. It has the
potentiality to act[25] when the thing acted on is present and is in a certain
state; and it will not have the potentiality to act without these conditions.
     For it is not necessary to add the condition 'if nothing external prevents
it'; for it has the potentiality insofar as it is a potentiality to act in a
particular way, and it is a potentiality, not to act in this way in all
conditions, but to act in this way in certain conditions, which exclude the
20   presence of external hindrances; for these are excluded by the presence of
some of the conditions mentioned in the definition. Hence even if one
has a wish or an appetite to act in two ways or in contrary ways at the
same time, one will not act in those ways. For that is not the sort of
potentiality one has for them, nor is it a potentiality to act in both ways
at the same time; for it will engage in its characteristic actions only in a
specific way <and hence it will not engage in both at the same time>.

23. **in the . . . potentialities**: Lit. 'in the way in which they are potential'. The
same phrase occurs in 1048a12, 18.

24. **overriding**: Lit. 'CONTROLLING'. This is the desire that controls and determines one's action.

25. **to act**: Read *echontos poiein* OCT deletes 'to act'. See POTENTIALITY #3.

6

Since we have now discussed the sort of potentiality that is spoken of   25
in relation to motion, let us discuss what, and what sort of thing, actuality
is. For our distinctions will also make potentiality clear at the same time;
we will see that what naturally initiates motion or is moved by something
else—either without qualification or in a certain way—is not the only
sort of thing that we take to have a potentiality. We also recognize
another sort of potentiality; and this is why we discussed the previous   30
cases in our investigation of it.[26]

Actuality, then, consists in something's being present <in a subject>,
but not in the same way as when we say something is present potentially.
We say something is present potentially when, for instance, we say
Hermes is in the block of wood, and a half-line in the whole line, because
it might be separated out; and we say that we have knowledge$_e$ even if
we are not attending to[27] what we know, as long as we have the potentiality to attend to it. The other case <attending to what we know, for   35
instance> is actuality.

What we mean to say is clear in particular cases by induction; we
must not seek a formula in every case, but in some cases we must grasp
the point by analogy. In this case, as the builder building is to the builder   1048b
who potentially builds, or how we are when awake compared to how
we are when asleep, or how we are when seeing compared to how we
are when we have our eyes shut but possess sight, or as the product
shaped from matter is to the matter, as the finished work is to the
unworked <material>—let actuality be defined by the first part of this   5
contrast, and the potential by the second.

Things are said to be actually <in some condition>, not all in the same
way, but by analogy—as A is in B or is related to B, so C is in D or is
related to D. For in some cases the actuality is that of motion in relation
to potentiality, and in other cases it is the actuality of substance in relation
to some matter.[28]

The sort of potentiality or actuality that belongs to the infinite, the   10

26. **and this . . . investigation of it**: See 1045b35–1046a2.

27. **attending to**: Or 'contemplating'. See STUDY.

28. **For in some . . . to some matter**: Lit. 'For some are as motion to potentiality,
and others as substance to matter'. Aristotle refers to the two types of potentiality
mentioned at the beginning of the chapter.

void, and all such things is different from the sort that belongs to many other things—to what sees or walks or is seen, for instance. For these latter things can also be truly said to be <actual> without qualification at some time—for instance, one thing is an object of sight because it is being seen, another because it can be seen. But the potentiality that

15 belongs to the infinite <in division> is not the sort that implies that it will be actually separable; it is <separable only> in knowledge. For the fact that further division is possible at every stage ensures that this actuality is potential, not that it is <ever> separate.[29]

[COMPLETE ACTUALITY DISTINGUISHED FROM MOTION]

20 No action that has a limit is an end; rather, all such actions promote an end as, for instance, slimming does. This is the sort of process[30] that <the bodily parts> are in when someone is slimming, since they are not in the condition that the motion aims at. Hence these things do not count as action* or, at least, not as complete* action; for none of them is a complete end,[31] whereas an action must have its end present in it.[32]

For instance, at the same time one is seeing and has seen, or is understanding and has understood, or is thinking and has thought; whereas it is false that at the same time one is learning and has learned,

25 or is being cured and has been cured. Similarly, at the same time one is living well and has lived well, is happy and has been happy. If this were not so, there would be some time at which one would have to stop <living well>, just as there is a time at which one has to stop slimming; in fact, however, there is no such time, but <at the same time> one is living and has lived.

Of these, then, one sort must be called processes, the other activities. Forevery process—for instance, slimming, learning, walking, building—

30 is incomplete; these are processes and are incomplete. For it is not true that at the same time a thing is walking and has walked,[33] or is building and has built, or is coming to be and has come to be, or is being moved and has been moved; rather, these <present-tense and perfect-tense

29. **For the fact . . . is <ever> separate**: See INFINITE #2.

30. **process**: See MOTION #2.

31. **complete end**: *telos*. This recalls 'COMPLETE (*teleia*) actions' just above.

32. **an action . . . in it**: For this strict conception of *praxis* see ACTUALITY, sense (4).

33. **is walking and has walked**: Aristotle must be referring to the distinction between (e.g.) 'is walking from London to Glasgow' and 'has walked from London to Glasgow' (rather than between 'is doing some walking' and 'has done some walking'). Cf. *EN* 1173a31–b4, 1174a14–b19.

statements> are true of different things. By contrast, the same thing at the same time has seen and is seeing, or is thinking and has thought. This latter sort of condition, then, I call an activity, and the former sort   35 I call a process. It should be clear for us, then, from these and similar considerations, what being in actuality is and what sort of thing it is.

[WHEN IS ONE THING POTENTIALLY ANOTHER?]

7

We must distinguish when a thing is potentially <something> and when it is not; for it is not potentially <something> at just any time. For   1049a example, is earth potentially a man or not? If not, is it potentially a man by the time it has become seed? Or perhaps not even then? Similarly, not everything can be healed by medical science or by luck; there is something which has the potentiality for it, and this is what is potentially   5 healthy.

In cases where thought causes an agent's potentiality to be realized, the definition is this: An agent is potentially F if whenever he wants to realize F, he realizes it, provided nothing external prevents it. In the case of the subject that is acted on—healed, for instance—the definition is this: The subject is potentially F whenever nothing in it prevents it <from realizing F>. The same is true of what is potentially a house; if nothing in it—i.e., in the matter—prevents it from becoming a house,   10 and nothing needs to be added or removed or changed, it is potentially a house. The same is true in all other cases where the principle of coming to be is external.

When the principle of coming to be is in the subject itself, the subject is potentially whatever it will be through itself if nothing external prevents it. For example, the seed is not yet <potentially the organism whose seed it is>, since it must be put in something else and changed;   15 but whenever it is in the appropriate condition[34] through a principle in itself, then it is potentially <the organism>. In the first condition, it needs another principle <outside itself>, just as earth is not yet potentially a statue, since it must change to become bronze.

[MATTER AND POTENTIALITY]

Sometimes we call the F not G but of-G.[35] A box, for example, is not wood, but of-wood, nor is wood earth, but of-earth, and again earth, if   20

34. **appropriate condition**: And so it will become the organism if nothing external prevents it.
35. **of-G**: Or 'G-en'. See 1033a17.

the same applies, is not that other thing, but of-that. In all these cases <where F is of-G>, it would seem that G is without qualification poten-tially F; a box, for instance, is neither of-earth nor earth, but of-wood, since it is wood that is potentially a box, and this is the matter of the box—wood in general of box in general, and this wood of this box. And

25   if there is a first thing which is no longer said of another thing or called of-that, this is the first matter; if earth, for instance, is of-air, and air is not fire but of-fire, then fire is the first matter, and the first matter is not a this.

For that of which <something else is said>, i.e., the subject, is of different sorts insofar as it is or is not a this.[36] The subject for attributes

30   is, for instance, a man, both body and soul, and the attributes are, for instance, musical and pale. When music is present in it, the subject is called not music but a musical thing, and the man is not paleness but a pale thing, and not walking or motion but a walking or moving thing— just as we say something is of-F, not that it is F. In these cases, then,

35   the last thing is substance. In other cases, when the thing predicated is a form and a this,[37] the last thing is matter, and material substance. And

1049b   we find that it is correct to apply 'of-F' both to matter and to attributes, since both matter and attributes are indefinite.[38]

We have said, then, when something should be said to be potentially and when it should not.

*   *   *   *   *   *   *

Book XII

[SUBSTANCE AS DIVINE INTELLECT]

[THERE MUST BE AN EVERLASTING, IMMATERIAL SUBSTANCE]

6

1071b3   Since we have found that there are three types of substance, two of them natural and one unmoved, we must discuss the third kind, to show

5   that there must be an everlasting unmoved substance. For substances are the primary[1] beings, and if all substances are perishable, then everything is perishable. But motion cannot come to be or perish (since it has always been), nor can time (since there cannot be a before and an after if there

36. **the subject . . . a this**: See 1038b4–6, 1042a26–29.

37. **the thing predicated . . . a this**: Cf. 1029a23.

38. **both . . . indefinite**. Neither matter nor an attribute satisfies the conditions for being a definite subject, i.e., a THIS.

1. **primary**: This is taken to imply asymmetrical existential dependence. See PRIOR #1.

is no time).[2] Motion is also continuous, then, in the same way that time   *10*
is, since time is either the same as motion or an attribute of it. But the
only continuous motion is local motion—specifically, circular motion.

Now if there is something that is capable of initiating motion or of
acting, but it does not actually do so, there will be no motion; for what
has a potentiality need not actualize it. It will be no use, then, to assume
everlasting substances, as believers in Forms* do, unless these include   *15*
some principle capable of initiating change.[3] And even this, or some
other type of substance apart from the Forms, is not sufficient; for if it
does not actualize its potentiality, there will be no motion. Nor yet is it
sufficient if it actualizes its potentiality, but its essence$_o$ is potentiality;
for there will be no everlasting motion, since what has a potentiality
need not actualize it. There must, then, be a principle of the sort whose   *20*
essence$_o$ is actuality. Further, these substances must be without matter;[4]
for they must be everlasting if anything else is to be everlasting, and
hence they must be actuality.

[PUZZLES ABOUT POTENTIALITY AND ACTUALITY]

Now a puzzle arises. For it seems that whatever actualizes a potentiality
must have it, but not everything that has a potentiality also actualizes
it; and so potentiality is prior. But now, if this is so, nothing that exists will   *25*
exist, since things can have the potentiality to exist without actualizing it.
And yet, if those who have written about the gods are right to generate
everything from night,[5] or if the natural philosophers are right to say
that 'all things were together',[6] the same impossibility results. For how
will things be moved if there is no cause <initiating motion> in actuality?
For surely matter will not initiate motion in itself, but carpentry, <for   *30*
instance, must initiate the motion>; nor will the menstrual fluid or the
earth initiate motion in themselves, but the semen and the seeds <must
initiate the motion>.

Hence some people—Leucippus and Plato, for instance—believe in
everlasting actuality; for they say that there is always motion. But they
do not say why there is this motion, or what kind of motion it is, and

2. **(since there . . . no time)**: If TIME came to be, then—in Aristotle's view—it
must have come to be at some time, and hence there must have been some time
before it existed, which is self-contradictory. See *Phys*. 251a8–252a5.

3. **It will be . . . change**: For this criticism of Plato cf. *GC* 336a7–24, *Met*. 991b3–
9.

4. **without matter**: Matter is what makes things perishable.

5. **from night**: HESIOD.

6. **all things were together**: ANAXAGORAS.

neither do they state the cause of something's being moved in this way
35   or that. For[7] nothing is moved at random,[8] but in every case there must
be some <cause>—as in fact things are moved in one way by nature
and in another by force or by the agency of mind or something else.
Further, what sort of motion is primary? For that makes an enormous
1072a   difference. Nor can Plato say that the principle is of the sort that he
sometimes thinks it is—what initiates its own motion. For he also says
that the soul is later <than motion> and comes into being at the same
time as the universe.[9]

[THE PRIORITY OF ACTUALITY TO POTENTIALITY]

The view that potentiality is prior to actuality is in a way correct and in
5   a way incorrect—we have explained[10] how this is so. The priority of
actuality is attested by Anaxagoras (since mind is actuality), and by
Empedocles (who makes love and strife prior), and by those who say
that there is always motion, as Leucippus does. And so chaos or night
did not exist for an infinite time, but the same things have always existed
(either in a cycle[11] or in some other way), if actuality is prior to potentiality.
10   If, then, the same things always exist in a cycle, something must
always remain actually operating in the same way. And if there is to be
coming to be and perishing, then there must be something else that
always actually operates, in one way at one time and in another way at
another time. This <second mover>, then, must actually operate in one
way because of itself and in another way because of something else,
and hence either because of some third mover or because of the first
mover. Hence it must be because of the first mover; for <otherwise>
15   the first mover will cause the motion of both the second and the third.[12]

7. **For . . .**: This sentence explains why Plato and Leucippus ought to have
considered the questions in the previous sentence.

8. **at random**: Lit. 'as it chanced'. See LUCK #2. Aristotle means that nothing
is moved purely by chance, with no other cause; see *Phys.* 197a12–18.

9. **Nor can Plato . . . universe**: Aristotle is probably thinking of *Timaeus* 34b.
Plato identifies what moves itself with soul, but he describes soul as coming
into existence when some sort of motion already exists.

10. **we have explained**: This probably refers to 1071b22–6, but it might refer to
ix 8.

11. **a cycle**: These are not the numerically same things (see ONE), but the same
sorts of things that keep recurring in regular cycles. See *GC* 338b11–19.

12. **Hence it must . . . and the third**: If we introduce a third mover, we will
have to appeal in any case to the first mover to explain the effects of the third

334

Then surely it is better if the first mover is the cause. For we have seen that it is the cause of what is always the same, and a second mover is the cause of what is different at different times. Clearly both together cause this everlasting succession. Then surely this is also how the motions occur. Why, then, do we need to search for any other principles?

[HOW THE FIRST MOVER INITIATES MOTION]

7

Since it is possible for things to be as we have said they are, and since the only alternative is for everything to come to be from night and from all things being together and from what is not, this may be taken as the solution of the puzzles. There is something, then, that is always being moved in a ceaseless motion, and this motion is circular (this is clear not only from argument but also from what actually happens);[13] and so the first heaven is everlasting. Hence there is also something that initiates motion. And since whatever both is moved and initiates motion is an intermediary, there is something[14] that initiates motion without being moved, something that is everlasting and a substance and actuality.

This is how an object of understanding or desire initiates motion; it initiates motion without being moved. The primary objects of desire and of understanding are the same. For what appears fine is the object of appetite, and what is fine[15] is the primary object of wish; and we desire something because it seems <fine>, rather* than its seeming <fine> because we desire it—for understanding is the principle.[16]

Understanding is moved by its object, and the first column* <of opposites> is what is understood in its own right. In this column substance is primary; and the primary substance is the substance that is simple and actually operating. (Being one and being simple are not the same; for being one signifies a measure, while being simple signifies that something is itself in a particular condition.)[17] Further, what is fine

---

mover on the second; so we might as well cut out the third mover and explain its alleged effects on the second as effects of the first mover on the second.

13. **from what actually happens)**: The contrast with argument (*logos*) is similar to that between the APPEARANCES (= observations) and argument.

14. **intermediary, there is something . . .** : Text uncertain. Read *kinoun meson, esti toinun*.

15. **what appears fine . . . what is fine**: Cf. *DA* 433a26–30, *EN* 1113a15–22.

16. **understanding is the principle**: Cf. *DA* 433a21, *EN* 1139a31–36.

17. **(Being one . . . a particular condition)**: A note explaining what is meant in saying that the primary substance is simple. Being one is just being one of something, and the something in question might be complex (e.g., one book is

35   and what is choiceworthy for itself are in the same column; and what
1072b is primary is in every case either the best or what is analogous to the
       best.

       Division[18] shows that what something is for is among the things that
       are unmoved. For it is either the end for some <beneficiary> or the end
       <aimed at> in some <process>;[19] the first of these is moved, and the
       second is unmoved. The <end> initiates motion by being an object of
       love, and it initiates motion in the other things by <something else's>
       being moved.[20]

5   If, then, something is moved, it can be otherwise. And so, if some-
       thing's actuality is the primary type of local motion,[21] it follows that
       insofar as it is in motion, in this respect it admits of being otherwise, in
       place if not in substance.[22] But since there is something that initiates
       motion without itself being moved, and this is actually operating, it
       cannot be otherwise in any respect at all. For local motion is the primary
       type of motion, and the primary type of local motion is circular motion;
10   and this is the sort of motion that the primary mover initiates. Hence
       the primary mover exists necessarily; and insofar as it exists necessarily,
       its being is fine, and insofar as its being is fine, it is a principle.[23] For
       what is necessary is spoken of in a number of ways—as what is forced
       because it is contrary to the subject's impulse, as that without which the
       good cannot be, and as what cannot be otherwise but is necessary with-
       out qualification.[24]

       [THE LIFE OF THE DIVINE SUBSTANCE]

       This, then, is the sort of principle on which the heaven* and nature
15   depend. Its way of life has the same character as our own way of life at
       its best has for a short time. For the primary mover is always in this

       ---

       not simple, but a complex of many pages). To attribute simplicity is to deny this
       internal complexity.

       18. **Division**: of the logical possibilities.

       19. **For it is either the end . . . <process>**: For this contrast see FOR SOMETHING
       #4.

       20. **and it . . . moved**: What is moved may be the second mover of 1072a9–26.
       But the text and interpretation are doubtful.

       21. **if something's . . . motion**: Read *ei phora prōtē hē energeia estin*.

       22. **if . . . substance**: This sort of change is ruled out for everlasting things,
       since the types of change belonging to the category of substance are coming to
       be and perishing.

       23. **it is a principle**: since it is an object of love.

       24. **necessary without qualification**: This is true of the primary mover.

state <of complete actuality>, whereas we cannot always be in it; for its actuality is also pleasure (that is why being awake, perceiving, and thinking are pleasantest, while expectations and memories are pleasant because of these).[25]

Understanding in its own right is of what is best in its own right, and the highest degree of understanding is of what is best to the highest degree in its own right. And understanding understands itself by sharing   *20* the character of the object of understanding; for it becomes an object of understanding by being in contact with and by understanding its object, so that understanding and its object are the same.[26] For understanding is what is capable of receiving the object of understanding and the essence$_o$, and it is actually understanding when it possesses its object; and so it is this <actual understanding and possession> rather than <the potentiality to receive the object> that seems to be the divine aspect of understanding, and its actual attention to the object of under-standing[27] is pleasantest and best.

If, then, the god[28] is always in the good state that we are in sometimes,   *25* that deserves wonder;[29] if he is in a better state, that deserves still more wonder. And that is indeed the state he is in. Further, life belongs to the god. For the actuality of understanding is life, and the god is that actuality; and his actuality in its own right is the best and everlasting life. We say, then, that the god is the best and everlasting living being,[30] so that continuous and everlasting life and duration belong to the god;   *30* for that is what the god is.

[DEFENCE AND SUMMARY]

Some, however, suppose, as the Pythagoreans and Speusippus do, that what is finest and best is not present in the principle, claiming that the principles[31] of plants and animals are their causes, whereas what is fine

---

25. **for its actuality . . . because of these)**: Pleasure is the result of the full actualization of one's capacities; see *EN* 1174b14–26. That is why the prime mover, having its capacities fully actualized all the time, has pleasure all the time. We cannot actualize our capacities continuously, and get tired, so that our pleasure is not continuous, *EN* 1175a3–10.

26. **so that . . . the same**: Cf. *DA* 430a3.

27. **actual . . . of understanding**: Lit. just 'studying' or 'contemplating', *theōria*.

28. **the god**: See GOD #2.

29. **wonder**: See ADMIRE.

30. **living being**: *zōon*, usually rendered 'animal'.

31. **principles**: They mean 'beginnings' (see PRINCIPLE #1), i.e., (as Aristotle's criticism shows) the seeds.

35
1073a
and complete is found in what results from these. Their view is mistaken. For the seed comes from other <principles> that are prior and complete*; and what is primary is not the seed, but the complete <organism>; for instance,[32] one would say that the man is prior to the seed (not the man who comes into being from the seed, but another one, from whom the seed comes).

5

10
It is evident from what has been said, then, that there is an everlasting, unmoved substance that is separated from perceptible things. It has also been proved that this substance cannot have any magnitude, but must be without parts and indivisible; for it initiates motion for an infinite time, but nothing finite has infinite potentiality. And since every magnitude is either infinite or finite, <the primary mover> cannot have a finite magnitude, and it cannot have an infinite magnitude, because there is no infinite magnitude at all. Besides, it has also been proved that this substance is not affected or altered, since all other motions depend on local motion.[33] It is clear, then, why these things are so.

[THERE MUST BE A PLURALITY OF UNMOVED MOVERS]

8

15

20
We must also consider, however, whether we should take there to be one such substance, or more than one, and, if more than one, how many; and we must remember that, on the question about how many there are, other people's views have contributed nothing that can be perspicuously stated. The views about the Ideas, for instance, include no special discussion of the question. For those who speak of Ideas say that the Ideas are numbers, but when they speak of numbers, they sometimes speak as though numbers were infinite, sometimes as though they were finite and went only as far as the number ten;[34] and they make no serious effort to demonstrate the reason why there should be just this many numbers. Let us, however, take what has been laid down and determined as a basis for discussion.

25
The principle and primary being is unmoved both in its own right and coincidentally, and it initiates the everlasting and single primary motion. Now, what is moved must be moved by something, but the primary mover is unmoved in its own right. Further, an everlasting motion is initiated by an everlasting mover, and a single motion is initiated by a single mover; but we see that, apart from the simple local

32. **for instance . . .:** Read *hoion proteron*.

33. **on local motion:** And since the primary mover is not subject to local motion, it cannot have any of these other motions either.

34. **as far as the number ten:** For Platonist views on numbers cf. 1084a12–b2, *Phys*. 206b27–33.

338

motion of the whole, which we say is initiated by the primary and   *30*
unmoved substance, there are also the everlasting local motions of the
planets[35] (for a body that moves in a circle has an everlasting and unceas-
ing motion, as was shown in our work on nature).[36] Hence it necessarily
follows that each of these motions is also initiated by the agency of some
substance that is unmoved in its own right and everlasting. For the nature
of the stars is everlasting and is a type of substance; and what initiates   *35*
motion is everlasting and prior to what is moved; and what is prior to a
substance must be a substance. It is evident, then, that there must be this
number of substances that are everlasting in their nature and unmoved in
their own right, and (for the reason given above) without magnitude.   *1073b*

[THEORIES ABOUT THE NUMBER OF HEAVENLY MOTIONS]

It is evident, then, that there are substances, and that one of them is
first and another second, in an order corresponding to the motions of
the stars. But when we come to the number of these motions, we must
examine it on the basis of the mathematical science that is closest[37] to   *5*
philosophy, i.e., astronomy. For astronomy studies a kind of substance
that is perceptible, but still everlasting, whereas the other mathematical
sciences—those concerned with numbers and with geometry, for instance—do not study any substance at all.[38]

Now it is evident, even on moderate acquaintance, that there are
more motions than there are bodies moved, since each of the planets   *10*
has more than one motion. On the question of how many motions there
are, we now state what some of the mathematicians say, in order to
form some conception <of an answer>, so that we can suppose some
definite number in our thinking. Beyond this <provisional answer> we
must on some points inquire ourselves and on other points find out
from other people's inquiries. If something different from what is now   *15*
said appears[39] correct to later students, we must be friends to both sides,[40]
but must follow the more exact investigators.

35. **planets**: Lit. 'wanderers', the moving as opposed to the fixed stars.

36. **on nature)**: See *Phys.* viii 8–9, *DC* i 2, ii 3–8.

37. **closest**: Or 'most PROPER', 'most akin'. Aristotle seems to refer here to closeness in its subject matter, rather than in its methods.

38. **do not . . . at all**: On the status of mathematical objects see ABSTRACTION
#2.

39. **appears**: *phainesthai*. Here APPEARANCES are tentative theories.

40. **both sides**: i.e., both current students and their successors. For this attitude
to inquirers and to the truth cf. *EN* 1096a14–17. Aristotle emphasizes the contrast
between his confidence about the existence of a divine substance and the uncer-
tainty of astronomers' speculations. On later investigators cf. *GA* 760b27–33.

Eudoxus thought that the motion of the sun and the moon in each case involves three spheres. The first is the sphere of the fixed stars; the second moves in the circle along the middle of the zodiac; the third moves in the circle inclined across the breadth of the zodiac; and the moon's circle is inclined at a greater angle than the sun's circle. The motion of each planet involves four spheres. The first and second of these are the same as for the sun and the moon; for the sphere of the fixed stars is the one that moves all the spheres, and the sphere placed under this, moving in the circle along the middle of the zodiac, is also common to all the spheres. But the third sphere of each of the planets has its poles in the circle along the middle of the zodiac; and the fourth moves along the circle inclined at an angle to the equator of the third sphere. And the poles of the third sphere are different for each of the planets, except that for Venus[41] and Mercury they are the same.

Callippus agreed with Eudoxus about the position of the spheres. On their number, he agreed with Eudoxus about Jupiter and Saturn, but, in the case of the sun and the moon, he thought two further spheres must be added in order to yield the appearances,[42] and that one must be added for each of the other planets.

In fact, however, it is necessary, if all the combined spheres together are to yield the appearances, to admit further spheres (one fewer <than those mentioned>) that counteract <the previous spheres>, and in each case restore to the same position the first sphere of the star that is placed beneath the given star. For only in that way is it possible for all the combined spheres to produce the motions of the planets.

And so the spheres in which the planets themselves move are eight and twenty-five;[43] and only the spheres in which the lowest-placed planet moves need no counteracting spheres. Hence the spheres counteracting the spheres of the first two planets will be six, and those counteracting the spheres of the next four will be sixteen. Hence the total number of the <forward->moving and counteracting spheres will be fifty-five. If we do not add to the moon and sun the motions we mentioned, then the total number of the spheres will be forty-seven.[44]

41. **Venus**: Aristotle uses the names of the corresponding Greek gods (Aphrodite, Hermes, Zeus, Cronus) where we have used the Latin equivalents. On the use of names of gods for planets see [Plato], *Epinomis* 987b, Plato, *Timaeus* 38d.

42. **yield the appearances**: See APPEARANCES #3.

43. **are eight**: i.e., four each for Jupiter and Saturn, as in 1073b34. The twenty-five are made up of five for each of the other bodies).

44. **If we do not . . . forty-seven**: Text and interpretation doubtful.

[THE NUMBER OF UNMOVED MOVERS]

Let this, then, be the number of the spheres. In that case the supposition   *15*
that this is also the number of unmoved substances and principles is
reasonable—we can leave talk of necessity to stronger people.[45]

And if every local motion <in the heaven> must contribute to the
motion of a star, and if every nature and every substance that is unaffected and that in its own right has achieved the best must be regarded   *20*
as an end, it follows that there can be no other natures apart from these,
and that this must be the number of substances. For if there were other
substances, they would have to initiate motions by being the end of
local motion; but there cannot be any other local motion apart from those
mentioned above. It is reasonable to infer this from the bodies that are   *25*
moved. For if everything that initiates local motion is for the sake of
what is moved, and if every motion is the motion of something that is
moved, then no motion is for its own sake or for the sake of some other
motion, but every motion is for the sake of the stars. For if every motion
were for the sake of some further motion, then that further motion would
have to be for the sake of something else; and so, since it cannot go on
to infinity, one of the divine bodies that is moved in the heaven must   *30*
be the end of every motion.

[THERE IS ONLY ONE UNIVERSE]

It is evident that there is only one heaven.* For if there were a number
of heavens, as there are a number of men, then the principle—one for
each heaven—would be specifically one but numerically many.[46] Now,
things that are numerically many all have matter; for many <particulars>
have one and the same account—that of man, for instance—but Socrates   *35*
is one <particular>. But the primary essence has no matter, since it is
actuality. Hence the primary and unmoved mover is one in number and
account; so also, then, is what is always and continuously moved; and
so there is only one heaven.

[THE TRUTH IN THE TRADITIONS ABOUT THE GODS]

There is a tradition handed down from the distant past to later genera-   *1074b*
tions, that these stars are gods and that the whole of nature is divine.

45. **stronger people**: This is perhaps intentionally ambiguous and ironical. It
might mean 'people who can find stronger arguments' or 'people who are rash
enough to make stronger assertions'. With Aristotle's caution here contrast the
claim about necessity just below.

46. **specifically one but numerically many**: See ONE #2.

5   The rest of the tradition is a mythical accretion, added to persuade the
       many and to use in upholding what is lawful and advantageous;[47] for
       those who handed it down say that the gods have human form or are
       similar to other animals, and they add other features following from
       these and similar to them. But if we separate the first point—that they
       thought the primary substances were gods—from these accretions, and
10   consider it alone, we will regard it as a divine insight,[48] on the assumption
       that every craft and philosophical discipline has probably often been
       discovered, as far as people could manage it, and has often been forgot-
       ten, and that this belief has survived like remains from earlier generations
       until the present.[49] And so <the truth of> the ancestral beliefs coming
       from the earliest times is evident[50] to us only to this extent.

       [PUZZLES ABOUT THE DIVINE UNDERSTANDING]

       9

15   The nature of <divine> understanding* raises a number of puzzles. For
       understanding seems to be the most divine of the things we observe,[51]
       but many difficulties arise about what state it must be in if it is to be so
       divine. For if it understands nothing, what is so impressive about it? It
       would be like someone asleep. If, on the other hand, it does understand,
20   but something else controls whether it understands (since its essence$_o$
       is not actual understanding, but the potentiality for it), it is not the best
       substance; for what makes it valuable comes from <actual> under-
       standing.[52]
          And in any case, whether its essence$_o$ is potential or actual understand-
       ing, what does it understand? It must understand either itself or some-
       thing else; if something else, then either always the same thing or else
       different things at different times. Then does it make any difference
       whether the object of its understanding is fine or is just any old thing?
25   Surely there are some things that it would be absurd for it to think about.

47. **lawful and advantageous**: Presumably Aristotle refers to the belief that the
gods are sufficiently concerned with human affairs to punish particular acts of
injustice.

48. **as a divine insight**: Lit. 'as being said divinely'.

49. **remains . . . present**: Cf. DC 270b5–20, Meteor. 339b27–30, Pol. 1329b25–33.

50. **is evident**: Aristotle stops short of saying—though he suggests—that the
rest of the traditional beliefs are false.

51. **things we observe**: Lit. 'things that appear', phainomena. See APPEARANCES.

52. **for what makes . . . understanding**: And so what controls actual understanding would be more valuable.

Clearly, then, it understands what is most divine and most valuable, and it does not change; for the change[53] would be to something worse, and it would thereby also be a motion.[54]

[ANSWERS TO PUZZLES]

First, then, if it is potential, not actual, understanding, it is reasonable to expect that the continuous <exercise of> understanding would be tiring for it. Moreover, clearly something other than understanding— namely the object of understanding—would be more valuable. For indeed both the potentiality and the activity of understanding[55] will belong even to someone who understands the worst thing; and if this is to be avoided (since there are also some things it is better not to see than to see), then the activity of understanding is not the best thing.

    <The divine understanding,> then, must understand itself, so that its understanding is an understanding of understanding. In every case, however, knowledge$_e$, perception, belief, and thought have something other than themselves as their object; each has itself as its object as a by-product. Further, if to understand and to be understood are different, which is responsible for the presence of the good? For to be an act of understanding is not the same as to be understood.

    Well, perhaps in some cases the knowledge is the object. In the productive <sciences, the knowledge is> the substance and essence <of the product> without the matter,[56] and in the theoretical sciences, the account is both the object and the understanding. In these cases, then, where the object of understanding does not differ from understanding— i.e., in cases where the object has no matter—the object and the understanding will be the same, and the activity of understanding will be one with its object.

    One puzzle still remains: Is the object of understanding composite? If it were composite, understanding would change in <understanding different> parts of the whole. Perhaps we should say that whatever has no matter is indivisible. <On this view, the condition of actual understanding is> the condition that human understanding (or rather, the understanding of any composite beings) reaches over a certain length of time; for it does not possess the good at this or that time, but achieves the best, which is something other than it, in some whole <period of

30

35

1075a

5

53. **change**: i.e., change from the most divine and valuable.

54. **a motion**: This is inconsistent with the substance's being unmoved.

55. **both the . . . of understanding**: Or 'both thinking (*noein*) and the act of thinking (*noēsis*)'.

56. **In the . . . matter**: Cf. 1032a32–b14.

10   time>. And this is the condition the understanding that understands
itself is in throughout all time.

[*DIVINE INTELLECT IN THE UNIVERSE*]

10

We should also consider the way in which the nature of the whole
<universe> possesses the good—i.e., the best good. Is this good some-
thing separated, itself in its own right, or is it the order <of the whole>?
Perhaps it is present in both ways, as in an army. For there the good is
in the order <of the whole army>, and it is also, and to a greater extent,

15   the general; for he does not exist because the order exists, but the order
exists because he does. All things—fishes, birds, and plants—are joined
in some order, but not all in the same way. Nor are they unrelated to
each other, but they have some relation; for all things are joined in some
order in relation to one thing. (It is like a household, where the free*

20   members are least of all at liberty to do what they like,[57] and all or most
of what they do is ordered, whereas only a little of what slaves and
beasts do promotes the common <good>, and mostly they do what
they like.) For the nature of each sort of thing is such a principle <that
aims at the good of the whole>. I mean, for instance, that everything
necessarily is eventually dissolved, and in this way there are other things
in which everything shares for <the good of> the whole. . . .[58]

*   *   *   *   *   *   *

Book XIII

[*KNOWLEDGE, UNIVERSALS, AND SUBSTANCE*]

[*ARE THE PRINCIPLES OF THINGS UNIVERSALS OR PARTICULARS?
BOTH VIEWS RAISE PUZZLES* [1]]

10

1086b14   There is a question that raises a puzzle both for those who say there are
15   Ideas and for those who do not. We have mentioned it before, at the
beginning, in the discussion of puzzles; let us discuss it now.

57. **what they like**: Or 'any old thing'. See LUCK #2.

58. **the whole**: The nature of plants and animals causes them to reproduce for
the good of the whole, though it does not determine each particular movement
of each particular plant or animal for the good of the whole.

1. Aristotle raises this puzzle in 994b24–1000a4. Bk vii might be taken to argue
(see FORM #9) both that (i) a primary substance is a particular form and that (ii)
knowledge is of universal substances. The combination of (i) and (ii) raises

If we do not take substances to be separated in the way in which particular beings are said to be separated, then we do away with substance as we intend to speak of it. But if we take substances to be separable,* how will we regard their elements and principles? For if the   *20* elements and principles are particulars and not universals, there will be as many elements as there are beings,[2] and the elements will not be knowable$_e$.[3]

For let the syllables in speech be substances, and their letters[4] the elements of substances. Then there must be only one BA, and only one   *25* of each of the other syllables—if they are not universals[5] (i.e., specifically the same),[6] but each is numerically one and a this; nor would any have the same name[7] <as any other>. (Further, <the believers in Ideas> believe that each what-it-is-itself[8] is one.) But if each syllable is one, then so is each of the letters it is composed of. If so, there will be only one A, and only one of any given letter, by the same argument that shows   *30* that there must be only one of any given syllable. But if this is so, there will be no other beings apart* from the elements, but only elements.

Further, the elements will not be knowable; for they are not universals, and knowledge is of universals, as is clear from demonstrations and definitions. For there cannot be a deduction*[9] that this triangle has angles   *35* equal to two right angles, unless every triangle has its angles equal to two right angles; and there cannot be a deduction that this man is an animal, unless every man is an animal.

If, on the other hand,[10] the principles are universals, then either the

---

difficulties if he also believes that (iii) primary substances are basic objects of knowledge. This chapter might be taken to explain how (iii) is consistent with (i) and (ii).

2. **there will . . . there are beings**: The paragraph beginning 'For let the syllables . . .' argues for this conclusion.

3. **the elements . . . knowable$_e$**: The paragraph beginning 'Further, the elements . . .' argues for this conclusion.

4. **letters**: Or ELEMENTS.

5. **if they are not universals**: This follows if we assume that they are 'separated in the way in which particular beings are said to be separated', as suggested above.

6. **specifically the same**: i.e., the same universal in all the particulars it belongs to. See ONE.

7. **have the same name**: *homōnumon*. See HOMONYMY.

8. **what-it-is-itself**: A phrase sometimes used (as, e.g., 'what good is itself' or 'the good itself') in Plato for the FORMS.

9. **cannot be a deduction**: See *APo* 71a29.

10. **If, on the other hand . . .**: This paragraph rests on the assumption that we

substances composed of them are also universals or else[11] nonsubstances will be prior to substances. For no universal is a substance, but an element and principle is universal, and an element and principle is prior to those things of which it is the element and principle.

5 All these things follow reasonably, when they make Ideas out of elements and also claim that there is a single separated thing apart from substances that have the same form.[12]

[SOLUTION OF THE PUZZLES]

If, however, just as with the elements of speech, it is quite possible for there to be many As and Bs, even though there is no A-itself and B-
10 itself apart* from the many, so also (as far as this goes) there will be infinitely many similar syllables. The claim that all knowledge is universal, so that the principles of beings are also necessarily universals and not separated substances, certainly raises a greater puzzle than any other claim we have mentioned; and yet the claim is true in one way, though not in another.

15 For knowledge, like knowing, is of two kinds, potential and actual. Since the potentiality, as being matter, is universal and indefinite, it is of the universal and indefinite. But since the actuality is definite, it is of what is definite, and, since it is a this, it is of a this.[13] It is <only>
20 coincidentally that sight sees universal color; it does so because this <particular instance of> color which it sees is <an instance of> color. And similarly, this <instance of> A that the grammarian studies is <an> A.

For if the principles must be universals, what comes from them must also be universal, as in demonstrations. But if this is so, nothing will be separable or a substance. It is clear, however, that in a way knowledge
25 is universal, and in a way it is not.

---

reject the supposition of the second paragraph of the chapter, that the elements must be particulars.

11. **or else**: Retain *ē kai . . . katholou*, 1086b37 (deleted in OCT), and read <*ē*> *estai*, 1087a1.

12. **form**: Or 'species', *eidos*.

13. **a this**: i.e., a particular.

NICOMACHEAN ETHICS

Book I

[HAPPINESS]

[THE HIGHEST GOOD]

1

Every craft and every investigation, and likewise every action and deci-   1094a
sion, seems to aim[1] at some good; hence the good has been well described
as that at which everything aims.

However, there is an apparent difference among the ends aimed at.
For the end is sometimes an activity, sometimes a product beyond the   5
activity; and when there is an end beyond the action, the product is by
nature better than the activity.

Since there are many actions, crafts and sciences, the ends turn out to
be many as well; for health is the end of medicine, a boat of boatbuilding,
victory of generalship, and wealth of household management.   10

But whenever any of these sciences[2] are subordinate to some one
capacity—as, for instance, bridlemaking and every other science producing equipment for horses are subordinate to horsemanship, while this
and every action in warfare are in turn subordinate to generalship, and
in the same way other sciences are subordinate to further ones—in each
of these the end of the ruling science is more choiceworthy than all the   15
ends subordinate to it, since it is the end for which those ends are also
pursued. And here it does not matter whether the ends of the actions
are the activities themselves, or some product beyond them, as in the
sciences we have mentioned.

1. **seems to aim**: Aristotle begins with an APPEARANCE.

2. **But . . . sciences**: In this paragraph 'sciences' is supplied (except in 'sciences
we have mentioned', a18). These 'actions, crafts and sciences' (a7) do not meet
Aristotle's most stringent conditions for a SCIENCE.

2

Suppose, then, that (a) there is some end of the things we pursue in our actions which we wish for because of itself, and because of which we wish for the other things; and (b) we do not choose everything because of something else, since (c) if we do, it will go on without limit, making desire empty and futile; then clearly (d) this end will be the good, i.e., the best good.

20

Then surely knowledge$_g$ of this good is also of great importance for the conduct of our lives, and if, like archers, we have a target to aim at, we are more likely to hit the right mark. If so, we should try to grasp, in outline at any rate, what the good is, and which science or capacity is concerned with it.

25

It seems to concern the most controlling science, the one that, more than any other, is the ruling science. And political science apparently has this character.

1094b

(1) For it is the one that prescribes which of the sciences ought to be studied in cities, and which ones each class in the city should learn, and how far.

(2) Again, we see that even the most honored capacities—generalship, household management and rhetoric, for instance—are subordinate to it.

5

(3) Further, it uses the other sciences concerned with action,[3] and moreover legislates what must be done and what avoided.

Hence its end will include the ends of the other sciences, and so will be the human good.

<This is properly called political science;> for though admittedly the good is the same for a city as for an individual, still the good of the city is apparently a greater and more complete good to acquire and preserve. For while it is satisfactory to acquire and preserve the good even for an individual, it is finer and more divine to acquire and preserve it for a people and for cities. And so, since our investigation aims at these <goods, for an individual and for a city>, it is a sort of political science.

10

3. **concerned with action**: *praktikais*. OCT deletes.

3

Our discussion will be adequate if its degree of clarity fits the subject matter;[4] for we would not seek the same degree of exactness in all sorts of arguments alike, any more than in the products of different crafts.

Moreover, what is fine and what is just, the topics of inquiry in   *15*
political science, differ and vary so much that they seem to rest on convention only, not on nature. Goods, however, also vary in the same sort of way, since they cause harm to many people; for it has happened that some people have been destroyed because of their wealth, others because of their bravery.

Since these, then, are the sorts of things we argue from and about,   *20*
it will be satisfactory if we can indicate the truth roughly and in outline; since <that is to say> we argue from and about what holds good usually <but not universally>, it will be satisfactory if we can draw conclusions of the same sort.

Each of our claims, then, ought to be accepted in the same way <as claiming to hold good usually>, since the educated person seeks exactness in each area to the extent that the nature of the subject allows;   *25*
for apparently it is just as mistaken to demand demonstrations from a rhetorician as to accept <merely> persuasive arguments from a mathematician.

Further, each person judges well what he knows$_g$, and is a good judge   *1095a*
about that; hence the good judge in a particular area is the person educated in that area, and the unqualifiedly good judge is the person educated in every area.

This is why a youth is not a suitable student of political science; for he lacks experience of the actions in life which political science argues from and about.

Moreover, since he tends to be guided by his feelings, his study will   *5*
be futile and useless; for its end is action, not knowledge$_g$. And here it does not matter whether he is young in years or immature in character, since the deficiency does not depend on age, but results from being guided in his life and in each of his pursuits by his feelings; for an immature person, like an incontinent person, gets no benefit from his knowledge$_g$.

If, however, we are guided by reason in forming our desires and in   *10*
acting, then this knowledge$_o$ will be of great benefit.

These are the preliminary points about the student, about the way our claims are to be accepted, and about what we intend to do.

---

4. **fits the subject matter**: See 1098a28, 1137b19.

4

Let us, then, begin again. Since every sort of knowledge$_g$ and decision
15   pursues some good, what is that good which we say is the aim of political
science? What <in other words> is the highest of all the goods pursued
in action?

As far as its name goes, most people virtually agree <about what the
good is>, since both the many and the cultivated call it happiness, and
20   suppose that living well and doing well are the same as being happy.
But they disagree about what happiness is, and the many do not give
the same answer as the wise.

For the many think it is something obvious and evident—for instance,
pleasure, wealth or honor—some thinking one thing, others another;
and indeed the same person keeps changing his mind, since in sickness
he thinks it is health, in poverty wealth. And when they are conscious
25   of their own ignorance, they admire anyone who speaks of something
grand and beyond them.

<Among the wise,> however, some used to think that apart* from
these many goods there is some other good that is something in itself,
and also causes all these goods to be goods.

Presumably, then, it is rather futile to examine all these beliefs, and
30   it is enough to examine those that are most current or seem to have
some argument for them.

We must notice, however, the difference between arguments from
principles* and arguments toward principles. For indeed Plato was
right to be puzzled about this, when he used to ask if <the argument>
1095b   set out from the principles or led toward them—just as on a race
course the path may go from the starting-line to the far end,[5] or back
again.

For while we should certainly begin from starting points that are
known$_g$, things are known in two ways; for some are known to us,
some known without qualification <but not necessarily known to us>.
Presumably, then, the starting point we should begin from is what is
known to us.

5   This is why we need to have been brought up in fine habits if we
are to be adequate students of what is fine and just, and of political
questions generally. For the starting point is the belief that something
is true, and if this is apparent enough to us, we will not <,at this
stage,> need the reason why it is true in addition; and if we have
this good upbringing, we have the starting points, or can easily

5. **far end**: Lit. 'limit'. See *Phys.* 239b35n.

acquire them.[6] Someone who neither has them nor can acquire them
should listen to Hesiod: 'He who understands everything himself is best   10
of all; he is noble also who listens to one who has spoken well; but he
who neither understands it himself nor takes to heart what he hears
from another is a useless man.'

5

But let us begin again from <the common beliefs> from which we   15
digressed. For, it would seem, people quite reasonably reach their conception of the good, i.e., of happiness, from the lives <they lead>; for   17, 18
there are roughly three most favored lives—the lives of gratification, of   19
political activity, and, third, of study.   16

The many, the most vulgar, would seem to conceive the good and   17
happiness as pleasure, and hence they also like the life of gratification.   19
Here they appear completely slavish, since the life they decide on is a   20
life for grazing animals; and yet they have some argument in their de-
fense, since many in positions of power feel the same way as Sardanapallus[7] <and also choose this life>.

The cultivated people, those active <in politics>, conceive the good
as honor, since this is more or less the end <normally pursued> in the
political life. This, however, appears to be too superficial to be what we
are seeking, since it seems to depend more on those who honor than   25
on the one honored, whereas we intuitively believe that the good is
something of our own[8] and hard to take from us.

Further, it would seem, they pursue honor to convince themselves
that they are good; at any rate, they seek to be honored by intelligent
people, among people who know$_g$ them, and for virtue. It is clear, then,
that in the view of active people at least, virtue is superior <to honor>.   30

Perhaps, indeed, one might conceive virtue more than honor to be
the end of the political life. However, this also is apparently too incomplete <to be the good>. For, it seems, someone might possess virtue
but be asleep or inactive throughout his life; or, further, he might suffer   1096a
the worst evils and misfortunes; and if this is the sort of life he leads, no
one would count him happy, except to defend a philosopher's paradox.
Enough about this, since it has been adequately discussed in the popular
works also.

6. **For the. . . acquire them**: Lit. 'For the *archē* is the that, and if this appears
adequately, he will not at all need in addition the because. Such a one has *archai*
or would get them easily.' Both 'PRINCIPLE' and 'starting point' translate *archē*.

7. **Sardanapallus**: An Assyrian king who lived in legendary luxury.

8. **our own** *oikeion*. See PROPER.

5   The third life is the life of study, which we will examine in what follows.

The money-maker's life is in a way forced on him <not chosen for itself>; and clearly wealth is not the good we are seeking, since it is <merely> useful, <choiceworthy only> for some other end. Hence one would be more inclined to suppose that <any of> the goods mentioned earlier is the end, since they are liked for themselves. But apparently
10   they are not <the end> either; and many arguments have been presented against them. Let us, then, dismiss them.

[THE PLATONIC FORM OF THE GOOD]

6

Presumably, though, we had better examine the universal good, and puzzle out what is meant in speaking of it. This sort of inquiry is, to be sure, unwelcome to us, when those who introduced the Forms were
15   friends of ours; still, it presumably seems better, indeed only right, to destroy even what is close to us if that is the way to preserve truth. And we must especially do this when we are philosophers, <lovers of wisdom>; for though we love both the truth and our friends, piety requires us to honor the truth first.

Those who introduced this view did not mean to produce an Idea for any <series> in which they spoke of prior and posterior <members>; that was why they did not mean to establish an Idea <of number> for
20   <the series of> numbers. But the good is spoken of both in what-it-is and in quality and relative;[9] and what is in itself, i.e., substance, is by nature prior to what is relative, since a relative would seem to be an appendage and coincident of being. And so there is no common Idea over these.

25   Further, good is spoken of in as many ways as being is spoken of. For it is spoken of in what-it-is, as god and mind;[10] in quality, as the virtues; in quantity, as the measured amount; in relative, as the useful; in time, as the opportune moment; in place, as the <right> situation; and so on. Hence it is clear that the good cannot be some common <nature of good things> that is universal and single; for if it were, it would be spoken of in only one of the predications,* not in them all.
30   Further, if a number of things have a single Idea, there is also a single

9. **But the good . . . and relative**: The categories (see PREDICATIONS) are introduced here and in the next two paragraphs. See BE #2.

10. **as god . . .**: Probably Aristotle means not just that these are examples of goods that are SUBSTANCES, but that they are what it is to be good in the category of substance.

science of them; hence <if there were an Idea of Good> there would also be some single science of all goods. But in fact there are many sciences even of the goods under one predication; for the science of the opportune moment, for instance, in war is generalship, in disease medicine. And similarly the science of the measured amount in food is medicine, in exertion gymnastics. <Hence there is no single science of the good, and so no Idea.>

One might be puzzled about what <the believers in Ideas> really   *35* mean in speaking of the So-and-So Itself, since Man Itself and man have   *1096b* one and the same account of man; for insofar as each is man, they will not differ at all. If that is so, then <Good Itself and good have the same account of good>; hence they also will not differ at all insofar as each is good, <hence there is no point in appealing to Good itself>.

Moreover, Good Itself will be no more of a good by being eternal; for a white thing is no whiter if it lasts a long time than if it lasts a day.   *5*

The Pythagoreans seemingly have a more plausible view about the good, since they place the One in the column of goods. Indeed, Speusippus seems to have followed them. But let us leave this for another discussion.

A dispute emerges about what we have said: 'The arguments <in   *10* favor of the Idea> are not concerned with every sort of good. Goods pursued and liked in themselves are spoken of as one species of goods, while those that in some way tend to produce or preserve these goods, or to prevent their contraries, are spoken of as goods because of these and in a different way; clearly, then, goods are spoken of in two ways, and some are goods in themselves, others goods because of these. <And it is claimed only that there is a single Form for all goods in themselves.>'

Let us, then, separate the goods in themselves from the <merely>   *15* useful goods, and consider whether goods in themselves are spoken of in correspondence to a single Idea.

Well, what sorts of goods may be regarded as goods in themselves? (a) Perhaps they are those that are pursued even on their own—for instance, intelligence, seeing, some types of pleasures, and honors; for even if we also pursue these because of something else, they may still be regarded as goods in themselves. (b) Or perhaps nothing except the   *20* Idea is good in itself.

<If (b) is true>, then the Form will be futile, <since it will not explain the goodness of anything. But if (a) is true>, then, since these other things are also goods in themselves, the same account of good will have to turn up in all of them, just as the same account of whiteness turns up in snow and in chalk. In fact, however, honor, intelligence and pleasure have different and dissimilar accounts, precisely insofar as they   *25* are goods. Hence the good is not something common which corresponds to a single Idea.

But how after all, then, is good spoken of? For <these goods have different accounts, i.e., are homonymous, and yet> are seemingly not homonymous by mere chance. Perhaps they are homonymous by all being derived from a single source, or by all referring to a single focus.[11] Or perhaps instead they are homonymous by analogy;* for example, as sight is to body, so understanding is to soul, and so on for other cases.

30   Presumably, though, we should leave these questions for now, since their exact treatment is more appropriate for another <branch of> philosophy. And the same is true about the Idea. For even if the good predicated in common is some single thing, or something separated, itself in itself, clearly it is not the sort of good a human being can pursue in
35   action or possess; but that is just the sort we are looking for in our present inquiry.

1097a   'But,' it might seem to some, 'it is better to get to know$_g$ the Idea with a view to the goods that we can possess and pursue in action; for if we have this as a sort of pattern,* we shall also know$_o$ better about the goods that are goods for us, and if we know about them, we shall hit on them.'

5   This argument does indeed have some plausibility, but it would seem to clash with the sciences. For each of these, though it aims at some good and seeks to supply what is lacking, proceeds without concern for knowledge$_g$ of the Idea; and if the Idea were such an important aid, surely it would not be reasonable for all craftsmen to be ignorant and not even to look for it.

    Moreover, it is a puzzle to know what the weaver or carpenter will
10   gain for his own craft from knowing$_o$ this Good Itself, or how anyone will be better at medicine or generalship from having gazed on the Idea Itself. For what the doctor appears to consider is not even health <universally, let alone good universally>, but human beings' health, since it is particular patients he treats.

    So much, then, for these questions.

[AN ACCOUNT OF HAPPINESS]

7

15   But let us return once again to the good we are looking for, and consider just what it could be, since it is apparently one thing in one action or craft, and another thing in another; for it is one thing in medicine, another in generalship, and so on for the rest.

    What, then, is the good in each of these cases? Surely it is that for
20   the sake of which the other things are done; and in medicine this is

11. **all referring . . . .**: See HOMONYMY #3.

health, in generalship victory, in housebuilding a house, in another case something else, but in every action and decision it is the end, since it is for the sake of the end that everyone does the other things.

And so, if there is some end of everything that is pursued in action, this will be the good pursued in action; and if there are more ends than one, these will be the goods pursued in action.

Our argument has progressed, then, to the same conclusion <as before, that the highest end is the good>; but we must try to clarify this still more.   25

Though apparently there are many ends, we choose some of them—for instance, wealth, flutes and, in general, instruments—because of something else; hence it is clear that not all ends are complete.* But the best good is apparently something complete. Hence, if only one end is complete, this will be what we are looking for; and if more than one are complete, the most complete of these will be what we are looking for.   30

An end pursued in itself, we say, is more complete than an end pursued because of something else; and an end that is never choicewor-thy because of something else is more complete than ends that are choiceworthy both in themselves and because of this end; and hence an end that is always <choiceworthy, and also> choiceworthy in itself, never because of something else, is complete without qualification.

Now happiness more than anything else seems complete without   1097b qualification, since we always <choose it, and also> choose it because of itself, never because of something else.

Honor, pleasure, understanding and every virtue we certainly choose because of themselves, since we would choose each of them even if it had no further result; but we also choose them for the sake of happiness,   5 supposing that through them we shall be happy. Happiness, by contrast, no one ever chooses for their sake, or for the sake of anything else at all.

The same conclusion <that happiness is complete> also appears to follow from self-sufficiency, since the complete good seems to be self-sufficient.

Now what we count as self-sufficient is not what suffices for a solitary person by himself, living an isolated life, but what suffices also for   10 parents, children, wife and in general for friends and fellow-citizens, since a human being is a naturally political <animal>.[12] Here, however, we must impose some limit; for if we extend the good to parents' parents and children's children and to friends of friends, we shall go on without limit; but we must examine this another time.

12. **solitary . . . political**: See 1142a9, 1157b18, 1158a23, 1169b16, 1170b12, 1172a6, 1178b5, *Pol.* 1253a7, 1280b33.

15   Anyhow, we regard something as self-sufficient when all by itself it makes a life choiceworthy and lacking nothing; and that is what we think happiness does.

Moreover, we think happiness is most choiceworthy of all goods, since it is not counted as one good among many. If it were counted as one among many, then, clearly, we think that the addition of the smallest of goods would make it more choiceworthy;[13] for <the smallest good> that is added becomes an extra quantity of goods <so creating a good larger than the original good>, and the larger of two goods is always more choiceworthy. <But we do not think any addition can make happiness more choiceworthy; hence it is most choiceworthy.>

20   Happiness, then, is apparently something complete and self-sufficient, since it is the end of the things pursued in action.

But presumably the remark that the best good is happiness is apparently something <generally> agreed, and what we miss is a clearer statement of what the best good is.

25   Well, perhaps we shall find the best good if we first find the function of a human being. For just as the good, i.e., <doing> well, for a flautist, a sculptor, and every craftsman, and, in general, for whatever has a function and <characteristic> action, seems to depend on its function, the same seems to be true for a human being, if a human being has some function.

30   Then do the carpenter and the leatherworker have their functions and actions, while a human being has none, and is by nature idle, without any function? Or, just as eye, hand, foot and, in general, every <bodily> part apparently has its functions, may we likewise ascribe to a human being some function apart* from all of theirs?

What, then, could this be? For living is apparently shared with plants,
1098a   but what we are looking for is the special function of a human being; hence we should set aside the life of nutrition and growth. The life next in order is some sort of life of sense-perception; but this too is apparently shared, with horse, ox and every animal. The remaining possibility, then, is some sort of life of action of the <part of the soul> that has reason.

Now this <part has two parts, which have reason in different ways>,
5   one as obeying the reason[14] <in the other part>, the other as itself having reason and thinking. <We intend both.> Moreover, life is also

---

13. **of all goods . . . more choiceworthy**: Less probably: '. . .of all goods, when it is not counted with other goods. When it is so counted, then, clearly, we think the addition of the smallest good to it makes it more choiceworthy. . .' (so that happiness does not embrace all intrinsic goods).

14. **obeying the reason** Cf. 1102b26.

356

spoken of in two ways <as capacity and as activity>, and we must take <a human being's special function to be> life as activity, since this seems to be called life to a fuller extent.

(a) We have found, then, that the human function is the soul's activity that expresses reason <as itself having reason> or requires reason <as obeying reason>. (b) Now the function of F, of a harpist, for instance, is the same in kind, so we say, as the function of an excellent F, an excellent harpist, for instance. (c) The same is true without qualification   *10* in every case, when we add to the function the superior achievement that expresses the virtue; for a harpist's function, for instance, is to play the harp, and a good harpist's is to do it well. (d) Now we take the human function to be a certain kind of life, and take this life to be the soul's activity and actions that express reason. (e) <Hence by (c) and (d)> the excellent man's function is to do this finely and well. (f) Each   *15* function is completed well when its completion expresses the proper virtue. (g) Therefore[15] <by (d), (e), and (f)> the human good turns out to be the soul's activity that expresses virtue.

And if there are more virtues than one, the good will express the best and most complete virtue. Moreover, it will be in a complete life.[16] For one swallow does not make a spring, nor does one day; nor, similarly,   *20* does one day or a short time make us blessed and happy.

This, then, is a sketch of the good; for, presumably, the outline must come first, to be filled in later. If the sketch is good, then anyone, it seems, can advance and articulate it, and in such cases time is a good discoverer or <at least> a good co-worker. That is also how the crafts   *25* have improved, since anyone can add what is lacking <in the outline>.

However, we must also remember our previous remarks, so that we do not look for the same degree of exactness in all areas, but the degree that fits the subject matter in each area and is proper to the investigation. For the carpenter's and the geometer's inquiries about the right angle   *30* are different also; the carpenter's is confined to the right angle's usefulness for his work, whereas the geometer's concerns what, or what sort of thing, the right angle is, since he studies the truth. We must do the same, then, in other areas too, <seeking the proper degree of exactness>, so that digressions do not overwhelm our main task.

Nor should we make the same demand for an explanation in all cases.   *1098b* Rather, in some cases it is enough to prove that something is true without

---

15. **Now we take . . . Therefore**: Deleted by OCT.

16. **complete life**: See 1101a6, 1177b25. Complete virtue needs a complete life (which need not, however, be a whole lifetime; see 1101a6–13) because virtuous activities need time to develop and to express themselves fully.

explaining why it is true. This is so, for instance, with principles, where the fact that something is true is the first thing, i.e., the principle.[17]

5   Some principles are studied by means of induction, some by means of perception, some by means of some sort of habituation, and others by other means. In each case we should try to find them out by means suited to their nature, and work hard to define them well. For they have a great influence on what follows; for the principle seems to be more than half the whole, and makes evident the answer to many of our questions.

[APPEAL TO COMMON BELIEFS]

8

10   However, we should examine the principle not only from the conclusion and premises <of a deductive argument>, but also from what is said about it; for all the facts harmonize with a true account, whereas the truth soon clashes with a false one.

Goods are divided, then, into three types, some called external, some
15   goods of the soul, others goods of the body; and the goods of the soul are said to be goods to the fullest extent and most of all, and the soul's actions and activities are ascribed to the soul. Hence the account <of the good> is sound, to judge by this belief anyhow—and it is an ancient belief agreed on by philosophers.

Our account is also correct in saying that some sort of actions and
20   activities are the end; for then the end turns out to be a good of the soul, not an external good.

The belief that the happy person lives well and does well in action also agrees with our account, since we have virtually said that the end is a sort of living well and doing well in action.

Further, all the features that people look for in happiness appear to be true of the end described in our account. For to some people it seems
25   to be virtue; to others intelligence; to others some sort of wisdom; to others again it seems to be these, or one of these, involving pleasure or requiring its addition; and others add in external prosperity as well.

Some of these views are traditional, held by many, while others are held by a few reputable men; and it is reasonable for each group to be not entirely in error, but correct on one point at least, or even on most points.

17. **Rather, in some . . . i.e., the principle**: Lit. 'But it is enough in some cases for the that to be proved well, e.g., in the case of principles, and the that is first and principle.' The principles provide the 'because', i.e., the reason, and so a further 'because' cannot be given for them.

First, our account agrees with those who say happiness is virtue <in   *30*
general> or some <particular> virtue; for activity expressing virtue is
proper to virtue. Presumably, though, it matters quite a bit whether we
suppose that the best good consists in possessing or in using, i.e., in a
state or in an activity <that actualizes the state>. For while someone
may be in a state that achieves no good, if, for instance, he is asleep or   *1099a*
inactive in some other way, this cannot be true of the activity; for it will
necessarily do actions and do well in them. And just as Olympic prizes
are not for the finest and strongest, but for the contestants, since it is   *5*
only these who win; so also in life <only> the fine and good people who
act correctly win the prize.

Moreover, the life of these <active people> is also pleasant in itself.
For being pleased is a condition of the soul, <hence included in the
activity of the soul>. Further, each type of person finds pleasure in
whatever he is called a lover of, so that a horse, for instance, pleases
the horse-lover, a spectacle the lover of spectacles, and similarly what   *10*
is just pleases the lover of justice, and in general what expresses virtue
pleases the lover of virtue. Hence the things that please most people
conflict, because they are not pleasant by nature, whereas the things
that please lovers of what is fine are things pleasant by nature; and
actions expressing virtue are pleasant in this way; and so they both
please lovers of what is fine and are pleasant in themselves.   *15*

Hence their life does not need pleasure to be added <to virtuous
activity> as some sort of ornament; rather, it has its pleasure within
itself. For besides the reasons already given, someone who does not
enjoy fine actions is not good; for no one would call him just, for instance,
if he did not enjoy doing just actions, or generous if he did not enjoy
generous actions, and similarly for the other virtues. If this is so, then   *20*
actions expressing the virtues are pleasant in themselves.

Moreover, these actions are good and fine as well as pleasant; indeed,
they are good, fine and pleasant more than anything else, since on this
question the excellent person has good judgement, and his judgement
agrees with our conclusions.

Happiness, then, is best, finest and most pleasant, and these three   *25*
features are not distinguished in the way suggested by the Delian inscrip-
tion: 'What is most just is finest; being healthy is most beneficial; but it
is most pleasant to win our heart's desire.' For all three features are
found in the best activities, and happiness we say is these activities, or   *30*
<rather> one of them, the best one.

Nonetheless, happiness evidently also needs external goods to be
added <to the activity>, as we said, since we cannot, or cannot easily,
do fine actions if we lack the resources.

For, first of all, in many actions we use friends, wealth and political   *1099b*
power just as we use instruments. Further, deprivation of certain <exter-

nals>—for instance, good birth, good children, beauty—mars our blessedness; for we do not altogether have the character of happiness if we
look utterly repulsive or are ill-born, solitary or childless, and have it
5   even less, presumably, if our children or friends are totally bad, or were
good but have died.

And so, as we have said, happiness would seem to need this sort of
prosperity added also; that is why some people identify happiness with
good fortune, while others <reacting from one extreme to the other>
identify it with virtue.

[*HAPPINESS AND EXTERNAL GOODS*]

9

This <question about the role of fortune> raises a puzzle: Is happiness
10   acquired by learning, or habituation, or by some other form of cultivation? Or is it the result of some divine fate, or even of fortune?

First, then, if the gods give any gift at all to human beings, it is
reasonable to give happiness more than any other human <good>,
insofar as it is the best of human <goods>. Presumably, however, this
question is more suitable for a different inquiry.

15   But even if it is not sent by the gods, but instead results from virtue
and some sort of learning or cultivation, happiness appears to be one
of the most divine things, since the prize and goal of virtue appears to
be the best good, something divine and blessed.

Moreover <if happiness comes in this way> it will be widely shared;
for anyone who is not deformed <in his capacity> for virtue will be
20   able to achieve happiness through some sort of learning and attention.

And since it is better to be happy in this way than because of fortune,
it is reasonable for this to be the way <we become> happy. For whatever
is natural is naturally in the finest state possible, and so are the products
of crafts and of every other cause, especially the best cause; and it
would be seriously inappropriate to entrust what is greatest and finest
to fortune.

25   The answer to our question is also evident from our account <of happi-
ness>. For we have said it is a certain sort of activity of the soul expressing
virtue, <and hence not a product of fortune>; and some of the other goods
are necessary conditions of happiness>, others are naturally useful and
cooperative as instruments <but are not parts of it>.

30   Further, this conclusion agrees with our opening remarks. For we
took the goal of political science to be the best good; and most of its
attention is devoted to the character of the citizens, to make them good
people who do fine actions, <which is reasonable if happiness depends
on virtue, not on fortune>.

It is not surprising, then, that we regard neither ox nor horse nor any
other kind of animal as happy, since none of them can share in this sort   *1100a*
of activity. And for the same reason a child is not happy either,[18] since
his age prevents him from doing these sorts of actions; and if he is called
happy, he is being congratulated because of anticipated blessedness,
since, as we have said, happiness requires both complete virtue and a   *5*
complete life.

<Happiness needs a complete life.> For life includes many reversals
of fortune, good and bad, and the most prosperous person may fall into
a terrible disaster in old age, as the Trojan stories tell us about Priam;
but if someone has suffered these sorts of misfortunes and comes to a
miserable end, no one counts him happy.

10

Then should we count no human being happy during his lifetime, but   *10*
follow Solon's advice to wait to see the end? And if we should hold that,
can he really be happy during the time after he has died? Surely that is
completely absurd, especially when we say happiness is an activity.

We do not say, then, that someone is happy during the time he is   *15*
dead, and Solon's point is not this <absurd one>, but rather that when
a human being has died, we can safely pronounce <that he was> blessed
<before he died>, on the assumption that he is now finally beyond
evils and misfortuncs.

Still, even this claim is disputable. For if a living person has good or   *20*
evil of which he is not aware, then a dead person also, it seems, has
good or evil when, for instance, he receives honors or dishonors, and
his children, and descendants in general, do well or suffer misfortune.
<Hence, apparently, what happens after his death can affect whether
or not he was happy before his death.>

However, this view also raises a puzzle. For even if someone has
lived in blessedness until old age, and has died appropriately, many
fluctuations of his descendants' fortunes may still happen to him; for   *25*
some may be good people and get the life they deserve, while the
contrary may be true of others, and clearly they may be as distantly
related to their ancestor as you please. Surely, then, it would be an
absurd result if the dead person's condition changed along with the
fortunes of his descendants, so that at one time he became happy <in
his lifetime> and at another time miserable. But it would also be absurd   *30*
if the condition of descendants did not affect their ancestors at all or for
any length of time.

18. **we regard neither . . . happy either**: Cf. 1177a8, 1178b27, *Phys.* 197b6.

But we must return to the previous puzzle, since that will perhaps also show us the answer to our present question.

If, then, we must wait to see the end, and must then count someone blessed, not as being blessed <during the time he is dead> but because
35   he previously was blessed, surely it is absurd if at the time when he is happy we will not truly ascribe to him the happiness he has.

1100b   <We hesitate> out of reluctance to call him happy during his lifetime, because of the variations, and because we suppose happiness is enduring and definitely not prone to fluctuate, whereas the same person's fortunes
5   often turn to and fro. For clearly, if we are guided by his fortunes, so that we often call him happy and then miserable again, we will be representing the happy person as a kind of chameleon insecurely based.

But surely it is quite wrong to be guided by someone's fortunes. For his doing well or badly does not rest on them; though a human life, as
10   we said, needs these added, it is the activities expressing virtue that control happiness, and the contrary activities that control its contrary.

Indeed, the present puzzle is further evidence for our account <of happiness>. For no human achievement has the stability of activities that express virtue,[19] since these seem to be more enduring even than
15   our knowledge of the sciences; and the most honorable of the virtues themselves are more enduring <than the others> because blessed people devote their lives to them more fully and more continually than to anything else—for this <continual activity> would seem to be the reason we do not forget them.

It follows, then, that the happy person has the <stability> we are looking for and keeps the character he has throughout his life. For
20   always, or more than anything else, he will do and study the actions expressing virtue, and will bear fortunes most finely, in every way and in all conditions appropriately, since he is truly 'good, foursquare and blameless'. However, many events are matters of fortune, and some are
25   smaller, some greater. Hence, while small strokes of good or ill fortune clearly will not influence his life, many great strokes of good fortune will make it more blessed, since in themselves they naturally add adornment to it, and his use of them proves to be fine and excellent. Conversely, if they are great misfortunes, they oppress and spoil his blessed-
30   ness, since they involve pain and impede many activities.

And yet, even here what is fine shines through, whenever someone bears many severe misfortunes with good temper, not because he feels no distress, but because he is noble and magnanimous.

And since it is activities that control life, as we said, no blessed person

19. **For no . . . express virtue**: Cf. 1105a33, 1140b29, 1156b12; 1159b2, 1164a12, 1172b9.

could ever become miserable, since he will never do hateful and base   *35*
actions. For a truly good and intelligent person, we suppose, will bear   *1101a*
strokes of fortune suitably, and from his resources at any time will do
the finest actions, just as a good general will make the best use of his   *5*
forces in war, and a good shoemaker will produce the finest shoe from
the hides given to him, and similarly for all other craftsmen.

If this is so, then the happy person could never become miserable.
Still, he will not be blessed either, if he falls into misfortunes as bad as
Priam's. Nor, however, will he be inconstant and prone to fluctuate,
since he will neither be easily shaken from his happiness nor shaken by   *10*
just any misfortunes. He will be shaken from it, though, by many serious
misfortunes, and from these a return to happiness will take no short
time; at best, it will take a long and complete length of time that includes
great and fine successes.

Then why not say that the happy person is the one who expresses   *15*
complete virtue in his activities, with an adequate supply of external
goods, not for just any time but for a complete life? Or should we add
that he will also go on living this way and will come to an appropriate
end?

The future is not apparent to us, and we take happiness to be the
end, and altogether complete in every way; hence we will say that a   *20*
living person who has, and will keep, the goods we mentioned is blessed,
but blessed as a human being is.[20] So much for a determination of this
question.

* * * * * * *

[INTRODUCTION TO THE ACCOUNT OF VIRTUE]

13

Since happiness is an activity of the soul expressing complete virtue, we   *1102a5*
must examine virtue; for that will perhaps also be a way to study happiness better.

Moreover, the true politician seems to have spent more effort on
virtue than on anything else, since he wants to make the citizens good   *10*
and law-abiding. We find an example of this in the Spartan and Cretan
legislators and in any others with their concerns. Since, then, the examination of virtue is proper for political science, the inquiry clearly suits
our original decision <to pursue political science>.

20. **Or should we . . . human being is.** This translation assumes that Aristotle's
answer to 'Or should we . . . ?' is 'No'. A less probable translation would be
'an appropriate end, since the future . . . every way? Hence . . .' (suggesting
that the answer to 'Or should we . . . ?' is 'Yes', contrary to a6–16).

15 It is clear that the virtue we must examine is human virtue, since we are also seeking the human good and human happiness. And by human virtue we mean virtue of the soul, not of the body, since we also say that happiness is an activity of the soul. If this is so, then it is clear that the politician must acquire some knowledge₀ about the soul, just as 20 someone setting out to heal the eyes must acquire knowledge about the whole body as well. This is all the more true to the extent that political science is better and more honorable than medicine—and even among doctors the cultivated ones devote a lot of effort to acquiring knowledge₈ about the body. Hence the politician as well <as the student of nature> must study the soul.

25 But he must study it for the purpose <of inquiring into virtue>, as far as suffices for what he seeks; for a more exact treatment would presumably take more effort than his purpose requires. <We> have discussed the soul sufficiently <for our purposes> in <our> popular works as well <as our less popular>, and we should use this discussion.

We have said, for instance, that one <part> of the soul is nonrational, 30 while one has reason. Are these distinguished as parts of a body and everything divisible into parts are? Or are they two only in account,[21] and inseparable by nature, as the convex and the concave are in a surface? It does not matter for present purposes.

Consider the nonrational <part>. One <part> of it, i.e., the cause 1102b of nutrition and growth, is seemingly plant-like and shared <with other living things>: for we can ascribe this capacity of the soul to everything that is nourished, including embryos, and the same one to complete living things, since this is more reasonable than to ascribe another capacity to them.

Hence the virtue of this capacity is apparently shared, not <specifi-5 cally> human. For this part and capacity more than others seem to be active in sleep, and here the good and the bad person are least distinct, which is why happy people are said to be no better off than miserable people for half their lives.

And this lack of distinction is not surprising, since sleep is inactivity of the soul insofar as it is called excellent or base, unless to some small 10 extent some movements penetrate <to our awareness>, and in this way the decent person comes to have better images <in dreams> than just any random person has. Enough about this, however, and let us leave aside the nutritive part, since by nature it has no share in human virtue.

Another nature in the soul would also seem to be nonrational, though in a way it shares in reason.

21. **two only in account**: Cf. *DA* 413b13–32, 432a15–b8, 433a31–b13. On 'two in account' see ESSENCE #2.

<Clearly it is nonrational.> For in the continent and the incontinent   *15*
person we praise their reason, i.e., the <part> of the soul that has
reason, because it exhorts them correctly and toward what is best;
but they evidently also have in them some other <part> that is by
nature something apart from reason, conflicting and struggling with
reason.

For just as paralyzed parts of a body, when we decide to move them   *20*
to the right, do the contrary and move off to the left, the same is true
of the soul; for incontinent people have impulses in contrary directions.
In bodies, admittedly, we see the part go astray, whereas we do not see
it in the soul; nonetheless, presumably, we should suppose that the soul
also has something apart from reason, contrary to and countering reason.   *25*
The <precise> way it is different does not matter.

However, this <part> as well <as the rational part> appears, as
we said, to share in reason. At any rate, in the continent person it
obeys reason; and in the temperate and the brave person it presumably
listens still better to reason, since there it agrees with reason in
everything.

The nonrational <part>, then, as well <as the whole soul> apparently has two parts. For while the plant-like <part> shares in reason   *30*
not at all, the <part> with appetites and in general desires shares
in reason in a way, insofar as it both listens to reason and obeys it.

It listens in the way in which we are said to 'listen to reason' from
father or friends, not in the way in which we <'give the reason'> in
mathematics.

The nonrational part also <obeys and> is persuaded in some way
by reason, as is shown by chastening, and by every sort of reproof and   *1103a*
exhortation.

If we ought to say, then, that this <part> also has reason, then
the <part> that has reason, as well <as the nonrational part> will
have two parts, one that has reason to the full extent by having it
within itself, and another <that has it> by listening to reason as to
a father.

The division between virtues also reflects this difference. For some   *5*
virtues are called virtues of thought, others virtues of character; wisdom,
comprehension and intelligence are called virtues of thought, generosity
and temperance virtues of character.

For when we speak of someone's character we do not say that he is
wise or has good comprehension, but that he is gentle or temperate.
<Hence these are the virtues of character.> And yet, we also praise the
wise person for his state, and the states that are praiseworthy are the   *10*
ones we call virtues. <Hence wisdom is also a virtue.>

Book II

[VIRTUES OF CHARACTER]

[HOW A VIRTUE OF CHARACTER IS ACQUIRED]

1

15 Virtue, then, is of two sorts, virtue of thought and virtue of character. Virtue of thought arises and grows mostly from teaching, and hence needs experience and time. Virtue of character results from habit; hence its name[1] 'ethical', slightly varied from 'ethos'.

Hence it is also clear that none of the virtues of character arises in us naturally.

20 For if something is by nature <in one condition>, habituation cannot bring it into another condition. A stone, for instance, by nature moves downward, and habituation could not make it move upward, not even if you threw it up ten thousand times to habituate it; nor could habituation make fire move downward, or bring anything that is by nature in one condition into another condition.

25 Thus the virtues arise in us neither by nature nor against nature. Rather, we are by nature able to acquire them, and reach our complete perfection through habit.

Further, if something arises in us by nature, we first have the capacity for it, and later display the activity. This is clear in the case of the senses;

30 for we did not acquire them by frequent seeing or hearing, but already had them when we exercised them, and did not get them by exercising them.

Virtues, by contrast, we acquire, just as we acquire crafts, by having previously activated them. For we learn a craft by producing the same product that we must produce when we have learned it, becoming builders, for instance, by building and harpists by playing the harp; so

1103b also, then, we become just by doing just actions, temperate by doing temperate actions, brave by doing brave actions.

What goes on in cities is evidence for this also. For the legislator

5 makes the citizens good by habituating them, and this is the wish of every legislator; if he fails to do it well he misses his goal. <The right> habituation is what makes the difference between a good political system and a bad one.

Further, just as in the case of a craft, the sources and means that develop each virtue also ruin it. For playing the harp makes both good

10 and bad harpists, and it is analogous in the case of builders and all the rest; for building well makes good builders, building badly, bad ones.

---

1. **hence its name**: Aristotle plays on the similarity between *ēthos* (long e: 'character') and *ethos* (short e: 'habit').

If it were not so, no teacher would be needed, but everyone would be born a good or a bad craftsman.

It is the same, then, with the virtues. For actions in dealings with <other> human beings make some people just, some unjust; actions in terrifying situations and the acquired habit of fear or confidence make some brave and others cowardly. The same is true of situations involving appetites and anger; for one or another sort of conduct in these situations makes some people temperate and gentle, others intemperate and irascible. *20*

To sum up, then, in a single account: A state <of character> arises from <the repetition of> similar activities. Hence we must display the right activities, since differences in these imply corresponding differences in the states. It is not unimportant, then, to acquire one sort of habit or another, right from our youth; rather, it is very important, indeed all-important. *25*

2

Our present inquiry does not aim, as our others do, at study; for the purpose of our examination is not to know₀ what virtue is, but to become good, since otherwise the inquiry would be of no benefit to us. Hence *30* we must examine the right way to act, since, as we have said, the actions also control the character of the states we acquire.

First, then, actions should express correct reason. That is a common <belief>, and let us assume it; later we will say what correct reason is and how it is related to the other virtues.

But let us take it as agreed in advance that every account of the actions *1104a* we must do has to be stated in outline, not exactly. As we also said at the start, the type of accounts we demand should reflect the subject matter; and questions about actions and expediency, like questions about health, have no fixed <and invariable answers>.

And when our general account is so inexact, the account of particular *5* cases is all the more inexact. For these fall under no craft or profession, and the agents themselves must consider in each case what the opportune action is, as doctors and navigators do.

The account we offer, then, in our present inquiry is of this inexact *10* sort; still, we must try to offer help.

First, then, we should observe that these sorts of states naturally tend to be ruined by excess and deficiency. We see this happen with strength and health, which we mention because we must use what is evident as a witness to what is not. For both excessive and deficient exercises ruin *15* strength; and likewise, too much or too little eating or drinking ruins health, while the proportionate amount produces, increases and preserves it.

20 The same is true, then, of temperance, bravery and the other virtues. For if, for instance, someone avoids and is afraid of everything, standing firm against nothing, he becomes cowardly, but if he is afraid of nothing at all and goes to face everything, he becomes rash. Similarly, if he gratifies himself with every pleasure and refrains from none, he becomes 25 intemperate, but if he avoids them all, as boors do, he becomes some sort of insensible person. Temperance and bravery, then, are ruined by excess and deficiency but preserved by the mean.

The same actions, then, are the sources and causes both of the emergence and growth of virtues and of their ruin; but further, the activities 30 of the virtues will be found in these same actions. For this is also true of more evident cases; strength, for instance, arises from eating a lot and from withstanding much hard labor, and it is the strong person who is most able to do these very things. It is the same with the virtues. 35 Refraining from pleasures makes us become temperate, and when we 1104b have become temperate we are most able to refrain from pleasures. And it is similar with bravery; habituation in disdaining what is fearful and in standing firm against it makes us become brave, and when we have become brave we shall be most able to stand firm.

3

But <actions are not enough>; we must take as a sign of someone's 5 state his pleasure or pain in consequence of his action. For if someone who abstains from bodily pleasures enjoys the abstinence itself, then he is temperate, but if he is grieved by it, he is intemperate. Again, if he stands firm against terrifying situations and enjoys it, or at least does not find it painful, then he is brave, and if he finds it painful, he is cowardly.

<Pleasures and pains are appropriately taken as signs> because virtue of character is concerned with pleasures and pains.

10 (1) For it is pleasure that causes us to do base actions, and pain that causes us to abstain from fine ones. Hence we need to have had the appropriate upbringing—right from early youth, as Plato says—to make us find enjoyment or pain in the right things; for this is the correct education.

(2) Further, virtues are concerned with actions and feelings; but every 15 feeling and every action implies pleasure or pain; hence, for this reason too, virtue is concerned with pleasures and pains.

(3) Corrective treatment <for vicious actions> also indicates <the relevance of pleasure and pain>, since it uses pleasures and pains; it uses them because such correction is a form of medical treatment, and medical treatment naturally operates through contraries.

(4) Further, as we said earlier, every state of soul is naturally related

to and concerned with whatever naturally makes it better or worse; and   20
pleasures and pains make people worse, from pursuing and avoiding
the wrong ones, at the wrong time, in the wrong ways, or whatever
other distinctions of that sort are needed in an account.

These <bad effects of pleasure and pain> are the reason why people
actually define[2] the virtues as ŵays of being unaffected and undisturbed   25
<by pleasures and pains>. They are wrong, however, because they
speak <of being unaffected> without qualification, not of being unaffected in the right or wrong way, at the right or wrong time, and the
added specifications.

We assume, then, that virtue is the sort of state <with the appropriate
specifications> that does the best actions concerned with pleasures and
pains, and that vice is the contrary. The following points will also make
it evident that virtue and vice are concerned with the same things.   30

(5) There are three objects of choice—fine, expedient and pleasant—
and three objects of avoidance—their contraries, shameful, harmful and
painful. About all these, then, the good person is correct and the bad
person is in error, and especially about pleasure. For pleasure is shared   35
with animals, and implied by every object of choice, since what is fine   1105a
and what is expedient appear pleasant as well.

(6) Further, since pleasure grows up with all of us from infancy on,
it is hard to rub out this feeling that is dyed into our lives; and we
estimate actions as well <as feelings>, some of us more, some less, by   5
pleasure and pain. Hence, our whole inquiry must be about these, since
good or bad enjoyment or pain is very important for our actions.

(7) Moreover, it is harder to fight pleasure than to fight emotion,
<though that is hard enough>, as Heracleitus says. Now both craft and
virtue are concerned in every case with what is harder, since a good result   10
is even better when it is harder. Hence, for this reason also, the whole
inquiry, for virtue and political science alike, must consider pleasures and
pains; for if we use these well, we shall be good, and if badly, bad.

In short, virtue is concerned with pleasures and pains; the actions   15
that are its sources also increase it or, if they are done differently, ruin
it; and its activity is concerned with the same actions that are its sources.

[VIRTUOUS ACTION AND VIRTUOUS CHARACTER]

4

However, someone might raise this puzzle: 'What do you mean by
saying that to become just we must first do just actions and to become

2. **people actually define**: Probably SPEUSIPPUS (cf. Plato, *Phil.* 42e–51a) or the
Cynics (see ANTISTHENES).

20 temperate we must first do temperate actions? For if we do what is grammatical or musical, we must already be grammarians or musicians. In the same way, then, if we do what is just or temperate, we must already be just or temperate.'

But surely this is not so even with the crafts, for it is possible to produce something grammatical by chance or by following someone else's instructions. To be a grammarian, then, we must both produce 25 something grammatical and produce it in the way in which the grammarian produces it, i.e., expressing grammatical knowledge that is in us.

Moreover, in any case what is true of crafts is not true of virtues. For the products of a craft determine by their own character whether they have been produced well;[3] and so it suffices that they are in the right state when they have been produced. But for actions expressing virtue to be done temperately or justly <and hence well> it does not suffice 30 that they are themselves in the right state. Rather, the agent must also be in the right state when he does them. First, he must know$_0$ <that he is doing virtuous actions>; second, he must decide* on them, and decide on them for themselves; and, third, he must also do them from a firm and unchanging state.

1105b As conditions for having a craft these three do not count, except for the knowing itself. As a condition for having a virtue, however, the knowing counts for nothing, or <rather> for only a little, whereas the other two conditions are very important, indeed all-important. And these 5 other two conditions are achieved by the frequent doing of just and temperate actions.

Hence actions are called just or temperate when they are the sort that a just or temperate person would do. But the just and temperate person is not the one who <merely> does these actions, but the one who also does them in the way in which just or temperate people do them.

10 It is right, then, to say that a person comes to be just from doing just actions and temperate from doing temperate actions; for no one has even a prospect of becoming good from failing to do them.

The many, however, do not do these actions but take refuge in arguments, thinking that they are doing philosophy, and that this is the way 15 to become excellent people. In this they are like a sick person who listens attentively to the doctor, but acts on none of his instructions. Such a course of treatment will not improve the state of his body; any more than will the many's way of doing philosophy improve the state of their souls.

3. **For the products . . . produced well.** Lit. 'the things coming to be by crafts have the well in themselves'. A better method of production is better because it is better at producing the right sort of product.

[VIRTUE OF CHARACTER AS AN INTERMEDIATE STATE]

5

Next we must examine what virtue is. Since there are three conditions   *20*
arising in the soul—feelings, capacities and states—virtue must be one
of these.

By feelings I mean appetite, anger, fear, confidence, envy, joy, love,
hate, longing, jealousy, pity, in general whatever implies pleasure or pain.

By capacities I mean what we have when we are said to be capable   *25*
of these feelings—capable of being angry, for instance, or afraid or feeling
pity.

By states I mean what we have when we are well or badly off in
relation to feelings. If, for instance, our feeling is too intense or slack,
we are badly off in relation to anger, but if it is intermediate, we are
well off;⁴ and the same is true in the other cases.

First, then, neither virtues nor vices are feelings. (a) For we are called   *30*
excellent or base insofar as we have virtues or vices, not insofar as we
have feelings. (b) We are neither praised nor blamed insofar as we have
feelings; for we do not praise the angry or the frightened person, and
do not blame the person who is simply angry, but only the person who   *1106a*
is angry in a particular way. But we are praised or blamed insofar as we
have virtues or vices. (c) We are angry and afraid without decision; but
the virtues are decisions of some kind, or <rather> require decision.
(d) Besides, in so far as we have feelings, we are said to be moved; but   *5*
insofar as we have virtues or vices, we are said to be in some condition
rather than moved.

For these reasons the virtues are not capacities either; for we are
neither called good nor called bad⁵ insofar as we are simply capable of
feelings. Further, while we have capacities by nature, we do not become   *10*
good or bad by nature; we have discussed this before.

If, then, the virtues are neither feelings nor capacities, the remaining
possibility is that they are states. And so we have said what the genus
of virtue is.

6

But we must say not only, as we already have, that it is a state, but also   *15*
what sort of state it is.

It should be said, then, that every virtue causes its possessors to be

---

4. **By states . . . well off.** A STATE is not *merely* a capacity (see POTENTIALITY).
Aristotle does not deny that a state is a *type* of capacity.

5. **called bad**: The mss add 'nor are we praised or blamed', retained by OCT.

in a good state and to perform their functions well;[6] the virtue of eyes,
for instance, makes the eyes and their functioning excellent, because it
20   makes us see well; and similarly, the virtue of a horse makes the horse
excellent, and thereby good at galloping, at carrying its rider and at
standing steady in the face of the enemy. If this is true in every case,
then the virtue of a human being will likewise be the state that makes
a human being good and makes him perform his function well.

25   We have already said how this will be true, and it will also be evident
from our next remarks, if we consider the sort of nature that virtue has.

In everything continuous and divisible we can take more, less and
equal, and each of them either in the object itself or relative to us; and
the equal is some intermediate between excess and deficiency.

30   By the intermediate in the object I mean what is equidistant from each
extremity; this is one and the same for everyone. But relative to us the
intermediate is what is neither superfluous nor deficient; this is not one,
and is not the same for everyone.[7]

If, for instance, ten are many and two are few, we take six as intermedi-
35   ate in the object, since it exceeds <two> and is exceeded <by ten> by
an equal amount, <four>; this is what is intermediate by numerical
1106b   proportion. But that is not how we must take the intermediate that is
relative to us. For if, for instance, ten pounds <of food> are a lot for
someone to eat, and two pounds a little, it does not follow that the
trainer will prescribe six, since this might also be either a little or a lot
for the person who is to take it—for Milo <the athlete> a little, but for
5   the beginner in gymnastics a lot; and the same is true for running and
wrestling. In this way every scientific expert avoids excess and deficiency
and seeks and chooses what is intermediate—but intermediate relative
to us, not in the object.

This, then, is how each science produces its product well, by focusing
10   on what is intermediate and making the product conform to that. This,
indeed, is why people regularly comment on well-made products that
nothing could be added or subtracted, since they assume that excess or

6. **It should ...**: The connection between virtue and FUNCTION was urged in
1098a7; cf. 1139a16; Plato, *Rep.* 352d. As i 13 argued, a virtue will require the
right relation among different parts of the soul, so that someone's actions are
guided by reason. Here Aristotle expands his earlier suggestion (see 1104a26)
that guidance by reason requires neither total repression nor total indulgence
of nonrational desires. Hence the connection between virtue and function leads
directly into the doctrine of the MEAN.

7. **But relative ... for everyone**: The appeal to a mean does not provide a
precise, quantitative test. To find the mean relative to us is to find the state of
character that correct reason requires, neither suppressing nor totally indulging
nonrational desires.

deficiency ruins a good <result> while the mean preserves it. Good craftsmen also, we say, focus on what is intermediate when they produce their product. And since virtue, like nature, is better and more exact *15* than any craft, it will also aim at what is intermediate.

By virtue I mean virtue of character; for this <pursues the mean because> it is concerned with feelings and actions, and these admit of excess, deficiency and an intermediate condition. We can be afraid, for instance, or be confident, or have appetites, or get angry, or feel pity, in general have pleasure or pain, both too much and too little, and in *20* both ways not well; but <having these feelings> at the right times, about the right things, toward the right people, for the right end, and in the right way, is the intermediate condition.

Now virtue is concerned with feelings and actions, in which excess *25* and deficiency are in error and incur blame, while the intermediate condition is correct and wins praise, which are both proper features of virtue. Virtue, then, is a mean, insofar as it aims at what is intermediate.

Moreover, there are many ways to be in error, since badness is proper *30* to what is unlimited, as the Pythagoreans pictured it, and good to what is limited; but there is only one way to be correct. That is why error is easy and correctness hard, since it is easy to miss the target and hard to hit it. And so for this reason also excess and deficiency are proper to *35* vice, the mean to virtue; 'for we are noble in only one way, but bad in all sorts of ways.'

Virtue, then, is (a) a state that decides, (b) <consisting> in a mean, *1107a* (c) the mean relative to us, (d) which is defined by reference to reason, (e) i.e., to the reason by reference to which the intelligent person would define it. It is a mean between two vices, one of excess and one of deficiency.

It is a mean for this reason also: Some vices miss what is right because they are deficient, others because they are excessive, in feelings or in *5* actions, while virtue finds and chooses what is intermediate.

Hence, as far as its substance and the account stating its essence are concerned, virtue is a mean; but as far as the best <condition> and the good <result> are concerned, it is an extremity.

But not every action or feeling admits of the mean. For the names of *10* some automatically include baseness—for instance, spite, shame-lessness, envy <among feelings>, and adultery, theft, murder, among actions. All of these and similar things are called by these names because they themselves, not their excesses or deficiencies, are base.

Hence in doing these things we can never be correct, but must invari- *15* ably be in error. We cannot do them well or not well—by committing adultery, for instance, with the right woman at the right time in the right way; on the contrary, it is true without qualification that to do any of them is to be in error.

20 <To think these admit of a mean>, therefore, is like thinking that unjust or cowardly or intemperate action also admits of a mean, an excess and a deficiency. For then there would be a mean of excess, a mean of deficiency, an excess of excess and a deficiency of deficiency.

Rather, just as there is no excess or deficiency of temperance or of bravery, since the intermediate is a sort of extreme <in achieving the good>, so also there is no mean of these <vicious actions> either, but whatever way anyone does them, he is in error. For in general there is 25 no mean of excess or of deficiency, and no excess or deficiency of a mean.

[*THE INDIVIDUAL VIRTUES OF CHARACTER*]

7

However, we must not only state this general account but also apply it 30 to the particular cases. For among accounts concerning actions, though the general ones are common to more cases, the specific ones are truer, since actions are about particular cases, and our account must accord with these. Let us, then, find these from the chart.[8]

1107b (1) First, in feelings of fear and confidence the mean is bravery. The excessively fearless person is nameless (and in fact many cases are nameless), while the one who is excessively confident is rash; the one who is excessively afraid and deficient in confidence is cowardly.

5 (2) In pleasures and pains, though not in all types, and in pains less than in pleasures, the mean is temperance and the excess intemperance. People deficient in pleasure are not often found, which is why they also lack even a name; let us call them insensible.

10 (3) In giving and taking money the mean is generosity, the excess wastefulness and the deficiency ungenerosity. Here the vicious people have contrary excesses and defects; for the wasteful person spends to excess and is deficient in taking, whereas the ungenerous person takes to excess and is deficient in spending. At the moment we are speaking 15 in outline and summary, and that suffices; later we shall define these things more exactly.

(4) In questions of money there are also other conditions. Another mean is magnificence; for the magnificent person differs from the generous by being concerned with large matters, while the generous person 20 is concerned with small. The excess is ostentation and vulgarity, and

8. **chart**: Presumably in Aristotle's lecture room. This chapter anticipates the detailed argument of Bks iii–v. The virtues are classified into groups, and Aristotle seeks to show that for every genuine virtue of character the doctrine of the mean explains why it is a virtue.

the deficiency niggardliness, and these differ from the vices related to generosity in ways we shall describe later.

(5) In honor and dishonor the mean is magnanimity, the excess something called a sort of vanity, and the deficiency pusillanimity.

(6) And just as we said that generosity differs from magnificence in its concern with small matters, similarly there is a virtue concerned with small honors, differing in the same way from magnanimity, which is concerned with great honors. For honor can be desired either in the right way or more or less than is right. If someone desires it to excess, he is called an honor-lover, and if his desire is deficient he is called indifferent to honor, but if he is intermediate he has no name. The corresponding conditions have no name either, except the condition of the honor-lover, which is called honor-loving.

This is why people at the extremes claim the intermediate area. Indeed, we also sometimes call the intermediate person an honor-lover, and sometimes call him indifferent to honor; and sometimes we praise the honor-lover, sometimes the person indifferent to honor. We will mention later the reason we do this; for the moment, let us speak of the other cases in the way we have laid down.

(7) Anger also admits of an excess, deficiency and mean. These are all practically nameless; but since we call the intermediate person mild, let us call the mean mildness. Among the extreme people let the excessive person be irascible, and the vice be irascibility, and let the deficient person be a sort of inirascible person, and the deficiency be inirascibility.

There are three other means, somewhat similar to one another, but different. For they are all concerned with association in conversations and actions, but differ insofar as one is concerned with truth-telling in these areas, the other two with sources of pleasure, some of which are found in amusement, and the others in daily life in general. Hence we should also discuss these states, so that we can better observe that in every case the mean is praiseworthy, while the extremes are neither praiseworthy nor correct, but blameworthy. Most of these cases are also nameless, and we must try, as in the other cases also, to make names ourselves, to make things clear and easy to follow.

(8) In truth-telling, then, let us call the intermediate person truthful, and the mean truthfulness; pretence that overstates will be boastfulness, and the person who has it boastful; pretence that understates will be self-deprecation, and the person who has it self-deprecating.

(9) In sources of pleasure in amusements let us call the intermediate person witty, and the condition wit; the excess buffoonery and the person who has it a buffoon; and the deficient person a sort of boor and the state boorishness.

(10) In the other sources of pleasure, those in daily life, let us call the person who is pleasant in the right way friendly, and the mean state

25

30

1108a

5

10

15

20

25

friendliness. If someone goes to excess with no <further> aim he will be ingratiating; if he does it for his own advantage, a flatterer. The

30   deficient person, unpleasant in everything, will be a sort of quarrelsome and ill-tempered person.

(11) There are also means in feelings and concerned with feelings: shame, for instance, is not a virtue, but the person prone to shame as well as the virtuous person we have described receives praise. For here also one person is called intermediate, and another—the person excessively prone to shame, who is ashamed about everything—is called

35   excessive; the person who is deficient in shame or never feels shame at

1108b all is said to have no sense of disgrace; and the intermediate one is called prone to shame.

(12) Proper indignation is the mean between envy and spite; these conditions are concerned with pleasure and pain at what happens to our neighbors. For the properly indignant person feels pain when some-

5   one does well undeservedly; the envious person exceeds him by feeling pain when anyone does well, while the spiteful person is so deficient in feeling pain that he actually enjoys <other people's misfortunes>.

There will also be an opportunity elsewhere to speak of these <means that are not virtues>.

We must consider justice after these other conditions, and, because it is not spoken of in one way only, we shall distinguish its two types and say how each of them is a mean.

10   Similarly, we must consider the virtues that belong to reason.

*   *   *   *   *   *   *

Book III

[VIRTUE, PRAISE, AND BLAME]

[VOLUNTARY ACTION]

1

1109b30   Virtue, then, is about feelings and actions. These receive praise or blame when they are voluntary, but pardon, sometimes even pity, when they are involuntary. Hence, presumably, in examining virtue we must define the voluntary and the involuntary. This is also useful to legislators, both

35   for honors and for corrective treatments.

1110a   What comes about by force or because of ignorance seems to be involuntary. What is forced has an external principle,* the sort of principle in which the agent or victim contributes nothing—if, for instance, a wind or human beings who control him were to carry him off.

5   But now consider actions done because of fear of greater evils, or because of something fine. Suppose, for instance, a tyrant tells you to do something shameful, when he has control over your parents and

children, and if you do it, they will live, but if not, they will die. These cases raise dispute about whether they are voluntary or involuntary.[1]

However, the same sort of thing also happens with throwing cargo   10
overboard in storms; for no one willingly throws cargo overboard, without qualification,[2] but anyone with any sense throws it overboard <under some conditions> to save himself and the others.

These sorts of actions, then, are mixed. But they would seem to be more like voluntary actions. For at the time they are done they are choiceworthy, and the goal of an action reflects the occasion; hence also we should call the action voluntary or involuntary with reference to the time when he does it. Now in fact he does it willingly; for in these sorts   15
of actions he has within him the principle of the movement of the limbs that are the instruments <of the action>, and when the principle of the actions is in him, it is also up to him to do them or not to do them. Hence actions of this sort are voluntary, though presumably the actions without <the appropriate> condition are involuntary, since no one would choose any action of this sort in itself.

For such <mixed> actions people are sometimes actually praised,   20
whenever they endure something shameful or painful as the price of great and fine results; and if they do the reverse, they are blamed, since it is a base person who endures what is most shameful for nothing fine or for only some moderately fine result.

In some cases there is no praise, but there is pardon, whenever some-   25
one does a wrong action because of conditions of a sort that overstrain human nature, and that no one would endure. But presumably there are some things we cannot be compelled[3] to do, and rather than do them we should suffer the most terrible consequences and accept death; for the things that <allegedly> compelled Euripides' Alcmaeon to kill his mother appear ridiculous.

It is sometimes hard, however, to judge what <goods> should be   30
chosen at the price of what <evils>, and what <evils> should be en-

1. **But now consider . . .**: Aristotle rejects two possible claims about these mixed actions: (1) they are forced, and hence involuntary; (2) they are not forced but they are involuntary. In 1110b1 ('What sorts of things, then . . .?'), Aristotle answers (1). He answers (2) by explaining how mixed actions can be voluntary. The case of the tyrant's threat is meant to appear an involuntary action. To show that the appearance is misleading, Aristotle counters with the case of the cargo, presented as a clearly voluntary action.

2. **without qualification**: Here and in a18 and b1 Aristotle contrasts simply doing F with doing F in specific conditions in which it is reasonable to do F. See WITHOUT QUALIFICATION #4.'In itself' (see IN ITS OWN RIGHT), a19, b3, marks the same contrast.

3. **compelled**: 'Compel' translates *anankazein* (see NECESSARY). 'FORCE' renders *biazein*.

dured as the price of what <goods>. And it is even harder to abide by our judgment, since the results we expect <when we endure> are usually painful, and the actions we are compelled <to endure, when we choose>
1110b   are usually shameful. That is why those who have been compelled or not compelled receive praise or blame.

What sorts of things, then, should we say are forced? Perhaps we should say that something is forced without qualification whenever its cause is external and the agent contributes nothing. Other things are involuntary in themselves, but choiceworthy on this occasion and as the
5   price of these <goods>, and their principle is in the agent. These are involuntary in themselves, but, on this occasion and as the price of these <goods>, voluntary. Still, they would seem to be more like voluntary actions, since actions involve particular <conditions>, and <in mixed actions> these <conditions> are voluntary. But what sort of thing should be chosen as the price of what <good> is not easy to answer, since there are many differences in particular <conditions>.

10   But suppose someone says that pleasant things and fine things force us, since they are outside us and compel us. It will follow that for him everything is forced, since everyone in every action aims at something fine or pleasant.

Moreover, if we are forced and unwilling to act, we find it painful; but if something pleasant or fine is its cause, we do it with pleasure.

It is ridiculous, then, for <our opponent> to ascribe responsibility to
15   external <causes> and not to himself, when he is easily snared by such things; and ridiculous to take responsibility for fine actions himself, but to hold pleasant things responsible for his shameful actions.

What is forced, then, would seem to be what has its principle outside the person forced, who contributes nothing.

Everything caused by ignorance is nonvoluntary, but what is involun-
20   tary also causes pain and regret. For if someone's action was caused by ignorance, but he now has no objection to the action, he has done it neither willingly, since he did not know₀ what it was, nor unwillingly, since he now feels no pain. Hence, among those who act because of ignorance, the agent who now regrets his action seems to be unwilling, while the agent with no regrets may be called nonwilling, since he is another case—for since he is different, it is better if he has his own special name.

25   Further, action caused by ignorance would seem to be different from action done in ignorance. For if the agent is drunk or angry, his action seems to be caused by drunkenness or anger, not by ignorance, though it is done in ignorance, not in knowledge.

<This ignorance does not make an action involuntary.> Certainly every vicious person is ignorant of the actions he must do or avoid, and
30   this sort of error makes people unjust, and in general bad. But talk of

involuntary action is not meant to apply to <this> ignorance of what is beneficial.[4]

For the cause of involuntary action is not <this> ignorance in the decision, which causes vice; it is not <in other words> ignorance of the universal, since that is a cause for blame. Rather, the cause is ignorance   *1111a* of the particulars which the action consists in and is concerned with; for these allow both pity and pardon, since an agent acts involuntarily if he is ignorant of one of these particulars.

Presumably, then, it is not a bad idea to define these particulars, and say what they are, and how many. They are: (1) who is doing it; (2) what he is doing; (3) about what or to what he is doing it; (4) sometimes   *5* also what he is doing with it—with the instrument, for example; (5) for what result—safety, for example; (6) in what way—gently or hard, for example.

Now certainly someone could not be ignorant of *all* of these unless he were mad. Nor, clearly, (1) could he be ignorant of who is doing it, since he could hardly be ignorant of himself. But (2) he might be ignorant of what he is doing, as when someone says that <the secret> slipped out while he was speaking, or, as Aeschylus said about the mysteries, that he did not know it was forbidden to reveal it; or, like the person with   *10* the catapult, that he let it go when he <only> wanted to demonstrate it. (3) Again, he might think that his son is an enemy, as Merope did; or (4) that the barbed spear has a button on it, or that the stone is pumice-stone. (5) By giving someone a drink to save his life we might kill him; (6) and wanting to touch someone, as they do in sparring, we might   *15* wound him.

There is ignorance about all of these <particulars> that the action consists in. Hence someone who was ignorant of one of these seems to have done an action unwillingly, especially when he was ignorant of the more important of them; these seem to be (2) what he is doing, and (5) the result for which he does it.

Hence it is action called involuntary with reference to *this* sort of   *20* ignorance <that we meant when we said that> the agent must, in addition, feel pain and regret for his action.

Since, then, what is involuntary is what is forced or is caused by ignorance, what is involuntary seems to be what has its principle in the agent himself when he knows the particulars that the action consists in.

---

4. **But talk of involuntary . . .:** Probably 'ignorance of what is beneficial', 'ignorance in the decision' and 'ignorance of the universal' all refer to the same thing. Aristotle is thinking of someone whose anger makes him think it is all right to shoot the offender, not of someone whose anger blinds him to the fact that he is shooting, or that he is shooting this person.

25   <Our definition is sound.> For, presumably, it is not correct to say
that action caused by emotion or appetite is involuntary.

For, first of all, on this view none of the other animals will ever act
voluntarily; nor will children. <But clearly they do.>

Next, among all the actions caused by appetite or emotion do we do
none of them voluntarily? Or do we do the fine actions voluntarily and
the shameful involuntarily? Surely <the second answer> is ridiculous
when one and the same thing <i.e., appetite or emotion> causes <both

30   fine and shameful actions>. And presumably it is also absurd to say
<as the first answer implies> that things we ought to desire are involun-
tary; and in fact we ought both to be angry at some things and to have
appetite for some things—for health and learning, for instance.

Again, what is involuntary seems to be painful, whereas what expresses our appetite seems to be pleasant.

Moreover, how are errors that express emotion any less voluntary

1111b   than those that express rational calculation? For both sorts of errors are
to be avoided; and since nonrational feelings seem to be no less human
<than rational calculation>, actions resulting from emotion or appetite
are also proper to a human being; it is absurd, then, to regard them as
involuntary.

[DECISION]

2

5   Now that we have defined what is voluntary and what involuntary, the
next task is to discuss decision; for decision seems to be most proper to
virtue, and to distinguish characters from one another better than actions
do.

Decision, then, is apparently voluntary, but not the same as what is
voluntary, which extends more widely. For children and the other animals share in what is voluntary, but not in decision; and the actions we

10   do on the spur of the moment are said to be voluntary, but not to express
decision.

Those who say decision is appetite or emotion or wish or some sort
of belief would seem to be wrong.

For decision is not shared with nonrational <animals>, but appetite
and emotion are shared with them.

15   Further, the incontinent person acts on appetite, not on decision, but
the continent person does the reverse and acts on decision, not on
appetite.

Again, appetite is contrary to decision, but not to appetite.

Further, appetite's concern is what is pleasant and what is painful,
but neither of these is the concern of decision.

Still less is emotion decision; for actions caused by emotion seem least of all to express decision.

But further, it is not wish either, though it is apparently close to it.   20

For, first, we do not decide to do what is impossible, and anyone claiming to decide to do it would seem a fool; but we do wish for what is impossible—for immortality, for instance—as well <as for what is possible>.

Further, we wish <not only for results we can achieve>, but also for results that are <possible, but> not achievable through our own agency—victory for some actor or athlete, for instance. But what we   25 decide to do is never anything of that sort, but what we think would come about through our own agency.

Again, we wish for the end more <than for what promotes it>, but we decide to do what promotes the end.[5] We wish, for instance, to be healthy, but decide to do what will make us healthy; and we wish to be happy, and say so, but could not appropriately say we decide to be happy, since in   30 general what we decide to do would seem to be what is up to us.

Nor is it belief.

For, first, belief seems to be about everything, no less about what is eternal and what is impossible <for us> than about what is up to us.

Moreover, beliefs are divided into true and false, not into good and bad, but decisions are divided into good and bad more than into true and false.

Now presumably no one even claims that decision is the same as   1112a belief in general. But it is not the same as any kind of belief either.

For it is our decisions to do what is good or bad, not our beliefs, that make the characters we have.

Again, we decide to take or avoid something good or bad. We believe   5 what it is, whom it benefits or how; but we do not exactly believe to take or avoid.

Further, decision is praised more for deciding on what is right, whereas belief is praised for believing rightly.

Moreover, we decide on something <even> when we know$_0$ most completely that it is good; but <what> we believe <is> what we do not quite know.

Again, those who make the best decisions do not seem to be the same as those with the best beliefs; on the contrary, some seem to have better   10 beliefs, but to make the wrong decisions because of vice.

We can agree that decision follows or implies belief. But that is irrelevant, since it is not the question we are asking; our question is whether decision is the *same* as some sort of belief.

---

5. **what promotes the end**: Lit. 'things toward the end', *ta pros to telos*.

15   Then what, or what sort of thing, is decision, since it is none of the things mentioned? Well, apparently it is voluntary, but not everything voluntary is decided. Then perhaps what is decided is the result of prior deliberation. For decision involves reason and thought, and even the name itself would seem to indicate that <what is decided, *prohaireton*> is chosen <*haireton*> before <*pro*> other things.

[*DELIBERATION*]

3

20   But do we deliberate about everything, and is everything open to deliberation, or is there no deliberation about some things? By 'open to deliberation', presumably, we should mean what someone with some sense, not some fool or madman, might deliberate about.
      Now no one deliberates about eternal things—about the universe, for instance, or about the incommensurability of the sides and the diagonal;
25   nor about things that are in movement but always come about the same way, either from necessity or by nature or by some other cause—the solstices, for instance, or the rising of the stars; nor about what happens different ways at different times—droughts and rains, for instance; nor
30   about what results from fortune—the finding of a treasure, for instance.[6] For none of these results could be achieved through our agency.
      We deliberate about what is up to us, i.e., about the actions we can do; and this is what is left <besides the previous cases>. For causes
33   seem to include nature, necessity and fortune, but besides them mind and everything <operating> through human agency.
28   However, we do not deliberate about all human affairs; no Spartan,
29   for instance, deliberates about how the Scythians might have the best
33   political system. Rather, each group of human beings deliberates about the actions *they* can do.
1112b   Now there is no deliberation about the sciences that are exact and self-sufficient, as, for instance, about letters, since we are in no doubt about how to write them <in spelling a word>. Rather, we deliberate about what results through our agency, but in different ways on different
5   occasions, as, for instance, about questions of medicine and money-making; more about navigation than about gymnastics, to the extent that it is less exactly worked out, and similarly with other <crafts>; and more about beliefs[7] than about sciences, since we are more in doubt about them.

6. **treasure, for instance**: Here the mss (followed by OCT) have b28–29 'However, we do not . . . best political system', which we have placed after b33 below.

7. **beliefs**: Read *doxas*. OCT: 'crafts'.

Deliberation concerns what is usually <one way rather than another>, where the outcome is unclear and the right way to act is undefined.   *10* And we enlist partners in deliberation on large issues when we distrust our own ability to discern <the right answer>.

We deliberate not about ends,[8] but about what promotes ends; a doctor, for instance, does not deliberate about whether he will cure, or an orator about whether he will persuade, or a politician about whether he will produce good order, or any other <expert> about the end <that   *15* his science aims at>.

Rather, we first lay down the end, and then examine the ways and means to achieve it. If it appears that any of several <possible> means will reach it, we consider which of them will reach it most easily and most finely; and if only one <possible> means reaches it, we consider how that means will reach it, and how the means itself is reached, until we come to the first cause, the last thing to be discovered.

For a deliberator would seem to inquire and analyze in the way de-   *20* scribed, as though analysing a diagram.[9] <The comparison is apt, since>, apparently, all deliberation is inquiry, though not all inquiry— in mathematics, for instance—is deliberation. And the last thing <found> in the analysis is the first that comes to be.

If we encounter an impossible step—for instance, we need money   *25* but cannot raise it—we desist; but if the action appears possible, we undertake it. What is possible is what we could achieve through our agency <including what our friends could achieve for us>; for what our friends achieve is, in a way, achieved through our agency, since the principle is in us. <In crafts> we sometimes look for instruments, some- times <for the way> to use them; so also in other cases we sometimes   *30* look for the means to the end, sometimes for the proper use of the means or for the means to that proper use.

As we have said, then, a human being would seem to be the principle of action; deliberation is about the actions he can do; and actions are for the sake of other things; hence we deliberate about what promotes an end, not about the end.

Nor do we deliberate about particulars, about whether this is a loaf,   *1113a* for instance, or is cooked the right amount; for these are questions for perception, and if we keep on deliberating at each stage we shall go on without end.

What we deliberate about is the same as what we decide to do, except

---

8. **not about ends**: See 1111b27, *Rhet.* 1355b10.

9. **analysing a diagram**: The geometer considers how to construct a complex figure by analysing it into simpler figures, until he finds the first one that he should draw.

that by the time we decide to do it, it is definite; for what we decide to
5   do is what we have judged <to be right> as a result of deliberation.
For each of us stops inquiring how to act as soon as he traces the principle
to himself, and within himself to the dominant part; for this is the part
that decides. This is also clear from the ancient political systems described
by Homer; there the kings would first decide and then announce their
decision to the people.
10   We have found, then, that what we decide to do is whatever action
among those up to us we deliberate about and desire to do. Hence also
decision will be deliberative desire to do an action that is up to us; for
when we have judged <that it is right> as a result of deliberation, our
desire to do it expresses our wish.[10]

So much, then, for an outline of the sort of thing decision is about;
it is about what promotes the end.

[RATIONAL WISH]

4

15   Wish, we have said, is for the end. But to some it seems that wish is
for the good, to others that it is for the apparent good.[11]
For those who say the good is what is wished, it follows that what
someone wishes if he chooses incorrectly is not wished at all. For if it
is wished, then <on this view> it is good; but what he wishes is in fact
20   bad, if it turns out that way. <Hence what he wishes is not wished,
which is self-contradictory.>
For those, on the other hand, who say the apparent good is wished, it
follows that there is nothing wished by nature. To each person what is
wished is what seems <good to him>; but different things, and indeed
contrary things, if it turns out that way, appear good to different people.
<Hence contrary things will be wished and nothing will be wished by
nature.>
If, then, these views do not satisfy us, should we say that, without
qualification and in reality, what is wished is the good, but to each
person what is wished is the apparent good?
25   To the excellent person, then, what is wished will be what is wished
in reality, while to the base person what is wished is whatever it turns
out to be <that appears good to him>. Similarly in the case of bodies,

---

10. **expresses our wish**: Read *boulēsin*. OCT: *bouleusin*, 'deliberation'.

11. **Wish . . . apparent good**: 'Wished' (*boulēton*, cf. CHOICEWORTHY) may mean
(a) what is wished or (b) what deserves to be wished. The proper object of
wish—i.e., the suitable object for the well-informed person—is the good, just
as what is known by nature (1095b3) is what the fully informed person thinks
he knows.

really healthy things are healthy to people in good condition, while other things are healthy to sickly people, and the same is true of what is bitter, sweet, hot, heavy and so on.

For the excellent person judges each sort of thing correctly, and in   *30* each case what is true appears to him. For each state <of character> has its own special <view of> what is fine and pleasant, and presumably the excellent person is far superior because he sees what is true in each case, being a sort of standard and measure of what is fine and pleasant.[12]

In the many, however, pleasure would seem to cause deception, since   *1113b* it appears good when it is not; at any rate, they choose what is pleasant because they assume it is good, and avoid pain because they assume it is evil.

[*VIRTUE AND VICE ARE IN OUR POWER*]

5

We have found, then, that we wish for the end, and deliberate and decide about what promotes it; hence the actions concerned with what   *5* promotes the end will express a decision and will be voluntary. Now the activities of the virtues are concerned with <what promotes the end>; hence virtue is also up to us, and so is vice.

For when acting is up to us, so is not acting, and when No is up to us, so is Yes. Hence if acting, when it is fine, is up to us, then not acting, when it is shameful, is also up to us; and if not acting, when it is fine, is up to   *10* us, then acting, when it is shameful, is also up to us. Hence if doing, and likewise not doing, fine or shameful actions is up to us; and if, as we saw, <doing or not doing them> is <what it is> to be a good or bad person;[13] then it follows that being decent or base is up to us.

The claim that no one is willingly bad or unwillingly blessed would   *15* seem to be partly true but partly false. For while certainly no one is unwillingly blessed, vice is voluntary. If it is not, we must dispute the conclusion just reached, that a human being originates and fathers his own actions as he fathers his children. But if our conclusion appears true, and we cannot refer <actions> back to other principles beyond   *20* those in ourselves, then it follows that whatever has its principle in us is itself up to us and voluntary.

There would seem to be testimony in favor of our view not only in what each of us does as a private citizen, but also in what legislators themselves do. For they impose corrective treatments and penalties on

12. **standard and measure of what is fine and pleasant**: See PROTAGORAS.

13. **and if . . . person**: Lit. 'and being good and bad people was this'. If Aristotle is right, then 'this' must refer to more than simply doing the right actions, since being virtuous requires the further conditions described in ii 4.

25   anyone who does vicious actions, unless his action is forced or is caused
      by ignorance that he is not responsible for; and they honor anyone who
      does fine actions; they assume that they will encourage the one and
      restrain the other. But no one encourages us to do anything that is not
      up to us and voluntary; people assume it is pointless to persuade us not
      to get hot or distressed or hungry or anything else of that sort, since
      persuasion will not stop it happening to us.

30   Indeed, legislators also impose corrective treatments for the ignorance
      itself,[14] if the person seems to be responsible for the ignorance. A drunk,
      for instance, pays a double penalty; for the principle is in him, since he
      controls whether he gets drunk, and his getting drunk is responsible
      for his ignorance.
            They also impose corrective treatment on someone who <does a
      vicious action> in ignorance of some provision of law that he is required
1114a to know$_e$ and that is not hard <to know>. And they impose it in other
      cases likewise for any other ignorance that seems to be caused by the
      agent's inattention; they assume it is up to him not to be ignorant, since
      he controls whether he pays attention.
            But presumably his character makes him inattentive. Still, he is himself
5   responsible for having this character, by living carelessly, and similarly
      for being unjust by cheating, or being intemperate by passing his time
      in drinking and the like; for each type of activity produces the corres-
      ponding character. This is clear from those who train for any contest or
10   action, since they continually practise the appropriate activities. <Only>
      a totally insensible person would not know$_g$ that each type of activity is
12   the source of the corresponding state;hence if someone does what he
13   knows will make him unjust, he is willingly unjust.[15]
11   Moreover, it is unreasonable for someone doing injustice not to wish
12   to be unjust, or for someone doing intemperate action not to wish to be
13   intemperate. This does not mean, however, that if he is unjust and
      wishes to stop, he will stop and will be just.
15   For neither does a sick person recover his health <simply by wish-
      ing>; nonetheless, he is sick willingly, by living incontinently and dis-
      obeying the doctors, if that was how it happened. At that time, then,
      he was free not to be sick, though no longer free once he has let himself
      go, just as it was up to us to throw a stone, since the principle was in
      us, though we can no longer take it back once we have thrown it.
20   Similarly, then, the person who is <now> unjust or intemperate was
      originally free not to acquire this character, so that he has it willingly,

14. **for the ignorance itself**: Aristotle supplements the treatment of ignorance
of fact at 1110b18–1111a2.

15. **hence if someone . . . willingly unjust**: The mss (followed by OCT) have
this after 'unjust or intemperate' in the next paragraph.

though once he has acquired the character, he is no longer free not to have it <now>.

It is not only vices of the soul that are voluntary; vices of the body are also voluntary for some people, and we actually censure them. For we never censure someone if nature causes his ugliness; but if his lack of training or attention causes it, we do censure him. The same is true for weakness of maiming; for everyone would pity, not reproach someone if he were blind by nature or because of a disease or a wound, but would censure him if his heavy drinking or some other form of intemperance made him blind.

Hence bodily vices that are up to us are censured, while those not up to us are not censured. If so, then in the other cases also the vices that are censured will be up to us.

But someone may say, 'Everyone aims at the apparent good, and does not control how it appears; on the contrary, his character controls how the end appears to him.'

First, then, if each person is in some way responsible for his own state <of character>, then he is also himself in some way responsible for how <the end> appears.

Suppose, on the other hand, that no one is responsible for acting badly, but one does so because one is ignorant of the end, and thinks this is the way to gain what is best for oneself. One's aiming at the end will not be one's own choice, but one needs a sort of natural, inborn sense of sight, to judge finely and to choose what is really good. Whoever by nature has this sense in a fine condition has a good nature. For this sense is the greatest and finest thing, and one cannot acquire it or learn it from another; rather, its natural character determines his later condition, and when it is naturally good and fine, that is true and complete good nature.

If all this is true, then, surely virtue will be no more voluntary than vice? For how the end appears is laid down, by nature or in whatever way, for the good and the bad person alike, and they trace all the other things back to the end in doing whatever actions they do.

Suppose, then, that it is not nature that makes the end appear however it appears to each person, but something also depends on him; or, alternatively, suppose that <how> the end <appears> is natural, but virtue is voluntary because the virtuous person does the other things voluntarily. In either case vice will be no less voluntary than virtue; for the bad person, no less than the good, is responsible for his own actions, even if not for <how> the end <appears>.[16]

Now the virtues, as we say, are voluntary, since in fact we are our-

25

30

1114b

5

10

15

20

---

16. **for the bad. . . .**: Lit. 'for similarly to the bad person also belongs the because of (*dia*) himself in the actions, even if not in the end'.

selves in a way jointly responsible[17] for our states of character, and by having the sort of character we have we lay down the sort of end we
25 do. Hence the vices will also be voluntary, since the same is true of them.

We have now discussed the virtues in general. We have described their genus in outline; they are means, and they are states. Certain actions produce them, and they cause us to do these same actions, expressing the virtues themselves, in the way that correct reason prescribes.[18] They are up to us and voluntary.

30 Actions and states, however, are not voluntary in the same way. For we are in control of actions from the beginning to the end, when we
1115a know$_o$ the particulars. With states, however, we are in control of the beginning, but do not know$_g$, any more than with sicknesses, what the cumulative effect of particular actions will be; nonetheless, since it was up to us to exercise a capacity either this way or another way, states are voluntary.

5 Let us now take up the virtues again, and discuss each singly. Let us say what they are, what sorts of thing they are concerned with, and how they are concerned with them; it will also be clear at the same time how many virtues there are.

[THE INDIVIDUAL VIRTUES OF CHARACTER]

[BRAVERY]

6

First let us discuss bravery.[19] We have already made it apparent that there is a mean about feeling of fear and confidence. What we fear, clearly, is what is frightening, and such things are, speaking without qualification, bad things; hence people define[20] fear as expectation of something bad.

10 Now while we certainly fear all bad things—for instance, bad reputation, poverty, sickness, friendlessness, death, they do not all seem to concern the brave person. For fear of some bad things, such as bad reputation, for instance, is actually right and fine, and lack of fear is

17. **jointly responsible**: We are not the sole CAUSES of our states; nature and upbringing contribute also.

18. **in the way . . . prescribes**: The mss, followed by OCT, place this at the end of the next sentence.

19. The discussion of bravery provides an example of Aristotle's treatment of the individual virtues of character.

20. **people define**: See Plato, *Prot.* 358d.

disgraceful; for if someone fears bad reputation, he is decent and properly prone to shame, and if he has no fear of it, he has no feeling of disgrace. Some, however, call this fearless person brave, by a transference <of   15 the name>, since he has some similarity to the brave person, in that the brave person is also a type of fearless person.

Presumably, though, it is wrong to fear poverty or sickness or, in general, <bad things> that are not the results of vice or caused by ourselves; still, someone who is fearless about these is not thereby brave. He also is called brave by similarity, since some people who are cowardly   20 in the dangers of war are nonetheless generous, and face with confidence the <danger of> losing money.

Again, if someone is afraid of committing wanton aggression on children or women, or of being envious or anything of that sort, that does not make him cowardly. Nor again, if someone is confident when he is going to be whipped <for his crimes> does that make him brave.

Then what sorts of frightening conditions concern the brave person?   25 Surely the most frightening; for no one stands firmer against terrifying conditions. Now death is most frightening of all, since it is a boundary, and when someone is dead nothing beyond it seems either good or bad for him any more. Still, not even death in all conditions—on the sea, for instance, or in sickness, seems to be the brave person's concern.

In what conditions, then, is death his concern? surely in the finest   30 conditions. Now such deaths are those in war, since they occur in the greatest and finest danger; and this judgment is endorsed by the honors given in cities and by monarchs. Hence someone is called brave to the fullest extent if he is intrepid in facing a fine death and the immediate dangers that bring death—and this is above all true of the dangers of   35 war.

Certainly the brave person is also intrepid on the sea and in sickness,   1115b but not in the same way as seafarers are. For he has given up hope of safety, and objects to this sort of death <with nothing fine in it>, but seafarers' experience makes them hopeful. Moreover, we act like brave men on occasions when we can use our strength, or when it is fine to   5 be killed; and neither of these is true when we perish on the sea.

7

Now what is frightening is not the same for everyone. We do say, however, that some things are too frightening for a human being to resist; these, then, are frightening for everyone, at least for everyone with any sense. What is frightening, but not irresistible for a human being, varies in its seriousness and degree; and the same is true of what   10 inspires confidence.

Now the brave person is unperturbed, as far as a human being can be. Hence, though he will fear even the sorts of things that are not irresistible, he will stand firm against them, in the right way, as prescribed by reason, for the sake of what is fine, since this is the end aimed at by virtue.

15 It is possible to be more or less afraid of these frightening things, and also possible to be afraid of what is not frightening as though it were frightening. The cause of error may be fear of the wrong thing, or in the wrong way, or at the wrong time, or something of that sort; and the same is true for things that inspire confidence.

Hence whoever stands firm against the right things and fears the right things, for the right end, in the right way, at the right time, and is correspondingly confident, is the brave person; for the brave person's actions and feelings reflect what something is worth and what reason <prescribes>.

20 Every activity aims at actions expressing its state of character, and to the brave person bravery is fine; hence the end it aims at is also fine, since each thing is defined by its end. The brave person, then, aims at what is fine when he expresses bravery in his standing firm and acting.

Consider now those who go to excess.

25 The person who is excessively fearless has no name—we said earlier that many states have no names. He would be some sort of madman, or incapable of feeling distress, if he feared nothing, neither earthquake nor waves, as they say about the Celts.

The person who is excessively confident about frightening things is 30 rash. The rash person also seems to be a boaster, and a pretender to bravery. At any rate, the attitude to frightening things that the brave person really has is the attitude that the rash person wants to appear to have; hence he imitates the brave person where he can. That is why most of them are rash cowards; for rash though they are on these <occa- 1116a7 sions for imitation>, they do not stand firm against anything frightening. 8 Moreover, rash people are impetuous, and wish for dangers before they 9 arrive, but shrink from them when they come; brave people, on the contrary, are eager when in action, but keep quiet until then.

1115b34 The person who is excessively afraid is the coward, since he fears the 35 wrong things, and in the wrong way, and so on. Though indeed he is 1116a also deficient in confidence, it is more his excessive pain that clearly distinguishes him. Hence, since he is afraid of everything, he is a despairing sort. The brave person, on the contrary, is hopeful, since <he is confident and> confidence is proper to a hopeful person.

5 Hence the coward, the rash person and the brave person are all concerned with the same things, but have different states related to 7 them; the others are excessive or defective, but the brave person has the intermediate and right state.

10 As we have said, then, bravery is a mean about what inspires confi-

dence and about what is frightening in the conditions we have described; it chooses and stands firm because that is fine or because anything else is shameful. Dying to avoid poverty or erotic passion or something painful is proper to a coward, not to a brave person; for trying to avoid   *15* burdens is softness, and such a person stands firm <in the face of death> to avoid an evil, not because it is fine.

* * * * * * *

Book V¹

[JUSTICE]

[THE DEFINITION OF JUSTICE]

1

The questions we must examine about justice and injustice are these: *1129a* What sorts of actions are they concerned with? What sort of mean is   *5* justice? What are the extremes between which justice is intermediate? Let us examine them by the same type of investigation that we used in the topics discussed before.

We see that the state everyone means in speaking of justice is the state that makes us doers of just actions, that makes us do justice and wish what is just. In the same way they mean by injustice the state that   *10* makes us do injustice and wish what is unjust. Let us also, then, <follow the common beliefs and> begin by assuming this in outline.

For what is true of sciences and capacities is not true of states. For while one and the same capacity or science seems to have contrary activities, a state that is a contrary has no contrary activities. Health, for   *15* instance, only makes us do healthy actions, not their contraries; for we say we are walking in a healthy way if <and only if> we are walking in the way a healthy person would.

Often one of a pair of contrary states is recognized from the other contrary; and often the states are recognized from their subjects. For if, for instance, the good state is evident, the bad state becomes evident   *20* too; and moreover the good state becomes evident from the things that have it, and the things from the state. For if, for instance, the good state is thickness of flesh, then the bad state will necessarily be thinness of flesh, and the thing that produces the good state will be what produces thickness of flesh.

It follows, usually, that if one of a pair of contraries is spoken of in   *25*

1. The three books *EN* v–vii are also, according to manuscripts of *EN* and *EE*, the three books *EE* iv–vi.

more ways than one, so is the other; if, for instance, what is just is spoken of in more ways than one, so is what is unjust.

Now it would seem that justice and injustice are both spoken of in more ways than one, but since the different ways are closely related, their homonymy is unnoticed, and is less clear than it is with distant
30   homonyms where the distance in appearance is wide (for instance, the bone below an animal's neck and what we lock doors with are called keys homonymously).

Let us, then, find the number of ways an unjust person is spoken of. Both the lawless person and the greedy and unfair person seem to be unjust; and so, clearly, both the lawful and the fair[2] person will be just.
1129b   Hence what is just will be both what is lawful and what is fair, and what is unjust will be both what is lawless and what is unfair.

Since the unjust person is greedy, he will be concerned with goods[3]— not with all goods, but only with those involved in good and bad fortune, goods which are, <considered> without qualification, always good, but for this or that person not always good. Though human beings pray for
5   these and pursue them, they are wrong; the right thing is to pray that what is good without qualification will also be good for us, but to choose <only> what is good for us.

Now the unjust person <who chooses these goods> does not choose more in every case; in the case of what is bad without qualification he
10   actually chooses less. But since what is less bad also seems to be good in a way, and greed aims at more of what is good, he seems to be greedy. In fact he is unfair; for unfairness includes <all these actions>, and is a common feature <of his choice of the greater good and of the lesser evil>.

[GENERAL JUSTICE]

Since, as we saw, the lawless person is unjust and the lawful person is just, it clearly follows that whatever is lawful is in some way just;[4] for the provisions of legislative science are lawful, and we say that each of
15   them is just. Now in every matter they deal with the laws aim either at

---

2. **fair**: *ison*. See EQUAL.

3. **goods**: On these goods see GOOD #3. Wealth, e.g., is good for a human being. By this Aristotle means not that it is good for every human being, but only that a human being can use wealth well, and if he uses it well, it will promote his happiness. See WITHOUT QUALIFICATION #3.

4. **whatever is lawful . . .**: Aristotle does not say here that every system of positive LAW is just. His reference to 'legislative science' ('science' supplied) shows that he has in mind only correct laws.

the common benefit of all, or at the benefit of those in control, whose control rests on virtue or on some other such basis.[5] And so in one way what we call just is whatever produces and maintains happiness and its parts for a political community.

Now the law instructs us to do the actions of a brave person—not to   20
leave the battle-line, for instance, or to flee, or to throw away our weapons; of a temperate person—not to commit adultery or wanton aggression; of a mild person—not to strike or revile another; and similarly requires actions that express the other virtues, and prohibits those that express the vices. The correctly established law does this correctly, and   25
the less carefully framed one does this worse.

This type of justice, then, is complete virtue, not complete virtue without qualification but complete virtue in relation to another. And this is why justice often seems to be supreme among the virtues, and 'neither the evening star nor the morning star is so marvellous', and the proverb says 'And in justice all virtue is summed up.'   30

Moreover, justice is complete virtue to the highest degree because it is the complete exercise of complete virtue. And it is the complete exercise because the person who has justice is able to exercise virtue in relation to another, not only in what concerns himself; for many are able to exercise virtue in their own concerns but unable in what relates to another.

And hence Bias seems to have been correct in saying that ruling will   1130a
reveal the man, since a ruler is automatically related to another, and in a community. And for the same reason justice is the only virtue that seems to be another person's good,[6] because it is related to another; for   5
it does what benefits another, either the ruler or the fellow-member of the community.

The worst person, therefore, is the one who exercises his vice toward himself and his friends as well <as toward others>. And the best person is not the one who exercises virtue <only> toward himself, but the one who <also> exercises it in relation to another, since this is a difficult task.

This type of justice, then, is the whole, not a part, of virtue, and the   10
injustice contrary to it is the whole, not a part, of vice.

At the same time our discussion makes clear the difference between virtue and this type of justice. For virtue is the same as justice, but what it is to be virtue is not the same as what it is to be justice. Rather, insofar as virtue is related to another, it is justice, and insofar as it is a certain sort of state without qualification, it is virtue.

5. **either at . . . such basis**: This refers to different POLITICAL SYSTEMS.
6. **another person's good**: See Plato, *Rep.* 343c.

[*SPECIAL JUSTICE*]

2

15   But we are looking for the type of justice, since we say there is one, that consists in a part of virtue, and correspondingly for the type of injustice that is a part <of vice>.

Here is evidence that there is this type of justice and injustice:

First, if someone's activities express the other vices—if, for instance, cowardice made him throw away his shield, or irritability made him revile someone, or ungenerosity made him fail to help someone with
20   money—what he does is unjust, but not greedy. But when one acts from greed, in many cases his action expresses none of these vices—certainly not all of them; but it still expresses some type of wickedness, since we blame him, and <in particular> it expresses injustice. Hence there is another type of injustice that is a part of the whole, and a way for a thing to be unjust that is a part of the whole that is contrary to law.
25   Moreover, if A commits adultery for profit and makes a profit, while B commits adultery because of his appetite, and spends money on it to his own loss, B seems intemperate rather than greedy, while A seems unjust, not intemperate. Clearly, then, this is because A acts to make a profit.
30   Further, we can refer every other unjust action to some vice—to intemperance if he committed adultery, to cowardice if he deserted his comrade in the battle-line, to anger if he struck someone. But if he made an <unjust> profit, we can refer it to no other vice except injustice.

Hence evidently (a) there is another type of injustice, special injustice, apart from the whole of injustice; and (b) it is synonymous with the
1130b   whole, since the definition is in the same genus. For (b) both have their area of competence in relation to another. But (a) special injustice is concerned with honor or wealth or safety, or whatever single name will include all these, and aims at the pleasure that results from making a
5   profit; but the concern of injustice as a whole is whatever concerns the excellent person.

Clearly, then, there is more than one type of justice, and there is another type apart from <the type that is> the whole of virtue; but we must still grasp what it is, and what sort of thing it is.

What is unjust is divided into what is lawless and what is unfair, and
10   what is just into what is lawful and what is fair. The <general> injustice previously described, then, is concerned with what is lawless. But what is unfair is not the same as what is lawless, but related to it as part to whole, since whatever is unfair is lawless, but not everything lawless is unfair. Hence also the type of injustice and the way for a thing to be
15   unjust <that expresses lawlessness>, but differ as parts from wholes. For this injustice <as unfairness> is a part of the whole of injustice, and similarly justice <as fairness> is a part of the whole of justice.

Hence we must describe special <as well as general> justice and injustice, and equally this way for a thing to be just or unjust.

Let us, then, set to one side the type of justice and injustice that   20
corresponds to the whole of virtue, justice being the exercise of the whole of virtue, and injustice of the whole of vice, in relation to another.

And it is evident how we must distinguish the way for a thing to be just or unjust that expresses this type of justice and injustice; for the majority of lawful actions, we might say, are the actions resulting from virtue as a whole. For the law instructs us to express each virtue, and forbids us to express each vice, in how we live. Moreover, the actions   25
producing the whole of virtue are the lawful actions that the laws pre- scribe for education promoting the common good.

We must wait till later,[7] however, to determine whether the education that makes an individual an unqualifiedly good man is a task for political science or for another science; for, presumably, being a good man is not the same as being every sort of good citizen.[8]

Special justice, however, and the corresponding way for something   30
to be just <must be divided>.

One species is found in the distribution of honors or wealth or any- thing else that can be divided among members of a community who share in a political system; for here it is possible for one member to have a share equal or unequal to another's.

Another species concerns rectification in transactions. This species has   1131a
two parts, since one sort of transaction is voluntary, and one involuntary. Voluntary transactions include selling, buying, lending, pledging, rent- ing, depositing, hiring out—these are called voluntary because the princi-   5
ple of these transactions is voluntary. Some involuntary ones are secret, such as theft, adultery, poisoning, pimping, slave-deception, murder by treachery, false witness; others are forcible, such as assault, imprison- ment, murder, plunder, mutilation, slander, insult.

* * * * * * *

[NATURAL JUSTICE]

7

One part of what is politically just is natural, and the other part legal.[9]   1134b18
What is natural is what has the same validity everywhere alike, indepen-   20
dent of its seeming so or not. What is legal is what originally makes

7. **later**: See x 9, *Pol.* vii.

8. **being a good man . . .**: On this distinction see *Pol.* iii 4.

9. **One part . . . other part legal**: On LAW (here related to convention) and NATURE cf. 1094b16.

no difference <whether it is done> one way or another, but makes a difference whenever people have laid down the rule—that a mina is the price of a ransom, for instance, or that a goat rather than two sheep should be sacrificed; and also laws passed for particular cases—that sacrifices should be offered to Brasidas,[10] for instance; and enactments by decree.

25 Now it seems to some people that everything just is merely legal, since what is natural is unchangeable and equally valid everywhere— fire, for instance, burns both here and in Persia—while they see that what is just changes <from city to city>.

This is not so, though in a way it is so. With us, though presumably

30 not at all with the gods, there is such a thing as what is natural, but still all is changeable; despite the change there is such a thing as what is natural and what is not.

What sort of thing that <is changeable and hence> admits of being otherwise is natural, and what sort is not natural, but legal and conventional, if both natural and legal are changeable? It is clear in other cases also, and the same distinction <between the natural and the unchangeable> will apply; for the right hand, for instance, is naturally superior,

35 even though it is possible for everyone to become ambidextrous.

1135a The sorts of things that are just by convention and expediency are like measures. For measures for wine and for corn are not of equal size everywhere, but in wholesale markets they are bigger, and in retail smaller. Similarly, the things that are just by human <enactment> and

5 not by nature differ from place to place, since political systems also differ; still, only one system is by nature the best everywhere.

[SUMMARY ACCOUNT OF JUSTICE]

1133b29 We have now said what it is that is unjust and just. And now that we have defined them, it is clear that doing justice is intermediate between doing injustice and suffering injustice, since doing injustice is having too little.

1134a Justice is a mean, not as the other virtues are, but because it concerns an intermediate condition, while injustice concerns the extremes. Justice is the virtue that the just person is said to express in the just actions expressing his decision, distributing good things and bad, both between himself and others and between others. He does not award too much

5 of what is choiceworthy to himself and too little to his neighbor (and

10. **Brasidas**: A Spartan general who after his death received sacrifices in Amphipolis as a liberator. His cult is a strictly local observance initiated by decree (cf. 1137b29).

the reverse with what is harmful), but awards what is proportionately equal; and he does the same in distributing between others.

Injustice, on the other hand, is related <in the same way> to what is unjust. What is unjust is disproportionate excess and deficiency in what is beneficial or harmful; hence injustice is excess and deficiency because it concerns excess and deficiency. The unjust person awards   10
himself an excess of what is beneficial, <considered> without qualification, and a deficiency of what is harmful, and speaking as a whole, he acts similarly <in distributions between> others, but deviates from proportion in either direction. In an unjust action getting too little good is suffering injustice, and getting too much is doing injustice.

*   *   *   *   *   *   *

[DECENCY]

10

The next task is to discuss how decency is related to justice and how   1137a31
what is decent is related to what is just.

For on examination they appear as neither the same without qualification nor as states of different kinds. Sometimes we praise what is decent   35
and the decent person, so that even when we praise someone for other   1137b
things we transfer[11] the term 'decent' and use it instead of 'good', making
it clear that what is more decent is better.

And yet, sometimes, when we reason about the matter, it appears absurd for what is decent to be something beyond what is just, and still praiseworthy. For <apparently> either what is just is not excellent or what is decent is not excellent, if it is something other than what is just,   5
or else, if they are both excellent, they are the same.

These, then, are roughly the claims that raise the puzzle about what is decent; but in fact they are all correct in a way, and none is contrary to any other. For what is decent is better than one way of being just, but it is still just, and not better than what is just by being a different genus. Hence the same thing is just and decent, and while both are   10
excellent, what is decent is superior.

The puzzle arises because what is decent is just, but is not what is legally just, but a rectification of it. The reason is that all law is universal, but in some areas no universal rule can be correct; and so where a   15
universal rule has to be made, but cannot be correct, the law chooses the <universal rule> that is usually <correct>, well aware of the error

---

11. **transfer**: See HOMONYMY. As the *EN* itself often makes clear, it is common to use 'DECENT' to refer, by meiosis, to goodness in general. In this chapter he refers more narrowly to what is often called 'equity'.

being made. And the law is no less correct on this account; for the source
of the error is not the law or the legislator, but the nature of the object
itself, since that is what the subject matter[12] of actions is bound to be
like.

20   Hence whenever the law makes a universal rule, but in this particular
case what happens violates the <intended scope of> the universal rule,
here the legislator falls short, and has made an error by making an
unqualified rule. Then it is correct to rectify the deficiency; this is what
the legislator would have said himself if he had been present there, and
what he would have prescribed, had he known$_o$, in his legislation.

25   Hence what is decent is just, and better than a certain way of being
just—not better than what is unqualifiedly just, but better than the error
resulting from the omission of any condition <in the rule>. And this
is the nature of what is decent—rectification of law insofar as the universality of law makes it deficient.

    This is also the reason why not everything is guided by law. For on
some matters legislation is impossible, and so a decree[13] is needed. For
30 the standard applied to what is indefinite is itself indefinite, as the lead
standard is in Lesbian building, where it is not fixed, but adapts itself
to the shape of the stone; likewise, a decree is adapted to fit its objects.

    It is clear from this what is decent, and clear that it is just, and better
35 than a certain way of being just. It is also evident from this who the
1138a decent person is; for he is the one who decides for and does such actions,
not an exact stickler for justice in the bad way, but taking less than he
might even though he has the law on his side. This is the decent person,
and his state is decency; it is a sort of justice, and not some state different
from it.

* * * * * * *

BOOK VI

[VIRTUES OF THOUGHT]

[THE DOCTRINE OF THE MEAN, CORRECT REASON, AND
VIRTUES OF THOUGHT]

1

1138b18 Since we have said previously that we must choose the intermediate
20 condition, not the excess or the deficiency, and that the intermediate

---

12. **subject matter**: See 1094b12, 1098a28.
13. **decree**: See 1134b23, 1141b27.

condition is as correct reason says, let us now determine this <i.e., what it says>.¹

For in all the states of character we have mentioned, as well as in the others, there is a target which the person who has reason focuses on and so tightens or relaxes; and there is a definition of the means, which we say are between excess and deficiency because they express correct reason.   25

To say this is admittedly true, but it is not at all clear. For in other pursuits directed by a science it is equally true that we must labor and be idle neither too much nor too little, but the intermediate amount prescribed by correct reason. But knowing only this, we would be none   30 the wiser about, for instance, the medicines to be applied to the body, if we were told we must apply the ones that medical science prescribes and in the way that the medical scientist applies them.

Similarly, then, our account of the states of the soul must not only be true up to this point; we must also determine what correct reason is, i.e., what its definition is.

After we divided the virtues of the soul we said that some are virtues   35 of character and some of thought. And so, having finished our discussion   1139a of the virtues of character, let us now discuss the others as follows, after speaking first about the soul.

Previously, then, we said there are two parts of the soul, one that   5 has reason, and one nonrational. Now we should divide in the same way the part that has reason.

Let us assume there are two parts that have reason: one with which we study beings whose principles do not admit of being otherwise than they are, and one with which we study beings whose principles admit of being otherwise. For when the beings are of different kinds, the parts of the soul naturally suited to each of them are also of different kinds,   10 since the parts possess knowledge_g by being somehow similar and appropriate <to their objects>.

Let us call one of these the scientific part, and the other the rationally calculating part, since deliberating is the same as rationally calculating, and no one deliberates about what cannot be otherwise. Hence the rationally calculating part is one part of the part of the soul that has reason.   15

Hence we should find the best state of the scientific and the best state of the rationally calculating part; for this state is the virtue of each of them. And since something's virtue is relative to its own proper function² <we must consider the function of each part>.

1. **let us ... it says>**: The general formula in the account of the virtues needs to be made more precise; cf. 1103b21. 1107a1 has already suggested that INTELLI-GENCE is relevant.

2. **function**: See 1106a15.

2

There are three <capacities> in the soul—perception, understanding, desire—that control action and truth. Of these three perception clearly
20   originates no action, since beasts have perception, but no share in action.*

As assertion and denial are to thought, so pursuit and avoidance are to desire. Now virtue of character is a state that decides; and decision is a deliberative desire. If, then, the decision is excellent, the reason
25   must be true and the desire correct, so that what reason asserts is what desire pursues.

This, then, is thought and truth concerned with action. By contrast, when thought is concerned with study, not with action or production, its good or bad state consists <simply> in being true or false. For truth
30   is the function of whatever thinks; but the function of what thinks about action is truth agreeing with correct desire.

Now the principle* of an action—the source of motion,[3] not the action's goal—is decision, and the principle of decision is desire together with reason that aims at some goal. Hence decision requires understanding
35   and thought, and also a state of character, since doing well or badly in action requires both thought and character.

Thought by itself, however, moves nothing; what moves us is thought
1139b   aiming at some goal and concerned with action.[4] For this is the sort of thought that also originates productive thinking; for every producer in his production aims at some <further> goal, and the goal without qualification is not the product, which is only the <conditional> goal of some <production>, and aims at some <further> goal. <A goal without qualification is> what we achieve in *action*, since doing well in action is the goal.

Now desire is for the goal. Hence decision is either understanding
5   combined with desire or desire combined with thought; and what originates movement in this way is a human being.

We do not decide to do what is already past; no one decides, e.g., to have sacked Troy. For neither do we deliberate about what is past, but only about what will be and admits <of being or not being>; and what is past does not admit of not having happened. Hence Agathon is correct
10   to say 'Of this alone even a god is deprived—to make what is all done to have never happened.'

Hence the function of each of the understanding parts is truth; and so the virtue of each part will be the state that makes that part grasp the truth most of all.

3. **source of motion**: Aristotle refers to the efficient and final CAUSES.

4. **concerned with action**: Here *praxis* (see ACTION) refers to action done for its own sake, as explained in vi 4.

[SCIENTIFIC KNOWLEDGE]

3

Then let us begin over again, and discuss these states of the soul. Let   15
us say, then, that there are five states in which the soul grasps the
truth in its affirmation or denials. These are craft, scientific knowledge,
intelligence, wisdom and understanding; for belief and supposition
admit of being false.

What science is is evident from the following, if we must speak exactly
and not be guided by <mere> similarities.

For we all suppose that what we know scientifically does not even   20
admit of being otherwise; and whenever what admits of being otherwise
escapes observation, we do not notice whether it is or is not, <and hence
we do not know about it>. Hence what is known scientifically is by
necessity. Hence it is everlasting; for the things that are by unqualified
necessity are all everlasting, and everlasting things are ingenerable and
indestructible.

Further, every science seems to be teachable, and what is scientifically   25
knowable is learnable. But all teaching is from what is already known$_g$, as
we also say in the *Analytics*;[5] for some teaching is through induction, some
by deductive inference, <which both require previous knowledge>.

Induction <reaches> the principle, i.e., the universal, while deductive inference proceeds from the universal. Hence deductive inference   30
has principles from which it proceeds, but which are not themselves
<reached> by deductive inference. Hence they are <reached> by in-
duction.

Scientific knowledge, then, is a demonstrative state, and has all the
other features that in the *Analytics*[6] we add to the definition. For someone
has scientific knowledge when he has the appropriate sort of confidence,
and the principles are known$_g$ to him; for if they are not better known$_g$ to him
than the conclusion, he will have scientific knowledge only coincidentally.   35

So much for a definition of scientific knowledge.

*   *   *   *   *   *   *

[INTELLIGENCE]

5

To grasp what intelligence is we should first study the sort of people   1140a25
we call intelligent.

It seems proper, then, to an intelligent person to be able to deliberate

5. **all teaching** . . .: See *APo.* i 1.
6. *Analytics*: See *APo.* i 3.

finely about what is good and beneficial for himself, not about some restricted area—about what promotes health or strength, for instance—but about what promotes living well in general.[7]

30   A sign of this is the fact that we call people intelligent about some <restricted area> whenever they calculate well to promote some excellent end, in an area where there is no craft.[8] Hence where <living well> as a whole is concerned, the deliberative person will also be intelligent.

Now no one deliberates about what cannot be otherwise or about what cannot be achieved by his action. Hence, if science involves demonstration, but there is no demonstration of anything whose principles

35   admit of being otherwise, since every such thing itself admits of being
1140b otherwise; and if we cannot deliberate about what is by necessity; it follows that intelligence is not science nor yet craft-knowledge.[9] It is not science, because what is done in action admits of being otherwise; and it is not craft-knowledge, because action and production belong to different kinds.

5   The remaining possibility, then, is that intelligence is a state grasping the truth, involving reason, concerned with action about what is good or bad for a human being.

For production has its end beyond it; but action does not, since its end is doing well itself, <and doing well is the concern of intelligence>.

Hence Pericles and such people are the ones whom we regard as
10   intelligent, because they are able to study what is good for themselves and for human beings; and we think that household managers and politicians are such people.

This is also how we come to give temperance (*sophrosune*) its name, because we think that it preserves intelligence, (*sozousan ten phronesin*). This is the sort of supposition that it preserves. For the sort of supposition that is corrupted and perverted by what is pleasant or painful is not
15   every sort—not, for instance, the supposition that the triangle does or does not have two right angles—but suppositions about what is done in action.

For the principle of what is done in action is the goal it aims at; and if pleasure or pain has corrupted someone, it follows that the principle will not appear to him. Hence it will not be apparent that this must be

7. **promotes living well in general**: For 'promotes' (*pros*) see 1111b27n. The intelligent person begins with the very indefinite conception of the end as 'living well', and his deliberation shows him the sorts of actions and states that living well consists in.

8. **no craft**: See 1112a34, *Rhet.* 1357a1. Since intelligence is concerned with living well in general, it must be concerned with action, not with PRODUCTION; hence it cannot be a craft (see CRAFT #4).

9. **craft-knowledge**: Lit. just 'CRAFT'.

the goal and cause of all his choice and action; for vice corrupts the   *20*
principle.

Hence <since intelligence is what temperance preserves, and what
temperance preserves is a true supposition about action>, intelligence
must be a state grasping the truth, involving reason, and concerned
with action about human goods.

Moreover, there is virtue <or vice in the use> of craft, but not <in
the use> of intelligence. Further, in a craft, someone who makes errors
voluntarily is more choiceworthy; but with intelligence, as with the virtues, the reverse is true. Clearly, then, intelligence is a virtue, not craft-   *25*
knowledge.

There are two parts of the soul that have reason. Intelligence is a
virtue of one of them, of the part that has belief; for belief is concerned,
as intelligence is, with what admits of being otherwise.

Moreover, it is not only a state involving reason. A sign of this is the
fact that such a state can be forgotten, but intelligence cannot.

[*UNDERSTANDING*]

6

Scientific knowledge is supposition about universals, things that are   *30*
by necessity. Further, everything demonstrable and every science have
principles, since scientific knowledge involves reason.

Hence there can be neither scientific knowledge nor craft-knowledge
nor intelligence about the principles of what is scientifically known. For   *35*
what is scientifically known is demonstrable, <but the principles are
not>; and craft and intelligence are about what admits of being other-   *1141a*
wise. Nor is wisdom <exclusively> about principles; for it is proper to
the wise person to have a demonstration of some things.

<The states of the soul> by which we always grasp the truth and never
make mistakes, about what can or cannot be otherwise, are scientific   *5*
knowledge, intelligence, wisdom and understanding. But none of the
first three—intelligence, scientific knowledge, wisdom—is possible
about principles. The remaining possibility, then, is that we have understanding about principles.

[*WISDOM*]

7

We ascribe wisdom in crafts to the people who have the most exact[10]   *10*
expertise in the crafts; for instance, we call Pheidias a wise stone-worker

10. **exact**: i.e., complete and finished in detail. See EXACT #2.

and Polycleitus a wise bronze-worker, signifying nothing else by wisdom than excellence in a craft. But we also think some people are wise in general, not wise in some <restricted> area, or in some other <specific>
15 way, as Homer says in the *Margites*: 'The gods did not make him a digger or a ploughman or wise in anything else.' Clearly, then, wisdom is the most exact <form> of scientific knowledge.

Hence the wise person must not only know$_0$ what is derived from the principles of a science, but also grasp the truth about the principles. Therefore wisdom is understanding plus scientific knowledge; it is scientific knowledge of the most honorable things that has received <understanding as> its copingstone.

20 For it would be absurd for someone to think that political science[11] or intelligence is the most excellent science, when the best thing in the universe is not a human being <and the most excellent science must be of the best things>.

Moreover, what is good and healthy for human beings and for fish is not the same, but what is white or straight is always the same. Hence
25 everyone would also say that the content of wisdom is always the same, but the content of intelligence is not. For the agent they would call intelligent is the one who studies well each question about his own <good>, and he is the one to whom they would entrust such questions. Hence intelligence is also ascribed to some of the beasts, the ones that are evidently capable of forethought about their own life.

30 It is also evident that wisdom is not the same as political science. For if people are to say that science about what is beneficial to themselves <as human beings> counts as wisdom, there will be many types of wisdom <corresponding to the different species of animals>. For if there is no one medical science about all beings, there is no one science about the good of all animals, but a different science about each specific good. <Hence there will be many types of wisdom, contrary to our assumption that it has always the same content>.

And it does not matter if human beings are the best among the animals.
1141b For there are other beings of a far more divine nature than human beings—most evidently, for instance, the beings composing the universe.

What we have said makes it clear that wisdom is both scientific knowledge and understanding about what is by nature most honorable. That
5 is why people say that Anaxagoras or Thales or that sort of person is wise, but not intelligent, when they see that he is ignorant of what benefits himself. And so they say that what he knows$_0$ is extraordinary,

---

11. **political science**: 'Science' is supplied here and until 1141b33 (except for 1141b3, 'scientific knowledge' (= *epistēmē*).

amazing, difficult and divine, but useless, because it is not human goods that he looks for.

[INTELLIGENCE COMPARED WITH THE OTHER VIRTUES OF THOUGHT]

Intelligence, by contrast, is about human concerns, about what is open   10
to deliberation. For we say that deliberating well is the function of the intelligent person more than anyone else; but no one deliberates about what cannot be otherwise, or about what lacks a goal that is a good achievable in action. The unqualifiedly good deliberator is the one whose aim expresses rational calculation in pursuit of the best good for a human being that is achievable in action.

Nor is intelligence about universals only. It must also come to know$_8$ 15
particulars,[12] since it is concerned with action and action is about particulars. Hence in other areas also some people who lack knowledge$_0$ but have experience are better in action than others who have knowledge. For someone who knows that light meats are digestible and healthy, but not which   20
sorts of meats are light, will not produce health; the one who knows that bird meats are healthy will be better at producing health. And since intelligence is concerned with action, it must possess both <the universal and the particular knowledge> or the <particular> more <than the universal>. Here too, however, <as in medicine> there is a ruling <science>.

8

Political science and intelligence are the same state, but their being is not the same.

One part of intelligence about the city is the ruling part; this is legisla-   25
tive science.

The part concerned with particulars <often> monopolizes the name 'political science' that <properly> applies to both parts in common. This part is concerned with action and deliberation, since <it is concerned with decrees and> the decree is to be acted on as the last thing <reached in deliberation>. Hence these people are the only ones who are said to be politically active; for these are the only ones who practise <politics> in the way that handcraftsmen practise <their craft>.

Now likewise intelligence concerned with the individual himself   30
seems most of all to be counted as intelligence; and this <part of intelligence often> monopolizes the name 'intelligence' that <properly> applies <to all parts> in common. Of the other parts one is household

12. **particulars**: Probably determinate types (e.g., bird meat as opposed to light meat in general). See PARTICULAR #2.

science, another legislative, another political, one part of which is deliberative and another judicial.

In fact knowledge$_o$ of what is <good> for oneself is one species <of
intelligence>. But there is much difference <in opinions> about it.

1142a   Someone who knows about himself, and spends his time on his own
concerns, seems to be intelligent, while politicians seem to be too active.
Hence Euripides says, 'Surely I cannot be intelligent, when I could have

5   been inactive, numbered among all the many in the army, and have had
an equal share. . . . For those who go too far and are too active. . . .'

For people seek what is good for themselves, and suppose that this
<inactivity> is the action required <to achieve their good>. Hence this
belief has led to the view that these are the intelligent people.

10   Presumably, however, one's own welfare requires household management and a political system.

Moreover, <another reason for the difference of opinion is this>: it
is unclear, and should be examined, how one must manage one's own
affairs.

A sign of what has been said <about the unclarity of what intelligence
requires> is the fact that whereas young people become accomplished
in geometry and mathematics, and wise within these limits, intelligent
young people do not seem to be found. The reason is that intelligence is
concerned with particulars as well as universals, and particulars become

15   known$_g$ from experience, but a young person lacks experience, since
some length of time is needed to produce it.

Indeed <to understand the difficulty and importance of experience>
we might consider why a boy can become accomplished in mathematics,
but not in wisdom or natural science. Surely it is because mathematical
objects are reached through abstraction, whereas the principles in these
other cases are reached from experience. Young people, then, <lacking

20   experience>, have no real conviction in these other sciences, but only say
the words, whereas the nature of mathematical objects is clear to them.

Moreover <intelligence is difficult because it is deliberative and>
deliberation may be in error about either the universal or the particular.[13]
For <we may wrongly suppose> either that all sorts of heavy water are
bad or that this water is heavy.

25   Intelligence is evidently not scientific knowledge; for, as we said, it
concerns the last thing <i.e., the particular>,[14] since this is what is done

13. **particular**: Probably particular instances (e.g., this water here) rather than
determinate types (contrast 1141b15).

14. **last thing**: i.e., last as we proceed from more general to more particular.
Intelligence is concerned with terms that come last in a practical science (not in
a DEMONSTRATIVE science) because they are the most particular.

in action. Hence it is opposed to understanding. For understanding is about the <first> terms, <those> that have no account of them; but intelligence is about the last thing, an object of perception, not of scientific knowledge.

This is not the perception of proper objects,[15] but the sort by which we perceive that the last among mathematical objects is a triangle; for it will stop here too. This is another species <of perception than percep-   30
tion of proper objects>; but it is still perception more than intelligence is.

* * * * * * *

[PUZZLES ABOUT INTELLIGENCE AND WISDOM]

12

Someone might, however, be puzzled about what use they <—wisdom   1143b1ℓ
and intelligence—> are.

For wisdom is not concerned with any sort of coming into being, and   20
hence will not study any source of human happiness.

Admittedly intelligence will study this; but what do we need it for?   25

For knowledge₀ of what is healthy or fit—i.e., of what results from   26
the state of health, not of what produces it—makes us no readier to act
appropriately if we are already healthy; for having the science of medicine   27
or gymnastics makes us no readier to act appropriately. Similarly, intelli-   21
gence is the science of what is just and what is fine, and what is good
for a human being; but this is how the good man acts; and if we are
already good, knowledge of them makes us no readier to act appropri-   25
ately, since virtues are states <activated in actions>.

If we concede that intelligence is not useful for this, should we say   28
it is useful for becoming good? In that case it will be no use to those   30
who are already excellent. Nor, however, will it be any use to those who
are not. For it will not matter to them whether they have it themselves
or take the advice of others who have it. The advice of others will be
quite adequate for us, just as it is with health: we wish to be healthy,
but still do not learn medical science.

Besides, it would seem absurd for intelligence, inferior as it is to   35
wisdom, to control it <as a superior. But this will be the result>, since
the science that produces also rules and prescribes about its product.

We must discuss these questions; for so far we have only gone through
the puzzles about them.

First of all, let us state that both intelligence and wisdom must be   1144a

---

15. **proper objects**: See *DA* ii 6.

choiceworthy in themselves, even if neither produces anything at all;
for each is the virtue of one of the two <rational> parts <of the soul>.

Second, they do produce something. Wisdom produces happiness,
not in the way that medical science produces health, but in the way that
health produces <health>.[16] For since wisdom is a part of virtue as a
whole, it makes us happy because it is a state that we possess and
activate.

Further, we fulfill our function insofar as we have intelligence and
virtue of character; for virtue makes the goal correct, and intelligence
makes what promotes the goal <correct>.[17] The fourth part of the soul,
the nutritive part, has no such virtue <related to our function>, since
no action is up to it to do or not to do.

[THE RELATION BETWEEN INTELLIGENCE AND VIRTUE OF CHARACTER]

To answer the claim that intelligence will make us no readier to do
fine and just actions, we must begin from a little further back <in our
discussion>.

Here is where we begin. We say that some people who do just actions
are not yet thereby just, if, for instance, they do the actions prescribed
by the laws, either unwillingly or because of ignorance or because of
some other end, not because of the actions themselves, even though
they do the right actions, those that the excellent person ought to do.
Equally, however, it would seem to be possible for someone to do each
type of action in the state that makes him a good person, i.e., because
of decision and for the sake of the actions themselves.[18]

Now virtue makes the decision correct; but the actions that are naturally to be done to fulfill the decision are the concern not of virtue, but
of another capacity. We must get to know$_0$ them more clearly before
continuing our discussion.

There is a capacity, called cleverness, which is such as to be able to
do the actions that tend to promote whatever goal is assumed and to
achieve it. If, then, the goal is fine, cleverness is praiseworthy, and if
the goal is base, cleverness is unscrupulousness; hence both intelligent
and unscrupulous people are called clever.

Intelligence is not the same as this capacity <of cleverness>, though
it requires it. Intelligence, this eye of the soul, cannot reach its fully

---

16. . . . **health produces** <health>: Less probably: 'health produces <hap-
piness>'.

17. **makes the goal. . .**: Cf. 1144a20, 1145a4.

18. **because of decision and . . .**: See 1105a32.

developed state without virtue,[19] as we have said and as is clear. For inferences about actions have a principle,[20] 'Since the end and the best good is this sort of thing', whatever it actually is—let it be any old thing for the sake of argument. And this <best good> is apparent only to the good person; for vice perverts us and produces false views about the   35 principles of actions.[21]

Evidently, then, we cannot be intelligent without being good.   1144b

13

We must, then, also examine virtue over again. For virtue is similar <in this way> to intelligence; as intelligence is related to cleverness, not the same but similar, so natural virtue[22] is related to full virtue.

For each of us seems to possess his type of character to some extent   5 by nature, since we are just, brave, prone to temperance, or have another feature, immediately from birth. However, we still search for some other condition as full goodness, and expect to possess these features in another way.

For these natural states belong to children and to beasts as well <as to adults>, but without understanding they are evidently harmful. At   10 any rate, this much would seem to be clear: just as a heavy body moving around unable to see suffers a heavy fall because it has no sight, so it is with virtue. <A naturally well-endowed person without understanding will harm himself.> But if someone acquires understanding, he improves in his actions; and the state he now has, though still similar <to the natural one>, will be virtue to the full extent.

And so, just as there are two sorts of conditions, cleverness and   15 intelligence, in the part of the soul that has belief, so also there are two in the part that has character, natural virtue and full virtue. And of these full virtue cannot be acquired without intelligence.

This is why some say that all the virtues are <instances of> intelligence, and why Socrates' inquiries were in one way correct, and in another way in error. For in that he thought all the virtues are <instances   20

19. **Intelligence . . . virtue**: Lit. 'The state comes to be for this eye of the soul not without virtue.' Until someone is virtuous he has only an aptitude for intelligence, not intelligence itself.

20. **For . . . principle**: See DEDUCTION #4, PRINCIPLE #3.

21. **For inferences . . .**: Only the good person has the correct conception of what the highest good consists in. On the effects of vice cf. 1140b11.

22. **natural virtue**: Cf. 1117a14, 1179b21–26. Aristotle refers to natural aptitudes, not to genuine virtues (cf. 1103a23). Without intelligence someone will lack full (see CONTROLLING #2) virtue.

of> intelligence,[23] he was in error; but in that he thought they all require intelligence, he was right.

Here is a sign of this: Whenever people now define virtue, they all say what state it is and what it is related to, and then add that it is the state that expresses correct reason. Now correct reason is reason that expresses intelligence; it would seem, then, that they all in a way intuitively believe that the state expressing intelligence is virtue.

But we must make a slight change. For it is not merely the state expressing correct reason, but the state involving correct reason,[24] that is virtue. And it is intelligence that is correct reason in this area. Socrates, then, thought that the virtues are <instances of> reason because he thought they are all <instances of> knowledge_e, whereas we think they involve reason.

What we have said, then, makes it clear that we cannot be fully good without intelligence, or intelligent without virtue of character.

In this way we can also solve the dialectical argument that someone might use to show that the virtues are separated from each other. For, <it is argued>, since the same person is not naturally best suited for all the virtues, someone will already have one virtue before he has got another.

This is indeed possible with the natural virtues. It is not possible, however, with the <full> virtues that someone must have to be called good without qualification; for as soon as he has intelligence, which is a single state, he has all the virtues as well.

And clearly, even if intelligence were useless in action, we would need it because it is the virtue of this part of the soul, and because the decision will not be correct without intelligence or without virtue. For virtue makes us reach the end in our action, while intelligence makes us reach what promotes the end.[25]

Moreover, intelligence does not control wisdom or the better part of the soul, just as medical science does not control health. For it does not use health, but only aims to bring health into being; hence it prescribes for the sake of health, but does not prescribe to health. Besides, <saying that intelligence controls wisdom> would be like saying that political science rules the gods because it prescribes about everything in the city.

23. <instances of> intelligence: Lit. 'intelligences'.

24. expressing . . . involving . . .: Probably Aristotle means to contrast (a) the actions that express the virtuous person's decision with (b) those (instinctive reactions and feelings) that do not express his decision, but still would not be what they are without his rational reflection and decision.

25. For virtue . . . end: Lit. 'for the one makes us do the end, the other the things toward the end.' Cf. 1144a8, 1178a16.

Book VII

[CONTINENCE AND INCONTINENCE]

[COMMON BELIEFS ABOUT CONTINENCE AND INCONTINENCE]

1

*   *   *   *   *   *   *

We must now discuss incontinence, softness and self-indulgence, and *1145a35*
also continence and resistance; for we must not suppose that continence *1145b*
and incontinence are concerned with the same states as virtue and vice,
or that they belong to a different kind.

As in the other cases we must set out the appearances,* and first of
all go through the puzzles. In this way we must prove the common   5
beliefs about these ways of being affected—ideally, all the common
beliefs, but if not all, then most of them, and the most important. For
if the objections are solved, and the common beliefs are left, it will be
an adequate proof.[1]

Continence and resistance seem to be good and praiseworthy conditions, while incontinence and softness seem to be base and blameworthy   10
conditions.

The continent person seems to be the same as one who abides by his
rational calculation; and the incontinent person seems to be the same
as one who abandons it.

The incontinent person knows₀ that his actions are base, but does
them because of his feelings, while the continent person knows that his
appetites are base, but because of reason does not follow them.

People think the temperate person is continent and resistant. Some   15
think that every continent and resistant person is temperate, while others
do not. Some people say the incontinent person is intemperate and
the intemperate incontinent, with no distinction; others say they are
different.

Sometime it is said that an intelligent person cannot be incontinent;
but sometimes it is said that some people are intelligent and clever, but
still incontinent.

Further, people are called incontinent about emotion, honor and gain.   20
These, then, are the things that are said.

---

1. **As in the other . . . adequate proof**: On the method described in this paragraph see DIALECTIC.

[PUZZLES ABOUT THE COMMON BELIEFS]

2

We might be puzzled about the sort of correct supposition* someone has when he acts incontinently.

First of all, some say he cannot have knowledge$_e$ <at the time he acts>. For it would be terrible, Socrates[2] thought, for knowledge to be in someone, but mastered by something else, and dragged around like a slave. For Socrates fought against the account <of incontinence> in general, in the belief that there is no incontinence; for no one, he thought, supposes while he acts that his action conflicts with what is best; our action conflicts with what is best only because we are ignorant <of the conflict>.

This argument, then, contradicts things that appear manifestly. If ignorance causes the incontinent person to be affected as he is, then we must look for the type of ignorance that it turns out to be; for it is evident, at any rate, that before he is affected the person who acts incontinently does not think <he should do the action he eventually does>.

Some people concede some of <Socrates' points>, but reject some of them. For they agree that nothing is superior to knowledge, but deny that no one's action conflicts with what has seemed better to him. Hence they say that when the incontinent person is overcome by pleasure he has only belief, not knowledge.

In that case, however, if he has belief, not knowledge, and what resists is not a strong supposition, but only a mild one, such as people have when they are in doubt, we will pardon failure to abide by these beliefs against strong appetites. In fact, however, we do not pardon vice, or any other blameworthy condition <and incontinence is one of these>.

Then is it intelligence that resists, since it is the strongest? This is absurd. For on this view the same person will be both intelligent and incontinent; and no one would say that the intelligent person is the sort to do the worst actions willingly.

Besides, we have shown earlier that the intelligent person acts <on his knowledge>, since he is concerned with the last things, <i.e., particulars>, and that he has the other virtues.

Further, if the continent person must have strong and base appetites, the temperate person will not be continent nor the continent person temperate. For the temperate person is not the sort to have either excessive or base appetites; but <the continent person> must have both.

For if his appetites are good, the state that prevents him from following them must be base, so that not all continence is excellent. If, on the

---

2. **Socrates**: See Plato, *Protagoras* 352–57.

412

Margin line numbers: 25, 30, 35, 1146a, 5, 10, 15

other hand, the appetites are weak and not base, continence is nothing impressive; and if they are base and weak, it is nothing great.

Besides, if continence makes someone prone to abide by every belief, it is bad, if, for instance, it makes him abide by a false as well <as true> belief.

And if incontinence makes someone prone to abandon every belief, there will be an excellent type of incontinence. Neoptolemus, for instance, in Sophocles' *Philoctetes* is praiseworthy when, after being persuaded by Odysseus, he does not abide by his resolve, because he feels pain at lying.   20

Besides, the sophistical argument is a puzzle. For <the sophists> wish to refute an <opponent, by showing> that his views have paradoxical results, so that they will be clever in encounters. Hence the inference that results is a puzzle; for thought is tied up,[3] since it does not want to stand still because the conclusion is displeasing, but it cannot advance because it cannot solve the argument.   25

A certain argument, then, concludes that foolishness combined with incontinence is virtue. For incontinence makes someone act contrary to what he supposes <is right>; but since he supposes that good things are bad and that it is wrong to do them, he will do the good actions, not the bad.   30

Further, someone who acts to pursue what is pleasant because this is what he is persuaded and decides[4] to do, seems to be better than someone who acts not because of rational calculation, but because of incontinence.

For the first person is the easier to cure, because he might be persuaded otherwise; but the incontinent person illustrates the proverb 'If water chokes us, what must we drink to wash it down?' For if he had been persuaded to do the action he does, he would have stopped when he was persuaded to act otherwise; but in fact, though already persuaded to act otherwise, he still acts <wrongly>.   35
                                                                      1146b

Further, is there incontinence and continence about everything? If so, who is simply[5] incontinent? For no one has all the types of incontinence, but we say that some people are simply incontinent.   5

These, then, are the sorts of puzzles that arise. We must undermine some of these claims, and leave others intact; for the solution of the puzzle is the discovery <of what we are seeking>.

3. **tied up**: See *Met.* 995a28.

4. **decides**: This is the intemperate person.

5. **simply**: *haplōs*. See WITHOUT QUALIFICATION #3. He is said simply to be incontinent, without mention of any specific area of incontinence.

3

First, then, we must examine whether the incontinent has knowledge$_o$
10   or not, and in what way he has it. Second, what should we take to
be the incontinent and the continent person's area of concern—every
pleasure and pain, or some definite subclass? Are the continent and the
resistant person the same or different? Similarly we must deal with the
other questions that are relevant to this study.

[THE SCOPE OF INCONTINENCE]

15   We begin the examination with this question: Are the continent and the
incontinent person distinguished <from others> (i) by their concerns
or (ii) by their attitudes to them? In other words, is the incontinent
person incontinent (i) only by having these concerns, or instead (ii) by
having this attitude: or instead (iii) by both? Next, is there continence
and incontinence about everything, or not?
20   <Surely (iii) is right.> For <(i) is insufficient> since the simple incontinent is not concerned with everything, but with the same things as
the intemperate person. Moreover, <(ii) is insufficient> since he is not
incontinent simply by being inclined toward these things—that would
make incontinence the same as intemperance. Rather <as (iii) implies>,
he is incontinent by being inclined toward them in this way. For the
intemperate person acts on decision when he is led on, since he thinks
it is right in every case to pursue the pleasant thing at hand; but the
incontinent person thinks it is wrong to pursue it, yet still pursues it.

[THE INCONTINENT PERSON'S KNOWLEDGE]

25   It is claimed that the incontinent person's action conflicts with the true
belief, not with knowledge$_e$. But whether it is knowledge or belief that
he has does not matter for this argument. For some people with belief
are in no doubt, but think they have exact knowledge$_o$.
If, then, it is the weakness of their conviction that makes people with
belief, not people with knowledge$_e$, act in conflict with their supposition,
it follows that knowledge will <for these purposes> be no different
30   from belief; for, as Heracleitus makes clear, some people's convictions
about what they believe are no weaker than other people's convictions
about what they know.
But we speak of knowing in two ways, and ascribe it both to someone
who has it without using it and to someone who is using it. Hence it
will matter whether someone has the knowledge that his action is wrong,
35   without attending to his knowledge, or both has and attends to it. For
this second case seems extraordinary, but wrong action when he does
not attend to his knowledge does not seem extraordinary.
1147a   Besides, since there are two types of premisses, someone's action may

well conflict with his knowledge if he has both types of premisses, but uses only the universal premiss and not the particular premiss.[6] For <the particular premiss states the particulars and> it is particular actions that are done.

Moreover, <in both types of premisses> there are different types of universal, (a) one type referring to the agent himself, and (b) the other   5
referring to the object. Perhaps, for instance, someone knows that (a1) dry things benefit every human being, and that (a2) he himself is a human being, or that (b1) this sort of thing is dry; but he either does not have or does not activate the knowledge that (b2) this particular thing is of this sort.

Hence these ways <of knowing and not knowing> make such a remarkable difference that it seems quite intelligible <for someone acting against his knowledge> to have the one sort of knowledge$_o$ <i.e., without (b2)>, but astounding if he has the other sort <including (b2)>.

Besides, human beings may have knowledge$_e$ in a way different from   10
those we have described. For we see that having without using includes different types of having; hence in some people, such as those asleep or mad or drunk, both have knowledge in a way and do not have it.[7]

Moreover, this is the condition of those affected by strong feelings.   15
For emotions, sexual appetites and some conditions of this sort clearly <both disturb knowledge and> disturb the body as well, and even produce fits of madness in some people.

Clearly, then <since incontinents are also affected by strong feelings>, we should say that they have knowledge in a way similar to these people.

Saying the words that come from knowledge$_e$ is no sign <of fully having it>. For people affected in these ways even recite demonstrations   20
and verses of Empedocles. Further, those who have just learned something do not yet know$_o$ it, though they string the words together; for it must grow into them, and this needs time.

Hence we must suppose that incontinents say the words in the way that actors do.

Further, we may also look at the cause in the following way, referring   25
to <human> nature.[8] One belief (a) is universal; the other (b) is about particulars, and because they are particulars perception controls them.

6. **particular premiss**: Lit. 'partial' (*kata meros*), mentioning PARTICULARS.

7. **both have . . .**: Someone may know French but have no access to his knowledge because of his condition; he does not apply the knowledge in the normal way.

8. **nature**: Aristotle discusses the question from a natural (i.e., specific to psychology, not merely LOGICAL) point of view, referring to the structure of practical inference; cf. *DA*. 431a15, *MA* 7. The letters interpolated in the translation express some controversial decisions about interpretation.

And in the cases[9] where these two beliefs result in (c) one belief, it is necessary in purely theoretical beliefs for the soul to affirm what has been concluded, and in beliefs about production (d) to act at once on what has been concluded.

30   If, for instance, (a) everything sweet must be tasted, and (b) this, some one particular thing, is sweet, it is necessary (d) for someone who is able and unhindered[10] also to act on this at the same time.

Suppose, then, that someone has (a) the universal belief, and it hinders him from tasting; he has (b) the second belief, that everything sweet is pleasant and this is sweet, and this belief (b) is active; and he also has

35   appetite. Hence the belief[11] (c) tells him to avoid this, but appetite leads him on, since it is capable of moving each of the <bodily> parts.

1147b   The result, then, is that in a way reason and belief make him act incontinently. The belief (b) is contrary to correct reason (a), but only coincidentally, not in itself. For it is the appetite, not the belief, that is contrary <in itself to correct reason>.

5   Hence beasts are not incontinent, because they have no universal supposition, but <only> appearance and memory of particulars.

How is the ignorance resolved, so that the incontinent person recovers his knowledge$_e$? The same account that applies to someone drunk or asleep applies here too, and is not special to this way of being affected. We must hear it from the natural scientists.

10   And since the last premiss[12] (b) is a belief about something perceptible, and controls action, this must be what the incontinent person does not have when he is being affected. Or rather the way he has it is not knowledge of it, but, as we saw, <merely> saying the words, as the drunk says the words of Empedocles.

Further, since the last term does not seem to be universal, or expressive

15   of knowledge in the same way as the universal term, even the result Socrates was looking for would seem to come about. For the knowledge that is present when someone is affected by incontinence, and that is dragged about[13] because he is affected, is not the sort that seems to be

9. **And in the cases . . .**: Lit. (following the Greek word-order) 'Whenever one comes to be from them, it is necessary that the thing concluded, in the one case the soul affirms, and in productive <beliefs> does at once.' 'The thing concluded' is the object both of 'affirms' and 'does'.

10. **unhindered**: Probably Aristotle has in mind external hindrances as in *Met.* 1048a10–24, *DA* 417a27.

11. **Hence the belief**: Less probably, this refers to (a).

12. **premiss**: (*protasis*) Or (less probably) 'proposition'—in which case (c) would be intended.

13. **dragged about**: It is detached from the correct principle (a), and attached to appetite.

knowledge to the full extent <in (c)>, but only perceptual knowledge <in (b)>.

So much, then, for knowing$_o$ and not knowing, and for how it is possible to know and still to act incontinently.

*   *   *   *   *   *   *

Book VIII

[VARIETIES OF FRIENDSHIP]

[THE PROBLEMS]

1

After that the next topic is friendship; for it is a virtue, or involves virtue,   *1155a* and besides is most necessary for our life.

For no one would choose to live without friends even if he had all   5 the other goods. For in fact rich people and holders of powerful positions, even more than other people, seem to need friends. For how would one benefit from such prosperity if one had no opportunity for beneficence, which is most often displayed, and most highly praised, in relation to   10 friends? And how would one guard and protect prosperity without friends, when it is all the more precarious the greater it is? In poverty also, and in the other misfortunes, people think friends are the only refuge.

Moreover, the young need it to keep them from error. The old need it to care for them and support the actions that fail because of weakness. And those in their prime need it, to do fine actions; for 'when two go   15 together . . .', they are more capable of understanding and acting.

Further, a parent would seem to have a natural friendship for a child, and a child for a parent, not only among human beings but also among birds and most kinds of animals. Members of the same race, and human   20 beings most of all, have a natural friendship for each other; that is why we praise friends of humanity. And in our travels we can see how every human being is akin and beloved to a human being.

Moreover, friendship would seem to hold cities together, and legisla-   tors would seem to be more concerned about it than about justice. For   25 concord would seem to be similar to friendship and they aim at concord among all, while they try above all to expel civil conflict, which is enmity.

Further, if people are friends, they have no need of justice, but if they are just they need friendship in addition; and the justice that is most just seems to belong to friendship.

However, friendship is not only necessary, but also fine.[1] For we   30 praise lovers of friends, and having many friends seems to be a fine

1. **also fine**: 'Fine' repeats the claim in 'a virtue or involves virtue' in 1155a4.

417

thing. Moreover, people think that the same people are good and also friends.

Still, there are quite a few disputed points about friendship.

For some hold it is a sort of similarity and that similar people are
35   friends. Hence the saying 'Similar to similar', and 'Birds of a feather', and so on. On the other hand it is said that similar people are all like the proverbial potters, quarreling with each other.
1155b   On these questions some people inquire at a higher level, more proper to natural science. Euripides says that when earth gets dry it longs passionately for rain, and the holy heaven when filled with rain longs
5   passionately to fall into the earth; and Heracleitus says that the opponent cooperates, the finest harmony arises from discordant elements, and all things come to be in struggle. Others, such as Empedocles, oppose this view, and say that similar aims for similar.

Let us, then, leave aside the puzzles proper to natural science, since they are not proper to the present examination; and let us examine the
10   puzzles that concern human <nature>, and bear on characters and feelings.

For instance, does friendship arise among all sorts of people, or can people not be friends if they are vicious?

Is there one species of frieendship, or are there more? Some people think there is only one species because friendship allows more and less.
15   But here their confidence rests on an inadequate sign; for things of different species also allow more and less.[2]

[GENERAL ACCOUNT OF FRIENDSHIP]

2

Perhaps these questions will become clear once we find out what it is that is lovable. For, it seems, not everything is loved, but <only> what is lovable, and this is either good or pleasant or useful. However, it
20   seems that what is useful is the source of some good or some pleasure; hence what is good and what is pleasant are lovable as ends.

Do people love what is good, or what is good for them? For sometimes these conflict; and the same is true of what is pleasant. Each one, it seems, loves what is good for him; and while what is good is lovable
25   without qualification, what is lovable for each one is what is good for him. In fact each one loves not what *is* good for him, but what *appears* good for him; but this will not matter, since <what appears good for him> will be what appears lovable.

---

2. **more and less**: The mss add: 'We have spoken about them previously.' These words are probably spurious; they may refer to *Catg.* 6b10–17.

Hence there are these three causes of love.

Love for a soulless thing is not called friendship, since there is no mutual loving, and you do not wish good to it. For it would presumably be ridiculous to wish good things to wine; the most you wish is its   30 preservation so that you can have it. To a friend, however, it is said, you must wish goods for his own sake.[3]

If you wish good things in this way, but the same wish is not returned by the other, you would be said to have <only> goodwill for the other. For friendship is said to be *reciprocated* goodwill.

But perhaps we should add that friends are aware of the reciprocated   35 goodwill. For many a one has goodwill to people whom he has not seen   1156a but supposes to be decent or useful, and one of these might have the same goodwill toward him. These people, then, apparently have goodwill to each other, but how could we call them friends when they are unaware of their attitude to each other?

Hence, <to be friends> they must have goodwill[4] to each other, wish   5 goods and be aware of it, from one of the causes mentioned above.[5]

[*THE THREE TYPES OF FRIENDSHIP*]

3

Now since these causes differ in species, so do the types of loving and types of friendship. Hence friendship has three species, corresponding to the three objects of love. For each object of love has a corresponding type of mutual loving, combined with awareness of it, and those who love each other wish goods to each other insofar as they love each other.[6]   10

Those who love each other for utility love the other not in himself, but insofar as they gain some good for themselves from him. The same is true of those who love for pleasure; for they like a witty person not because of his character, but because he is pleasant to themselves.

And so those who love for utility or pleasure are fond of a friend   15

3. **for his own sake**: Apparently this does not apply to wine because it has no choices, desires or aims of its own.

4. **must have goodwill**: The definition of goodwill implies that in all friendships A must wish good for B for B's sake. Contrast 1156a10.

5. **from one . . .**: Lit. 'because of (*dia*) one of the three things mentioned above'. The different types of friendship are 'for' (*dia*) character, utility and pleasure. Here '*dia*' probably refers to both the final and the efficient CAUSE. Cf. 1156a31, 1172b21.

6. **insofar as . . .**: Probably Aristotle means to restrict the extent of goodwill in the incomplete friendships (those for utility and pleasure). In these A wishes good to B only insofar as B is useful or pleasant to A, not for B's own sake.

because of what is good or pleasant for themselves, not insofar as the beloved is who he is, but insofar as he is useful or pleasant.

Hence these friendships as well <as the friends> are coincidental, since the beloved is loved not insofar as he is who he is, but insofar as he provides some good or pleasure.

20 And so these sorts of friendships are easily dissolved, when the friends do not remain similar <to what they were>; for if someone is no longer pleasant or useful, the other stops loving him.

What is useful does not remain the same, but is different at different times. Hence, when the cause of their being friends is removed, the friendship is dissolved too, on the assumption that the friendship aims at these <useful results>. This sort of friendship seems to arise especially 25 among older people, since at that age they pursue what is advantageous, not what is pleasant, and also among those in their prime or youth who pursue what is expedient.

Nor do such people live together very much. For sometimes they do not even find each other pleasant. Hence they have no further need to meet in this way if they are not advantageous <to each other>; for each 30 finds the other pleasant <only> to the extent that he expects some good from him. The friendship of hosts and guests[7] is taken to be of this type too.

The cause of friendship between young people seems to be pleasure. For their lives are guided by their feelings, and they pursue above all what is pleasant for themselves and what is near at hand. But as they 35 grow up <what they find> pleasant changes too. Hence they are quick to become friends, and quick to stop; for their friendship shifts with 1156b <what they find> pleasant, and the change in such pleasure is quick. Young people are prone to erotic passion, since this mostly follows feelings, and is caused by pleasure; that is why they love and quickly stop, often changing in a single day.

5 These people wish to spend their days together and to live together; for this is how they gain <the good things> corresponding to their friendship.

But complete friendship is the friendship of good people similar in virtue; for they wish goods in the same way to each other insofar as they are good, and they are good in themselves. <Hence they wish 10 goods to each other for each other's own sake.> Now those who wish goods to their friend for the friend's own sake are friends most of all; for they have this attitude because of the friend himself, not coincidentally.

7. **hosts and guests**: (*xenikē*) If A is an Athenian and B is a Spartan, each is the *xenos* of the other if A provides B with hospitality in Athens and B does the same for A in Sparta, and they provide each other with other sorts of reciprocal mutual aid.

Hence these people's friendship lasts as long as they are good; and virtue is enduring.

Each of them is both good without qualification and good for his friend, since good people are both good without qualification and advantageous for each other. They are pleasant in the same ways too, since *15* good people are pleasant both without qualification and for each other. <They are pleasant for each other> because each person finds his own actions and actions of that kind pleasant, and the actions of good people are the same or similar.

It is reasonable that this sort of friendship is enduring, since it embraces in itself all the features that friends must have. For the cause of *20* every friendship is good or pleasure, either unqualified or for the lover; and every friendship reflects some similarity. And all the features we have mentioned are found in this friendship because of <the nature of> the friends themselves. For they are similar in this way <i.e., in being good>. Moreover, their friendship also has the other things—what is good without qualification and what is pleasant without qualification; and these are lovable most of all. Hence loving and friendship are found most of all and at their best in these friends.

These kinds of friendships are likely to be rare, since such people are *25* few. Moreover, they need time to grow accustomed to each other; for, as the proverb says, they cannot know₀ each other before they have shared the traditional <peck of> salt, and they cannot accept each other or be friends until each appears lovable to the other and gains the other's confidence. Those who are quick to treat each other in friendly ways *30* wish to be friends, but are not friends, unless they are also lovable, and know this. For though the wish for friendship comes quickly, friendship does not.

*   *   *   *   *   *   *

[FRIENDSHIP IN COMMUNITIES]

9

As we said at the beginning, friendship and justice would seem to have *1159b25* the same area of concern and to be found in the same people. For in every community there seems to be some sort of justice, and some type of friendship also. At any rate, fellow-voyagers and fellow-soldiers are called friends, and so are members of other communities. And the extent of their community is the extent of their friendship, since it is also the *30* extent of the justice found there. The proverb 'What friends have is common' is correct, since friendship involves community. But while brothers and companions have everything in common, what people have in common in other types of community is limited, more in some

35 communities and less in others, since some friendships are also closer than others, some less close.

1160a What is just is also different, since it is not the same for parents toward children as for one brother toward another, and not the same for companions as for fellow-citizens, and similarly with the other types of friendship. Similarly, what is unjust toward each of these is also different, and becomes more unjust as it is practised on closer friends.

5 It is more shocking, for instance, to rob a companion of money than to rob a fellow-citizen, to fail to help a brother than a stranger, and to strike one's father than anyone else. What is just also naturally increases with friendship, since it involves the same people and extends over an equal area.

10 All communities would seem to be parts of the political community.[8] For people keep company for some advantage and to supply something contributing to their life. Moreover, the political community seems both to have been originally formed and to endure for advantage; for legislators also aim at advantage, and the common advantage[9] is said to be just.

15 The other types of community aim at partial advantage. Sea-travellers, for instance, seek the advantage proper to a journey, in making money or something like that, while fellow-soldiers seek the advantage proper to war, desiring either money or victory or a city; and the same is true of fellow-tribesmen and fellow-damesmen. Some communities—

20 religious societies and dining clubs—seem to arise for pleasure, since these are, respectively, for religious sacrifices and for companionship.

All these communities would seem to be subordinate to the political community, since it aims not at some advantage close at hand, but at advantage for the whole of life . . . <For> in performing sacrifices and

25 arranging gatherings for these, people both accord honors to the gods and provide themselves with pleasant relaxations. For the long-established sacrifices and gatherings appear to take place after the harvesting of the crops, as a sort of first-fruits, since this was the time when people used to be most at leisure <and the time when relaxation would be most advantageous for the whole of life>.

30 All the types of community, then, appear to be parts of the political community, and these sorts of communities imply the appropriate sorts of friendships.

---

8. **All communities . . . community**: The other communities are parts of the political community because each is affected by its relation to other social institutions and the political community regulates them for the common good.

9. **common advantage**: Cf. 1129b14–19. Aristotle does not say here that the city aims only at advantage. For a further aim see *Pol.* 1280a25–1281a4.

* * * * * * *

BOOK IX

[THE SOURCES AND JUSTIFICATION OF FRIENDSHIP]

[FRIENDSHIP COMPARED TO SELF-LOVE]

4

The defining features of friendship that are found in friendships to one's   1166a
neighbors would seem to be derived from features of friendship toward
oneself.

For a friend is taken to be (1) someone who wishes and does goods
or apparent goods to his friend for the friend's own sake; or (2) one who
wishes the friend to be and to live for the friend's own sake—this is   5
how mothers feel toward their children, and how friends who have been
in conflict feel <toward each other>. (3) Others take a friend to be one
who spends his time with his friend, and (4) makes the same choices;
or (5) one who shares his friend's distress and enjoyment—and this also
is especially true of mothers. And people define friendship by one of
these features.

Each of these features is found in the decent person's relation to   10
himself, and it is found in other people, insofar as they suppose they
are decent. As we have said, virtue and the excellent person would seem
to be the standard in each case.[1]

(4) The excellent person is of one mind with himself, and desires the
same things in his whole soul.

(1) Hence he wishes goods and apparent goods to himself, and does   15
them in his actions, since it is proper to the good person to achieve the
good. He wishes and does them for his own sake, since he does them
for the sake of his thinking part, and that is what each person seems to
be.

(2) He wishes himself to live and to be preserved. And he wishes this
for the part by which he has intelligence more than for any other part.
For being is a good for the good person, and each person wishes for   20
goods for himself. And no one chooses to become another person even
if that other will have every good when he has come into being; for, as
it is, the god has the good <but no one chooses to be replaced by a
god>. Rather <each of us chooses goods> on condition that he remains
whatever he is; and each person would seem to be the understanding
part, or that most of all. <Hence the good person wishes for goods for
the understanding part.>

(3) Further, such a person finds it pleasant to spend time with himself,

---

1. **As we have said**: See 1113a29, PROTAGORAS.

25 and so wishes to do it. For his memories of what he has done are agreeable, and his expectations for the future are good, and hence both are pleasant. And besides, his thought is well supplied with topics for study.

(5) Moreover, he shares his own distresses and pleasures, more than other people share theirs. For it is always the same thing that is painful or pleasant, not different things at different times. This is because he practically never regrets <what he has done>.[2]

30 The decent person, then, has each of these features in relation to himself, and is related to his friend as he is to himself, since the friend is another himself. Hence friendship seems to be one of these features, and people with these features seem to be friends.

Is there friendship toward oneself, or is there not?[3] Let us dismiss

35 that question for the present. However, there seems to be friendship insofar as someone is two or more parts. This seems to be true from

1166b what we have said, and because an extreme degree of friendship resembles one's friendship to oneself.

The many, base though they are, also appear to have these features. But perhaps they share in them only insofar as they approve of them-

5 selves and suppose they are decent. For no one who is utterly bad and unscrupulous either has these features or appears to have them.

Indeed, even base people hardly have them.

(4) For they are at odds with themselves, and, like incontinent people, have an appetite for one thing and a wish for another.

(1) For they do not choose things that seem to be good for them, but

10 instead choose pleasant things that are actually harmful. And cowardice or laziness causes others to shrink from doing what they think best for themselves.

(2) Those who have done many terrible actions hate and shun life because of their vice, and destroy themselves.

15 (3) Besides, vicious people seek others to pass their days with, and shun themselves. For when they are by themselves they remember many disagreeable actions, and expect to do others in the future; but they manage to forget these in other people's company. These people have nothing lovable about them, and so have no friendly feelings for themselves.

20 (5) Hence such a person does not share his own enjoyments and distresses. For his soul is in conflict, and because he is vicious one part is distressed at being restrained, and another is pleased <by the intended

2. **never regrets**: Since he could not reasonably have made past decisions different from those he made, he will have nothing to blame or reproach himself for.

3. **Is there . . .** : We can speak of friendship between different parts of the SOUL.

action>; and so each part pulls in a different direction, as though they were tearing him apart. Even if he cannot be distressed and pleased at the same time, still he is soon distressed because he was pleased, and wishes these things had not become pleasant to him; for base people *25* are full of regret.

Hence the base person appears not to have a friendly attitude even toward himself, because he has nothing lovable about him.

If this state is utterly miserable, everyone should earnestly shun vice and try to be decent; for that is how someone will have a friendly relation to himself and will become a friend to another.

* * * * * * *

[ACTIVE BENEVOLENCE AND FRIENDSHIP]

7

Now benefactors seem to love their beneficiaries more than the benefi-   *1167b17* ciaries love them <in return>, and this is discussed as though it were an unreasonable thing to happen.

Here is how it appears to most people. It is because the beneficiaries   *20* are debtors and the benefactors creditors: the debtor in a loan wishes the creditor did not exist, while the creditor even attends to the safety of the debtor. So also, then, a benefactor wants the beneficiary to exist because he expects gratitude in return, while the beneficiary is not   *25* attentive about making the return.

Now Epicharmus might say that most people say this because they 'take a bad person's point of view'. Still, it would seem to be a human point of view, since the many are indeed forgetful, and seek to receive benefits more than to give them.

However, it seems that the cause is more proper to <human> nature, and the case of creditors is not even similar. For they do not love their   *30* debtors, but in wishing for their safety simply seek repayment; whereas benefactors love and like their beneficiaries even if they are of no present or future use to them.

The same is true with craftsmen; for each likes his own product[4] more   *35* than it would like him if it acquired a soul. Perhaps this is true of poets   *1168a* most of all, since they dearly like their own poems, and are fond of them as though they were their children. This, then, is what the case of the benefactor resembles; here the beneficiary is his product, and hence he   *5* likes him more than the product likes its producer.

The cause of this is as follows:

4. **his own product**: (*ergon*) see FUNCTION. The connection between *ergon* as product and *ergon* as function is important in the argument.

1. Being is choiceworthy and lovable for all.

2. We are insofar as we are actualized, since we are insofar as we live and act.

3. The product is, in a way, the producer in his actualization.[5]

4. Hence the producer is fond of the product, because he loves his own being. And this is natural, since what he is potentially is what the product indicates in actualization.

10   At the same time, the benefactor's action is fine for him, so that he finds enjoyment in the person he acts on; but the person acted on finds nothing fine in the agent, but only, at most, some advantage, which is less pleasant and lovable.

What is pleasant is actualization in the present, expectation for the
15   future, and memory of the past; but what is pleasantest is the <action we do> insofar as we are actualized, and this is also most lovable. For the benefactor, then, his product endures, since what is fine is long-lasting; but for the person acted on, what is useful passes away.

Besides, memory of something fine is pleasant, while memory of <receiving> something useful is not altogether pleasant, or is less pleas-ant—though the reverse would seem to be true for expectation.

20   Moreover, loving is like production, while being loved is like being acted on; and <the benefactor's> love and friendliness is the result of his greater activity.

Besides, everyone is fond of what has needed effort to produce it; for instance, people who have made money themselves are fonder of it than people who have inherited it. And while receiving a benefit seems to take no effort, giving one is hard work.

25   This is also why mothers love their children more <than fathers do>, since giving birth is more effort for them, and they know₀ better that the children are theirs. And this also would seem to be proper to benefactors.

[SELF-LOVE AND FRIENDSHIP]

8

There is also a puzzle about whether one ought to love oneself or some-
30   one else most of all; for those who like themselves most are criticized and denounced as self-lovers, as though this were something shameful.

Indeed, the base person does seem to go to every length for his own sake, and all the more the more vicious he is; hence he is accused, for

5. **actualization**: (*energeia*) See ACTUALITY. Both the exercise of skill in the produc-tive activity and the product resulting from this exercise actualize the agent's capacities, and so express his being.

instance, of doing nothing of his own accord.[6] The decent person, on the contrary, acts for what is fine, all the more the better he is, and for his friend's sake, disregarding his own good.

The facts, however, conflict with these claims, and that is not unreasonable.

For it is said that we must love most the friend who is most a friend; and one person is most a friend to another if he wishes goods to the other for the other's sake, even if no one will know₀ about it. But these are features most of all of one's relation to oneself; and so too are all the other defining features of a friend, since we have said that all the features of friendship extend from oneself to others.

All the proverbs agree with this too, speaking, for instance, of 'one soul', 'what friends have is common', 'equality is friendship' and 'the knee is closer than the shin'. For all these are true most of all in someone's relations with himself, since one is a friend to himself most of all. Hence he should also love himself most of all.

It is not surprising that there is a puzzle about which view we ought to follow, since both inspire some confidence; hence we must presumably divide these sorts of arguments, and distinguish how far and in what ways those on each side are true.

Perhaps, then, it will become clear, if we grasp how those on each side understand self-love.

Those who make self-love a matter for reproach ascribe it to those who award the biggest share in money, honors and bodily pleasures to themselves. For these are the goods desired and eagerly pursued by the many on the assumption that they are best; and hence they are also contested.[7]

Those who are greedy for these goods gratify their appetites and in general their feelings and the nonrational part of the soul; and since this is the character of the many, the application of the term <'self-love'> is derived from the most frequent <kind of self-love>, which is base. This type of self-lover, then, is justifiably reproached.

And plainly it is the person who awards himself these goods whom the many habitually call a self-lover. For if someone is always eager to excel everyone in doing just or temperate actions or any others expressing the virtues, and in general always gains for himself what is fine, no one will call him a self-lover or blame him for it.

However, it is this more than the other sort of person who seems to

6. **of his own accord**: Lit. 'from himself'. Less probably, 'away from himself', i.e., separated from his selfish interest.

7. **contested**: Or 'fought over', i.e., the objects pursued in competition. See Plato, *Rep.* 586b–c.

30   be a self-lover. At any rate he awards himself what is finest and best of all, and gratifies the most controlling part of himself, obeying it in everything. And just as a city[8] and every other composite system seems to be above all its most controlling part, the same is true of a human being; hence someone loves himself most if he likes and gratifies this part.

35
1169a   Similarly, someone is called continent or incontinent because his understanding is or is not the master, on the assumption that this is what each person is. Moreover, his own voluntary actions seem above all to be those involving reason. Clearly, then, this, or this above all, is what each person is, and the decent person likes this most of all.

    Hence he most of all is a self-lover, but a different kind from the self-

5   lover who is reproached, differing from him as much as the life guided by reason differs from the life guided by feelings, and as much as the desire for what is fine differs from the desire for what seems advantageous.

    Those who are unusually eager to do fine actions are welcomed and praised by everyone. And when everyone contends to achieve what is

10   fine and strains to do the finest actions, everything that is right will be done for the common good, and each person individually will receive the greatest of goods, since that is the character of virtue.

    Hence the good person must be a self-lover, since he will both help himself and benefit others by doing fine actions. But the vicious person must not love himself, since he will harm both himself and his neighbors by following his base feelings.

15   For the vicious person, then, the right actions conflict with those he does. The decent person, however, does the right actions, since every understanding chooses what is best for itself and the decent person obeys his understanding.

    Besides, it is true that, as they say, the excellent person labors for his

20   friends and for his native country, and will die for them if he must; he will sacrifice money, honors and contested goods in general, in achieving what is fine for himself. For he will choose intense pleasure for a short time over mild pleasure for a long time; a year of living finely over many

25   years of undistinguished life; and a single fine and great action over many small actions.

    This is presumably true of one who dies for others; he does indeed choose something great and fine for himself. He is ready to sacrifice money as long as his friends profit; for the friends gain money, while he gains what is fine, and so he awards himself the greater good. He

    8. **a city and . . .**: Cf. 1166a17, 1178a2. A complex system is most of all its most CONTROLLING (or important) part because this part represents the interests of the whole.

428

treats honors and offices the same way; for he will sacrifice them all for   30
his friends, since this is fine and praiseworthy for him. It is not surprising,
then, that he seems to be excellent, when he chooses what is fine at the
cost of everything. It is also possible, however, to sacrifice actions to his
friend, since it may be finer to be responsible for his friend's doing
the action than to do it himself. In everything praiseworthy, then, the   35
excellent person awards himself what is fine.

In this way, then, we must be self-lovers, as we have said. But in the   1169b
way the many are, we ought not to be.

[THE JUSTIFICATION OF FRIENDSHIP]

9

There is also a dispute about whether the happy person will need friends
or not.

For it is said that blessedly happy and self-sufficient people have no
need of friends. For they already have <all> the goods, and hence,   5
being self-sufficient, need nothing added. But your friend, since he is
another yourself, supplies what your own efforts cannot supply. Hence
it is said, 'When the god gives well, what need is there of friends?'

However, in awarding the happy person all the goods it would seem
absurd not to give him friends; for having friends seems to be the greatest   10
external good.

And it is more proper to a friend to confer benefits than to receive
them, and proper to the good person and to virtue to do good; and it
is finer to benefit friends than to benefit strangers. Hence the excellent
person will need people for him to benefit. Indeed, that is why there is
a question about whether friends are needed more in good fortune than
in ill-fortune; for it is assumed that in ill-fortune we need people to   15
benefit us, and in good fortune we need others for us to benefit.

Surely it is also absurd to make the blessed person solitary.[9] For no
one would choose to have all <other> goods and yet be alone, since a
human being is political, tending by nature to live together with others.
This will also be true, then, of the happy person; for he has the natural   20
goods, and clearly it is better to spend his days with decent friends than
with strangers of just any character. Hence the happy person will need
friends.

Then what are the other side saying, and in what way is it true?
Surely they say what they say because the many think that it is the
useful people who are friends. Certainly the blessedly happy person   25
will have no need of these, since he has <all> goods. Similarly, he will

9. **solitary**: See 1097b9.

have no need, or very little, of friends for pleasure; for since his life is pleasant, it has no need of imported pleasures. Since he does not need these sorts of friends, he does not seem to need friends at all.

However, this conclusion is presumably not true:

30   (1) For we said at the beginning that happiness is a kind of activity; and clearly activity comes into being, and does not belong <to someone all the time>, as a possession does. Being happy, then, is found in living and being active.

(2) The activity of the good person is excellent, and <hence> pleasant in itself, as we said at the beginning.

(3) Moreover, what is our own is pleasant.

35   (4) We are able to observe our neighbors more than ourselves, and to observe their actions more than our own.

(5) Hence a good person finds pleasure in the actions of excellent
1170a   people who are his friends, since these actions have both the naturally pleasant <features, i.e., they are good, and they are his own>.

(6) The blessed person decides to observe virtuous actions that are his own; and the actions of a virtuous friend are of this sort.

(7) Hence he will need virtuous friends.

5   Further, it is thought that the happy person must live pleasantly. But the solitary person's life is hard, since it is not easy for him to be continuously active all by himself; but in relation to others and in their company it is easier, and hence his activity will be more continuous. It is also pleasant in itself, as it must be in the blessedly happy person's case. For the excellent person, insofar as he is excellent, enjoys actions
10   expressing virtue, and objects to actions caused by vice, just as the musician enjoys fine melodies and is pained by bad ones.

Further, good people's life together allows the cultivation of virtue, as Theognis says.

If we examine the question more from the point of view of <human> nature, an excellent friend would seem to be choiceworthy by nature for an excellent person.

15   (1) For, as we have said, what is good by nature is good and pleasant in itself for an excellent person.

(2) For animals life is defined by the capacity for perception; for human beings it is defined by the capacity for perception of understanding.

(3) Every capacity refers to an activity, and a thing is present to its full extent in its activity.

(4) Hence living to its full extent would seem to be perceiving or understanding.

(5) Life is good and pleasant in itself. For it has definite order, which   *20*
is proper to the nature of what is good.

(6) What is good by nature is also good for the decent person. That
is why life would seem to be pleasant for everyone. Here, however, we
must not consider a life that is vicious and corrupted, or filled with
pains; for such a life lacks definite order, just as its proper features do.   *25*
(The truth about pain will be more evident in what follows.)

(7) Life itself, then, is good and pleasant. So it looks, at any rate,
from the fact that everyone desires it, and decent and blessed people
desire it more than others do; for their life is most choiceworthy for
them, and their living is most blessed.

(8) Now someone who sees perceives that he sees; one who hears   *30*
perceives that he hears; and one who walks perceives that he walks.

(9) Similarly in the other cases also there is some <element> that
perceives that we are active.

(10) Hence, if we are perceiving, we perceive that we are perceiving;
and if we are understanding, we perceive that we are understanding.

(11) Now perceiving that we are perceiving or understanding is the
same as perceiving that we are, since we agreed <in (4)> that being is
perceiving or understanding.

(12) Perceiving that we are alive is pleasant in itself. For life is by   *1170b*
nature a good <from (5)>, and it is pleasant to perceive that something
good is present in us.

(13) And living is choiceworthy, for a good person most of all, since
being is good and pleasant for him; for he is pleased to perceive some-   *5*
thing good in itself together <with his own being>.

(14) The excellent person is related to his friend in the same way as
he is related to himself, since a friend is another himself.

(15) Therefore, just as his own being is choiceworthy for him, his
friend's being is choiceworthy for him in the same or a similar way.

We agreed that someone's own being is choiceworthy because he
perceives that he is good, and this sort of perception is pleasant in itself.   *10*
He must, then, perceive his friend's being together <with his own>,
and he will do this when they live together[10] and share conversation
and thought. For in the case of human beings what seems to count as
living together is this sharing of conversation and thought, not sharing
the same pasture, as in the case of grazing animals.

If, then, for the blessedly happy person, being is choiceworthy, since   *15*
it is naturally good and pleasant; and if the being of his friend is closely
similar to his own; then his friend will also be choiceworthy. Whatever

10. **live together**: See 1095b30, 1097b9.

431

is choiceworthy for him he must possess, since otherwise he will to this extent lack something, <and hence will not be self-sufficient>.[11] Anyone who is to be happy, then, must have excellent friends.

* * * * * * *

[LIVING TOGETHER AND FRIENDSHIP]

12

1171b29 What the erotic lover likes most is the sight of his beloved, and this is
30 the sort of perception he chooses over the others, supposing that this above all is what makes him fall in love and remain in love. In the same way, surely, what friends find most choiceworthy is living together. For friendship is community, and we are related to our friend as we are related to ourselves. Hence, since the perception of our own being is
35 choiceworthy, so is the perception of our friend's being. Perception is
1172a active when we live with him; hence, not surprisingly, this is what we seek.

Whatever someone <regards as> his being, or the end for which he chooses to be alive, that is the activity he wishes to pursue in his friend's company. Hence some friends drink together, others play dice, while
5 others do gymnastics and go hunting, or do philosophy. They spend their days together on whichever pursuit in life they like most; for since they want to live with their friends, they share the actions in which they find their common life.

Hence the friendship of base people turns out to be vicious. For they
10 are unstable, and share base pursuits; and by becoming similar to each other, they grow vicious. But the friendship of decent people is decent, and increases the more often they meet. And they seem to become still better from their activities and their mutual correction. For each molds the other in what they approve of, so that '<you will learn> what is noble from noble people'.

15 So much, then, for friendship. The next task will be to discuss pleasure.

---

11. **Whatever is . . .**: Aristotle appeals to the COMPLETE and SELF-SUFFICIENT character of happiness, taking it to include everything good and choiceworthy; cf. 1097b6, 1097b16–20.

Book X

*   *   *   *   *   *   *

[PLEASURE]

[PLEASURE IS AN ACTIVITY, NOT A PROCESS]

4

What, then, or what kind of thing, is pleasure? This will become clearer   *1174a13*
if we take it up again from the beginning.

Seeing seems to be complete at any time, since it has no need for   *15*
anything else to complete its form[1] by coming to be at a later time. And
pleasure is also like this, since it is some sort of whole, and no pleasure
is to be found at any time that will have its form completed by coming
to be for a longer time. Hence pleasure is not a process either.

For every process, such as constructing a building, takes time, and   *20*
aims at some end, and is complete when it produces the product it seeks,
or, <in other words, is complete> in the whole time <that it takes>.

Moreover, each process is incomplete during the processes that are
its parts, i.e., during the time it goes on; and it consists of processes
that are different in form from the whole process and from each other.[2]

For laying stones together and fluting a column are different processes;
and both are different from the <whole> production of the temple. For   *25*
the production of the temple is a complete production, since it needs
nothing further <when it is finished> to achieve the proposed goal;
but the production of the foundation or the triglyph is an incomplete
production, since <when it is finished> it is <the production> of a
part.

Hence <processes that are parts of larger processes> differ in form;
and we cannot find a process complete in form at any time <while it is
going on>, but <only>, if at all, in the whole time <that it takes>.

The same is true of walking and the other <processes>. For if locomo-   *30*

---

1. **its form**: Here the FORM is closely associated with essence and DEFINITION;
something achieves its form to the extent that it acquires the character that makes
it the kind of thing that it is. The building of a temple takes time to acquire all
that makes it a complete building of a temple; hence it takes time to achieve its
form. An enjoyment does not take time to acquire all that makes it a complete
enjoyment. Though certainly I might prefer my enjoyment to be prolonged, it
is no more an enjoyment by being prolonged.

2. **Moreover . . . each other.** Lit. 'And in the parts and in the time they are all
incomplete, and they differ in form from the whole and from each other.' The
words 'they are all' must apparently refer to (a) processes such as temple-
building, and 'they differ in form' must refer to (b) the parts of (a). The next
sentence relies on the distinction between (a) and (b).

tion is a process from one place to another, it includes locomotions differing in form—flying, walking, jumping and so on. And besides these differences, there are differences in walking itself. For the place from which and the place to which are not the same in the whole race-course as they are in a part of it, or the same in one part as in another;

1174b nor is traveling along one line the same as traveling along another, since what we cover is not just a line, but a line in a <particular> place, and this line and that line are in different places.

Now we have discussed process exactly elsewhere. But, at any rate, a process, it would seem, is not complete at every time; and the many

5 <constituent> processes are incomplete, and differ in form, since the place from which and the place to which make the form of a process <and different processes begin and end in different places>.

The form of pleasure, by contrast, is complete at any time. Clearly, then, it is different from a process, and is something whole and complete. This also seems true because a process must take time, but being pleased need not; for what <takes no time and hence is present> in an instant is a whole.[3]

10 This also makes it clear that it is wrong to say there is a process or a coming-to-be of pleasure. For this is not said of everything, but only of what is divisible and not a whole; for seeing, or a point, or a unit, has no coming to be, and none of these is either a process or a becoming. But pleasure is a whole; hence it too has no coming to be.

[PLEASURE COMPLETES AN ACTIVITY]

15 Every faculty of perception[4] is active in relation to its perceptible object, and completely active when it is in good condition in relation to the finest of its perceptible objects. For this above all seems to be the character of complete activity, whether it is ascribed to the faculty or to the subject that has it. Hence for each faculty the best activity is the activity of the subject in the best condition in relation to the best object of the faculty.

20 This activity will also be the most complete and the pleasantest. For every faculty of perception, and every sort of thought and study, has its pleasure; the pleasantest activity is the most complete; and the most complete is the activity of the subject in good condition in relation to the most excellent object of the faculty. Pleasure completes the activity.

25 But the way in which pleasure completes the activity is not the way

---

3. **instant**: Lit. 'now'; cf. *Phys.* 218a6, 220a18. There is no coming into being of pleasure because coming into being requires the parts to come into being one after the other, and pleasure is present as a whole all at once.

4. **faculty of perception**: *aisthēsis*. On 'objects' see PERCEPTION #1.

in which the perceptible object and the faculty of perception complete it when they are both excellent—just as health and the doctor are not the cause of being healthy in the same way.[5] For clearly a pleasure arises that corresponds to each faculty of perception, since we say that sights and sounds are pleasant; and clearly it arises above all whenever the faculty of perception is best, and is active in relation to the best sort of object. When this is the condition of the perceptible object and of the perceiving subject, there will always be pleasure, when the producer and the subject to be affected are both present.

Pleasure completes the activity—not, however, as the state does, by being present <in the activity>, but as a sort of consequent end, like the bloom on youths.[6]

Hence as long as the objects of understanding or perception and the subject that judges or attends are in the right condition, there will be pleasure in the activity. For as long as the subject affected and the productive <cause> remain similar and in the same relation to each other, the same thing naturally arises.

Then how is it that no one is continuously pleased? Is it not because we get tired? For nothing human is capable of continuous activity, and hence no continuous pleasure arises either, since pleasure is a consequence of the activity.

Again, some things delight us when they are new to us, but less alter, for the same reason. For at first our thought is stimulated and intensely active toward them, as our sense of sight is when we look closely at something; but later the activity becomes lax and careless, so that the pleasure fades also.

We might think that everyone desires pleasure, since everyone aims at being alive. Living is a type of activity, and each of us is active toward the objects he likes most and in the ways he likes most. The musician, for instance, activates his hearing in hearing melodies; the lover of learning activates his thought in thinking about objects of study; and so on for each of the others. Pleasure completes their activities, and hence completes life, which they desire. It is reasonable, then, that they also aim at pleasure, since it completes each person's life for him, and life is choiceworthy.

5. **health and . . . same way**: The doctor is the efficient CAUSE, and health the formal cause, of being healthy. The different ways of completing an activity, however, seem to be final causes.

6. **Pleasure completes . . .**: Perceiving is good as an end in itself, as the activity of a desirable capacity. The pleasure is an added end, another good in itself, which is consequent on our choosing the action as a good in itself. Similarly, the 'bloom' of a youth (the attractiveness that makes a youth an object of desire and pleasure to an older man) is added to his youth.

20 Do we choose life because of pleasure, or pleasure because of life? Let us set aside this question for now, since the two appear to be yoked together, and to allow no separation; for pleasure never arises without activity, and, equally, it completes every activity.

[PLEASURES DIFFER IN KIND]

5

Hence pleasures also seem to be of different species. For we suppose that things of different species are completed by different things. That is how it appears, both with natural things and with artifacts—for instance,
25 with animals, trees, a painting, a statue, a house or an implement; and similarly, activities that differ in species are also completed by things that differ in species. Activities of thought differ in species from activities of the faculties of perception, and so do these from each other; so also, then, do the pleasures that complete them.
30 This is also apparent from the way each pleasure is proper to the activity that it completes. For the proper pleasure increases the activity. For we judge each thing better and more exactly when our activity is associated with pleasure. If, for instance, we enjoy doing geometry, we become better geometers, and understand each question better; and
35 similarly lovers of music, building and so on improve at their proper function when they enjoy it.
1175b Each pleasure increases the activity; what increases it is proper to it; and since the activities are different in species, what is proper to them is also different in species.

This is even more apparent from the way some activities are impeded by pleasures from others. For lovers of flutes, for instance, cannot pay attention to a conversation if they catch the sound of someone playing
5 the flute, because they enjoy flute-playing more than their present activity; and so the pleasure proper to flute-playing destroys the activity of conversation.

The same is true in other cases also, whenever we are engaged in two activities at once. For the pleasanter activity pushes out the other
10 one, all the more if it is much pleasanter, so that we no longer even engage in the other activity. Hence if we are enjoying one thing intensely, we do not do another very much. It is when we are only mildly pleased that we do something else; for instance, people who eat nuts in theatres do this most when the actors are bad.
15 Since, then, the proper pleasure makes an activity more exact, longer and better, while an alien pleasure damages it, clearly the two pleasures differ widely.

For an alien pleasure does virtually what a proper pain does. The proper pain destroys activity, so that if, for instance, writing or rational calculation has no pleasure and is in fact painful for us, we do not write or calculate, since the activity is painful. Hence the proper pleasures   *20* and pains have contrary effects on an activity; and the proper ones are those that arise from the activity in itself. And as we have said, the effect of alien pleasures is similar to the effect of pain, since they ruin the activity, though not in the same way as pain.

[WHICH PLEASURES ARE GOODS?]

Since activities differ in degrees of decency and badness, and some are   *25* choiceworthy, some to be avoided, some neither, the same is true of pleasures; for each activity has its own proper pleasure. Hence the pleasure proper to an excellent activity is decent, and the one proper to a base activity is vicious; for, similarly, appetites for fine things are praiseworthy, and appetites for shameful things are blameworthy.

And in fact the pleasure in an activity is more proper to it than the   *30* desire for it. For the desire is distinguished from it in time and in nature; but the pleasure is close to the activity, and so little distinguished from it that disputes arise about whether the activity is the same as the pleasure.

Still, pleasure is seemingly neither thought nor perception, since that   *35* would be absurd. Rather, it is because <pleasure and activity> are not separated that to some people they appear the same.

Hence, just as activities differ, so do the pleasures. Sight differs from   *1176a* touch in purity, as hearing and smell do from taste; hence the pleasures also differ in the same way. So also do the pleasures of thought differ from these <pleasures of sense>; and both sorts have different kinds within them.

Each kind of animal seems to have its own proper pleasure, just as it has its own proper function; for the proper pleasure will be the one that corresponds to its activity.

This is apparent if we also study each kind. For a horse, a dog and   *5* a human being have different pleasures; and, as Heracleitus says, an ass would choose chaff over gold, since asses find food pleasanter than gold. Hence animals that differ in species also have pleasures that differ in species; and it would be reasonable for animals of the same species to have the same pleasures also.

In fact, however, the pleasures differ quite a lot, in human beings at   *10* any rate. For the same things delight some people, and cause pain to others; and while some find them painful and hateful, others find them pleasant and lovable. The same is true of sweet things. For the same things do not seem sweet to a feverish and to a healthy person, or hot to an enfeebled and to a vigorous person; and the same is true of other   *15* things.

But in all such cases it seems that what is really so is what appears
so to the excellent person. If this is correct, as it seems to be, and virtue,
i.e., the good person insofar as he is good, is the measure of each thing,
then what appear pleasures to him will also *be* pleasures, and what is
pleasant will be what he enjoys.

20   And if what he finds objectionable appears pleasant to someone, that
is nothing surprising, since human beings suffer many sorts of corruption
and damage. It is not pleasant, however, except to these people in these
conditions.

Clearly, then, we should say that the pleasures agreed to be shameful
are not pleasures at all, except to corrupted people.[7]

25   But what about those pleasures that seem to be decent? Of these,
which kind, or which particular pleasure, should we take to be the
pleasure of a human being? Surely it will be clear from the activities,
since the pleasures are consequences of these.

Hence the pleasures that complete the activities of the complete and
blessedly happy man, whether he has one activity or more than one,
will be called the human pleasures to the fullest extent. The other pleasures will be human in secondary and even more remote ways corresponding to the character of the activities.

[HAPPINESS AND INTELLECTUAL ACTIVITY]

[HAPPINESS AND VIRTUOUS ACTION]

6

30   We have now finished our discussion of the types of virtue; of friendship;
and of pleasure. It remains for us to discuss happiness in outline, since
we take this to be the end of human <aims>. Our discussion will be
shorter if we first take up again what we said before.

We said, then, that happiness is not a state.[8] For if it were, someone
35   might have it and yet be asleep for his whole life, living the life of a
1176b   plant, or suffer the greatest misfortunes. If we do not approve of this,
we count happiness as an activity rather than a state, as we said before.

Some activities are necessary, i.e., choiceworthy for some other end,
while others are choiceworthy in themselves. Clearly, then, we should
5   count happiness as one of those activities that are choiceworthy in themselves, not as one of those choiceworthy for some other end. For happi-

7. The good person is the standard of what is really a pleasure. Vicious people
mistake what appears pleasant to them for what is really pleasant (really pleasant
for them too though not pleasant for them in their depraved condition). Cf.
1113a27, PROTAGORAS.

8. **not a state**: See 1095b31.

ness lacks nothing, but is self-sufficient; and an activity is choiceworthy in itself when nothing further beyond it is sought from it.

This seems to be the character of actions expressing virtue; for doing fine and excellent actions is choiceworthy for itself.

But pleasant amusements also <seem to be choiceworthy in them-   *10* selves>. For they are not chosen for other ends, since they actually cause more harm than benefit, by causing neglect of our bodies and possessions.

Moreover, most of those people congratulated for their happiness resort to these sorts of pastimes. Hence people who are witty participants in them have a good reputation with tyrants, since they offer themselves   *15* as pleasant <partners> in the tyrant's aims, and these are the sort of people the tyrant requires. And so these amusements seem to have the character of happiness because people in supreme power spend their leisure in them.

However, these sorts of people are presumably no evidence. For virtue and understanding, the sources of excellent activities, do not depend on holding supreme power. Further, these powerful people have had   *20* no taste of pure and civilized⁹ pleasure, and so they resort to bodily pleasures. But that is no reason to think these pleasures are most choiceworthy, since boys also think that what they honor is best. Hence, just as different things appear honorable to boys and to men, it is reasonable that in the same way different things appear honorable to base and to decent people.

As we have often said, then, what is honorable and pleasant is what   *25* is so to the excellent person; and to each type of person the activity expressing his own proper state is most choiceworthy; hence the activity expressing virtue is most choiceworthy to the excellent person <and hence is most honorable and pleasant>.

Happiness, then, is not found in amusement; for it would be absurd if the end were amusement, and our lifelong efforts and sufferings aimed   *30* at amusing ourselves. For we choose practically everything for some other end—except for happiness, since it is <the> end; but serious work and toil aimed <only> at amusement appears stupid and excessively childish. Rather, it seems correct to amuse ourselves so that we can do something serious, as Anacharsis says; for amusement would seem to be relaxation, and it is because we cannot toil continuously that we   *35* require relaxation. Relaxation, then, is not <the> end, since we pursue it <to prepare> for activity.   *1177a*

Further, the happy life seems to be a life expressing virtue, which is a life involving serious actions, and not consisting in amusement.

Besides, we say that things to be taken seriously are better than funny

9. **civilized**: See FREE.

5   things that provide amusement, and that in each case the activity of the
      better part and the better person is more serious and excellent; and the
      activity of what is better is superior, and thereby has more the character
      of happiness.
          Moreover, anyone at all, even a slave, no less than the best person,
      might enjoy bodily pleasures; but no one would allow that a slave shares
      in happiness, if one does not <also allow that the slave shares in the
      sort of> life <needed for happiness>.[10] Happiness, then, is found not
10   in these pastimes, but in the activities expressing virtue, as we also said
      previously.

[THEORETICAL STUDY AND HAPPINESS]

7

If happiness, then, is activity expressing virtue, it is reasonable for it to
express the supreme virtue, which will be the virtue of the best thing.
15   The best is understanding, or whatever else seems to be the natural
      ruler and leader, and to understand what is fine and divine, by being
      itself either divine or the most divine element in us.
          Hence complete happiness will be its activity expressing its proper
      virtue; and we have said that this activity is the activity of study. This
      seems to agree with what has been said before, and also with the truth.
20   For this activity is supreme, since understanding is the supreme ele-
      ment in us, and the objects of understanding are the supreme objects
      of knowledge$_g$.
          Besides, it is the most continuous activity, since we are more capable
      of continuous study than any continuous action.
          We think pleasure must be mixed into happiness; and it is agreed
25   that the activity expressing wisdom is the pleasantest of the activities
      expressing virtue. At any rate, philosophy seems to have remarkably
      pure and firm pleasures; and it is reasonable for those who have knowl-
      edge$_o$ to spend their lives more pleasantly than those who seek it.
          Moreover, the self-sufficiency we spoke of will be found in study
      above all.
          For admittedly the wise person, the just person and the other virtuous
30   people all need the good things necessary for life. Still, when these are
      adequately supplied, the just person needs other people as partners and
      recipients of his just actions; and the same is true of the temperate person
      and the brave person and each of the others.
          But the wise person is able, and more able the wiser he is, to study
1177b even by himself; and though he presumably does it better with col-

10. **if one . . . for happiness**>: On SLAVES and happiness see 1099b32.

leagues, even so he is more self-sufficient than any other <virtuous person>.

Besides, study seems to be liked because of itself alone,[11] since it has no result beyond having studied. But from the virtues concerned with action we try to a greater or lesser extent to gain something beyond the action itself.

Happiness seems to be found in leisure, since we accept trouble so   5
that we can be at leisure, and fight wars so that we can be at peace. Now the virtues concerned with action have their activities in politics or war, and actions here seem to require trouble.

This seems completely true for actions in war, since no one chooses to fight a war, and no one continues it, for the sake of fighting a war;   10
for someone would have to be a complete murderer if he made his friends his enemies so that there could be battles and killings.

But the actions of the politician require trouble also. Beyond political activities themselves those actions seek positions of power and honors; or at least they seek happiness for the politician himself and for his fellow-citizens, which is something different from political science itself,   15
and clearly is sought on the assumption that it is different.

Hence among actions expressing the virtues those in politics and war are preeminently fine and great; but they require trouble, aim at some <further> end, and are choiceworthy for something other than themselves.[12]

But the activity of understanding, it seems, is superior in excellence   20
because it is the activity of study, aims at no end beyond itself and has its own proper pleasure, which increases the activity. Further, self-sufficiency, leisure, unwearied activity (as far as is possible for a human being), and any other features ascribed to the blessed person, are evidently features of this activity.

Hence a human being's complete happiness will be this activity, if it   25
receives a complete span of life,[13] since nothing incomplete is proper to happiness.

Such a life would be superior to the human level. For someone will live it not insofar as he is a human being, but insofar as he has some divine element in him. And the activity of this divine element is as much superior to the activity expressing the rest of virtue as this element is superior to the compound. Hence if understanding is something divine   30

11. **because of itself alone**: Cf. 1176b2. Study is not chosen for any end wholly external to it. Less probably, 'it is the only virtue chosen because of itself'.

12. **and are . . . themselves**: Lit. 'and are choiceworthy not because of themselves'. Less probably, 'and are not choiceworthy because of themselves'.

13. **complete span**: See 1098a18, 1101a16.

in comparison with a human being, so also will the life that expresses understanding be divine in comparison with human life.

We ought not to follow the proverb-writers, and 'think human, since you are human', or 'think mortal, since you are mortal.' Rather, as far as we can, we ought to be pro-immortal,[14] and go to all lengths to live a life
1178a   that expresses our supreme element; for however much this element may lack in bulk, by much more it surpasses everything in power and value.

Moreover, each person seems to be his understanding, if he is his controlling and better element; it would be absurd, then, if he were to choose not his own life, but something else's.

5   And what we have said previously will also apply now. For what is proper to each thing's nature is supremely best and pleasantest for it; and hence for a human being the life expressing understanding will be supremely best and pleasantest, if understanding above all is the human being. This life, then, will also be happiest.

[THEORETICAL STUDY AND VIRTUES OF CHARACTER]

8

The life expressing the other kind of virtue <i.e., the kind concerned
10   with action> is <happiest> in a secondary way because the activities expressing this virtue are human.

For we do just and brave actions, and the others expressing the virtues, in relation to other people, by abiding by what fits each person in contracts, services, all types of actions, and also in feelings; and all these appear to be human conditions.

15   Indeed, some feelings actually seem to arise from the body; and in many ways virtue of character seems to be proper to feelings.

Besides, intelligence is yoked together with virtue of character, and so is this virtue with intelligence.[15] For the principles of intelligence express the virtues of character; and correctness in virtues of character
20   expresses intelligence. And since these virtues are also connected to feelings, they are concerned with the compound. Since the virtues of the compound are human virtues, the life and the happiness expressing these virtues is also human.

The virtue of understanding, however, is separated <from the compound>. Let us say no more about it, since an exact account would be too large a task for our present project.

25   Moreover, it seems to need external supplies very little, or <at any rate> less than virtue of character needs them. For grant that they both need necessary goods, and to the same extent, since there will be only

14. **pro-immortal**: *athanatizein*. Less probably, 'make oneself immortal'.

15. **Besides . . . with intelligence**: See 1145a4.

a very small difference even though the politician labors more about the body and suchlike. Still, there will be a large difference in <what is needed> for the <proper> activities <of each type of virtue>.

For the generous person will need money for generous actions; and   *30*
the just person will need it for paying debts, since wishes are not clear, and people who are not just pretend to wish to do justice. Similarly, the brave person will need enough power, and the temperate person will need freedom <to do intemperate actions>, if they are to achieve anything that the virtue requires. For how else will they, or any other virtuous people, make their virtue clear?

Moreover, it is disputed whether it is decision or actions that is more   *35*
in control of virtue, on the assumption that virtue depends on both.[16]   *1178b*
Well, certainly it is clear that what is complete depends on both; but for actions many external goods are needed, and the greater and finer the actions the more numerous are the external goods needed.

But someone who is studying needs none of these goods, for that activity at least; indeed, for study at least, we might say they are even hindrances.

Insofar as he is a human being, however, and <hence> lives together   *5*
with a number of other human beings, he chooses to do the actions expressing virtue.[17] Hence he will need the sorts of external goods <that are needed for the virtues>, for living a human life.

In another way also it appears that complete happiness is some activity of study. For we traditionally suppose that the gods more than anyone   *10*
are blessed and happy; but what sorts of actions ought we to ascribe to them? Just actions? Surely they will appear ridiculous making contracts, returning deposits and so on. Brave actions? Do they endure what <they find> frightening and endure dangers because it is fine? Generous actions? Whom will they give to? And surely it would be absurd for them to have currency or anything like that. What would their temperate   *15*
actions be? Surely it is vulgar praise to say that they do not have base appetites. When we go through them all, anything that concerns actions appears trivial and unworthy of the gods.

However, we all traditionally suppose that they are alive and active,   *20*
since surely they are not asleep like Endymion. Then if someone is alive, and action is excluded, and production even more, what is left but study? Hence the gods' activity that is superior in blessedness will be an activity of study. And so the human activity that is most akin to the gods' will, more than any others, have the character of happiness.

16. **it is disputed . . . both**: Aristotle usually takes decision to be the crucial aspect; see 1111b5.

17. **Insofar . . . expressing virtue**: See 1097b9. Aristotle seems to concede that a human being's happiness includes the activity of other virtues besides study.

25   A sign of this is the fact that other animals have no share in happiness, being completely deprived of this activity of study. For the whole life of the gods is blessed, and human life is blessed to the extent that it has something resembling this sort of activity; but none of the other animals is happy, because none of them shares in study at all. Hence happiness

30   extends just as far as study extends, and the more someone studies, the happier he is, not coincidentally but insofar as he studies, since study is valuable in itself. And so <on this argument> happiness will be some kind of study.

However, the happy person is a human being, and so will need

35   external prosperity also; for his nature is not self-sufficient for study, but he needs a healthy body, and needs to have food and the other services provided.

1179a   Still, even though no one can be blessedly happy without external goods, we must not think that to be happy we will need many large goods. For self-sufficiency and action do not depend on excess, and we can do fine actions even if we do not rule earth and sea; for even from

5   moderate resources we can do the actions expressing virtue. This is evident to see, since many private citizens seem to do decent actions no less than people in power do—even more, in fact. It is enough if moderate resources are provided; for the life of someone whose activity expresses virtue will be happy.

10   Solon surely described happy people well, when he said they had been moderately supplied with external goods, had done what he regarded as the finest actions, and had lived their lives temperately. For it is possible to have moderate possessions and still to do the right actions.

And Anaxagoras would seem to have supposed that the happy person

15   was neither rich nor powerful, since he said he would not be surprised if the happy person appeared an absurd sort of person to the many. For the many judge by externals, since these are all they perceive.

Hence the beliefs of the wise would seem to accord with our arguments.

These considerations do indeed produce some confidence. The truth,

20   however, in questions about action is judged from what we do and how we live, since these are what control <the answers to such questions>. Hence we ought to examine what has been said by applying it to what we do and how we live; and if it harmonizes with what we do, we should accept it, but if it conflicts we should count it <mere> words.

The person whose activity expresses understanding and who takes care of understanding would seem to be in the best condition, and most

25   loved by the gods. For if the gods pay some attention to human beings, as they seem to, it would be reasonable for them to take pleasure in what is best and most akin to them, namely understanding; and reasonable for them to benefit in return those who most of all like and honor

444

understanding, on the assumption that these people attend to what is beloved by the gods, and act correctly and finely.

Clearly, all this is true of the wise person more than anyone else;   *30* hence he is most loved by the gods. And it is likely that this same person will be happiest; hence the wise person will be happier than anyone else on this argument too.

[ETHICS AND POLITICS]

[MORAL EDUCATION]

9

We have now said enough in outlines about happiness and the virtues, and about friendship and pleasure also. Should we then think that our   *35* decision <to study these> has achieved its end? On the contrary, the   *1179b* aim of studies about action, as we say, is surely not to study and know$_0$ about each thing, but rather to act on our knowledge. Hence knowing about virtue is not enough, but we must also try to possess and exercise virtue, or become good in any other way.

Now if arguments were sufficient by themselves to make people decent,   *5* the rewards they would command would justifiably have been many and large, as Theognis says, and rightly bestowed. In fact, however, arguments seem to have enough influence to stimulate and encourage the civilized ones among the young people, and perhaps to make virtue take possession of a well-born character that truly loves what is fine;   *10* but they seem unable to stimulate the many toward being fine and good.

For the many naturally obey fear, not shame; they avoid what is base because of the penalties, not because it is disgraceful. For since they live by their feelings, they pursue their proper pleasures and the sources of them, and avoid the opposed pains, and have not even a notion of what   *15* is fine and <hence> truly pleasant, since they have had no taste of it.

What argument could reform people like these? For it is impossible, or not easy, to alter by argument what has long been absorbed by habit; but, presumably, we should be satisfied to achieve some share in virtue when we already have what we seem to need to become decent.

Some think it is nature that makes people good; some think it is habit;   *20* some that it is teaching.

The <contribution> of nature clearly is not up to us, but results from some divine cause in those who have it, who are the truly fortunate ones.

Arguments and teaching surely do not influence everyone, but the   *25* soul of the student needs to have been prepared by habits for enjoying and hating finely, like ground that is to nourish seed. For someone whose life follows his feelings would not even listen to an argument turning him away, or comprehend it <if he did listen>; and in that state how could he be persuaded to change? And in general feelings seem to yield to force, not to argument.

30   Hence we must already in some way have a character suitable for virtue, fond of what is fine and objecting to what is shameful.

[*LEGISLATION*]

But it is hard for someone to be trained correctly for virtue from his youth if he has not been brought up under correct laws, since the many, especially the young, do not find it pleasant to live in a temperate and

35   resistant way. Hence laws must prescribe their upbringing and practices; for they will not find these things painful when they get used to them.

1180a   Presumably, however, it is not enough to get the correct upbringing and attention when they are young; rather, they must continue the same practices and be habituated to them when they become men. Hence we need laws concerned with these things also, and in general with all of

5   life. For the many yield to compulsion more than to argument, and to sanctions more than to what is fine.

This, some think, is why legislators should urge people toward virtue and exhort them to aim at what is fine, on the assumption that anyone whose good habits have prepared him decently will listen to them, but should impose corrective treatments and penalties on anyone who

10   disobeys or lacks the right nature, and completely expel an incurable. For the decent person, it is assumed, will attend to reason because his life aims at what is fine, while the base person, since he desires pleasure, has to receive corrective treatment by pain, like a beast of burden; that is why it is said that the pains imposed must be those most contrary to the pleasures he likes.

15   As we have said, then, someone who is to be good must be finely brought up and habituated, and then must live in decent practices, doing nothing base either willingly or unwillingly. And this will be true if his life follows some sort of understanding and correct order that has influence over him.

20   A father's instructions, however, lack this influence and compelling power; and so in general do the instructions of an individual man, unless he is a king or someone like that. Law, however, has the power that compels; and law is reason that proceeds from a sort of intelligence and understanding. Besides, people become hostile to an individual human being who opposes their impulses even if he is correct in opposing them; whereas a law's prescription of what is decent is not burdensome.

25   And yet, only in Sparta,[18] or in a few other cities as well, does the

---

18. **And yet . . . Sparta**: On Sparta see *Pol.* 1333b5–35.

legislator seem to have attended to upbringing and practices. In most other cities they are neglected, and each individual citizen lives as he wishes, 'laying down the rules for his children and wife', like a Cyclops.

It is best, then, if the community attends to upbringing, and attends   30
correctly. If, however, the community neglects it, it seems fitting for each individual to promote the virtue of his children and his friends— to be able to do it, or at least to decide to do it.

[LEGISLATIVE SCIENCE]

From what we have said, however, it seems he will be better able to do it if he acquires legislative science. For, clearly, attention by the community   35
works through laws, and decent attention works through excellent laws;   1180b
and whether the laws are written or unwritten, for the education of one or of many, seems unimportant, as it is in music, gymnastics and other practices. For just as in cities the provisions of law and the <prevailing> types of character have influence, similarly a father's words and habits   5
have influence, and all the more because of kinship and because of the benefits he does; for his children are already fond of him and naturally ready to obey.

Moreover, education adapted to an individual is actually better than a common education for everyone, just as individualized medical treat- ment is better. For though generally a feverish patient benefits from rest and starvation, presumably some patient does not; nor does the boxing   10
instructor impose the same way of fighting on everyone. Hence it seems that treatment in particular cases is more exactly right when each person gets special attention, since he then more often gets the suitable treatment.

Nonetheless a doctor, a gymnastics trainer and everyone else will give the best individual attention if they also know$_o$ universally what is   15
good for all, or for these sorts. For sciences are said to be, and are, of what is common <to many particular cases>.

Admittedly someone without scientific knowledge may well attend properly to a single person, if his experience has allowed him to take exact note of what happens in each case, just as some people seem to be their own best doctors, though unable to help anyone else at all.   20
Nonetheless, presumably, it seems that someone who wants to be an expert in a craft and a branch of study should progress to the universal, and come to know$_g$ that, as far as possible; for that, as we have said, is what the sciences are about.[19]

19. **Nonetheless . . .:** Though experience may make someone competent in a restricted range of cases, general competence and understanding require the grasp of the UNIVERSAL. See *Met.* i 1.

25   Then perhaps also someone who wishes to make people better by his
attention, many people or few, should try to acquire legislative science,
if we will become good through laws. For not just anyone can improve
the condition of just anyone, or the person presented to him; but if
anyone can it is the person with knowledge₀, just as in medical science
and the others that require attention and intelligence.

[WHO SHOULD TEACH LEGISLATIVE SCIENCE?]

30   Next, then, should we examine whence and how someone might acquire
legislative science? Just as in other cases <we go to the practitioner>,
should we go to the politicians? For, as we saw, legislative science seems
to be a part of political science.
       But is the case of political science perhaps apparently different from
the other sciences and capacities? For evidently in others the same people, such as doctors or painters, who transmit the capacity to others
35   actively practice it themselves. By contrast, it is the sophists who adver-
1181a   tise that they teach politics but none of them practices it. Instead, those
who practice it are the political activists, and they seem to act on some
sort of capacity and experience rather than thought.
       For evidently they neither write nor speak on such questions, though
5   presumably it would be finer to do this than to compose speeches for
the law courts or the Assembly; nor have they made politicians out of
their own sons or any other friends of theirs. And yet it would be
reasonable for them to do this if they were able; for there is nothing
better than the political capacity that they could leave to their cities, and
nothing better that they could decide to produce in themselves, or,
therefore, in their closest friends.
10   Certainly experience would seem to contribute quite a lot; otherwise
people would not have become better politicians by familiarity with
politics. Hence those who aim to know₀ about political science would
seem to need experience as well.
       By contrast, those of the sophists who advertise <that they teach
political science> appear to be a long way from teaching; for they are
altogether ignorant about the sort of thing political science is, and the
15   sorts of things it is about. For if they had known₀ what it is, they would
not have taken it to be the same as rhetoric, or something inferior to it,
or thought it an easy task to assemble the laws with good reputations
and then legislate. For they think they can select the best laws, as though
the selection itself did not require comprehension, and as though correct
judgment were not the most important thing, as it is in music.
20   It is those with experience in each area who judge the products correctly and who comprehend the method or way of completing them,
and what fits with what; for if we lack experience, we must be satisfied

with noticing that the product is well or badly made, as with painting. Now laws would seem to be the products of political science; how, then, could someone acquire legislative science, or judge which laws are best, from laws alone? For neither do we appear to become experts in medicine by reading textbooks.

And yet doctors not only try to describe the <recognized> treatments, but also distinguish different <physical> states, and try to say how each type of patient might be cured and must be treated. And what they say seems to be useful to the experienced, though useless to the ignorant.

Similarly, then, collections of laws and political systems might also, presumably, be most useful if we are capable of studying them and of judging what is done finely or in the contrary way, and what sorts of <elements> fit with what. Those who lack the <proper> state <of experience> when they go through these collections will not manage to judge finely, unless they can do it all by themselves <without training>, though they might come to comprehend them better by going through them.

[TRANSITION TO POLITICS]

Since, then, our predecessors have left the area of legislation uncharted, it is presumably better to examine it ourselves instead, and indeed to examine political systems in general, and so to complete the philosophy of human affairs, as far as we are able.

First, then, let us try to review any sound remarks our predecessors have made on particular topics. Then let us study the collected political systems,[20] to see from them what sorts of things preserve and destroy cities, and political systems of different types; and what causes some cities to conduct politics well, and some badly.

For when we have studied these questions, we will perhaps grasp better what sort of political system is best; how each political system should be organized so as to be best; and what habits and laws it should follow.[21]

Let us discuss this, then, starting from the beginning.

20. **collected political systems**: Aristotle and his students collected 158 of them. Only one, the *Constitution of Athens*, largely survives.

21. **For when . . . should follow**: In this and the previous paragraph Aristotle outlines the *Pol.*, as the natural completion of the *EN*.

449

POLITICS

Book I

[THE HUMAN GOOD AND THE POLITICAL COMMUNITY]

[THE CITY IS THE HUMAN COMMUNITY AIMING AT THE ULTIMATE GOOD]

1

1252a We see that every city is some sort of community,* and that every community is constituted for the sake of some good, since everyone does everything for the sake of what seems good.[1] Clearly, then, while all communities aim at some good, the community that aims most of all
5 at the good—at the good that most of all controls all the other goods— is the one that most of all controls and includes the others; and this is the one called the city, the political community.[2]

[THE DIFFERENCE BETWEEN POLITICAL RULE AND OTHER FORMS OF RULE]

It is wrong, then, to suppose, as some do,[3] that the character of the politician,* the king, the household manager, and the slave-master is
10 the same. People suppose this because they think the difference is not a difference in kind, but only in the number who are ruled, so that the ruler of a few is a master, the ruler of more people is a household-manager, and the ruler of still more people is a politician or a king—on the assumption that a large household is no different from a small city. And all they can say to distinguish a king from a politician is that someone
15 who directs things himself is a king, whereas someone who follows the principles[4] of political science, ruling and being ruled in turn, is a politician. These views are not true.

What we mean will be clear if the investigation follows our recognized

---

1. **everyone . . . what seems good**: Cf. EN 1094a1–3, 1102a2–3.

2. **the city, the political community**: Aristotle relies, as he often does (cf. 1253a2–3) on the connection between *polis* and the adjective *politikos*.

3. **as some do**: See Plato, *Statesman* 259b. On the importance of distinguishing different types of rule see 1278b32, 1324b32.

4. **principles**: *logoi*. See REASON.

line* of inquiry.[5] Just as in other cases we must divide the composite into incomposites, since these are the smallest parts of the whole, so 20 also in this case we must investigate the components of the city; for then we will also see better the difference between these rulers, and the prospect of finding any sort of scientific treatment[6] of the questions we have mentioned.

[THE ELEMENTARY COMMUNITIES LEADING TO A CITY]

2

The best way to study this as well as other matters is to trace things 25 back to their beginnings[7] and observe their growth. First, then, those who cannot exist without each other have to form pairs, as female and male do for reproduction. And they do this not because of any decision,* but from the natural impulse that they share with other animals and with plants to leave behind another of the same kind as oneself.[8] 30

Self-preservation <rather than reproduction> is the basis of the natural division between ruler and subject. For the capacity for rational foresight makes one a natural ruler and natural master, and the capacity to execute this foresight by bodily labor[9] makes another a subject and a natural slave; that is why the interests of master and slave coincide.

Now there is a natural distinction between the female and the slave. 1252b For nature makes nothing stingily, like a smith making a Delphic knife,[10] but makes one thing for one function, since the best instrument for a particular function is made exclusively for it, not for many others. Among 5 foreigners,* however, female and slave have the same rank; the reason is that no foreigners are natural rulers, and so their community consists of a female slave and a male slave. Hence the poets say 'It is to be expected that Greeks rule over foreigners', assuming that the foreigner and the slave are naturally the same.

And so from these two communities <between female and male and 10 between slave and master> the first community that results is the household. Hesiod[11] was right when he said 'Get first of all a house, a wife,

5. **line of inquiry**: For this method cf. *HA* 486a5–14, *PA* 646a13.

6. **scientific treatment**: Lit. 'belonging to a craft', *technikon*.

7. **beginnings**: *archai*. See PRINCIPLE #1.

8. **natural impulse . . . oneself**: Cf. *DA* 415a26.

9. **to execute . . . labor**: Read *tauta tōi sōmati poiein*. (OCT: 'to labor with one's body'.)

10. **a Delphic knife**: Like a Swiss army knife, with several different functions.

11. **Hesiod**: *Works and Days* 406.

and a plough-ox'—for the poor use an ox in place of a slave. Hence the community naturally formed for every day[12] is a household of 'breadbin-mates' (as Charondas* calls them) or (as Epimenides* the Cretan says) 'manger-mates'.

15

The first community formed from a number of households for long-term advantage is a village, and the most natural type of village would seem to be an extension of a household, including children and grand-children, sometimes called 'milkmates'. That is why cities were also originally ruled by kings and some nations are ruled by kings even at present; they were formed from communities ruled by kings—for in every household the oldest member rules as its king, and the same is true in its extensions,[13] because the villagers are related by kinship. Homer[14] describes this when he says 'Each rules over his children and wives', because they were isolated, as households were in ancient times. And for the same reason everyone says the gods are ruled by a king; it is because we were all ruled by kings in ancient times, and some still are, and human beings ascribe to the gods a human way of life, as well as a human form.

20

25

The complete* community, formed from a number of villages, is a city. Unlike the others, it has the full degree of practically every sort of self-sufficiency;* it comes to be for the sake of living, but remains in being[15] for the sake of living well. That is why every city is natural, since the previous communities are natural. For the city is their end, and nature is an end; for we say that something's nature (for instance, of a human being, a horse, or a household) is the character it has when its coming to be is complete.[16] Moreover, the final cause and end is the best <good>, and self-sufficiency is both the end and the best <good>.

30

1253a

[*THE CITY FULFILLS HUMAN NATURE*]

It is evident, then, that the city exists by nature, and that a human being is by nature a political animal.[17] Anyone without a city because of his nature rather than his fortune is either worthless or superior to a human

---

12. **for every day**: i.e., for more than a short period. Or perhaps 'for day to day needs'.

13. **extensions**: i.e., villages.

14. **Homer**: *Odyssey* ix 114, referring to the Cyclopes.

15. **remains in being**: Lit. just 'is'. For the contrast with COMING TO BE see BEING #3. For the contrast between living and living well (i.e., HAPPINESS) cf. 1280a31.

16. **for we say ... is complete**: Cf. *Phys.* 193b12n.

17. **political animal**: See MAN #4.

being. Like the man reviled by Homer,[18] 'he has no kin, no law, no   5
home'. For his natural isolation from a city gives him an appetite for
war, since, like <a solitary piece> in a game of checkers, he has no
partner.

It is evident why a human being is more of a political animal than is
any bee or any gregarious animal; for nature, we say, does nothing
pointlessly,[19] and a human being is the only animal with rational dis-   10
course.[20] A voice signifies pleasure and pain, and so the other animals,
as well as human beings, have it, since their nature is far enough advanced for them to perceive pleasure and pain and to signify them to
one another. But rational discourse is for making clear what is expedient
or harmful, and hence what is just or unjust. For this is distinctive of   15
human beings in contrast to the other animals, that they are the only
ones with a perception of good and evil, and of just and unjust, and so
on; and it is community in these that produces a household and a city.

Further, the city is naturally prior* to the household and to the individual, since the whole is necessarily prior to the part.* For if the whole   20
animal is dead, neither foot nor hand will survive, except homonymously,* as if we were speaking of a stone hand—for that is what a
dead hand will be like. Now everything is defined by its function[21] and
potentiality; and so anything that has lost them should not be called the
same thing, but a homonymous thing.   25

Clearly, then, the city is also natural and is prior to the individual.
For if the individual separated from the city is not self-sufficient, his
relation to it corresponds to that of parts to wholes in other cases;[22] and
anyone who is incapable of membership in a community, or who has
no need of it because he is self-sufficient, is no part of a city, and so is
either a beast or a god.

Everyone has a natural impulse, then, toward this sort of community,   30
and whoever first constituted it is the cause of the greatest goods. For
just as a human being is the best of the animals if he has been completed,
he is also the worst of them if he is separated from law and the rule of
justice. For injustice is most formidable when it is armed, and a human
being naturally grows up armed and equipped for intelligence and virtue,   35

18. Homer, *Iliad* ix 63.

19. **nature . . . pointlessly**: See NATURE #6.

20. **rational discourse**; *logos*. See REASON #2, *Met.* 1006a13–15, *Rhet.* 1355b1.
Having *logos* is contrasted with simply having a voice.

21. **everything . . . function**: For the appeal to FUNCTION cf. *EN* 1097b24.

22. **For if . . . cases**: Aristotle argues that since the city is naturally PRIOR to the
individual (since without it individuals cannot fulfill their nature), it is also
natural (as claimed in 1253a2).

but can most readily use this equipment for ends that are contrary to intelligence and virtue;[23] hence without virtue he is the most unscrupulous and savage of animals, the most excessive in pursuit of sex and food. Justice, however, is political; for the rule of justice is an order in the political community, and justice is the judgment of what is just.[24]

[THE HOUSEHOLD]

3

1253b   Since it is evident what parts constitute the city, we must first discuss household* science, since every city is constituted of households. The parts of household management are the constituent parts of the household, and a complete household is constituted of slaves and free people.

5   Since we should begin our inquiry with the smallest parts of a thing, and since the primary and smallest parts of a household are master and slave, husband and wife, father and children, we should investigate these three things to see what each of them is and what its character ought to be. The three are: the combination ruled by the master; the

10   marital combination (since the combination of woman and man has no established name[25]); and, third, the child-producing combination (since this has no distinctive name either). Let these, then, be <the names of> the three we mentioned. There is also a fourth part, which some people think is <the whole of> household management, and which others think is the greatest part of it; and we should study what is true of this—I refer to what is called money-making.

[SLAVERY]

15   First, let us discuss master and slave, to see what is useful for the necessities of life, and to see if we can reach knowledge$_o$ that improves on current views about them.[26] For some suppose that rule over slaves is a science, and that household management, rule over slaves, political

20   science, and kingly science, are all the same, as we said at the beginning.[27]

23. **contrary . . . virtue**: Cf. *EN* 1103a23–26, 1144b1–14.

24. **Justice, however . . . just**: This sentence explains why justice, and therefore the city, is the cause (as claimed above) of great benefits; it guards against the bad effects of injustice.

25. **no established name**: Lit. 'no NAME'.

26. **to see what is useful . . . current views about them**: For these two purposes of the *Politics* cf. 1279b12.

27. **beginning**: Aristotle returns to correct the error mentioned at 1252a7 above.

Others, however, suppose that ruling over slaves is against nature, since (they say) law* makes one free and another a slave, whereas nature draws no distinction between them; that is why such rule (they say) is also unjust, since it rests on force.[28]

4

Possession is a part of the household, and acquisition of possessions is a part of household management, since we can neither live nor live well without the necessities; and so, just as the well-defined crafts need their   *25* proper tools if they are to complete their work, the same is true of the household manager. Some tools are inanimate, others animate; the pilot, for instance, uses the rudder as an inanimate tool, and the lookout as an animate tool (since in the practice of the crafts a servant serves as a   *30* tool). In the same way, then, a possession is a tool for living, and one's possessions are a collection of tools; a slave, then, is a particular sort of animate tool, and every servant is a tool prior to <other> tools.[29]

For suppose that each tool could follow orders, or could itself perceive in advance what is needed, and so could complete its work by itself,   *35* like the statues of Daedalus, or the tripods of Hephaestus, which, according to the poet, 'moved by themselves into the assembly of gods';[30] if, in the same way, a shuttle worked by itself and a plectrum struck the chords of a lyre by itself, master-craftsmen would have no need of   *1254a* servants, and masters would have no need of slaves.

What we <normally> call tools are in fact tools for production, while a possession is a tool for action;[31] for a shuttle results in something apart from its use, whereas a garment or a bed results only in the use of it. Further, since action and production differ in species, and tools are   *5* needed for both, tools must also differ correspondingly. Now a way of life is action, not production; that is why a slave is a servant in what promotes action.[32]

We speak of a possession in the same way as we speak of a part; for a part is not only a part of another thing, but belongs altogether to the   *10* other thing; and the same is true of a possession. That is why a master

---

28. **rests on force**: Since it is contrary to NATURE, it rests on FORCE.

29. **prior . . . tools**: As the next paragraph explains, a slave is needed in order to use the other tools.

30. **'moved . . . gods'**: Homer, *Iliad* ix 376.

31. **action**: *praxis*. Here Aristotle contrasts *praxis* with the production of artifacts in particular. Elsewhere he contrasts it with all production by CRAFTS (not just those that produce physical artifacts). See ACTION, *Rhet.* 1360b16.

32. **that is why . . . action**: since he is a tool for living.

is only a master of a slave, and does not also belong to the slave, whereas the slave not only is the slave of a master, but also belongs altogether to the master.

It is clear from this, then, what the nature and capacity of a slave is. Someone is a natural slave if, though a human being, he belongs to another, not to himself; a human being belongs to another if, though a human being, he is a possession; and a possession is a tool that is for action and is separable.[33]

[ARE THERE ANY NATURAL SLAVES?]

5

We must next consider whether there are any natural slaves[34]—any for whom it is better and just to be slaves—or there are none, so that all slavery is against nature; this is easy both to study from arguments and to grasp from the things that happen.[35]

For ruling and being ruled are not only necessary, but also expedient; and right from birth some <members of a species> are suited for[36] ruling, and are divided from those suited for being ruled. There are many species of rulers and ruled, and in every case rule over the better is better—for instance, rule over a human being is better than rule over a beast; for the function fulfilled by better agents is a better function, and where one rules and another is ruled, both have a function.

For whenever things are constituted from a number <of parts>—continuous or divided—and one common whole results, the ruler and the ruled are discernible in every case. Animate things receive this order from the nature of the universe; for even things without life—for instance, a musical harmony—have some sort of ruling principle.[37] But presumably this is a topic for a more popular* investigation than the present one.

An animal, first of all, is constituted primarily of soul and body; and the soul is the natural ruler, whereas the body is ruled. In investigating

33. **tool that is . . . separable**: Aristotle relies on the use of *organon* (see INSTRUMENT) both for a tool and for a bodily organ. A bodily organ is part of its possessor, and so inseparable, whereas a slave is not actually part of his owner.

34. **whether . . . natural slaves**: Cf. Alcidamas, quoted at *Rhet.* 1373b18.

35. **things that happen**: This is the sort of evidence that Aristotle sometimes calls 'APPEARANCES'. For the contrast between appearances and arguments see REASON #3.

36. **suited for**: Lit. 'toward', *epi*.

37. **ruling principle**: *archē*. See PRINCIPLE. Aristotle relies on the use of *archē* both for political rule and for a first principle or CAUSE.

what is natural, we should attend to things in the natural condition, not
in a corrupt condition; hence we should also study human beings in the
best condition of body and soul. In this case it is clear <that the soul is
the natural ruler>; for in depraved people, or those in a depraved condi-   *1254b*
tion, the body often seems to rule the soul, because their condition is
base and unnatural.

As we say, then, it is in an animal first of all that we can observe a
master's rule and political rule. For the rule of soul over body is a master's   *5*
rule, and the rule of intellect over desire is political, or rather kingly,[38]
rule. And here it is evident* that it is natural and expedient for the body
to be ruled by the soul, and for the affective part to be ruled by intellect,
by the part that has reason,[39] whereas equality or the reverse order is
harmful for all.

The same applies to the rule of human beings over other animals. For   *10*
the tame animals are naturally better than the wild, and it is better for
all the tame ones to be ruled by a human being, since that is how they
are preserved. Further, the male is naturally superior, the female inferior,
and the male is naturally the ruler and the female the ruled; and this   *15*
must be true of all human beings as well <as of other animals>.

Hence those who are as different <from normal human beings> as
body is from soul, or beast from human being—and this is the condition
of those whose function and best product is the use of their body—these
are natural slaves, and it is better for them, just as for the others we   *20*
have mentioned, to be ruled by a master's rule.

For someone is a natural slave if he is capable of belonging to another[40]
(that is why he belongs to another[41])—if, that is to say, he shares in
reason enough to perceive it <in another> without having it himself.
For the other animals obey feelings, not reason;[42] and moreover, the use
of slaves differs little from the use of tame animals, since both provide   *25*
bodily help in securing necessities.

Now, nature tends[43] to distinguish the bodies as well <as the souls>
of the free and the slaves, so that slaves' bodies are strong for use in

38. **or rather kingly**: since intellect (see UNDERSTANDING) and DESIRE are not
equals.

39. **part that has reason**: See SOUL #4.

40. **capable of belonging to another**: i.e., he has no rational part of his own.

41. **belongs to another**: in the sense specified in 1254a8–13, in the comparison
with parts of a body.

42. **obey feelings, not reason**: To this extent they are like slaves (though they
differ in being unable to perceive *logos*—REASON or rational discourse—in another).

43. **tends**: Or 'aims' (*bouletai*).

30

securing necessities, whereas free people's bodies are upright, and so useless for such work, but useful for political life (which is divided into use in war and use in peace). In fact, however, the contrary <of the natural tendency> often happens too, so that some have free people's bodies, and others have their souls. For at any rate it is evident that if

35

some people's bodies turned out to be as superior as the images of the gods are, everyone would say that the inferior are appropriately slaves to the superior. And if this is true in the case of the body, it is much

1255a

more justifiable to draw the distinction in the case of the soul; but the beauty of the soul is less easily seen than the beauty of the body.

It is evident, then, that some are naturally free, others natural slaves; and for natural slaves slavery is both expedient and just.

[REASONS FOR DOUBT ABOUT THE EXISTENCE OF NATURAL SLAVES [44]]

6

On the other hand, it is easy to see that those who take the contrary view <that slavery is unjust> are also in a way correct. For we speak

5

in two ways of slavery and a slave. <Apart from the natural slave>, there is also a legal slave, and legal slavery; for this law is a sort of agreement declaring that the losers in war belong to the winners. Now many students of law impeach this <allegedly> just <provision> as unlawful, as if it were a speaker;[45] for they find it shocking that if one

10

side is strong enough to force the other and is superior in power, the victim of the force is to be ruled as a slave. Some take this view, and others, among the wise as well <as among the many>, take the other view.

This dispute arises, and the arguments overlap,[46] because virtue, if supplied with resources, also, in a way, has the most power to

15

force, and moreover, in every case the winner excels in *some* good. This makes it seem that superior force always implies virtue, and that only a question of justice is in dispute.[47] This is why some think

44. Having put forward his own view, Aristotle now shows that it avoids the objections that might seem to refute belief in natural slavery.

45. **as if it were a speaker**: Aristotle refers to the Athenian provision allowing a speaker in the Assembly to challenge the legality (in American terms, the 'constitutionality') of any provision proposed by another speaker.

46. **overlap**: The arguments share a common premiss, that superior virtue gives a basis for ruling (see next note).

47. **This dispute . . . in dispute**: Both sides agree that (1) superior virtue gives a basis for ruling. The defenders of slavery by conquest also believe that (2) superior force implies superior virtue. In 'because virtue . . . in *some* good'

justice is goodwill,[48] while others think that precisely this rule by the
superior in power is just. For when these arguments are taken in separation,[49] neither has any strong or persuasive reply to the view that it is   20
right for the one who is better in virtue to rule.

And in general some cling to what they take to be a sort of justice
(since law is a sort of justice) when they take enslavement in war to be
just. But at the same time they say it is not just.[50] For the wars may
begin unjustly, and one would never say that someone who does not   25
deserve to be enslaved is a slave. If we disagree with this, it will turn
out that those who seem most nobly born are slaves or the sons of slaves,
if it happens that they <or their fathers> are captured and sold into
slavery. That is why the people they mean to call slaves are not these
<nobly born> people, but only foreigners; but in saying this, they are   30
looking for the natural slaves[51] we referred to at the beginning, since
one must concede that some are slaves everywhere, some nowhere.

The same is true of noble birth. People count themselves nobly born
not only at home, but everywhere, but the foreigners only at home—
assuming that they, unlike the foreigners, are free and nobly born with-   35
out qualification, as Theodectes'* Helen says: 'I am from divine stock
on both father's and mother's side. Who then would think it fitting to
call me a servant girl?' Whenever they say this, they distinguish slave   40
and free, and the nobly born and the baseborn, precisely by appeal to
virtue and vice; for they think it fitting for a good person to be born of   1255b
good people, just as a human being is born of a human being and a
beast of beasts. Often, however, though nature tends toward this result,
it is unable to achieve it.

It is clear, then, that there is some reason for the dispute, and that   5
<those enslaved> are not invariably natural slaves, nor are <the en-
slavers> naturally free. It is also clear that in some cases the natural
slave and the free person are distinguished; in these cases it is expedient
for the natural slave to be enslaved and for the naturally free person to

---

Aristotle explains why people believe (2). He then resolves the dispute by rejecting (2).

48. **goodwill**: Read *eunoia*. (OCT: 'foolishness', *anoia*.) This is the goodwill shown
by the victors in not enslaving the vanquished. On this view, enslavement is
unjust.

49. **taken in separation**: i.e., separated from the assumption that force implies
virtue.

50. **say it is not just**: They imply this because of the other things they believe.

51. **they . . . slaves**: In claiming that only foreigners are genuine slaves as a
result of conquest, they admit that natural inferiority determines whether someone ought to be enslaved.

be master. It is right for one to be ruled and for the other to rule, in the way that is natural for both of them, so that it is right for one to be master <and the other the slave>. To rule badly is to rule inexpediently

10 for both of them. For the same thing is expedient for the part as for the whole, and for the body as for the soul, and the slave is a sort of part of the master, since, though he is separated from his master's body, he is a sort of animate part of it. Hence the same thing is expedient for slave and master, and there is friendship[52] between them, if they are naturally worthy of these positions; but the contrary is true of those who

15 are slaves only by convention and force and do not deserve to be slaves.

* * * * * * *

BOOK II

[CRITICISMS OF PROPOSALS FOR IDEAL STATES [1]]

[THE AIM OF THE INQUIRY]

1

1260b27 Our decision is to study the best political community for those who are capable of living, as far as possible, in the conditions they would aspire

30 to live in;[2] hence we must also investigate the political systems that are found in cities said to be well governed,[3] and also any systems other people have proposed that seem well conceived. Our aim is to see what the correct condition is for a city and what is useful, and also to show that, in searching for something different from these systems, we are not behaving like people who want above all to play the sophist,*[4] but are undertaking this line of inquiry in response to the inadequacies of current systems. . . .

* * * * * * *

52. **friendship**: Cf. *EN* 1161a32–b8.

1. Bk ii is concerned with the proposals of various theorists and with the actual states (e.g., Sparta and Crete) that some people have presented as models. The extracts translated come from the criticism of Plato's *Republic*.

2. **aspire to live in**: Lit. 'would pray to live in'. Cf. 1288b23, 1295a39, 1325b36. Aristotle assumes favorable external circumstances for his ideal state, though he does not intend his assumptions to be so unrealistic that his ideal state becomes a mere utopia.

3. **well governed**: See GOOD GOVERNMENT.

4. **play the sophist**: by irrelevant displays of novelty and cleverness, with no good reasons for rejecting other views. Cf. *EN* 1146a21–27.

[SOME DIFFERENCES BETWEEN CITIZENS ARE ESSENTIAL TO A CITY]

2

The proposal that all <the rulers'> women should be shared[5] raises   *1261a10*
many objections. In particular Socrates' arguments do not make it apparent why he thinks this legislation is needed. Moreover, the end he
prescribes for the city is impossible, taken literally, and he has not explained how else we should take it.[6] I refer to Socrates' assumption that   *15*
it is best if all the city is as unified as possible. It is evident, on the
contrary, that as the city goes further and further in the direction of
unity, it will finally not even be a city. For a city is by nature a mass[7] of
people; as it becomes more and more unified, first the city will turn into
a household, and then the household will turn into just one person[8]—
for we would say that a household is more unified than a city, and one   *20*
person more unified than a household. And so, even if someone were
capable of completely unifying a city, he should not do it, since he would
destroy the city.

Besides, a city is composed, not merely of a number of human beings,
but of those different in kind—for similar people do not constitute a
city. For a city is different from an alliance; for since an alliance naturally   *25*
aims at assistance, the added quantity, even of something the same in
kind, makes the ally useful (like a weight that pulls a balance down
further). A city differs in the same way from a nation* that is not scattered
in separate villages but <is all together>, as the Arcadians[9] are. <In
contrast to these cases,> the parts from which a unity[10] comes to be
must differ in kind.   *30*

This is why reciprocal equality preserves a city, as we said before in
the *Ethics*.[11] Even free and equal people need this, since they cannot all
rule at the same time, but must rule for a year, or some other fixed
length of time. Such an arrangement ensures that they all rule—just as   *35*
if cobblers and carpenters were to change occupations, and the same
people were not cobblers or carpenters all the time. Since <the normal

5. **The proposal . . . shared**: Plato, *Rep.* 457d.

6. **taken . . . take it**: Lit. 'as he states it, and how we should divide <the
reasonable from the unreasonable interpretations> is not at all defined'. This is
a frequent line of objection to PLATO.

7. **mass**: i.e., a large number. See 1274b41.

8. **just one person**: This, then, results from taking Plato's advice literally.

9. **Arcadians**: Their villages formed a federation, without the structure that
Aristotle takes to be necessary for a *polis*.

10. **a unity**: Cf. *Met.* 1040b5–16.

11. *Ethics*: 1132b33.

practice in the crafts> is also better in the political community, it is clearly better if the same people are, if possible, always rulers. But in 1261b some circumstances this is not possible, because all are naturally equal, and moreover it is just for all to take part in ruling—whether it is a benefit or a burden. This arrangement—where equals yield office to each other in turn and are similar when they are not holding office—at least imitates <the practice of the crafts>; some rule and others are ruled, 5 taking turns, as though they had become other people. In the same way, among the rulers themselves, different ones rule in different ruling offices.[12]

It is evident, then, from what we have said, that a city is not naturally unified in the way that some claim it is and that the unity alleged to be the greatest good for cities in fact destroys them, whereas a thing's good preserves it.

10 It is evident in another way too that attempts at excessive unification do not benefit a city. For a household is more self-sufficient than an individual person is; and a community of a mass of people counts as a city only if it proves to be self-sufficient. Since, then, what is more self-15 sufficient* is more choiceworthy, what is less unified is <in this case> more choiceworthy than what is more unified.

[PLATO UNDERESTIMATES THE IMPORTANCE OF
EXCLUSIVE ATTACHMENT TO INDIVIDUALS]

3

But even if it is indeed best if the community is as unified as possible, <Socrates'> argument does not seem to demonstrate that this will be the effect of agreement in saying 'mine' and 'not mine'[13]—though Socrates 20 regards this agreement as a sign of the city's being completely unified.

For 'all' is said in two ways. If all, taken each one at a time, <speak of what is 'mine'>, then perhaps the <unity> that Socrates wants to produce would be more likely to result; for each one will call the same person his own son, and the same person his own wife, and will speak in the same way of property, and whatever else he has. In fact, however, 25 those who share wives and children will not speak in this way. They will, all together, not each taken one at a time, regard <wives and

12. **This arrangement . . . ruling offices**: Aristotle suggests rather awkwardly that even among free and equal people the principle of division of labor is observed to some degree, so that this case confirms his claim that the city requires different sorts of people.

13. **agreement . . . 'not mine'**: Lit. 'saying "mine" and "not mine" at the same time'. See Plato, *Rep.* 462c.

children as theirs>; and similarly, all together, not each taken one at a time, will regard property <as theirs>. Evidently, then, speaking of 'all' is a fallacious inference;[14] for 'all', 'both', 'odd', and 'even' also produce contentious* deductions in discussions, because they are spoken of in these two ways. Hence if all say the same thing, the result is in one case fine, but not possible,[15] and in the other case contributes nothing to concord.

Besides this, the proposal mentioned involves a further harm. For what is common to the largest number of people gets least attention, since people think most about what is private to them and think less about what is common, or else think about what is common only to the extent that it applies to each of them. They care less about it because, in addition to other reasons, they assume that someone else is thinking about it—as in household service many attendants sometimes serve worse than a few. <In Socrates' city> each citizen will have a thousand sons, but not as sons of each taken one at a time; any given son will be the son of this father no more than of any other, and so all the fathers alike will care little about them. . . .

* * * * * * *

[THE BAD RESULTS OF ELIMINATING PRIVATE PROPERTY AND PRIVATE ATTACHMENTS]

4

. . . And in general the results of this sort of law <eliminating private property> are bound to be contrary to the results to be expected from correctly established laws, and contrary to Socrates' aim in prescribing these arrangements about children and women. For we think friendship is the greatest good for cities, since it best prevents civil conflict in them;[16] indeed Socrates himself praises the unity of the city more than anything else, and, like other people, he takes unity to be the result of friendship. In the same way, as we know, in the discussions of erotic love,[17] Aristophanes says that erotic lovers love so intensely that they long to grow together and make one person out of two. But whereas this union requires the perishing of one or both of the lovers, sharing of wives and

14. **fallacious inference**: The fallacy Aristotle has in mind is illustrated by the difference between: (a) If all ('taken each one at a time') are human beings, each is a human being; and (b) If all ('all together') fill an airplane, each fills an airplane. For fallacies involving 'all' see also 1281b4, 1307b35, 1332a36.

15. **not possible**: since we cannot (in Aristotle's view) expect each father to say 'my own son' about someone else's son.

16. **For we . . . in them**: On the importance of friendship see EN 1155a22–28.

17. **erotic love**: See Plato, *Symp.* 192de.

children will merely make friendship in the city watery, and it will be least true that a father speaks of 'my son' or a son of 'my father'. For just as a little of something sweet mixed into a lot of water makes the mixture imperceptible, the same is true of the mutual closeness resulting
20 from these names <'father' and 'son'>, since this sort of political system is the least likely to ensure that a father is especially concerned for his son, or a son for his father, or one brother for another. For the two most important sources of care and friendship among human beings are the fact that something is one's own and the fact that one likes* it; neither can be true of those living under such a political system. . . .

* * * * * * *

[*THE BENEFITS OF PRIVATE PROPERTY* [18]]

5

1263a21 . . . These, then, and others like them, are the disagreeable results of common ownership. The present arrangement would be far better, if it were improved by good habits and ordered by correct laws. For in that
25 case it would have the advantages of both arrangements, i.e., of common and of private ownership. For ownership ought to be common in a way, but basically[19] private; if different people attend to different things, no mutual accusations result, and they will together contribute more, since each person keeps his mind on his own proper concerns. On the other hand, virtue will make friends' possessions common (as the proverb
30 says) for their use.

Even now there are traces of this arrangement in outline in some cities, suggesting that it is not impossible, and, especially in well-managed cities, some aspects are already there, and others might arise. For while each has his own possessions, he offers his own for his friends
35 to use and uses <his friends'> possessions as common possessions. In Sparta, for instance, they use one another's slaves practically as their own and do the same with horses and dogs and with the fields around the countryside, if they need food for a journey.

Evidently, then, it is better if we own possessions privately, but make
40 them common by our use of them. And it is the legislator's proper task to see that the right sort of people develop.

Further, it is unbelievably more pleasant to regard something as one's

18. This section follows Aristotle's attack on Plato's abolition of private property among the ruling class in the *Republic*.

19. **basically**: *holōs* (see IN GENERAL). It is a system of private property, taken as a whole, but with provision for common use.

own. For each person's love of himself[20] is not pointless, but a natural   *1263b*
tendency.[21] Certainly, selfishness is quite rightly blamed; but selfishness
is not love of oneself, but excessive self-love. The same distinction applies
to love of money, since practically everyone loves himself and loves   *5*
money. Moreover, the pleasantest thing is to please or to help our friends
or guests or companions, and we can do this when ownership is private.

These, then, are the results for those who unify the city excessively.
Moreover, they evidently remove any function for two virtues—temperance* toward women (since it is a fine action to refrain because of temper-   *10*
ance from a woman who is someone else's wife) and generosity* with
our possessions (since no one's generosity will be evident, and no one
will do any generous action—for generosity has its function in the use
of possessions). . . .

* * * * * * *

Book III

[CITIZENSHIP AND THE CITY[1]]

[THE DEFINITION OF A CITIZEN]

1

In investigating a political system* and asking what, and of what sort,   *1274b*
each system is, our first question should be to ask what the city is. For
as things are, this is disputed; some assert that the city has done some   *35*
action, while others assert that it was not the city, but the oligarchy or
the tyrant that did it.[2] Moreover, we see that the politician's and the
legislator's whole concern is with the city, and that the political system
is a particular sort of ordering of those who live in the city.

Since the city is a composite, and we must proceed as we do with
other wholes that are constituted of many parts, it is clear that we must   *40*
first of all inquire into the citizen, since a city is a particular sort of mass
of citizens. And so we should examine who ought to be called a citizen   *1275a*
and who the citizen is. For in fact there is often dispute about the citizen
as well <as about the city>, since not everyone agrees that the same

---

20. **love of himself**: See *EN* 1168a22–b10.

21. **natural tendency**: See NATURE #6.

1. In Bk iii Aristotle turns to his own constructive theory, beginning with
questions about who is appropriately a member of the political association. This
is the foundation both for his analysis of existing states (Bks iv–vi) and for his
own account of the ideal state (Bk vii).

2. **it was not the city . . . did it**: They assume that some regimes fail to represent
the city.

5   person is a citizen; someone who is a citizen in a democracy is often not a citizen in an oligarchy.

We should omit those who acquire the title of citizen in some other way <than by birth>—those who are created citizens,[3] for instance. Someone is not a citizen if he simply lives in a particular place; for resident aliens and slaves live in the same place <as the citizens, but are not citizens>. Nor is someone a citizen if he simply shares in the

10   judicial system[4] to the extent of claiming justice and submitting to it; for this is also true of those who share judicial arrangements by treaty.[5] (In many cities, indeed, resident aliens do not share fully in the judicial system, but must find a representative <to take up their case>, so that their share in this sort of community is in a way incomplete.)

What we say about these cases is similar to what we say about boys

15   who are not yet of an age to be enrolled and about old men who have been released <from active participation>. For we say that these are citizens in a way, but not without qualification; we add the qualification that boys are incomplete[6] citizens and that the old men are citizens past the proper age, or something like that (it does not matter exactly what we say, since what we mean is clear). For we are inquiring about those who are citizens without qualification, in such a way that their claim

20   admits of no ground for objection needing to be rectified. Similar puzzles and solutions apply to the dishonored[7] and to exiles.

[*THE PRIMARY TYPE OF CITIZENSHIP*]

A citizen without qualification is defined, above all, as one who shares in judging and ruling.[8] Some types of rule are limited in time, so that

25   some ruling offices can never be held by the same person twice or can be held again only after a specified interval. Another type of ruler, however, is indefinite <in time>—for instance, the juryman* or the assemblyman. Now, perhaps someone might say that these people are

3. **We should . . . created citizens**: These should not be the focus of discussion, because they are not the cases that raise the disputes; if a decision by the state were the only way for someone to be a citizen, then there would be no room for dispute about who is really a citizen.

4. **judicial system**: Lit. 'just things'.

5. **share judicial arrangements by treaty**: i.e., different states that agree to recognize the jurisdiction of each other's courts in certain (e.g., commercial) cases.

6. **incomplete**: Or 'immature'.

7. **dishonored**: See HONOR.

8. **ruling**: *archē*. See PRINCIPLE #5.

not rulers at all and that these functions do not count as sharing in ruling. Surely, however, it is ridiculous to deny that those with the most complete control[9] are rulers. Still, we need not suppose that this matters; it is simply an argument about a name, since the common feature applying to the juryman and the assemblyman has no name. And so, to make clear the distinction, let us call it indefinite[10] rule. We take it, then, that those who share in ruling on these terms are citizens.

30

[THE DEFINITION FITS DIFFERENT POLITICAL SYSTEMS]

This, then, is more or less the definition of citizen that best fits all those called citizens. We must notice, however, that in cases where the subjects <of a property F> differ in species, and one is the primary F, another secondary, and so on in order,[11] their common feature, insofar as they are F, is nothing, or only slight. Now, we see that political systems differ in species and that some are prior and some posterior, since the erroneous and deviant systems must be posterior to the correct ones (the meaning of 'deviant systems' will be clarified later); and so a different type of citizen must also correspond to each political system.

35

1275b

    That is why the citizen fitting our definition is a citizen in a democracy more than in the other systems, and in the other systems the citizen may <have these functions>, but need not have them. For some systems have no popular body, or recognized assembly <of all the people>, but only convocations <of selected members>, and different judicial cases are decided by different select bodies. (In Sparta, for instance, different types of cases arising from treaties are decided by a different Overseer, cases of homicide by the Elders, and other cases presumably by some other ruling official. The same is true in Carthage, where ruling officials judge all the cases.[12])

5

10

    Our way of distinguishing a citizen can still be corrected.[13] In the nondemocratic political systems the assemblyman or juryman exercises a definite, not an indefinite, rule; for either all or some of these are

15

9. **those . . . control**: Or 'most sovereign', *kurios*. See CONTROLLING.

10. **indefinite**: *ahoristos*. See INFINITE #3.

11. **in cases . . . in order**: See DEFINITION #7.

12. **In Sparta . . . judge all the cases**: Aristotle contrasts these cases with the practice in Athens, where nearly all legal cases came before popular jury-courts.

13. **corrected**: to fit the cases mentioned in the previous paragraph. The incomplete citizens of nondemocratic states count as citizens to the extent that they share the functions of a citizen in a democracy; hence they need not exercise 'indefinite rule' in order to count as citizens to some extent. The previous definition remains correct, however, for the complete citizen.

assigned the task of deliberating and sitting on juries, either on all questions or on some. From this, then, it is clear who the citizen is; if it is open[14] to someone to share in deliberative and judicial rule, we say he

20 is thereby a citizen of this sort of city; and a city (to speak without qualification[15]) is the collection of such people that is adequate for self-sufficient life.

* * * * * * *

[THE GOOD MAN AND THE GOOD CITIZEN SEEM TO BE DIFFERENT]

4

1276b16 The next question to be examined among those we have just mentioned is whether or not we must take the virtue of a good man and of an excellent* citizen to be the same or different. And if we must search for this, we must first grasp in some rough outline the virtue of a citizen.

20 Well, then, we say that a citizen, like a sailor, is one of a number of associates. Now, sailors are dissimilar in their capacities—for one is an oarsman, one a pilot, one a lookout, and another has some other name—

25 and clearly the most exact account of each one's virtue will be special to him, but similarly some common account will also fit them all, since the function of them all is to secure a safe voyage, and that is what each sailor aims at. Similarly, then, the function of citizens, despite their dissimilarity, is to secure the safety of the community; the political system

30 is the community; hence the virtue of the citizen must be relative to the political system.

If, then, there are several species of political system, there clearly cannot be one virtue—complete virtue—of the excellent citizen. The good man, by contrast, is good precisely insofar as he has one virtue—complete virtue. Evidently, then, someone can be an excellent citizen

35 without having the virtue that makes someone an excellent man.

Moreover, we can raise a further puzzle in approaching the same discussion about the best political system. If a city cannot be composed entirely of excellent men, still each must perform his own function

40 well, and this requires virtue; and since the citizens cannot all be
1277a similar, the virtue of a citizen cannot be the same as that of a good man. For all must have the virtue of the excellent citizen, since that is needed if the city is to be best; but they cannot all have the virtue

14. **it is open**: *exeinai* (abstract noun *exousia*). In contexts such as this 'have a right' would be appropriate.

15. **without qualification**: We omit the qualification (needed for strict accuracy) that we are defining the city only with reference to an incomplete type of citizen.

of the good man, if the citizens in the excellent city cannot all be   5
good men.[16]

Further, a city is constituted of dissimilar people, just as an animal
is necessarily constituted of soul and body, a soul is constituted of reason
and desire, a household is constituted of husband and wife, and possession is constituted of master and slave. A city is constituted of all of
these, and moreover of different kinds of people; and so the citizens   10
cannot all have the same virtue, any more than the chorus-leader and an
ordinary member of the chorus can have the same virtue.

This makes it evident why <the virtue of an excellent man and of an
excellent citizen> are not the same without qualification. But will the
virtue of one type of excellent citizen be the same as the virtue of an
excellent man? We say that an excellent ruler is good and intelligent,*   15
but that a citizen need not be intelligent, so that (in some people's view)
a ruler should have a different type of education (just as we see the sons
of kings educated in horsemanship and warfare, and Euripides[17] says,
'For me none of these subtleties ... but what the city needs', on the   20
assumption that there is a type of education proper to a ruler).

Now, if the virtue of a good ruler and of a good man are the same,
and both the ruler and the ruled are citizens, it follows that the virtue
of a man is not the same without qualification as the virtue of a citizen
but is the same as the virtue of a certain kind of citizen <—a ruler>;
for the virtue of a ruler is not the same as the virtue of a citizen, and
presumably that is why Jason said he was starving when he was not
tyrant, suggesting that he did not know how to be a private citizen.   25

[*IN SOME CASES, HOWEVER, THE GOOD CITIZEN ALSO HAS
THE VIRTUES OF THE GOOD MAN*]

And yet someone is praised for being able both to rule and to be ruled,
and the virtue of an estimable citizen seems to be the ability both to rule
and to be ruled finely.[18] If, then, we take the good man's virtue to be a
virtue in ruling, and the citizen's virtue to be both <in ruling and being
ruled>, the two abilities cannot be praiseworthy in the same way. Since,
then, they seem to be different in some cases, and it seems that the ruler 30

16. **if the citizens ... men**: Or 'unless it is necessary for all the citizens ...'.
For Aristotle's view on this question see vii 13.

17. **Euripides**: in a lost tragedy. This passage is also quoted in Plato, *Gorg.* 485e–
486a.

18. **And yet ... ruled finely**: Aristotle now challenges a premiss of the previous
argument, by showing that the virtue of a good citizen is not entirely separate
from the virtue of a ruler, and so is not separate from the virtue of a good man.

and the ruled must learn different things, while the citizen must know and share in both ruling and being ruled, we may see what follows from that.

One type of rule is a master's rule over slaves. We say that this is
35 concerned with necessities; the ruler needs the knowledge of how to use these, not the knowledge of how to produce them, which would actually be slavish—I mean the ability to perform the actions of a servant. We speak of several types of slaves, since there are several types of work. One type of work belongs to manual workers; as the name itself
1277b indicates, these are the ones who live by the work of their hands, and they include the menial* craftsmen. That is why some cities gave the manual workers no share in ruling offices, before the extreme type of democracy arose. Hence neither the good politician nor the good citizen
5 must learn the functions of people who are ruled in this way, unless he needs them for himself (for then it no longer involves a master and a slave).[19]

However, there is a type of rule that is exercised over people who are free and similar in kind <to the ruler>; this is called political rule.
10 A ruler must learn this type of rule by being ruled himself—for instance, he must be ruled by a cavalry officer to learn to rule as a cavalry officer, and ruled by a general or troop-leader or squadron-leader to learn to rule in these positions. Hence this is also a sound maxim, that you cannot rule well until you have been ruled. These virtues of ruler and ruled are different, but the good citizen must have the knowledge and
15 ability both to be ruled and to rule; and the virtue of a citizen is this knowledge of rule over free people, from both points of view.

Hence the good man has both virtues, even if the ruler has a different kind of temperance and justice. For, clearly, if a good person is ruled, but is a free citizen, his virtue—justice, for instance—is not of only one
20 kind, but includes one kind for ruling and another for being ruled. Similarly, a man and a woman have different kinds of temperance and bravery—for a man would seem cowardly if he were <only> as brave as a brave woman, and a woman would seem talkative if she were <only> as restrained as the good man is; and similarly household man-agement is different for a man and a woman, since it is the man's task
25 to acquire the goods and the woman's task to preserve them. Intelligence is the only virtue that is distinctive of the ruler; for all the others, it would seem, must be common to rulers and ruled, but true belief, not

19. **for himself . . . slave):** He may want to learn (e.g.) to cook for himself, in case he needs to do it; but it would be slavish to cook for other people for a living. (Alternative translation: 'for himself; for <if he does not practice them only for his own use,> there is no longer a distinction between master and slave.')

intelligence, is the virtue of the ruled, since they correspond to flute-
makers, whereas the rulers correspond to flute-players who use the   *30*
flutes.[20]

From this, then, it is evident whether the virtue of the good man and
of the excellent citizen are the same or different, and in what ways they
are the same, and in what ways different.

*   *   *   *   *   *   *

[THE VARIETY OF POLITICAL SYSTEMS]

6

Now that these points have been determined, the next question to inves-   *1278b6*
tigate is whether we should suppose there is one type or several types
of political system, and, if there are several, what and how many they
are, and what features differentiate them.

A political system is the ordering in a city of the various ruling offices,
and especially of the one that controls everything. For in every city the   *10*
controlling* element is the political body,[21] and the political body is the
political system. I mean, for instance, that in democracies the common
people* are in control, and, by contrast, in oligarchies* the few are in
control, and we take the political systems of these cities to be different—
and we will give the same account of the other political systems as well.   *15*

First, then, we should state our assumption about what end the city
is constituted for, and how many types of rule are concerned with human
beings and with community of life.

[THE GOAL OF A CITY]

In our first discussions, when we determined the features of rule over
households and over slaves, we also said that a human being is by nature
a political animal.[22] That is why, even when they have no need of mutual   *20*
help, they desire nonetheless to live together; at the same time common
advantage draws them together, to the extent that it contributes something to living finely for each person. Living finely, then, most of all is
the goal of a city, both for all the citizens in common and for each
separately. Still, they also combine and maintain the political community   *25*

---

20. **use the flutes**: The user knows what the flute should be like, whereas the
flute-maker takes the standards for a good flute on trust from the player. Cf.
Plato, *Rep.* 601de.

21. **political body**: *politeuma*. 'Government' would also be a suitable rendering;
cf. 1279a25.

22. **political animal**: See MAN #4.

for the sake of life itself. For presumably even life itself includes something fine in it, as long as its adversities are not overwhelming; and, clearly, most human beings still cling to life even if they must endure much suffering, finding that simply being alive is a source of some well-
30   being and natural delight.

[*THE DIFFERENT TYPES OF RULE*]

Further, it is easy to distinguish the types of rule we have mentioned—indeed we often distinguish them in popular* discussions. First comes the rule of master over slave, where the advantage of the natural slave
35   and of the natural master are in fact the same, but nonetheless the master rules for his own advantage, and for the slave's advantage <only> coincidentally (since the master cannot maintain his rule if the slave is being ruined).

By contrast, rule over children and wife and the whole household—called household-rule—is for the benefit of the ruled, or <coinciden-
40   tally> for some benefit common to ruler and ruled, but in itself for the
1279a   benefit of the ruled. In the same way we see that the crafts[23]—medicine and gymnastics, for instance—may also be coincidentally for the benefit of the craftsman as well as the subject, since the gymnastics trainer may sometimes be one of the people in training, just as the pilot is always
5   one of the sailors; and so the trainer or pilot considers the good of those he rules, but whenever he turns out to be one of them, he shares coincidentally in the benefit, since the pilot is a sailor, and the trainer is at the same time in training.

[*THE PROPER AIM OF POLITICAL RULE*]

10   Hence, when a city is constituted on the basis of equality and similarity among the citizens, they think it right to take turns at ruling.[24] In the past each did this in the naturally suitable way, thinking it right to take his turn in public service, and then in return to have someone else consider his advantage afterwards, just as he previously was a ruler and considered the other's advantage. These days, however, people want

23. **the crafts**: Lit. 'the other crafts', probably meaning 'the other things, the crafts', i.e., 'the crafts besides'.

24. **Hence . . . at ruling**: Aristotle assumes that political rule is one of the types of rule that aim at the benefit of the ruled (like the crafts just mentioned). In this section he emphasizes the similarity among citizens as a hallmark of political society; contrast his previous (not inconsistent) emphasis on differentiation. See 1261a22, 1276b20–31, 1328a35.

to be rulers continuously, to gain the benefits of ruling and holding public office, and so they pursue it as eagerly as they would if they were all sick and would all invariably recover their health if they became rulers.

It is evident, then, that all the political systems that consider the common advantage are correct types, conforming to what is just without qualification, whereas all those that consider only the advantage of the rulers are erroneous types, deviations from the correct political systems— for these are the types of rule that a master exercises over slaves, whereas a city is a community of free citizens.

[THE CLASSIFICATION OF POLITICAL SYSTEMS]

7

Now that this has been determined, the next task is to investigate how many political systems there are and what they are. First we consider the correct systems; for when we have determined these, we will have made the deviant systems evident.

A political system and a political body[25] signify the same thing; the political body controls a city, and either one person or a few or the many must be in control. If, then, the one person or the few or the many rule for the common advantage, these political systems must be correct; and the systems that aim at the special advantage of the one or the few or the mass of people[26] must be deviations—for either those who do not participate <in the political system> should not be called citizens, or they must <at least> share in the advantage.[27]

The type of monarchy that considers the common advantage is usually called kingship. The corresponding type of rule by a few people, but more than one, is called aristocracy,[28] either because the best people are the rulers or because it aims at what is best for the city and those associated in it. Whenever the masses conduct political life for the common advantage, that system is called a polity*—the name that is common to all the political systems. And this <name> is reasonable; for while one person or a few people may excel in virtue, it is not easy for a larger number to be accomplished in every virtue, but they are accomplished

25. **political body**: *politeuma*. Cf. 1278b11.

26. **mass of people**: *plēthos*. Or 'the majority'. Cf. 1274b41. The term normally refers (as *dēmos* does, in one of its uses; see PEOPLE) to the lower classes, not necessarily with any unfavorable suggestion.

27. **or they must . . . advantage**: i.e., at least this much must be true if they are to be called citizens in cases where they have no share in the government.

28. **aristocracy**: i.e., 'best-rule'. Aristotle offers two interpretations.

in the virtue of war, since that requires a mass of people. That is why the controlling element in the political system consists of those who fight in wars, and those who own their own weapons are those who participate in the political system.

5   The deviations from these systems are tyranny, a deviation from kingship; oligarchy, a deviation from aristocracy; and democracy, a deviation from polity. For tyranny is rule by one person, aiming at the advantage of the ruler himself; oligarchy aims at the advantage of the prosperous; and democracy aims at the advantage of the disadvantaged;[29]

10   and none of these aims at what benefits the community.

[FURTHER QUESTIONS ABOUT THE CLASSIFICATION OF POLITICAL SYSTEMS]

8

We must spend a little longer, however, in saying what each of these political systems is. For the question raises some puzzles: and if we approach a line* of inquiry from a philosophical point of view, not simply focussing on what is useful for action,[30] it is appropriate not

15   to overlook or omit any point, but to make clear the truth about each question.

A tyranny, as we have said, is rule by one person who rules the political community as a master rules slaves. There is an oligarchy whenever possessors of property control the political system, and a democracy, by contrast, whenever those in control are the disadvantaged, those possessing no large property.

20   The first puzzle arises about this distinction. For suppose that the majority are prosperous and that they control the city, and it is a democracy whenever the masses are in control; and again suppose that in some city the disadvantaged are fewer in number than the prosperous, but are stronger and control the political system, and there is said to be an

25   oligarchy whenever a small number are in control. In these cases we do

29. **prosperous**: *euporoi*. Lit. 'well provided'. The Greek is cognate with 'disadvantaged' (*aporoi*, lit. 'unprovided'). Aristotle's argument (e.g., in iii 8) shows that he does not use the terms simply as relative classifications. He does not mean, e.g., that the minority who are best-off in a given city are *euporoi*, irrespective of how well off they are absolutely; for he considers the possibility of a city in which most people are *euporoi* (iii 8), and though he denies the possibility of a city in which all the citizens are *aporoi* (1283a18), he does not treat this as a logical impossibility. See also 1296a12.

30. **from a philosophical . . . for action**: On these two purposes of Aristotle's treatise cf. 1253b15.

474

not seem to have drawn the right distinction between these political systems.[31]

We might, then, combine being prosperous with small numbers, and being disadvantaged with large numbers, and hence classify the political systems by saying that an oligarchy is the system in which the prosperous are few in number and hold the ruling offices, and that a democracy is   *30* the system in which the disadvantaged are many and hold the ruling offices. But these definitions raise another puzzle; what are we to call the systems we have just mentioned—the one in which the prosperous are in control of the system and are more numerous, and the one in which the disadvantaged are in control but are fewer in number—if there is no other political system apart from the ones we listed?

This argument, then, would seem to show that control by the few is   *35* coincidental to oligarchies, and control by the many to democracies, because in every city the prosperous are few in number and the disadvantaged are many. Hence the reasons we mentioned do not turn out to be reasons for distinguishing the systems <by the number in the ruling group>. What really differentiates democracy from oligarchy is poverty   *40* and wealth.[32] If the rulers rule because they are wealthy, whether they   *1280a* are few or many, the system must be an oligarchy, and if the disadvantaged rule, it must be a democracy; it comes about coincidentally, as we said, that the prosperous are few and the disadvantaged are many. For only a few are well off, but all <wealthy and poor> alike share free   *5* citizenship; wealth and freedom cause[33] the struggle between the two <groups> for control of the political system.

[*DIFFERENT VIEWS OF JUSTICE UNDERLIE DIFFERENT POLITICAL SYSTEMS*]

9

First we must understand the received formulae* of oligarchy and democracy, and the oligarchic and democratic <views of> justice; for everyone touches on some sort of justice, but they make only limited progress   *10*

31. **In these cases . . . political systems**: Aristotle rejects the proposed distinction between democracy and oligarchy because he regards it as absurd to claim that the rule of the poor could ever count as oligarchy. His belief that this is an absurd classification underlies the rest of his argument as well.

32. **poverty and wealth**: Aristotle assumes that this is what explains political antagonisms, and therefore it is the ESSENTIAL difference between the two systems.

33. **wealth and freedom cause**: Aristotle does not mean that the classes fight to gain wealth or freedom, but that the difference between the rich and the poor is the basis for the different aims and interests that result in political struggle.

and do not describe the whole of what is fully just. Justice seems to be equality, for instance, and indeed it is—but for equals, not for everyone. Again, inequality seems to be just; and so it is—but for unequals, not for everyone. But these <partisans of each view> omit this part—equality or inequality for whom—and so make the wrong judgment. The reason is that they are giving judgment in their own case, and most people are practically always bad judges in their own cases.

Justice is justice *for* certain people, and the division in the things <to be distributed> corresponds to the division in those to whom <they are distributed>, as we have said before in the *Ethics*.[34] Hence all sides agree about the equal amount of the thing <to be distributed> but dispute about who should receive it. They do this mainly for the reason we have just given, that people are bad judges in their own cases, but also because each side makes some progress in describing a sort of justice and so thinks it describes unqualified justice. For <supporters of oligarchy> think that if they are unequal in some aspects—wealth, for instance—they are altogether unequal, whereas <supporters of democracy> think that if they are equal in some aspect—free status, for instance—they are altogether equal.

[A CORRECT VIEW OF JUSTICE RESTS ON A CORRECT VIEW OF THE GOAL OF A CITY]

But they fail to mention the most important[35] aspect. For if people combined and formed a <political> community in order to acquire possessions, then someone's share in the city would correspond to his possessions, and the supporters of oligarchy would seem to have a strong argument; for, they say, if A has contributed one out of a hundred minas and B has contributed the other ninety-nine, it is not just for A to get the same return as B, either of the original sum or of any later profits.[36]

In fact, however, the <political> community does not aim simply at staying alive, but aims predominantly at a good life.[37] For if it aimed simply at staying alive, then slaves and nonhuman animals would be members of a city, whereas in fact they are not, since they do not participate in happiness or in a life guided by decision.*

[THE GOAL OF A CITY MUST BE DISTINGUISHED FROM THE GOAL OF AN ALLIANCE]

Nor does the city aim at an alliance, to prevent anyone from doing injustice to anyone; or at exchange and dealings between its members.

34. *Ethics*: 1131a14–24.

35. **important**: *kurion*. Or 'CONTROLLING'.

36. **for, they say . . . profits**: According to Aristotle, then, oligarchs mistakenly treat the city as if it were a business partnership.

37. **In fact . . . good life**: Cf. 1252b29, 1278b24.

For if this were the aim, then the Etruscans and the Carthaginians—and any other peoples related by treaty—would all count as citizens of a single city; at any rate, these have made conventions about imports, treaties to prohibit doing injustice, and written articles of alliance. These *40* peoples, however, have no common government, but each has its own *1280b* government.[38] Moreover, neither people is concerned about the right character to form in the citizens of the other city, or about how to remove injustice or any other vice from the other city that is bound by the agreements; each is concerned only to prevent the other city from doing *5* injustice[39] to it. By contrast, those who are concerned with good* government consider the virtues and vices of citizens.

Hence it is evident that whatever is correctly called a city, not just for the sake of argument, must be concerned with virtue. For <otherwise> the community turns out to be <merely> an alliance, differing only in the proximity of its members from the other alliances with more *10* distant members. In that case law turns out to be an agreement and, as Lycophron* the sophist said, a mutual guarantor of just treatment, but unable to make the citizens good and just.[40]

To make it evident that we are right, suppose that we actually joined the territories <of two allied states>, so that the cities of the Megarians and the Corinthians had their walls adjacent; even so, they would not *15* be one single city, even if their citizens intermarried—though that is one sort of community that is distinctive of a city. Similarly, suppose people lived apart, though not too far to prevent community, but had laws prohibiting unjust treatment in exchanges (if, for instance, one was a *20* carpenter, another a farmer, another a cobbler, and so on), and there were ten thousand of them, but their community extended no further than such matters as commerce and alliance; that would still not be enough to make a city.

Why is this? Surely it is not because their community is scattered. For *25* if they even lived closer together but in the same sort of community, each treating his own household as a city, and they formed a purely defensive alliance against unjust actions—even so, an exact study would not count this as a city, if their intercourse when they live closer together is no different from what it was when they lived apart.

---

38. **government**: Or 'ruling offices', *archai*. See PRINCIPLE.

39. **doing injustice**: This does not necessarily manifest an unjust state of character. See *EN* 1105b5–9, 1135b19–25.

40. **In that case . . . and just**: LYCOPHRON apparently put forward a version of a 'social contract' theory of the state. Aristotle rejects this version on the ground that it fails to distinguish a political COMMUNITY from a mere alliance.

[THE TRUE GOAL OF A CITY]

30 Evidently, then, a city is not a community for living in the same place, for preventing the unjust treatment of one member by another, and for exchange. All these are necessary conditions for a city, but their presence does not make a city. Rather, the city is a community for living well for both households and families, aiming at a complete

35 and self-sufficient* life (but this requires them to live in the same place and to intermarry).[41] That is why kinship-groups, brotherhoods, religious societies, and pursuits that involve living together[42] have developed in cities; these are the product of friendship, since the decision to live together is friendship.

40 The end of a city, then, is living well, and these <pursuits> are for

1281a the sake of the end. A city is the community of families and villages in a complete and self-sufficient life. This sort of life, as we say, is a happy and fine life; hence we should suppose that a city aims at fine actions, not <merely> at living together.[43]

[CONSEQUENCES FOR RIVAL CONCEPTIONS OF JUSTICE]

5 That is why someone who contributes most to this sort of community has a greater share in the city than that of someone who is equal or superior in free status or in family, but unequal in a citizen's virtue, and a greater share than that of someone who excels in wealth but is excelled in virtue.

It is evident, then, from what we have said that each of the parties

10 disputing about political systems is describing a part of justice.

[QUESTIONS OF JUSTICE ARISE ABOUT THE BEST FORM OF GOVERNMENT]

10

A puzzle arises about which element ought to control the political system; for it must be either the masses, or the wealthy, or the decent* people, or the single best person, or a tyrant. Each of these answers appears to raise difficulties.

41. **(but this . . . intermarry)**: This clause shows why it is understandable that people mistakenly suppose that physical proximity and intermarriage constitute a city.

42. **living together**: This refers (as the examples show) to shared activities and pursuits rather than to sharing living quarters.

43. **living together**: This is used in a narrower sense (excluding the pursuit of fine actions and living well) than in the previous paragraph referring to friendship (where it included these pursuits).

For if the poor, since they are more numerous, divide up the posses-   *15*
sions of the rich, is that not unjust? 'Well, <they might say,> it seemed
just to the controlling body.' But what could be a clearer case of extreme
injustice? Again, if the majority take everything and divide up the possessions of the minority, evidently they are ruining the city; but a virtue
does not ruin its possessor and justice does not ruin a city, and so this   *20*
law clearly cannot be just. Moreover, <if such distributions are just,>
all the tyrant's actions must have been just too; for he is the stronger,
and forces compliance, just as the masses force the rich.

Then is it just for the rulers to be the minority and the rich? If, then,   *25*
they do these things, and plunder and confiscate the possessions of the
masses, this will be just. And if this is just, the corresponding action by
the masses is just too. Evidently, then, all these actions are base and
not just.

Then ought the decent people to be rulers and in control of everything?
If they are, then surely all the others will necessarily be dishonored,[44]   *30*
since they are denied the honor of holding political ruling offices. For
we say that ruling offices are positions of honor, and if the same people
are rulers all the time, the others will necessarily be dishonored. Then
should the single most excellent person be ruler? But that is an even
narrower oligarchy, since those dishonored are still more numerous.

Now, presumably someone might say that it is a bad arrangement if   *35*
a human being rather than law is in control at all, since any human
being has the feelings that normally arise in a human soul.[45] If, then,
the law is in control, but it is oligarchic or democratic, how will that
help to avoid the puzzles? For the previous objections will arise in just
the same way.

[THE CASE FOR RULE BY THE MAJORITY]

11

Most of these puzzles must be postponed to another discussion. But it   *40*
seems that the claim that the masses rather than the few best people
must be in control is generally accepted,[46] and it seems that, though it
raises a puzzle, it perhaps contains some truth.

For even though each one among the many is not an excellent man,   *1281b*
still it is possible that when they combine they are collectively, though

44. **dishonored**: See HONOR.

45. **Now, presumably . . . human soul**: The suggestion is that the rule of law
avoids personal prejudice, and so avoids injustice. Aristotle replies that if the
laws have an oligarchic or a democratic bias, the rule of law does not ensure
avoidance of injustice.

46. **generally accepted**: Lit. just 'said'. Text uncertain.

not individually,[47] better than the few best people, just as a dinner
provided by many people's contributions is better than one provided at
an individual's expense; for (on this view) they are many, and each has
5   some part of virtue and intelligence, so that when they combine, the
masses become like one human being, with many feet, many hands,
and many senses, and similarly for characters and for intellect. That is
why the many are also better judges of the products of music and of
10 poets; different individuals are better judges of different parts, and all
of them together are better judges of the whole.[48]

Indeed it is this <combination of qualities> that makes an excellent
man better than an ordinary individual among the many, just as it
(supposedly) makes handsome people more handsome than plain people
and makes a statue more handsome than the real things; for <in the
statue> the dispersed features are gathered together in one figure, even
15 though, taken separately, this person's eye and some other part of someone else might be more handsome than <the corresponding parts of>
the statue.[49]

Now, it is not clear whether this claim about the superiority of the
many over the few excellent ones could be true of every sort of common
people and every sort of mass of people. Indeed, presumably, there are
some of which it cannot be true; for if it were true of them, it would
20 also be true of beasts; and indeed there are some who are practically no
better than beasts. But the claim may still be true for masses of a certain
sort.

Hence we can use this argument to solve the previous puzzle, and
the next one—which things should be controlled by the free citizens and
25 the mass of the citizens, those who have neither wealth nor any other
claim to reputation for virtue? For it is not safe for them to share in the
highest ruling offices, since an unjust character is bound to cause unjust
actions, and lack of intelligence is bound to cause errors. On the other
hand, if they are given nothing and have no share, that is dangerous;

47. **collectively . . . individually**: Cf. 1261b27n.

48. **That is why . . . the whole**: In Athens the prizes for the three best tragedies
and comedies in the annual festivals were awarded by a panel chosen by lot;
see OCD p. 1087b.

49. **Indeed it is . . . statue**: The handsomest person is not the one whose eyes,
nose, etc. are handsomest, taken individually, but the one whose features are
handsomest, taken collectively. Similarly, the best person, everything considered, is the one who has the best combination of qualities. Aristotle argues that
we already apply to individuals the standard of appraisal that he applies (with
what he takes to be necessary qualifications, mentioned in the next paragraph)
to the collective qualities of the majority of people.

for any city that holds many poor people in dishonor is bound to be full   30
of enemies.

The remaining option, then, is for them to share in deliberating and
judging. That is why both Solon* and some other legislators assign them
the election of ruling officials and the scrutinizing of officials,[50] but do
not allow them to hold office individually. For all combined have ade-   35
quate sense, and when they are mixed with the better people, they
benefit cities (just as impure food mixed with pure makes the whole
more useful than the smaller amount <of pure food>), but each taken
separately is incompletely equipped for judging.

[PUZZLES ABOUT THE JUSTIFICATION OF MAJORITY RULE]

The first puzzle raised by this organization of the political system is this:
The task of judging who has applied medicine correctly seems to belong   40
to the person who also has the task of applying the medicine and curing
the patient from his present illness; and this is the medical expert. And
the same is true for the other empirical techniques[51] and for the crafts.   1282a
And so just as a medical expert should submit his conduct to scrutiny
by medical experts, other experts should also be scrutinized by their
peers.[52]

Medical experts, however, include not only the practitioners and the
supervising experts, but also those who are educated* about the craft—
for in practically every craft there are people educated about it. And we   5
assign the task of judging to the educated people no less than to those
who know₀ the craft.

The same puzzle seems to arise about selection <as about judging>.
For selection is also properly a task for those who know₀ the craft; it is
the task of geometers, for instance, to select a geometer, and of pilots   10
to select a pilot.[53] For even if laymen have some share in selection for

---

50. **scrutinizing of officials**: At Athens their conduct during their year of office
was subject to a 'scrutiny' (*euthuna*) by a jury-court (chosen by lot from the
citizens) after they had held office. This is the sort of power that Aristotle has
in mind when he calls the office of a JURYMAN a form of political rule. See 1275a13,
OCD p. 424b.

51. **empirical techniques**: *empeiriai*. See EXPERIENCE.

52. **And so just as . . . their peers**: This is the argument against scrutiny by the
many. The next sentence, however, suggests that the previous argument does
not accurately represent the role of 'experts'. If 'experts' is understood in an
appropriately wide sense, to include users as well as providers, then medical
'experts' include others besides those with specialized medical training.

53. **it is the task . . . a pilot**: Cf. Plato, *Prot.* 318bc.

some types of production and craft, their share is no greater than that of people who know the craft. Hence, on this argument, the masses should not be given control either of selecting rulers or of scrutinizing them.

15   Presumably, however, this argument is not completely correct. First, it is refuted by our earlier argument, as long as the masses are not too slavish; for though each one individually is a worse judge than one who knows the craft, all combined are better, or no worse. Second,[54] the argument is mistaken because in some cases the producer is neither the only judge nor the best judge; this is so whenever laymen also know$_g$[55]

20   the products of a craft. It is not only the builder of the house, for instance, who knows$_g$ it; its user—the householder—is an even better judge. Similarly, a pilot is a better judge of a rudder than a carpenter is, and the diner, not the cook, is the judge of a feast. This, then, might seem to be an adequate solution of the puzzle.

25   There is another puzzle, however, following this one. For it seems absurd for base people to control issues that are more important than the ones controlled by decent people; but scrutinies and elections to ruling offices are the most important thing, and in some political systems, as we have said, these functions are assigned to the common people, since the assembly[56] controls all of these. And yet participation in the

30   assembly, deliberative council, and jury-court[57] requires only a small property-qualification[58] and no minimum age,[59] whereas a large qualification is needed to be a financial officer or general or to hold the highest ruling offices.

Well, the same solution applies to this puzzle also. For presumably this <policy that raises the puzzle> is also correct. For the ruler is not

54. **Second . . .**: This second argument does not rely, as the first did, on any appeal to the collective judgment of the masses. It suggests that individual nonexperts may be appropriate judges. Hence the two arguments against the objection support each other.

55. **know$_g$**: Or perhaps 'recognize' (see KNOW #1). The user can tell whether an artifact is doing what it ought to do, even if he does not know about the process of making it.

56. **assembly**: All citizens were eligible to attend and vote in the assembly (at Athens and in other democracies).

57. **deliberative council and jury-court**: At Athens the members of these were chosen by lot from the citizens. See OCD p. 178, 342–43.

58. **property-qualification**: *timēma*, from *timē*, ('honor', 'value').

59. **no minimum age**: They did require their members to be adults. Aristotle is contrasting them with bodies (e.g., the Spartan council of Elders) that were confined to people of advanced age.

the individual juryman or councilman or assemblyman, but the jury-   *35*
court, the council, and the assembly; each individual councilman, assemblyman, or juryman is a part of the <collectives> we have mentioned.
Hence it is just for the masses to control the most important things, since
the common people, the council, and the jury-court are all composed of
many members. Moreover, the property of all these <collectively> is   *40*
greater than the property of those who, one at a time or a few at a time,
hold the high ruling offices. This, then, is how we settle these questions.   *1282b*
    The puzzle that was raised first[60] makes it especially evident that the
laws, when they are correctly framed, must be in control, and that the
ruler, either one or many, must be in control where the laws are incapable
of giving the exactly correct guidance, since it is not easy to determine   *5*
these cases in a universal rule.[61] But what sorts of laws are the correctly
framed ones? This is not yet clear, and the previous puzzle remains
unsolved. For the baseness or excellence, and justice or injustice, of laws
depends on, and matches, the character of political systems. It is evident,   *10*
however, that the laws must at any rate be framed to fit the political
system.[62] And if this is so, then, clearly, the laws corresponding to correct
systems will necessarily be just, and those corresponding to deviant
systems not just.

[JUSTICE IN POLITICAL DISTRIBUTION [63]*]*

12

In all types of science and craft the end is a good, and the greatest and   *15*
best good is the end of the science that most controls all the others, and
this is the political capacity.[64] The political good is justice,[65] and justice
is the common benefit.[66] Everyone thinks justice is some sort of equality,
and hence to some extent they all agree with the philosophical discus-

60. **The puzzle that was raised first**: at 1281a14ff. 1281a34 raised the specific
question about the rule and character of the laws.

61. **it is not easy . . . universal rule**: Cf. *EN* 1137b12–19.

62. **to fit the political system**: See 1289a13.

63. This discussion is concerned explicitly with the distribution of political functions and offices, though it is also relevant to the distribution of other benefits.

64. **In all . . . political capacity**: See 1252a1–7, *EN* 1094a24–b7.

65. **The political good is justice**: Hence justice is the good pursued by POLITICAL
SCIENCE as its distinctive contribution to HAPPINESS, which is its more ultimate
end.

66. **justice . . . benefit**: Or 'the political good is the common benefit'.

20   sions in which we have determined ethical questions;[67] for they say that
what is just is relative to the people involved and that it must be equality
for equals. But we must find the relevant respect of equality or inequality;
for this question raises a puzzle that concerns political philosophy.

For presumably someone might say that ruling offices ought to be
unequally distributed in accordance with superiority in any good at all,
25   if people are alike and not at all different in all of the other goods; for,
it will be argued, superior people justly deserve to get more than other
people get. In that case, however, anyone who excels in complexion,
size, or any other good at all, will have a politically just <claim> to get*
more <goods>.

30   Surely the falsity in this view is easy to spot, and is evident in the
other sciences and capacities. If two flute-players are at the same level
in their craft, we ought not to assign more flutes to the better-born one,
since his birth does not make him a better flute-player; rather, the one
who excels in the relevant function must be assigned the extra instruments.

35   If our point is not yet clear, it will become still more evident if we
develop it further. Suppose that A is superior to B in the flute-playing
craft, but far inferior to B in birth or beauty. Suppose even that each of
these other goods—i.e., good birth and beauty—is a greater good than
the flute-playing craft, and that B's superiority <in these respects> over
40   A's flute-playing is proportionately greater than A's superiority over B
in the flute-playing craft. Even in this case A should be given the better
1283a   flutes. For if superiority in birth and wealth is relevant <to a distribu-
tion>, it ought to contribute to the relevant function, but in this case it
contributes nothing to it.

Moreover, the argument we are opposing implies that every good is
comparable with every other; for if some particular size competes <with
5   some other good>, then size in general will also compete with wealth
and free status. And so if A's superiority over B in size is greater than
B's superiority over A in virtue, even though virtue in general is a greater
good than size, then all goods will be comparable; for if some amount
is greater than some other, clearly some amount is equal to it.[68]

67. **ethical questions**: See *EN* v.

68. **And so if . . . equal to it**: According to the view that Aristotle rejects, if x
and y are goods (in any respect at all), then there is some amount of x that is
a greater good than a given amount of y. And so if, e.g., A's superior wisdom
gives him a claim to hold office in preference to B, we can say how much richer
or more handsome than A B would have to be in order to have a superior good
to A's wisdom and hence a claim to hold office in preference to A. Aristotle
points out that this appeal to 'goods' without reference to what particular goods
are good for leads to these sorts of absurd results.

But since this is impossible, clearly it is also reasonable that in politics   *10*
not every sort of inequality is a ground for dispute about ruling offices.
For if A is quick and B is slow, it does not follow that A should have
more and B less; this sort of superiority receives its honor in gymnastic
contests. The goods that are grounds for dispute must be those that   *15*
constitute the city.

Hence it is reasonable that the well-born and the free citizens and the
rich lay claims to honor. For <citizens> must be freemen, with some
property-qualification, since a city could not be composed entirely of
disadvantaged people, any more than it could be composed of slaves.
And yet, if the city needs these, clearly it also needs justice and political   *20*
virtue, since these are also necessary conditions of living in a city. The
difference is that birth, free status, and wealth are <simply> necessary
for a city to exist, whereas justice and political virtue are necessary for
living finely in a city.

*   *   *   *   *   *   *

Book IV

[POLITICAL SCIENCE AND NONIDEAL STATES]

[WE MUST NOT LIMIT OUR INVESTIGATION TO IDEAL STATES [1]]

1

In all crafts and sciences that are not concerned only with a part of any   *1288b10*
genus, but study the whole genus completely, it is a task for one and
the same discipline to study these questions: (1) What suits a particular
kind of thing? What sort of exercise, for instance, benefits what sort of
body? (2) What is the best exercise? For the best exercise will necessarily   *15*
suit the body with the best nature and resources. (3) What one type of
exercise best suits most bodies? For this is also a task for the gymnastic
craft. (4) Further, if someone has no desire for the best bodily condition
or for the science that is most appropriate for competitive sport, even
so it is the trainer's and gymnastic teacher's task to develop <in his
client> the degree of ability <that the client wants>—and we see that
the same is true of the crafts concerned with medicine, shipbuilding,
and dress, and of every other craft.   *20*

Clearly, then, it is the task of one and the same science to study these
questions: (1) What is the best political system, the sort that would best

---

1. Bk iv begins the 'empirical' books of the *Politics* (iv–vi), in which Aristotle
analyzes existing states, their structure and the changes in their political systems,
in preparation for his own normative account of a city in Bk vii.

25

suit our aspirations,[2] assuming no external obstacles? (2) Which system suits which people? For, presumably, many are unable to achieve the best system; and so the good legislator and the true politician must consider both the unqualifiedly best system and the best one that can be made from the given situation. (3) What is the best system, given certain assumptions? The politician must be able to study how a given system might come to be from the beginning, and once it has come to

30

be, how it might be preserved for the longest time. I mean, for instance, that a city might not have the best political system and might lack the necessary resources for it, or, alternatively, might not have the best that is possible in the prevailing circumstances, but some inferior system. (4) Apart from all these, he must know the one type of system that best

35

suits all cities.

[HENCE WE MUST AVOID THE USUAL APPROACH TO POLITICAL QUESTIONS]

And so most of those who discuss the political system fail to give useful advice, even if what they say on other points is good. For we must study not only the best system, but also the system that is possible <for a particular city>, and equally the one that is easier <to establish> and more suitable for all cities alike. But as things are, some people inquire

40

only into the best system, the one that requires large resources, while those who instead describe a common system for all cities do away with

1289a

the existing systems, in favor of the Spartan or some other system.

In contrast to these inquiries, we should describe the sort of political order that people will easily, in the prevailing circumstances, endorse and introduce; for it is no less important a task to correct a political system than to construct it from the beginning, just as it is no less

5

important to correct what we have learned than to learn it from the beginning. That is why the politician must be able, besides the things we have mentioned, to help <to improve> existing political systems, as we also said earlier.

[TO GIVE USEFUL ADVICE, WE MUST UNDERSTAND THE
VARIETY OF POLITICAL SYSTEMS]

We cannot do this, however, if we do not know how many species[3] of political systems there are; but, as things are, some people think there

2. **aspirations**: Cf. 1260b29n.

3. **species**: *eidē*. See FORM #8. The more technical term is perhaps better than 'type' or 'sort' here, to suggest the parallel with Aristotle's classification of biological species.

is only one type of democracy and one of oligarchy, which is not true.   *10*
And so we must notice the ways political systems differ and are constituted.

Further, it is the task of the same intelligence* both to see what the
best laws are and to see which ones fit each political system, since the
laws must be framed (and in fact everyone frames them) to fit the system,[4]
not the system to fit the laws. For the political system is the ordering   *15*
that determines the allocation of ruling offices in cities, the controlling
element in the system, and the goal of a particular community;[5] laws,
by contrast, apart from those that declare the type of political system it
is,[6] are what the rulers must follow in their ruling and in their precautions
against violators of them.   *20*

Clearly, then, we must grasp the differentiae and definition of each
type of political system <both for our other aims> and for the aim of
framing laws; for the same laws cannot benefit all types of oligarchy or
all types of democracy, if there are a number of types, and not just one
type, both of democracy and of oligarchy.

* * * * * * *

[DIFFERENT POLITICAL SYSTEMS ASSIGN POWER TO DIFFERENT PARTS OF A CITY]

3

The reason for the number of political systems is that every city has a   *1289b27*
number of parts.[7]

(1) For, first of all, we see that every city is composed of households.   *30*
(2) Next, we see that in the mass of people <in a city> some must
be prosperous, some disadvantaged, some in the middle, and that the
prosperous possess armor,[8] while the disadvantaged do not. And we
see that the common people in some states are occupied in agriculture,
elsewhere in commerce, elsewhere in menial* work. The people of reputation[9] also differ in their wealth and in the size of their property. They   *35*

4. **to fit the system**: Cf. 1282b10, 1286a33.

5. **the political system . . . community**: Democratic and oligarchic systems,
e.g., have different goals. See 1310a29.

6. **those that declare . . . system it is**: i.e., the laws defining the constitution.

7. **The reason . . . number of parts**: Aristotle offers a number of explanations
for the variety in political systems. See 1280a7, 1301a25, 1328a27.

8. **armor**: The armor and weapons of heavy infantry ('hoplites') were the backbone of a Greek army in the Classical period; see OCD p. 526b.

9. **people of reputation**: See KNOW #6.

differ, for example, in the number of horses they breed, since it is not easy to do this without wealth. That is why in ancient times all the cities whose strength depended on their horses had oligarchies; and these used their horses for wars against neighboring cities. This is true, for 40 example, of the Eretrians, the Chalcidians, the Magnesians on the Maeander, and many others in Asia.

1290a (3) Further, besides differences in wealth, there are differences in birth, in virtue, and in anything else that we counted as a part of the city in our discussion of aristocracy (for there we distinguished the number of parts of which any city must consist).[10]

5 For in some cases all of these parts participate in the political system, and in other cases not all parts participate—in some fewer and in some more. Evidently, then, there must be a number of political systems of different species, since these parts are of different species.

For a political system is the ordering of the ruling offices; and everyone distributes these either in accordance with the degree of power of those 10 who participate in the system, or in accordance with some common feature that they share equally—for instance, equality among the disadvantaged or the prosperous,[11] or equality common to both parts. Hence there must be as many political systems as there are types of superiority and of difference between the parts. . . .

* * * * * * *

[THE BEST POLITICAL SYSTEM IN NONIDEAL CONDITIONS]

11

1295a25 What is the best political system, and the best way of life for most cities and for most human beings? We are not judging by reference to a type of virtue that is beyond a private citizen's capacity, or by reference to a type of education that requires <a suitable> nature and a level of resources that depends on good fortune, or by reference to a political 30 system that is the best we could aspire to,[12] but by reference to a way of life that most people are able to share and a political system that most

10. **in our . . . consist)**: in 1283a14.

11. **equality . . . prosperous**: Equality among the poor would be in accordance with free birth. Equality among the rich would be in accordance with some property-qualification.

12. **aspire to**: See 1260b29n.

cities can achieve. For the so-called aristocracies[13] we discussed just now are in some ways beyond the capacity of most cities, and some ways are close to the so-called polity,* so that we can treat <this type of aristocracy and the polity> as one.

[THE DOCTRINE OF VIRTUE AS A MEAN JUSTIFIES A PREFERENCE FOR CITIZENS OF INTERMEDIATE WEALTH]

A judgment on all these questions depends on the same elementary   35
principles.[14] For if we were right to say in the *Ethics*[15] that the happy life is the one that conforms to unimpeded virtue, and that virtue is a mean*, then the intermediate life—achieving the mean that is possible for a given type of person—is the best. Moreover, these same formulae that   40
apply to the virtue and vice <of an individual> must also apply to a city and a political system, since the political system is a sort of way of   1295b
life of a city.

Now, in every city there are three parts—the extremely prosperous, the extremely disadvantaged, and, third, those intermediate between them. And so, since it is agreed that what is moderate and what is intermediate is best, it is also evident that the possession of an intermedi-   5
ate amount of goods of fortune is best of all; for it is easiest in this condition to obey reason. But if one is exceedingly handsome, strong, well born, or rich, or, on the contrary, exceedingly poor or feeble or extremely dishonored, it is hard to follow reason. For <the exceedingly well-favored> turn out to be wantonly* aggressive and wicked on a   10
grand scale, while the exceedingly ill-favored turn out crooked and exces- sively wicked on a small scale; and wanton aggression causes some acts of injustice, while crookedness causes others. Further, the intermediate people are least prone either to shirk or to covet ruling offices; and each of these two tendencies is harmful to cities.

[THE DANGERS OF EXTREME WEALTH AND POVERTY]

Besides, those who have exceedingly good fortune—strength, wealth, friends, and so on—neither wish nor know how to submit to being   15
ruled—indeed, this begins even when they are children at home, since their luxurious upbringing makes them unused to being ruled even at

13. **so-called aristocracies**: They are not aristocracies in the sense defined in 1279a3–5.

14. **elementary principles**: *stoicheion*, usually rendered 'element'.

15. *Ethics*: See *EN* 1108b11, 1153b9–12, *EE* 1222b12.

school. On the other hand, the exceedingly needy are excessively abased.
20 And so the needy do not know how to rule but only how to submit to being ruled as slaves, while the fortunate do not know how to submit to any kind of rule but only how to rule as masters over slaves. The result is a city of masters and slaves, not of free citizens, and, moreover, of slaves looking spitefully* on their masters and of masters despising their slaves. And this is furthest of all from friendship and a political
25 community. For community involves friendship; people are unwilling even to share the road with their enemies.

Now, the city aims to consist as far as possible of citizens who are equal and similar; these features are most frequent in the intermediate people. And so the city composed of these people, who we say are the naturally <appropriate> constituents of cities, is bound to have the best political system.

Moreover, these are the citizens who most frequently survive in cities.
30 For they do not covet other people's possessions, as the poor do, nor do others covet theirs, as the poor covet those of the rich. And since they are neither victims of plots nor plotters themselves, they pass their lives without danger. And so Phocylides* was right in his wish, 'Many things go best for the intermediate people; I want to be intermediate in the city.'

[A CITY BENEFITS WHEN THE INTERMEDIATE ELEMENT IS NUMEROUS AND POWERFUL]

35 Clearly, then, the political community that is in the hands of the intermediate people is best, and the cities capable of having a good system are those in which the intermediate <part> is numerous and superior, preferably to both the other <parts> together, but at least to either one of them—for if it is added <to either one> it tips the balance and tends to prevent the contrary excesses.
40 Hence it is the greatest good fortune <for a city> if the politically
1296a active citizens have intermediate and adequate property. For if some possess an extremely large amount and others possess nothing, the result is either an extreme democracy or an unmitigated oligarchy, or a tyranny resulting from either of these excesses; for tyranny arises from
5 the most thorough democracy or oligarchy, but far less often from the intermediate systems and those that are close to them. We will explain this in our account of changes in political systems.

Evidently, then, the intermediate system is best. For it is the only one free from civil conflicts,* since the cities that have a large intermediate <part> are least likely to have civil conflicts and divisions among the citi-
10 zens. And for the same reason large cities are less prone to civil conflict, since their intermediate <part> is numerous; in small cities, by contrast,

it is easy to divide all the citizens into two groups, so as to leave no intermediate <part>, and they are virtually all either prosperous or disadvantaged.[16]

Moreover, the intermediate people make democracies more secure
and lasting than oligarchies; for they are more numerous and more   15
likely to share in honors in democracies than they are in oligarchies. For
whenever the disadvantaged overcome by weight of numbers, without
the intermediate people, things turn out badly, and <the city is> soon
ruined.

And we must see further evidence <for our claim> in the fact that
the best legislators have come from the intermediate citizens. For Solon*
was one of them, as he shows in his poetry; so was Lycurgus,* since he   20
was not a king; so was Charondas;* and so were virtually most of the
other legislators.

[THE STRUGGLE BETWEEN RICH AND POOR]

From this it is also evident why most political systems are either democratic or oligarchic; for since the intermediate <part> is often small in
these cities, those outside the intermediate <part> who are on top at   25.
the time (either those with property or the common people) lead the
system in the direction they prefer, so that the result is either a democracy
or an oligarchy.

Besides, civil conflicts and struggles arise between the common people
and the prosperous. The result is that the side that happens to beat the   30
opposition does not establish a system that all can share in fairly,[17] but
grabs the top places in the political system as a prize of victory, so that
one side establishes a democracy, and the other side an oligarchy.

Further, the same applies to those cities[18] that once achieved leadership over Greece. Each city was guided by its own political system, so
that one of them set up democracies in the cities, and the other set up   35
oligarchies; each considered its own advantage, not the advantage of
the cities.

For these reasons, then, the intermediate system has either never
been established or only on a few occasions in a few cities. For only one

16. **in small cities . . . or disadvantaged**: There are not enough intermediate
people to form a strong group with recognized common interests, and so they
go toward the two extremes. On prosperous and disadvantaged classes see
1279b8n.

17. **that all . . . fairly**: Lit. 'common and equal'.

18. **those cities**: Athens and Sparta. They also regarded control over the political
system as a prize for the winning side.

40   man in earlier times among those who reached a position of leadership
1296b   was persuaded to introduce this sort of order; and by now it has become
a habit in cities not even to wish for a fair system, but either to seek to
rule or to submit to domination by others.

[THE INTERMEDIATE SYSTEM PROVIDES A CRITERION FOR OTHER SYSTEMS]

It is evident, then, from this what the best political system is, and why
it is best. But among the other systems, since we say there are several
5   types of democracy and of oligarchy, which should we put first, which
second, and which next in the order of better and worse? This is not
hard to see once we have determined the best system. For in each case
the system that is nearer to the best must be better, and the one further
from the intermediate must be worse, unless our judgment is relative
10   to an assumption.[19] By 'relative to an assumption' I mean that though
one system may be preferable <in general>, a different system may
well be more beneficial for some cities.

*   *   *   *   *   *   *

Book V

[THE CAUSES OF POLITICAL CHANGE]

[DIFFERENT POLITICAL SYSTEMS ARISE FROM
DIFFERENT CONCEPTIONS OF JUSTICE AND EQUALITY]

1

1301a19   We have now discussed most of the questions we decided to discuss.
20   Next in order we should examine the nature, number, and character of
the sources of change in political systems; what destroys each system;
what system most often changes into what; further, what conditions
preserve political systems in general and each system separately; and
what measures will best produce these conditions in each particular
system.
25   The principle we must accept at the outset is that many different
political systems have arisen because, while all agree on justice, i.e.,
proportionate equality, they are in error about proportionate equality,
as we said before.[1] For democracy has arisen from the supposition that
30   people who are equal in some aspect are equal without qualification; for

19. **an assumption**: We assume the continuation of the present regime.

1. **said before**: See 1280a7, 1289a27n.

since they are all free citizens in the same way, <democrats> suppose that they are equal without qualification. Oligarchy has arisen from the supposition that people who are unequal in some one aspect are unequal altogether; for since they are unequal in property, they suppose they are unequal without qualification. The result is that the democrats, taking themselves to be equal, claim an equal share in everything, while the   35 oligarchs, taking themselves to be unequal, seek to get* more, since that is unequal.

Hence all these systems have something just about them, but, speaking without qualification,[2] they are in error. And for this reason whenever the two sides participate in a system that does not fit both <partisan> views <of justice>, there is civil conflict.*

Those who would most justifiably start a civil conflict, but who in fact   40 do it least, are the people who are superior in virtue; for it is most   1301b reasonable for these alone to be unqualifiedly unequal. But some people of superior birth suppose, because of this inequality, that they deserve more than an equal share; for people seem to be well-born when they have ancestral virtue and wealth.[3]

[*DIFFERENT TYPES OF POLITICAL CHANGE RESULT FROM
CONFLICTING CONCEPTIONS OF JUSTICE*]

These, then, we may say, are the origins and springs of civil conflicts.   5 This is also why changes come about in two ways. Sometimes they are aimed at the political system, in order to change the established system to another—to change a democracy, for instance, into an oligarchy, or an oligarchy into a democracy, or to change either of these into a polity* or an aristocracy, or either of these into a democracy or an oligarchy.   10 Sometimes, however, instead of trying to change the established system, people decide to retain it, but want the oligarchy or monarchy, for instance, to be more in their control.

There are also conflicts about degree, about making an oligarchy, for instance, more or less oligarchic, or a democracy more or less democratic,   15 and so on with the others; or <there may be conflicts> about relaxing or tightening the system.

Again, there are conflicts about changing some part of the system—

2. **without qualification**: i.e., not relative to a particular political system or a particular aspect of equality.

3. **But some people . . . and wealth**: These people suppose they are entitled to more, because they believe they have the sort of superiority that, in Aristotle's view, belongs only to superior virtue.

about establishing or abolishing some ruling office, for instance. They
20   say, for instance, that Lysander tried to abolish the Spartan kingship,
and king Pausanias the office of Overseer. In Epidamnus also the system
changed partially; they established a council to replace the tribal rulers;
25   and the ruling officials among those in the political body are still required
to come to the popular court[4] when someone is elected to a ruling office,
whereas the single ruler is an oligarchical feature in that system.

For everywhere conflicts arise because of inequality, whenever unequals do not receive the proportionate amount—for lifetime kingship,
for instance, is unequal and unfair[5] if it is held among equals. For in
general civil conflicts arise from the pursuit of equality.

30   Equality is of two types, numerical equality and equality in worth.
By numerically equal I mean what is the same and equal in numerousness
or magnitude, and by equal in worth I mean what is proportionately[6]
equal. For instance, three exceeds two by an amount numerically equal
to that by which two exceeds one, but four exceeds two by an amount
35   proportionately equal to that by which two exceeds one, since two and
one are equal parts, i.e., halves, of four and of two.

But though people agree that what is unqualifiedly just is what conforms to worth, they still disagree (as we said earlier); for some, if they
are equal in some aspect, think they are equal altogether, while others,
if they are unequal in some aspect, think they deserve unequal shares
of everything.

[THESE DISAGREEMENTS MAKE DEMOCRACY AND OLIGARCHY
THE PREVALENT POLITICAL SYSTEMS]

40   Hence the two political systems that arise most frequently are democracy
1302a   and oligarchy; for while good birth and virtue are found only in a few
people, <wealth and free citizenship> are more widespread—for no
city has as many as a hundred well-born and good people, but many
cities have prosperous and disadvantaged people.

But it is bad to have the political system organized unqualifiedly and
altogether to conform to either sort of equality. This is evident from
5   what actually happens, since not a single system of that sort is stable.
The reason for this is that if they begin from an erroneous beginning,
they cannot avoid a bad end. Hence in some cases it is right to use
numerical equality, in others equality in worth.

---

4. **come . . . court**: Examination of officials, before their term of office, by a
popular JURY-court is characteristic of democracy.

5. **unequal and unfair**: *anison*, Lit. 'unequal'. See EQUAL.

6. **proportionately**: Lit. 'in *logos*'. See REASON #6.

[THE ADVANTAGES OF DEMOCRACY]

Still, democracy is more secure than oligarchy and less prone to civil conflicts. For in oligarchies there are two sorts of civil conflict—of oli-   10
garchs against each other and of oligarchs against the common people. In democracies there is conflict only with the oligarchs, and no internal conflict worth mentioning arises within the common people themselves. Moreover, the intermediate system is closer to democracy than to oligar-   15
chy, and this is the most secure of systems of this sort.

*   *   *   *   *   *   *

[THE PRESERVATION OF POLITICAL SYSTEMS [7]]

[EVEN SMALL CHANGES SHOULD BE CAREFULLY WATCHED]

8

Next we must discuss how to preserve political systems in general and   1307b27
how to preserve each system in particular. It is clear, first of all, that if we have found what destroys political systems, we have also found the ways to preserve them; for contrary causes produce contrary effects,   30
and destruction is contrary to preservation.

Hence in well mixed systems, just as they must be on guard against any other sort of lawlessness, they must especially beware of small offenses; for lawlessness insinuates itself unobserved, just as small but frequent expenses do away with the whole of someone's property. The   35
expense is not noticed because it does not come all at once; for the frequent small expenses lead the mind into fallacy, as does the sophistical argument, 'If each is small, then all are small'.[8] This is true in a way, but in a way false; for the whole and all of them <together> are not small, but are composed of small amounts. This, then, is one precaution   40
to be taken against this beginning <of disturbance>.

[TRICKS SHOULD BE AVOIDED]

Next, no confidence should be placed in the tricks aimed at the masses;   1308a
for these are discredited by the actual results. (We have previously said what we mean by tricks in political systems.)[9]

7. In this section Aristotle fulfills his promise to go beyond mere theory (ethical or sociological) and to give practical advice for different political systems. The section illustrates Aristotle's view of the significant features of political life and the sources of political change.

  8. **sophistical . . . small'**: Cf. 1261b27n.

  9. **(We have . . . systems)**: in 1297a14.

[THE DOMINANT PART SHOULD BEHAVE WELL IN INTERNAL
AND EXTERNAL RELATIONS]

Further, we must notice that some systems, oligarchies as well as aristocracies, are stable, not because the systems themselves are secure, but
because the ruling officials behave well both toward those outside the
political system and toward those within it. They avoid injustice against
the outsiders and promote their best leaders into the political system;
they avoid injustices that deny honor to the lovers of honor, or that
deny profit to the many. Toward fellow-rulers and those who participate
in the political system they behave democratically.

For the equality that democrats seek to apply to the masses is beneficial
as well as just if it is practiced among similar people. And so if there is
a large number in the political body, many features of democratic legislation are expedient—six-month terms of office, for instance—so that all
the similar people can share in them. For in this case the similar people
correspond to the common people <in a democracy>, so that indeed
popular leaders[10] often arise here too, as we said earlier.

Moreover, <if terms of office are short,> oligarchies and aristocracies
are less likely to lapse into ruling cliques,[11] since wrongdoing is not as
easy in a short term of office as in a long term. Indeed, long terms of
office are the source of tyrannies in oligarchies and democracies. For
those who aim at tyranny are either the more prominent in a given
system—in democracies the popular leaders and in oligarchies the members of the ruling clique—or those who hold the highest offices, in cities
where they hold them for a long time.

[DANGERS SHOULD NOT BE FORGOTTEN]

Political systems are preserved, not only because sources of destruction
are distant, but sometimes even because they are close at hand, since
fear makes people keep tighter control over the political system. Hence
those concerned about the system must instill fears, so that people will
be vigilant and will not be slack, as in a night watch, in guarding the
political system; they must make the distant danger present.[12]

10. **popular leaders**: *dēmagōgoi*. The term is sometimes pejorative, but need not
be.

11. **ruling cliques**, *dunasteiai*: a group of rulers with the extra-legal status of a
tyrant.

12. **they must . . . present**: i.e., bring it to people's attention. Aristotle does not
suggest that the rulers should deceive people into fearing imaginary dangers,
but that they should make them vividly aware of real dangers.

[CONFLICTS MUST BE AVOIDED]

Further, they must try by legislation to prevent competitions and conflicts among the people of reputation and to keep watch on those standing outside a competition, before they are also drawn in. For to spot a growing evil at its beginning is a task not for just anyone, but for a man   35
with political science.

[CHANGES IN MATERIAL CONDITIONS]

To avoid the change from oligarchy and polity that results when the property-qualification remains the same but the money-supply is increasing, it is expedient to examine the total amount[13] of property compared   40
with the past amount. This should be examined annually in cities where the qualification is assessed annually; in the larger cities it should be   1308b
examined triennially or quinquennially. If the total is many times larger or smaller than at the time when the qualification for participation in the political system was fixed, the qualification should be raised or lowered by legislation; if the total has risen, the qualification should be   5
raised in the same ratio, and if it has fallen, the qualification should be correspondingly relaxed and reduced. For in oligarchies and polities where they fail to do this, the result <when the total falls> is a change from polity to oligarchy or from oligarchy to a ruling clique, and <when the total rises> from polity to democracy or from oligarchy to polity or   10
democracy.

[DISTRIBUTION OF HONORS]

A <safeguard> that applies equally to democracy, oligarchy, and every political system is to avoid raising anyone beyond due measure, and instead to try to assign small honors over a long period rather than large ones all at once; for <people who receive large honors all at once> are corrupted, and not every man can bear good fortune. If <legislators>   15
cannot arrange this, at least they should try to avoid giving honors all at once and then removing them all at once, but they should give and remove them gradually. And, best of all, they should adjust things by legislation so as to prevent anyone from reaching ascendancy by the

13. **total amount**: Aristotle appears to be assuming without warrant that a higher total level of property implies that more people will meet a property-qualification; he does not mention the possibility that the increased wealth may be concentrated in a few hands. (An alternative text gives: 'the new valuation of property'.)

power of friends or wealth; or at least they should make such people go abroad when out of office.[14]

[REGULATION OF PRIVATE LIFE]

20 And since people's private ways of life also lead them to revolution, a ruling office must be introduced to oversee those who live in ways that are damaging to the political system—damaging to democracy in a democracy, to oligarchy in an oligarchy, and so on for each of the other
25 systems.

[DISTRIBUTION OF MATERIAL PROSPERITY]

For the same reasons, we must beware of prosperity confined to a part of the city. The remedy against this in each case is to assign public business and ruling offices to both the opposed parts (I mean that the decent people are opposed to the mass of people, and the prosperous to the disadvantaged), and to try either to combine the mass of the
30 disadvantaged with the prosperous or to increase the intermediate part, since this resolves the conflicts caused by inequality.

[RULING OFFICES SHOULD NOT BE SOURCES OF PROFIT]

The greatest safeguard in every political system is to order the laws and the rest of the organization so as to prevent ruling officials from making a profit. This precaution is especially necessary in oligarchies. For the
35 many are less offended by exclusion from ruling (indeed they are even pleased to have leisure for their own affairs) than by the thought that the rulers are stealing public funds, with the result that the many are offended by being excluded both from honors and from profits.
40   Indeed, this arrangement <that prevents profit> is the only one that
1309a allows democracy and aristocracy at the same time. For then both the people of reputation and the masses can have what they want. Making ruling offices open to everyone is democratic, and the holding of them by people of reputation is aristocratic, and both results are achieved
5 when no one can profit from holding office. In such cases the disadvan-

14. **go abroad when out of office**: There is no known constitutional precedent for Aristotle's advice. He is perhaps thinking of the Athenian practice of ostracism; see OCD p. 762.

taged will not want to hold office, since it offers no profit, but will prefer to stick to their private affairs, whereas the prosperous will be able to hold office because they need no extra income from public funds; hence the disadvantaged will become prosperous by occupying themselves with their work, while the people of reputation will not have just anyone ruling over them.

And so, to prevent theft of public funds, they should be transferred *10* when all the citizens are present, and copies of the list should be given to each brotherhood, company, and tribe.[15] And to encourage people to hold ruling offices without profit, honors must be provided by law for officials who win a good reputation.

[PROTECTION OF THE LOSING SIDE]

In democracies the prosperous must be spared. Not only must their *15* property not be redistributed, but the income should not be redistributed either, which happens inadvertently in some political systems.[16] And it is better to prohibit them, even against their will, from undertaking the public services that are costly but useless—for instance, equipping *20* choruses,[17] torch races, and everything of that sort.

Oligarchies should take great care of the disadvantaged, and assign them the ruling offices that yield a profit. If a prosperous person commits wanton* aggression on a disadvantaged person, his penalty should be greater than if he commits it against another like himself. Inheritance should not be by bequest, but by family relations, and one person should *25* not inherit more than one person's property; for <if only one person's property is inherited,> different people's property will be more nearly equal, and more of the disadvantaged will become prosperous.

Both in a democracy and in an oligarchy, it is expedient to allow those with a smaller share in the political system—in a democracy the *30* prosperous and in an oligarchy the disadvantaged—to have equality or precedence in everything, except for the ruling offices that control the political system; these should be committed exclusively or predominantly to those who belong to the system.

15. **brotherhood, company, and tribe**: political subdivisions of the city, in Athens and elsewhere.

16. **happens inadvertently in some political systems**: At Athens rich people were assessed, according to their property, for providing ships for the navy and for other 'public services' (*leitourgiai*; see OCD p. 613b). Aristotle goes on to mention less necessary contributions imposed on, or expected of, the rich.

17. **choruses**: for dramatic performances at state festivals (cf. *EN* 1123a18–27).

[POLITICAL EXTREMES MUST BE AVOIDED]

9

*   *   *   *   *   *   *

1309b18   . . . Apart from all these things, we must not overlook what the deviant
20   political systems overlook now—the intermediate <part of the city>.
For many measures that seem democratic or oligarchic in fact destroy
these systems, but the <partisans> think <the tendency they favor>
is the only virtue, and so take it to excess. They do not realize that,
though a nose may still be handsome and pleasing to look at even if it
is not optimally straight, but deviates in a hooked or snub direction,
25   someone who deviates further will first lose the proper proportion of
that part <of the body> and finally will deviate so far that he will not
even appear to have a nose, because one feature is so excessive and
30   contrary features are so deficient; and the same applies to the other parts
<of the body>.

This, then, is the result in political systems as well. For an oligarchy
or a democracy may be in a good enough condition even though it has
lapsed from the best order; but if someone takes either system to further
extremes, he will first make the political system worse and finally make
35   it cease to be a political system at all.

That is why the legislator and the politician must know which democratic or oligarchic measures preserve or destroy the corresponding system. For neither system can exist and endure without both the prosperous and the disadvantaged, but whenever equality of property is
1310a   introduced, that is bound to change the political system; and so by
destroying <one part> by laws that go to extremes, they destroy the
political system.

Both democracies and oligarchies make mistakes. In democracies the
5   popular leaders make the mistakes, in cities where the masses control
the laws; for they invariably split the city in two with their attacks on
the prosperous, when in fact they should always make it seem that they
are speaking on behalf of the prosperous. In oligarchies the oligarchs
should always make it seem that they are speaking on behalf of the
common people, and should swear oaths contrary to those they swear
10   now. For in some systems they swear: 'And I will hate the common
people, and devise any evil I can against them', whereas they ought
both to accept and to display the opposite view, adding to their oaths
the clause 'I will not do injustice to the common people'.

[EDUCATION MUST FIT THE POLITICAL SYSTEM]

But the most important measure of all those that we have mentioned
for the survival of the political system is the one that at present everyone

pays little heed to—education to fit the political system. For the most   15
beneficial laws agreed by all who participate in the system are of no
benefit unless people are habituated and educated in the political system—in a democratic way if the laws are democratic, and in an oligarchic
way if the laws are oligarchic. For if an individual can be incontinent,*
so can a city.[18]   20

However, education to fit the political system is not doing what pleases
the oligarchs or the democratic partisans; it is doing what will allow
them to maintain oligarchy or democracy. In oligarchies at present, however, the sons of the rulers live in idle luxury, while the sons of the
disadvantaged come to be trained and seasoned by hard labor, so that   25
they are both more eager for revolution and more capable of it.[19] And
in the democracies that are most thoroughly democratic, the custom is
the contrary of what is expedient; the reason for this is that they define
freedom wrongly.

For democracy seems to be defined by two features—control by the
majority, and freedom. For equality seems to be justice, and control by   30
what seems good to the masses seems to conform to equality; and freedom
seems to be doing what one wishes. And so in democracies of this sort
everyone lives as he wishes, and 'pursues whatever he likes', as Euripides
says. This, however, is bad; for we ought to think that living in the way   35
that fits the political system is not slavery, but preservation. . . .[20]

Book VII

[THE BEST STATE AND THE BEST SYSTEM [1]]

[THE POLITICAL SCIENTIST MUST BEGIN FROM A CONCEPTION OF HAPPINESS]

1

Anyone who is inquiring along the appropriate lines into the best political   1323a15
system must first determine what the most choiceworthy life is. If it is
left unclear what this is, it must also be unclear what the best political
system is; for those who have the best political system in their circum-

18. **so can a city**: by failing to act on laws that it has enacted and accepted.

19. **capable of it**: Cf. Plato, *Rep.* 556b–d.

20. **but preservation**: Aristotle does not deny that freedom is doing what one
wishes. He denies instead the (alleged) democratic claim that freedom is identical
to following one's whims or inclinations, however irrational. Cf. Plato, *Rep.*
557b.

1. Aristotle now returns to the topics of Bks ii–iii, after his discussion of the
shortcomings of actual states; these shortcomings are to be avoided in the ideal
state.

20   stances will characteristically be best-off, if nothing unexpected happens.[2] That is why we must first agree on what sort of life is most
choiceworthy for (we may say)[3] everyone, and then agree on whether
such a life is or is not the same for an individual as for a community.
We may take it then, that the best life is discussed at sufficient length
even in <our> popular* discussions; and so we should use those now.

[DIFFERENT KINDS OF GOODS ARE IMPORTANT IN HAPPINESS]

25   For certainly no one would dispute one classification <of goods>, at
least, into external goods, goods in the body, and goods in the soul,[4] or
would deny that blessedly happy people ought to possess them all. For
no one would count a person blessedly happy if he had no part of
30   bravery, temperance, justice, or wisdom, but was afraid of every passing
fly, sank to any depth to satisfy his appetite for food or drink, ruined
his closest friends for some trivial gain, and had his mind as full of
senseless illusion as a child's or a madman's.[5]

[VIRTUE IS THE MOST IMPORTANT GOOD]

35   Everyone would agree with these statements, but people disagree about
how much <of each good is needed> and about large amounts of them.
For whereas they think any slight degree of virtue is quite enough, they
seek extreme abundance of wealth, valuables, power, reputation, and
all such things,[6] without limit. We will tell them, on the contrary, that
40   it is easy to reach a confident belief about these questions, by simply
attending to the facts.
        For we see that people possess and keep external goods by having
1323b   the virtues, not the other way round. Further, as we see, a happy life—
whether such a life for human beings consists in enjoyment or in virtue
or in both—belongs to those who go to extremes in well-ordered charac-
5   ter and intellect, but possess a moderate level of external goods, rather

2. **if nothing unexpected happens**: As usual, Aristotle does not claim that virtue
by itself ensures happiness; good fortune (see LUCK) and favorable external
conditions must also be assumed.

3. **(we may say)**: i.e., it may not be best for absolutely everyone. Cf. *Met.*
1009b16n.

4. **one classification . . . the soul**: For this threefold classification of goods
(accepted in Aristotle's POPULAR works) cf. *EN* 1099a12–20.

5. **but was afraid . . . madman's**: These actions indicate the total absence of
the four cardinal virtues just listed.

6. **such things**: i.e., external goods.

than to those who have more external goods than they can use, but are deficient in character and intellect.

Moreover, the same point is easy to notice if we approach the question by argument.[7] For externals, like instruments, and everything useful for some purpose, have a limit, and excess of them is bound to harm, not to benefit, the possessor;[8] but each good of the soul becomes more useful   10
as it exceeds[9] (if we are to attribute usefulness as well as fineness even to these goods).

And in general, clearly we will say that the best condition of one thing surpasses the best condition of another in proportion to the superiority   15
of the first thing over the second. And so, if the soul is more honorable,* both without qualification and in relation to us, than possessions and the body, it follows that its best condition must be proportionately better than theirs. Further, these other things are naturally choiceworthy for the sake of the soul, and every intelligent person must choose them for   20
its sake, not the soul for their sake.

[THE DIFFERENCE BETWEEN HAPPINESS AND GOOD FORTUNE]

Let us, then, take it as agreed that each person achieves happiness to the extent that he achieves virtue and intelligence, and acts in accordance with them. We appeal to the god as evidence; for he is happy and blessed, because of himself and the character that is naturally his, not   25
through any external good. Indeed this is also why good fortune cannot be the same as happiness; for chance and fortune produce goods external to the soul, whereas no one is just or temperate from fortune or because   30
of fortune.

[HAPPINESS FOR AN INDIVIDUAL AND A COMMUNITY]

The next point, relying on the same arguments, is that the happy city is also the best one, the one that acts finely. But no one can act finely without doing fine actions,[10] and neither a man nor a city does any fine

---

7. **by argument**: The contrast between 'facts' (lit. 'things done', *erga*; see FUNC-TION) and 'argument' (*logos*; i.e., appeal to general principles) matches the usual contrast between APPEARANCES and *logos*; see REASON #3.

8. **For externals . . . possessor**: On the proper use of external GOODS see *EN* 1129b1–6.

9. **each good of the soul . . . exceeds**: This claim does not seem to be true of all intellectual gifts. Cleverness, for instance, could be used in planning a robbery as well as in helping one's neighbor. Aristotle seems to be confining goods of the soul to the virtues of character.

10. **acts finely . . . doing fine actions**: *kalōs prattein . . . prattein ta kala*.

35   actions without virtue and intelligence. Moreover, the bravery, justice, intelligence, and temperance of a city have the same capacity[11] and form$_m$ that belongs to a human being who is called brave, just, intelligent, and temperate.

    So much, then, for a preface to our argument; for we can neither leave these questions untouched nor go through all the appropriate 40 arguments, since this is a task for another discipline.[12] For now, let us simply assume that the best life for an individual by himself, and the 1324a best common life for cities, is the life involving virtue that has sufficient <external> resources to share in actions expressing virtue. In our present line* of inquiry we must leave aside objections, and consider them later, if someone turns out to be unpersuaded by what we have said.

2

5   It remains to be said, however, whether we should or should not take happiness to be the same for an individual human being and for a city. But the answer to this is also evident; for everyone would agree that it is the same. For those who think an individual lives well in being rich 10 also count a whole city blessed if it is rich, whereas those who honor the tyrant's way of life above all others would say that the happiest city is the one that rules over the most people; and if anyone thinks that virtue makes an individual happy, he will also say that the more excellent city is happier.

[POLITICAL ACTIVITY AND PHILOSOPHICAL STUDY]

15   But now there are two questions to be investigated. First, which of these two lives is more choiceworthy—the one that involves taking part in political activities and sharing in the city, or the life of an alien, released from the political community? Second, what political system and what condition of the city should we regard as best (no matter whether we decide that participation in the city is choiceworthy for everyone, or 20 only for most people, not for everyone)? This second question—not the question about what is choiceworthy for the individual—is the task of political thought and study; and since we have decided to undertake a political investigation now, that first question will be a side-issue, and the second will be the main issue for this line* of inquiry.

11. **same capacity**: They are capacities (see POTENTIALITY) for the same sorts of actions.

12. **discipline**: *scholē*, usually rendered 'LEISURE'. Probably the relevant discipline is ethics.

First, then, it is evident that the best political system must be the order that guides the life of anyone at all who does best and lives blessedly. *25* But even those who agree that the life involving virtue is the most choiceworthy disagree about whether the active life of the citizen is choiceworthy, or the life of someone released from all externals—some life of study,* which some people think is the only life for a philosopher— is more choiceworthy.[13] For practically all those, both in the past and *30* now, who have most eagerly pursued virtue have evidently decided on one or other of these two lives, the political and the philosophical; and it is quite important to decide which view is correct, since the intelligent *35* individual, and the intelligent political system no less, will necessarily order life to aim at the best goal.

[DOES POLITICAL ACTIVITY HARM INDIVIDUAL HAPPINESS?]

Some people, however, think that ruling over one's neighbors as a master over slaves involves one of the worst injustices, and that even rule as a citizen over citizens, though it has nothing unjust about it, still interferes with the ruler's well-being. Others take just about the contrary view, supposing that the only life for a man is the life of political activity, *40* since, in their view, the actions resulting from each virtue are open to *1324b* those who undertake political action for the community, no less than to a private individual.

[DOES HAPPINESS REQUIRE DOMINATION OVER OTHERS?]

Some, then, hold this view. But still others say that only the form of political system that rules as a master and a tyrant is happy. And so in some cities the very aim of the political system and laws is to rule over *5* neighboring peoples as slaves.[14]

And so, while most laws in most cities are pretty haphazard, still any city that has laws aiming to any extent at some end has them all aiming at domination, as in Sparta and Crete both the education and most of the laws are organized for war. Moreover, all the <non-Greek> nations *10* that have the power to get* more <at the expense of others> honor this sort of power. For in some places there are even laws that incite them to this sort of virtue. The Carthaginians, for example, so it is said, decorate soldiers with bracelets for the number of campaigns they have *15* served in. Once the Macedonians had a law that someone who had not

13. **more choiceworthy**: Or perhaps 'choiceworthy rather than the citizen's life'. See MORE.

14. **And so . . . slaves**: Aristotle has Sparta especially in mind.

killed an enemy should wear a rope around his waist[15] instead of a belt.
The Scythians used to pass around a cup at feasts and forbade it to
20   anyone who had not killed an enemy. And the warlike Iberian nation
place around someone's grave a number of stakes to mark the number
of enemies he has killed. Many peoples have many similar practices
established by laws or customs.

[SUCH A VIEW IS MISTAKEN]

If we are willing to examine this question, however, we will find it utterly
25   absurd to suppose that the politician's task is the ability to study ways
of ruling over neighboring peoples as willing or unwilling slaves. For
how could this be a politician's or lawgiver's task, since it is not even
lawful?[16] It is unlawful to rule without regard to justice or injustice, and
30   domination may quite possibly be unjust. Moreover, we never see this
in the other sciences; it is not the doctor's or pilot's task to force his
patients or passengers if he fails to persuade them.

Most people, however, would seem to think the science of mastery
over slaves is political science;[17] and they are not ashamed to treat other
peoples in ways that they reject as unjust and harmful among individu-
35   als. For among themselves they seek to rule justly, but in relations with
other peoples they are indifferent to justice.

It is absurd, however, to deny that some creatures are, and some are
not, naturally suited to be ruled by masters. And so, if this is true, we
must try to rule as masters only over those suited to be ruled, not over
40   everyone, just as we must not try to hunt human beings for a feast or
sacrifice, but only animals that are suitable to be hunted; these are the
1325a wild animals that are suitable to eat.

Besides, a single city even by itself—if it has a fine political system,
of course—can be happy, if it is possible for a city to live in isolation
somewhere, governed by excellent laws. The organization of this political
5   system will not aim at war or at domination over enemy states, since it
is assumed to have no enemies or wars.[18]

15. **a rope around his waist**: Lit. 'a halter'.

16. **not even lawful?**: Aristotle does not mean that there is any positive law
against it, but that it is contrary to the rule (*nomos*) of JUSTICE. Many would regard
the fact that there is no law against inter-state aggression as a reason for thinking
it is not unjust (see 1324b33), but Aristotle rejects this argument.

17. **Most people . . . political science**: On the importance of distinguishing these
two disciplines see 1252a7n.

18. **The organization . . . enemies or wars**: Aristotle means that it is possible
(in favorable external circumstances) for a city to be complete (with reference to
happiness) without domination over other cities.

Clearly, then, all the ways of training for war should be regarded as fine—not, however, as the ultimate end of everything, but as promoting that end. The excellent legislator's task is to consider how a city, or people, or any other community, is to participate in a good life and in   *10* the happiness available to it. However, some prescriptions of law will vary; and it is the task of legislative science, if a city has neighbors, to see what practices should be cultivated in relations with different sorts of neighbors and how to apply the suitable ones to dealings with each neighboring city.

This question, however, about the right aim for the best political   *15* system, will receive the proper discussion later.

3

We must reply to the two sides who agree that the life involving virtue is the most choiceworthy but differ about the right way to practice it. For those on one side refuse to hold any rule over citizens, since they suppose that the free person's way of life is both different from the life   *20* of political activity and the most choiceworthy of all lives. Those on the other side, on the contrary, hold that the politically active life is the best of all, since, in their view, someone who is inactive cannot possibly be acting well, and good action is the same as happiness. In reply we say that each side is partly right and partly wrong.

The one side is right to say that the free person's way of life is better than the life of a master ruling slaves. This is true; for employing a slave,   *25* insofar as he is a slave, is quite unimpressive, since there is nothing fine about giving orders for the provision of necessities. But to suppose that every sort of rule is the rule of a master over slaves is wrong. For there is just as great a difference between rule over free people and rule over slaves as there is between being naturally free and being naturally a   *30* slave. We have determined this sufficiently in the first discussions.[19] Moreover, it is incorrect to praise inactivity over activity; for happiness is activity, and, further, the actions of just and temperate people achieve many fine goals.[20]

And yet, someone might perhaps take this conclusion to imply that   *35* control over everyone is the best thing, thinking that this is the way to

19. **first discussions**: See 1255b16.

20. **achieve many fine goals**: Lit. 'have the end of many and fine things'.

be in control of the largest number of the finest actions.[21] And so, on this view, anyone capable of ruling must not resign rule to his neighbor, but must seize it from him; a father must have no consideration for his sons, nor sons for their father, nor in general one friend for another, 40 nor consider them at all in comparison to this goal <of ruling>, since what is best is most choiceworthy, and good action is best.

1325b Now, presumably this claim <about ruling> is true, if brigands who rob and use force get the most choiceworthy thing there is. But presumably they cannot, and this assumption is false. For <the actions of an absolute ruler> cannot be fine if he is not as far superior to his subjects 5 as a man is to his wife, or a father is to his children, or a master to his slaves. And so someone who deviates from virtue can never achieve a great enough success thereby to outweigh his previous deviation.

[THE POLITICAL LIFE PROMOTES HAPPINESS IN THE RIGHT CONDITIONS]

For what is fine and just for people who are similar is <holding office> in turn. For this is equal and similar treatment, whereas unequal treatment for equal people and dissimilar treatment for similar people are 10 against nature, and nothing that is against nature is fine. That is why, if another person is superior in virtue and in the capacity for the best actions, it is fine to follow him, and just to obey him; but he must have not only virtue but also the capacity for the actions.

15 If this is right, and we should take happiness to be good action, then the life of action is best both for a whole city in common and for the individual.

[BUT PURE THOUGHT IS ALSO A GOOD ACTIVITY]

However, the life of action need not, as some think, involve relations to others, and the thoughts concerned with action need not be only 20 those carried out for the sake of the results of the action. On the contrary, the studies and thoughts that include their own end and are carried out for their own sakes must be far more concerned with action; for <their> end is good action,[22] and hence it is a kind of action. And in fact, even

21. **And yet, someone . . . finest actions**: These people wrongly suppose that the good aspects of ruling make ruling an unqualified good to be pursued without restriction, whereas Aristotle suggests that it is good for an agent only if it is regulated by the VIRTUES.

22. **good action**: Or 'doing well', *eupraxia*. This is the sort of ACTION that does not involve motion (*kinēsis*) at all.

in the case of external actions, those whom we regard as acting most fully are the master craftsmen whose plans <direct production>.

Nor, moreover, are cities necessarily inactive if their position is isolated   25
and they have decided to live in isolation. For a city can still have activities involving parts of itself, since the parts of the city have many communities with each other. And the same is also true of any individual human being; otherwise the god and the whole universe would hardly be in a fine condition, since they have no actions directed outside them,   30
but only their own proper actions involving themselves.

It is evident, then, that the same sort of life must be the best one both for an individual human being and for cities and human beings in common.[23]

*   *   *   *   *   *   *

[THE COMPOSITION OF THE IDEAL CITY]

[THE PARTS OF THE CITY CONTRASTED WITH THE NECESSARY CONDITIONS]

8

Just as the conditions necessary for the existence of anything else consti-   1328a21
tuted by nature are not <thereby> parts of its whole constitution, so also it is clear that we must not count a necessary condition as a part of a city or of any other community composing a whole that is one in kind;   25
for the community must share in some one thing common to them, whether their shares in it are equal or unequal—in food, for instance, or amount of land, or anything of that sort.

Now, when one thing is the end and the other is for the sake of the end, these have nothing in common[24] apart from the fact that one acquires   30
what the other produces. This is true of an instrument or a workman in relation to the resulting product; for the house and the builder have nothing in common, but the builder's craft is for the sake of the house.

Hence, though a city needs possessions, they are no part of a city,   35

23. **It is evident . . . in common**: What was Aristotle's answer to his original question about the nature of the best life? He has argued that the life of study counts as ACTION, and so deserves to be counted among lives of good action. But he has not shown that this life achieves the COMPLETE good, or that it is the only life that achieves it; and therefore he has not shown (and apparently has not attempted to show) that it is to be identified with happiness. The life of study is discussed further in *EN* x 6–8.

24. **nothing in common**: They have no common interest, insofar as they are related only as producer and beneficiary (they may of course have common interests, if they are related in some other way as well).

and many animate creatures[25] are included among possessions, whereas a city is a community of similar people,[26] aiming at the best life possible.

40

1328b

Now the best good is happiness, which is some complete activity and exercise of virtue; and the fact is that some can share in it, while others can have little or no share in it. Clearly, then, this is why different types of cities and a number of political systems arise;[27] for different sorts of people pursue happiness in different ways, and through different means, and so form different ways of life and different political systems.

[THE REQUIREMENTS OF SELF-SUFFICIENCY]

We must consider how many things are necessary conditions for a city; for the things we call parts of the city must also be included among these. And so we must enumerate the required functions, since these will make clear the necessary conditions.

5

First, then, a city needs a supply of food; second, crafts (since life needs many tools); third, arms (since the members of the community need arms belonging to themselves as well <as to noncitizen auxiliaries>, for maintenance of their rule, by restraining the disobedient, and for warding off attempts by outsiders to treat the city unjustly); fourth, a good supply of money (to use for internal purposes and for wars); fifth, and first <in honor>, observance of divine matters, called priesthood; sixth, and most necessary of all, some judicial procedure for settling questions of expediency and justice in the members' relations with each other.

10

15

These, then, are the functions needed, we may say,[28] by every city. For a city is not just any chance mass of people, but is self-sufficient, as we say, for its life; a community that lacks any of these functions cannot be self-sufficient without qualification. Hence the composition of the city must correspond to these functions; and so there must be a number of farmers to supply food; craftsmen; a military force; a prosperous <class>; priests; and judges of what is necessary and expedient.

20

25. **animate creatures**: i.e., both animals and slaves.

26. **similar people**: In different places Aristotle stresses the similarities and the differences needed among citizens. See 1279a8n.

27. **Clearly . . . systems arise**: Aristotle offers different explanations of the variety of political systems; see 1289b27n.

28. **we may say**: Cf. *Met.* 1009b16n.

[THE DIVISION OF FUNCTIONS SHOULD REFLECT OUR VIEW
OF VIRTUE AND HAPPINESS]

9

Now that this has been determined, the next question to consider is this: Should everyone share in all these functions, since it is possible for   25
all the same people to be at once farmers, craftsmen, councillors, and jurymen? Or should different people be assumed for each of the functions we have listed? Or is it necessary for some to be confined to some people and for others to be shared by everyone?

It is not the same in every political system. For, as we said, it is   30
possible either for all to share in every function, or for all not to share in every function, but particular people in particular functions. For indeed this is what makes systems different, since in democracies all participate in every function, while in oligarchies the contrary is true.

We, however, are investigating the best political system, and this is   35
the one that will result in the greatest happiness for the city; and, as we have said, happiness cannot be separate from virtue. From this it is evident that in a city with the finest system, possessing men who are just without qualification, not <merely> just in relation to the assumption <of this city>, the citizens must not live the life of menial workers or tradesmen, since it is ignoble and contrary to virtue; and if they are   40
to be citizens, they must not be farmers, since they need leisure both   1329a
to develop virtue and for political actions.

We have found that a military <force> and a <body> that deliberates about what is expedient and judges about what is just are present in the city, and that they, most of all, are evidently parts of the city. Should   5
we, then, assign different functions to different people in this case also, or should we assign both functions to the same people?

The answer to this is also evident, because in one way they should be assigned to the same people, in another way to different people. Insofar as each function is appropriate to a different period of life, and one function needs intelligence, the other strength, in this respect they   10
should be assigned to different people. But insofar as it is impossible that people who are able to force and hinder others should accept permanent rule by others, in this respect they must be assigned to the same people, since those who control the arms also control the survival or collapse of the political system.

The remaining option, then, is for the political system to assign both of these functions to the same people, but not at the same time of   15
life. Rather, since strength is naturally found in younger people, and intelligence in older people, that would seem to be the just and expedient assignment of functions to each group—for this division corresponds to the worth of each.

20   Moreover, these must also own the possessions, since the citizens must have property, and these are the citizens. For the menial <class> has no share in the political system, nor has any other class that does not produce virtue.[29] This is clear from our <basic> assumption. For happiness must involve virtue; and in calling a city happy we must

25   consider all the citizens, not just a part of the city.[30] Moreover, it is also evident that these citizens must own the possessions, since the farmers must be slaves or foreign serfs.[31]

Among the classes previously listed there remains the class of priests. It is also evident how they should be organized. For neither a farmer

30   nor a menial worker should be constituted priest, since it is appropriate for citizens to be the ones who honor the gods. And since the citizens have been divided into two parts, military and deliberative, and since it is appropriate for those who have retired because of age to attend duly on the gods and have a time of rest, the priesthoods of the gods must be assigned to these people.

35   We have now described the necessary conditions and the parts of a city; for farmers, craftsmen, and the whole laboring <class> are necessary for the city, while the military and the deliberative <classes> are the parts of the city. And each of these is separated from the others, some permanently, others by taking functions in turns.

*   *   *   *   *   *   *

[OUR CONCEPTION OF HAPPINESS AND VIRTUE DETERMINES OUR CONCEPTION OF THE GOOD CITIZEN [32]]

13

1331b24   We should now discuss the political system itself and say which people,
25   and of what character, must constitute a city if it is to be blessedly happy and to have a fine political system.

29. **does not produce virtue**: Aristotle does not explain why the argument that he has just applied to the military functions in a state could not also be applied to the laboring classes.

30. **in calling . . . of the city**: Aristotle rejects Plato's (alleged) view that the city as a whole is happy if the ruling class is happy (see 1264b17). His response, however, is not to ensure that the members of the laboring classes will be individually as happy as possible, but to deny them citizenship (so that their happiness or lack of it does not count in determining the happiness of the citizens).

31. **foreign serfs**: The natural inferiority, as Aristotle conceives it (see FOREIGNER), of non-Greeks makes them suitable for the work of slaves.

32. Here Aristotle answers his puzzle about the relation between the good man and the good citizen. Cf. iii 4.

Everyone's welfare depends on two conditions; the goal and end of actions must be correctly laid down, and the actions promoting the end *30* must be found. For these may either conflict or harmonize with each other. Sometimes the goal has been finely laid down, but we fail to obtain it in our actions; sometimes we attain everything that promotes our end, but have laid down a bad end; and sometimes we fail on both counts (as in medicine, for instance, when sometimes they neither make *35* a correct judgment about the character of a healthy body nor manage to find the right productive process relative to the standard[33] that has been laid down). In crafts and sciences we must master both the end and the actions advancing toward it.

It is evident, then, that everyone aims at living well and at happiness. *40* In fact, however, these are open to some and not to others, because of *1332a* something in fortune or nature—for living finely also needs resources, fewer if our condition is better, and more if it is worse. Others again, though happiness is open to them, seek it in the wrong way from the start. Our task is to see the best political system, the one that will result *5* in the best political life in the city; this will be the one that most of all results in happiness for the city. Hence we must not be ignorant of what happiness is.

We say, then—as we define it in the *Ethics*,[34] if those discussions are of any benefit—that happiness is complete activity and exercise of virtue, *10* complete without qualification, not conditionally.[35] By 'conditionally' I mean what is necessary, and by 'without qualification' I mean what is done finely. For in the case of just actions, for instance, penalties and corrective treatments result from virtue, but are necessary, and are done finely only to the extent that is possible for necessary actions,[36] since it is more choiceworthy if neither a man nor a city needs any such thing. By *15* contrast, actions leading to honors and prosperity are the finest actions without qualification; for while the other type of action involves merely the removal of some evil, these, on the contrary, construct and generate goods.

Now, certainly the excellent man will act finely in response to poverty *20* or disease or any other ill fortune.[37] Still, blessedness consists in the contrary of these. For we have determined this also in our ethical discussions, that the excellent person is the sort whose virtue makes unqualified

33. **standard**: See FORMULA.

34. **Ethics**: Cf. *EN* 1098a16, *EE* 1219a38.

35. **conditionally**: Lit. 'on an ASSUMPTION'. See NECESSITY #4.

36. **only . . . necessary actions**: Lit. just 'necessarily'.

37. **in response . . . ill fortune**: Lit. 'in the use of . . . ill fortune'. Aristotle speaks of 'use' both in referring to one's use of good circumstances and in referring to one's attitude to bad circumstances.

goods good for him;[38] and clearly the ways in which he uses them must
25 also be excellent and fine without qualification. Indeed this is why human
beings think external goods cause happiness; it is as though they took
the lyre rather than the performer's craft to be the cause of a splendidly
fine performance.

It follows, then, from what has been said, that some conditions must
30 be presupposed, but some must be provided by the legislator. That is
why, in establishing the city, we assume that the goods we want that
are controlled by fortune (since we take fortune to control <externals>)
are provided at the level we aspire to, but when we come to making the
city excellent, it is a task not for fortune, but for science and decision.

Moreover, a city is excellent because the citizens who participate in
35 the political system are excellent; and in our city all the citizens participate
in the political system. Hence we must consider how an excellent man
comes to be; for even if it is possible for the citizens to be excellent all
together without being so individually,[39] still it is more choiceworthy for
each to be excellent individually, since being excellent individually also
implies being excellent all together <but the converse is not true>.

[THE ROLES OF NATURE AND EDUCATION]

40 Now, people come to be good and excellent through three means—
nature, habit, and reason. For, first of all, we must be born with the
nature of a human being, not of some other animal; and then we must
1332b have the appropriate sort of body and soul. But in some cases being
born with a given quality is no help, since habits alter it; for nature
makes some things able to go either way, and habits change them for
the worse or the better.[40]

Now, whereas the other animals live mostly by nature, while some
5 live to some slight extent by habit, a human being also lives by reason,
since he is the only animal who has it. And so these three ought to be
in accord; for people do many actions contrary to habituation and nature
because of reason, if they are persuaded that another way is better.

We have previously defined, then, the sort of nature that is needed
10 if people are to be easily handled by the legislator. Thereafter the task
falls to education, since some things are learned by habituation, others
by instruction.

38. **makes . . . for him**: Cf. *EN* 1129b1–6, *EE* 1248b26.

39. **all . . . individually**: For the distinction see 1261b29n.

40. **for nature . . . the better**: On the contributions of nature and of habituation
see *EN* 1103a28, 1179b21.

* * * * * * *

[HAPPINESS REQUIRES THE VIRTUES APPROPRIATE FOR DIFFERENT CIRCUMSTANCES]

15

The goal appears to be the same for a community of human beings as   *1334a11*
for an individual, and the best political system must conform to the same
standard* that the best man conforms to. Evidently, then, it must possess
the virtues applying to leisure; for, as we have often said, the goal of   *15*
war is peace, and the goal of labor is leisure.

The virtues that are useful for leisure and for spending one's leisure
time are those whose function applies to leisure and those whose function applies to labor; for many necessary <goods> must be presupposed
if leisure is to be open to us. Hence it is fitting for the city to be temperate,   *20*
brave, and resistant; for, as the proverb says, slaves have no leisure,
and those who cannot face dangers bravely are slaves of their attackers.

Now, bravery and resistance are needed for labor, philosophy for
leisure, and temperance and justice in both circumstances—indeed, even   *25*
more in peace and leisure. For war compels us to be just and temperate,
but enjoyment of good fortune and of peacetime makes people wantonly*
aggressive instead. Much justice and temperance, then, are needed by
those who seem to do best and to enjoy the <external> goods that bring   *30*
congratulation for blessedness. This will be true, for instance, of the
people in the Isles of the Blessed, if there are any, as the poets say there
are; for these will have most need of philosophy, temperance, and justice,
to the extent that they more than anyone else are at leisure, with abundance of all those <external> goods.

It is evident, then, why the city that is to be happy and excellent   *35*
needs to share in the virtues. For it is shameful to be incapable of using
goods <properly>; it is even more shameful to be incapable of using
them in leisure, so that we appear good when we are laboring and
fighting wars, but slavish when we are at leisure in time of peace.

That is why we must not cultivate virtue as Sparta[41] does. For the   *40*
Spartans are superior to other people not by rejecting other people's   *1334b*
view that the <externals> are the greatest goods, but by believing that
a particular virtue is the best way to secure these goods. But since they
esteem these goods and the enjoyment of them more highly than the
enjoyment of the virtues[42] . . . and that <virtue is to be cultivated> for   *5*
itself, is evident from this. The next thing to attend to, then, is the means
and method of acquiring virtue.

41. **Sparta**: For similar comments on Spartan militarism see 1324b7.

42. **virtues . . .**: There seems to be a passage missing from the manuscripts at
this point.

[HOW VIRTUES ARE ACQUIRED]

We have previously determined, then, that the acquisition of virtue depends on nature, habit, and reason; and among these we have previously determined the sort of natural characteristics people should have. The remaining question to study is whether education by reason or by habit should come first.

For reason and habit must achieve the best sort of harmony, since it is possible both for reason to fall short of the best basic assumption[43] and for upbringing by habits to fail similarly. This at least, then, is evident first of all, as in other cases, that coming to be has some starting point, and the end resulting from one starting point is itself the starting point of another end. Now, the goal of nature for us is reason and understanding; hence the coming to be and the practice of habits must be arranged to aim at these.

Further, just as soul and body are two, so also we see that the soul has two parts,[44] the nonrational and the rational, and these have two <characteristic> states, desire and understanding <respectively>. And just as the body comes to be before the soul, so also the nonrational part of the soul comes to be before the rational. This also is evident from the fact that emotion, wish, and also appetite[45] are present in children as soon as they are born, whereas reasoning and understanding naturally arise in the course of growth.

First of all, then, attention to the body must precede attention to the soul, and, next, attention to desire must precede attention to understanding. Nonetheless, attention to desire must be for the sake of understanding, just as attention to the body must be for the sake of the soul.

43. **assumption**: i.e., the general principles determining the character of a political system.

44. **two parts**: See SOUL #4.

45. **emotion, wish, and also appetite**: Usually these are the names of the DESIRES of different parts of the soul. In this passage, however, Aristotle suggests that wish (normally the desire of the rational part of the soul) can be present in children before their rational part develops.

RHETORIC[1]

[*THE STUDY OF RHETORIC*]

Book I

[THE PROPER SCOPE OF RHETORIC]

1

Rhetoric is a counterpart of dialectic. For both of them are about questions   *1354a*
which, in a way, it is everyone's concern to know$_g$ about and which do
not belong to any definite science. Hence everyone, in a way, participates
in both <pursuits>; for everyone tries to some extent both to examine   *5*
and to give an account, and tries both to defend and to denounce.[2]

Now, among most people, some do these things at random, while
others do them a particular way because of habit, from a <firm> state.
And since these things can be done in either of these two ways, clearly
they can also be done methodically. For we can study why some succeeded because of habit and others at random; everyone would agree   *10*
that this sort of study is a function of a craft.

[MOST WRITERS FOCUS ON PERIPHERAL QUESTIONS,
NOT ON THE PROPER TASK OF RHETORIC]

As things are, those who have compiled treatises on the craft of speaking
have supplied us with (we may say[3]) no part of the craft. For convincing*

---

1. Aristotle's treatise on rhetoric discusses (1) the forms of rhetorical argument,
in comparison and contrast with DEMONSTRATION and DIALECTIC; (2) the sorts of
moral assumptions that the public speaker ought to appeal to; (3) the kinds of
emotions that the speaker ought to try to arouse in the audience. We have
translated only a brief selection to illustrate these three themes.

Public speaking played an important part in the Athenian democracy, which
made many important decisions in mass meetings of the popular Assembly and
in large jury-courts. A large body of rhetorical theory and technique (some of it
criticized in Plato's *Gorgias*; cf. *Top.* 183b26–184b3) had been built up by Aristotle's
time. See OCD p. 920b.

2. **everyone . . . and denounce**: Examining is the questioner's role in dialectic,
and giving an account is the respondent's role. Defending and denouncing are
characteristic of rhetoric.

3. **we may say**: Cf. *Met.* 1009b16n.

arguments are the only genuine constituents of the craft, and everything else is an accessory; but these people say nothing about argumentations,* which are the main body of convincing arguments, but they devote most of their concern to questions that are external to the subject. For <the exciting of> hostility, pity,* and such feelings of the soul is not relevant to the subject matter of rhetoric but is directed to the juryman.*

If, then, legal judgments were reached in every city as they now are in some cities, especially those that are well governed,[4] these <orators> would have nothing left to say. For while everyone thinks the laws ought to prescribe this, some states actually put the view into practice and forbid speakers to say anything extraneous to the subject. This is what they do in the Council of the Areopagus,[5] and their view is quite correct. For it is wrong to pervert the juryman by provoking him to anger or spite* or pity; that is like bending a rod before we use it to measure.

Moreover, the disputant's task is evidently confined to showing that the fact is so or that it is not so, or that something has happened or that it has not. Whether it is serious or trivial, just or unjust, to the extent that the legislator has not determined it, presumably the juryman must find this out[6] for himself, and not learn it from the disputants.

[A CORRECT LEGAL SYSTEM WOULD LEAVE NO ROOM FOR THE DIVERSION OF RHETORIC FROM ITS PROPER TASK]

Hence it is most appropriate for correctly established laws to determine everything themselves, as far as possible, and to leave as little discretion as possible to the judges.* This is true because, first of all, it is easier to find one or a few people of sound intelligence who are capable of legislating and reaching judicial verdicts than to find many. Further, legislative provisions are the result of examination over a long time, whereas a court's judgments are reached in a short time, so that it is difficult for the judges to reach the right view of what is just and expedient. And the most important reason of all is that the legislator's judgment is not for a particular case, but is concerned with future cases and has a universal scope, whereas the assemblymen or jurymen judge about some definite present case. For them, friendship, hatred, and their own special interest are often involved, so that they can no longer attend adequately to the truth, but what is pleasant or painful to themselves obscures their judgment.

4. **well governed**: See GOOD GOVERNMENT.

5. **Council of the Areopagus**: This was the Athenian 'Senate' (composed of ex-officials), which also served as a court to try some offenses. See OCD pp. 102–3.

6. **find this out**: *gignōskein*. See KNOW #1.

On these other questions,[7] then, as we say, the least possible control must be allowed to the judge. But questions about whether something has or has not happened, or will or will not be, or is or is not so, must be left up to the judges, since the legislator cannot foresee all these   *15* things.

[MISTAKES ABOUT RHETORIC EXPLAIN THE PREVALENT PREFERENCE FOR
FORENSIC OVER POLITICAL SPEECHES]

If this is so, then evidently people who claim to be expounding the craft but discuss the other issues—for instance, what the introduction or the exposition or any other part of a speech must include—are in fact expounding matters that are extraneous to the real subject. For here their whole concern is to mold the judge in a particular way. They offer   *20* no account of the convincing arguments that are proper to the craft, that is, what makes someone good at argumentation.

This <neglect of the essentials of the craft> also explains <another error>. The same line* of inquiry applies both to political and to forensic speeches, and a treatment of political speaking is finer and more proper for a citizen than a treatment of <private> transactions; and yet <stu-   *25* dents of rhetoric> have nothing to say about political speaking, but they all try to expound the craft with reference to forensic speeches. The reason is that it is less useful to bring extraneous matters into political speeches, and political speaking tends to be less dishonest than forensic speaking, because it is about more common interests. For in listening to political speeches the judge reaches a verdict about his own interest,[8]   *30* and so nothing else is needed besides a demonstration that things are as the proponent says they are. In forensic cases, by contrast, this is not enough; what matters is to win over the juryman who hears the speech. For his verdict is about other people's interests; hence he keeps his eye on his own interest, and listens to the speeches with favor to one side or the other, so that he does not really judge between the disputants   *1355a* but gives in to one or the other of them.

This is why the law in many cities, as I said before, forbids extraneous matters <in forensic speeches>, whereas in political speeches the judges themselves keep adequate guard against them.[9]

[RHETORIC IS PROPERLY CONCERNED WITH CONVINCING ARGUMENTS]

It is evident, then, that the line of inquiry proper to this craft is concerned with convincing arguments. A convincing argument is a sort of demon-   *5*

7. **these other questions**: These concern justice and expediency.

8. **his own interest**: sc. as well as everyone else's.

9. **the judges . . . against them**: sc. without any need for legislation.

stration,* since we are convinced of a point most of all when we suppose it has been demonstrated. A rhetorical demonstration is an argumentation;* and this, speaking without qualification, is the most important among convincing arguments.

Now, an argumentation is a sort of deduction and it is the task of dialectic—either of dialectic as a whole or of a part of it—to consider every sort of deduction equally. Clearly, then, the person who can best study the sources and methods of deduction will also be the best at argumentation, if he has also grasped the subject matter of argumentation and the ways it differs from logical deductions.[10] For the same capacity has the task of seeing what is true and of seeing what is similar to what is true. Moreover, human beings have a sufficient natural tendency toward what is true, and they mostly reach the truth. Hence the one who is good at aiming at the truth is also the one who is good at aiming at what is commonly believed.[11]

It is evident, then, both that other people who write about the craft are really concerned with extraneous matters and why they have inclined more toward forensic oratory.

[*THE USES OF RHETORIC*]

Rhetoric is useful for the following reasons:

(1) What is true and what is just are by nature superior to their contraries. Hence if judgments do not reach the appropriate verdict, the speakers must have been defeated through their own mistakes,[12] and this deserves censure.

(2) Moreover, even if we have the most exact scientific knowledge, there are some audiences who will not be easily persuaded if we rely on it in speaking to them. For a discourse expressing scientific knowledge is for teaching <the science>, but <with these audiences> such teaching is impossible. Instead we must use what is commonly believed[13] in constructing our convincing arguments and our discourses, as we also said in the *Topics*,[14] when we discussed the way to encounter the many.

10. **if he has . . . deductions**: On rhetoric and DEDUCTION see *APr* 68b9–14.

11. **Moreover, human beings . . . commonly believed**: This is Aristotle's reason for believing that the study of rhetorical argument should be a branch of the study of argument—especially of valid and sound argument—in general.

12. **their own mistakes**: They have failed to present the inherent superiority of their case, because they did not use rhetoric effectively.

13. **what is commonly believed**: Lit. 'the common things'.

14. *Topics*: 101a30.

(3) Further, we must be able to persuade an audience of each of two   *30*
contrary positions, just as in the case of deductions.[15] This is not for the
purpose of persuading people of both sides, since we must not persuade
them of what is base. Rather, the purpose is to see clearly how things
are, and to be able to destroy someone else's arguments if he uses them
unjustly. Now, no other craft argues deductively for each of the two
contrary positions; only dialectic and rhetoric do this, since they are both   *35*
concerned in the same way with contraries. Still, the underlying subjects
are not on an equal footing; in every case what is true and what is better
are by nature more readily deduced and more persuasive, to speak
without qualification.[16]

(4) Besides, if it is shameful to be unable to defend ourselves physically, it must obviously be shameful to be unable to defend ourselves   *1355b*
by rational discourse,[17] which indeed is more distinctive* of a human
being than the use of his body is.

(5) And if it is true that someone who uses this ability in discourse
unjustly might do great harm,[18] still, this feature is common to all goods
except virtue. Indeed, it is especially true of the most useful goods,   *5*
such as strength, health, wealth, generalship; for by using these justly
someone might do the greatest benefit and by using them unjustly do
the greatest harm.

[SUMMARY OF THE DISCUSSION]

It is evident, then, that rhetoric, like dialectic, has no distinct subject
matter and that it is useful. It is also evident that its function is not to   *10*
persuade but to discover the persuasive <arguments> available on each
topic. The same is also true of all the other crafts. For it is not the function
of medical science to make people healthy, but to lead them as close to
it as possible; for it is possible to provide good treatment to people who
are incapable of sharing in health.

Moreover, it is evidently also a task for the same craft to see both   *15*
what is persuasive and what appears persuasive, just as, in the case of
dialectic, the same craft sees both what is a deduction and what appears
to be one—for sophistry <differs from dialectic> not in its capacity, but

15. **in the case of deductions**: We must be able to find deductions on both sides
of a question.

16. **to speak without qualification**: Aristotle implicitly concedes that what is
true and what is better may not invariably be more persuasive in fact, in face
of an especially ignorant or especially prejudiced audience.

17. **rational discourse**: See REASON #2.

18. **someone who . . . harm**: Cf. Plato, *Gorg.* 456c.

20 in <the sophist's> decision.[19] In the case of rhetoric, however, one person is an orator because he has the appropriate knowledge$_e$, and another is a <sophistical> orator because of his decision, whereas a sophist is so called because of his decision, and a dialectician is so called because of his capacity, not because of his decision.[20]

Let us now try to discover the line of inquiry proper to rhetoric, and find the means and sources for achieving what we seek. Let us, then, define over again what it is, as though making a fresh start, and then discuss the remaining points.

[THE DIFFERENT SOURCES OF CONVINCING ARGUMENTS]

2

25 Let us, then, take rhetoric to be the capacity to observe the available means of persuasion on a given question. For this is the function of no other craft. Each of the other crafts teaches and persuades about its own subject matter[21] (medical science, for instance, about what promotes
30 health or sickness, geometry about the properties coincident to magnitudes,[22] arithmetic about numbers, and so on for the other sciences and crafts), whereas rhetoric seems to be able to observe what is persuasive on any question presented to it, one might say—that is why we say it practices its craft on no special determinate genus.
35 Among means of conviction,[23] some are external to the craft, others internal. By 'external' I mean those that we do not supply from our own resources but are given in advance—for instance, witnesses, inquisitions,[24] and such like. By 'internal' I mean those that we can establish through the line of inquiry <proper to the craft> and from our own

19. **decision**: Cf. *Met.* 1004b22–26. The SOPHIST decides to use some of the dialectician's abilities, in order to produce apparent deductions, with the aim of deceiving the hearer.

20. **In the case . . . not because of his decision**: Someone who uses rhetoric for sophistical purposes is still called an orator, but someone who uses dialectic for sophistical purposes is not called a dialectician.

21. **Each . . . own subject matter**: Aristotle takes up a question raised by Plato at *Gorg.* 453d.

22. **coincident to magnitudes**: i.e., intrinsic coincidents. See COINCIDENT #2.

23. **means of conviction**: This term (*pistis*) is usually translated 'convincing argument'; but that rendering does not readily apply to such means of conviction as torture. Cf. 1356a13, 21.

24. **inquisitions**: These examinations of slaves under torture were standard Athenian practice.

resources. Hence we must use the external means but find the internal means for ourselves.

The convincing arguments supplied through speech are of three species: (1) Some are found in the character of the speaker, (2) some in the condition of the hearer, (3) some in the speech itself, through proving or appearing to prove.   1356a

They are secured through character whenever the speech is delivered   5
in such a way as to make the speaker deserve our confidence. For we have more confidence, and come to have it more quickly, in decent* people; this is true, speaking without qualification,[25] on all topics, but it is altogether true on topics where there is variation of opinion rather than an exact answer.[26] This also, however, must result from the speech itself, not from the hearer's previous views about the character of the   10
speaker. For we do not follow some writers expounding this craft, who exclude the character of the speaker from the scope of the craft, on the supposition that it contributes nothing to the persuasiveness of the speech.[27] On the contrary, character provides almost, one might say, the most important means of conviction.

Conviction is secured through the hearers whenever the speech arouses some feeling in them. For we do not give the same verdicts   15
when we feel distress and when we feel enjoyment, or when we are friendly and when we are hostile; indeed writers on rhetoric at present, as we say, try to focus their whole treatment on this alone. We will clarify these questions, taking the feelings one at a time, when we come to discuss the feelings.

People are convinced through the speech itself whenever we prove   20
what is true or appears true from whatever is persuasive on each topic.

[THE RELEVANCE OF RHETORIC TO DIALECTIC AND ETHICS]

Since these are the means of conviction, it is evident that the person who will find them must reason deductively and also observe what is true of characters and virtues and, thereby, of feelings—what and of what sort each feeling is, and from what source and in what ways it   25

25. **without qualification**: Here what is true without qualification is contrasted with what is true without exception. See WITHOUT QUALIFICATION #3.

26. **but it is . . . answer**: It is especially true that we rely on the speaker's character in cases where there is no agreed effective method of finding the right answer (if there were, we would not have to take the speaker's word for it).

27. **For we . . . speech**: Presumably these writers fail to draw the distinction that was drawn in the previous sentence, and so they fail to recognize that the speech itself can present the speaker as a person of good character.

arises. Hence it follows that rhetoric is a sort of appendage of dialectic and of the study of character, which is rightly called political* science.

This is why rhetoric and those who claim to practice it actually masquerade in the guise of political science.[28] In some cases the reason is
30   lack of education, in other cases boastfulness, and in other cases some other human <weaknesses>. For in fact rhetoric is a part of dialectic and a likeness of it, as we also said at the beginning; for neither of them is scientific knowledge of how any definite subject matter is, but both are capacities for finding arguments.

We have said practically enough, then, about the capacity of rhetoric and dialectic, and about how they are related to each other.

[DEDUCTIVE AND INDUCTIVE ARGUMENT IN RHETORIC]

Now we turn to the convincing arguments that result through proving
1356b   or appearing to prove. In dialectic one type of such arguments is induction, one deduction, and another apparent deduction. The same is true in rhetoric; for illustration is induction, argumentation is deduction, and apparent argumentation is apparent deduction.
5   By 'argumentation' I mean rhetorical deduction, and by 'illustration' rhetorical induction. Now, everyone produces convincing arguments by presenting either illustrations or argumentations, and in no other way apart from these. Hence, if a proof must proceed either by deduction
10   or by induction (and this is clear to us from the Analytics),[29] each of these <rhetorical forms of argument> must be the same as each of those <dialectical forms>.

The difference between illustration and argumentation is evident from the Topics,[30] where we have previously discussed deduction and induc-
15   tion. We can see that a proof that something is so by appeal to many similar instances is induction, in the case of dialectic, and illustration, in the case of rhetoric. A proof that, when certain things are so, something else apart* from these follows because of them, by their being so, either necessary or usually,* is called a deduction,[31] in the case of dialectic, and an argumentation, in the case of rhetoric.
20   It is also evident that each type of rhetoric has its advantages; for the same thing is true here as we said in the work on lines of inquiry.[32] For

28. **masquerade . . . science**: Cf. *Met.* 1004b18; Plato, *Gorg.* 464bc.

29. **(and this . . . Analytics)**: Cf. *APo* 71a1–11.

30. *Topics*: See *Top.* i 12.

31. **A proof . . . deduction**: For this definition of a DEDUCTION see *APr* 24b18–20.

32. **the work on lines of inquiry**: Presumably a lost work. See also *Top.* 105a16.

some types of rhetoric rely on illustrations, others on argumentations, and similarly some orators deal in illustrations, others in argumentations. While certainly speeches using illustrations are no less persuasive, those   *25* using argumentations win more applause. Later we will state the reason for this and describe the right use of each <procedure>. For the moment let us define the two kinds of argument more clearly.

[*THE SUBJECTS OF RHETORICAL ARGUMENT*]

What is persuasive is persuasive to someone; and some things are immediately persuasive and convincing, while other things are persuasive and convincing because they seem to be proved through things that are   *30* immediately so. Now, no craft examines the particular; medicine, for instance, does not examine what it is that is healthy for Socrates or Callias, but what is healthy for this type or these types of person—for this is the concern of crafts, whereas the particular is unlimited[33] and not an object of scientific knowledge.[34] Nor, therefore, will rhetoric study the particular thing that is believed,[35] for instance, by Socrates or Hippias, but what is believed by these people,[36] just as dialectic does. For neither   *35* does dialectic carry out its deductions from just any random beliefs— for some things appear true to madmen;[37] rather, dialectic begins from beliefs that need some argument, while rhetoric begins from the habitual   *1357a* questions for deliberation.

The function of rhetoric is to deal with the sorts of questions we deliberate about, where we have no crafts, before the sorts of audiences who cannot keep many steps in mind at once or keep track of a long argument. And we deliberate about what appears to admit of being one   *5* way or the other; for if something does not admit of becoming or being otherwise than it is, no one deliberates about it, if that is what he supposes, since he gains nothing from it.[38]

*   *   *   *   *   *   *

33. **unlimited**: i.e., indefinite. See INFINITE #3.

34. **whereas . . . knowledge**: Cf. *Met*. 981b5–30, KNOWLEDGE #4, PARTICULAR #3.

35. **believed**: *endoxon*, usually translated 'COMMON BELIEF'.

36. **these people**: i.e., the many and the wise.

37. **for some . . . madmen**: These do not concern DIALECTIC. Cf. *Top*. 104a5, 170b6.

38. **And we deliberate . . . nothing from it**: Cf. *DI* 18b31, *EN* 1112a21.

[RHETORIC AND ETHICS]

[HAPPINESS AND ITS PARTS [39]]

5

1360b4   Practically every individual and all people in common have some target
   5   that they aim at in their choosing and avoiding; this target, to state it
         in summary, is happiness and its parts. Let us then, by way of illustra-
         tion, grasp what happiness is, speaking without qualification,[40] and what
   10   things constitute its parts. For all advice for or against <a course of
         action> is concerned with happiness and the things relevant to it, or
         with their contraries. For we must do what provides happiness or some
         part of it, or produces a greater part at the cost of a smaller; and we must
         avoid whatever destroys or impedes a part of happiness or produces its
         contrary.

         Let us, then, take happiness to be doing well with virtue; or self-
   15   sufficiency* of life; or the pleasantest life with safety; or prosperity of
         possessions and slaves[41] with the capacity to keep them and to use them
         in action.[42] For everyone more or less agrees that happiness is one or
         more of these.

   20   If, then, happiness is this sort of thing, its parts must be good birth,
         many friends, good friends, wealth, good children, many children, pros-
         perous old age. They must also include bodily excellences (for instance,
         health, beauty, strength, size, athletic ability), honor, good fortune, and
   25   virtue.[43] For this is the way for someone to be most self-sufficient, by
         having both the goods internal to himself and the external goods,[44] since
         there are no other goods apart from these. The internal goods are those
         in the soul and body, and the external are good birth, friends, money,
         and honor. We also think it suitable for him to have power and good
   30   fortune, since that makes life safest. Let us, then, also grasp in the same
         way what each of these <parts of happiness> is.

39. This chapter should be compared with the discussion of HAPPINESS in *EN* i
1–5, 8–12, *Pol.* vii 1–3. The *Rhet.* gives specific examples to illustrate the COMMON
BELIEFS from which Aristotle begins his argument in the *EN* and *Pol.*

40. **speaking without qualification**: i.e., without the qualifications that would
be necessary for a more accurate account. See EXACT #2, WITHOUT QUALIFICATION
#3.

41. **slaves**: Lit. 'bodies'.

42. **to use them in action**: On ACTION see *Pol.* 1254a2.

43. **bodily excellences (*aretai*) . . . virtue (*aretē*)**: Though Aristotle uses the same
word (in the plural) for bodily excellences and (in the singular) for VIRTUE of
character, he clearly expects his readers to know what difference he has in mind.

44. **the goods internal . . . external goods**: For this division see GOOD #3.

First, then, a nation* or city is well-born if <its members> are indige-
nous or ancient inhabitants, and if their earliest ancestors were illustrious
leaders and had many descendants who were illustrious for their admired qualities. An individual is well-born on the male or the female   35
side if he is a legitimate citizen on each side and, as in the case of a city,
if his earliest ancestors were renowned for virtue or wealth or any other
honored quality and if the family has many illustrious members, male
and female, young and old.

It is clear what it means to have good children and to have many
children. In the case of the community, this means that its youth are   1361a
numerous and good. They are good by having bodily excellence, such
as size, beauty, strength, and athletic ability; in the soul, temperance
and bravery are the virtues of a youth. An individual has good children
and many children if his own children, both female and male, are numer-   5
ous and have these qualities. But for females bodily excellence is beauty
and size, and virtue of the soul is temperance and a love of their work
that is not excessive for a free person.[45] And we must seek to acquire
each of these qualities no less for the community than for individuals,
and no less for women than for men; for if the condition of women is   10
poor, as it is in Sparta,[46] then happiness is lacking in practically half
<the community>.

The parts of wealth are: a large amount of money and land; the
possession of lands outstanding in number, size, and beauty; further,
the possession of implements, slaves, and domestic animals outstanding   15
in number and beauty; and all these must be our own and safely pos-
sessed, both the civilized[47] and the useful possessions. The ones that
are more useful are the productive ones, and the civilized ones are those
that contribute to gratification. By 'productive' I mean those that yield
a return; by 'sources of gratification' I mean those that have no result
worth mentioning beyond the use of them.

Safety is defined as possession in such a place and in such a way that   20
the use of the possessions is up to us. They are defined as being our
own or not our own according to whether it is up to us to alienate them.
By 'alienation' I mean lending and selling. And in general wealth consists
in use more than in possession; for it is the active use of possessions
that is wealth.

45. **a love . . . free person**: They must avoid the complete absorption that Aristotle takes to be characteristic of the manual craftsman who does not live the
life of a FREE citizen. See *Pol.* 1340b31.

46. **for if . . . Sparta**: Aristotle believes Spartan women have too much freedom.
Cf. *Pol.* 1269b12.

47. **civilized**: See GENEROUS. Cf. *EN* 1125a11.

25   Good reputation consists in being supposed by everyone to be excellent; or in having something of the sort that is pursued by everyone, or by most people, or by the good or the intelligent people.

    Honor is the sign of a good reputation as a benefactor. The people who are justly and most highly honored are those who have conferred
30 benefits; but someone who is capable of conferring them is also honored. Conferring benefit refers to safety and to the causes of being alive; or to wealth; or to one of the other goods that are not easy to acquire, either not easy at all or not easy at this place or time—since many people win honor for actions that seem small, but this is explained by the places and times.

35   The parts of honor are: sacrifices;[48] memorials in verse or prose; privileges; grants of land; seats of honor; tombs; statues; meals at public expense;[49] foreign* customs such as prostration and stepping aside; the gifts honored by each people. For a gift is both the giving of a possession and a sign of honor. That is why both the money-lover and the honor-
1361b lover pursue gifts, since gifts provide both of them with what they want; for a gift is the possession pursued by the money-lover, and provides the honor pursued by the honor-lover.

    Bodily excellence is health, but health of the sort that allows us to
5 exert our bodies without falling ill; for, as Herodicus[50] says, there are many healthy people whom no one would congratulate as happy for their health, because they refrain from all or most human affairs.

    Beauty is different for different periods of life. A youth's beauty consists in having a body that is serviceable for exertions in running and
10 physical force, and pleasant to look at for gratification.[51] This is why the all-round athletes are the most beautiful, since they are naturally suited both for physical force and for speed. Beauty in someone in the prime of life consists in having his body serviceable for exertions in war, and in being both pleasant and formidable to look at. Beauty in an old man is having a body adequate for necessary exertions, and not painful to look at, because it has none of the deformities that mar old age.

15   Strength is the power to move something[52] else as we wish. To move something we must either pull or push or raise or pin down or grip. Hence someone is strong if he is strong in all or some of these ways.

    Excellence in size consists in being superior to most people in height,

---

48. **sacrifices**: i.e., cult sacrifices (in honor of a god or hero). See *EN* 1134b23, OCD p. 506a.

49. **meals at public expense**: Cf. Plato, *Ap.* 36de.

50. **Herodicus**: a physician (fifth century B.C.). See Plato, *Rep.* 406a.

51. **gratification**: i.e., (probably) for gratification of the sense of sight.

52. **something**: Or 'someone'.

thickness, and width, to an extent that makes us no slower in our move-   20
ments.

Athletic bodily excellence is composed of size, strength, and speed—
for the speedy person is also strong. For someone who can propel his
legs in the right way and move them far and fast is good at running; if
he can grip his opponent and pin him down, he is good at wrestling; if   25
he can repel the opponent with a blow, he is good at boxing; if he can
both wrestle and box, he is a good all-round fighter; if he can do all
these things, he is a good all-round athlete.

Good old age is the slow and painless onset of old age; for it is not
a good old age either if we age rapidly or if we age slowly but painfully.
It involves both bodily excellences and fortune; for we will not be free   30
of suffering and pain if we are not strong and free of disease, and we
will not last long without good fortune. There is another ability, the
ability to live long, that is separated from strength and health; for many
people have long lives without bodily excellences. But exact discussion
of this is of no use for our present purposes.

Having many friends and having good friends are clear enough once   35
we have defined a friend. A friend is the sort of person who does for
another's sake whatever he thinks is good for the other.[53] Hence, whoever has many of this sort has many friends, and whenever they are
also decent men, he has good friends.

We have good fortune* whenever we acquire and possess all or most   1362a
or the greatest of the goods caused by fortune. Fortune causes some
things that are also <of the sort> caused by the crafts, but also many
things that are not subject to crafts—for instance, the <sort of> thing
caused by nature, though it is also possible for some <fortunate events>
to occur contrary to nature. For craft causes health, but nature causes   5
beauty and size. And in general the sorts of goods that result from
fortune are those that provoke envy.

Fortune is also a cause of goods that happen contrary to reason.[54]
Suppose, for instance, that the other brothers are all ugly, but this one
is handsome; or the other people did not see the treasure, but this one
found it; or the missile hit his neighbor, but missed him; or he always   10
frequented the place, but <this time> was the only one who did not
go, while the others went there for the first time and were killed. For
all these sorts of things seem to be strokes of good fortune.

The most appropriate place to discuss virtue is the discussion of praise;
hence we will define it when we discuss praise.

53. **A friend . . . the other**: Cf. the descriptions of friendship at 1380b36, *EN*
1155b27.

54. **contrary to reason**: i.e., contrary to reasonable expectation.

[*DIFFERENT TYPES OF GOODS*]

6

15 It is evident, then, what present or future result we must aim at in advocating a course of action[55] and what we must aim at in dissuading from it—i.e. the contrary of the former. Now, the target set for the proponent is advantage, since deliberation is not about the end, but about what promotes the end,[56] and this is what is advantageous in 20 action; moreover, the advantageous is good; we must therefore grasp the elementary points about what is good and advantageous without qualification.

Let us say, then, that something is good if it is choiceworthy for its own sake; we choose something else for its sake; everything, or everything that has perception, aims at it; everything would aim at it if it 25 acquired understanding; understanding would assign it to an individual; his individual understanding assigns it to him, since this is what is good for each individual; its presence produces a good and self-sufficient condition in the recipient; it is self-sufficient; it produces or preserves such conditions; such conditions follow on it; it prevents or destroys the contrary conditions.[57]

30 One thing follows on another in two ways—either at the same time, as being alive follows on being healthy, or later, as knowing follows on learning.

One thing produces another in three ways—either as being healthy produces health, or as food produces health, or as exercising produces health, because it usually produces health.[58]

35 Once these things are assumed, it necessarily follows that getting a good thing and avoiding a bad thing are good; for it follows, in the latter case, that at the same time we do not have the bad thing, and, in the former case, that later we have the good thing. Moreover, getting a greater good instead of a lesser, and a lesser bad thing instead of a 1362b greater, are good; for we get one thing and avoid another to the extent that the one exceeds the other.

Again, the virtues must be a good thing; for these produce a good

55. **what present . . . action**: i.e., we must show that it promotes happiness.

56. **since deliberation . . . promotes the end**: Cf. *EN* 1111b26, 1112b11.

57. **Let us say . . . contrary conditions**: Some of the features listed in this paragraph seem to be different features of the same things; others seem to be features of different things.

58. **One thing . . . usually produces health**: Health seems to be the formal CAUSE, food a necessary condition, and exercise a condition that USUALLY promotes health without being a necessary condition.

condition in their possessor, produce good results, and are active in
good actions; we must say separately what and of what sort each is.   5
Pleasure must also be a good; for all animals by nature aim at it.[59] Hence
both pleasant things and fine things must be goods; for pleasant things
produce pleasure, and among fine things some are pleasant, while others
are choiceworthy in themselves.

The following, listing them individually, must be goods: 10

Happiness. For it is choiceworthy in itself and self-sufficient, and,
moreover, we choose the other things for its sake.

Justice, bravery, temperance, magnanimity, magnificence, and the
other such states. For these are virtues of the soul.

Health, beauty, and such things. For these are excellences of the body   15
and produce many goods. Health, for example, produces both pleasure
and life. That, indeed, is why it seems to be the best good, because it
causes the two goods that most people honor more than anything else—
pleasure and life.

Wealth. For it is excellence of possession and produces many goods.

A friend and friendship. For a friend is choiceworthy in himself and   20
moreover produces many goods.

Honor and reputation. For these are pleasant and also produce many
goods, and usually they imply the presence of the qualities for which
people are honored.

Ability in speaking and acting. For all such things produce goods.

Further, natural aptitude, good memory, ability to learn, sharp wits,
all such things. For these abilities produce goods. The same is true of   25
all the sciences and the crafts.

Life. For even if no other good followed on it, it would still be choiceworthy in itself.

Justice. For it is an advantage for the community.

These, then, we may say, are the agreed goods.

[ARGUMENTS ABOUT GOODS AND EVILS]

In disputable cases, the following are the sources of inferences: 30

If the contrary of x is evil, then x is good.

If the contrary of x is an advantage for the enemy, then x is good. If,
for instance, our cowardice is the enemy's greatest advantage, then
clearly bravery is the greatest benefit to our citizens. And, in general,
whatever the enemy wish for or are pleased by, its contrary appears   35
beneficial. Hence it is said, 'Indeed Priam would rejoice . . .'.[60] This is

59. **Pleasure . . . aim at it**: Cf. *EN* 1172b9.
60. **'Indeed . . . rejoice'**: Homer, *Iliad* i 235.

1363a

not always so, however, but only usually. For it is quite possible that the same thing is an advantage for both opponents; hence it is said that evils draw human beings together, whenever the same thing is harmful to both sides.

If something cannot be taken to excess, then it is good. But if something is greater than it ought to be, then it is evil.

Something is good if we have worked hard or spent much for its sake. For it is thereby an apparent good; such a thing is regarded as an end, the end of many <labors>, and an end is a good. Hence it is said, 'And indeed a boast for Priam . . .' and 'It is shameful to remain so long'.[61] Hence also the proverb about stumbling at the last fence.[62]

Something is good if most people aim at it and if it appears to be fought over. For, as we agreed, if everyone aims at something, it is a good; and the majority give the appearance of being everyone.[63]

If something is praiseworthy,[64] it is good. For no one praises what is not good. And it is good if <even> our enemies[65] praise it; for if even those who have suffered from something agree in praising it, it is as though it amounted to everyone's agreement—for they would agree in praising it because it is evidently good. Similarly, people are base if their friends reproach them and their enemies do not. That is why the Corinthians thought the Spartans had insulted them by writing, 'Troy has no complaint against the Corinthians'.

Again, something is good if some wise or good man or woman has shown special favor to it, as Athena did to Odysseus, Theseus to Helen, the goddesses to Paris, and Homer to Achilles.

And in general, something is good if it is what we[66] decide to do. For the things we decide to do are the things already mentioned, and also what is bad for our enemies, what is good for our friends, and what we are able to do. What we are able to do is of two sorts—what might come about, and what might come about easily. Things are easy if they can be done without trouble or in a short time, since difficulty is defined either by amount of trouble or by length of time.

Something is good if it is as we wish. What we wish is either nothing bad or less bad than good—and the second will occur if the bad aspect is unnoticed or the penalty is slight.

61. **'And indeed . . . so long'**: Homer, *Iliad* ii 260, ii 298.

62. **stumbling . . . fence**: Lit., breaking the water-jar at the door.

63. **the majority . . . everyone**: Lit. 'the many appear as all'.

64. **praiseworthy**: Or perhaps 'praised'.

65. **our enemies**: OCT adds *kai hoi phauloi*.

66. **we**: The first person plural, here and in the rest of the chapter, corresponds either to nothing or to a third person plural ('people in general') in Greek.

Something is good if it is distinctive of us, if no one else has it, or if it is outstanding; for that sort of thing wins more honor.

Something is good if it suits us. This includes what suits our family background or ability and what we think we are deprived of, even if it   30
is small (for that does not stop people from deciding to get it).

Something is good if it is easily achieved; for that is within our ability and easy for us. Something is easily achieved if everyone or most people, or people of similar or inferior ability <to ours> have succeeded at it.

Something is good if our friends will be gratified by it and our enemies will hate it.

Something is good if the people we admire decide to achieve it.   35

Something is good if we are naturally adapted for it and experienced with it. For then we think we will more easily succeed.

Something is good if no base person <has it>; for then it is more praiseworthy.

Something is good if we find that we have an appetite for it; for then it appears better as well as pleasant. This is true most of all when some   1363b
type of person is a lover of something; a lover of victory, for instance, seeks victory, a lover of honor seeks honor, a lover of money seeks money, and the same is true for the others.

These, then, are the sources from which we must draw convincing arguments about good and advantage.

*   *   *   *   *   *   *

[JUSTICE: WRITTEN AND UNWRITTEN LAW [67]*]*

13

Let us classify all unjust and just acts, beginning first from this point.   1373b
First, then, what is just or unjust is divided into two types according to the type of law, and into two types according to the type of victim.

By this I mean that one type of law is local[68] and the other universal. Local law is the law that each <city> has laid down to apply to itself;   5
one part of this is written, one unwritten. Universal law is the law that is in accordance with nature. For there is something that everyone intuitively believes, a universal justice and injustice by nature, even if people share no association or agreement.

This is the sort of justice that Sophocles' Antigone evidently refers

---

67. On the subject of this chapter, cf. *EN* v 7. Aristotle is giving advice for a speaker who cannot claim support in the written law. He points out that appeals to justice need not rest solely on appeal to the written law, or even to the laws and customs of a particular state.

68. **local**: Lit. 'DISTINCTIVE' (i.e., confined to a particular state and legal system).

10 to, when she says it was just for her to have buried Polyneices, even though it was forbidden, claiming that it was just by nature: 'For this does not live today and yesterday, but forever, and no one knows whence it appeared.'[69] Empedocles* speaks in similar terms about not killing

15 whatever has a soul. For, he says, this is not merely just for some people and not for others; 'No; this is a law for all, a law that stretches through the broad sky and through the immense ray of the sun.'[70] And, similarly, in his Messenian speech Alcidamas[71] says: 'The god has left everyone free; nature has made no one a slave.' . . .

* * * * * * *

Book II

[RHETORIC AND THE EMOTIONS]

[THE IMPORTANCE OF MOLDING ATTITUDES AND EMOTIONS]

1

1377b16 These, then, are the sources from which we must argue for or against a proposal, praise or blame, accuse or defend; these are the beliefs and premises that are useful for constructing convincing arguments on these questions. For these are the subjects and the sources of argumentations,

20 taking each type of speech in turn.

Now rhetoric aims at a judgment; for the members of the audience <in the Assembly> reach a judgment about the advice given them, and a jury's verdict is also a judgment. Hence we must attend not only to making our argument demonstrative and convincing, but also to shaping

25 our own attitude[1] and the judge's. For how convincing we are (especially in giving advice but also before a jury) is greatly affected by what the speaker's attitude appears to be, what his hearers take his attitude toward them to be, and moreover what their attitude turns out to be.

30 The speaker's attitude is more useful in giving advice, and the hearer's in court cases. For things do not appear the same to a friendly and to a hostile hearer, or to an angry and to a calm hearer; they appear either

1378a completely different or different in degree. For if the juryman is friendly to the accused, he thinks the accused has done no injustice at all or only

69. **'For this . . . appeared'**: Sophocles, *Antigone* 456–57.

70. **'No . . . the sun'**: Empedocles, DK 31 B 135.

71. **Alcidamas**: A rhetorician (fourth century).

1. **attitude**: 'Attitude' is perhaps too narrow. The Greek (lit. 'what one is like' or 'one's quality') also includes CHARACTER (*ēthos*), a more permanent QUALITY (cf. *Catg.* 8b26–9a13, 9a28–10a10). Sometimes Aristotle has this in mind, but sometimes he refers to a more transient condition.

a slight injustice; but if he is hostile, quite the contrary is true. And if someone is eager for and looks forward to something that will be pleasant if it happens, then it appears to him that this will both happen and be good; but if he is indifferent or discontented, the contrary will be true.   5

There are three causes that make a speaker convincing; for these are the things that convince us of something apart from a demonstration of it, namely, intelligence, virtue, and goodwill.[2] For someone's speech or advice may be mistaken for some or all of these three reasons; either   10 his beliefs are mistaken from lack of intelligence, or his beliefs are correct but because of vice he does not say what he believes, or he is both intelligent and decent but he lacks goodwill, so that he may fail to give the best advice even though he knows what it is. And these are all the reasons there are. Hence someone who seems to have all these good qualities is bound to appear convincing to his hearers.   15

The ways of appearing intelligent and excellent must be gathered from the discussion of the virtues; for the same means can be used to form one's own attitude and to form another's. We must consider goodwill and friendship in our discussion of the feelings.

Feelings are all those conditions that cause us to change and alter   20 our attitude to judgments, conditions that imply pain or pleasure[3]—for instance, anger, pity, fear, and all other such things and their contraries. In each case we must distinguish three aspects; in the case of anger, for instance, we must say what condition makes people prone to anger, against whom they normally get angry, and about what. For if we secure one or two of these three aspects, but not all of them, we will be unable   25 to arouse anger; and the same is true in the other cases. And so, just as in our previous discussions we described the different types of premisses, let us do the same in this case also and follow the divisions we have mentioned.

*   *   *   *   *   *   *

[FRIENDLINESS]

4

Let us say what sorts of people we[4] are friendly to, or hate, and why;   1380b35 but first let us define friendship and friendliness.[5]

---

2. **goodwill**: See *EN* 1155b33, ix 5.

3. **conditions . . . pleasure**: On feelings see ATTRIBUTE #3.

4. **we**: Again this renders a vague third person plural; cf. 1363a20n.

5. **friendship . . .**: *philia*. 'Friendliness' translates *philein*. See FRIENDSHIP.

Let us take[6] friendliness to be wishing to another what one thinks
good,[7] for his sake and not for one's own,[8] and also being disposed to
do these things as far as one can. One person is a friend to another if
he is friendly to the other and the other is friendly to him in return; and
we think we are friends if we think that this is our relation to each other.

If these assumptions are accepted, then necessarily one is a friend to
another person if one shares the other's pleasure in good things and his
distress at painful things, not because of something else, but because of
the other person himself. For we all enjoy getting what we wish for,
and we suffer pain in the contrary cases, so that pains and pleasures
are signs of what we wish. People are also friends[9] if the same things
are good or bad for them or if they are friends to the same people and
enemies to the same people. For necessarily these people wish the same
things; and so, since one wishes the same things for the other as one
wishes for oneself, one appears to be a friend to him.

We are also friendly to those who have benefited us or those we care
about, or if the benefits were great or given eagerly, or if they were
given on some difficult occasion, and for our own sake, or if we think
the other person wishes to benefit us.

Also to those who are friends of our friends and to those who are
friendly to the people to whom we ourselves are friendly; and also to
those to whom the people we ourselves are friendly to are friendly.

Also to those who are enemies to and hate the people we hate, and
to those who are hated by the people we hate. For it appears to us that
what is good for these people is the same as what is good for ourselves,
so that we wish what is good for them,[10] which is characteristic of a
friend.

Also to those who tend to benefit us by providing money or safety;
that is why we honor generous, brave, and just people. We suppose
that these are people who do not make their livings from other people;
these are the ones who make their livings by their own work, and among
these the ones who make their living by farming, especially those who

6. **Let us take**: Aristotle puts forward a definition to be taken for granted in
the rest of the discussion; he neither endorses nor rejects the definition.

7. **thinks good**: i.e., what one thinks good for the other.

8. **for his sake and not for one's own**: In the *Rhet*. Aristotle regards this disinter-
ested concern as a feature of all friendship. In the *EN* his attitude is more
complicated. See 1155b31, 1156a10, b7–12, 1167a10–14.

9. **People are also friends**: Read *ēdē* (OCT: *dē*).

10. **For it appears . . . what is good for them**: Or: 'For the same things appear
good to these people as appear good to ourselves, so that they wish the things
that are good for us'.

work with their own hands. We are also friendly to temperate people, because they are not unjust, and to people who are not busybodies, for the same reason.   *25*

We are also friendly to those whose friends we wish to be, if they appear to wish to be our friends. This includes those who are good by having virtue, as well as those who have a good reputation, either among all, or among the best people, or among those whom we admire, or among those who admire us.

Also to those who are pleasant to pass the time with and spend our days with. These are good tempered, not eager to expose our mistakes,   *30* not competitive, and not quarrelsome (for all such people easily start fights, and people who are fighting appear to have contrary wishes). They are also dexterous in making jokes and taking them; for in both ways they have the same aims as their neighbor, since they are both able to take a joke and able to make the appropriate sort of joke.   *35*

We are also friendly to people who praise the good points we have, especially those who praise the ones we are afraid we lack.   *1381b*

Also to people who are neat in their appearance, their dress, and their way of life in general.

Also to those who do not reproach us either because of <our> mistakes or because of the good turns <they have done for us>; for both sorts of people are eager to expose shortcomings.

Also to those who do not bear grudges or keep track of grievances   *5* but are easily reconciled. For we suppose they will treat us in the way they treat others.

Also to those who do not slander and who know good things, not bad things, about their neighbors or about ourselves; for this is what the good person does.

Also to those who do not pick quarrels with[11] someone who is angry or eager for something; for people who pick such quarrels are the sort   *10* who are prone to fight.

We are also friendly to those who have some favorable attitude toward us—if, for instance, they admire us, take us to be virtuous, or enjoy our company. This is especially true if they take this attitude toward the qualities for which we ourselves most of all wish to be admired or to be thought virtuous or pleasant.

Also to those who are similar to us and who engage in the same   *15* pursuits, provided that they do not obstruct us or make their living from the same sort of work—for that is a case of 'potter <quarrels with> potter'.[12] We are also friendly to those who desire the same things as

---

11. **pick quarrels with**: Lit. 'oppose'.
12. **'potter . . . potter'** A proverb; cf. *EN* 1155a35.

we desire, provided that it is possible for both us and them to get these things; if it is not possible, the same thing happens here as in the previous case.

20 Also to those who do not make us feel ashamed of doing something unconventional—provided that this is not because we look down on them[13]—and to those who make us feel ashamed of doing what is really wrong.

Also to our rivals, and to those whom we want to feel emulation rather than spite* toward us; and to those with whom we cooperate in securing some benefit to them, provided that a worse harm to ourselves will not result.

25 Also to those who remain friends to someone when he is absent as well as when he is present. That is why everyone is also friendly to someone who is loyal to a dead friend. And in general we are friendly to those who have intense friendships and do not abandon their friends; for among good people we are friendly most of all to those who are good friends.

30 Also to those who do not put on a false front toward us. These are people who admit their own faults to us—for we have said that we are not ashamed in front of our friends of doing something unconventional. If, then, one who is ashamed <in these cases> is not friendly to us, one who is not ashamed is like someone who is friendly to us.

Also to those whom we do not find frightening and to those who give us confidence; for no one is friendly to someone he is afraid of.

The species of friendship are companionship, intimacy, kinship, and
35 so on. The causes of friendship are doing kindnesses, doing them without being asked, and doing them without announcing it afterwards. For in this way someone appears to be doing something for our own sake, not because of something else.

1382a It is evident that we must study enmity and hatred from the things contrary to those we have described. The causes of enmity are anger, malicious opposition,[14] and slander.

Now, anger is provoked by offenses against oneself, but enmity may arise without them; for we hate someone if we <simply> suppose that
5 he has a bad character. Moreover anger is always directed at a particular, at Callias or Socrates, for instance, whereas hatred may also be directed at kinds of people; for everyone hates the thief and the informer. Further,

13. **not because we look down on them**: If we looked down on them, we would not care what they thought about us, and we would not be friendly toward them.

14. **malicious opposition**: i.e., my thwarting someone just for the fun of it, even without any further advantage to myself.

anger is curable by lapse of time, whereas hatred is incurable. Anger is a desire to inflict pain, whereas hatred is a desire to inflict evil; for if we are angry, we want someone to suffer and to be aware of it;[15] but if we hate him, we do not care about that. Everything painful is perceptible   10 to its possessor, but the worst evils, injustice and foolishness, are the least perceptible to their possessor, since the presence of the evil gives him no pain. Again, anger involves pain, whereas hatred does not; for if we are angry, we feel pain, but this is not true for hatred. Moreover, if the person we are angry with suffers a great deal, we may take pity[16] on him, but no amount of suffering changes our mind if we hate someone; for if we are angry with someone, we <only> want him to suffer   15 in return, but if we hate <some type of person>, we want <that type of person> not to exist at all.

It is evident from this, then, that it is possible, when people are enemies or friends, to prove that they are; when they are not, to make them out to be so;[17] when they say they are, to refute the assertion;[18] and if they are disputing about whether anger or enmity <was the source of some offense>, to trace it back to whichever source one decides.

*   *   *   *   *   *   *

[STRATEGIES OF ARGUMENT]

[THE SELECTION OF APPROPRIATE ARGUMENTS AND PREMISSES]

22

Let us say first of all how we must search for argumentations, and then   1395b21 what the forms of argument[19] are; for each of these is a different type <of question>.

We have previously said[20] that an argumentation is a deduction, and in what way it is one, and how it is different from dialectical deduction.   25 For in argumentation we should not proceed from remote premisses or through all the intermediate steps in reaching our conclusion; for the first results in obscurity, because of the length of the argument, and the second results in redundancy, because it states what is evident.

This indeed is the reason why uneducated speakers are more persua-

15. **we want . . . aware of it**: Or 'we want to be aware of his suffering'.

16. **if the person . . . we may take pity**: Or 'in many circumstances an angry person may take pity'.

17. **to make them out to be so**: Or 'to make them so'.

18. **to refute the assertion**: Or 'to dissolve the friendship'.

19. **forms of argument**: Lit. 'places', *topoi*. See *Topics*, note on title.

20. **previously said**: See 1355a3, b34.

30   sive than educated speakers are in speaking to a crowd;[21] as the poets
say, their words are better adapted to the crowd's taste. For educated
speakers appeal to general principles of broad application,[22] whereas the
uneducated argue from what the audience know$_0$ and what bears closely
on the question.[23]

    We should not, then, argue from all the premises that seem true,
but from a limited selection of them—for instance, from those that seem
1396a   true to the jurymen or to those whose opinions they accept; for this is
the way to make something appear plain to everyone or to most people.
Further, we must draw our conclusions not only from necessary premisses, but also from premises that hold usually.

[ARGUMENT FROM THE APPROPRIATE FACTS]

    First, then, we must grasp that, whatever the subject on which we must
5   speak and argue, in a deduction in a political context or any other context,
we must possess all or some of the facts relevant to the subject. For if
we have none of these, we will have no basis for drawing our conclusions.
I mean, for instance, how can we advise the Athenians about whether
or not to go to war, if we do not know what forces they have, military
10   or naval or both, and in what strength; what revenues, allies, and enemies they have; and, moreover, what wars they have fought and with
what success, and so on? And how can we praise them if we do not
know about the naval battle of Salamis, or about the battle of Marathon,
or what the sons of Heracles did, and so on? For everyone's praise is
15   based on the actual or supposed facts about the fine actions of those
they praise. Similarly, our blame is based on the contrary sorts of actions;
we consider the actual or supposed facts about actions of this type—
that, for instance, they enslaved the Greeks, and that they enslaved the
20   allies—the Aeginetans and Poteidaeans—who had distinguished themselves in fighting with them against the foreigner,[24] and any other incidents of this sort, if the facts show any other fault of theirs. In the same
way accusers and defenders rely on consideration of the facts to construct
their cases.

21. **uneducated . . . crowd**: Cf. Plato, *Gorg.* 459bc.

22. **general . . . application**: Lit. 'common and universal things', too abstract
for some audiences.

23. **what bears . . . question**: Lit. 'close things'. Perhaps 'what is close <to the
audience's experience>'.

24. **the allies . . . the foreigner**: The 'foreigner' refers to the Persian Empire.
Aristotle refers to the period (described in Thucydides Book i) between the
Persian Wars (480–78) and the outbreak of the Peloponnesian War (431).

We must do the same in dealing with Athenians or Spartans, with a human being or a god. For if we are advising Achilles, or praising or 25 blaming him, or accusing or defending him, we must grasp the actual or supposed facts, so that we can construct our case from them, praising or blaming if the facts show any fine or shameful action, defending or accusing if they show any just or unjust action, giving advice if the facts 30 show that something is advantageous or harmful. The same applies to any subject whatever. If, for instance, we are being asked whether justice is or is not a good, we must argue from the facts about justice and the good.

This, then, is evidently the way in which everyone argues demonstratively, by a more exact or a looser form of deduction; one argues not 1396b from just any facts, but from the ones that are relevant to the subject in question. Moreover, it is also clear from argument[25] that it is impossible to prove something in any other way. Evidently, then, we must, as in the *Topics*, have selected in advance premisses concerning issues that may possibly arise and are opportune for us, and we must look in the 5 same way for points relevant to a question that arises without advance warning. We must rely, not on an indeterminate* range of premisses, but on the facts about the subject of our arguments, and we must pick out the largest possible number of the most clearly relevant facts. For the more facts we possess, the easier it is to prove our point; and the more clearly relevant they are, the more appropriate they are and the 10 fewer generalities they involve.[26]

By generalities I mean, for instance, praise of Achilles for being a human being, or for being a demigod, or for having been in the expedition against Troy; for these things are true of many others too, so that a speaker who appeals to them is praising Achilles no more than Diomede. The distinctive facts are those that apply to no one except Achilles, 15 that, for instance, he killed both Hector, the best of the Trojans, and the invulnerable Cycnus, who prevented them all from landing, that he was the youngest in the expedition, that he joined it though he was not obliged by an oath, and so on.

This, then, is the first method of selection involving forms of argument. Let us now state the elements of argumentations; I mean the same 20 by 'element' and by 'form of argumentation'. And let us state first the things that should be stated first. There are two types of argumentation; for some of them prove that something is so or is not so, and others are refutative. The two types differ in the way that, in dialectic, refutation

---

25. **from argument**: On the contrast between argument and appeal to particular facts or APPEARANCES see REASON #3.

26. **the fewer . . . involve**: Lit. 'the less common they are'. Cf. *EN* 1107a28.

25   and deduction differ. A probative argumentation draws a conclusion
      from agreed premisses; a refutative argumentation draws a conclusion
      that is not agreed <previously>.

          We are now more or less in possession of the forms of argument for
30   each type of necessary or useful subject. For we have selected the prem-
      isses about each subject; hence we already have the forms of argument
      from which we must construct argumentations about good or evil, fine
      or shameful, just or unjust, and similarly about characters, feelings, and
1397a states <of character>. But let us grasp these matters generally in still
      another way. Let us indicate in our remarks the forms of argument that
      are refutative and those that are demonstrative, and those belonging to
      apparent argumentations that really are not argumentations,[27] because
5   they are not deductions either. When we have made this clear, let us
      determine how we must find refutations and objections to bring against
      argumentations.

27. **apparent . . . not argumentations**: This corresponds to the treatment of
sophistic reasoning in *Top*. ix.

POETICS

[THE ORIGINS OF POETRY]

4

It would seem that in general poetry[1] is the product of two causes, both   *1448b4*
of them natural to human beings. First, imitating comes naturally to   *5*
human beings from childhood, and in this point they differ from the
other animals, in that they are most prone to imitation and what they
learn first of all is through imitation. Secondly, enjoyment of the products
of imitation also comes naturally to everyone. What actually happens is
evidence of this. For even if we find the real things painful to see, we   *10*
enjoy looking at the most exactly* executed copies of them—for instance,
the shape of the most repulsive beasts or of corpses.

The cause of this <enjoyment> is the fact that learning is pleasantest
not only to philosophers,[2] but also in the same way to everyone else,
though they have only a small share in it. For this is why they enjoy   *15*
seeing pictures, because looking at <a picture> causes them to learn
and infer what a thing is—that, for instance, this man <in the picture>
is that <actual> man.[3] For if they happen not to have previously seen
the thing imitated, the picture produces pleasure, not insofar as it is an
imitation, but because of the execution or the color or some similar cause.

Since, then, imitation, harmony, and rhythm arise naturally (for it is   *20*
evident that meters are part of rhythm), those with the greatest natural
aptitude for them developed them from the beginning by gradual progress, and so produced poetry out of improvisation. . . .

*   *   *   *   *   *   *

1. **poetry**: *poiētikē* (sc. *technē*). Lit. 'the productive (sc. craft)'. See PRODUCE.

2. **philosophers**: Aristotle alludes to the etymology, 'lovers of wisdom'.

3. <**actual**> **man**: This, then, is the source of our specific pleasure in the picture
as an imitation, as opposed to the sorts of pleasure mentioned in the next
sentence.

[*THE ELEMENTS OF TRAGEDY*]

6

1449b21   We will discuss imitative hexameter poetry and comedy later. Let us now discuss tragedy, after recapitulating the definition of its essence, that emerges from what we have said.

25   Tragedy, then, is an imitation of an action that is serious and complete, one that has some greatness. It imitates in words with pleasant accompaniments, each type belonging separately to the different parts <of the work>. It imitates people performing actions and does not rely on narration. Through pity and fear it achieves purification[4] from[5] such feelings.

   By 'words with pleasant accompaniments' I mean words with rhythm, 30 harmony, and song.[6] By 'the type belonging separately' I mean that some parts are executed in verse alone, and other parts in song.

   Since the imitation is produced by action, the parts of the tragedy must include, first of all, the visual display, and second, song and speech; 35 for in these the imitation is produced. By 'speech' I mean the composition of the verses, and what I mean by 'song' is clear to everyone.

   It is an imitation of action, and action is done by agents. These must have some qualities of character and thought, since it is through these 1450a that we attribute qualities to the action also. Hence there are[7] by nature two causes of actions—intellect and thought—and actions are what make every agent succeed or fail.

   The story is the imitation of the action; for by 'story'[8] I mean the 5 combination of actions;[9] By 'characters' I mean whatever makes us attribute some quality to an agent. By 'thought' I mean the ways in which the agents demonstrate[10] a position or express a view.

   Every tragedy, then, must have six parts, which give the tragedy its

---

4. **purification**: *katharsis*. Or 'purgation'.

5. **from**: Or 'of'. Aristotle might have in mind: (a) A purification that consists in or works through pity and fear. (b) A purgation, i.e., removal, of pity and fear. (c) A purification from excessive pity and fear, i.e., their replacement with feelings closer to the MEAN. (d) A purification, i.e., making purer, of pity and fear.

6. **and song**: OCT deletes.

7. **Hence there are**: Read *pephuke dē*. OCT deletes 'Hence . . . character'.

8. **story**: *muthos*. Or 'plot'. This is often but not always (see 1451b19) a traditional 'myth'. A *muthos* is not necessarily taken to be unhistorical; see 1451b15.

9. **actions**: *pragmata*. The unifying action of a play is the *praxis* (singular). The *pragmata* are the actions (plural) done in the course of this single action.

10. **demonstrate**: This is presumably the less rigorous sort of DEMONSTRATION that is described in *Rhet.* 1355a5. See ARGUMENTATION.

quality. These are story, characters, speech, thought, visual display, and   10
song. For two of these are the means by which we imitate, one is the
way we imitate, three are the things we imitate, and there is nothing
besides these six. Quite a few dramatists, we may say, have used these
different kinds of parts. For every drama has visual displays,[11] character,
story, speech, song, and thought likewise.

[THE IMPORTANCE OF ACTION]

The most important of these is the combination of actions. For tragedy   15
is an imitation, not of human beings, but of an action[12] and a way of
life and of happiness* and unhappiness. Happiness and unhappiness[13]
are found in action, and the end <we aim at> is a type of action, not
a quality <of character>; people's characters make them people of a
certain sort, but it is their actions that make them happy or unhappy.[14]   20
Hence they do not perform the actions <in a drama> to imitate characters, but rather include the characters in order to imitate[15] the actions.
And so it is the actions and <hence> the story that are the end of a
tragedy, and the end is most important of all.

Further, there can be no tragedy without action, but there can be one
without <presentation of> characters.[16] For the ones by most of the   25
recent authors are without character; and in general this is true of many
poets. It is similar to the difference between Zeuxis and Polygnotus
among painters; for Polygnotus is a good painter of character, whereas
Zeuxis's painting contains no presentation of character. Moreover, a
poet will not achieve what we have seen to be the function* of a tragedy   30
simply by arranging in order discourses that present character, well
composed in their speech and thought. He will achieve it much better
in a tragedy that is inferior in these points but has a story and a combination of actions.

Besides, the main aspects by which a tragedy appeals to our feelings[17]

11. **visual displays**: Read *opseis*. OCT: 'visual display'.

12. **an action**: Read *praxeōs*. OCT: 'actions'.

13. **of happiness . . . and unhappiness**: Read *kai eudaimonias <kai kaekodaimonias, hē d'eudaimonia> kai hē kakodaimonia*. OCT: *kai eudaimonia kai kakodaimonia*.

14. **Happiness . . . or unhappy**: OCT deletes the whole sentence.

15. **in order to imitate**: Lit. 'because of'.

16. **characters**: Aristotle does not speak as we do of 'a character' as simply a figure in a play, one of the dramatis personae. (Hence the plays 'without characters' still have figures playing different roles.) By 'character', *ēthos*, he means the character (good, bad, etc.) of a person, as depicted by a figure in a play.

17. **appeals to our feelings**: *psuchagōgein*. Lit. 'leads souls'.

35   are parts of the story—the reversals and the recognition. Further evidence is the fact that beginners in composition are able to get the speech and characters exactly right before they can correctly combine the actions; this was true, for instance, of practically all the earliest poets.

1450b   The story, then, is the principle* and, we might say, the soul of the tragedy, and the characters are secondary. For it is similar in the case of painting also; for if a painter covered the canvas with the most beautiful colors in no order, he would please us less than if he produced a black and white sketch. Similarly, the story is an imitation of action; it imitates agents[18] primarily in order to imitate the action.[19]

5   The third part is thought. This is the capacity to say what is involved in the situation and suitable to it, which, in the case of speeches, is the task of political* science and rhetoric. For the early poets presented people speaking in a politician's manner, whereas contemporary poets present them speaking them in a rhetorician's manner.[20]

Character is the sort of thing that makes clear what sort of decision* is made when it is not clear whether someone is deciding for or against

10   an action;[21] that is why the speeches that do not present anything to be decided for or against do not present any character. Thought, by contrast, is that in which someone demonstrates* that something is so or is not so, or makes some general pronouncement.

The fourth of the elements found in discourse is speech. By 'speech' I mean, as I said before, the expression <of thought> through the use

15   of words,[22] which has the same force in meter and <prose> discourses.

Among the remaining parts, the song is the most important of the pleasant accompaniments. The visual display appeals most to our feelings[23], but involves the least craft* and is the least proper to poetry. For the power of tragedy can be achieved without a performance and actors;

20   moreover the equipment-maker's craft, more than the poet's, is properly in control of the production of visual display.

18. **imitates agents**: It does this by imitating their characters.

19. **in order to imitate the action**: Lit. 'because of the action'.

20. **in a rhetorician's manner**: They use the more elaborately constructed speeches characteristic of rhetorical technique.

21. **when it . . . an action**: OCT deletes.

22. **expression . . . words**: Lit. 'interpretation (see *Top.* 160b10–16, note 1 to *DI*) through naming'.

23. **appeals . . . feelings**: See 1450a33n.

[THE CONSTRUCTION OF THE PLOT]

7

Now that we have determined this, let us say next what the combination of actions should be like, since this is the first and most important aspect of a tragedy.

Well, we have laid it down that a tragedy is an imitation of a whole and complete* action that has some greatness (for it is possible for some-   25
thing to be a whole and yet to have no greatness). A whole has a beginning, middle, and ending. A beginning[24] is whatever itself is not necessarily after something else but has something that by nature is or comes to be after it. An ending, on the contrary, is whatever itself is naturally after something else, either necessarily or usually, but has   30
nothing else after itself. A middle is whatever is both itself after something else and has something else after it. Those who have composed stories well must, then, neither begin nor end at just any old place, but must observe the character <of beginning and ending> that has been described.

[THE PROPER LENGTH]

Moreover, if an animal or anything composite is to be beautiful, it not   35
only must have its parts in an orderly arrangement, but also must itself have some appropriate greatness, not just any old size. For beauty is found in greatness and order. This is why an extremely small animal could not turn out to be beautiful; for when our observation[25] takes a nearly imperceptible length of time, it becomes confused. Nor can something be beautiful if it is extremely large; for we cannot observe it   1451a
all at the same time, but in the course of observing it we lose the unity and the whole from our observation—if, for instance, an animal were a thousand miles long. And so, in the case of animals as of all composites, it must have some greatness, but one that can be easily surveyed. Similarly, then, a story must have some length, but one that can be easily remem-   5
bered.

The proper limit of length, as far as it concerns performing and seeing a drama is not a question for the poet's craft.[26] For if a hundred tragedies had to be performed,[27] the performances would be limited by the water

24. **beginning**: *archē*. See PRINCIPLE #1.

25. **observation**: See STUDY.

26. **not a . . . craft**: Questions about length depend on external circumstances. A limited time was allowed for plays in the public festivals at which Greek plays were performed.

27. **performed**: sc. at a single public festival.

clock, as they are said to have been in other times.[28] The limit, as far as
10   it concerns the nature of the thing, is this: the longer it is, as long as it
remains clear, its beauty is greater in proportion to its size. But—to
define it without qualification[29]—whatever size allows things happening
in a necessary or likely sequence to pass from bad to good fortune or
15   from good to bad, that is a sufficient standard[30] for its size.

[THE UNITY OF THE PLOT]

8

A story is not a unity, as some people think it is, simply by being about
a single person. For many things, indeed an indefinite number, happen
to a single person, and some of them do not constitute any unity; and
similarly a single person does many actions that constitute no unified
20   action. That is why all the poets, it would seem, who have written poems
on 'The Life of Heracles' or 'The Life of Theseus', and so on, have been
in error. For they think that since Heracles was one person, his story
can be expected to be one story also.

    Homer, by contrast, is superior in this way as in others and, it would
seem, saw this point well, whether because of his skill in the craft or
25   because of his natural gifts. For in composing the *Odyssey* he did not
include everything that happened to Odysseus. (For instance, he was
wounded on Mount Parnassus; and he feigned madness when he was
summoned to join the expedition;[31] but neither of these events forms
any necessary or likely sequence with the other.) Instead Homer composed the *Odyssey*, and likewise the *Iliad*, about a single action of the
sort we are describing.
30   And so, just as in the other imitative crafts a single imitation is of one
object, the same should be true of a story. Since it is an imitation of action,
it should imitate a single whole action and the parts of the <constituent>
actions should be combined in such a way that if one part were placed
elsewhere or removed, the whole would be disturbed and ruined. For
35   if the addition or nonaddition of something has no clear effect, that thing
is no part of the whole.

28. **as they . . . times**: Text uncertain.

29. **without qualification**: Aristotle acknowledges that he is omitting qualifications needed for an EXACT statement. See WITHOUT QUALIFICATION #3.

30. **standard**: See FORMULA #3.

31. **expedition**: i.e., the expedition that resulted in the Trojan War.

[THE PROPER CONCERN OF TRAGEDY IS THE UNIVERSAL]

9

It is also evident from what we have said that it is the poet's function to describe not what has happened, but the sorts of things that would happen[32] and are possible, in a necessary or likely sequence. For the difference between a historian[33] and a poet is not that one writes in verse and the other in prose; for you could put Herodotus' work into verse, and it would be a history[34] in verse no less than it would be in prose. The difference is that the historian describes what has happened, whereas the poet describes the sorts of things that would happen.   *1451b*

5

This is why poetry is more philosophical* and more serious[35] than history; for it speaks more of what is universal, whereas history speaks of what is particular. What is universal is, for instance, that in a necessary or likely sequence the result is that this sort of person says or does things of this sort; this is what poetry aims at, attaching names[36] to it. What is particular is, for instance, what actions Alcibiades did or what things happened to him.   *10*

[THIS CONCERN WITH THE UNIVERSAL EXPLAINS
THE ROLE OF TRADITIONAL STORIES]

The case of comedy makes this difference clear at once. For there the poet first composes his story, relying on likely sequences, and then supplies any old names; his work is not about a particular person, as a lampoon is.[37] In the case of tragedy, however, the poet retains names of actual people of the past. The reason for this is that what persuades us is <what we find> convincing,[38] and if something has not happened,   *15*

---

32. **would happen**: The following explanation shows that Aristotle means 'what might reasonably be expected to happen', not something that is merely possible (which might be highly unlikely).

33. **historian**: *historikos*.

34. **history**: *historia*. Lit. 'INQUIRY'.

35. **more serious**: since SCIENCE is concerned with UNIVERSALS.

36. **names**: i.e., proper names. Poets use 'Oedipus' or 'Hamlet' for a person of a certain character, not merely to name an actual historical person.

37. **lampoon**: Lit. 'iambic poem'. Aristotle's remarks on comedy presumably refer mainly to later comedy, rather than to, e.g., Aristophanes (some of whose plays include historical figures such as Cleon and Lamachus).

38. **convincing**: If a tragedy presents some incident as the sort of thing that happens, we must be convinced that it is possible. Aristotle assumes that a contemporary audience would take the traditional myths to be historically accurate (at least in outline).

we are not yet convinced that it is possible, whereas if it has happened, then evidently it is possible (since it would not have happened if it had been impossible).

20 Still, some tragedies have one or two names of known~g~ people, while the other names are fictitious. And some tragedies even have no <names of actual people>, as is true in the *Antheus* of Agathon; for in this both the actions and the names are alike fictitious, and nonetheless pleasing for that.

We must not seek, then, to retain at all costs the traditional stories
25 that tragedies are about. Indeed, it would be ridiculous to seek to do this, since even the <incidents> that are known are known to few people, but still are pleasing to everyone.

[THE BEST STRUCTURE FOR A PLOT]

Hence it is clear that the poet must be a composer[39] of stories rather than verses, insofar as it is his imitating that makes him a poet, and the things he imitates are actions. And so even if it happens that the incidents
30 in his composition have actually happened, it does not follow that he is any less a composer. For it is quite possible for some things that have happened to be the sorts of things that are likely to happen, and capable of happening;[40] and insofar as they are <likely and capable of happening>, he is the composer of them.

Among simple stories and actions the episodic ones are the worst.
35 By 'episodic story' I mean one in which the episodes follow in neither a necessary nor a likely sequence. Bad poets compose such stories because of their own incompetence. But good poets also compose such stories, for the sake of the actors;[41] for since they are composing plays for a competition and stretching the story beyond its capacity, they are
1452a often compelled to distort the sequence.

Now, a tragedy imitates not only a complete action, but also incidents arousing fear and pity. And incidents have this effect most of all when
5 they happen unexpectedly because of each other. For this <causal connection> will make them more amazing[42] than if they happened by chance and luck.* For even among things happening by luck the ones

---

39. **poet . . . composer**: Both words translate *poiētēs* (lit. 'producer'). The poet must actually compose a story, not simply versify a ready-made story.

40. **and capable of happening**: OCT deletes.

41. **for . . . actors**: They write parts that will allow the actors to show off (as operas are written not with the aim of a good plot, but with the aim of providing suitable arias for the singers).

42. **amazing**: See ADMIRE.

that seem most amazing are those that appear to have happened as though on purpose. That is true, for instance, of the statue of Mitys in Argos that killed the man responsible for Mitys' death, by falling on him when he was looking at it; for such things look as though they do not   *10* happen at random. Hence stories of the same sort are bound to be better.

[SIMPLE AND COMPLEX PLOTS]

10

Some stories are simple and others are complex. For it is immediately clear that the actions imitated by stories are of these two types. By 'simple actions' I mean that the change <of fortune> results from an action that   *15* is continuous and single in the way we have defined,[43] without a reversal or recognition. A complex action is that from which the change results with a recognition or a reversal or both. These, however, must result from the structure of the story itself, in such a way that the later events   *20* follow the earlier in either a necessary or a likely sequence. For there is a great difference between one thing's happening because of another[44] and its <merely> happening after another.

[ASPECTS OF A PLOT]

11

A reversal is the change of what is done to the contrary condition, as we said, in a likely or necessary sequence, as we are saying. It is the sort of thing that happens in the Oedipus,[45] where <the messenger>   *25* intends to relieve Oedipus and to free him from his fear about his mother, by revealing who he is, but produces the contrary result. In the Lynceus Lynceus is being led off to be put to death, and Danaus is following to put him to death, but then it comes about, as a result of what was done previously, that Danaus is put to death and Lynceus is saved.

A recognition, as the name itself signifies, is a change from ignorance   *30* to knowledge$_g$, or to friendship or to enmity, in the people marked[46] for good or bad fortune. The best type of recognition is the one that is accompanied by a reversal, as is true of the one in the Oedipus. Certainly, there are also other types of recognition. For it is possible for the sort   *35* of thing we mentioned to happen with inanimate objects, indeed with

43. **we have defined**: See 1450b24.
44. **because of another**: as it should in a tragedy.
45. *Oedipus*: Sophocles, *Oedipus Tyrannus* 911–1085.
46. **marked . . . fortune**: Lit. 'defined in relation to good or bad fortune'.

any old thing, and it is possible to come to recognize whether someone
has or has not done an action. But still, the type of recognition most
appropriate for the story and the action is the type we have mentioned.
1452b   For this is the type of recognition and reversal that will arouse either
pity or fear, and we assume that this is the sort of action that tragedy
imitates; moreover, bad or good fortune will result in such cases.

Since, then, a recognition is a recognition of particular people, some
of them simply involve one person recognizing another, whenever it is
5   made clear who the other is. Sometimes, however, each has to recognize
the other; for instance, Orestes recognized Iphigeneia from her sending
the letter, but it took another recognition for her to recognize him.[47]

And so two parts of the story—reversal and recognition—are about
10   these things. A third part is suffering.[48] We have already said what
reversal and recognition are. Suffering is a destructive or painful action—
for instance, death in front of other people,[49] torture, wounding, and so
on.

* * * * * * *

[THE AIMS AND STRUCTURE OF A TRAGEDY]

13

1452b28   After what we have said, our next task is to say what the poet should
aim at and what he should avoid in constructing his stories, and how
to achieve the function* of a tragedy.
30   Now, the construction of the finest tragedy must be complex, not
simple, and must imitate things that arouse fear and pity; for this is
distinctive of this type of imitation. First of all, then, it is clear that decent
35   men must not be shown passing from good to bad fortune. For this is
not an object of fear or pity, but of abhorrence.[50] Nor must vicious people
be shown passing from bad fortune to good. For this process is the most
untragic of all; it has none of the features needed <in a tragedy>, since
1453a   it arouses neither our feeling for humanity[51] nor our pity nor our fear.

47. **Orestes . . . to recognize him**: Euripides, *Iphigeneia in Tauris* 760–826.

48. **suffering**: *pathos*. See ATTRIBUTE #1.

49. **in front of other people**: *en tō(i) phanerō(i)* (see EVIDENT). Or perhaps 'before
our eyes' (i.e., on the stage) or 'made vivid to us' (by the play).

50. **not an . . . abhorrence**: Perhaps Aristotle means that it is not *merely* an object
of fear or pity (1453a4 suggests that it satisfies at least the conditions for being
pitied, since the good person does not deserve bad fortune).

51. **feeling for humanity**: This might refer either to (1) our sympathy for the
victims (good or bad) of ill fortune, or (2) our feeling that people have got what
they deserved (good fortune if they are good, ill fortune if they are bad).

Nor must an extremely base person be shown falling from good fortune
to bad. For though this construction appeals to our feeling for humanity,
it arouses neither pity nor fear. For pity is felt for someone suffering ill
fortune who does not deserve it, and fear for someone like <ourselves>.   5
Hence the result <of this sort of story> arouses neither pity nor fear.

The remaining case is the person between these. He is a person who
is not superior in virtue and justice who passes into ill fortune, not
because he is bad and vicious, but because he makes some error[52]—   10
someone in high esteem and good fortune, such as Oedipus, Thyestes,
and the <other> illustrious men of such <noble> families.

And so a story that is well constructed must be single,[53] not, as some
say, double. It must involve passing from good fortune to bad, not the   15
other way round, and this must happen because of some great error by
an agent who is either the sort of person we have described or better
than that rather than worse. What actually happens is evidence for our
claim. For in the earliest times poets used just any old story, but at
present the finest tragedies are composed about a few families—for
example, about Alcmaeon, Oedipus, Orestes, Meleager, Thyestes, Tele-   20
phus, and all the others for whom it turned out that they did terrible
things or had terrible things happen to them.

And so the tragedy that counts as finest on the principles prescribed
by the craft[54] has this structure. That is also why Euripides' critics are
in error when they make it a ground of accusation against him that he   25
does this in his tragedies, so that[55] many of them end with ill fortune.
For, as we have said, this is the correct sort of ending. The best evidence
of this is the fact that on the stage and in performance these sorts of
plays appear the most tragic, if they are successfully executed, and even
if Euripides does not arrange the other things well, still he appears the   30
most tragic of the poets.

The second-best type of structure is the one that some people say is
best, the one that has a double structure, such as the *Odyssey* has, that
ends with contrary results for the better and the worse people. This is
regarded as best because of the weakness of the audiences; for the poets
follow them and compose what will please the audience. But the pleasure   35
<resulting from this structure> is not the pleasure from tragedy, but is
more proper to comedy. For there the bitterest enemies in the story—

52. **error**: *hamartia*. Different interpretations: (1) A fault of character (the 'tragic
flaw'). (2) A mistake of fact that is not blameworthy. (3) A blameworthy mistake.
Probably (3) is preferable.

53. **single**: i.e., it must have just one result.

54. **tragedy . . . craft**: Lit. 'finest tragedy in accordance with the craft'.

55. **so that**: Lit. 'and'.

Orestes and Aegisthus, for instance—become friends at the end and walk off <together>, and no one kills anyone.

[*HOW PITY AND FEAR SHOULD BE AROUSED BY ACTIONS*]

14

1453b Fear and pity may be aroused by the visual display, but it may also be aroused by the actual structure of the actions. This second method is preferable, and shows the better poet. For even without our seeing it,

5 the story should be constructed so that when we hear what is going on, we tremble and feel pity at the result; this is what would happen to someone hearing the story of Oedipus. To achieve this effect visually is a mark of inferiority in the <poet's> craft, and requires equipment. Those who use visual display not to arouse fear, but only to produce

10 freakish effects, have nothing in common with tragedy; for we must not seek every type of pleasure from tragedy, but only the type of pleasure that is proper to it.

Since it is the pleasure resulting from pity and fear that the poet must produce through imitation, it is evident that this <capacity to arouse pity and fear> must be incorporated into the actions. Let us, then, find the sorts of events that appear terrible or worthy of pity.

15 Well, such actions must involve people who are friends[56] or enemies or neither. If an enemy does something to an enemy, his doing it or being about to do it arouses no pity, except in the actual suffering <of the victim>. The same is true if they are neither friends nor enemies.

20 But when these sufferings arise among friends—when, for instance, a brother kills, or is about to kill, his brother, or a son his father, or a mother her son, or a son his mother, or something else of this sort— these are the situations we should seek. We cannot, then, tamper with the traditional stories—I mean, for instance, that Orestes kills Clytaem-

25 nestra, and Alcmaeon kills Eriphyle; but the poet must find ways to use[57] the traditional stories well. Let us say more clearly what we mean by 'using them well'.

It is possible for the action to come about, as the early poets used to present it, so that it is done by someone who knows <what he is doing> and recognizes <the victim>, as Euripides presented Medea killing her

30 children. Secondly, it is possible to do it, but to do it in ignorance of the terrible thing <one is doing>, and then afterwards to come to recognize

---

56. **friends**: In this passage Aristotle uses *philos* to include members of the same family, whether or not they are FRIENDS in the sense of having friendly feelings to one another.

57. **find ways to use**: Lit. 'find (object unexpressed), and use'.

the friendship; this is true of Sophocles' Oedipus. In his case <the terrible thing> happens outside the drama, but sometimes it happens within the tragedy itself, as with Astydamas' Alcmaeon, or Telegonus in *The Wounding of Odysseus*. A third possibility is that someone is about to do   35
something abominable, because he is ignorant, and comes to recognize the facts before he does it. And besides these there is no other possibility; for the agent must either act or not, and either in knowledge or in ignorance.

Among these possibilities, the worse is the one in which the agent is about to act in full knowledge, and then does not act. For it arouses abhorrence and is not tragic, since it involves no suffering. Hence no one composes a drama along such lines, except occasionally, as in the   1454a
case of Haemon against Creon in the *Antigone*. Actually doing it <in full knowledge> is second worst. It is better to act in ignorance and to recognize the truth after doing it; for then the abhorrent aspect[58] is not added, and the recognition arouses amazement. But the best is the last   5
possibility.[59] I mean, for instance, what Merope does in the *Cresphontes*; she is about to kill her son, but does not kill him, but instead has recognized him. The same is true of sister and brother in the *Iphigeneia*;[60] and in the *Helle* the son is about to hand over his mother <to the enemy> when he recognizes her.

This is why, as we said some time ago, tragedies are about a small number of families. For the poets in their searching found, by good   10
fortune rather than by craft, how to achieve this sort of effect in the <traditional> stories; hence they have to recur to those families that were the victims of such events.

We have said enough, then, about the structure of the actions and about the proper characteristics of the stories.   15

[*THE PRESENTATION OF CHARACTER IN TRAGEDY*]

15

There are four points to aim at in presenting types of character.

The first and primary point is that they must be estimable.[61] Someone in a tragedy has a character if, as we said, the words or the action make

---

58. **abhorrent aspect**: sc. of being about to commit an abominable crime knowingly.

59. **But the best . . . possibility**: Aristotle does not explain why this is best.

60. *Iphigeneia*: Euripides' *Iphigeneia in Tauris*.

61. **estimable**: *chrēstos*. It is not clear whether this is equivalent to 'good', *agathos*.

some decision[62] evident; he has an estimable character if it is an estimable
20   decision. But an estimable character must fit a given type of person; for
a woman or a slave may be estimable, but still, presumably, the woman
is inferior <to an estimable man> and the slave is altogether base.
Secondly, the characters must fit the people. For a character may be
brave, but such bravery or cleverness does not fit a woman. Thirdly,
they must be like <the people who are imitated>;[63] for this is different
25   from making the character estimable and appropriate, as we have described it. Fourth, they must be consistent. For even if the person being
imitated is inconsistent and that is the sort of character he displays, still
he must be <presented as> consistently inconsistent.

An example of unnecessary depravity of character is Menelaus in the
30   *Orestes*. An inappropriate and unfitting character is shown by the lament[64] of Odysseus in the *Scylla*, and the speech of Melanippe.[65] Inconsis-
tency is displayed by Iphigeneia in the *Iphigeneia at Aulis*; for <her charac-
ter> when she is a suppliant is not at all like her later <character>. In
characters, as in the structure of actions, we must always seek either
35   what is necessary or what is likely, so that it is necessary or likely that
this sort of person will say this sort of thing, and that this event will
follow that.

1454b   It is evident, then, that the resolution of the story must arise from
the story itself, and not from an artificial contrivance,[66] as in the *Medea*,
and as the incident about sailing home happens in the *Iliad*. Such a
device should be used for what is outside the drama, for earlier events
5   that a human being cannot know, or for later events that need to be
foretold and announced (for we attribute the power of seeing everything
to the gods). There should be nothing unreasonable in the actions; if
there is anything, it should be outside the tragedy, as in Sophocles'
Oedipus.

Since tragedy is an imitation of better people,[67] we must imitate good
10   painters. For they render each person's distinctive features and retain
the likeness, but still make him handsomer than he is. Similarly, the

62. **decision**: Or perhaps 'attitude', 'outlook'. Aristotle may not be thinking of
anything as precise as the sort of DECISION he describes in the *Ethics*.

63. **they must . . . imitated>**: Aristotle seems to mean that an Achilles, say, in
a play must have a character that fits the main historical facts (as we conceive
them) about the actual Achilles.

64. **lament**: Perhaps this particular lament strikes Aristotle as excessively
womanly.

65. **of Melanippe**: Perhaps Aristotle thinks it was too clever for a woman.

66. **artificial contrivance**: See *Met*. 985a18n.

67. **better people**: OCT: 'better people than we are'.

poet imitates irascible and lazy people and people with other <faults> of character; but in presenting them as people with such characters he should make them decent, as Homer made Achilles good even while making him an example of inflexibility.[68]

The points to be observed are these, and besides these the visual   15
displays that necessarily depend on the poetic craft; for here too it is possible to make frequent errors. But we have discussed these adequately in our published works.

68. **as Homer . . . inflexibility**: Read *hoion ton Achillea agathon kai paradeigma sklērotētos Homēros*. Text uncertain.

ON IDEAS[1]

[THE ARGUMENTS FROM THE SCIENCES [2]]

(79.3–80.6)

They used the sciences in many ways to establish that there are Ideas, as he <Aristotle> says in the first book of *On Ideas*. And the arguments he seems to have in mind here are the following:

79.5

If every science does its work by referring to some one and the same thing, and not to any of the particulars, then for each science there would be some other thing apart* from perceptible things, which is everlasting and a pattern* of the things that come to be within that science. And this sort of thing is the Idea.

Further, the things the sciences are of exist. And the sciences are of some other things apart from particulars; for particulars are indefinite and indeterminate, whereas the sciences are of determinate things. Therefore there are some things apart from particulars, and these things are the Ideas.

79.10

Further, if medicine is the science not of this health but of health without* qualification, there will be such a thing as health itself. And if geometry is the science not of this equal and of this commensurate but of equal without qualification and of commensurate without qualification, there will be such a thing as equal itself and as commensurate itself. And these things are the Ideas.

79.15

Now these arguments do not prove what they set out to prove, that there are Ideas; but they do prove that there are some things apart from particulars and perceptible things. But it does not immediately follow that, if there are some things that are apart from particulars, they are

---

1. This is excerpted from Alexander of Aphrodisias' *Commentary on the Metaphysics of Aristotle*, which preserves fragments of Aristotle's lost work *On Ideas*. The excerpt translated here is to be found in G. Fine, *On Ideas: Aristotle's Criticism of Plato's Theory of Forms* (Oxford, 1993). Aristotle lays out various arguments for the existence of Platonic FORMS and then criticizes them. The arguments and criticisms are briefly mentioned in *Metaphysics* i 9.

2. Or: The Arguments from the Branches of Knowledge; see KNOWLEDGE #1.

Ideas; for there are common things apart from the particulars, and we say that the sciences are in fact of them.[3]

Further, there is also the objection that if these arguments succeeded, they would prove that there are also Ideas of the things that fall under 79.20 the crafts. For every craft also refers the things that it produces to some one thing; and the things the crafts are of exist, and the crafts are of some other things apart from the particulars. And this last argument, in addition to the fact that, like the other arguments, it does not prove that there are Ideas, seems to establish that there are also Ideas of things for which they do not want Ideas <as well as of things for which they want Ideas>. For if, because medicine is the science not of this health but of health without qualification, there is some health itself, then this 80 will also apply to each of the crafts. For none of them is of the particular or the this either, but each is of the thing without qualification that it is about. For example, carpentry is of bench without qualification, not of this bench, and of bed without qualification, not of this bed. And sculpture, painting, house-building, and each of the other crafts is related in 80.5 a similar way to the things that fall under it. Therefore, there will be an Idea of each of the things that fall under the crafts as well <as of the things that fall under the sciences>, which they do not want.[4]

[THE ONE OVER MANY]

(80.8–81.22)

They also use the following argument to establish that there are Ideas:

If each of the many men is <a> man, and if each of the many animals is <an> animal, and the same applies in the other cases; and if in the 80.10 case of each of these it is not that something is predicated of itself but that there is something which is predicated of all of them and which is not the same as any of them, then this is some being apart from particular beings, which is both separated from them and everlasting. For it is in every case predicated in the same way of all the numerically successive particulars. And what is a one over many, separated from them, and everlasting is an Idea. Therefore there are Ideas. 80.15

3. **for there are . . . of them**: The Arguments from the Sciences prove that something APART FROM perceptible particulars exists; but (Aristotle objects) this something need not be a Platonic Form, as opposed to an Aristotelian universal (which he here calls a common thing, because each universal is common to, predicated of, many things). See UNIVERSAL #2, #4.

4. **Therefore . . . do not want**: Here Aristotle objects that the Arguments from the Sciences prove the existence of Forms in cases where the Platonists do not want them; though they want Forms for things falling under the sciences (e.g., virtue), they do not want Forms for things falling under the crafts (e.g., bench).

He says that this argument establishes that there are Ideas both of negations and of things that are not. For one and the same negation is predicated of many things, including things that are not, and it is not the same as any of the things of which it is true. For not-man is predicated of horse and of dog and of everything apart from man, and for this reason it is a one over many and is not the same as any of the things of which it is predicated. Further, it always remains, since it is true in the same way of similar things <i.e. of the numerically successive particulars>. For not-musical is true of many things (of all those things that are not musical) in the same way, and similarly not-man is true of all those things that are not men. Therefore there are also Ideas of negations.

This is absurd. For how could there be an Idea of not being? For if one accepts this, there will be one Idea of things that are different in genus and different in every way, such as line and man, since all these are not-horses. And there will also be one Idea of indeterminate and indefinite things; and also of things of which one is primary, the other secondary (for man and animal, of which one is primary and the other secondary, are both not-wood). And of such things they did not want genera or Ideas.

And it is clear that neither does this argument validly deduce[5] that there are Ideas. Rather, it too tends to prove that what is predicated in common is something other than the particulars of which it is predicated.[6]

Further, the same people who want to prove that what is predicated in common of a plurality of things is some one thing and that it is an Idea, establish this from negations. For if someone denying something of a plurality of things denies it by referring to some one thing (for someone saying 'man is not white', and 'horse is not <white>', does not deny something peculiar to each of them; rather, by referring to some one thing, he denies the same white of all of them), then someone affirming the same thing of a plurality of things will not be affirming something different of each of them. Rather, there will be some one thing he affirms—e.g. man—referring to some one and the same thing. For as with negation, so with affirmation. Therefore, there is some other being apart from that which is in perceptible things, which is the cause of the affirmation that is both true of a plurality of things and also common; and this is the Idea.

This argument, then, he says, produces Ideas not only of things that

5. **validly deduce**: *sullogizesthai*. See DEDUCTION.

6. **Rather, it too . . . predicated**: Aristotle objects that the One over Many Argument proves that there is something apart from perceptible particulars, but not that this something is a Platonic Form as opposed to an Aristotelian universal.

are affirmed but also of things that are denied. For in both cases <there is a reference to> one thing in the same way.

[THE OBJECT OF THOUGHT ARGUMENT]

(81.25–82.7)

The argument that establishes from thinking that there are Ideas is the following: 81.25

   If, whenever we think of man, footed, or animal, we are thinking (a) of something that is and (b) of none of the particulars (for the same thought remains even when they have perished), then clearly there is something, apart from particulars and perceptibles, which we are thinking of whether or not they are. For surely we are not then thinking of something that is not. And this is a Form and Idea.   82

   He says, then, that this argument also establishes that there are Ideas of perishing and perished things, and in general of particular and perishable things, such as Socrates and Plato. For (a) we also think of them, and (b) we retain and preserve an appearance of them even when they no longer are.   82.5

   Indeed, we also think of things that in no way are, such as hippocentaur and chimera.

   So neither does this argument validly deduce that there are Ideas.[7]

[THE ARGUMENT FROM RELATIVES]

(82.11–83.33)

The argument that establishes from relatives that there are Ideas is the following: 82.11

   In cases where some same thing is predicated of a plurality of things not homonymously, but so as to reveal some one nature, it is true of them either (a) because they are fully what is signified by the thing predicated, as when we call Socrates and Plato man; or (b) because they   83.1 are likenesses of the true ones, as when we predicate man of pictured

---

   7. **So neither . . . Ideas**: Like the Arguments from the Sciences and the One over Many Argument, this argument is an invalid argument for the existence of Platonic Forms. Aristotle does not say here, as he does in the preceding two cases, that the argument is a valid argument for the existence of Aristotelian universals. Some mss, however, add (LF 82.7–9): 'So neither does this argument validly deduce that there are Ideas, but <it does validly deduce> that there is something else apart from particulars. Now the universal which is in particulars also fits this <description—i.e., it is something apart from particulars>, and it does not necessarily introduce an Idea.'

83.5

<men> (for in their case we reveal the likenesses of man, signifying some same nature in all of them); or (c) because one of them is the pattern, the others likenesses, as if we were to call Socrates and the likenesses of him men.

And when we predicate the equal itself of the things here, we predicate it of them homonymously. For (a) the same account does not fit them all. (b) Nor do we signify the truly equals. For the quantity in perceptible

83.10 things changes and continuously shifts and is not determinate. (c) But neither do any of the things here accurately receive the account of the equal.

But neither <can they be called equal nonhomonymously> by one of them's being a pattern, another a likeness. For one of them is not a pattern or a likeness any more than another.

And indeed, if someone were to accept that the likeness is not homonymous with the pattern, it always follows that these equals are equals by being likenesses of what is fully and truly equal.

83.15 But if this is so, then there is something which is the equal itself and which is fully <equal>, in relation to which the things here, by being likenesses, both come to be and are called equal. And this is an Idea, being a pattern and likeness of the things that come to be in relation to it.

This, then, is one argument that he says establishes that there are Ideas even of relatives. It seems more carefully and more accurately and more directly to aim at the proof of the Ideas. For this argument does not, like the ones before it, seem to prove simply that there is some

83.20 common thing apart from the particulars, but rather <it seems to prove> that there is some pattern of the things here which is fully. For this seems to be especially characteristic of the Ideas.[8]

He says, then, that this argument establishes that there are Ideas even of relatives. At least, the present proof has proceeded from the equal, which is a relative. But they used to say that there are no Ideas of

83.25 relatives. For in their view the Ideas subsist in themselves, being kinds of substances, whereas relatives have their being in their relation to one another.

Further, if the equal is equal to an equal, there will be more than one Idea of equal. For the equal itself is equal to an equal itself. For if it were not equal to anything, it would not be equal at all.

Further, by the same argument there will also have to be Ideas of unequals. For opposites are alike in that there will be Ideas corresponding

---

8. **For this . . . Idea**: Unlike the preceding arguments, the Argument from Relatives is a valid argument for the existence of Platonic Forms. Aristotle goes on to argue, however, that it is not sound.

to both or to neither; and the unequal is also agreed by them to be in   *83.30*
more than one thing.

Again, he made this opinion common ground when he spoke of it
as his own, saying 'of which things we say there is no in itself genus',
speaking of 'genus', instead of 'reality' or 'nature', if a relative* is indeed
like an appendage, as he said elsewhere.   *83.33*

[*THE THIRD MAN ARGUMENT*]

(84.21–85.3)[9]

The third man is also[10] proved in this way:

If what is predicated truly of some plurality of things is also some other
thing apart from the things of which it is predicated, being separated from
them (for this is what those who posit the Ideas think they prove; for   *84.25*
this is why, according to them, there is such a thing as man-itself, because
the man is predicated truly of the particular men, these being a plurality,
and it is other than the particular men)—but if this is so, there will be   *85*
a third man. For if the <man> being predicated is other than the things
of which it is predicated and subsists on its own, and <if> the man is
predicated both of the particulars and of the Idea, then there will be a
third man apart from the particular and the Idea. In the same way, there
will also be a fourth <man> predicated of this <third man>, of the
Idea, and of the particulars, and similarly also a fifth, and so on to
infinity.

9. On the Third Man Argument see FORM (PLATONIC) #3.

10. **is also**: Alexander also records Third Man Arguments by other authors.

GLOSSARY

ABSTRACTION, *aphairesis*

1. If x is F, G, and H, but I want to examine what is true of x INSOFAR AS it is F (x qua F), then I 'abstract' or 'remove' G and H from x in thought. My claims and arguments about x do not rely on the assumption that x is G and H. See *APo* 74a32–b4, *DA* 429b18–20.

2. This is Aristotle's account of how (contrary to Plato) mathematics can be true of material objects (and so does not need SEPARATED objects), though not qua material; the mathematician makes true judgments about material objects by focussing on their purely mathematical properties and abstracting from their matter. See *Phys.* 193b31–194a12, *DA* 403b15, *Met.* 1073b3–8, 1077b17–1078a31.

3. Aristotle also recognizes a place for abstraction in metaphysics, *Met.* 1004b10–17, 1029a16; but he believes it is a mistake (characteristic of Plato) to suppose that we can find the ESSENCE and FORM of natural organisms if we abstract their MATTER altogether. The mathematician ignoring the physical body that has a surface does not thereby reach false conclusions about the character of the surface as such; but ignoring the material character of natural organisms does lead to false conclusions about the study of natural organisms. This is why the study of nature differs from mathematics in its relation to matter. See *PA* 641b10–12, *Met.* 1036b21–30, SNUB.

ACCOUNT: see REASON

ACHIEVEMENT: see FUNCTION

ACT, ACT ON: see PRODUCE

ACTED ON: see ATTRIBUTE

ACTION, *praxis*

Aristotle uses *praxis* and the verb *prattein* (1) in a broad sense parallel to 'do'; (2) to distinguish VOLUNTARY actions from things that happen to us or things over which we have no control (e.g., *DI* 19a8, *EN* 1096b34); (3) for rational action on a DECISION, which is not open to nonrational animals or to children (*Phys.* 197b1–8, *EN* 1139a18–20); (4) for rational action in which the action itself is the end, as opposed to PRODUCTION, in which the end is some product distinct from the action (*Met.* 1048b22, *EN* 1139a35–b4, 1140b6–7, 1326a21; cf. *Pol.* 1254a2n)— in this sense *praxis* is a complete ACTUALITY, in contrast to MOTION. Since ethics and politics are concerned with action in sense (4), they are 'practical' disciplines, in contrast to productive CRAFTS such as shoemaking, building, rhetoric, and poetics.

ACTUALITY, ACTUALIZATION, ACTIVITY, REALIZATION, *energeia*

1. *Energeia* is contrasted with POTENTIALITY, as actually walking, e.g., is contrasted with merely having the potentiality to walk, *DI* 19a9, *Phys.* 201a9–15, *Met.* 1048a25–b9. It seems to be equivalent to *entelecheia*, which is therefore also translated 'actuality' (except that when the two terms occur together in contexts that require different translations, 'realization' translates *entelecheia*, and 'actuality' translates *energeia*; see *Met.* 1045b36n).

2. Aristotle sometimes distinguishes (a) first actuality (sometimes equivalent to STATE, *hexis*) from (b) second actuality, as in (a) knowing French, but not thinking or speaking in French at the time, in contrast to (b) speaking or thinking in French at the time, and so having actualized the potentiality still present in (a). *DA* 412a22–27, 417a21–b9, *EN* 1098a5–7.

3. Sometimes the verb *energein* is rendered by 'be active' and *energeia* by 'activity', e.g., *Phys.* 201a28, *DA* 416b2, *EN* 1094a4, 1174a4. See PLEASURE #1.

4. On the contrast between complete and incomplete actuality see MOTION.

ADMIRE, WONDER, BE AMAZED, *thaumazein*

Thaumazein may indicate (a) finding something surprising or unexpected; (b) finding it admirable and wonderful; (c) finding it unbelievable, and so likely to be false. See *DA* 402a3, *PA* 645a17, *Met.* 981b14 ff, 982b13, 983a20, 1072b25, *Poet.* 1452a6.

ADMIT OF, *endechesthai*: see POTENTIALITY

AFFECT, AFFECTION: see ATTRIBUTE

aisthēsis: see PERCEPTION

aition, aitia: CAUSE

akrasia: INCONTINENCE

ALTERATION, *alloiōsis*

This is MOTION or CHANGE in the category of QUALITY, *Phys.* 226a26–29, *GC* i 4, *MA* 701b12, *Met.* 1010a22–25, 1020b8–12, 1069b12.

ALTOGETHER: see IN GENERAL

ALWAYS, *aiei*; EVERLASTING, *aidion*

1. *Aiei* serves as a universal quantifier, and hence is often rendered 'in every case'; e.g., 'Clever politicians are always unscrupulous' means 'If a politician is clever, he is unscrupulous'.

2. What is always the case is sometimes identified with what is NECESSARY; see especially *GC* 337b35–338a5. Aristotle need not mean, however, that necessity is reducible to purely temporal concepts (see *APo* 73a28–b28); probably he intends 'always' and 'everlasting' to have a modal sense. He probably also intends this modal sense when he contrasts what holds always with the USUAL; this is not simply a contrast between regularities that have no exceptions and those that have exceptions, but a contrast between different kinds of lawlike regularities. See *Phys.* 196b10–13, 198b25.

GLOSSARY

ANALOGY, *analogia*

This applies to cases where no single definition usefully explains the nature of the thing or property, but it is not a case of pure HOMONYMY without any connection. See *Phys.* 191a8, *Met.* 1048a37, *EN* 1096b28.

ANALYTICS: see LOGICAL

ANAXAGORAS

Anaxagoras (500–428?; cf. *Met.* 984a11–16)) is one of the later Presocratic NATURAL-ISTS. He rejects atomist (see DEMOCRITUS) views of the composition of matter, believing instead that every division of any piece of matter is division into uniform (homoeomerous) PARTS (hence his view that there is 'a portion of everything in everything'), *Phys.* 187a23–b7, *DC* 302a28–b5, *GC* 314a11–b6. See also *Met.* 1007b25 (cf. Plato, *Phaedo* 72c), 1009a22–30, b26–28, 1069b20–21, 1071b28. He recognizes a place for intelligent design, and hence for something like FINAL CAUSATION, in the universe; but he does so only half-heartedly, *Phys.* 250b23–26, *Met.* 985a18–21 (cf. Plato, *Phaedo* 98b7–c2).

ANAXIMANDER

An early Presocratic NATURALIST (c. 610–c. 545). He believes that everything, including the four elements, comes from the 'unbounded' (*apeiron*; see INFINITE). Aristotle mentions him only rarely by name, *Phys.* 187a21, 203b10–15, *DC* 295b1–16, *Met.* 1069b22. It is uncertain how often he refers to him without naming him (e.g., *Phys.* 204b22–29, *GC* 332a20–23).

ANAXIMENES

An early Presocratic NATURALIST (fl. 546), probably a younger contemporary of ANAXIMANDER. He regards air as the basic material subject and substance, *Met.* 984a5 (cf. *DC* 294b13–17, *Metr.* 365b6–13).

ANIMAL, *zō(i)on*

Animals differ from plants in having PERCEPTION and DESIRE, *DA* 414a31–b6. There are nonrational animals (*DA* 433a11, 434a5), and rational animals—human beings, who share rationality with the GODS. See *EN* 1111b12, 1118b1, *Pol.* 1253a3.

ANIMATE, *empsuchos*: see SOUL

ANTIPHON

A sophist, rhetorician, and natural philosopher (?480–411?). His major work 'On Truth' dealt especially with the contrast between NATURE and convention (*nomos*; see LAW). See *Phys.* 193a12.

ANTISTHENES

A follower of Socrates (c. 445–c. 360), and a reputed founder of Cynic philosophy. See *Top.* 104b20, *Met.* 1043b24.

ANY OLD THING: see LUCK #2.

APART FROM, *para*

1. Sometimes 'x is *para* y' (with accusative) just means that x exists in addition to y. Sometimes it suggests that x is independent of y. See, e.g., *APo* 74a7, 29,

Phys. 200b32, 218b13, 251b25, 259a4, *DA* 414b21, 424b17, *PA* 641a35, *Met.* 1010b36, 1086b31, *EN* 1095a26.

2. A special problem arises about *para* in statements about UNIVERSALS and PARTIC-ULARS. Sometimes Aristotle allows that the universal is a 'one apart from the many', *APo* 100a7; but sometimes he uses such phrases to indicate the Platonic doctrine of SEPARATION, which he rejects, *APo* 77a5, 85b19, *Top.* 178b37 (ambiguous), *Met.* 1033b20, 1038b33, 1087a9.

APPETITE, *epithumia*; see DESIRE

apodeixis: DEMONSTRATION

aporia: see DIALECTIC

APPEARANCE, *phantasia*

1. In its most general sense '*phantasia*' is simply the abstract noun corresponding to *phainesthai*, 'appear'. Hence my *phantasia* of x (the tree, Pythagoras' Theorem) is simply how x appears to me (whether x is sensible or nonsensible), and every APPEARANCE expresses a *phantasia*, *DA* 402b23.

2. In its more specific sense *phantasia* is more closely connected to the senses, as opposed to the intellect. Hence Aristotle describes it as the product of PERCEP-TION and memory, *DA* 428b10–17. (Here 'imagination' would be, in some ways, a suitable rendering, though it would often be misleading.) On perception and appearance see *DA* 428a11–12, *Met.* 1010b1–3. On appearance and UNDERSTAND-ING: *DA* 403a8–10, 428a16–24, 431a14–17, 432a9–13. Appearance is present in all or most ANIMALS, *DA* 413b22–24, 414b16, 428a9–11, 433a9–11, *MA* 701b17. This sort of appearance is perceptual, as distinct from rational appearance, 434a5–10.

APPEARANCES, *phainomena*

1. *Phainomena* are literally 'things appearing', cognate with *phainesthai*, 'appear'. Two senses of *phainesthai* are marked by different grammatical constructions: (a) 'x appears to be F' (with the infinitive), or (b) 'x is evidently F' (with the participle; lit. 'x, being F, appears so'). Sense (b) implies, but sense (a) does not imply, that what appears F is F. Sometimes the Greek does not make it clear which construction is intended; to preserve the ambiguity of the Greek in these cases, 'F *phainetai* to me' is sometimes translated 'I have the appearance of F' (i.e., I have an impression of F); see *Met.* 1009b7. Sometimes (e.g., *DC* 287b23, *PA* 644a5, *Met.* 1073b15), but not always, the *phainomena* are tentative observations or beliefs.

2. Aristotle believes that both empirical INQUIRY and dialectic should begin from the appearances, *APr* 46a17–27, *PA* 639b5–10, *EN* 1145b2–7. In a dialectical inquiry these appearances are also COMMON BELIEFS, *endoxa*.

3. Aristotle does not assume that all appearances are true; but a theory must respect and account for the most reasonable ones, *Phys.* 189a16, *DC* 306a6–17, *Met.* 1073b36, 1074b6, *EN* 1145b2–7, 28.

APPETITE, *epithumia*; see DESIRE

archē: see PRINCIPLE

ARCHYTAS

A writer (1st half, 4th cent.) on mathematics and harmonics. See *Met.* 1043a21.

aretē: see VIRTUE

ARGUMENT: see REASON

ARGUMENTATION, *enthumēma*

The translation 'argumentation' is somewhat misleading, since an *enthumēma* is a single argument, not (as 'argumentation' might suggest) a series of arguments; but no English rendering is completely satisfactory. The term is derived from *enthumeisthai*, which means 'have in mind' or 'consider' generally, and sometimes refers to what we should have in mind as a result of considering something else; here 'infer' or 'conclude' is an appropriate translation, and this use of *enthumeisthai* may be the origin of Aristotle's technical term. An *enthumēma* is the sort of DEDUCTION (or approximation to it) that is appropriately used in rhetoric, while argument by example, *paradeigma*, is the rhetorical form of INDUCTION. An *enthumēma* is a 'deduction from likelihoods or signs', *APr* 70a2; cf. *APo* 71a9–11, *Rhet.* 1354a14, 1355a3–14, 1356a35–b18, 1395b23, 1402b13. The modern use of 'enthymematic' for an argument with some premises unexpressed seems to lack Aristotelian authority (though cf. *APr* 70a19–20, *Rhet.* 1395b25).

ASSUMPTION, *hupothesis*

The term (derived from *hupotithesthai*, 'lay down'; cf. Plato, *Rep.* 510b–e) refers to assumptions in general (cf. NECESSITY #4, *Pol.* 1271a41, 1317a40). Sometimes 'x is F on an assumption' is contrasted with 'x is F WITHOUT QUALIFICATION (*APo* 72b15, *Pol.* 1278a5). It is also used in a narrower sense for the PRINCIPLES of a SCIENCE, from which all the other propositions in a DEMONSTRATIVE system are derived. These are prior to all the derived propositions of the science, and cannot themselves be proved within the science, but must be grasped by UNDERSTANDING. See *APo* 72a18–20, 76b23–34, *Met.* 1005b14–16. See also CONDITIONAL.

atomon: INDIVIDUAL

ATTEND TO: see STUDY

ATTRIBUTE, AFFECTION, FEELING, *pathos*; **BE ACTED ON, BE AFFECTED, UNDERGO,** *paschein*

1. The verb *paschein* is correlative to *poiein* ('act on', 'PRODUCE'), *Catg.* 2a3–4, *GC* 329b21, *Met.* 1048a6–8. Hence what someone *paschei* is what happens to him, in contrast to what he does, *Poet.* 1451b11. (Hence *pathos* = 'suffering', *Poet.* 1452b10.)

2. In a wide sense (rendered by 'attribute', e.g., *GC* 314b17, 317b11) a *pathos* of x is something that 'happens to' x quite generally, i.e., something that is true of x. In some cases (though not always) a mere *pathos* of x is contrasted with x's essence, and so is more or less equivalent to COINCIDENT, *Top.* 145a3–12 (cf. Plato, *Euthyphro* 11a8).

3. In a narrower sense (rendered by 'affection' or 'feeling') a *pathos* is an 'affection' or 'passion', a mental state involving pleasure or pain, *EN* 1105b21, *Rhet.* 1378a19, and especially a state belonging to the nonrational parts of the SOUL, *EN* 1151a20–

24. These states are especially closely connected with ways in which the body is affected, *DA* 403a3–10, *MA* 701b22. See DESIRE. It would often be reasonable (especially in *Rhet*. ii) to translate *pathos* by 'emotion', but *pathē* extend more widely than emotions as normally conceived.

automaton: see LUCK

AXIOM, *axioma*

Axioms include the Principles of Noncontradiction and Excluded Middle discussed in *Met*. iv, and the Axiom of Equals; see *APo* 72a17, 75a41, 76a38. 76b10, 77a29, 88a36–b3, *Met*. 995b9, 1005a20, 1008a3. They are PRINCIPLES common to all the SCIENCES, in contrast to the PROPER principles of each science.

BAD: see VICIOUS

barbaros: FOREIGNER

BASE: see VICIOUS

BE, EXIST, *einai*

1. Aristotle uses the same word to indicate predication ('x is F') and existence ('x is', i.e., x exists). It is sometimes difficult to know which rendering suits a given context better (since Aristotle does not always supply the 'F', even in places where he seems to intend it); see *Catg*. 14b12, *DI* 16b15, *APo* 71a12n, 93a4, *Met*. 985b6. He does not distinguish the concept of existence from the general concept of being F, perhaps because he assumes that to be (= exist) is to be (= be predicatively) something or other.

2. Aristotle claims that being (*to on*, present participle) and beings (or things that are; *ta onta*) are SPOKEN OF IN MANY WAYS, corresponding to the categories (see PREDICATIONS). See *Top*. 103b27–39, *Met*. 1003a31-b10, 1017a22–30, 1028a10–20, 1042b25–1043a1, *EN* 1096a23–29. This raises two questions: (1) Is Aristotle speaking of predication or of existence? (2) Is he claiming that 'be' (predicative or existential) has ten different senses (see HOMONYMY) corresponding to the categories?

3. Being (the result of a process of becoming) is sometimes contrasted with (the process of) coming to be, *PA* 640a10–19, *Met*. 1041a31–33, *Pol*. 1252b29 (cf. Plato, *Rep*. 485b1–3, *Phil*. 53e4–7). See also SUBSTANCE.

4. 'Being F' (e.g., 'being a man') is used to translate *to anthrōpō(i) einai* (etc.). See ESSENCE #2.

BEAUTIFUL: see FINE

BEING$_\text{O}$; see SUBSTANCE #1

BELIEF, *doxa*

Unlike KNOWLEDGE, *doxa* (cognate with *dokein*, 'seem'; see COMMON BELIEFS) may be either true or false. It requires some rational and conceptual SUPPOSITION or judgment, and therefore is not possible for nonrational ANIMALS, *DA* 428a18–24, 434a10–11.

BELONG: see PREDICATION

BETTER KNOWN: see KNOWN

BODY, *sōma*

Aristotle uses 'body' to refer to (1) solids in the geometrical sense, *DC* 268a7, *Met.* 1020a14, 1029a13; (2) 'natural' or 'perceptible' bodies, i.e., masses of matter (including the four elements and compounds of them), *DC* 275b5, *DA* 416a28, *Met.* 1017b10, 1028b10, 1042a8; (3) the organic bodies of animals, *DA* 412a15. The difference between (2) and (3) is sometimes especially important; see MATTER, SOUL.

BRAVERY, *andreia*; **COWARDICE,** *deilia*

See *EN* iii 6–9.

CALLIPPUS

An astronomer (fl. 330), said to have collaborated with Aristotle. See *Met.* 1073b32.

CAPABLE, CAPACITY; see POTENTIALITY

CATEGORIES: see PREDICATIONS

CAUSE, REASON, EXPLANATION, *aition, aitia*

1. In *Phys.* ii 3, *GC* 335a28–336a12, *PA* 639b12, *Met.* 983a24–b6, Aristotle distinguishes the four types of *aition*: MATTER, FORM, the PRINCIPLE of MOTION (see *Phys.* 194b29n), and the FOR SOMETHING. These are standardly known as the 'four causes'—material, formal, efficient, and final. (Aristotle himself does not use the last two labels.)

2. We cite an *aition* in answer to the question 'Why?', *Phys.* 194b19; hence 'reason' and 'explanation' sometimes render *aition* and *to dihoti* (lit. 'the why', *APo* 93a17, *DA* 413a13, *EN* 1095b7), in contrast to *to hoti* ('the fact', lit. 'the that' (i.e., that so and so is the case)). Some examples (e.g., the mathematical one, *Phys.* 194b27) show that an *aition* need not be a causal explanation, but 'cause' is appropriate in most instances, and has been used in the translation.

3. In stating the *aition* Aristotle mentions different kinds of things: a substance, *Phys.* 194b20; an event, *APo* 93b36–94a2; a state, *Phys.* 194b33; a substance performing or failing to perform an action, *Phys.* 195a13, 195b5–6. In these cases the substance can be said to be 'responsible' (*aitios*) for the action; the nature of this causal responsibility will vary with the type of agent involved (see VOLUNTARY).

4. The four *aitia* are not always mutually exclusive, *Phys.* 193a28–31 (both matter and form may be efficient causes), *DA* 415b8–28 (one and the same thing may have the different explanatory roles appropriate to the different types of cause).

5. Aristotle's claims about whether one thing is the *aition* of another often rely on his distinction between intrinsic (*kath'hauto*; see IN ITS OWN RIGHT) and COINCIDENTAL *aitia*; see *Phys.* 195a32–35, 196b23–29, *Met.* 1026b37. We can truly say, e.g., that (1) Polycleitus made (is the cause of) the statue, or that (2) the baker made the statue (if Polycleitus is a baker). But both of these state a purely coincidental cause. We state the intrinsic cause only if we say that (3) the sculptor made the statue. In Aristotle's view, Polycleitus INSOFAR AS he is a sculptor produces the statue; in other words, it is Polycleitus' being a sculptor, not his being Polycleitus or his being a baker, that explains the production of the statue.

6. On *aitia* and KNOWLEDGE see *APo* 71b9–12, *Phys.* 194b17–19, *Met.* 981a24–b6, 983a25.

CHANCE: see LUCK

CHANGE: see MOTION

CHARACTER, *ēthos*

Character is a STATE formed by habituation, *ethismos*, *EN* 1103a14–26, of DESIRES, feelings (see ATTRIBUTE), PLEASURES, and pains, so that they are rightly guided by the rational part of the SOUL. A well formed state of character is a VIRTUE, 1105b25–28.

CHARONDAS

A Sicilian lawgiver (6th cent. B.C.?); *Pol.* 1252b14, 1295a21.

CHOICEWORTHY, *haireton*

The Greek term is ambiguous (as are other words ending in 'ton'; see SEPARABLE) between 'chosen', 'capable of being chosen', and 'deserving to be chosen'. ('Eligible' illustrates an ambiguity parallel to that between the last two senses of *haireton*.)

chōriston: SEPARABLE

CITY, STATE, *polis*

A typical Greek *polis* of the sort that Aristotle was familiar with had the area and population of a modern city (cf. *EN* 1170a3), but a degree of political independence more characteristic of a modern state. Hence 'city' and 'state' (in contrast to NATION) are appropriate in different contexts. For Aristotle the city is the complete COMMUNITY, the association of citizens, *politikē koinōnia*, *Pol.* 1252a1–7, 1252a37–1253a7, 1280a25–1281a4. Aristotle often relies on the verbal connections between *polis*, *politikē* (see POLITICAL SCIENCE), and *politēs* (citizen).

CIVIL CONFLICT, *stasis*

Greek cities were often subject to party strife carried on by legal and illegal means, not necessarily going as far as open civil war. See *Pol.* 1262b28, 1296a8, 1301a37.

CIVILIZED: see GENEROUS

CLOAK, *himation*

Aristotle uses this term simply as a dummy (where we might use 'x'), e.g., *Met.* 1029b27, 1045a26. Contrast the example at *DI* 19a12 and elsewhere.

COINCIDENT, *sumbebēkos*

1. *Sumbebēkos* is derived from *sumbainein*, 'come about together', which often just means 'happen' or 'turn out'; and hence it has a wide range of uses. This makes 'accident' a misleading translation, since *sumbebēkota* include many things that are not, in the ordinary sense, accidents. 'Coincidence' is also too narrow, but 'coincide' is fairly close to the Greek term (to say 'your view coincides with mine' does not imply that our agreement is an accident or a coincidence).

2. Aristotle recognizes two sorts of coincidents: (1) G is a coincident of F if (a) G belongs to F IN ITS OWN RIGHT, but (b) G is not the ESSENCE of F; e.g., a triangle has two right angles in its own right, but this is not the essence of a triangle (since a triangle is essentially a three-sided plane figure, from which it follows that a triangle has two right angles), *Met.* 1025a30–34 (cf. *DA* 402b18, *Rhet.* 1355b29). (2) G is a coincident of F if (a) G belongs to F, but (b) F is not essentially G (or: if F is not necessarily G; for different statements of clause (b) see *Met.* 1025a14–16, *Top.* 102b4–9). In this case F's being G does not follow from the essence of F.

3. Coincidents of type (1) are especially important in the theory of DEMONSTRA-TION. For demonstration begins with a DEFINITION of F, stating the essence of F, and proceeds to demonstrate the coincidents of F in its own right, *APo* 75a42–b2, *DA* 402b16–28, *Met.* 995b20.

4. When Aristotle mentions coincidents without further specification, he usually has (2) in mind; see *APo* 83a10, *Phys.* 188a34, *Met.* 1017a7–13, 1031b22–28, *Pol.* 1279b36. In contrast to (1), coincidents of type (2) are not NECESSARY or USUAL, but matters of chance (see LUCK; *Phys.* 196b24, 198b23, *Met.* 1025a14), and so they are not open to demonstration, *APo* 75a18–22, *Met.* 1027a19–26.

5. On coincidental v. intrinsic causes see CAUSE.

COLUMN, *sustoichia*

Aristotle speaks of the Pythagorean columns of opposites (e.g., *Met.* 986a23–27), and also recognizes pairs of positive and negative properties in a broader sense (not confined to the Pythagorean list); see *Phys.* 201b25, *GC* 319a15, *Met.* 1004b27, 1046b14, 1072a31. The positive properties are PRIOR, because the negative properties have to be understood by contrast with the positive.

COME TO BE, *gignesthai*; COMING TO BE, *genesis*

1. Aristotle distinguishes unqualified (see WITHOUT QUALIFICATION) from qualified coming to be, *Phys.* 190a31–33. (a) In unqualified coming to be a SUBSTANCE did not exist at time t1, but exists at t2; hence we can say 'the tree came to be (= came into being)'. (b) In qualified coming to be one and the same substance remains in existence and changes in one of its nonessential properties; cf. *Catg.* 4a10–13. Hence from 'The tree came to be taller (= became taller)' we cannot infer 'The tree came to be (= came into being)'. Cf. *GC* 318a25–319a22. Analogous distinctions apply to perishing, *phthora*.

2. On the relation between coming to be and BEING see *PA* 640a10–19. On MATTER, FORM, and coming to be see *Met.* 1033b16–1034a5, 1041a26–b32.

3. Coming to be distinguishes the material, sublunary world from the heavens; and in the sublunary world coming to be is always going on, *GC* 338a4–b19, *Met.* 1072a9–25.

4. Sometimes Aristotle distinguishes 'F comes to be' from 'there is a coming to be of F'. In some cases we can say that F exists at time t1 and no longer exists at t2, even though it is not F itself, but something else G to which F belongs, that has really undergone the process of destruction. (We might say that when Jane has a child, Jane's brother John becomes an uncle, but John himself does not go through a process of becoming an uncle.) See *Phys.* 258b18–20, *Met.* 1027a29–30, 1033b6, 1039b20–27.

COMMON BELIEFS, *endoxa*

These are the starting point of DIALECTIC, *Top.* 100a29–30, 104a8–20, 105b30–31, *Rhet.* 1356b34. They are one type of APPEARANCES, *EN* 1145b3, 20, 28. Aristotle often reports the *endoxa* by using 'seems' (*dokei*, cognate with *doxa*, 'belief'), e.g., *Phys.* 189a31–32, *EN* 1097b8 (cf. 'appear', 1097a25). In these contexts 'seems' does not necessarily indicate tentativeness or hesitation, but simply the fact that the claim is a starting point for the construction of a theory (or sometimes a belief against which a theory can be tested) rather than a conclusion of a theoretical argument.

COMMUNITY, *koinōnia*

Koinōnia is cognate with *koinon*, 'common'. Aristotle believes that a *koinōnia* is created by every type of FRIENDSHIP. Hence the term includes both loose alliances and relatively casual relationships, close-knit communities and societies. 'Association' is sometimes a more natural rendering than 'community' would be, since a *koinōnia* may be looser and more temporary than 'community' would suggest, *EN* 1161b11, 1170b11, *Pol.* 1252b12–34. However, 'community' is suitable (since it retains the connection with 'common' suggested by the Greek terms), especially with reference to the stable and comprehensive political *koinōnia*, the CITY. Sometimes (see e.g., *Pol.* iii 9, esp. 1280b15 ff) Aristotle's argument is easier to understand if the great variety of types of *koinōnia* is kept in mind.

COMPLETE, *teleion*

Teleion is cognate with *telos*, 'end' (see FOR SOMETHING). It applies to something that has reached its *telos*, and hence to a mature, adult organism, *Met.* 1072b24. 'Final' and 'perfect' are other possible translations. Aristotle explains completeness in *Met.* v 16. He attributes it to HAPPINESS, *EN* 1097a25–b21, 1098a18, 1101a13, and to the CITY, *Pol.* 1252b27–30 (cf. 1281a1). MOTION is an incomplete rather than complete ACTUALITY, *Phys.* 201b31. On a 'complete deduction' see DEDUCTION.

COMPOUND; see FORM

COMPREHEND, *sunienai*

Sunienai is used for understanding in a broad sense, as opposed to the more specialized type of UNDERSTANDING involved in *nous*. See *APo* 71a13, *EN* vi 10.

CONDITIONAL, *ex hupotheseōs*

Lit. 'on an assumption'. See NECESSITY #4, KNOW #5.

CONTENTIOUS, *eristikon*

Contentious argument involves 'talking for victory' without regard to the truth of one's premises or the legitimacy of one's arguments (see Plato's *Euthydemus*). See *Top.* 100b23, 165b7, *Pol.* 1261b30.

CONTINENT: see INCONTINENCE

CONTRARY, *enantion*: see OPPOSITE

CONTROLLING, FULL, STRICT, AUTHORITATIVE, OVERRIDING, IMPORTANT, *kurion*

1. To be *kurion* of x is to be in control of x, or to have authority over x, or both. See *GC* 335b34, *PA* 640b28 ('important'), *EN* 1113b32, 1114a32; for 'authoritative'

see *Met*. 981b11, 1010b13. For 'overriding' see *Met*. 1003b16, 1048a12. The two aspects are often connected in political contexts, where 'sovereign' would often be an appropriate translation. See *Pol*. 1252a5, 1275a28 1281a11, 40, 1281b23, 1282a25.

2. The *kurion* use or application of a word controls its other uses, which are derived from it; here 'fully', or 'strictly', or 'full sense' is used. See *Catg*. 2a11, *Phys*. 191b7, *GC* 314a10, 317a33, *DA* 412b9, 418a3, 24, *EN* 1144b4.

CONVENTION: see LAW

CONVICTION, CONVINCING ARGUMENT, *pistis*

1. *Pistis* is the source of BELIEF (which may fall short of KNOWLEDGE, *DC* 270b13), and is peculiar to rational beings, *DA* 428a19–24. See also *Top*. 100b2, 103b3, *DA* 402a11.

2. Hence the term is also applied to arguments resulting in rational conviction. Sometimes it is applied especially to arguments that fall short of DEMONSTRATION. See *APo* 72a25, *Rhet*. 1354a13, b21, 1355a3–5 (cf. 1355b35).

CRAFT, CRAFT-KNOWLEDGE, *technē*

1. A craft is a rational discipline, distinct from a theoretical science (see KNOW) insofar as (1) it aims at PRODUCTION, and (2) it does not provide DEMONSTRATIONS. See *APo* 100a9, *Met*. 980b25–981a30, 1025b18–28, 1070a7, *EN* 1140b2, 34. For a more general sense, applying to any rational and systematic treatment of a subject, see *Pol*. 1252a22.

2. Craft imitates NATURE, *Phys*. 194a21, 199a8–20 (see FORM #7), especially in being FOR SOMETHING. Aristotle often uses examples of crafts to explain points about matter and form in natural organisms; but he is careful to distinguish the two cases. See *DA* 412b10–17, *Met*. 1032a27–b14.

3. Aristotle usually speaks as though the products of crafts (statues, beds etc.) are SUBSTANCES, e.g., *Phys*. 190b6; but sometimes he expresses doubts, *Met*. 1041b28–30, 1043b21–23.

4. Since craft involves inquiry and deliberation, Aristotle sometimes refers to it to illustrate the operations of VIRTUE and INTELLIGENCE. But he also points out a basic difference, insofar as craft is concerned with PRODUCTION and intelligence with ACTION. See *EN* 1104a5–11, 1112a34–b31, 1141b14–22. Moreover, a craft is a rational POTENTIALITY that can be used in different ways, whereas a virtue requires the right use of one's capacities and cannot be used well or badly. See *Top*. 101b6, *Met*. 1046b4–22, 1048a8–11, *EN* 1106a4–10, 1140b21–25, *Rhet*. 1355b2–7.

CRATYLUS

A contemporary of Socrates, and an extreme Heracleitean. See Plato, *Cratylus* 402a, 439b–440a, *Met*. 987a32, 1010a12.

DECENT, *epieikēs*

The term is cognate with *eikos*, 'likely', and means 'reasonable, plausible'. Aristotle uses it interchangeably with 'GOOD' in moral contexts, *EN* 1137a15, *Pol*. 1308b27, *Rhet*. 1356a6. The term often has social ('the better classes') as well as moral implications, *Pol.* 1281a12. It is used in a more specialized sense for the decency (or 'equity') that corrects the rigors of the written LAW, *EN* v 10, *Rhet.* 1374a18–b22.

DECISION, *prohairesis*

A decision results from wish (i.e., rational DESIRE) for some end, focussed by DELIBERATION about what promotes the end; the result is a rational choice about what to do here and now to achieve the end. See *Phys.* 196b18, 197b8, *EN* iii 2–3, 1139a22–26. The decision to do the virtuous action for its own sake is essential to VIRTUE; see 1105a32, 1144a19.

DEDUCTION, INFERENCE, *sullogismos*

1. The English derivative 'syllogism' is too narrow to capture the meaning of '*sullogismos*', which applies to inference more generally, and specifically to valid deductive inference proceeding from more general principles rather than from particular cases (in contrast to INDUCTION). See *APr* 24b18–20, *APo* 71b23, *Top.* 100a25–27, 105a12–19, *EN* 1144a31, 1149a33, *Rhet.* 1356b13–18, ARGUMENTATION.

2. A 'syllogism' in the technical sense is a valid deductive argument with one of the formal structures that Aristotle describes in the *APr*; in these arguments the conclusion follows necessarily from the premises, *APr* 24b18–20 (this is necessitas consequentiae; see NECESSITY #7). Aristotle presents a syllogism in this form: A belongs to (or 'is predicated of' or 'follows') every B; B belongs to every C; therefore A belongs to every C. He names the terms according to the order of their occurrence; hence A is the first, B the middle, C the last, and A and C are the extremes. (Hence A is also called the 'major extreme' term, since it is the extreme term occurring in the major premiss; and analogously C is the 'minor extreme' term. See *APr* 26a21.) The formulation standard in post-Aristotelian syllogistic is: All B is A; all C is B; therefore all C is A. The translation, however, keeps Aristotle's formulation, which often makes his claims easier to grasp. On middle terms see also *APo* 75a2, 75b11, 93a7. The different types of syllogism are its FIGURES, *APr* 26a13.

3. A COMPLETE deduction (often called a 'perfect syllogism') is one that has all the elements of a valid inference present and needs nothing to be supplied or reformulated. See *APr* 24b22, 25b35, 27a16, 28a3, 29a30.

4. The term 'practical syllogism' (cf. *EN* 1144a31) is sometimes used (by modern students, not by Aristotle, and not in this translation) for the kind of inference that Aristotle describes in *DA* 434a16–21, *MA* 7, *Met.* 1032b6–9, *EN* 1147a25. Though this lacks the features of a proper deduction (e.g., some of its premisses mention particulars), Aristotle applies some of his technical syllogistic terminology to it.

DEFINE, DETERMINE, DISTINGUISH, *dihorizein*

Dihorizein (cognate with *horismos*; see DEFINITION) is used both for (a) marking a distinction between different species of a genus or different senses or different interpretations of a statement, *GC* 317b14, 318b1, 323a16, *EN* 1130b8; and for (b) finding a solution to puzzles or deciding between different solutions, *Phys.* 196a10, 200b15, *GC* 315b2, *Met.* 1029a1, 1037a14.

DEFINE, *horizein*; **DEFINITION**, *horismos*; see also FORMULA

1. The definition of F can replace the name 'F' while preserving truth, by saying what F is, and thereby stating the ESSENCE of F, *Top*. 101b38–102a5, 141a35.

2. A 'nominal definition' (not an Aristotelian term) says what we take a name to SIGNIFY (e.g., 'thunder is a noise in the clouds') when we begin an inquiry, but does not state the essence. A 'real definition' states the essence. See *APo* ii 10, *DA* 413a13–20.

3. DEMONSTRATIONS begin with a definition of the subject whose intrinsic COINCI-DENTS are demonstrated, *APo* 72a18–24, 74b5–12, 75a28–b2.

4. The correct statement of a definition should involve terms that are better KNOWN by nature, not terms that are merely better known to us, *Top*. 141a26–b16.

5. PARTICULARS do not have definitions (or at least do not have definitions of the primary sort), *Met*. 1039b27–1040a7.

6. Aristotle also speaks of the *horismos* when he means (as we would be inclined to put it) what the definition is of, i.e., the essence. He speaks of the *logos* in the same way; see *Phys*. 200a35, REASON.

7. In artifacts and natural organisms definitions involve reference to FORM and FUNCTION, *Metr*. 390a20, *DA* 412a10–20, *PA* 640b17–641a6, *Met*. 1035b14, 1036b28, *Pol*. 1253a23.

8. Aristotle denies that one definition invariably corresponds to one name. See HOMONYMY. On definitions of serially ordered items see *DA* 414b20–33, *EN* 1096a17–23, *Pol*. 1275b34.

DELIBERATION, *bouleusis*; see DECISION

DEMOCRACY, *dēmokratia*; see PEOPLE

DEMOCRITUS

Aristotle often mentions Democritus (c. 460–c. 360?) together with Leucippus (whom he seems to regard as the founder of Atomism, *GC* 325a23–29). He regards Atomism as the most sophisticated and detailed rival to his own account of the nature of the physical world and its explanatory principles.

1. The Atomists identify SUBSTANCE with MATTER, and in particular with physically indivisible (*atoma*; see INDIVIDUAL) bodies, *Phys*. 184b21, *DC* 275b29–276a1, *GC* 314a12, 21, 315a34–b11, 316a13, *Met*. 985b4–20, 1039a7–11.

2. They do not recognize formal and FINAL CAUSES, *Phys*. 194a21–22, *DA* 406b15–25, *PA* 640b29–641a6, 642a25–28, *GA* 788b9–12, 789b2–15, *Met*. 1042b11–13, 1078b19–21. Hence they recognize only material NECESSITY in nature.

3. Democritus raises skeptical doubts about the veracity of PERCEPTION, *Met*. 1009b11–17 (cf. *GC* 315b9–10).

4. The Atomists recognize no beginning of MOTION or TIME, *Phys*. 251b15–17, 252a32–b1, *GA* 742b17–23.

DEMONSTRATION, *apodeixis*

Scientific KNOWLEDGE has to be expressed in a demonstration—the particular sort of DEDUCTION from ASSUMPTIONS, with appropriately NECESSARY, explanatory, and better known premisses, that is described in *APo* 71b16–25. See also *APo* 72b5–73a6, 76a37-b22, i 30, 93a1–15, b15–20, 100b9–14, *DA* 402b25, *Met.* 1006a6–18, 1039b27–1040a5. See also COINCIDENT #3.

DESIRE, *orexis*

Aristotle recognizes three types of desire (cf. Plato, *Rep.* 435ff): (1) Rational desire or wish, *boulēsis*, directed at some end regarded as GOOD, *Met.* 1072a28, *EN* 1111b26, 1113a15. (2) Appetite, *epithumia*, nonrational desire directed at an object regarded as PLEASANT, 1103b18, 1111a31. (3) Emotion, *thumos* (which might also be rendered by 'spirit'), connected especially with shame, honor, and anger, 1111b18, 1116b23, 1149a25. The second and third types of desire are feelings, *pathē* (see ATTRIBUTE). For this tripartite division see *DA* 414b2, 432b4–7, *EN* 1111a27, b10–30, *Pol.* 1334b22–28, *Rhet.* 1368b37–1369a7.

DETERMINE; see DEFINE

DIALECTIC, *dialektikē*

Dialektikē (an adjective with *technē* or *methodos* understood; cf. POLITICAL SCIENCE) is cognate with *dialegesthai*, 'discuss', and *dialogos*, 'dialogue' (at *APo* 78a12 *dialogos* is used for dialectical discussions in contrast to strictly mathematical arguments). Dialectic is the method Aristotle ascribes to SOCRATES in Plato's dialogues, *Met.* 1078b17–25. He speaks as though Socrates especially practiced the aspect of dialectic that Aristotle calls 'testing', *peirastikē*, *Top.* 159a25–37, 169b24, 171b8, 183b1, *Met.* 1004b25 (dialecticians can test someone's claim to knowledge even though they lack that knowledge themselves). The *Topics* is devoted to a description of dialectical methods and arguments; see 100a18–30, 101a25–b4, 159a25–37, 165a38–b11. Aristotle practices dialectic constructively in his major philosophical works; see *Phys.* 184a16–b14, *Met.* 1004b17–26, *EN* 1145b2–7.
The main stages of a constructive dialectical argument (cf. *EN* 1145b2–7) are: (1) We set out the APPEARANCES, i.e., the COMMON BELIEFS (including the views of Aristotle's predecessors). (2) Since common beliefs tend to result in puzzles, *aporiai* (which arise from 'the equality of contrary reasonings', *Top.* 145b17), an important part of dialectic consists of 'expounding the puzzles' (*diaporein*) on a given question, *Phys.* 191b30–34, 217b29–218a31, *GC* 321b11, *Met.* iii, esp. 995a24–b7, *EN* vii 2, esp. 1145b2–7, *Pol.* iii 10–11. (3) We look for a solution that retains the most important appearances, *GC* 321b10–16. (4) We show how the solution resolves the puzzles, *Phys.* 211a6–11, *EN* 1154b22–25. *Phys.* iv 10–14 displays these stages quite clearly.

DIFFERENTIA, *diaphora*

A differentia divides a GENUS into its SPECIES, *Catg.* 3a21–28, *Top.* 122b12–24, 128a20–37, 145a3–12, *GC* 314b18, *Met.* 1020a33–b1, 1038a18–21. Aristotle mainly refers to differentiae not with abstract nouns (e.g., 'footedness') but with adjectives agreeing in gender with the (often unexpressed) genus-term (e.g., he takes 'Man is biped' to abbreviate 'Man is [a] biped [sort of] animal'). See *Catg.* 3a23, 14b33–15a7.

dihorizein: see DETERMINE

DISCRIMINATE, JUDGE, *krinein*

Aristotle recognizes *krinein* as one of the functions of the senses (see PERCEPTION), *DA* 418a14, 424a5, 425b21, 427a20, 428a3. *Krinein* does not always require reasoning or intellectual awareness, and so 'discriminate' is often a more suitable rendering than 'judge' (cf. *Phys.* 219b4). Sometimes, however, 'judge' and 'judgment' are suitable (e.g., *Met.* 995b4, 1009b2), and they are needed in specifically legal contexts (see also JURYMAN).

DISHONORED: see HONOR

DISTINCTIVE, PROPER, PRIVATE, *idion*

1. *Idion* refers to what is private as opposed to what is public (e.g., private as opposed to public property (*Pol.* 1269a26) or a private citizen as opposed to a public official). Hence 'one's own' is used at *Pol.* 1263a41.

2. Aristotle uses *idion* as a technical term (Latin 'proprium') for a nonESSENTIAL but necessary property of F, belonging to all and only Fs, *Catg.* 3a21, 4a10, *Top.* 102a18–30 (discussed fully in *Top.* v). He also uses the term less strictly, so that it includes essential properties, *APo* 73a7, 75b18, 76a17, *DA* 402a9, *Met.* 1004b11, *EN* 1097b34.

3. *Idion* is rendered by 'proper' where Aristotle uses it for the object that is peculiar to each sense (e.g., color for sight, sound for hearing, and so on), *DA* 418a10.

4. On the distinctive PRINCIPLES of each science, in contrast to common principles (the AXIOMS), see PROPER.

DISTINGUISH; see DEFINE

dunamis, dunaton: see POTENTIALITY

EDUCATION, *paideia*

On general education and education in a particular discipline see *Top.* 183b37, 184a3, *PA* 639a1–15, *Met.* 1006a6, 1043b24, *EN* 1094b22–1095a2, *Pol.* 1282a4. On moral education see *EN* 1102a5–10, 1104b11–13, 1130b25, 1180a1, *Pol.* 1280a40–b8, 1310a12–36, 1334b16–17. See also CHARACTER.

eidos: see FORM

ELEMENT, LETTER, *stoicheion*

The term refers originally to a letter of the alphabet (an element of a syllable). Aristotle also uses it to refer to elements (e.g., the four primary BODIES) of other sorts of compound; *GC* 314a15, *Met.* 985b15n, 992b18, 1034b26, 1035a14, 1041b11–33, 1086b20; the original use of *stoicheion* naturally suggests the comparison between elements and letters to him.

EMOTION, *thumos*; see DESIRE

EMPEDOCLES

Aristotle often cites and discusses Empedocles (c. 495–35; see *Met.* 984a11), especially on these points:

1. Empedocles believes in four 'roots' or 'ELEMENTS', and two forces, Love and

Strife, explaining their interaction. Aristotle tends to see a partial anticipation of his own views on formal and FINAL CAUSES. See *Phys.* 187a22–26, 188a17–18, 194a20, 250b26–251a5, 252a7, 20, *GC* 314a11–315a25, ii 6–7, *DA* 408a19–23, *Met.* 984a8–11, 985a21–b3, 988a27, 989a18–30, 993a17–24, 1072a6, 1075b1–7.

2. Aristotle criticizes, but also develops, Empedocles' biological speculations, *Phys.* 198b31–32, *DA* 415b28–416a9, *PA* 640a19–25, 642a18–24, *GA* 722b6–30, 731a4–9.

3. Empedocles' epistemology and theory of perception rely on the assumption that like is known by like. Aristotle thinks this assumption is false, but points toward the truth. See *DA* 404b11–15, 409b29–410a11, 410b4, 418b20–23, 422a21–25, *PN* 437b23–438a5, *Met.* 1009b15–20.

4. On Empedocles' cosmological poems see *EN* 1147a20, b12, *Rhet.* 1373b14, *Poet.* 1447b18.

EMULATION, *zēlos*: see SPITE

END, *telos*: see FOR SOMETHING

endoxa: COMMON BELIEFS

energeia: ACTUALITY

entelecheia: ACTUALITY

enthumēma: ARGUMENTATION

ENVY, *phthonos*: see SPITE

epagōgē: INDUCTION

EPIMENIDES
A Cretan religious teacher (6th cent. B.C.?); *Pol.* 1252b14.

epistēmē, epistasthai: see KNOW

epithumia; see DESIRE

EQUAL, FAIR, *isos*
The term may be used to mean either (a) neither more nor less than a given quantity, or (b) neither more nor less than the right quantity. When Aristotle describes JUSTICE as a sort of equality (*EN* 1129a33, 1131b31, *Pol.* 1280a11–25), he normally has (b) in mind, and in these cases 'fair' is often the better rendering; see *Pol.* 1301b28.

ergon: see FUNCTION

ESSENCE
1. To state the essence of F is to answer the question 'What is F?', and to state the (real) DEFINITION of F.

2. Aristotle uses different phrases to refer to the essence: (a) 'Being F' (*to einai F*, also referring more generally to the definition or concept of F). He often says 'the F and the G are the same, but their being (or form, or account) is not the same', *Phys.* 190a17, 191a1, 201a29–b3, 202a18–21, 219a20, *GC* 319b4, *DA* 424a25,

426a16, 429b10, *Met*. 1003b24, 1006a32, 1029b14, *EN* 1102a30, 1130a12–13. See ONE. (b) 'What F is' (*ti esti F*) or in general 'the what-it-is' (*to ti esti*). (c) 'What it is to be F' (*to ti ēn F einai*). This phrase probably means 'What it is for F to be F', indicating that one wants to know what F is INSOFAR AS it is F (e.g., one wants to know that the man is qua man, not qua musician). See *Top*. 101b38, *Met*. 1029b14n, 1030a30–31. Aristotle uses *to einai F* equivalently with *to ti ēn einai F*, except that he seems to regard the first phrase as easier to understand, and therefore useful for explaining the second phrase. (d) 'F is essentially G' renders 'F is *hoper* G' (i.e., 'F is precisely what is G', especially where G is the GENUS of F); *APo* 83a7, *Top*. 141b35 (translated 'essence'), *Met*. 1006b13, 1030a3, 5.

3. An essential property of F is part of what F is IN ITS OWN RIGHT, not COINCIDEN-TALLY. The essential property is the starting point for a DEMONSTRATION, because it is the one that explains why the subject has the coincidents that it has in its own right, *APo* 75a42–b2.

4. This connection between essence and explanation (see CAUSE) shows why Aristotle claims that the FORM of a natural organism is its essence, *Met*. 1032b1–2, 1041a25–32.

5. SUBSTANCES have essences in the primary way, *Met*. 1028a34–b2, 1030a2–b13 (cf. *Top*. 103b22, 27).

ESSENCE$_O$; see SUBSTANCE #2

eudaimonia; see HAPPINESS

EUDOXUS
Eudoxus was a leading mathematician, astronomer, and philosopher contemporary with Aristotle (c. 390–c. 340). See *Met*. 991b17, 1073b17. On his views about PLEASURE and the GOOD see *EN* 1101b27, 1172b9.

eunomia: see GOOD GOVERNMENT

EURIPIDES
Athenian tragic dramatist (c. 485–c. 406), a younger contemporary of SOPHOCLES.

EVERLASTING: see ALWAYS

EVIDENT, *phaneron, phainesthai*
Both empirical and dialectical inquiry should start from the APPEARANCES that seem clearest and least open to dispute. We do not necessarily understand at the start, however, why they are clear and reliable; we discover that as a result of inquiry that makes our beliefs more explicit and PERSPICUOUS. See *Pol*. 1254b6, 34. 'Evident' is also used to translate *phainesthai* in its veridical sense, *APr* 24b24; see APPEARANCES #1.

EXACT, *akribēs*
A statement is exact insofar as it needs nothing added or qualified (cf. WITHOUT QUALIFICATION) in order to tell the whole truth. This conception of exactness is used in two different types of contrast:

1. The statement (a) 'The angles in a triangle add up to 180 degrees' is more exact

than (b) 'Human beings live for under 100 years'. While (a) is a generalization with no exceptions, (b) is USUALLY true, but has exceptions. Aristotle has this contrast in mind when he contrasts the degrees of exactness found in different disciplines, *APo* 87a31–37, 100b8–9, *DC* 306a27, *Met.* 982a13, 25, *EN* 1094b13, 1141a16.

2. On the other hand, the statement (c) 'You should keep your promise unless you will save someone's life by breaking it' is more exact than (d) 'You should keep your promises'. While (d) is only roughly true, (c) spells out more of the circumstances that qualify the truth of (d). Aristotle has this contrast in mind when he contrasts the more exact with the more general statement, *APr* 46a28–30, *Met.* 1030a16, or an outline with an exact account, *Top.* 101a21, *Met.* 1029a7, *EN* 1098a20–33.

EXAMPLE, *paradeigma*: see ARGUMENTATION

EXCELLENCE: see VIRTUE

EXCELLENT, *spoudaios*

In ethical contexts *spoudaios* (lit. 'serious', hence worth taking seriously) is equivalent to GOOD (as a property of persons); see *EN* 1177a1–6.

EXIST: see BE

EXPERIENCE, EMPIRICAL TECHNIQUE, *empeiria*

Empeiria is the product of PERCEPTION and memory, and a necessary, though insufficient, condition for the KNOWLEDGE that is characteristic of both CRAFTS and theoretical sciences, *APr* 46a18, *APo* 100a5, *Met.* 980b25–981a30, *EN* 1143b14, *Pol.* 1282a1.

EXPLANATION: see CAUSE

FAIR: see EQUAL

FEELING: see ATTRIBUTE

FIGURE, *schēma*

In many cases, something's *schēma* is its shape, *PA* 640b29, 34, 641a20, *Met.* 985b16, 1042b15; hence different geometrical figures are called *schēmata*, *DA* 414b21. *Schēma* also has two extended uses: (1) It is used for the 'figures' (i.e., different forms) of the syllogism (see DEDUCTION), *APr* 26a13. (2) It is sometimes used for the FORM, *PA* 640b27, 641a8, *Met.* 1029a4. See esp. FORM #5.

FINAL CAUSE: see FOR SOMETHING

FINE, BEAUTIFUL, *kalos*

The term is applied generally to whatever deserves admiration, and so includes aesthetic beauty (e.g., *EN* 1099b3). In moral contexts it is used for what is praiseworthy and admirable, 1104b31, 1162b35, *Rhet.* 1366a33; hence the virtuous person is expected to choose fine action for its own sake, 1115b12, 1116a28, 1120a12, 23. Its opposite is *aischros* (ugly, shameful, disgraceful).

FIRST PHILOSOPHY: see PHILOSOPHY

FOR SOMETHING, WHAT SOMETHING IS FOR, FINAL CAUSE, *heneka tou, hou heneka*

1. Aristotle uses 'for something' (*heneka tou*) for a goal-directed process. He uses 'what something is for' (or 'that for the sake of which' (*to hou heneka*)) for the goal or end (*telos*) to which the process is directed, *Phys.* 194a35, *Met.* 1072b2. 'Final cause' (from Latin 'finis', 'end') is a convenient technical term. Aristotle believes that the final cause is found in natural processes as well as in the products of CRAFT, *Phys.* ii 8, *GC* 336b27–28, *DA* 415b28–416a18, *PA* 639b12–21, 640a12–b5. Since he contrasts final causation with mere LUCK or chance, *Phys.* 197b11–22, he must believe that in final causation, the end, *telos* (hence 'teleology'), contributes causally to the result. If, e.g., the result of my idly chipping at a piece of rock is a shape that looks very like Pericles, it does not follow that I was chipping at the rock in order to make a likeness of Pericles; if I was doing it in order to make the likeness, my goal of making the likeness must have played some causal role in the production of that result.

2. Different kinds of ends are relevant to production by crafts (and nonproductive intentional ACTION) and to natural processes. (a) In production the end that plays a causal role is the result aimed at by a designer or producer (e.g., the designer's intention to produce something suitable for cutting explains the production of a knife with a sharp edge; hence it has a sharp edge in order to cut). (b) In natural processes there is (in Aristotle's view) no intention or design (*Phys.* 199a20–30). Nonetheless some processes in natural organisms happen for the sake of a beneficial result to the organisms. This is true in cases where the fact that the process benefits the organism contributes to the causal explanation of why the process happens. Certain kinds of animals, for instance, have sharp teeth for the sake of their survival; this is true because the fact that sharp teeth contribute to the survival of those animals explains why the animals have sharp teeth. On final causes in nature see *Phys.* 198b23–199a8 and notes.

3. In production and in natural processes, final causation requires material causation too. In relation to the end (*telos*) the material processes are conditionally NECESSARY.

4. In nature many of the laws about final causation hold only USUALLY.

5. Sometimes Aristotle remarks that 'what something is for' may refer either to the goal or to the beneficiary of an action. If I want to give you a present, your getting the present is what the action is for, since it is the goal, but you are also what it is for, since you are the beneficiary. See *Phys.* 194a35, *DA* 415b2, 20, *Met.* 1072b2.

FORCE, *bia*

Forced motion is necessitated by something contrary to a subject's NATURE or internal principle (i.e., DESIRE) and caused by something external to the subject; *Phys.* 254b13, 255a3, *Met.* 1015a26–b3, 1046a35, 1072b12, *EN* 1110a1–4, *EE* 1224a15–23, *Pol.* 1253b20. See VOLUNTARY.

FOREIGNER, *barbaros*

A *barbaros* is literally someone who does not speak Greek (and so the sounds he makes sound like 'bar-bar'). Hence it normally has the sense of 'foreigner'. Unlike the English 'barbarian', it does not suggest anything primitive or crude or uncivilized (since it includes, e.g., the Egyptians and Persians); but it certainly often suggests inferiority of nature and character. See *EN* 1145a30, *Pol.* 1252b5, 1329a26, *Rhet.* 1361a36.

FORM, SPECIES, SORT, *eidos*

1. In the most general sense, something's *eidos* is its character, sort, or type. Aristotle sometimes uses the term more narrowly, so that the *eidos* is what the MATTER acquires in COMING TO BE, (when, e.g., the bronze is made into a statue, or the wood composes a tree); see *Phys.* i 7. Here the form is PREDICATED of the matter, and is the formal CAUSE.

2. Aristotle argues that the form, rather than the matter or the compound of form and matter, is the primary sort of SUBSTANCE, *Met.* 1029a5–7. Form is a THIS, *Met.* 1042a29, 1049a35. It is the ACTUALITY that realizes the POTENTIALITY of the matter, *DA* 412a10, *Met.* 1038b6, 1042b10. It is also the primary subject of growth; we need to refer to the form to explain why a process counts as growth in the organism, rather than mere quantitative increase, *GC* 321b22–322a4, 322a28–33.

3. The form of F is what is defined in the DEFINITION or account of F, stating the ESSENCE of F, *Met.* 1032b1–2, 1035a7–9, 1035b33–1036a2, 1037a21–25. Hence 'account', *logos*, is often used interchangeably with 'form'. In such cases 'form₁' is sometimes used to translate *logos*, where 'account' would be misleading (see also REASON #5).

4. The relation between the form, the matter, and the definition of things that are compounds of matter and form is not always clear; it is discussed at length in *Met.* vii 10–11. Sometimes Aristotle seems to assume that the form itself includes matter, *DC* 278a9, 14, *DA* 412b7–8. This matter is presumably the 'proximate' matter whose existence depends on the existence of the form (see MATTER #5).

5. In some cases (e.g., when a block of wood is made into a statue) the form is closely connected with the shape acquired by the matter. And so Aristotle readily uses *morphē* (lit. 'shape') to refer to the form, e.g., *Phys.* 190b15n, 30, 192a13, 193a30n. But since *morphē* is also applied to cases where functional properties rather than mere physical shape are intended, 'shape' would often be a misleading rendering; in these cases 'form' is used (marked as 'form_m' (e.g., at *GC* 335b35, *PA* 640b30) where it seems important to indicate an occurrence of *morphē*). Aristotle also uses '*morphē* and *eidos*' as a phrase referring to the form, with no obvious difference of meaning between the two terms, e.g., *GC* 335b6. See also FIGURE.

6. Nonsensible substances are form without matter, *Met.* 1037a10–16, 1042a31.

7. In reproduction of animals form is transmitted by the male parent, *Phys.* 192a13, *GA* 727b31–33, 729a9–11, 28–33. The role of form is indicated by the general rule that 'a man comes to be from a man', *Phys.* 193b8, 198a26, *Met.* 1033b32. Production by CRAFTS begins from form without matter and results in form in matter, *DA* 424a17–19, *PA* 640a32, *Met.* 1032a30–b14.

8. Aristotle uses '*eidos*' for the species (e.g., man, horse), in contrast to both the PARTICULARS (e.g., this man) and the GENUS (e.g., animal). In these contexts it is translated 'species', e.g., *Catg.* 2a14. When the contrast between *eidos* and

matter is involved, 'form' is used. Sometimes, however, it is difficult to choose between the two renderings, e.g., at *Met.* 1034a5–8. It is especially difficult to be sure whether Aristotle intends to distinguish the species from the species form (see *Met.* 1033b31n).

9. These different uses of '*eidos*' make it difficult to decide (i) what Aristotle means by identifying substance with form; (ii) whether he thinks a substantial form (i.e., the sort of form that is a substance) is also a PARTICULAR; (iii) what he means by claiming that a substantial form is a THIS. Some of the most relevant and controversial passages are *Met.* 1028a27, 1029a1–7, 26–33, 1032a4–11, 1032b1–2, 1034a5–8, 1035a1–9, 1036b21–1037a2, 1037a21–b7, 1038b1–16, 1038b34–1039a2, 1040b21–27, 1042a25–b11, 1043a29–b4, 1045b17–23, 1049a27–36, xiii 4, *DA* 412a1–22, b6–9. Two possible answers are these: (a) Aristotle identifies primary substance with a particular form, one that is peculiar to each particular substance (hence in living organisms it will be an individual SOUL; on artifacts as substances see CRAFT #3). The particular form is a this, in contrast to a species form (e.g., man, horse) which is a UNIVERSAL. (b) He identifies primary substance with the species form (different views have been taken on whether or not he regards this as a universal); hence his conception of a this does not exclude species forms from being thises.

10. Sense-PERCEPTION involves the reception of the perceptible form (not the form that is identified with the substance) without the matter it is embodied in, *DA* 424a18 (cf. *Met.* 1032b1).

11. For similar reasons, UNDERSTANDING is the reception of intelligible forms without matter, *DA* 429a15–18, *Met.* 1072b18–21.

FORM$_l$; see REASON #5.

FORM$_m$; see FORM #5.

FORM, IDEA (PLATONIC), *eidos, idea*

1. As well as using *eidos* for the substantial forms and species that he believes in, Aristotle uses the term (interchangeably with *idea*, following Plato's practice; for the more general use of *idea* as 'character' see *Met.* 1029a4) for the Forms or Ideas recognized by Plato (in these cases an initial capital is used for convenience, when it seems clear that Aristotle is talking about Platonic Forms).

2. Aristotle describes the origin of the Theory of Forms, and the arguments offered for Forms in *On Ideas*, *Met.* 987a29–b10, 1078b12–32, 1086a31–b13. He criticizes the theory in *On Ideas*, *APo* 77a5–9, 83a32–35, 85a18–22, *Top.* 178b36–179a10, *Met.* i 9, vii 6, 1033b19–29, vii 13–15, 1045a16, xiii 4–5, 10, *EN* i 6.

3. Many of these criticisms are concerned especially with the SEPARATION of Forms. Aristotle argues that Plato fails to grasp the distinction between PARTICULARS and UNIVERSALS, *Met.* 1038b34–1039a3, 1040b27–30; and he argues that this mistake underlies the 'Third Man' regress, on which see *On Ideas* 84.21, *Top.* 178b36, *Met.* 990b17, 1039a2 (cf. Plato, *Parmenides* 132a–c). See also ABSTRACTION, PATTERN.

FORMULA, TERM, STANDARD, *horos*

1. Sometimes *horos* (lit. 'boundary', 'limit', cognate with *horizein*, 'define'; see *Phys.* 218b15n) is used for a term in a deduction, *APr* 24b16, *EN* 1142a26. 'Term'

might suggest a linguistic or semantic item; but (as with other words for apparently linguistic or semantic items; cf. DEFINITION) Aristotle sometimes seems to take the *horos* to be the thing (e.g., man) signified by the term as well as the term itself (e.g., the word 'man').

2. Sometimes it is used for something more complex than a single word, and is often equivalent to *horismos*, 'DEFINITION', e.g., *Top.* 101b22, 141a27, *Phys.* 194a2, *DA* 413a11, *Met.* 987b6, 1030a8, 1038a21, 1039a20, 1040a6, 1045a26, *Pol.* 1280a7.

3. Sometimes the *horos* is the standard that defines or formulates the criteria appropriate to an activity or discipline. See *PA* 639a13, *EN* 1138b23, *Pol.* 1331b36, 1334a12, *Poet.* 1451a15.

FORTUNE: see LUCK

FREE, *eleutheros*

Aristotle takes the difference in legal status between a free citizen and a SLAVE to be correlated (not exactly; see *Pol.* 1255b4) with a difference of nature and character, *Met.* 982b26, *EN* 1176b20, *Pol.* 1254a11, 1325a29. The free person takes a more 'civilized', *eleutherios*, attitude to life, *Met.* 1075a19, whereas the slavish person is absorbed in the satisfaction of bodily needs, and the pursuit of physical pleasures connected with satisfying these needs. See GENEROUS, MENIAL.

FRIENDSHIP, *philia;* **LOVE,** *philein*

'Friendship' is the best single translation of *philia*, but it does not sound equally natural for all the different types of cooperative relations that Aristotle classifies as types of *philia* (for the cognate verb *philein* 'love' has to be used); see *EN* viii–ix. *Philiai* include business partnerships and family relations (see *Poet.* 1453b15) that we might not readily recognize as constituting friendships in their own right. While Aristotle sees some common or overlapping features (e.g., 1155b32–1156a10, 1158a7, ix 5), he is mainly concerned to show the ethical differences between types of *philia* in individual and political relations (cf. viii 10–11).

The cognate verb *philein* is best rendered 'love' in the *Ethics*, where Aristotle is primarily concerned with relatively close and stable relations between people. In *Rhet.* ii 4, however, the discussion of *philia* is not concerned primarily with ways of establishing close and lasting affectionate relations between individuals, but with arousing friendly or hostile feelings or attitudes. In this context 'friendliness' seems the best rendering. The rendering 'love' runs the risk of misleading the reader (and even of making Aristotle's claims sound quite odd—e.g., his remark that we tend to *philein* people who dress neatly, 1381b1).

FULL, FULLY; see CONTROLLING

FUNCTION, TASK, ACTIVITY, ACHIEVEMENT, *ergon*

Ergon has the range of uses of the English 'work'. It is applied to an activity ('this is hard work') as well as to the result ('a great work of art'; see *Phys.* 202a24, *Met.* 993b21, *Poet.* 1452b30). Often 'function' is suitable, e.g., *EN* 1097b25, *Pol.* 1253a23; sometimes 'task' (*Met.* 1029b5) and 'activity' (*Met.* 1045b35; see ACTUALITY) are used.

GENEROUS, *eleutherios*

This is cognate with *eleutheros*, 'FREE'. It is used (a) in a general sense for a 'free' or 'civilized' outlook, *EN* 1176b20, 1179b8, *Rhet.* 1361a16; (b) in a more specialized sense, for the virtue of generosity (or 'liberality') described in *EN* 1107b9, iv 1–2.

genesis: COMING TO BE

GENUS, *genos*

The term is cognate with *gignesthai*, 'COME TO BE', and originally means 'family' or 'race', *Met.* 1024a29–36. Aristotle uses it in a broader sense for a sort or kind (not always sharply distinguished from *eidos*, e.g., at *PA* 645a30; see FORM), and in a narrower, technical sense. In the technical sense a genus is a secondary SUBSTANCE (e.g., animal) and a UNIVERSAL, divided by DIFFERENTIAE (e.g., biped, quadruped) into species (e.g., man, horse; see FORM #9), *Catg.* 2a17–19, *Top.* 102a31–35, *Met.* 1024b4–9. Aristotle discusses in several places the proper way of dividing genera into species, and the relation of the genus to the differentiae and species; see *Met.* 1038a5–9, vii 14. On the highest genera (the categories) see PREDICATIONS.

GET MORE, *pleonektein*; **GREED,** *pleonexia*

The verb *pleonektein* sometimes has a neutral sense, of getting more of some good than someone else. It often has the unfavorable sense that the noun *pleonexia* normally has, of getting (or being disposed to get) more than one is entitled to of some good, to someone else's disadvantage. See *EN* 1129a32–b10, *Pol.* 1282b29, 1324b10.

gignesthai: COME TO BE

gignōskō: KNOW

GOD, *theos*

1. Aristotle mentions the traditional Olympian gods, without committing himself to acceptance of the traditional conception of them, *Met.* 1074a38–b14, *Pol.* 1252b24, 1254b35.

2. Sometimes he refers generally to 'the god' when he has no particular god in mind (it is not necessarily an expression of monotheism), *GC* 334b32, *Met.* 983a8, 1072b35, *Pol.* 1323b23.

3. He rejects anthropomorphizing views of the nature of the gods, *EN* 1101b18, 1178b9.

4. He believes that there is something divine about the order and workings of nature, *Phys.* 192a16, *DA* 415a29, and still more divine in the heavenly substances, *PA* 644b22–645a7. The primary divine substance is discussed in *Met.* xii 7–10.

GOOD, *agathos*

Aristotle connects 'good' (and the corresponding adverb *eu*, 'well') closely with ends (see FOR SOMETHING).

1. A good F (e.g., knife, horse, person) has a VIRTUE that is defined by reference to the FUNCTION of F, and therefore to the ESSENCE of F, *EN* 1098a8, 1106a15.

2. Something is good for a substance F insofar as it promotes F's good or welfare,

Pol. 1261b9; F's good is determined by F's function and essence, *EN* 1094a18–22, 1097a15–24, 1097b22–1098a5. The good for human beings is their HAPPINESS, which is their ultimate end.

3. External goods (wealth, security, etc.) are not in an agent's control (see LUCK #3). See *EN* 1098b13, 1099a31, 1129b2, *Pol.* 1323a25, b7, 1323b27, *Rhet.* 1360b25.

GOOD GOVERNMENT, *eunomia*

This term is derived from *nomos* (see LAW) and *eu* ('well', the adverb corresponding to *agathos*). It implies (i) having good laws, and (ii) observing them (so that it includes, but is not confined to, 'law and order'). See *Pol.* 1260b30, 1280b6, *Rhet.* 1354a20.

GROWTH: see FORM #2.

HABITUATION, *ethismos*: see CHARACTER

haplōs: see WITHOUT QUALIFICATION

HAPPINESS, *eudaimonia*

1. The term is derived from *eu*, 'well' (see GOOD), and *daimōn*, 'divine being', and so suggests a life favored by the gods. Following common beliefs, Aristotle identifies happiness with the highest good, also described as 'living well', 1095a18, 1097a15–b21. Happiness is the COMPLETE end fully satisfying a person's correct rational DESIRE.

2. The English 'happiness' may mislead, if it suggests that Aristotle thinks PLEASURE or contentment or 'feeling happy' is the highest good. In fact he denies (*EN* x 1–5) that pleasure is the same as *eudaimonia*; he thinks *eudaimonia* consists in living and acting (in accordance with VIRTUE), not simply in having a certain kind of pleasure (though he certainly thinks that the best sort of life includes pleasure in the appropriate actions).

3. The *EN* discusses the nature of happiness for an individual, and the *Politics* discusses its political and social aspects. On the components of happiness see *EN* x 6–8, *Pol.* vii 1–3.

HEAVEN, *ouranos*

Aristotle uses *ouranos* both for the upper universe in contrast to the earth, as in *Met.* 1072b14, and for the universe including the earth, as in 1074a31. See *Phys.* 196a25, 251b18, *GC* 338a19, *PA* 641b16, *Met.* 1042a10.

HERACLEITUS

Heracleitus (fl. 500?) is usually but not always supposed to precede PARMENIDES. In Aristotle's view, he is one of the early materialist NATURALISTS. He identifies the basic substance with fire, *Met.* 984a7–8. Aristotle, following Plato (*Cratylus* 402a), also ascribes to Heracleitus the belief in universal flux in the sensible world, *Met.* 987a32–b1, 1010a10–15. This belief in radical flux and instability includes belief in the unity of opposites (expressed, e.g., in his view that 'day and night are one', 'the road up and the road down are one and the same', and so on). Heracleitus' belief in this strong form of universal flux is probably the basis of Aristotle's view that he denies the Principle of Noncontradiction, *Phys.* 185a5–7, *Met.* 1005b23–25, 1012a24–26. For aspects of his life and character see *PA* 645a17, *EN* 1146b27–31.

HERODOTUS

Historian (c. 484–c. 427). See *Poet.* 1451b2.

HESIOD

Aristotle uses Hesiod (8th cent.) rather similarly to the way he uses HOMER, especially as representing the predecessors of the NATURALISTS. See *Met.* 984b23, 989a10, 1000a9, 1071b27, *EN* 1095b10, *Pol.* 1252b10.

holōs: see IN GENERAL

HOMER

Aristotle often quotes Homer (8th cent.); the slight inaccuracy of some of the quotations suggests that he relies on memory. He uses Homer (1) for the ornamental effect of familiar phrases from the best known of Greek poets; (2) to illustrate the mythological as opposed to the NATURALIST world-view (see HESIOD); (3) as a source of familiar and respectable ethical or political views. See *Met.* 1009b28, 1076a4, *EN* 1109b8, 1113a8, 1116a21, *Pol.* 1253a5, *Poet.* 1451a23.

HOMONYMOUS, *homōnumon*; SPOKEN OF IN MANY WAYS, *pollachōs legomenon*

1. *Homōnuma* are, literally, 'things that have the same NAME (*onoma*)', and the word is sometimes used in this nontechnical sense, *Met.* 987b10, 990b6, 1034a22. In Aristotle's technical sense, two or more F things are F homonymously if and only if (a) they share the name 'F', but (b) they do not share the DEFINITION or ACCOUNT corresponding to 'F', *Catg.* 1a1–6, *Top.* 106a1–8, 107a3–12. Hence 'homonymy' is often used equivalently to 'spoken of in many ways'. Clause (b) above might be taken to mean (1) homonyms have no common element at all in their definitions; or (2) homonyms cannot have the whole of their definitions in common. According to (1), definitions of homonymous Fs cannot have any common elements. According to (2), the definitions may (though they need not) have some common elements. Probably (2) captures Aristotle's intention in clause (b) (since some of his examples of definitions of homonyms seem to contain common elements).

2. We may speak of 'extreme' homonymy when the definitions have little or nothing in common, and of 'moderate' homonymy when they have more in common. In cases of extreme homonymy, the homonymy is very clear (cf. *EN* 1129a26–31), and it may simply be 'chance homonymy' (e.g., 'horse' applied to racehorses and clothes horses; cf. *EN* 1096b26). In some cases homonymous Fs are all perfectly genuine Fs; but in some cases homonymy indicates Fs that have only the name 'F' but are not genuine Fs, and in these cases Aristotle sometimes says 'not F, except homonymously'. Hence a statue of a horse is called a horse merely homonymously, *Met.* 991a6, and (in Aristotle's view) a dead hand or arm is a hand or arm merely homonymously (see PART, MATTER).

3. When Aristotle has cases of extreme homonymy in mind, he sometimes contrasts homonymy with being spoken of in many ways. When he has this contrast in mind, he mentions cases where Fs are all called F 'with reference to one thing' (*pros hen*); this relation may be called 'focal connection'. Healthy things, e.g., have different definitions of 'healthy', but they are all called healthy by reference to health, since healthy diets are healthy because they promote

health, and healthy appetites are healthy because they indicate health. Aristotle sometimes says that these focally connected things are spoken of in many ways (since they have no single definition), but are nonhomonymous (i.e., not completely homonymous, since their definitions all refer to one thing), *Met.* 1003a3–b10, 1004a23–25, 1028a10–13, 1030a32–b3, *EN* 1096b26–29. (If one accepts interpretation (1) of the definition of homonymy in #1 above, one will explain the relation of focal connection to homonymy differently.)

4. Homonymy and being spoken of in many ways are primarily relations between the things that have the names, not between the names themselves. Hence Aristotle usually says that horses (e.g.) are homonymous, not that the word 'horse' is homonymous. Sometimes, though, he attributes homonymy to names; see *GC* 322b29–30.

5. On the importance of noticing homonymy see *Top.* 108a18–37.

HONOR, *timē*

A's *timē* expresses other people's view of A's FINE or GOOD qualities. See *EN* 1095a22, 1101b11–34, 1123b13–22, 1159a12. The adjective *timios* is rendered by 'honorable' or 'valuable'; see *DA* 402a1, *PA* 639a2, 644b24, *Pol.* 1323b17. 'Dishonored', *atimos*, is the technical term for those deprived of civil rights (as a penalty for certain crimes); hence the dishonored are mentioned together with exiles as being deprived of the normal functions of a citizen. See *Pol.* 1275a21, 1281a34, 1281b29, 1295b8.

horismos: DEFINITION

horos: see FORMULA

hōs epi to polu: USUAL

HOUSEHOLD MANAGEMENT, *oikonomia*

This concerns the provision of material resources for a household, or, more properly, the use of these resources, *Pol.* 1253b2. It may also deal with provision for a city, *Pol.* 1256a1–10, 1263a32 ('managed'), 1285b33; hence it may include something closer to 'economics' in a modern sense.

hupokeimenon: SUBJECT

hupolēpsis: see SUPPOSITION

idea: see FORM, IDEA

idios: DISTINCTIVE

IN GENERAL, ALTOGETHER, *holōs*

The translation 'in general' may sometimes be misleading. We might take 'in general' to mean 'as a general rule but not always'; for this Aristotle uses 'USUAL'. *Holōs* normally means 'in general' in the sense of 'speaking quite generally, and without exception'; and so its sense (in, e.g., *Met.* 1029b6, *Pol.* 1280a23) is often close to that of WITHOUT QUALIFICATION. See *DA* 403a7, 412b7, *Met.* 1033b11, *EN* 1140a25–31, *Pol.* 1254a10, 1263a26, 1301a31.

IN ITS OWN RIGHT, IN ITSELF, INTRINSIC, *kath'hauto*

1. G may belong to F in its own right (per se; lit. 'in accordance with itself') in either of two ways: (a) G is part of, or derivable from, the ESSENCE and DEFINITION of F, and G belongs to F INSOFAR AS it is F (belongs to F qua F), *APo* 73a34–b24, *Met.* 1029b13–19; or (b) G contains F in its definition (as odd belongs to number in its own right, though not every number is odd), *APo* 73a37–b5, *Met.* 1030b16–26.

2. Because of its connection with the essence, what belongs to F in F's own right is often contrasted with what belongs to F coincidentally, *Met.* 1017a7–8. Aristotle, however, also recognizes coincidents of F in its own right; see COINCIDENT #2.

3. On intrinsic causation see CAUSE.

4. Something that is (i.e., exists) in its own right is not dependent on anything else, *APo* 73b5–10, *Met.* 1031a28, 1032a5, *EN* 1095a27, 1096a20.

5. On intrinsic objects of PERCEPTION see *DA* 418a8.

INCONTINENCE, *akrasia*

Incontinent or 'uncontrolled' people lack control (*kratein*) over their nonrational DESIRES; hence they act on appetite in opposition to their correct DECISION, and choose what they know (in some way that Aristotle tries to describe more precisely) is worse for them. Incontinence is fully discussed in *EN* vii 1–10, esp. vii 3. See also *DA* 434a10–21, *EN* 1102b14–28, 1111b13–15, 1168b34.

INDEFINITE: see INFINITE

INDETERMINATE: see INFINITE #3

INDIVIDUAL, INDIVISIBLE, *atomon*

1. What is *atomon* is in some way indivisible (lit. 'uncuttable'). Aristotle applies the term to mathematical points, *Phys.* 232a24, and to the 'atoms' recognized by DEMOCRITUS, *Phys.* 265b29, *DA* 404a2, *Met.* 1039a19. Aristotle himself rejects indivisible magnitudes, *GC* 315b26 ff.

2. Aristotle says that x is an *atomon* F when he means that x is not divisible into further Fs. Hence Socrates is *atomon* insofar as he is a man and is not divisible into further men. In these cases an *atomon* is a PARTICULAR, *Catg.* 1b6, 3a38, b12, *Met.* 995b30.

3. A species (see FORM #9) (e.g., man) is also said to be *atomon*, since—in contrast to the GENUS (e.g., animal), which is divisible into species—the species is not divisible into further species, though it is divisible into particulars. See *DA* 414b27, *Met.* 1034a8.

4. 'The individual man' etc. is also used to translate *ho tis anthrōpos*, lit. 'the some man', *Catg.* 1a22 etc. The indefinite *tis* ('some') is the nearest thing in Greek to an indefinite article; cf. *APo* 93a23.

INDUCTION, *epagōgē*

1. Induction and DEDUCTION are the two ways of reaching rational CONVICTION, *APr* 68b13, *APo* 71a5, *EN* 1139b26–31. In contrast to deduction, induction proceeds from PARTICULAR to UNIVERSAL, *APr* 68b27–29, 35–37, *APo* 72b29, 100b4,

Top. 105a11–19. On the use of induction in rhetoric see ARGUMENTATION. On the advantages and disadvantages of induction and deduction see *Top.* 105a16, *Rhet.* 1356b23.

2. Aristotle speaks of induction not only where we form some general conclusion on the basis of EXPERIENCE of particular instances, but also where we come to understand some general principle or concept on the basis of some particular illustrations, *Top.* 105b27, *Phys.* 210b8, 229b3, *Met.* 1048a36 (cf. *Phys.* 191a8).

INFERENCE, *sullogismos*: see DEDUCTION

INFINITE, UNLIMITED, INDEFINITE, *apeiron*; **INDEFINITE, INDETERMINATE,** *ahoriston*

1. Aristotle uses *apeiron* for infinity, discussed in *Phys.* iii 4–8 (esp. 206a27–29)—a series in which there is always another member besides those previously counted. See also *DI* 23a25, *Phys.* 207a7–8, 218a21, 263a28, *GC* 318a19, *Met.* 1048b9–17.

2. Aristotle rejects the possibility of some types of infinite series. He rejects, for instance, any form of argument or DELIBERATION that requires an infinite regress of actual steps, and any sort of causal explanation that requires the completion of an infinite series of actual events. See *APo* 72b7–11, 84a29–b1, *Phys.* 256a17–19, 263a6, *Met.* ii 2, *EN* 1094a20–21. But he believes, against ZENO, that an infinite series of the sort required by MOTION is acceptable, *Phys.* vi 9, 263a15–b9. He believes that every length is infinitely divisible, *Phys.* 206a27, 233a13–21, *Met.* 1048b14, and hence that time is infinitely divisible, *Phys.* 218a20–21. The infinite divisibility of a length consists in the fact that any part of the length is further divisible; it does not imply that complete division (with no further possible division left) will ever be actual.

3. Sometimes Aristotle seems to make a less definite claim about something that is *apeiron*—not that a series can never be completed, but that there is no reason to suppose that it stops at any definite place. Here 'unlimited' is suitable, and the sense of *apeiron* is close to that of *ahoriston*, 'indeterminate' or 'indefinite'. See *DI* 16a28, b14, *Phys.* 187b7, 196b27–29, *DA* 416a15, *Met.* 987b25, 1006a34–b11, 1007a13–15, b1, b26–29, *Pol.* 1275a32, *Rhet.* 1356b32, 1396b7. In some of these passages he may have infinity in mind also, but he focusses primarily on indefiniteness. He is probably also thinking of qualitative (rather than purely numerical) indefiniteness, arising from the difficulty of specifying something's properties in any determinate way, *Met.* 1006b5–7, 1026b2–14.

INQUIRE: see SEARCH

INQUIRY, *historia*

This is Aristotle's normal term for the empirical investigation of APPEARANCES, in preparation for the formation of a theory that can be expressed as a demonstrative science (see KNOW #3). Aristotle uses the term for his own inquiry into the behavior of characteristics of animals (the *Peri ta zōa historia* or *Historia Animalium*, literally 'Inquiry about Animals') and for 'history' in the narrower sense; see *APr* 46a24, *HA* 491a12, *PA* 639a13, 644a8, *Poet.* 1451a38. He also uses it occasionally for dialectical inquiry (see *DA* 402a4).

INQUIRY, LINE OF: see LINE OF INQUIRY

INSOFAR AS, *hē(i)*

This is the dative of the relative pronoun, and means literally 'by which' or 'in the respect in which', often Latinized as 'qua'. When Aristotle says that x is G insofar as x is F, he means that x is G because x is F; x's being F is the basis for correctly predicating G of x. Socrates, e.g., is both a man and a musician; but it is qua man that he is an animal, and qua musician that he is incompetent. Aristotle often uses 'insofar as' to identify the intrinsic cause (see CAUSE #5). See *APo* 73b27, *Phys.* 191b4, 193b32, 201a29, 219b2, *Met.* 1003a21, 1004b10–17, 1035a8, *EN* 1096b24, 1130a12–13.

INSTRUMENT, TOOL, ORGAN, *organon*

Organon refers to a craftsman's tools or instruments, which are designed for achieving the craftsman's end. Since Aristotle believes in FINAL CAUSATION, he applies the same term to parts of the body, since they also work (though without design) for an end—the benefit of the whole organism. See *DA* 412a28, 433b19, *PA* 642a12, *MA* 701b8, *Pol.* 1254a17.

INTELLECT: see UNDERSTANDING

INTELLIGENCE, UNDERSTANDING, *phronēsis*

Aristotle uses '*phronēsis*' (1) in a wider sense, referring to intelligent consciousness or understanding in general, *DA* 417b8, *Met.* 980b1, 982b24, 1009b30; (2) in his own specialized sense, for the deliberative VIRTUE of practical intellect, discussed in *EN* vi, esp. vi 5, 7–8, 12–13 (vi 7 contrasts *phronēsis* with theoretical WISDOM, *sophia*); cf. *Pol.* 1277a15, b23, 1281b5, 1324a34, 1329a9, 15. POLITICAL SCIENCE is a branch of *phronēsis*; see *Pol.* 1289a12.

JUDGE: see DISCRIMINATE, JURYMAN

JURYMAN, *dikastes*

Most Athenian trials were decided by a large panel of jurymen (often several hundred), who reached their verdict without the authoritative legal guidance of any 'judge' (of the sort found in modern courts). Hence Aristotle often (and especially in the *Rhet.*, e.g., 1354a18, 24, 32) refers to the same person both as 'juryman' and as 'judge' (*kritēs*; see DISCRIMINATE). Since many Athenian trials and court sittings were political in character (see *Pol.* 1281b33n, 1301b23n) it is reasonable for Aristotle to regard the juryman's office as a sort of 'rule' (*archē*; see PRINCIPLE #5), *Pol.* 1275a22. See OCD p. 342b.

JUSTICE, *dikaiosunē*

Justice is the other-regarding virtue especially associated with the CITY, or political COMMUNITY. Aristotle distinguishes 'general' justice from the special virtue of 'partial' justice, in *EN* v 1–2, and analyzes the types of partial justice in v 3–5. On political justice see *Pol.* iii 9, 12. On LAW and justice see *EN* 1134b18–1135a5.

kalos: see FINE

katēgorein: PREDICATE

kath'hauto: IN ITS OWN RIGHT

kath'hekaston: PARTICULAR

katholou: UNIVERSAL

kinein, kinesis: see MOTION

KNOW, *epistasthai, gignōskein, eidenai;* **KNOW SCIENTIFICALLY**, *epistasthai;* **KNOWLEDGE**, *gnōsis, epistēmē;* **SCIENCE, SCIENTIFIC KNOWLEDGE**, *epistēmē;* **KNOWN**, *gnōrimon, epistēton*

1. The occurrences of Aristotle's different epistemic verbs are marked by subscript initial letters (the same verb is used until a different subscript letter appears). 'Know$_e$' is used for *epistasthai*, 'know$_g$' for *gignōskein*, and 'know$_o$' for *eidenai* (since the first person singular is *oida*). The relations between the different verbs are not always clear (see *DA* 402a1n). But in general: (1) *epistasthai* (cognate noun *epistēmē* = 'knowledge' or 'science') is most frequently associated with demonstrative science, or at any rate with a systematic discipline that is the source of the knowledge (hence 'science', 'scientific knowledge', and 'know scientifically' often seem appropriate). (2) *gignōskein* and its cognates (*gnōrizein*, 'know' or 'come to know'; *gnōsis*, 'knowledge'; *gnōrimon*, 'known'; *gnōrimōteron*, 'better known') often seem rather weaker (hence 'find out', *Rhet.* 1354a30). It is appropriate to apply *gignōskein* to knowing or recognizing people and ordinary perceptible objects, but it would be odd to use *epistasthai* in such a context (though cf. *EN* 1113b34, vii 3). See *Pol.* 1282a19n. (3) *eidenai* seems less specialized than either of the other two terms. (4) In English 'S knows that p' implies that (i) p is true and (roughly) (ii) S is justified in believing that p. The first implication holds for *epistasthai* and *eidenai*, but it may not hold for *gignōskein* (and certainly does not hold in the phrase translated 'known to us'; see below). Something like the second implication holds (as Aristotle makes clear in *APo* i 2) for *epistasthai* and probably for *eidenai*, but it is less clear that it holds for *gignōskein*.

2. Aristotle often contrasts what is better known (*gnōrimon*) 'to us' with what is better known 'by nature' or 'WITHOUT QUALIFICATION', *APo* 71b33–72a5, *Top.* 141b3–14, *Phys.* 184a16–23, *Met.* 1029b3–12, *EN* 1095b2–4 (cf. *APr* 68b35–37, *Top.* 105a16–19). The contrast is connected to the difference between types of *archai* (see PRINCIPLE #4). What is 'known to us' (i.e., 'known as far as we are concerned', or 'known in our view', and hence need not be true) is our *archē* insofar as it is the starting point; this consists of the APPEARANCES. What is 'known by nature' (i.e., is the sort of thing that makes it an appropriate object of knowledge, and hence must be true) is the result of successful investigation; this is the *archē* insofar as it is the first principle. The distinction between 'known to us' and 'known by nature' applies not only to different propositions that may be known, but also to the things known about; see PRINCIPLE.

3. Sometimes (e.g., *APo* 71b9–25) Aristotle takes DEMONSTRATION to be necessary for *epistēmē*. But he does not always use '*epistēmē*' so narrowly; sometimes 'sciences' seem to include CRAFTS as well as strictly demonstrative sciences, *EN* 1094a28, 1180b13–16.

4. General features of a demonstrative science: (1) It must be about what is NECESSARY, *APo* 71b12, 75a18–22, or about the necessary and the USUAL, *APo* 87b19–27, *Met.* 1026b27–1027a5. (2) It must be about UNIVERSALS, not (or not primarily) about PARTICULARS, *Met.* 981a5–30, 1039b27–1040a7 (but see 1087a10–

25), *Rhet*. 1356b30–35. (3) It does not require Platonic FORMS, *APo* 77a5–9, 83a32–35, 85b15–22.

5. On conditional knowledge in contrast to unqualified (see WITHOUT QUALIFICATION) knowledge see *APo* 72b15, 83b29.

6. In political contexts the upper classes are referred to as the 'well-known' or 'notables' (*gnōrimoi*; cf. Latin 'nobiles'); the term is translated 'people of reputation'. See *Pol*. 1289b33 (cf. *Poet*. 1451b20).

koinōnia: COMMUNITY

kurios: see CONTROLLING

LAW, CONVENTION, *nomos*

Nomos is the product of human enactment or belief, or a norm for guiding behavior; it is not confined to positive law enacted by some legislature (see esp. *Pol*. 1324b27n). It is sometimes contrasted with NATURE. See *Phys*. 193a15, *EN* 1094b16, 1129b12, 1134b19, *Pol*. 1253b20, 1255a5, 1282b1–13, 1289a11–15, *Rhet*. 1373b4–24. Aristotle insists on the importance of rule by law rather than by individual decisions, *Pol*. 1287a28–b8; but he also argues that DECENCY is needed to avoid the bad results of rigid observance of the written law. On law and moral EDUCATION, see *EN* 1179b34–1180a24.

LEISURE, *scholē*

People are at leisure when they need not spend all their time and effort on the satisfaction of basic needs, and so can engage in activities that are directed at some end other than the satisfaction of these needs. See *Met*. 981b23, *EN* 1177b4, *Pol*. 1329a1, 1334a14. In *Pol*. 1323b39 'discipline' renders *scholē*.

LEUCIPPUS: see DEMOCRITUS

LIFE, *zōē*: see NATURE #1

LIKE, BE SATISFIED, *agapan*

This may, but need not, be a weaker attachment than is conveyed by *philein*, 'love' (see FRIENDSHIP). See *EN* 1094b19, 1156a13, 1167b32, *Pol*. 1262b23.

LINE OF INQUIRY, *methodos*

See *APr* 68b12, *Top*. 100a18, *Phys*. 200b13, 251a7, *Met*. 983a23, *EN* 1094b11, *Rhet*. 1354b23, 1355a4. The term is used not only for an approach or procedure (*Top*. 100a18, *DA* 402a14), but also for the branch of study or inquiry that embodies that procedure; hence 'discipline' (e.g., *Top*. 101b3, *Phys*. 184a11, *PA* 639a1, *EN* 1094b1) or even 'treatise' (e.g., *Top*. 184b4) is appropriate.

LOCAL MOTION: see TRAVEL

LOGICAL, *logikos*

'Logical' problems are a subset of DIALECTICAL problems, distinguished from problems about nature and about ethics. They have no specific subject matter, but may be expected to apply generally to inquiries in different specific areas, *Top*. 105b19–29. When Aristotle mentions 'logical' arguments, he usually contrasts them with those that are specific to the subject matter at hand (and rely on its PROPER principles), *APo* 83b35, 84a7–8, 88a19, 30, 93a15, *Phys.* 202a21, 204b4, 10, *Met.* 1005b22, 1029b13n, 1030a27–28, 1041a27–28, *EN* 1147a24. These passages show that 'logical' argument is not confined to formal 'logic' in the modern sense. Aristotle refers to his formal logic as 'analytics'; *APo* 84a8, *Met.* 1005b4, 1037b8; this term refers to the analysis of arguments to reveal the basic patterns of deductive argument that they display (see *APr* 47a2–5, 49a11–18).

logos: see REASON

LOVE: see FRIENDSHIP

LUCK, CHANCE, FORTUNE, tuchē; CHANCE, *to automaton*

1. In Aristotle's strictest use, *to automaton* refers to an event that is of the right sort to have a FINAL CAUSE, but does not actually have one. The subset of these events that come about from a DECISION are matters of *tuchē*, *Phys.* 196b21–29, 197b18–22, *Poet.* 1452a5. In these cases *tuchē* is rendered by 'luck', and *to automaton* by 'chance'.

2. When Aristotle does not have this contrast between luck and chance in mind, he tends to use *tuchē* (and cognates) to refer more broadly to *to automaton*, and still more broadly to COINCIDENTAL results (where no special similarity to events with final causes is implied), *DI* 18b7, 19a19, 38, *APo* 87b19, *Met.* 1027b13. In the threefold division of NECESSARY, USUAL, and *tuchē*, the term has this broad reference, with no particular suggestion of similarity to events with final causes. The cognate verb *tunchanein* ('happen') is often used to cover both luck and chance (e.g., *Met.* 1071b34). 'Any old thing' translates *to tuchon* (lit. 'what happens' or 'what happens by chance'), which Aristotle uses (e.g., *Phys.* 188a33, *Met.* 1075a20) to refer to what happens on no definite principle or rule. The phrase is also used to mean 'anything picked out at random' and so 'nondescript', 'undistinguished'.

3. In ethical contexts (cf. *Phys.* 197a25–30) *tuchē* refers to what is outside an agent's rational control; this need not be a matter of chance or coincidence in any other sense. Here 'fortune' is used (and 'good fortune' for *eutuchia*); see *Phys.* 197a26, *EN* 1096a1, 1099a31–b8, 1101a28, 1129b3, *Rhet.* 1361b39.

4. *To automaton* is also used for 'spontaneous' generation, which does not have the normal sort of final and efficient causes, *DA* 415a28, *PA* 640a27, *Met.* 1034b4. It is used in a sense close to 'automatic' at *Met.* 983a14, and hence for puppets, *MA* 701b2.

LYCOPHRON

A SOPHIST of unknown date. See *Met.* 1045b10, *Pol.* 1280b10, fr. 91 (see ROT p. 2422).

LYCURGUS

A Spartan king and lawgiver (8th cent.?). See *Pol.* 1296a20.

MAN, HUMAN BEING, *anthrōpos*

1. *Anthrōpos* corresponds to the Latin 'homo' (referring to the human species), as opposed to 'vir' (adult male), for which Aristotle uses *anēr* (e.g., *Phys.* 184b13). In contexts where *anthrōpos* is used as a species term coordinate with 'horse', 'tree' etc., 'man' is the best rendering (since the grammatical form of 'human

being' makes it unsuitable for understanding some of Aristotle's linguistic points). In other contexts (e.g., ethical) 'human being' is a better rendering, and 'man' is used for *anēr*.

2. On the differences between men and women see *EN* 1162a19–27, *Pol*. 1259b28–1260a24, 1277b20.

3. On human beings and other animals see REASON #1.

4. Human beings are 'political' animals (i.e., suitable for life in a *polis*; see CITY), since they have their NATURE fulfilled, and reach their natural END, by living in a *polis*. See *EN* 1097b11, 1169b17, *Pol*. 1253a2, 1278b19.

MATHEMATICS: see ABSTRACTION, MATTER #6

MATTER, *hulē*

1. In ordinary Greek *hulē* means 'wood'. Aristotle extends this use to raw material in general, *Phys*. 191a8–12, 195a16 (cf. Plato, *Philebus* 54c2). Matter is the SUBJECT of COMING TO BE and perishing, and so it is the subject from which a substance comes to be; for instance, the bronze from which a statue is made, and the material elements of which an organism is composed, are the matter, *Phys*. 190b3–10. Since matter explains some features of artifacts and organisms by reference to their composition, it is a CAUSE.

2. Different types of matter are relative to different levels of organization, *Phys*. 193a10, 29, 194b8–9. Wood is the 'proximate' (or 'closest'; cf. *Met*. 1044b1–3) matter of the box, but earth is the matter of the wood, and only indirectly the matter of the box, *Met*. 1023a26–29, 1044a15–20, 1044b1–3, 1049a18–24.

3. It is usually (though not always) believed that at the lowest level of organization Aristotle recognizes 'prime' (i.e., first) matter. This is the subject of the most basic qualities, and it remains throughout changes of one element into another. It has none of the qualities of the elements essentially, but is capable of having all of them at different times, and necessarily has the qualities of some element or other at any given time (i.e., it cannot exist without being hot or cold or . . . , but it is neither necessarily hot nor necessarily cold nor . . .). See *Phys*. 193a17–21, GC 332a17–20, 35.

4. Since matter is a subject, it seems to count as a SUBSTANCE. Aristotle sometimes suggests that matter is needed to make something a PARTICULAR subject at all. But he also insists that it is neither the only nor the primary sort of substance, *Phys*. 191a12–14, 193a9–12, *Met*. 1029a10–33, 1035a1–4, 1040b5–10, 1042a25–b8, 1049a34–36. It is substance because of its POTENTIALITY, DA 412a9, *Met*. 1042a28, b10.

5. In speaking of the matter of a living organism Aristotle distinguishes its proximate from its nonproximate matter: (1) The living BODY and its organic PARTS are the proximate matter of the organism (DA 412a17–19), and do not exist—except HOMONYMOUSLY—after the death of the organism, DA 412b13–15, 20–22, PA 640b35–641a6, 645a35, *Met*. 1035b23–25, 1036b30–32, *Pol*. 1253a18–25. (2) By contrast, the material constituents of the living body and of its parts still exist after the death of the organism, DA 412b25–26, *Met*. 1035a18–19, 31–33. On the two types of matter, see GC 321b19–22, *Metr*. 389b29–390a16. On the relation of different types of matter to form, see FORM #4.

6. Most of Aristotle's remarks on matter apply to PERCEPTIBLE matter, which

belongs to things that undergo coming to be, perishing, and MOTION, *Met.* 1037a10–13, 1044b27–29. (A different sort of perceptible matter belongs to the imperishable heavenly bodies.) Mathematical objects are sometimes said to have intelligible matter (i.e., the extension that is determined by a specific geometrical figure), *Met.* 1036a9–12.

7. Aristotle claims that matter does not admit of scientific KNOWLEDGE or of DEFINITION, *Met.* 1036a8–9, 1037a27. This claim may be intended to apply to only some of the types of matter distinguished above.

MEAN, *mesotēs*; INTERMEDIATE, *meson*

Aristotle identifies VIRTUE of character with a mean, i.e., an intermediate state between excess and deficiency. The point of this doctrine, and the strict limits of the quantitative analogy, are explained in *EN* 1106a26–b27. His appeal to a mean does not by itself commit him to endorsing moderation in behavior or feelings. He suggests that his conception of virtue as a mean tends to support his view that the 'intermediate' or middle class in a city ought to have political power; see *Pol.* 1295a35–b5.

MELISSUS

Melissus (fl. 441) defends PARMENIDES' monism by somewhat different arguments. Aristotle usually mentions him together with Parmenides, regarding Melissus as the inferior of the two. See *Phys.* 184b16, 185a8–12, b16–19, 186a10–13, 207a15–17, 213b12–14, *Met.* 986b18–21.

MENIAL, *banausos*

Menial occupations are especially those that involve some forms of manual work, and, more generally, those that involve servile dependence on others to a degree that is damaging to a person's character. (See FREE.) The bad effects of menial occupations imply, in Aristotle's view, that menial workers should not be citizens in the best state. See *Pol.* 1258b37–39, 1277b1, 1282a15, 1289b33, 1328b29, 1329a20, 1337b8–15.

mesotēs; see MEAN

metabolē: see MOTION

methodos: LINE OF INQUIRY

MIDDLE TERM: see DEDUCTION

MIND: see UNDERSTANDING

MORE, RATHER, *mallon*

To say that x is *mallon* F than y can mean (a) 'x rather than y is F' (i.e., x is F and y is not F), or (b) 'x is F more than y' (i.e., x is F to a higher degree than y is—without implying that either x or y either is or is not F). In some cases it is not obvious whether Aristotle has (a) or (b) in mind, e.g., *DI* 19a20, 38, *Phys.* 193b6, *Met.* 1029a29, *Poet.* 1451b7.

morphē: see FORM #5

MOTION, PROCESS, CHANGE, *kinēsis*; MOVE, *kinein*

1. In many ways 'change' would be the best rendering of *kinēsis*, which extends more widely than motion, as we normally conceive it; see the types of *kinēsis*

distinguished in *Phys.* 225a5–9, 226a23–b8. But 'change' seems most suitable for *metabolē*, which is often hard to distinguish from *kinēsis* (e.g., *Phys.* 218b20, 226a35), but sometimes is distinguished from it (*Phys.* 225a34–b3, 229a30–32, *Met.* 991a11); moreover, 'changer' and 'unchanged changer' seem awkward. 'Change' has been used to translate both *kinein* and *metaballein* (and cognates) in passages (e.g., *Catg.* 4a35) where this resulted in more natural English and it seemed unimportant to mark the different Greek terms; but where it seemed important to distinguish them, 'move' has been used for *kinein* and 'change' for *metaballein*. The active voice *kinein* means 'move' in the sense of 'initiate motion', and the passive *kineisthai* means 'move' in the sense of 'be moved' or 'undergo motion' or 'be in motion'; this distinction has been marked in the translation at places where it seems important. 'Mover' is used in the active sense (i.e., initiator of motion); see e.g., *Phys.* 202a8, 254b7–12.

2. Motion is contrasted with complete actuality, *Met.* 1048b18–36, and hence *kinēsis* (here rendered 'process') is contrasted with *energeia*, *EN* 1174a14–b4 (see PLEASURE). The definition of motion as the actuality of what is potentially F, insofar as it is potentially F (*Phys.* 201b5) may be interpreted in different ways: (a) Motion is the actualizing (i.e., the process of making actual) that exists while the house is being built, as opposed to the complete actuality of the potentiality to be built (this complete actuality exists only when the bricks have been built into a house. (b) Motion is the actuality of the potentiality of the bricks to be being built (i.e., to be in the process of being built), as opposed to their potentiality to be built (this latter potentiality has been actualized only when a house exists). (c) Motion is the actuality of the potentiality of the bricks to be built (a potentiality which has been actualized only when it ceases to exist and the house exists), to the extent that this actuality is compatible with the continued existence of the potentiality.

3. Aristotle rejects a HERACLEITEAN view about change, by arguing that every motion requires some stability in its subject, *Met.* 1010a15–25.

4. Motion has no beginning, *Phys.* viii 1.

5. Motion requires an unmoved mover, *Phys.* viii 4–6. Among living organisms, animals (whose SOUL includes PERCEPTION) are 'self-movers'; see *Phys.* 255a1–10, 256a4–21, 259b1–11.

6. On motion and TIME see *Phys.* 218b21–219b3.

NAME, *onoma*

At *DI* 16a19–21 Aristotle uses *onoma* for nouns in contrast to verbs and other parts of speech. Sometimes, however, he uses it to include verbs and other parts of speech no less than nouns; his account of HOMONYMY ('having the same *onoma*'), for instance, is not confined to nouns.

Aristotle often signals the fact that he is coining a term for something that has no established name, *DI* 16b14, *EN* 1108b16, 1125b17, *Pol.* 1253b9, 1275a30.

NATION, *ethnos*

An *ethnos* is a COMMUNITY of people regarding themselves as sharing a common ancestry, but lacking the specific aims and institutions of a CITY. See *Pol.* 1261a27, *Rhet.* 1360b31.

NATURALIST, *phusiologos*

Aristotle uses this term (as opposed to the broader term *phusikos*; see NATURE #3–4) to refer to those who concentrate on the material side of the study of nature. They include the 'Presocratics', the natural philosophers before and during the lifetime of Socrates. See *PA* 641a7, *Met.* 986b14, 989b30, 990a2, *EN* 1147b8 (translated 'natural scientists').

NATURE, *phusis*

1. Aristotle (relying, as often, on dubious etymology) takes *phusis* to be the abstract noun cognate with *phuesthai*, 'grow' or 'be born' (cf. English 'native' and 'nativity'). The process of growth (*phusis*) is for the sake of the resulting growth (*phusis*, as we speak of a new branch as 'a new growth'), i.e., the nature. (The two senses of *phusis* are 'focally' connected; cf. *Met.* 1003b7, *Pol.* 1252b32, HOMONYMY #3.) See *Phys.* 193b12–13, *GC* 314b7, *Met.* 1014b16–18.

2. Something has a nature if and only if it has an internal PRINCIPLE initiating the subject's own MOTION and rest, *Phys.* 192b13–15, *Met.* 1015a13–15, 1070a6–9. This definition includes (a) the four ELEMENTS, which, in Aristotle's view, have their own natural local motion, *Phys.* 255a1–5, *DC* 301b16–30; (b) living organisms, i.e., those natural objects whose internally caused motions include self-nourishment and reproduction, *DA* 412a11–15.

3. Aristotle also uses 'nature' to refer to nature in general—the natural world of material SUBSTANCES that have natures. Since Greek has no indefinite article, it is sometimes difficult to know whether to translate *phusis* (without an article) by 'nature' (in general) or by 'a nature' (of some kind of thing). Moreover, when *phusis* occurs with a definite article, it is often difficult to choose between 'the nature' (of a particular thing or kind of thing) and 'nature' (in general), since Greek uses a definite article in both cases. Usually (see, e.g., *Phys.* 192b21n) Aristotle seems to be primarily concerned to say what it is for something (a tree or a dog, for instance) to have a nature, rather than to describe nature (the natural order) as a whole—though the two concerns are certainly connected. Nature, both general and specific, is studied by natural philosophy (*phusikē*, literally just 'natural', with 'science' (see KNOWLEDGE) or 'LINE OF INQUIRY' left unexpressed), to which the *Physics* is devoted. See *Phys.* 193b22–194a12, *DA* 403a27–b19, *PA* 641a18–642a2, i 5, *Met.* 1005a29–b2, 1025b25–1026a6, 1037a13–20.

4. Aristotle believes that the study of nature requires study of the FORM as well as the MATTER; and so it requires study of FINAL CAUSES, and of conditional as well as unqualified necessity (see NECESSITY #4), *Phys.* ii 8–9, *PA* i 1. This is why the 'student of nature', *phusikos*, cannot be confined to the study of empirical details of material processes; the less empirical questions discussed in the *Physics* are also the proper concern of the student of nature. The Presocratic NATURALISTS were mistaken in not recognizing the importance of form.

5. The USUAL as well as the necessary is characteristic of nature, *GA* 727b29–30.

6. Nature does nothing 'pointlessly', *matēn*, *DA* 415b16–17, 434a30–b8, *PA* 641b12–15, *Pol.* 1252b1–3, 1253a9–18, 1263a41; for something done *matēn* has no point or end (*Phys.* 197b28–30, *EN* 1094a21, *Pol.* 1255b1–4), but it is characteristic

of nature to act for an end. (*Matēn* might also, though less probably, be taken to mean 'in vain', i.e., 'unsuccessfully'.)

NATURE, STUDENT OF: see NATURE #3–4

NECESSITY, *anankē;* **NECESSARY,** *anankaion*

1. This is sometimes rendered by 'must' (which also renders *dei;* see RIGHT).

2. Aristotle often suggests that it is necessary that p if and only if it is not possible that not-p, *DI* 22b3–10, *APo* 71b15, 73a22, *Met.* 1015a33–36.

3. Sometimes, however, he seems to imply that the formula just given provides a necessary but not a sufficient condition (*APo* 73b25–32—if the necessary must also be universal). Occasionally he suggests that it does not even provide a necessary condition (*Phys.* 198b5–6—if the USUAL is treated as a case of necessity).

4. Aristotle contrasts unqualified (see WITHOUT QUALIFICATION) with conditional (lit. 'on an ASSUMPTION') necessity. He has different sorts of conditions or 'assumptions' in mind in different contexts, so that what he treats as unqualified necessity (i.e., not relative to one sort of condition) in one passage may be described as a type of conditional necessity (i.e., relative to another sort of condition) in another passage. See *DI* 19a26, *Phys.* 199b34–200a30, *DC* 281b2–18, *GC* 337b13–338a3, *DA* 415b28–416a18, *PA* 639b21–640a8, 642a3–13, *Met.* v 5, 1072b11. On the relation between the two types of necessity, see *PA* 642a31–b4.

5. The necessary is contrasted both with the USUAL and with matters of chance (see LUCK) and COINCIDENCE, *APo* 87b19–27, *Met.* 1026b27–1027a5.

6. Human VOLUNTARY action is not necessary, because its external circumstances do not by themselves make it impossible for the agent to do otherwise; the agent's own choice and DECISION also play a crucial role. See *DI* 18b26–19a18, *EN* 1112a18–34.

7. In a DEDUCTION the conclusion follows necessarily from the premises (necessitas consequentiae), but the conclusion itself need not be necessary (necessitas consequentis), unless the premises are also necessary (if they are necessary, the deduction satisfies a further condition for being a DEMONSTRATION). See *APr* 24b19, *APo* 71b3–5, 75a25–27, *Top.* 100a25–27. For a possible application of this distinction, see *DI* 19a23–32.

8. Some kinds of necessity belong to a subject's NATURE, and some do not; see FORCE.

9. Aristotle takes not only some propositions and states of affairs, but also some SUBSTANCES, to be necessary. Their existence is necessary, insofar as they are everlasting (see ALWAYS) and essential to the universe. See *DC* 281b20–25, *GC* 337b35–338a2, *Met.* 1072b10–13.

nomos: see LAW

nous: see UNDERSTANDING

NUMBER, *arithmos*

Aristotle distinguishes 'the number we count' from 'the number we count with'. If we count four horses, the number (what we enumerate with) is four. But there are four of them insofar as they are a number of horses, so that their being horses is what makes them numerable as four. If we counted them as horse-parts, their number would be much larger than four, and if we counted them as a team of horses, there would be only one. See *Phys.* 219b5, 220b14, *Met.* 991b20n, 1044a2n, 1052b18–24.

OBSERVE: see STUDY

OLIGARCHY, *oligarchia*
The term literally means 'rule (see PRINCIPLE) by the few (*oligoi*)'; but Aristotle uses it in a more restricted sense, referring to a ruling class determined by wealth, in contrast to a hereditary aristocracy. See *Pol.* 1279b5, and esp. iii 8.

ONE
1. Different kinds of sameness and oneness are distinguished in *Top.* i 7; see also *Phys.* 202b14–16, *GC* 338b17, *DA* 412b8–9, *Met.* 1003b22–34, v 6, 1040b16–19, x 1, 1072a32.

2. On numerical (v. specific) unity, attributed especially to PARTICULARS, see *Catg.* 1b6, 3b12–18, *Phys.* 190a15, 220b20–22, *DA* 415b4, *Met.* 999b33–1000a1, 1040b8–10, 25–26, 1074a32, 1086b26.

3. On 'F and G are one (the same), but being F is not the same as being G', see ESSENCE #2.

OPPOSITE, *antikeimenon*
Opposites include contradictories (e.g., pale and not-pale) as well as contraries, *enantia* (e.g., pale and dark). Aristotle believes that the Principle of Excluded Middle (*Met.* iv 7) applies to contradictories, but not to contraries. (The number 9, e.g., must be either pale or not-pale, but it is neither pale nor dark.) Contraries must be in the same GENUS, but contradictories need not be; see *Catg.* 11b7, 14a19, *DI* 17b16, 20, 19b1, *Phys.* 188a35–b3, *Met.* 1004a9, 1011b34, 1018a25.

ORGAN: see INSTRUMENT

ORIGIN: see PRINCIPLE

ousia: see SUBSTANCE

OUTLINE: see EXACT

PALE; see WHITE

para: APART FROM

PARMENIDES
Parmenides (c. 515–after 450) wrote a poem in two parts. In the first part, the 'Way of Truth', he denies the existence of plurality and of all forms of change. In his view, only what is can be spoken or thought of; but plurality and change require us to speak and think of what is not, and so they cannot be spoken or thought of. Hence at most one subject—'the One'—is, and only the One can be spoken or thought of. Having rejected NATURALIST views in the first part of his poem, Parmenides constructs a naturalist cosmology in the second part of his poem, the 'Way of Opinion' (or seeming or belief, *doxa*; see COMMON BELIEFS).

He seems to believe that this is at least as plausible as any other naturalist cosmology, though he maintains it is false (since it assumes the reality of change and plurality). Aristotle refers to both parts of Parmenides' poem. See *Phys.* i 2–3 (esp. 185a5–12), 188a20, 191b36–192a2, *GC* 318b2–7, 330b13–16, *Met.* 984b1–5, 25, 986b18–987a2, 1009b20–25, 1089a2–6.

PART, *meros, morion*

1. Aristotle distinguishes uniform from nonuniform parts. 'Uniform', *homoiomerēs*, means 'having parts similar (sc. to the whole)'. Flesh or water is divisible into more flesh or water; but arms are not divisible into more arms. Hence Aristotle calls flesh etc. uniform parts, and arms etc. nonuniform parts, *GC* 314a20, *Metr.* 389b23–29, *PA* 640b20, *GA* 715a8–11.

2. The nonuniform parts of organisms depend on the whole, *Met.* 1035b18–27, 1036b30–32 (see MATTER #5 and HOMONYMY), *Pol.* 1253a10–29.

3. Quantitative parts are distinguished from logical parts (i.e., parts of the FORM or DEFINITION), *Phys.* 200b4–8, 218a6–7, *Met.* v 25, vii 10–11, esp. 1034b20–1035a23.

4. Sometimes Aristotle seems to assume that parts of substances are themselves substances, *Catg.* 3a29–32, *DC* 298a29–32. But contrast *Met.* 1017b10–14, 1028b8–13, 1040b5–16.

5. On parts of the soul see SOUL.

PARTICIPATE, *metechein*

Usually *metechein* is translated 'share'. 'Participate' is used for the relation of particulars to Platonic FORMS, *Met.* 987b9, 990b31, 991a21, 1031b8 (cf. 1039b2).

PARTICULAR, *kath'hekaston*

1. The preposition *kata* in *kath'hekaston* means roughly 'taking one at a time' or 'by' (as in 'counting the army by regiments'). Hence 'taking Fs *kath'hekaston*' means 'taking Fs each one at a time', or 'taking Fs in turn' (*Phys.* 233a23), and so Aristotle uses the phrase *kath'hekaston* as a noun for each of the particular Fs taken one at a time. A particular is defined, in contrast to a UNIVERSAL, as what is not predicated of many things (lit. 'what is not of a nature to be predicated in the case of many things', *DI* 17a39–40). Hence particulars include substances (e.g., Callias) and nonsubstances (e.g., the individual white, *Catg.* 1a25). It is characteristic of a particular to be INDIVIDUAL and numerically ONE, *Catg.* 1b6–7, 2b3. See also THIS.

2. Aristotle sometimes uses 'particular' and 'universal' to mark a contrast between the more and less specific or determinate; hence the 'particulars' are sometimes, e.g., the species (and hence universals) of a genus, rather than particulars such as Callias (for in dividing a genus, the things we take 'each one at a time' are the species); *Phys.* 189b30, 195a32, *PA* 639b6. Sometimes (e.g., *EN* 1107a28–31) it is not clear what sort of *kath'hekaston* Aristotle has in mind. See also INDIVIDUAL #3. Sometimes *kata meros* (see PART) is used similarly to *kath'hekaston*; see *APr* 24a16n, 66b33, 67a19, 24.

3. Particulars (in the sense in which no universal is a particular) as such are not the objects of DEFINITION or scientific KNOWLEDGE, *Met.* 1035b34–1036a9, 1039b27–1040a7, *Rhet.* 1356b30–35, *Poet.* 1451b7. Contrast *Met* xiii 10.

***pathos*: see ATTRIBUTE**

PATTERN, *paradeigma*

Aristotle uses this term in speaking of the formal CAUSE in CRAFT and production, *Phys.* 194b26. According to Plato, FORMS are patterns for the perceptible things that participate in them. Aristotle criticizes this aspect of Forms in *Met.* 991b20, 1034a2, *EN* 1097a2, and *On Ideas*.

PEOPLE, COMMON PEOPLE, *dēmos*

Like 'the people' in English, *dēmos* may be applied both to the people as a whole (Latin 'populus') and to the lower classes (Latin 'plebs'). Hence *dēmokratia* ('democracy', i.e., 'rule by the *dēmos*') may be understood in two ways, corresponding to the two uses of *dēmos*. See *Pol.* 1275b7, 1277b3, 1278b12.

PERCEPTION, SENSE, SENSE-PERCEPTION, *aisthēsis*

1. *Aisthēsis* includes the five senses and the cognitive activity we perform with them, *DA* ii 6. Each sense has its own proper (see DISTINCTIVE) object (e.g., color for sight), *DA* 418a11–16, and the senses taken together have common objects, *DA* 425a14–b11. When we see an ordinary physical object (e.g., a chair, the son of Cleon), that is COINCIDENTAL perception, resulting from perceiving the perceptible qualities of the object, *DA* 418a20–25, 425a24–27.

2. On the reliability of the senses, see *DA* 418a11–16, 428b17–25, *Met.* 1010b14–26.

3. Aristotle values sense-perception highly as a means to KNOWLEDGE (*APo* i 18, 99b34–100a1, *Met.* 980a21–27), though it is not a sufficient condition for scientific knowledge (*epistēmē*) (*Met.* 1009b12–17). He relies on it as a source of APPEARANCES and empirical INQUIRY, *APr* 46a17–21, *GC* 316a5–10; in some cases he thinks it should be preferred over more general arguments (*logoi*; see REASON) as a source of reliable conclusions, *Phys.* 189a29, *GC* 314b13, 336b15, *PA* 639b5–14.

4. Perception primarily makes us aware of PARTICULARS, as opposed to UNIVERSALS, *APo* 87b28–88a2, 100a16–b1, *Met.* 1036a2–8, 1039b28–31, 1087a19–20.

5. On perception in ethics, see *EN* 1109b20–23, 1112b34–1113a2, 1142a23–30, 1143a35–b5.

PERISHING, *phthora*: see COMING TO BE

PERSPICUOUS, *saphēs*

Normally Aristotle reserves 'perspicuous' for the explicit and EXACT understanding that we achieve as the result of inquiry. See *Top.* 111a9, *DA* 413a11–13, *EN* 1138b26, *EE* 1216b33. He does not normally use the term for what seems EVIDENT at the beginning of inquiry (but see *Phys.* 184a21).

phainomena: APPEARANCES

phantasia: APPEARANCE

PHILOSOPHY, *philosophia*

1. Aristotle uses '*philosophia*' in a general sense (in keeping with its etymology, 'love of WISDOM') for studies concerned with the truth, apart from any immediate practical application, *APr* 46a3, *Top.* 101a17, 105b30, 163b4–16, *PA* 640b5, 642a30, 645a10, *Met.* 982b13, 983b20, 993b20, 1009b33–1010a1, *Pol.* 1279b11–15. Hence he takes DEMONSTRATIVE sciences to belong to philosophy, *Poet.* 1451b5.

2. He also uses the term in a narrower sense for the discipline—also called 'the science of being' or 'first philosophy'—that is introduced in the *Met*. See 1003a21, b19, 1004a6, 34, b9, b25–26; cf. and perhaps contrast *Phys*. 192a35, 194b14, *GC* 318a6, *DA* 403a16. First philosophy is contrasted with 'second philosophy', which is the study of nature, *Met*. 1037a15 (cf. *PA* 641a35, NATURE #3–4). The traditional title of Aristotle's treatise on first philosophy is *ta meta ta phusika*, 'the things beyond natural things'; it is probably not Aristotle's title, but it may go back to his immediate successors. It indicates that first philosophy goes 'beyond' the study of nature in either or both of two senses: (1) It studies entities outside the natural order. (2) It starts from the study of nature (treating it as better KNOWN to us) and goes beyond it to its foundations and presuppositions. Sense (1) suits the inquiry into divine substance in *Met*. xii. Sense (2) suits the inquiry in *Met*. iv–ix.

PHOCYLIDES
Poet (fl. 540s B.C.). See *Pol*. 1295b33.

phora: see TRAVEL

phusiologos: see NATURALIST

phusis, phusikos: see NATURE

pistis: see CONVICTION

PITY, *eleos*
Pity is defined and discussed in *Rhet*. ii 8; cf. *Rhet*. 1382a14, *Poet*. 1453a4. It is inappropriate to arouse and exploit pity in a jury, *Rhet*. 1354a17. Pity is an important element in the proper emotional reaction to tragedy, *Poet*. 1449b27, 1452a3, b1, b32, 1453b1.

PLATO
Aristotle's works show the pervasive influence of Plato (428–347); but when he refers to him explicitly, he usually sets out to examine and criticize some Platonic doctrine. He often refers to Plato's dialogues (e.g., *GC* 335b10, *Met*. 991b3, 1025a6, *Pol*. 1261a6, 1264b25), sometimes without naming them (e.g., *Met*. 1039a2, *EN* 1145b33). Sometimes he also cites Plato's 'unwritten teachings' (*Phys*. 209b11–16; cf. 192a6, *Met*. 987b18–29). Aristotle claims to interpret Plato strictly, without giving him the benefit of the doubt; see *Pol*. 1261a13. Among the fuller discussions of Plato are (1) The criticism of the Theory of FORMS. (2) The criticism of the Form of the Good, *EN* i 6. (3) The criticism of Plato's ideal states, *Pol*. ii 1–6. See also *GC* 335b10, *Met*. 1010b12, 1019a4, *EN* 1095a32, 1104b11, 1172b28.

PLEASURE, *hēdonē*
1. In *EN* x 4–5 Aristotle explains why he thinks pleasure is not a process (*kinēsis*; see MOTION #2), but a complete *energeia* (activity or ACTUALITY), an end that supervenes on the achievement of the end of an action. Since the nature of a pleasure depends essentially on the nature of the activity it supervenes on, Aristotle argues that the goodness or badness of a given pleasure depends on the goodness or badness of the underlying action, *EN* 1176a10.
2. Pleasure is the object of appetite, the nonrational DESIRE that explains action

by nonrational animals, *DA* 414b5–6. It is also important in human action, and especially in moral EDUCATION, *EN* 1104b30, 1109b7, 1113a33, 1140b13, 1144a3. The virtuous person is expected to take pleasure in virtuous action, 1099a7–21, 1104b3.

3. Pleasure is not identical to the good, but it is one important good, and therefore an element of HAPPINESS, 1095b16, 1098b25, 1099a7, 1172b26–1173a5.

pleonektein: GET MORE

POETRY: see PRODUCE

poiein: see PRODUCE

POINTLESS, *matēn*; see NATURE #4

poion: see QUALITY

polis: CITY

POLITICAL SCIENCE, *politikē*

Politikē is the discipline concerned with politics. (Aristotle normally just uses the adjective omitting the understood noun, which might be 'science' or 'LINE OF INQUIRY'; cf. NATURE #3); cf. *EN* 1094a26–b5). It is not a science (see KNOW) in the strictest sense, since it does not produce DEMONSTRATIONS, *EN* 1094b19–27. Its concern is the good both for the individual and for the CITY, *EN* 1094b7–11, 1141b23–1142a10, *Rhet.* 1356a27. This concern includes both the *Ethics* and the normative sections of the *Politics*; and since Aristotle believes that study of actual political systems is necessary for discovery of the best system, he also engages in the empirical study of political systems. On the different concerns of political science, see *EN* 1181b12–23, *Pol.* iv 1.

POLITICAL SYSTEM, POLITY, *politeia*

Oligarchy, democracy, aristocracy, and so on are different forms of *politeia*. See *Pol.* 1274b38, 1278b8–10, 1289a15, 1295a40. 'Constitution' is sometimes appropriate, but suggests something more narrowly legal than Aristotle has in mind; the character of the *politeia* depends on who controls the institutions, not simply on the constitutional character of the institutions themselves. The connection between *politeia*, *polis* ('city'), and *politēs* ('citizen') is lost in translation.

Aristotle also uses *politeia* for the restricted democracy described at *Pol.* 1279a38. Here it is translated by 'polity'.

POLITICIAN, *politikos*

The term covers both the student of POLITICAL SCIENCE and the participant in political activity (who, in Aristotle's view, should try to put the results of political science into practice). Hence 'statesman' and 'political scientist' are also sometimes suitable renderings. See *EN* 1102a8, 1142a3, 1180b13–28, 1181a1.

POPULAR

When Aristotle refers to 'popular' (*exōterika*) works he might refer (a) to his own works written for more general circulation than the lectures that have been preserved, or, less probably, (b) to other people's works. See *Phys.* 217b31,

DA 407b29, *Met.* 1076a28, *EN* 1096a13, 1102a26, 1140a3, *Pol.* 1254a33, 1278b31, 1323a22.

POSSIBILITY: see POTENTIALITY

POTENTIALITY, CAPACITY, *dunamis;* **POSSIBILITY, POSSIBLE, CAPABLE, POTENTIALLY,** *dunaton*

1. (a) 'Possible' translates *dunaton* applied to a state of affairs ('it is possible that it will rain tomorrow'). (b) 'Can' or 'capable' translates *dunaton* and the cognate verb *dunasthai* applied to substances. (c) 'Potentiality' (or 'potentially') or 'capacity' translates the cognate noun *dunamis* applied to substances (see #3). This broad application of *dunaton* and its cognates sometimes creates some ambiguity in Aristotle's claims (e.g., *DI* 21b12, *Met.* ix 3–4). 'Admit of', *endechesthai*, normally applies only to states of affairs, and does not appear to differ significantly in meaning from the use of *dunaton* for possibility.

2. What is possible is defined as (i) what is not impossible ('one-sided' possibility) or as (ii) what is neither NECESSARY nor impossible ('two-sided' possibility), *DI* 21b13–14, *APr* 25a37, 32a18–20, *Met.* 1047a24–25.

3. x has a potentiality for F (in the primary way) by having an internal PRINCIPLE of F, *Phys.* 251a11, *Met.* 1019a15–16, 1046a9–11; in that case F is the ACTUALITY of the potentiality. Every such potentiality is a potentiality for F not in all circumstances, but in the appropriate circumstances, *Phys.* 251b1–5, *DA* 417a28, *Met.* 1048a13–16. This might mean either (1) x has a potentiality for F if and only if (if favorable circumstances obtain, then x Fs); or (2) it is only if favorable circumstances obtain that x has the potentiality for F. Here (2) implies that (e.g.) if no combustible material is present, fire lacks the potentiality to burn, whereas (1) implies that even when no combustible material is present the fire retains its potentiality to burn. Probably (1) is preferable, in the light of *Met.* 1048a16–24. If (1) is right, then not everything for which x has a potentiality is also possible for x. Conversely, not everything that is possible for x is something for which x has a potentiality, *Met.* 1044b29.

4. Different levels of potentiality correspond to different degrees of closeness of the potentiality to the actuality, *DA* 417a21-b16, *Met.* 1048b37–1049a18. (The right combination of flour, water, and yeast has a higher-level potentiality for becoming bread, since it is closer to being bread; the wheat from which the flour is milled has a lower-level potentiality for becoming bread, since it is further from being bread.) This doctrine of degrees of potentiality underlies Aristotle's claim that the organic BODY of a living organism is potentially alive; see MATTER, SOUL.

5. On rational and nonrational potentialities and their different relations to contrary actualizations see *DI* 22b38, *Met.* 1046b4, 1048a12, CRAFT.

PRACTICAL SYLLOGISM; see DEDUCTION

PREDICATIONS, *katēgoriai*

1. Aristotle usually refers to the ten 'categories' (listed in, e.g., *Catg.* 4, *Top.* 103b20–27, *Phys.* 200b33, 225b5–9, *GC* 317b5–11, 319a11–12, *Met.* 1017a22–27, 1028a10–13, *EN* 1096a19–29) as 'the figures (i.e., types) of predication', or 'the GENERA of PREDICATIONS', *genē tōn kategoriōn*, *APo* 83b16, *Top.* 103b20. Sometimes

he speaks of 'the predications', *katēgoriai*, GC 317b6, 9, 319a11, *DA* 402A25, *Met.* 1032a15; this is the basis for the traditional label 'categories'.

2. The categories exemplify the fact that being is spoken of in many ways (see BE, HOMONYMOUS). Each category answers the question 'What is it?' at the most general level about items of a certain sort (e.g., this man, this white color etc., *Top.* 103b27–39). The items seem to be sorted (rather unsystematically) by the different sorts of questions that might be asked about a substance (e.g., 'What is he?' (a man); 'How big is he?' (six feet tall), etc., *Catg.* 1b27–2a4).

3. The names for the nonsubstance categories are usually rendered by the abstract nouns 'quality', 'quantity', etc.; but the Greek terms are neuter adjectives ('of what sort', 'how much', etc.; Latin 'quale', 'quantum') corresponding to interrogative adjectives. The items placed into categories are particulars (e.g., the individual white or a particular length) or universals (e.g., white, six feet long).

PREDICATE, *katēgorein*; THING PREDICATED, PREDICATION

1. Roughly speaking, F is predicated of x if and only if x is F; in this case x (e.g., this man) is the SUBJECT and F (e.g., man) is the thing predicated, *Catg.* 1b10–15. Hence predication is normally a relation between nonlinguistic items, not between words (though cf. *Catg.* 2a19–34). Aristotle uses 'F belongs (*huparchei*) to x' equivalently with 'F is predicated of x', *APr* 24a16–22.

2. The grammatical subject and predicate of a sentence need not always identify the actual subject and thing predicated in the nonlinguistic relation that is signified by the sentence. For instance, 'the musician' is the grammatical subject of 'the musician is a man'; but in Aristotle's view the man is the genuine subject and the musician is predicated of him. The grammatical structure, therefore, does not always correspond to the ontological subject and thing predicated. See *APo* 83a1–23, *Met.* 1025a7–19, 1025a25–29.

3. In most cases the thing predicated is a universal, *Catg.* 1b10, 2a12–13, *DI* 17a39–40, *Met.* 1038b16–17. Contrast, however, *Met.* 1049a34–36.

4. On the most general forms of predication, see PREDICATIONS.

PREMISS, PROPOSITION, *protasis*

'*Protasis*' means literally 'thing put forward', and sometimes is best rendered by 'proposition'. Often, however, and especially in discussing syllogisms (see DEDUCTION), Aristotle seems to have premisses specifically in mind. See *APr* 24a12, *APo* 72a8, *Top.* 104a8, *EN* 1143b3, 1147b9. Sometimes a *protasis* may even be interrogative in form, *Top.* 101b28–34.

PRINCIPLE, ORIGIN, BEGINNING, SOURCE, STARTING POINT, RULE, RULING OFFICE, *archē*

1. *Archē* (Latin 'principium') is cognate with *archein* ('begin, rule'), and the *archē* of x is in some way or other first in relation to x (cf. PRIOR). Hence it is the beginning or origin, *Top.* 183b22, *Met.* 1072b33, *EN* 1098b7, *Pol.* 1252a24, *Poet.* 1450b27.

2. Each of the four CAUSES is an *archē*, *Met.* 1013a16–17. In these cases the *archē* is something nonlinguistic and nonpropositional. The use of 'principle' in these

cases sometimes results in slightly archaic English, and sometimes 'source' is used.

3. In an argument, description, or theory, the *archē* is 'that from which primarily a thing is known', *Met.* 1013a14–15. (On different types of principles see AXIOMS, PROPER.) Similarly, in practical inferences (see DEDUCTION #4) the universal premiss is the *archē*, *MA* 701a21, *EN* 1144a32. In such contexts the sense of 'beginning' is also prominent; see *APo* 84a31, 100a13, *PA* 640a4n. In these cases the principle is a proposition or a belief. But it should not be assumed that Aristotle always intends a sharp distinction between this and the type of *archē* mentioned in #2. See *Phys.* 184a11n, *Met.* 1034a21.

4. The *archē* that we try to discover is prior 'by nature' or 'prior WITHOUT QUALIFICATION' to the truths that are derived from it. What we begin our inquiry from is also called an *archē*; this sort of *archē* is 'prior to us' but not 'prior by nature' (see KNOW #2). In the case of what is prior to us, 'starting point' is sometimes the best translation (e.g., *EN* 1095a30–b8).

5. In political contexts (cf. 'first secretary', 'prime minister') *archē* refers to rule in general (as in 'the rule of the few') or to specific ruling offices (judge, general, etc.). See *Pol.* 1275a24, 1278b9.

PRIOR, *proteron*

1. On different types of priority see *Catg.* 13, *DI* 23a25, *Top.* 141a16–b2, *GC* 329b14, *Met.* v 11, 1028a32–b2, 1038b27, 1049b4–12, 1071b5, *Pol.* 1253a19. Aristotle usually mentions (a) priority by nature (x can exist without y (and so is SEPARABLE from y), but y cannot exist without x); (b) priority in knowledge (x can be known without y, but knowledge of y requires knowledge of x); (c) priority in definition (the definition of x does not include mention of y, but the definition of y includes mention of x). But the lists of types of priority are somewhat different, and Aristotle sometimes uses the same term (e.g., 'prior by nature') for different distinctions in different places.

2. The distinction between (a) what is prior to us and (b) what is prior by nature is identified with the distinction between (a) what is better KNOWN to us, and (b) what is better known by nature or better known WITHOUT QUALIFICATION. In these cases 'prior by nature' refers to priority in knowledge. See *APo* 71b33–72a5.

PRIVATE: see DISTINCTIVE

PRIVATION, *sterēsis*

The privation is the contrary (see OPPOSITE) of FORM in a process of COMING TO BE. 'Uneducated' indicates the privation that is present before someone is educated; 'shapeless' indicates the privation in the bronze before it receives the specific shape of a statue. See *Phys.* 188a36–b26, 189b34–190a13, 190b23–191a3, *Met.* 1004a14–16, v 22, 1038a8–23, 1042b3.

PROCESS; see MOTION

PRODUCE, *poiein;* **PRODUCTION,** *poiēsis*

1. Sometimes *poiein* is rendered 'act on' in contrast to *paschein* ('be acted on', 'undergo', 'be affected'; see ATTRIBUTE), *Catg.* 2a3.

2. 'Producer' and 'productive' are used for the agent in contrast to the object affected, e.g., *Met.* 1046a17. On productive v. passive intellect (see UNDERSTAND-ING) see *DA* iii 5.

3. *Poiēsis* is production, action that has some end (e.g., a house) external to the productive action itself, in contrast to *praxis* (see ACTION) that is its own end, *EN* 1140b6–7. Production is characteristic of CRAFT, whereas action is characteristic of VIRTUE.

4. Aristotle also uses *poiētikē* (sc. *technē*) (lit. 'productive (sc. craft)') for what we call poetry. See esp. *Poet.* 1447b13–25.

PROPER, OWN, *oikeios*

1. The proper PRINCIPLES of each SCIENCE are DISTINCTIVE of it, in contrast with the AXIOMS, which are common principles. See *APo* 71b23, 72a6, 74b16–26, 75a38–b11, 76a17, 38, *Top.* 101a6, 14, 37, LOGIC.

2. In ethical contexts, what is *oikeion* to us is what belongs to us (*EN* 1095b26) and what we are close to. Hence it is connected with FRIENDSHIP. See *EN* 1155a21, 1161b21, 1169b33.

3. On 'proper sensibles' see DISTINCTIVE.

PROPERTY

This usually corresponds either to nothing in the Greek (Aristotle uses fewer abstract nouns than it is natural to use in English) or to some term of general scope, such as *pragma*, 'thing'.

PROTAGORAS

Protagoras (?485–415?) was a leading SOPHIST (cf. *EN* 1164a20). He maintained that 'a human being is the measure of all things', meaning that 'as things appear to each person, so they are to him' (Plato, *Theaetetus* 152a). Aristotle explores the connection between Protagoras' doctrines and the denial of the Principle of Noncontradiction, *Met.* 1007b22, 1009a5. He rejects the Protagorean view of moral properties, by affirming that the good person, not just anyone, is the measure of what is good and bad, *EN* 1113a29, 1166a12, 1170a21, 1176a16.

PROVE, *deiknunai*; PROOF, *deixis*

Deiknunai literally means 'show' (see esp. *PA* 642a32, where 'showing' or 'exposition' might be appropriate). Not all proofs need meet the stricter conditions imposed on *apodeixis*, 'DEMONSTRATION'; a demonstration requires the specific sort of DEDUCTION that meets the conditions in *APo* i 2 (cf. *EN* 1145b7, *Rhet.* 1356a35–b11).

PUZZLE, *aporia*: see DIALECTIC

PYTHAGORAS

Pythagoras (fl. 530?) became a subject of legend and fable, and it is difficult to find reliable evidence on his life and teaching. Aristotle may already have faced this difficulty; for he ascribes specific doctrines not to Pythagoras himself, but to 'the Pythagoreans'. He attributes to them an elaborate account of reality in numerical terms, and takes it to anticipate some aspects of Plato's Theory of

FORMS. See *DA* 407b20–24, *Met.* 985b22–986b8, 987a9–28, b10–13, 23, 31, 996a6, 1036b18, 1072b30–34, *EN* 1096b5–7, 1106b29–30.

QUA: see INSOFAR AS

QUALITY, SORT OF THING, *poion*

Aristotle normally uses the adjective *poion* rather than the abstract noun *poiotēs* for the name of the category of quality (see PREDICATIONS). The question '*poion estin x?*' may be translated 'What sort of thing is x?'. But Aristotle uses *poion* in two different cases, corresponding to two different ways of understanding this question: (a) It refers to the category of quality. (Cf. 'What sort of meal was it?' 'Terrible.') (b) But it need not refer to the category of quality; it sometimes refers to the species in any category, including the category of substance. (Cf. 'What sort of car is it?' 'A Mercedes.') Here (a) characterizes the subject, by predicating a quality, whereas (b) classifies the subject by mentioning a secondary SUBSTANCE (or other SPECIES; see FORM #8). See *Catg.* 3b15–21, ch. 8, *Top.* 178b31–179a10, *GC* 319a12, *DA* 415b7, *Met.* 1010a25, 1020a33–b18, 1038b23–1039a2. Plato's use of *poion* anticipates Aristotle's; see *Euthyphro* 11a6–b1, *Charmides* 159a, 160d7, *Protagoras* 312d5, *Meno* 71b, 74c3. The cognate term *toionde* is translated by 'this sort of thing'; see *Top.* 179a2n, *GC* 319a12, *Met.* 1033b22, 1039a2.

RATHER: see MORE

RATIO: see REASON #6

REALIZATION: see ACTUALITY

REASON, ACCOUNT, ARGUMENT, RATIONAL DISCOURSE, SENTENCE, STATEMENT, RATIO, *logos*

1. *Logos* refers to reason, as distinct from nonrational affection, *pathos* (see ATTRIBUTE), *EN* 1147b16. It is characteristic of human beings, in contrast to nonrational animals, who cannot grasp UNIVERSALS, *DA* 415a7–11, 428a22–24, *EN* 1147b3–5. *Logos* belongs to one part of the SOUL, *EN* 1098a3–5.

2. One characteristic expression of *logos* is significant rational discourse, formed by the combination of thoughts. The smallest such combination is a sentence. See *Catg.* 2a4–7, *DI* 16b26–32, *APr* 24a16 (translated 'sentence'), *Met.* 1006a13–15, 22–24, 1008b10–12 *Pol.* 1253a9–18, 1332b3–6, *Rhet.* 1355b1.

3. The combination of thoughts and sentences produces a *logos*, i.e., argument, *Top.* 100a25–27. *Logos* refers especially to DEDUCTIVE argument, in contrast to appeal to APPEARANCES, *Phys.* 210b8–10, *GC* 336b15, *Pol.* 1254a21, 1323b6, *Rhet.* 1396b2.

4. The *logos* of F is a verbal formula corresponding to (i.e., capable of replacing) the name 'F', *Catg.* 1a2, *Top.* 107a36–b5, *Phys.* 191a33, *Met.* 983a28, 1006b1. (Hence 'a horse is a quadruped' can be replaced by 'a horse has four legs'.) It is often equivalent to a DEFINITION.

5. *Logos* is sometimes used for the thing or property defined rather than for the defining formula itself, e.g., *Phys.* 193a31, *GC* 335b7, *Met.* 1035a4, 1042a28; and in Aristotle's view, the thing defined by a definition of x is the FORM of x rather than the MATTER of x. Hence 'the *logos* of x' is often equivalent to 'the form of

x'. In these cases 'form$_i$' is used to indicate an occurrence of *logos*; see *Phys.* 194b27, 200a35, *DA* 412b16, 414a27 (cf. 414a13), 424a24, 27, 31, *PA* 639b15, 642a20.

6. In mathematical contexts the *logos* is the ratio or proportion, *Phys.* 194b27, *DA* 407b32, 416a7, *Met.* 991b15, *Pol.* 1301b32.

7. On VIRTUE and correct reason see *EN* 1103b31, 1107a1, 1144b23–28.

REASON: see CAUSE

REASONABLE, *eulogos*

The term is derived from *eu*, 'well', and *logos* (see REASON). If something is *eulogos*, a good case, though not necessarily a conclusive one, can be made for it; if a convincing case could be made for something, it would not normally be said to be *eulogos* (cf. our normal use of 'probable', which we would not apply to something we thought was certain). See *DA* 429a26, *GA* 763a3–7, *Met.* 1074a14–17, *EN* 1097a8, 1098b28. Sometimes a state of affairs is said to be *eulogon* not (or not primarily) because it is probable, but because it is the sort of thing we might reasonably expect to happen. In these cases 'it is *eulogon* that x happens' means 'it is not surprising that x happens' (see *Phys.* 197a30).

RELATIVE, *pros ti*

This category (see PREDICATIONS) is discussed fully in *Catg.* 7. It includes, e.g., half (because it is half of something), larger (because it is larger than something), and slave (because he is the slave of someone). See also *Phys.* 251b7, *Met.* 990b16 (cf. *On Ideas* 83.31), 1011a17, v 15, 1088a21, *EN* 1096a21.

REPUTATION, PEOPLE OF: see KNOW #6

RESPONSIBLE, *aitios*: see CAUSE #3, VOLUNTARY

REVEAL, *dēloun*: see SIGNIFY

RIGHT, MUST, REQUIRE, NEED, OUGHT, *dein, chrēnai*

These terms are used for a wide range of requirements or obligations, including the requirements of self-interest (one's own HAPPINESS) and those of VIRTUE (expressed especially in the doctrine of the MEAN, e.g., *EN* 1106b21).

RULE, RULING OFFICE: see PRINCIPLE

SAME: see ONE

saphēs: PERSPICUOUS

SAY, SPEAK OF, *legein*

Aristotle uses *legein* both with a 'that . . .' clause (so that 'say that' is the appropriate rendering) and with a nonlinguistic direct object (hence '*legein* the tree' means 'speak of the tree'). Cf. the English use of 'mean' in both 'When I say it's hot, I mean that we should open the window', and 'That's the window I mean'. When Aristotle says that G is 'said of' F, G is usually not a linguistic or semantic item, but a nonlinguistic UNIVERSAL, *Catg.* 1a20–21, 1b10–11, *DI* 17a39, *Met.* 1028b36. (See also PREDICATE.) Sometimes it is not clear what sort of item is the object of *legein*; see *Met.* 1006a22.

SCIENCE: see KNOW

SEARCH, ASK, INVESTIGATE, SEEK, *zētein*

This verb covers looking for (an object), inquiring into (some subject matter or issue), and asking (a question). Sometimes it is not clear which of these Aristotle has in mind. See *APo* 93a26, *DA* 402a12, *Met.* 1041a10.

SEEM: see COMMON BELIEFS

SELF-SUFFICIENT, *autarkēs*

Something is self-sufficient if it can supply what it needs without resort to anything outside itself. Aristotle speaks of (1) of HAPPINESS as a self-sufficient good, because it is COMPLETE, *EN* 1097b6, 1169b3, *Pol.* 1280b34, *Rhet.* 1360b14, 24, (2) of the CITY as the complete and self-sufficient COMMUNITY, *Pol.* 1252b27, 1261b11, and (3) of some people or cities as more self-sufficient than others insofar as they are less dependent on external supplies, *Pol.* 1326b3, 24.

SENSE: see PERCEPTION

SENTENCE: see REASON

SEPARABLE, *chōriston*

1. *Chōriston* is formed from *chōrizein*, 'to separate'; it is hard to know whether in a given context it means 'separate' (i.e., is actually separated from something) or 'separable' (i.e., can be separated from something). (The same difficulty arises with many '-ton' endings; see CHOICEWORTHY.)

2. When Aristotle speaks of separability, he normally means that x is separable from y if and only if it is possible for x to exist without y (i.e., x does not depend on y for its existence), *GC* 317b10, 329a25, *DA* 403b9–19, 413a4, 31. If x is separable from y and y is not separable from x, then x is naturally PRIOR to y, *Met.* 1019a1–4, 1028a33–34.

3. Sometimes, however, he describes this sort of separability as separability WITHOUT QUALIFICATION, and contrasts it with separability in account, *logos* (see REASON), i.e., definitional independence (cf. the varieites of PRIORITY); see *Phys.* 193b34, *DA* 413b13–16, 429a11, 432a20, 433b24, *Met.* 1042a29, *EN* 1102a28–32. See also *Phys.* 194b12–15.

4. Aristotle criticizes Plato for separating the FORMS, and claiming that they are separated, *kechōrismena* (perfect passive participle of *chōrizein*), *Phys.* 193b35–194a1, *Met.* 1040b26–30, 1078b31, 1086a32–b13. See also APART FROM.

5. He objects to the positing of separated parts of the SOUL, *DA* 432a22–b3.

SHAMEFUL; see FINE

SHAPE; see FORM #5

SIGN, *sēmeion*

A sign is an indication (see SIGNIFY #1) of one thing by a second, where the second is in some way more EVIDENT than the first. DEDUCTIONS from signs include arguments from effects to causes, which do not give us the appropriate explanations (since the effect does not explain the cause). See *APr* 70a7–b6, *APo* 75a33.

SIGNIFY, *sēmainein*

1. *Sēmainein* is cognate with *sēmeion* ('SIGN', 'indication'), and so means 'indicate'. Aristotle also uses 'reveal', *dēloun*, which does not seem to be sharply distinguished from *sēmainein*, *Catg.* 3b10–21, *DI* 16a19, 28, *APo* 85b19–20, *Met.* 1003b27.

2. Aristotle standardly uses *sēmainein* where we would be inclined to speak of the meaning of a word. See, e.g., *DI* 16a17, 19, *APo* 71a15, 93b30.

3. However, not only words (e.g., 'man'), but also the corresponding things (e.g., man) are said to signify (as we say that spots signify measles), *Catg.* 3b12, *APo* 73b8, 76a32.

4. Moreover, not every meaningful word signifies something, so that signification is not the same as meaning. Words that do not signify some one essence do not signify one thing, *DI* 18a19–26.

5. These features of signification, especially (3), sometimes make it difficult to decide what sort of thing Aristotle takes to be signified in a particular context; see *Met.* 1006a21–b28, 1007a25, 1043a29.

SIMONIDES

Poet (?556–468). A source of familiar tags and proverbs. See *Met.* 982b30, *EN* 1100b21, 1121a7.

SIMPLE: see WITHOUT QUALIFICATION

SLAVE, *doulos*

Aristotle believes that slavery is just and beneficial to 'natural slaves' (*Pol.* i 5), who are not exactly nonhuman, but lack the capacity of REASON that is essential to adult human beings, *Pol.* 1254b20–24, 1260a12; cf. *EN* 1099b32, 1161a32–b8, 1177a8, 1178b27. This fact about natural slaves explains (according to Aristotle) why a slave exists purely for the sake of the master, as an 'animate tool'; cf. *Pol.* 1253b32. The slave's way of life produces a 'slavish' outlook (concerned exclusively with the satisfaction of basic bodily needs), which is also present in people who are not slaves. Aristotle contrasts the slavish outlook with the more civilized and generous outlook that he takes to be proper to a FREE person.

SNUB, *simon*

Aristotle often uses this as an example of something whose definition refers to a specific sort of SUBJECT (a nose) that has the property signified by the word. (Snubness is one sort of property that belongs to a nose IN ITS OWN RIGHT.) He offers it as a partial illustration of the reference to MATTER that is appropriate in the DEFINITION of natural things. See *Top.* 181b35–182a6, *Phys.* 194b6, *DA* 429b14, *Met.* 1025b28–1026a6, 1030b14–1031a5, 1035a5–26, 1037a31.

SOCRATES

Aristotle sharply distinguishes the doctrines and concerns of the historical Socrates (469–399) from those of Plato; see *Top.* 183b7, *PA* 642a28–31, *Met.* 987b1, 1078b17–31, 1086b3. When he is thinking of the character called 'Socrates' in a particular Platonic dialogue, he sometimes refers to the character as 'the Socrates in the *Phaedo*' or something similar, *GC* 335b10, *Pol.* 1261a6. Aristotle agrees with Socrates against Plato on the nature of UNIVERSALS. On the other hand, he sharply criticizes some of Socrates' ethical doctrines; here he agrees more closely with Plato; see *EN* 1116b4, 1144b18, 1145b23, 1147b15. See also DIALECTIC.

SOCRATES THE YOUNGER

An associate of Socrates. See *Met.* 1036b25, Plato, *Theaetetus* 147d1, *Sophist* 218b2.

SOLON

An Athenian legislator and poet (fl. 594). See *EN* 1100a11, 1179a9, *Pol.* 1281b32, 1296a19.

SOPHIST, *sophistēs*

Sophistēs is cognate with *sophos*, 'wise', and the sophists (who first appear in the mid-fifth century) were primarily concerned with higher education, especially for public life. See *EN* 1164a31, *Pol.* 1280b11, Plato, *Protagoras* 310a–314c, Usually, however, Aristotle uses 'sophist' in a less neutral sense, to refer to those who use fallacious arguments that seem convincing when they are not. *Top.* ix is devoted to the exposure of sophistical fallacies. See *APo* 71b10, 74a28, 74b23, *Top.* 183b2, *Phys.* 219b20, *Met.* 1004b22, 1032a6, *EN* 1146a21, *Pol.* 1260b34, *Rhet.* 1355b17–21.

SOPHOCLES

An Athenian tragic dramatist (c. 496–406). His plays strongly influence Aristotle's conception of tragedy.

SORT: see QUALITY

SOUL, *psuchē*

1. To attribute soul to something is not, in the view of Aristotle and his contemporaries, to make a disputable metaphysical claim about it. Aristotle assumes general agreement that animals (on plants see *DA* 402a6, 409a9–10, 410b22–24, 411b27) have souls, and he takes the dispute to be about the nature of soul. On the connection between life, MOTION, and soul see *DA* 403a3–8, b25–7, 412a13–15, *EN* 1098a3–8. The adjective *empsuchos*, lit. 'ensouled', is translated by 'animate' or by 'having a soul' (in contexts where Aristotle clearly relies on the connection between *empsuchos* and *psuchē*).

2. Aristotle's account of the soul as the form and actuality of the BODY relies heavily on his views about (i) SUBSTANCE as SUBJECT and as ESSENCE; (ii) FORM and MATTER; (iii) ACTUALITY and POTENTIALITY. He believes that an understanding of these views shows us why the soul is neither straightforwardly identical to a material body nor SEPARABLE from body. See *DA* 403a24–b9, 412b6–9, 413a3–10, 430a22–25, *PA* 641a17–b10, *Met.* 1035b14–27, 1036b28–32, 1043a34–b4.

3. On individual souls, see *GA* 767b29, *Met.* 1037a7, 1071a28.

4. The soul is divided into PARTS, corresponding to different POTENTIALITIES; see *DA* 413a4, 415a1–13, 432a19–b7, *EN* 1098a3, 1102a26–b2, *Pol.* 1254b5, 1260a5–14, 1334b18. The division between rational and nonrational parts sometimes marks a division between different types of DESIRE.

5. Different kinds of souls in different kinds of living organisms form a hierarchy. See *DA* 414b20–415a13, *HA* 588b4–27, *PA* 681a12–28, *GA* 731a29–b8, *EN* 1097b32–1098a7.

6. On the role of the soul in reproduction, see *GA* 736a27–b29.

7. On the relation of the soul to the four CAUSES, see *DA* 412a16–21, 414a4–28, 415b8–28, *PA* 641a17–32.

SOURCE: see PRINCIPLE

SPECIAL: see DISTINCTIVE

SPECIES: see FORM

SPEUSIPPUS

Speusippus (?407–339) succeeded Plato as head of the Academy. Aristotle criticizes his views at *Met.* 1028b21–24, 1072b31, *EN* 1096b7, 1153b5.

SPITE, ENVY, *phthonos*

Generally, A feels spiteful, *phthonos*, toward B if A wants B to do worse than B is doing (without necessarily thereby wanting A to do better than A is doing). By contrast A feels emulation, *zēlos*, toward B if A wants to do as well as B is doing (without thereby wanting B to do badly). See *Met.* 982b32, *Pol.* 1295b23, *Rhet.* 1354a25, 1381b22. (The less clearly malevolent 'envy' seems better in *Rhet.* 1362a6.)

SPOKEN OF IN MANY WAYS: see HOMONYMOUS

STANDARD: see FORMULA

STARTING POINT: see PRINCIPLE

STATE, *hexis*

Hexis is the abstract noun from *echein* 'have', which together with an adverb means 'be disposed in some way' (*echein pōs*); and so a *hexis* is a relatively fixed and permanent way a subject is disposed, *Catg.* 8b25–9a13, *EN* 1105b25–28 (it is a first, as opposed to a second, ACTUALITY, *DA* 412a21–28, 417a21–b16). Hence Aristotle identifies the VIRTUES of CHARACTER with states that involve the right tendencies to appropriate DECISION, FEELING, and ACTION (these components are summed up in the definition at 1106b36). A person's character is constituted by the states that have been formed by habituation; and Aristotle claims that it is up to us (see VOLUNTARY) to form our states of character, *EN* iii 5.

STATE: see CITY

STUDENT OF NATURE, *phusikos*: see NATURE #3–4.

STUDY, ATTEND TO, OBSERVE, *theōrein*

1. *Theōrein* (lit. 'view', 'gaze on') is the second ACTUALITY of knowing, i.e., actually attending to an item of one's knowledge, *DA* 412a23, 417a28, *Met.* 1048a34, 1072b24, 1087a20, *EN* 1146b33.

2. *Theōria* is the life of intellectual activity that Aristotle recognizes as the highest element of HAPPINESS for a human being, *EN* 1177a18.

3. The adjective *theōrētikos* sometimes refers to theoretical pursuits, as opposed to practical (concerned with *praxis*) or productive (concerned with *poiēsis*) pursuits, *PA* 640a2, *Met.* 1075a2. Hence 'theoretical' is used at *Met.* 982a1, 993b20.

SUBJECT, *hupokeimenon*

1. A subject (lit. 'underlying thing') is what has things PREDICATED of it, *Catg.* 2b15–16, *Met.* 1028a36–37. Predication is not a grammatical relation, and the subject referred to in a predication need not be what is named by the grammatical subject of a sentence; see *APo* 83a6–7.

2. A subject also underlies every change (see MOTION), both in nonsubstance categories (see PREDICATIONS), *Catg.* 4a10–12, and in the category of SUBSTANCE. In the first case the subject is (e.g.) the man who changes from pale to dark. In the second case the subject is MATTER, *Phys.* 190a13–15, 190a31–b5, 191a7–20, *GC* 314b3, *DA* 412a19, *Met.* 983b16–18.

3. Aristotle does not sharply distinguish the uses of 'subject' in #1 and #2. He seems to have both in mind when he considers the claim of the subject to be substance. Matter has an obvious claim to count as the relevant sort of subject; but Aristotle argues (according to one interpretation of *Met.* vii) that FORM counts as a THIS and a particular subject as well. See *Phys.* 191a19–20, 192b33–34, *Met.* 1017b23–26, 1028a5–9, 1029a7–9, 1038b4–6, 1042a26–b3, 1049a27–36.

4. The term is also used (cf. the English 'subject' = 'subject matter') for what a science (see KNOWLEDGE) or CRAFT or LINE OF INQUIRY studies, *APo* 75a42, 76a12, *EN* 1094b12.

5. It is used for external things in contrast to APPEARANCES, *DA* 425b14, *Met.* 1010b24.

SUBSTANCE, ESSENCE₀, *ousia*

1. *Ousia* is the abstract noun formed from the verb 'to BE', and sometimes 'being' is the right translation (hence 'being₀' at e.g., *GC* 336b33, *PA* 640a18, *Met.* 983a27). But 'being' is normally reserved for *to on*, the participle (= something that is) or for *einai* (the infinitive 'to be'). Aristotle sometimes (e.g., *Pol.* 1279b18) uses *ousia* with its ordinary Greek sense of 'property' (as in 'private property').

2. *Ousia* is the first of the ten categories (see PREDICATIONS). Aristotle seems to pick it out in two ways: (a) *Ousia* is the SUBJECT of the other categories. It is either a primary substance, which is a THIS and a PARTICULAR, and so a basic subject, or a secondary substance, which is a species (see FORM #8) or GENUS of primary substances. (b) *Ousia* is what something is; the answer to the question 'What is F?' tells us the *ousia* of F. In these cases it is rendered by 'essence₀' (which is required when the *ousia* of a nonsubstance is being considered, *Catg.* 1a1, *APo* 73a26, 93b26). This is a standard Platonic use; see *Euthyphro* 11a7–b1, *Meno* 72b1–2. On (a) and (b) see *Catg.* 3a11–18, 3b10–22, *Top.* 103b26, *GC* 317b9, *Met.* 1017b23–26, 1028a11–22. It is often difficult to be sure which aspect of *ousia* Aristotle has in mind in a particular context (see, e.g., *DA* 412b13, 415b11); and it is often important, since (b) applies to nonsubstances as well as to substances. Some of the passages cited above suggest, however, that Aristotle thinks there is some systematic connection between (a) and (b), and in particular that substances (according to (a)) are primary bearers of essences; see esp. *Met.* 1030a21–b13. Hence it is not always clear whether the distinction between (a) and (b) is meant to be (i) a distinction between two kinds of substance (or two senses of the word 'ousia') or (ii) a distinction between two criteria that (in Aristotle's view) are satisfied by one and the same thing.

3. Aristotle's elaborate discussion of substance in *Met* vii raises several questions (see FORM #9): (a) Does he maintain, as he does in the *Catg.*, that a primary substance must be a PARTICULAR (see also THIS)? (b) In what sense, if any, does he believe that a substance must be a SUBJECT? (c) What does he mean by identifying form (or some sort of form) with substance? Is the substantial form a universal or a particular? (d) How can a substance be, as Aristotle claims, an object of scientific KNOWLEDGE and DEFINITION? One series of answers results in the view that he identifies substances with particular forms; another series of answers implies that he identifies substances with species forms.

4. On the SEPARABILITY of substance and the inseparability of nonsubstances from substance, see *Catg.* 2b3–6, GC 317b8–11, *Met.* 1028a33–34, 1029a27–29, 1038b27–29, 1042a26–31.

5. On some doubtful examples of substances, see CRAFT, PART.

sullogismos: DEDUCTION

sumbebēkos: COINCIDENT

SUPPOSITION, VIEW, *hupolēpsis*

This is a general term covering both KNOWLEDGE and BELIEF, and so confined to rational animals; see *DA* 427b28, 428b3, *Met.* 1008b26, *EN* 1140b13, 1147b4. Where 'supposition' would sound misleadingly tentative, 'view' is used. See *Met.* 981a7, *Pol.* 1253b17, 1301a37.

SYNONYMOUS, *sunōnumon*

Etymologically *sunōnumon* means 'being named together', i.e., having the same NAME. (Hence in ordinary Greek it is sometimes used interchangeably with 'homonymous'; Aristotle, however, fixes sharply distinct senses for the two terms.) Like 'HOMONYMOUS' and 'said in many ways', it is applied primarily to things and not to words; x and y are synonymously F if and only if they have both the same name 'F' and the same DEFINITION of F. See *Catg.* 1a6–12, GC 314a20, *Met.* 1003b12–15, 1006b18.

technē: CRAFT

TEMPERANCE, *sōphrosunē*

Temperance (for Aristotle's dubious etymology see *EN* 1140b11; the term is probably derived from *sōs*, 'sound', and *phronein*, 'thought' (see INTELLIGENCE)) is the virtue concerned with the DESIRES and PLEASURES of the appetitive part of the soul. See *EN* iii 10–11.

TERM: see FORMULA

TESTING, *peirastikē*: see DIALECTIC

THALES

Aristotle regards Thales (fl. 585) as the first of the Presocratic NATURALISTS. Thales recognizes only the material cause, and treats water as the basic subject, *DC* 294a28–b15, *Met.* 983b6, 984a5. On his views about the soul see *DA* 405a19–21. See also *EN* 1141b4.

thaumazein: see ADMIRE

THEODECTES

Orator and tragedian (c. 375–c. 334 B.C.). See *EN* 1150b9, *Pol.* 1255a36.

theōria: STUDY

THIRD MAN: see FORM (PLATONIC)

THIS, *tode ti*

1. The Greek might be rendered: (1) 'this something' (e.g., this dog); (2) 'some this', i.e., either (2a) some particular thing or (2b) something of some kind (e.g., some dog).

2. 'This' is a standard way of referring to the category of substance, and being a this is especially characteristic of substance (though perhaps not confined to substance; cf. *Catg.* 1b6, 3b10, *GC* 318b15). See *APo* 73b7, *GC* 317b9, 21, 319a12, *DA* 402a24, *Met.* 1017b24–26, 1029a28.

3. A this is numerically ONE, in contrast to a 'such' (see QUALITY), *Catg.* 3b10–13, *Top.* 178b38, *Phys.* 190b25n, *Met.* 1039a1. Aristotle often seems to assume that if a this is numerically one, it is also a PARTICULAR. Since he requires a SUBSTANCE to be a this, he seems to imply that a substance must be a particular (see *Met.* 1029a28, 1038b5, 1042a29). But the claim that substance is a particular is sometimes thought to be inconsistent with Aristotle's view (in *Met.* vii) that substance is to be identified with form. See further FORM #9, SUBSTANCE #3.

THIS SORT OF THING, *toionde*: see QUALITY

THOUGHT: see UNDERSTANDING

ti esti: see ESSENCE

ti ēn einai: see ESSENCE

TIME, *chronos*

Time is discussed fully in *Phys.* iv 10–11. It is defined at 219b1–2. On the close connection of time with MOTION, see esp. 218b21–219b3. On the everlastingness of time, see 222a29–b7, 251a8–252a5, *Met.* 1071b7.

tode ti: THIS

TRAVEL, LOCAL MOTION, *phora*

Phora is change of place, one of the types of MOTION distinguished at *Phys.* 201a3–9, 226a23–b8.

tuchē: see LUCK

UNDERSTANDING, MIND, THOUGHT, INTELLECT, *nous*; **INTELLIGIBLE,** *noēton*

1. Aristotle applies *nous* to the faculty or capacity (see POTENTIALITY) of rational thought (e.g., *Met.* 985a19; see also REASON) and to its exercise in acts of rational thinking. Hence the term is applied to both the first and the second ACTUALITY. See *DA* iii 4. In many contexts (e.g., *MA* 701a7, *Met.* 1074b15) 'thought' would be a suitable rendering.

2. Often, however, *nous* is a cognitive state that includes more than mere think-

ing. I can think (= have the thought) of going to the moon, without thinking that I will go the moon; but when Aristotle says I have *nous* that p, he means that I believe (and indeed KNOW) that p. For these contexts 'understanding' is more suitable. In *DA* iii 4, e.g., Aristotle seems to treat *noein* as a form of knowledge, not simply as thinking about things; but it is not always clear which he has in mind.

3. In its broadest use, *nous* that p is any intellectual, as opposed to perceptual, grasp of the truth of p, e.g., *APr* 68b27–29, *APo* 88a15–17. In its narrowest use, *nous* applies to the nondemonstrative grasp of the PRINCIPLES that are premises for a DEMONSTRATION; in this case it is superior to *epistēmē* (see KNOW). See *APo* 72b13–15, 100b5–17n, *DA* 429a13n, *GA* 742b29–33.

4. On theoretical v. practical intellect, see *EN* 1143a35–b5.

5. On passive v. productive intellect, see *DA* iii 5 (cf. *GA* 736b5–28).

UNIFORM, *homoiomerēs*; see PART

UNIVERSAL, *katholou*

1. Aristotle's term is derived from the prepositional phrase *kata holou*, meaning 'taken as a whole' (cf. Plato, *Meno* 77a6), as opposed to 'taking each in turn' (*kath'hekaston*; see PARTICULAR #1). Sometimes it is appropriately rendered by 'generally' (equivalent to *holōs*; see GENERAL), *DA* 417a1, 424a17, *Met.* 1032a22.

2. A universal is 'what is of a nature to be predicated in the case of many things', *DI* 17a39; cf. *APo* 100a7, *Met.* 1038b16, 1040b25–27, 29–30. This might be taken to mean that (a) a universal is the sort of thing that can be predicated of many things, or (b) any universal must actually be predicated of many things. If Aristotle means (b), he denies the possiblity of uninstantiated universals, and insists that if (e.g.) the universal horse exists, there must be a plurality of horses that it is predicated of. If he means (a), he need not deny the possibility of uninstantiated universals.

3. It is not clear whether Aristotle thinks it is possible for a universal to exist at one time and not to exist at another; see *Catg.* 14a6–10, *APo* 85b16–18.

4. Universals are the primary objects of DEFINITION and scientific KNOWLEDGE, *Met.* 999b1–3, 1035b34–1036a9, 1039b27–1040a27, 1059a24–26 (but cf. *Met.* xiii 10), *Poet.* 1451b7.

5. Though Aristotle believes in the real (extra-mental, extra-linguistic) existence of universals APART FROM particulars (though cf. *DA* 417b23), he denies that they are SEPARABLE. Hence he thinks it important to distinguish them from separated Platonic FORMS, which (in his view) inconsistently combine features of particulars with features of universals. See *APo* 77a5–9, 83a32–35, 85b18–22, *Top.* 178b39–179a10, *Met.* 987b1–7, 1033b26–29, 1038b34–1039a3, 1040b27–1041a5, 1078b30–32, 1086a30–b13.

UNQUALIFIED: see WITHOUT QUALIFICATION

USUAL, *hōs epi to polu*

1. The phrase means 'for the most part' or 'as a general rule'. It is applied to what happens in most but not all cases of a given sort, *APr* 32b4–10. Sometimes Aristotle seems to identify a usual regularity with a mere statistical frequency.

2. On the other hand, the usual is contrasted with both NECESSITY and CHANCE, *DI* 19a18–22, 37–39, *Phys.* 196b12–17, 196b36–197a1, 197a18–20 (but cf. 198b6), 198b35, *Rhet.* 1362a33. The usual is even a legitimate object of SCIENCE, *Met.* 1026b27–1027a15, and is open to scientific DEMONSTRATION, *APo* i 30 (but cf. *EN* 1094b19–27, 1139b14–19).

3. The passages in #2 suggest that Aristotle sometimes conceives a usual regularity as something more than a simple rule about what happens more often than not. It is an instance of what happens by NATURE (*GA* 727b29–30, 777a19–21), i.e., as an instance of a final-causal regularity (and so not a mere statistical frequency) that may have exceptions, *Phys.* 199b22–26. For exceptions to such regularities see *Phys.* 198b34–199a5n, *GA* 767b13–15, *Met.* 1032a28–32.

VICIOUS, BAD, BASE, *kakos, phaulos, mochthēros*

These all indicate the state opposite to VIRTUE. The vicious person differs from the merely INCONTINENT person in having an erroneous DECISION; see *EN* 1146b19–24, 1148a4–11, 1150a19–24.

VIEW: see SUPPOSITION

VIRTUE, *aretē*

1. Something has an *aretē* insofar as it is GOOD at or for something; hence *aretē* is closely related to FUNCTION, and the term may refer to all sorts of excellences (see *DA* 408a3, *EN* 1098a8–12, *Rhet.* 1360b21–23, 1361b3, 1362a13).

2. More narrowly understood, the virtues are the praiseworthy STATES of CHARACTER and intellect that are discussed in the *EN*; these order the different parts of the SOUL so that they are properly suited to fulfill the human function in achieving the human good; see 1103a3–10, 1106a14–24, 1139a15–17, 1144a6–9, *Rhet.* 1366a23–b22.

3. The virtues of character involve both rational and nonrational elements; see 1106b36, DECISION, DESIRE, FINE, MEAN, PLEASURE, STATE.

4. On virtue and INTELLIGENCE, see *EN* vi 13.

5. On the relation of virtue to HAPPINESS, see *EN* 1100b7–1101a21, *Pol.* vii 1, *Rhet.* 1360b19–30.

VOLUNTARY, *hekousion*; WILLING, *hekōn*

In ordinary Greek these terms (used interchangeably by Aristotle) have the range of uses suggested by 'volunteer', 'voluntary' (as opposed to 'compulsory'), 'willing' (as opposed to 'against my will'). Aristotle, however, applies them to all actions that an agent can be praised or blamed for (including those that are done 'unwillingly' or 'reluctantly' or 'against one's will' in the ordinary sense; see esp. *EN* 1110a4–b9). In his view, agents are fairly held 'responsible' (*aitios*; see CAUSE #3) for their voluntary actions. Voluntary agents are 'in CONTROL' of their actions, and the actions are 'up to' (*epi*) the agents. Aristotle develops his views on voluntariness and responsibility for actions and for STATES of character in *EN* iii 1, 5. Such responsibility implies that human actions are not completely subject to NECESSITY (see #6); for human choice and DECISION play a crucial role in determining human actions.

WANTON AGGRESSION, *hubris*

An act of *hubris* is an insult or attack by A on B, aimed at B's humiliation and dishonor and at A's pleasure. See *EN* 1115a20, 1129b32, 1148b30, *Pol.* 1295b9, 1309b22.

WHAT-IT-IS: see ESSENCE

WHAT SOMETHING IS FOR: see FOR SOMETHING

WHITE, PALE, *leukon*

Leukon and *melan* seem to indicate a range of (respectively) light and dark colors; hence 'pale' is often the best rendering (e.g., in *Catg.* 4a15 and in 'pale man', *Met.* 1029b27). But sometimes its grammatical features are closer to those of 'white', making this the better rendering (e.g., *Catg.* 2a31).

WISDOM, *sophia*

In ordinary Greek *sophia* is applied to all sorts of CRAFT and other types of KNOWLEDGE (cf. *Met.* 981a25, 27, b1, *EN* 1141a9). Aristotle, however, confines it to theoretical wisdom, contrasted with practical INTELLIGENCE, *EN* vi 7. It is the general understanding of reality that Aristotle seeks in the *Met.*; see 981b10–982a3.

WISH, *boulēsis*; see DECISION, DESIRE.

WITHOUT QUALIFICATION, UNQUALIFIED, SIMPLY, UNCONDITIONALLY, WITHOUT EXCEPTION, *haplōs*

1. The adjective *haplous* is translated 'simple' (in contrast to compound), *Phys.* 189b33, *DA* 429b23, *Met.* 1072a31–34.

2. To say that x is F without qualification ('simpliciter') is to say that x is F without some addition; see *Top.* 115b29–35 (cf. *Met.* 1039b22). Hence being F without qualification is contrasted with being a sort of F (*APr* 24a28) or being F only in a particular way, or in a particular respect, or on an ASSUMPTION (see CONDITIONAL). This contrast is important in Aristotle's views about, e.g., BEING (e.g., *Phys.* 190b2, *Met.* 1028a30–31), CAUSE (e.g., *Phys.* 197a14), COMING TO BE (e.g., *Phys.* 190a32, 193b21), GOOD (e.g., *Phys.* 198b9, *EN* 1129b3), KNOWLEDGE (e.g., *Phys.* 184a19), NECESSITY (e.g., *Phys.* 199b35).

3. In different contexts 'x is F without qualification' may imply (a) that 'x is F' is true entirely without exception, so that no qualification is needed (see *Catg.* 1b6, 4b10, *APr* 68b12, *Phys.* 197a34–35, 198b6) or (b) that 'x is F' is true in standard, or appropriately understood, conditions, so that the relevant qualification is taken for granted (*Met.* 1030a16, *EN* 1129b1–6, *Rhet.* 1355a38, 1360b8).

4. Sometimes 'doing F without qualification' refers to the action-type described by 'doing F', as opposed to its particular action-tokens, which are described by 'doing F in these particular circumstances'. See *Phys.* 197b18–20, and perhaps *EN* 1110a18.

WONDER: see ADMIRE

WORK: see FUNCTION

XENOPHANES

Xenophanes (c. 570–c. 475) emigrated from Ionia to Elea in S. Italy. Aristotle regards him as the originator of the Eleatic monism of PARMENIDES and MELISSUS. He believes in one god, who is identified with the world as a whole. See *Met.* 986b18, 1010a6, *Poet.* 1460b35–1461a1, Plato, *Sophist* 242d.

ZENO

Plato regards Zeno (c. 490–?) as a follower of PARMENIDES, seeking to show that COMMON BELIEFS in plurality are self-contradictory (Plato, *Parmenides* 127d–128e). Aristotle comments in detail on the paradoxes purporting to show the impossibility of motion (*Phys.* vi 9, viii 8). He also mentions other paradoxes put forward by Zeno, or refers to his paradoxes in general terms; see *APr* 65b16–21, *Top.* 160b6–10, 172a8–9, 179b17–21, *Phys.* 209a23–25, 210b22–27, 233a21–b15, 250a19–26, *Met.* 1001b7–13.

FURTHER READING

Abbreviations used below:

[C] = volume in the Clarendon Aristotle Series.
[G] = commentary on the Greek text.
[E] = collection of essays (usually including bibliography).
[B] = especially useful for beginners.

This list of further reading is confined to books, and does not attempt to cover the large quantity of important work that has appeared in journals. Many important papers, however, are reprinted in some of the collections of essays listed below.

TEXTS

The first modern text of Aristotle (which is the source of the page and line references standardly used) is

    1. *Aristotelis Opera*, ed. I. Bekker (Berlin, 1831–70).

Many of Aristotle's works are most conveniently available in

    2. Oxford Classical Texts (Oxford, various editors and dates).

The OCT is not always the best available text of a particular work, but since these texts are generally good and generally accessible, we have thought it best to take them as the basis for our translation. Works not available in the OCT series are available in

    3. Teubner texts (Leipzig, various editors and dates).

The OCT and Teubner series present the Greek text with a short apparatus of variant readings, but no notes. The Greek text with a facing English translation is included in

    4. The Loeb Classical Library (Cambridge, Mass., various editors and dates).

The Loeb texts and translations are of varying quality. For the biological works, they are generally good; for the *Ethics* and *Politics*, adequate; for other works, often to be avoided.

TRANSLATIONS

The standard English translation is

    5. Barnes, J., ed., *The Complete Works of Aristotle*. 2 vols. (Princeton, 1984).

This is mostly a revision of the Oxford Translation:

    6. Ross, W. D., and Smith, J. A., eds., *The Works of Aristotle* (12 vols., Oxford, 1908–54).

Several of these volumes have useful notes.

A convenient selection from the unrevised Oxford Translation (without the notes) is

    7. McKeon, R., ed., *The Basic Works of Aristotle* (New York, 1941).

COMMENTARIES

A translation (often fairly literal) and philosophical commentary will be found in the different volumes (some of them excellent) of

    8. The Clarendon Aristotle Series (Oxford, since 1962; volumes indicated by '[C]' below).

We also list below some of the most important commentaries on the Greek text (marked by '[G]'). These can often be useful to readers without Greek. Those by W. D. Ross, e.g., contain helpful summaries of the argument.

The Greek commentaries on Aristotle (from the second century A.D. onwards) are often valuable. They are now being translated into English in a series still in progress:

    9. *Ancient Commentaries on Aristotle*, ed. R. Sorabji (London: various translators and dates).

A companion volume to this series is

    10. Sorabji, R., ed., *Aristotle Transformed* (London, 1990).

INTRODUCTORY AND GENERAL

Good short introductory books on Aristotle:

    11. [B] Ackrill, J. L., *Aristotle the Philosopher* (Oxford, 1981).

    12. [B] Barnes, J., *Aristotle* (Oxford, 1982).

A useful description and summary of Aristotle's works:

    13. Ross, W. D., *Aristotle* (London, 1923).

A good collection of important essays on many aspects of Aristotle's philosophy, with well-arranged bibliographies (up to the mid-1970s):

    14. [E] J. Barnes, M. Schofield, R. Sorabji, eds., *Articles on Aristotle*, 4 vols. (London, 1975–79).

Other essays, including some more recent ones, are collected in

    15. [E] Irwin, T. H., ed., *Classical Philosophy* (8 vols., New York, 1995). Vols. 5–7 are on Aristotle.

An earlier collection of essays:

    16. [E] Moravcsik, J.M.E., ed., *Aristotle* (Garden City, N.Y., 1967).

Essays on Aristotle, with useful bibilographies, are included in the different volumes of

    17. [E] Everson, S., ed., *Companions to Ancient Thought* (Cambridge, 1990 onwards).

Beginning in 1960, volumes of essays resulting from triennial meetings of the Symposium Aristotelicum have been published; many of these essays are important. The different volumes are listed in [77], p. vii.

Some influential essays on Aristotle appear in:
18. [E] Owen, G.E.L., *Logic, Science, and Dialectic* (Ithaca, 1986).
19. [E] Frede, M., *Essays on Ancient Philosophy* (Oxford, 1987).
Books covering several aspects of Aristotle's thought:
20. Lear, J., *Aristotle: The Desire to Understand* (Cambridge, 1988).
21. Irwin, T. H., *Aristotle's First Principles* (Oxford, 1988).
For readers who know Greek, a masterly and indispensable work is:
22. Bonitz, H., *Index Aristotelicus* (Berlin, 1870; vol. 5 of [1]).
An attempt to construct an index to the Oxford Translation is:
23. Organ, T. W., *An Index to Aristotle* (Princeton, 1949).
Volume 2 of ROT contains a brief index.

BACKGROUND TO ARISTOTLE

Fragments of the Presocratics are collected in:
24. Diels, H., and Kranz, W., eds. *Die Fragmente der Vorsokratiker* (Greek and German; the standard collection of fragments) (Berlin, 6th ed., 1951).
25. Kirk, G. S., Raven, J. E., and Schofield, M., *The Presocratic Philosophers* (Greek and English) (Cambridge, 1983).
26. McKirahan, R., *Philosophy Before Socrates* (English only) (Indianapolis, 1994).
Translations (not always the best) of most of Plato's dialogues are collected in:
27. E. Hamilton and H. Cairns, eds., *Plato: The Collected Dialogues* (Princeton, 1961).
Synoptic essays on different aspects of Plato are included in:
28. [B] [E] Kraut, R. (ed.), *The Cambridge Companion to Plato* (Cambridge, 1992).
Aristotle's criticisms of Plato are discussed by:
29. Fine, G., *On Ideas* (Oxford, 1993).

NATURAL PHILOSOPHY (*Phys., GC, PA, MA*)

Commentaries on the main texts:
30. [G] Ross, W. D., ed., *Aristotle's Physics* (Oxford, 1936).
31. [G] Joachim, H. H., ed., *Aristotle on Coming-to-be and Passing-away* (Oxford, 1922).
32. [C] Charlton, W., tr., *Physics I and II* (Oxford, 1970).
33. [C] Hussey, E. L., tr., *Physics III–IV* (Oxford, 1983).
34. [C] Williams, C.J.F., tr., *De Generatione et Corruptione* (Oxford, 1982).
35. [C] Balme, D. M., tr., *De Partibus Animalium* (Oxford, 1972).
Collections of essays:
36. [E] Judson, L., ed., *Aristotle's Physics* (Oxford, 1991).
37. [E] Gotthelf, A., and Lennox, J., eds., *Philosophical Essays on Aristotle's Biology* (Cambridge, 1987).
Some useful books:
38. Waterlow, S., *Nature, Change, and Agency* (Oxford, 1982).

39. [B] Sorabji, R., *Necessity, Cause, and Blame* (London, 1980).

40. [E] Hintikka, J., *Time and Necessity* (Oxford, 1973).

41. Waterlow, S., *Passage and Possibility* (Oxford, 1982).

METAPHYSICS, SUBSTANCE, MATTER, AND FORM (*Catg., Met.*)

Commentaries on the main texts:

42. [B] [C] Ackrill, J. L., tr., *Categories and De Interpretatione* (Oxford, 1963).

43. [G] Ross, W. D., ed., *Metaphysics*, 2 vols. (Oxford, 1924).

44. [C] Kirwan, C. A., tr., *Metaphysics IV, V, VI* (Oxford, 1971, 2nd ed., 1993).

45. [C] Bostock, D., tr., *Metaphysics VII–VIII* (Oxford, 1994).

46. [C] Annas, J., tr., *Metaphysics XIII, XIV* (Oxford, 1976).

Some recent books on substance, focussing especially on the *Metaphysics*, give an idea of the main issues:

47. [B] Witt, C., *Substance and Essence in Aristotle* (Ithaca, 1989).

48. Loux, M. J., *Primary Ousia* (Ithaca, 1991).

49. Lewis, F. A., *Substance and Predication in Aristotle* (Cambridge, 1991).

50. Furth, M., *Substance, Form, and Psyche* (Cambridge, 1988).

51. Gill, M. L., *Aristotle on Substance: The Paradox of Unity* (Princeton, 1989).

See also [14] vol. 3.

KNOWLEDGE (*Posterior Analytics*)

52. [G] Ross, W. D., ed. *Prior and Posterior Analytics* (Oxford, 1949).

53. [C] Barnes, J., tr., *Posterior Analytics*, 2nd ed. (Oxford, 1993).

54. [E] Berti, E., ed., *Aristotle on Science* (Padua, 1981).

See also [14] vol. 1.

SOUL (*De Anima*)

55. [G] Hicks, R. D., ed., *De Anima* (Cambridge, 1907).

56. [C] Hamlyn, D. W., tr., *De Anima II–III* (Oxford, 1968).

57. [G] Ross, W. D., ed., *Parva Naturalia* (Oxford, 1955).

58. [E] Nussbaum, M. C., and Rorty, A. O., eds., *Essays on Aristotle's De Anima* (Oxford, 1992).

59. Hartman, E. M., *Substance, Body, and Soul* (Princeton, 1977).

See also [14] vol. 4.

ETHICS

Commentaries:

60. [G] Stewart, J. A., *Notes on the Nicomachean Ethics*, 2 vols. (Oxford, 1892).

61. [G] Burnet, J., ed., *The Ethics of Aristotle* (London, 1900).

A short introduction:

62. [B] Urmson, J. O., *Aristotle's Ethics* (Oxford, 1988).

A useful collection of essays:

63. [E] Rorty, A. O., ed., *Essays on Aristotle's Ethics* (Berkeley, 1980).
See also [14] vol. 2.

General books on the *Ethics*:

64. Hardie, W.F.R., *Aristotle's Ethical Theory*, 2nd ed. (Oxford, 1980).

65. Broadie, S. W., *Ethics with Aristotle* (Oxford, 1991).

66. Kraut, R., *Aristotle on the Human Good* (Princeton, 1989).

POLITICS

67. [G] Newman, W. L., ed., *The Politics of Aristotle*, 4 vols., (Oxford, 1887–1902).

68. Barker, E., tr., *Aristotle's Politics* (Oxford, 1946).

69. [E] Keyt, D., and Miller, F. D., eds., *A Companion to Aristotle's Politics* (Oxford, 1991).

70. [E] Patzig, G., ed., *Aristoteles' Politik* (Göttingen, 1990). (Several essays are in English.).

RHETORIC AND POETICS

71. [G] Cope, E. M., ed., *The Rhetoric of Aristotle*, 3 vols., (Cambridge, 1877).

72. [G] Grimaldi, W.M.A., *A Commentary on Aristotle's Rhetoric, Books I–II*, 2 vols. (New York, 1980 and 1988).

73. Kennedy, G., tr., *Aristotle on Rhetoric* (Oxford, 1991).

74. [G] Lucas, D. W., ed., *Aristotle's Poetics* (Oxford, 1968).

75. Janko, R., tr., *Aristotle's Poetics* (Indianapolis, 1987).

76. [E] Rorty, A. O., ed., *Essays on Aristotle's Poetics* (Princeton, 1992).

77. [E] Furley, D. J., and Nehamas, A., eds., *Philosophical Essays on Aristotle's Rhetoric* (Princeton, 1994).